Digital Multimedia

Third Edition

Nigel Chapman and Jenny Chapman

John Wiley & Sons, Ltd

Other Wiley Editorial Offices

British Library Cataloguing in Publication Data

A catalogue record for this book is available from the British Library

ISBN-13 978-0-470-51216-6 (PB)

Produced from the authors' own PDF files.
Printed and bound in Italy by Printer Trento.
This book is printed on acid-free paper responsibly manufactured from sustainable forestry
in which at least two trees are planted for each one used for paper production.

Digital Multimedia

Third Edition

Contents

Preface

We know that publishers and authors are often criticized for producing new editions of well-established course texts such as this one. A new edition means that instructors have to rewrite lectures and – for a while, at least – students cannot purchase second-hand copies of the recommended text. We have not, therefore, undertaken the extensive revisions in this edition lightly. It is the nature of computing in general and multimedia especially to change at a fast rate. It had become essential that the book was changed too – outdated information is of no use to anyone studying a technical subject.

Looking back at the 2nd edition of *Digital Multimedia* (published in 2004) is an exercise in history now. There was little mention of digital cameras or MP3 players, but much about scanning photographs and using DAT recorders and tape decks. Video was not assumed to be digital and the idea of casually sharing video clips on the World Wide Web would have seemed fanciful. Flash was considered an unnecessary luxury in many cases. There were no podcasts or P2P downloads, broadband Internet access was something that was only just becoming available and we thought that some readers might not know what a URL was. And so on.

Advances in hardware and networks may be the most visible changes affecting the subject matter of this book, but many other technological changes have occurred, which have also contributed to the 2nd edition's obsolescence. For example, new codecs have been developed and adopted for still images and video, and we finally have broadly implemented standards governing Web scripting. New technologies such as "widgets" and Adobe AIR allow desktop applications incorporating multimedia to be created relatively easily using Web technologies.

Evidently a great deal has changed since the 2nd edition of this book was published, and – as a result of these many technological advances – multimedia has ceased to be a specialist subject to be studied in isolation and has become an accepted part of mainstream computing. Graphical user interfaces have been taken for granted for a long time (in computing terms). Multimedia interfaces are beginning to take over as the norm for interaction. Our main aim in revising *Digital Multimedia* has been to reflect multimedia's changed status while at the same time bringing all the information in the book up to date.

Every chapter has been brought up to date, and we have made countless revisions to the text and illustrations. Some chapters have been reorganized to improve the book's structure, and the page layout has been improved. The most significant changes to individual chapters can be found in Chapter 14 (Scripting) which has been updated to cover ActionScript 3 and DOM scripting for the Web, and Chapter 15 (XML and Multimedia) which has been shortened to reflect XML's failure to achieve broad acceptance. SMIL has been omitted and SVG incorporated into Chapter 15. The chapter on design (Chapter 11) has been rewritten to reduce the emphasis on the Web and to include new sections on gestalt and semiotics. The material on interactivity and accessibility has been expanded and placed in two new chapters (Chapters 12 and 13) in response to the growing importance of interactive multimedia. The chapters on video and animation (Chapters 6 and 7) have been rewritten to reflect the substantial changes in both technology and distribution for digital time-based media. Instructors who have been using the 2nd edition of *Digital Multimedia* can find a detailed list of changes on the book's supporting Web site.

The importance of the World Wide Web as a means of distributing multimedia has only grown in the years since the 2nd edition, but in this 3rd edition we also look at other multimedia formats besides World Wide Web Consortium standard technologies. We have also emphasized the emerging role of multimedia as an interface to applications and services. That is, when considering interactivity, we look at interaction *through* multimedia as well as interaction *with* multimedia. If your interest in multimedia is confined to Web-standard technologies, you might prefer to read our book dedicated to the subject. *Web Design: A Complete Introduction* (John Wiley & Sons, 2006) describes the interconnected collection of media that is the Web in greater detail than you will find here in *Digital Multimedia*.

This book continues to be the primary text for introductory courses on digital multimedia around the world. Taking account of recent developments has led to the book's becoming a little more technical than previous editions, so readers with no background in computing may find some chapters quite demanding. However, we have arranged the book so that the most technical material is at the end, providing a sensible stopping point (at the end of Chapter 13) for less technically inclined readers or courses which do not cover programming.

The arrangement of chapters is designed to provide an account of each of the individual media first, as a basis for appreciating the issues arising from combining them and adding interactivity, which are described in the later chapters.

The book includes various features to assist teaching and learning.

■ To aid revision, key points are presented in distinctive tinted boxes at the end of each section. These key points are also available on illustrated slides which you may download from the supporting Web site.

■ Important terms, marked in **_bold italics_** on their first occurrence in the text, are defined in the Glossary, which is also available in interactive form on the supporting Web site.

■ Distinctive boxes, marked "In Detail", appear throughout the text. These contain extra detail on some subjects for the benefit of technically inclined readers.

■ Every chapter ends with a collection of exercises, divided into three sets. First are routine test questions, which assess understanding of the text. Next, we offer some discussion topics, which require more thought and some additional research. These could be suitable as essay titles, or used as the basis of class discussions. Finally, we suggest some practical tasks. The proportion of these three types of exercise varies according to the subject of each chapter. Answers to the test questions and notes on the others are available on the supporting Web site.

You can find additional supporting material for teaching and learning, including working practical examples where relevant, on the book's Web site at **www.digitalmultimedia.org**.

Where necessary, we make reference to specific software. We have tried to refer only to widely used programs which students are likely to encounter in their practical work. It is inappropriate to offer detailed practical instruction in proprietary software in this book, but this may be found – together with many practice exercises – in our companion book, *Digital Media Tools*, the 3rd edition of which was published by John Wiley & Sons in 2007.

Acknowledgements. We are most grateful to Robert Gill, of GeoSec Slides, for allowing us to use material from his Web site **www.geosecslides.co.uk** and his multimedia CDs as examples in this book. We also thank Adobe Systems for permission to reproduce screenshots of Kuler, and Jonathan Shipley and Georgia King of John Wiley & Sons, Ltd for their assistance with this project.

Introduction

- **Media**
- **Multimedia**
- **Digital Multimedia in Perspective**

Suppose you had created a new computer program to display images of geological microscope slides interactively. Your program would offer people without a microscope the chance to examine rock samples under different lighting, rotate them and take measurements, almost as if they were working with the real thing. How would you provide the people who were going to use your program with instructions about how to operate it?

Until fairly recently, you probably would have had no hesitation in answering that question. You would write a manual. If your program was simple enough, you would just write a brief introduction and supplement it with a quick-reference card. If your program was more elaborate you might write a tutorial and a reference manual, and if appropriate, a developer's guide. However extensive the documentation needed to be, it would still have consisted of pages of text, like the one shown in Figure 1.1, composed and laid out in a way that best conveyed the information.

Measuring Angles

You can measure the angle between a reference point and some other position using the cross-hairs and the angle readouts.

1. Click on the button with an upright cross (+) on it to show the cross-hairs. This will cause a new button, labelled Set to appear, together with two text fields: the one to the left of the Set button (the base angle read-out) will be blank. The other (the angular difference readout) will show a copy of the current angle of rotation.

2. Use the slider or stepping arrows to rotate the slide to the position you want to use as the reference for your measurement.

3. Click the Set button. The current angle will be copied to the base angle readout and the angular difference readout will be set to zero.

4. Use the slider or stepping arrows to rotate the slide to the position where you want to measure the angle.

5. Read the angle in the angular difference readout.

Figure 1.1. *Text*

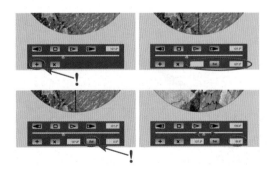

Figure 1.2. *Images*

If your program had a graphical user interface (which in our example it certainly would have) you might think that the most direct way to convey your instructions was by using screenshots and other illustrations. A written manual often includes images. For a simple program, you might consider it best to dispense with all or most of the text and rely solely on pictures – such as those shown in Figure 1.2 – to provide the instructions, the way the manufacturers of flat-packed furniture do.

If you had the means, you could also consider creating an instructive Web site. Here you could combine text and images to be displayed in a Web browser. Where you needed to provide cross-references from one section of the manual to another you could use links, so that a visitor to the site could click on some text and go to the linked page which described the cross-referenced topic. Figure 1.3 shows what a page from such a site could look like. You might be able to take advantage of the possibilities offered by server-side computation to provide a community help service, allowing users of the program to add their own advice to the instructions you had supplied, for the benefit of other users.

Alternatively, you might choose to prepare a slide presentation in PowerPoint or some similar program. Again, you could combine textual instructions with relevant illustrations, but in this case the material would be divided into short pieces, intended to be shown in sequence one after another. You could present the slides to an audience or make them available for people to download and view on their own computers, stepping forwards and backwards to read and re-read each slide. Possibly, you might include animated transitions and effects between each slide, to emphasize the sequential development of the material and to add visual interest.

If you felt that the users of your program would be likely to understand information presented as video more easily than any other form of instruction, you could go beyond the slide presentation and create an instructional video. This could be made available either for distribution on DVD or for watching on a Web site using a video player plug-in, like the one shown in Figure 1.4. A video presentation can include dynamic screen recordings, showing exactly what happens on screen when you perform some operation such as measuring an angle of rotation. This type of screen recording could usefully be supplemented by a spoken commentary explaining what was happening.

Sound on its own would probably not be a very good medium for conveying how to use your program, but it could be used to provide supplementary tips. A sound recording in the form of a conversation between expert users of the program can be an effective means of conveying knowledge in an informal way that captures some of the character of personal conversations in which this sort of information is passed on. (We are assuming here that you are only concerned with instructing sighted users, as people who cannot see would not be able to examine rock samples in the way described, but of course for many other applications sound would play a much more important role, in providing an alternative mode of instruction for people who are blind or partially sighted. We will discuss this in much greater detail later on.)

Geo*Player* Manual

GeoPlayer Home

Contents

Useful Links

Community

Measuring Angles

You can measure the angle between a reference point and some other position using the cross-hairs and the angle readouts.

Click on the button with an upright cross (+) on it to show the cross-hairs. This will cause a new button, labelled Set to appear, together with two text fields: the one to the left of the Set button (the base angle readout) will be blank. The other (the angular difference readout) will show a copy of the current angle of rotation.

+enlarge

Use the slider or stepping arrows to rotate the slide to the position you want to use as the reference for your measurement.

Click the Set button. The current angle will be copied to the base angle readout and the angular difference readout will be set to zero.

Use the slider or stepping arrows to rotate the slide to the position where you want to measure the angle.

Read the angle in the angular difference readout.

< previous   next >

Figure 1.3. *A Web page*

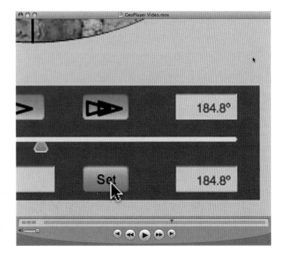

Figure 1.4. *Video*

But perhaps you don't feel that the instructions about using the program should be separate from the program itself. You might feel that a user should have help readily available while they were actually using the program. In that case, you might arrange for some information about each element in the program's user interface to pop up in the form of a short "tool tip" when the cursor moved over it, as shown in Figure 1.5. You might even consider embedding a little instructional animation within a dialogue or panel, indicating what a user should do to achieve a particular result.

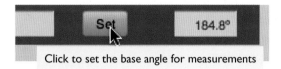

Figure 1.5. *A tool tip*

Media

The different media – text, image, sound, video, and so on – in which we have proposed that you give instructions about your program, each possess distinctive characteristics, which allow them to communicate your message in different ways.

There is a fundamental distinction between media that are ***time-based*** and those which, for want of a better name, we will call ***static media***. Time is an essential part of what video, animation and sound are. Of course time does pass when you look at a still image or read a piece of text, but the image and the text do not change in any way during that time. Time-based media are those media which themselves exhibit some change over time. Without time, animation, video and sound do not exist.

Another way of looking at this is by observing that when time-based media are presented on screen, they are usually supplied with player controls, which start, stop and pause them, just as DVD and music players are. These operations are only meaningful because of the way time-based media extend through time. You can't start or stop a still image.

Time-based media take up time – they take up your time. If you watch a video demonstration of some operation being carried out in a program, it will take just as long as the operation took when it was recorded, unless the maker of the video performed some editing. In that case, though, the way time passes within the video determines the time you spend watching it. You can skip forwards and backwards, but each time you press the play button the video's time takes over.

A still image isn't like this. You can look at it for as long or short a time as you like. You can concentrate on different parts of it, you can return to others. Static media impose no time. If you have a collection of images – for example, a set of screenshots, each illustrating a step in some complex operation – you must look at them in some order, but that order is up to you, and whenever you look at an image you can choose how long to spend on it.

Text is written language. It communicates through words, usually presented in sentences which are arranged to be read in a certain order. You might argue that text is more like a time-based medium than a static one, because it can be considered as a way of recording speech, so reading is like listening. This is a naïve sort of reading, though. Experienced readers use many strategies, such as skimming, skipping and re-reading, that do not respect the order of presentation of text. For their part, the authors and publishers of books and magazines use many techniques of visual presentation and organization, such as headings, call-out boxes, tables, indexes and cross-references, which allow text to be approached more like a static medium than a time-based one.

When you have a choice of which medium to use – when you are deciding how to document a computer program, for example – you should bear in mind that each medium has its own strengths and weaknesses, and choose only appropriate media. For instance, images are good at showing people what something looks like. Few writers are capable of producing written descriptions that can convey something's appearance with the same clarity as a photograph or illustration. However, images only show the surface characteristics of something. For explaining how something works or why it is the way it is, text is a superior medium. Instructions for assembling flat-packed furniture that consist only of pictures have the advantage from the manufacturer's point of view of not needing translation for an international market, but their uselessness as instruction is internationally notorious.

It may be tempting to believe that video should always be preferred whenever using it is feasible. Video consists of moving images, so like still images it is excellent at showing what things look like, with the added dimension of showing how they move or change over time. It is usual to combine video with sound, which can be recorded speech, so language can be used to comment on and explain the images. The success of film and television as mass media testifies to the popularity of moving images combined with sound. Why would you need to use a different medium?

Remember that video takes up your time and imposes its own. Often, as in the case of a feature film watched at leisure, this is exactly what you want. But when consulting reference material you need to control how you use your time. Instead of waiting while somebody demonstrates how to do something, you will often want to go to some clearly laid-out summary or choose a precise detail of the instructions to refer to. Text is ideal for this. Even if summaries are included in a video, picking out just one essential piece of information that you have forgotten is rarely straightforward. More likely, you will either have to waste time watching and listening to a complete presentation, or you will have to fast-forward and rewind until you find the fragment you need.

Besides being inconvenient and inefficient, choosing to use an inappropriate medium may have insidious effects on the content. Video needs to maintain a continuous flow of images, even when there is nothing to illustrate. Suppose, for example, you were making a video documentary about the musical development of Louis Armstrong as a cornet and trumpet player and a scat singer. The focus of the documentary is the music. Presumably, though, in choosing to make a video, you would be trying to add something that sound alone could not convey. You could certainly include footage of live performances, where it existed, but for many famous recordings there is no extant footage. This would tend to lead the film maker to concentrate on those performances that have been recorded on film, which would tend to exaggerate their importance in Armstrong's œuvre. Similarly, if you wanted to supply background information in your video you would need to concentrate on aspects for which photographic or film records existed, or which you could film yourself. For instance, you would probably shoot some footage in various locations that played an important part in the musician's life. Again, this would have a tendency to exaggerate the influence of place, and would distract from the true focus of the documentary – the music itself.

When all else fails, film makers resort to "talking heads". The picture here is largely superfluous, though, and speakers often fail to hold the viewer's attention, so interviews tend to be cut into short segments, which are interwoven with other material, thereby breaking up the speaker's flow and possibly misrepresenting their ideas. (Sometimes this is done deliberately.) If you simply want to present people talking, a sound recording may serve better.

You might conclude that video is not the best medium for a documentary about the musical development of Louis Armstrong. You might also conclude that a book was not the best medium either, for the obvious reason that the reader would not be able to hear any music. Perhaps a short illustrated booklet accompanying a CD? One drawback of this option is that there is no easy way of correlating the tracks on the CD with the text and images, except by including relatively clumsy references in the text. A Web site would allow this to be done more easily, but it would demand that the images and text be broken down and presented in short chunks, such as would fit comfortably in a browser window, and arranged in a structure that could be navigated by means of links.

It should be clear that each medium has its drawbacks as well as its own advantages, and for many projects it may be the case that no medium is perfect. The important thing is to try to choose the most appropriate medium or combination of media for the task in hand, and not to try to make everything into television.

It isn't always obvious what constitutes an appropriate medium, though. The ventriloquist Edgar Bergen enjoyed great popularity on the radio for nearly two decades. Cricket fans often prefer listening to a radio commentary to watching a cricket match on television. Conversely, popular music has become almost inseparable from promotional videos, while an earlier generation often enjoyed their music in the context of films.

We have emphasized their differences, but the various media do have some things in common. All but sound are visual media – they are perceived by sight. Therefore, it is clear that communication via these media raises problems for people who do not have good eyesight. In a similar way, communication using sound causes problems for people who are wholly or partially deaf. It is also clear that the visual characteristics of work in each visual medium may affect how well it communicates its message. For instance, text may be more or less easy to read, depending on how large the print is, what combination of colours are used on the page, how the typographic properties, such as type size and weight, are used to identify headings, how white space and alignment are used to lay out sections, and so on.

Accessibility is concerned with making it straightforward for the many people with physical limitations, such as poor eyesight, blindness, deafness or impaired motor control, to use computer systems, including multimedia and the Web. Graphic design and visual communication are the disciplines most relevant to ensuring that visual media communicate their message effectively. We discuss accessibility issues, design and visual communication in much greater depth later on.

Multimedia

We usually consider text, still images, sound, video and animation to be separate media. When we describe the digital representation of media in Chapter 2, it will be clear that they each must be stored in a different way on a computer system. However, it will also be clear that when media are represented in a digital form that can be stored and manipulated in a computer they can readily be combined, and it is often desirable to do so.

When media are combined, the result is *multimedia*. The most familiar example of digital multimedia is the World Wide Web, which combines text, images and time-based media in a network of pages connected by links. However, multimedia is not a new phenomenon that required computers to make it possible. On the contrary, older forms mix media routinely. Illustrated books and magazines combine text with still images. A TV news bulletin might include sound and moving pictures – both live and recorded – still images, such as photographs of politicians, graphic illustrations, such as a histogram showing the trend in unemployment, and text, in the form of subtitles, captions, quotations and credits, which will usually be accompanied by suitable annunciatory music. A contemporary live theatrical performance may incorporate two- or three-dimensional artwork and design (sets, backdrops, costumes), sound, which may be a mixture of speech and live music, perhaps with tape recordings and synthesized sounds, projected still and moving images, and sometimes text in the form of surtitles (written texts displayed above the stage, which are often used for translation, especially in opera).

Book: physical arrangement of text and pages implies a linear reading order.

Film: fixed order of frames defines a single playback sequence.

Figure 1.6. *Linear structures in conventional media*

What is it, then, if not the combination of media, that distinguishes digital multimedia from previous forms of combined media? It is the fact that the bits that represent text, sound, pictures, and so on can be treated as data by computer programs. This means that users can interact with media elements in novel ways, particularly by manipulating objects directly using the mouse. For instance, returning to our original example, instead of just showing what happens when a micro-scope slide is rotated under polarized light, as a video presentation would, a program can allow a user to drag the slide round using the mouse. In this way users gain control over the extent, direction and rate of rotation, instead of passively watching a recording of the slide moving under somebody else's control.

One pervasive consequence of the ability to manipulate multimedia by way of a program is ***non-linearity***. In many conventional media there is an obvious sequence from a well-defined beginning to the end. A play or film is usually watched from its first scene to its last; a novel or magazine article is usually read from beginning to end, as shown in Figure 1.6. We can, if we choose, depart from this linear sequence, by jumping to a chapter marker on a DVD or skipping pages in a book, but the intention of the work's creator is that it should be experienced linearly. In contrast, non-linearity is the essence of interactive multimedia. By clicking or dragging, the user can move about a structure or timeline arbitrarily.

Broadly speaking, there are two models currently in use for combining elements of different media types: page-based and time-based.

In the page-based model, text, images and video are laid out in a two-dimensional arrangement that resembles the way that text and images are laid out in books and magazines. Time-based elements, such as video clips and sound, are embedded in the page as if they were images, occu-pying a fixed area; controls may be provided within the page to start and stop their playback.

Individual pages can be combined using links, which connect pages, allowing the user to jump from one page to another – not necessarily the next page in any fixed order – by clicking on a representation of the link, such as an underlined word or phrase. Linked pages of text are called *hypertext*. When other media can be embedded in the linked pages the combination is called *hypermedia*. The best known example of a hypermedia system is the World Wide Web.

Hypermedia takes its inspiration from paper-based media that are essentially static, and grafts time-based features onto a spatially organized framework. In contrast, time-based multimedia makes time the central organizing principle. Elements are arranged in time, often using a time-line, so that they are presented as a sequence. The elements of the sequence may be frames – like those of a film or video clip, which are played back at a sufficient speed to provide the illusion of continuous motion in real time – or they may be discrete pages, presented one after another, like slides in a slide show.

With interactive time-based media, this linear flow can be disrupted by user interactions. Visible or invisible controls that respond to users' actions can cause jumps in the sequence. At present, Flash is the most commonly used time-based multimedia system. A Flash movie may include self-contained "movie clips" . These are movies-within-the-movie which may play independently of the main movie, introducing additional non-linearity by way of parallelism. Figures 1.7 illustrates how non-linearity arises on the Web and in Flash.

Like multimedia, non-linearity is not new. Many books are organized for non-linear reading: encyclopædias, dictionaries and other reference books are the most familiar examples of books that are usually accessed in a non-linear fashion. Tables of contents, indexes and cross-references are textual devices that are used in such works to help readers find their way around. A performance of a play demonstrates that the distinction between linearity and non-linearity is not entirely clear-cut. Although the play is performed in the linear sequence of scenes, the audience's attention can move around the stage, allowing them to concentrate on different aspects of the action (or the set). This is in contrast to a film, where the camera forces you to look at each scene in a particular way determined by the director.

The digital nature of multimedia permits users to interact with it in a non-linear way. Equally importantly, digital multimedia can interact with other sorts of data and computation. Most interesting Web sites are not composed of static pages which are always the same. They display information that has been retrieved from a database, usually in response to input received from the user, so each page is different. For instance, the page of results that is displayed when you enter a term in the search box on a Web site is generated dynamically, and the results depend on the search term. Here, the Web page is acting as an interface to the search engine, accepting input from users and displaying the results of the computation it performs to retrieve appropriate values

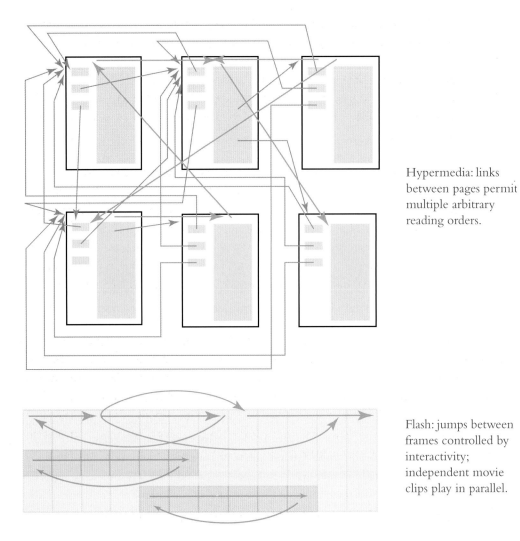

Hypermedia: links
between pages permit
multiple arbitrary
reading orders.

Flash: jumps between
frames controlled by
interactivity;
independent movie
clips play in parallel.

Figure 1.7. *Non-linear structures*

from its database. Most Web pages only offer simple interfaces, but increasingly a wider range of media and forms of interaction is being incorporated into user interfaces.

Many readers will be familiar with interactive multimedia from playing computer games. In some ways, games are among the most ambituous applications of multimedia, because of the demands they place on hardware by requiring graphics to be updated in real time in response to almost continuous input. Much of what distinguishes games from other applications of multimedia is their use of rules, narrative and artificial intelligence. However, the essentials of storing and displaying media and interacting with users are no different from our interactive microscope simulation.

The distinctive features of game design are beyond the scope of this book, but games enthusiasts should be able to see how the principles we describe are applied in that particular area.

The increasing use of multimedia has been made possible by the improved performance and falling costs of hardware and software. Formerly, the creation of multimedia demanded high-end computers with specialized peripherals. Nowadays, even inexpensive consumer systems are powerful enough for both playing and making multimedia.

The rapid rise in the use of digital still and video cameras has simplified the process of acquiring digital media. Video capture cards for converting analogue video signals to digital form are more or less obsolete, and the formerly essential scanner is now only required for relatively specialized digitization tasks, such as scanning original artwork, old photographs or documents. Consumer-level software for simple image manipulation, video editing, sound processing and DVD mastering is available for a nominal charge, and the price of at least some professional media software has tumbled, bringing multimedia production within the budget of many small independent studios and individuals.

Powerful hardware and cheaper software has made the widespread use of digital multimedia technically possible, but sharing multimedia between programs and platforms also requires that standards be developed and adhered to. Without agreed specifications for file formats, markup languages and network protocols, it would be impossible to exchange data between different programs and platforms. The development of standards is the responsibility of various national and international bodies. We will mention relevant standards at appropriate points in the main chapters of the book. A short account of the main bodies that set standards relevant to multimedia can be found in the Appendix.

Digital Multimedia in Perspective

Compared with established forms such as film or the novel, interactive digital multimedia is still in its infancy. As a measure of its youth, consider that the World Wide Web became publicly available outside CERN at the start of 1992, in the form of a line-based browser giving access to a handful of servers. In January 1997, when the HTML 3.2 specification was adopted as a World Wide Web Consortium Recommendation, audio and video were only supported in Web pages through the use of proprietary extensions. Ten years later, these media had become so commonplace and widely supported on Web sites that users all over the world were uploading their own audio and video presentations to share with other people. We have become so accustomed to the high speed of technological change in computing that multimedia is already seen as an established feature of the computing landscape. But, on the time-scale of cultural change, it has barely arrived, which in turn means that in reality it is still in an early stage of development.

The history of film and animation, for example, demonstrates that it takes time – much longer than the time digital multimedia has existed – for conventions about content and consumption to become established.

The very first films exhibited to the public, by the Lumière brothers at the Grand Café on the Boulevard des Capucines in Paris in 1895, showed such mundane subjects as workers going home from a factory, and a train arriving at a station. The films lasted for just a few minutes, but the audience was overcome with excitement. When no photographed moving images had been seen before, to be able to reproduce movement was enough, without the farrago of plot, character, or message we have come to associate with films.

The early "trick films" of Georges Méliès were shown as part of his magic show, in the same way as the magic lantern projections he used to create illusions. In a similar vein, Winsor McCay's *Gertie the Dinosaur*, one of the first short animations made in America (in 1909), was used as an integral part of his live vaudeville act. While Gertie did tricks, McCay stood in front of the screen on stage and talked to her, telling her what to do, and scolding her when she got it wrong, in response to which Gertie started to cry. At the end of the performance McCay appeared to walk into the frame and ride off on the dinosaur's back.

In the same early years of the twentieth century, films, including narrative and animation, were already being shown – particularly in Europe – as entertainments in their own right, purely to be watched on a screen. The diversity of early ways of using film shows that there was originally no consensus about a "right" way to present moving pictures. Only a few years later on, anything other than a cinema screening would be seen as eccentric. Even films that attempted to use the medium in original ways would mainly do so within the cinema context, and a film shown in other ways, for example projected onto the floor of a gallery, would be re-defined – for example, as an "installation".

Another notable feature of early cinema which has parallels in the development of digital multimedia is the way in which established forms were translated into the new medium. In particular, the newsreels shown around the time of the First World War were based on the same principles as a newspaper, even to the extent of including an animated cartoon corresponding to a comic strip. Characters were transported from the popular newspaper comic strips to film, and the animators who brought them to life were often (but not always) the artists who had drawn the strips. Perhaps more to the point, one of the most succesful studios producing newsreels and animations was the International Film Service, owned by the newspaper proprietor William Randolph Hearst – who also owned the syndication rights to many popular comic strips of the period.

Digital multimedia has also looked back to older forms. The first generation of succcessful multimedia products were reference works, such as encyclopædias, distributed on CD-ROM. These had the same form as their paper equivalents − a series of short articles, accessible through one or more indexes − and were often published by the same organization following the distinctive house style of their print originals.

Web news sites provide a more recent example of new media following the forms of old. Sites are divided into sections that correspond to those in the printed newspaper, with features and editorials as well as news stories. There are headlines and a front page. Often, the Web news site is owned by a print newspaper and uses the same livery. However, news sites are not just facsimiles of their printed counterparts, they must make concessions to the medium. In particular, they must take account of the limited size and low resolution of monitors, so, for example, the front page of a typical Web news site will contain only headlines and short synopses of the main stories, with links to the full story, which will be found on another page. Increasingly, news on the Web is beginning to shake off its print heritage, by incorporating video and audio.

One of the things that was needed before film could acquire its distinct character as a medium was an appreciation of the way the movie camera and film could be used to create new sorts of images, by framing, movement, editing and special effects. In multimedia, part of what is presently missing is a real understanding of how we can take advantage of the fact that digital multimedia is data. For the moment, we are largely confined to controlling the presentation interactively, and to moving the data across networks.

It is also important to remember that although films were first made and projected in 1895, there was no film distributed with synchronized sound until 1929, nearly 35 years later. Until that time all films were silent. They depended upon live musical accompaniment or commentory for their sound, and upon intertitles with short textual commentary to explain the action. The lack of synchronized sound profoundly affected the way in which action was represented and the film was constructed. For example, characters could be seen talking to each other on screen, sometimes quite rapidly, but no-one could hear what they said, and the intertitles only provided a short summary after (or sometimes before) the conversation took place. It took almost 35 years of development in the medium of film before it reached the form that we now consider "normal", with sychronized sound as well as incidental music, and without interruptions in the visual flow caused by static intertitle cards. Only a technological breakthrough could enable this fundamental change in the medium.

An equivalent technological breakthrough could perhaps fundamentally alter the nature of digital multimedia in the future in ways which we cannot yet foresee. However, the most significant recent development in digital multimedia has not been directly concerned with technology. It is the realization that Web applications can allow users to contribute to Web sites as well as consume their contents. This has led to the rise of popular media-sharing sites, such as Flickr for images and YouTube for video, and to a whole range of mechanisms for people to comment on, organize and even modify the contents of Web sites. This idea is taken to its extreme in social networking sites, whose only purpose is to provide a framework and venue for interaction between their users.

It remains to be seen whether the enthusiasm for user-contributed content and social networking will prove to be a short-lived fad or the expression of a new understanding of the fundamental nature of the medium. Even if they prove to be only a passing fashion, these recent developments on the Web serve to demonstrate that digital multimedia is capable of moving beyond old media and has the potential to develop its own distinctive forms and functions.

KEY POINTS

Information can be conveyed in the form of text, still images, Web pages, slideshow presentations, video, sound or interactive tooltips.

There is a fundamental distinction between time-based and static media: time-based media exhibit change over time; static media do not.

Video, animation and sound are time-based media.

Still images and text are usually considered to be static media.

Each medium has its own characteristics, leading to distinctive strengths and weaknesses.

Always choose the most appropriate medium for your purpose.

Media may be combined into multimedia.

Digital media can be manipulated as data by programs.

Users can interact with digital multimedia in novel ways, leading to non-linear structures.

Digital multimedia can interact with other sorts of data and computation, serving as a user interface to databases and applications.

Multimedia is a relatively immature technology, although its adoption is accelerating with the increasing power of computer systems.

The history of the development of film demonstrates that it takes much more time than multimedia has existed for new media forms to develop fully.

Most multimedia adapts the forms of older media, but unique new forms are beginning to emerge.

Exercises

Discussion Topics

1   How is multimedia used in lectures and other kinds of teaching in your college? Suggest how its use could be improved.

2   If you were hoping to sell a computer program you had created to an international market, what steps could you take to make the documentation as widely comprehensible as possible?

3   Do you consider a lecture to be an example of time-based media?

4   Why does the idea of a ventriloquist performing on the radio seem absurd? How could such a performance be successful (which it certainly was, in Bergen's case)?

5   Explain how a collection of Web pages could be arranged in a linear structure. In what contexts do you encounter linear structures on the Web?

Practical Tasks

1   Make a note of all the different media and combinations of media you are exposed to in the course of a single day.

2   Write a short set of instructions describing how to make an avocado and tomato sandwich. (Assume you have all the ingredients.) Create a second set of instructions for the same task, using only images – photographs, drawings or some combination of the two. Finally, create a third set of instructions that uses both text and images. How do you need to change the text and images when you combine them? Which version of the instructions do you find most easy to follow?

2

Fundamentals

■ **Digital Data**

Digitization. Compression.

■ **Digital Representation of Media**

Images. Video and Animation. Sound. Text. Interactivity. Metadata.

The production and consumption of digital multimedia depends on the ability of computers to perform operations at high speed. In order to benefit from this ability, media data must be in digital form. That is, the rich variety of sensory inputs that make up images, text, moving pictures and sound must be reduced to patterns of binary digits inside a computer. Once this remarkable transformation has been effected, programs can be used to change, combine, store, display and interact with media of all types. Furthermore, the same data can be transmitted over networks, to be distributed anywhere in the world – or beyond it – or conveyed to remote destinations on removable storage such as CD-ROMs, DVDs or Flash drives.

General-purpose computers provide the fullest range of possibilities for working with digital media, but more specialized devices can also interpret the data. Digital video can be played by DVD players, digital TV will soon be the standard for broadcast to domestic televisions, and digital audio can be transferred to a portable music player or written to CD and played by any CD player.

Digital Data

Computers are built out of devices that can only be in one of two states. Physically, this means that certain points in the devices' circuits are only stable at one of two well-defined voltages. In more abstract terms, we can say that these devices store and operate on *bits*, units of data that can only have one of two values. We might call these values 0V and 3.5V, or on and off, true and false, yin and yang, but conventionally we denote them by 0 and 1. Bits are usually grouped into larger units such as *bytes*, which consist of an ordered sequence of eight bits, or *words*, whose length depends on the particular model of computer, but is often four bytes, that is, 32 bits.

Adopting the convention that a bit is either 0 or 1 suggests an interpretation of these larger groups: they can be read as numbers to base 2, whose digits are the component bits. Thus, the byte containing the eight bits 0, 1, 1, 0, 1, 0, 1, and 0 can be read as the binary number 01101010, which is equal to 106 $(0 \times 2^7 + 1 \times 2^6 + 1 \times 2^5 + 0 \times 2^4 + 1 \times 2^3 + 0 \times 2^2 + 1 \times 2^1 + 0 \times 2^0)$ in decimal. Not only can we interpret bytes and words in this way, we can also build electronic devices that perform the basic arithmetic operations of addition, subtraction, multiplication and division, and produce an answer in the same format.

There is, however, nothing intrinsically numerical about bits and bytes, which is why computers are more than just very powerful calculators. It is only the way that we choose to interpret them, and the operations that we build into our computers, that make these bits and bytes into numbers.

We can choose to interpret patterns of bits in different ways, and this is how the data belonging to different media can be represented digitally. For instance, the pattern 01101010 might denote a particular shade of grey occurring in an image, if we wrote software and built display hardware to interpret it in that way.

It is easiest to make sense of digital representations if we describe the interpretation of bit patterns in terms of the interpretation of numbers, though, since we know how numbers and bit patterns can be associated, and numbers are easier to write down, and have familiar properties. Thus, we would prefer to say that 106 represents our particular shade of grey, on the understanding that what is stored in the computer will be the bit pattern 01101010. Sometimes it is more convenient to use a number representation that is related more directly to the bit pattern. **Hexadecimal** (base 16) numbers are often used for this purpose, with the letters A to F standing for the decimal numbers 10 to 15. Each hexadecimal digit corresponds to a group of four bits. Our example pattern would be 6A ($6 \times 16^1 + 10 \times 16^0$) in hexadecimal.

The representation of text provides an easily understood example of how numbers can be interpreted as values of some other type: we can represent characters of text by associating a unique number with each letter, digit or other sign we need, in the manner of a code. The widely used ASCII character set, for example, is an association between characters and numbers; it assigns the value 65 to the upper-case letter A, 66 to B, and so on, making 106 the code for lower-case j. For this association to mean anything, we must arrange that hardware − such as keyboards and printers − and software behave in a way that is consistent with it. For example, when you press the key labelled j on an ASCII keyboard without holding down the shift key, the number 106 (or rather a sequence of electrical pulses that can be interpreted as the corresponding pattern of bits) is sent to your computer.

As we shall see later, a similar association can be made between numbers and quantities such as the brightness of an image at a point, or the instantaneous amplitude of a sound wave. Although the association is essentially arbitrary, there will normally be some structure to the way numbers are assigned to the quantities they represent: e.g. numbers denoting high brightness have greater values than those denoting low brightness. Such properties tend to fall out naturally from the nature of the quantities represented.

Bits are arranged into bytes, and in the memory of a computer, bytes are arranged in a linear sequence so that each byte can be identified by its position in the sequence, which we usually call its **address**. Addresses behave like numbers, so they too can be represented by bit patterns and stored and manipulated like other quantities. This makes it possible to organize collections of bytes into **data structures**. For example, a black and white image is often represented by the values corresponding to the brightness at each point on a fine rectangular grid. We can store these values in a sequence of bytes and then use the address of the first byte to access the image data; a simple computation allows us to work out the address of the byte corresponding to any grid point, and access the stored value. If we need a sequence of such images, representing successive frames in an animation, for example, we can store with each image the address of the next and previous ones, so that we can easily traverse the sequence in either direction.

The most important interpretation of bit patterns in a computer is only incidentally related to multimedia: bit patterns can represent instructions that cause the processor to carry out operations on values stored in memory. Again, this interpretation relies on the fact that the hardware is constructed so that the intended effect is achieved when the instruction is presented to the processor. Because instructions are bit patterns, sequences of instructions – programs – can be stored in memory and executed. This is the defining characteristic of a computer: it is a stored program machine. This is what makes it possible for the same machine to be used for many diverse tasks, from the computation of tax allowances to the precise editing of video footage.

Since data is stored in bytes, any collection of data will occupy a certain number of them, often a large number, so we need a convenient way of talking about large numbers of bytes. The terms *kilobyte* and *megabyte* are used for this purpose. The prefix kilo- (abbreviated k) usually means one thousand: a kilometre is a thousand metres, a kilogram is a thousand grams, and so on. Similarly, mega- (M) means one million, as in megahertz and megawatts. In computing, with its physical basis in binary devices, a thousand and a million are not particularly significant numbers. It is the powers of two that have significance, since they correspond to the number of values that can be stored in a particular number of bits. (For example, 32 is 2^5, so you can store 32 different values in five bits.)

It so happens that 2^{10} is equal to 1024, which is close to 1000. When talking about memory sizes, it is customary to use kilo- to mean this value. Thus, a kilobyte (kB) is 1024 bytes. Similarly, mega- is used to mean 1024^2, so a megabyte (MB) is 1048576 bytes. (Although sometimes hard disk manufacturers use megabyte to mean a million bytes, even though file sizes use mega- in the binary sense, to make their disks appear to hold more megabytes than they do.)

In data communications, however, the conventional (decimal) meaning is used for these prefixes. A bit rate of 8 kilobits per second means 8000 bits per second, not 8192. Thus, a connection with that speed would take more than a second to transmit a kilobyte of data.

┌─IN DETAIL──
│   Some authors use K to stand for kilo- meaning 1024 and k for kilo- meaning 1000,
│   but this usage is not standard and there is no equivalent for mega-, so we will
│   use k for both and state explicitly which we mean when there is ambiguity.
└──

Digitization

Multimedia data sometimes originates in digital form – for example, when images are made using a painting program – but it is frequently necessary to convert a continuous physical phenomenon into a digital representation. For example, when a photograph is taken using a digital camera, the intensity and colour of the light in the external scene focussed by the lens vary continuously. The light is converted into a continuously varying electrical charge in the camera's sensor. An electrical signal that varies continuously so that it mimics a physically changing phenomenon is an example of an analogue representation. Similarly, when a sound is recorded on to a memory card, a microphone first converts the sound to an analogue electrical signal. In almost all cases, digital media data is obtained by converting some such analogue representation to digital form.

A banal illustration of the differences between analogue and digital representations is provided by the two ways in which the time of day is commonly displayed. Figure 2.1 shows two on-screen time displays: an analogue one, where the time is indicated by the angles of the three hands, and a more modern-looking digital clock, in which the hours, minutes and seconds are displayed as numbers. The second hand of the analogue clock moves steadily, and can point anywhere on the rim of the clock face; it is not constrained to point only at the marks indicating exact minutes. In contrast, the digital clock can only display whole numbers of seconds. As a result, the value it displays changes abruptly, once every second.

Figure 2.1. *Analogue and digital representations*

We are only considering ways of representing time values, not ways of computing them. In fact, since both the displays are running on a computer, the time is calculated digitally in both cases, but to a much greater precision than is shown. Thus, to all intents and purposes, the actual time value is a continuous one that is being displayed in two different ways. The important distinction between these two is that the digital representation can only take on certain exact values, whereas the analogue representation can vary continuously, within the limits of the screen's resolution.

---IN DETAIL---

You might argue that there can be no such thing as a truly continuous variation in the real world, because all physical media are ultimately made out of finite particles, even if these are sub-atomic; the infinitesimally small is a mathematical abstraction. However, as in the case of the clock, a continuous (analogue) model of behaviour is often more tractable than a digital one, and provides a more accurate description of what is going on than any manageable discrete (digital) model could do.

In multimedia, we encounter values of several kinds that change continuously, either because they originate in physical phenomena or because they exist in some analogue representation. For example, the amplitude (volume) of a sound wave varies continuously over time, as does the amplitude of an electrical signal produced by a microphone in response to a sound wave. The colour of the image formed inside a camera by its lens varies continuously across the image plane. As you see, we may be measuring different quantities, and they may be varying either over time or over space (or perhaps, as in the case of moving pictures, both). For this general discussion, we will follow tradition, and refer to the value we are measuring, whatever it may be, as a "signal", not usually distinguishing between time-varying and space-varying signals.

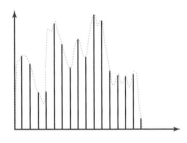

Figure 2.2. *An analogue signal*

When we have a continuously varying signal, such as the one shown in Figure 2.2, both the value we measure, and the intervals at which we can measure it, can vary infinitesimally. In contrast, if we were to convert it to a digital signal, we would have to restrict both of these to a set of discrete values that could be represented in some fixed number of bits. That is, **digitization** – the process of converting a signal from analogue to digital form – consists of two steps: **sampling**, when we measure the signal's value at discrete intervals, and **quantization**, when we restrict the value to a fixed set of levels. Sampling and quantization can be carried out in either order; Figure 2.3 shows a signal being first sampled and then quantized. In the sampling step, you see the continuous signal reduced to a sequence of equally spaced values; in the quantization step, some of these values are chopped off so that every one lies on one of the lines defining the allowed levels.

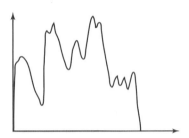

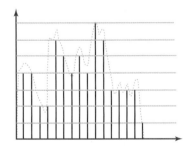

Figure 2.3. *Sampling and quantization*

These processes are normally carried out by special hardware devices, called **analogue to digital converters (ADCs)**, whose internal workings we will not examine. We will only consider the (almost invariable) case where the interval between successive samples is fixed; the number of samples in a fixed amount of time or space is known as the **sampling rate**. Similarly, we will generally assume that the levels to which a signal is quantized – the **quantization levels** – are equally spaced.

One of the great advantages that digital representations have over analogue ones stems from the fact that only certain signal values – those at the quantization levels – are valid. If a signal is transmitted over a wire or stored on some physical medium such as magnetic tape, inevitably some random noise is introduced, either because of interference from stray magnetic fields, or simply because of the unavoidable fluctuations in thermal energy of the transmission medium. This noise will cause the signal value to be changed. If the signal is an analogue one, these changes will not be detectable – any analogue value is legitimate, and so a signal polluted by noise cannot be distinguished from a clean one. If the signal is a digital one, though, any minor fluctuations caused by noise will usually transform a legal value into an illegal one that lies between quantization levels. It is then a simple matter to restore the original signal by quantizing again. Only if the noise is sufficiently bad to alter the signal to a different level will an error in the transmission occur. Even then, because digital signals can be described numerically, schemes to detect and correct errors on the basis of arithmetic properties of groups of bits can be devised and implemented. Digital signals are therefore much more robust than analogue ones, and do not suffer degradation when they are copied, or transmitted over noisy media.

However, looking at Figure 2.3, you can see that some information must have been lost during the digitization process. How can we claim that the digitized result is in any sense an accurate representation of the original analogue signal? The only meaningful measure of accuracy must be how closely the original can be reconstructed. In order to reconstruct an analogue signal from a set of samples, what we need to do, informally speaking, is decide what to put in the gaps between the samples. We can describe the reconstruction process precisely in mathematical terms, and that description provides an exact specification of the theoretically best way to generate the required signal. In practice, we use methods that are simpler than the theoretical optimum but which can easily be implemented in fast hardware.

One possibility is to "sample and hold": that is, the value of a sample is used for the entire extent between it and the following sample. As Figure 2.4 shows, this produces a signal with abrupt transitions, which is not really a very good approximation to the original (shown dotted). However, when such a signal is passed to an output device – such as a monitor or a loudspeaker – for display or playback, the lags and imperfections inherent in the physical device will cause these discontinuities to be smoothed out, and the result actually approximates the theoretical optimum quite well. (However, in the future, improvements in the technology for the playback of sound and picture will demand matching improvements in the signal.)

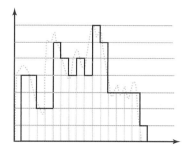

Figure 2.4. *Sample and hold reconstruction*

Clearly, though, if the original samples were too far apart, any reconstruction is going to be inadequate, because there may be details in the analogue signal that, as it were, slipped between samples. Figure 2.5 shows an example: the values of the consecutive samples taken at s_i and s_{i+1} are identical, and there cannot possibly be any way of inferring the presence of the spike in between those two points from them – the signal could as easily have dipped down or stayed at

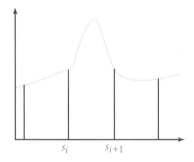

Figure 2.5. *Undersampling*

Figure 2.6. *A periodic fluctuation of brightness*

the same level. The effects of such **undersampling** on the way in which the reconstructed signal will be perceived depend on what the signal represents – sound, image, and so on – and whether it is time-varying or space-varying. We will describe specific instances later. Suffice it to say, for now, that they are manifested as distortions and artefacts which are always undesirable.

It is easy enough to see that if the sampling rate is too low some detail will be lost in the sampling. It is less easy to see whether there is ever any rate at which we can be sure that the samples are close enough together to allow the signal to be accurately reconstructed, and if there is, how close is close enough. To get a better understanding of these matters, we need to consider an alternative way of representing a signal. Later, this will also help us to understand some related aspects of sound and image processing.

You are probably familiar with the idea that a musical note played on an instrument consists of waveforms of several different frequencies added together. There is the fundamental, which is the pitch associated with the note, but depending on the instrument, different numbers of harmonics, or overtones, are also present, and these give the note its distinctive timbre. The fundamental and each harmonic are pure tones – sine waves of a single frequency, so the note is made from the superposition of a set of sine waves.

Any periodic waveform can be decomposed into a collection of different frequency components, each a pure sine wave, in a similar way; in fact, with a little clever mathematics, assuming you don't mind infinite frequencies, any waveform, periodic or not, can be decomposed into its frequency components. We are using the word "frequency" in a generalized sense, to go with our generalized concept of a signal. Normally, we think of frequency only in the context of time-varying signals, such as sound, radio, or light waves, when it is the number of times a periodic signal repeats during a unit of time. When we consider signals that vary periodically in space, such as the one shown in Figure 2.6, it makes equal sense to consider its frequency as the number of times it repeats over a unit of distance, and we shall often do so. Hence, in general discussions, frequencies, like signals, may be either temporal or spatial.

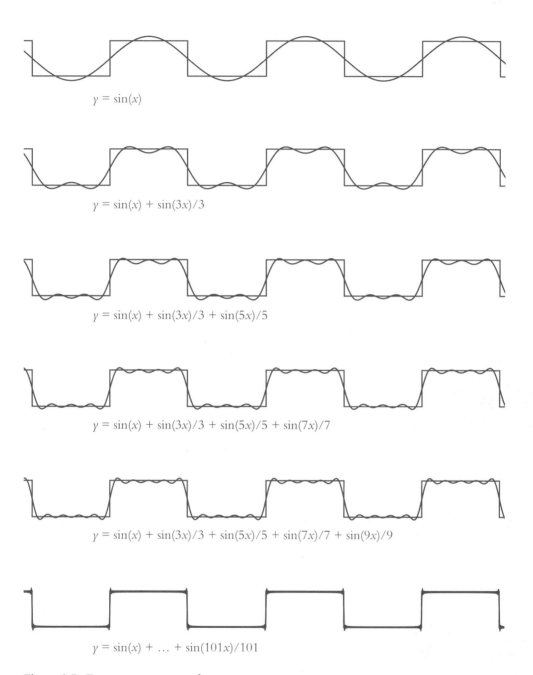

$y = \sin(x)$

$y = \sin(x) + \sin(3x)/3$

$y = \sin(x) + \sin(3x)/3 + \sin(5x)/5$

$y = \sin(x) + \sin(3x)/3 + \sin(5x)/5 + \sin(7x)/7$

$y = \sin(x) + \sin(3x)/3 + \sin(5x)/5 + \sin(7x)/7 + \sin(9x)/9$

$y = \sin(x) + \ldots + \sin(101x)/101$

Figure 2.7. *Frequency components of a square wave*

A spatially varying signal may vary in two dimensions, not just one. We will consider this complication in Chapter 4, but it can safely be ignored for now.

Figure 2.7 shows one of the classic examples of how pure sine waves at different frequencies combine to produce more complex waveforms. Starting with a pure sine wave of frequency f, we successively add components to it with frequencies of $3f$, $5f$, $7f$, and so on, whose amplitudes are one third, one fifth, one seventh,… of the amplitude of the original signal. As you can see, as we add more "harmonics", the signal begins to look more and more like a square wave; the more frequency components we add, the better the approximation.

We could use the frequencies and amplitudes of its components to represent our signal instead of showing directly how the amplitude varies with time or space. This is not as easy to grasp, but it is often a more useful representation. The collection of frequencies and amplitudes is the signal's representation in the **frequency domain**.[†] It can be computed using a mathematical operation known as the **Fourier Transform**. The result of applying the Fourier Transform to a signal can be displayed, like the original signal itself, in the form of a graph, but in the frequency domain the horizontal axis represents frequency and the vertical axis amplitude. A typical signal's **frequency spectrum**, as this representation is called, will consist of a set of spikes at different frequencies, corresponding to the different components. Figure 2.8 shows our square wave in the frequency domain. You will notice that it includes negative frequencies. There is no need to worry about this: negative frequencies are a notational convenience that allow us to deal with phase shifts. Where none is present, as here, the representation will be symmetrical, with the negative frequencies matching positive ones. There is also a spike at a frequency of zero, which is called the **DC component**, from the long-standing use of frequency domain representations in electrical engineering. It is equal to the integral of the signal, and provides a measure of its average value.

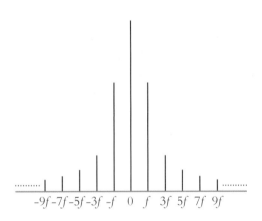

Figure 2.8. *Square wave transformed into the frequency domain*

The **Inverse Fourier Transform**, as its name suggests, performs the opposite operation to the Fourier Transform, taking a signal from the frequency domain to the time domain.

The square wave example in Figure 2.7 demonstrates a phenomenon that can be shown to be generally true: higher-frequency components are associated with abrupt transitions. As we add higher frequencies, the leading and falling edges of the waveform become more nearly vertical. Looking at this from the other end, as we omit high-frequency components such abrupt changes get smoothed out. Hence, operations such as sharpening or smoothing an image can be described

† *Strictly speaking, we also need to know the phase of the components, since it is sometimes necessary to displace them relative to each other, but we will ignore this complication.*

and implemented in terms of filters that remove certain frequencies – this is of fundamental importance in the processing of graphics, as we will see in Chapter 4.

Returning to the question of whether there is a sampling rate that guarantees accurate reconstruction of a signal, we can now give a precise answer. The **Sampling Theorem** states that, if the highest-frequency component of a signal is at f_h, the signal can be properly reconstructed if it has been sampled at a frequency greater than $2f_h$. This limiting value is known as the **Nyquist rate**.

┌ IN DETAIL ────────────────────────────────────

Some authors, especially in the field of audio, use the term "Nyquist rate" to denote the highest-frequency component that can be accurately reproduced. That is, if a signal is sampled at f_s, their Nyquist rate is $f_s/2$. The fact that the term is used with both meanings is unfortunate, but any ambiguity is usually easily resolved by context. We will always use the term in the sense of the lowest sampling rate for proper reconstruction.

The proof of the Sampling Theorem is technical, but the essence of the underlying effect can be illustrated simply. Suppose we have a circular disk, with a single radial line marked on it, which is spinning in a clockwise direction at a rate of n rotations per second, and suppose that we "sample" this rotation as a movie camera would, by taking snapshots of the disk at equal time intervals. The top row of Figure 2.9 shows the snapshots we would obtain by sampling $4n$ times a second. Looking at this sequence it is clear that the disk is rotating clockwise, and you can imagine that if these images were successive frames of a film, we would see the disk rotating in its proper direction when the film was projected. Considered as a periodic signal, the rotating disk has a frequency of n (it comes round to the same position n times every second) and we have sampled at $4n$, comfortably above the Nyquist rate.

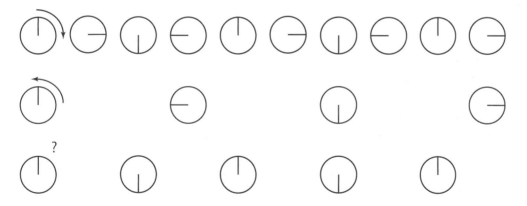

Figure 2.9. *Sampling and undersampling*

Consider now what happens if we sample at a rate of $4n/3$; the samples we obtain are the ones shown in the middle row of Figure 2.9. Looking at the sequence comprising only those samples, it appears from the successive positions of the line more as if the disk is rotating anti-clockwise at a rate of $n/3$. (The phenomenon may be familiar to you from Western movies, in which stagecoach wheels frequently appear to rotate backwards, because the rate at which the film frames were shot is less than the Nyquist rate relative to the actual rotational speed of the wheels.) Note that we must go beyond the Nyquist rate to make the disk appear to rotate clockwise: if we sample our disk at a rate of exactly $2n$, we get samples in which the line alternates between the 12 o'clock and 6 o'clock positions (the bottom row), so that it is impossible to determine whether the disk is rotating clockwise or anti-clockwise.

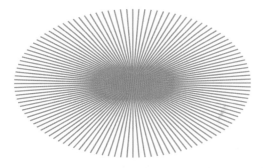

Figure 2.10. *Moiré patterns*

In general, if we ***undersample*** a signal – sample it at less than the Nyquist rate – some frequency components in the original will get transformed into other frequencies when the signal is reconstructed, just as our rotating disk's frequency was transformed from $4n$ to $-n/3$ when we undersampled it. This phenomenon is known as ***aliasing***, and is perceived in different ways in different media. With sound, it is heard as distortion; in images, it is usually seen in the form of jagged edges, or, where the image contains fine repeating details, Moiré patterns (see Figure 2.10 – the image is made up purely of radial lines); in moving pictures, temporal undersampling leads to jerkiness of motion, as well as phenomena similar to the appearance of the wheels spinning backwards, as just described.

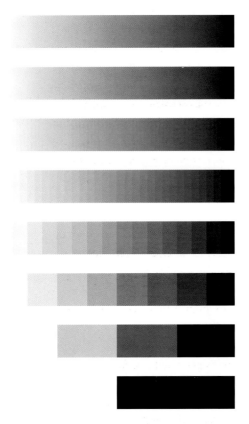

Figure 2.11. *256, 128, ..., 2 grey levels*

The effects of an insufficient number of quantization levels are generally easier to grasp intuitively than those of inadequate sampling rates. If we can only represent a limited number of different values, we will be unable to make fine distinctions among those that fall between. In images, it is as if we were forced to make do with only a few different colours, and so had to use, say, crimson for every shade of red we needed. The difference between scarlet and carmine would be lost, and any boundaries

Figure 2.12. *Posterization*

between areas of those colours would be elided. The effect on black and white images can be seen clearly in Figure 2.11, which shows a gradient swatch using 256, 128, 64, 32, 16, 8, 4, and 2 different grey levels. The original gradient varies linearly from pure white to pure black, and as we reduce the number of different greys, you can see how values band together as they are quantized increasingly coarsely. In a less regular image, the effect manifests itself as *posterization*, more formally known as brightness contouring, where coloured areas coalesce, somewhat like a cheaply printed poster. Figure 2.12 shows how posterization manifests itself on a colour image: the version on the left is a digital photograph with millions of colours; on the right, we have reduced it to just four colours, and the posterization effect can be seen clearly, especially in the background, where nearly all detail of the landscape has been lost. (Sometimes you may want to posterize an image deliberately – the result can be quite pleasing.)

The numbers of grey levels in our first example were not chosen at random. The most common reason for limiting the number of quantization levels (in any type of signal) is to reduce the amount of memory occupied by the digitized data by restricting the number of bits used to hold each sample value. Here we have used 8, 7, 6, 5, 4, 3, and 2 bits, and finally a single bit. As you can see, although the effect is just about visible with 128 (7 bits) greys, it only becomes intrusive when the number of levels falls to 32 (5 bits), after which deterioration is rapid.

When sound is quantized to too few amplitude levels, the result is perceived as a form of distortion, sometimes referred to as *quantization noise*, because its worst manifestation is a coarse hiss. It also leads to the loss of quiet passages, and a general fuzziness in sound (rather like a mobile phone in an area of low signal strength). Quantization noise is clearly discernible when sound is sampled to 8 bits (256 levels), but not (except in the opinion of some audiophiles) at the 16 bits (65536 levels) used for audio CDs.

Compression

You will learn, as we examine the individual media types in detail, that a characteristic property of media data is that it occupies a lot of storage. This means, in turn, that it needs a lot of bandwidth when it is transferred over networks. Storage and bandwidth are limited resources, so the high demands of media data can pose a problem. The common response to this problem is to apply some form of *compression*, which means any operation that can be performed on data to reduce the amount of storage required to represent it. If data has been compressed, an inverse *decompression* operation will be required to restore it to a form in which it can be displayed or used. Software that performs compression and decompression is often called a *codec* (short for compressor/decompressor), especially in the context of video and audio.

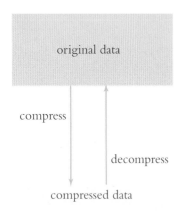

Figure 2.13. *Lossless compression*

Compression algorithms can be divided into two classes: *lossless* and *lossy*. A lossless algorithm has the property that it is always possible to decompress data that has been compressed and retrieve an exact copy of the original data, as indicated in Figure 2.13. Any compression algorithm that is not lossless is lossy, which means that some data has been discarded in the compression process and cannot be restored, so that the decompressed data is only an approximation to the original, as shown in Figure 2.14. The discarded data will represent information that is not significant, and lossy algorithms which are in common use do a remarkable job at preserving the quality of images, video and sound, even though a considerable amount of data has been discarded. Lossless algorithms are generally less effective than lossy ones, so for most multimedia applications some lossy compression will be used. However, for text the loss of even a single bit of information would be significant, so there is no such thing as lossy text compression.

It may not be apparent that any sort of data can be compressed at all without loss. If no information is being discarded, how can space be saved? In the case of text, lossless compression works because the usual representation of characters does not make the most efficient use of storage – it's efficient for the operations most often applied to text, but wasteful of storage. As we explained earlier, text can be represented just by arbitrarily mapping characters to numbers. It is normal to store each of these numbers in the same number of bits. If, instead, we were to use a different number of bits for each character, and assign fewer bits to the most commonly encountered characters, the total amount of space required would be less. Lossless compression works by reorganizing data in this and other ways. The resulting compressed files are not at all convenient to work with directly, so storage schemes which make less than optimal use of the available bits are used most of the time instead.

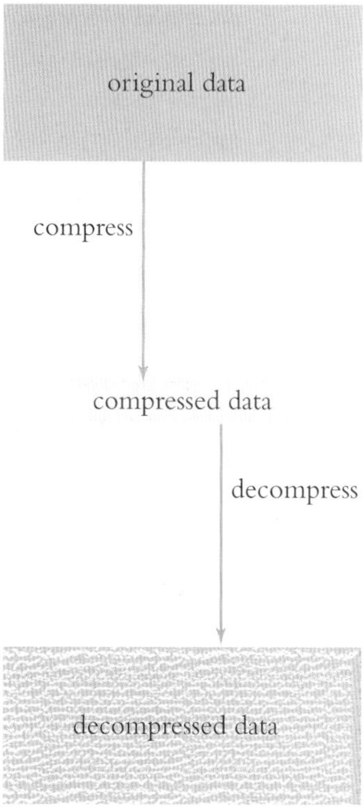

Lossless and lossy compression are not entirely separate techniques. Most lossy algorithms make use of some lossless technique as part of the total compression process. Generally, once insignificant information has been discarded, the resulting data is more amenable to lossless compression. This is particularly true in the case of image compression, as we will explain in Chapter 4.

Ideally, lossy compression will only be applied at the latest possible stage in the preparation of the media for delivery. Any processing that is required should be done on uncompressed or losslessly compressed data whenever possible. There are two reasons for this. When data is lossily compressed the lost information can never be retrieved, which means that if data is repeatedly compressed and decompressed in this way its quality will gradually deteriorate. Additionally, some processing operations can exaggerate the loss of quality caused by some types of compression. For both these reasons, it is best to work with uncompressed data, and only compress it for final delivery.

This ideal cannot always be achieved. Video data is usually compressed in the camera, and although digital still cameras that produce uncompressed images are increasingly common, many cheaper cameras will compress photographs fairly severely when the pictures are being taken. It may be necessary for a photographer to allow the camera to compress images, in order to fit them onto the available storage. Under these circumstances, data should be decompressed once, and an uncompressed version should be used for working. This may not, however, be practical for video.

The differing characteristics of different types of media mean that the sort of data that can be discarded is different for each type. There are therefore lossy algorithms specific to each type – JPEG for image compression, MP3 for audio compression, and so on. Lossless algorithms can be applied to any type of data but the amount of compression they lead to will depend on the type of data, any structure it may have and the actual data. For instance, lossless compression is usually fairly ineffective when applied to photographs, but computer-generated images that feature large areas of flat single colour will compress well. We will expand on this point in Chapter 4.

No compression algorithm can work magic. It is a general property of any compression scheme that there will be some data for which the "compressed" version is actually larger than the

Figure 2.14. *Lossy compression*

uncompressed version. This must be so: if we had an algorithm that could always achieve some compression, no matter what input data it was given, it would be possible to apply it to its own output to achieve extra compression, and then to the new output, and so on, arbitrarily many times, so that any data could be compressed down to a single byte (assuming we do not deal with smaller units of data). Even though this is clearly absurd, from time to time people claim to have developed such an algorithm, and have even been granted patents for the process.

KEY POINTS

Bits are units of data that can only have one of two values.

A byte is eight bits.

Groups of bits can be interpreted as numbers to base 2, but can also be treated as characters, colours, etc.

Analogue data must be converted to digital form before it can be manipulated by a computer program.

Digitization comprises two operations: sampling and quantization.

The sampling rate is the number of samples in a fixed amount of time or space.

The quantization levels are the set of values to which a signal is quantized.

Spatial and temporal signals are made up of pure sine wave components at different frequencies.

The Fourier Transform operation can be used to compute a signal's representation in the frequency domain.

Higher-frequency components are associated with abrupt transitions.

The Sampling Theorem states that, if the highest-frequency component of a signal is at f_h, the signal can be properly reconstructed if it has been sampled at a frequency greater than the Nyquist rate $2f_h$.

Undersampling leads to aliasing.

Using too few quantization levels leads to posterization and Moiré effects in images, or quantization noise in sound.

Compression must often be applied to media data.

Compression may be lossless or lossy.

Different compression algorithms are applicable to different types of media data. Their effectiveness depends on the characteristics of the data itself.

Digital Representation of Media

Their common representation as collections of bits means that data belonging to all media can be manipulated by programs, combined and integrated into user interfaces. There are established ways of representing images, video, animation, sound and text in bits. We will describe the data representations of all these types of media in detail in later chapters, but we will begin with a summary of their main characteristics.

A media object, such as an image, must be represented in memory while it is being manipulated by a program. It must also be represented on disk, while it is being stored. The internal representations used by programs are of little interest to most users of these programs, as long as they work, but dealing with file formats is something that you will find yourself doing every day.

Earlier we indicated how text can be represented by mapping characters to bit patterns. Text has a special role to play in representing media. It can be considered a medium itself, but because it can carry meaning, text can also be used to represent information in some other medium. For instance, as we will demonstrate shortly, a text file with a particular structure can be used to describe an image. Textual representations are based on languages, which define the allowable form they may take and their meaning. Conforming to a language's well-defined syntax ensures that textual representations can be processed by computer programs. In particular, textual representations can be edited using any general-purpose text editor (although this may not always be the most efficient means of doing so).

Some types of data are better represented by bit patterns that are not intended to be interpreted as characters. Direct representations of this sort, which do not involve an intermediate text-based language, are called **binary** representations. Although they are not linguistic in nature, binary representations invariably have some structure. For example, the first four bytes of a file might be used to store the length of the media data, the second two the version of the format specification applying to the file, and so on. Binary data stored on disk must conform to some *file format* in order to be processed by software, in the same way that textual data must obey the syntax rules of some language.

As a result, there is some imprecision in the way people talk about the types of file containing media data. It is common, for example, to talk about "an SVG file", meaning a file containing text conforming to the syntax of the SVG language, or "a TIFF file", meaning a binary file laid out according to the TIFF format for images. This usually causes no confusion, but you should be aware that what makes a file a TIFF file is the interpretation of its individual bytes, but what makes a file an SVG file is the interpretation of the text that its bytes represent.

Many of the most important file formats are associated with particular programs. For example, one of the most important formats for images is the Photoshop (PSD) file. Other formats are not tied to a particular program in the same way, but can be used as interchange formats, or common standards that can be read by many programs. For example, most image manipulation programs can read JPEG files.

Images

Monitors display pictures as a rectangular array of *pixels* – small, usually square, dots of colour, which merge optically when viewed at a suitable distance to produce the impression of continuous tones. Figure 2.15 shows a digital photograph, together with a detail that has been enlarged so that the pixels making up the image are visible. To display an image on the monitor, the program must set each pixel to an appropriate colour or shade of grey, in order that the pattern of pixels on the screen produces the desired image.

Figure 2.15. *An image made up of pixels*

Different output devices are capable of displaying pixels of different sizes. The pixels printed by a phototypesetter are much smaller than those displayed by an ordinary computer monitor, for example. This means that the phototypesetter will be able to print more pixels per inch (or per millimetre) than the monitor can display. The number of pixels that a device can display in a unit of length is called its *resolution*. (Actually, resolution is a bit more complicated, as we will explain in Chapter 4.) Monitors do not all have the same resolution; many can be adjusted to use a range of resolutions. We often refer to the resolution of an image, by which we mean the resolution at which it will be displayed at its natural or original size. The resolution is often stored with the image data.

A graphics application program must somehow keep an internal model of the image to be displayed. The process of generating a pattern of pixels from a model is called *rendering*. The graphic model will usually take the form of an explicit data structure that holds a description of the image, but it may be implicit in the sequence of calls to the graphics library which are made as the program executes. Where picture data must be persistent (i.e. must live on after the execution of the program, so that the image can be displayed again at a later time, possibly by a different program), a similar model must be kept in a file.

The sequence of events for displaying an image stored in a file begins with a program reading the data from the image file. Image files are often compressed, so the data may have to be decompressed while it is being read. The program then constructs an internal data structure corresponding to the image's description in the file. The low-level operations required to set pixel values are usually performed by a graphics library, which communicates with the display hardware and provides a higher-level interface to the application program, so a program will typically render the image for display by calling functions from a graphics library, supplying arguments derived from its image model.

It is usual to distinguish between two different approaches to graphical modelling: *bitmapped graphics* and *vector graphics*. (You will sometimes see the term *raster graphics* used instead of bitmapped graphics, especially in North America.)

In bitmapped graphics, the image is modelled directly by an array of pixel values. Where it is necessary to emphasize the distinction between these stored values and the physical dots on a display screen, we will call the former *logical pixels* and the latter *physical pixels*. In the simplest case, the logical pixels correspond one-to-one to the physical pixels: the model is a map of the displayed image, as illustrated in Figure 2.16. (We have used 24-bit values, written in hexadecimal notation, to represent the bit patterns for the logical pixels, for reasons that will be made clear in Chapter 5.) Strictly speaking, the array of values is the bitmap, but we often use the name "bitmap" for the image as well.

logical pixels   physical pixels

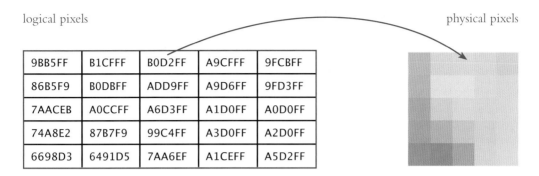

9BB5FF	B1CFFF	B0D2FF	A9CFFF	9FCBFF
86B5F9	B0DBFF	ADD9FF	A9D6FF	9FD3FF
7AACEB	A0CCFF	A6D3FF	A1D0FF	A0D0FF
74A8E2	87B7F9	99C4FF	A3D0FF	A2D0FF
6698D3	6491D5	7AA6EF	A1CEFF	A5D2FF

Figure 2.16. *Simple bitmapped image representation*

In vector graphics, the image is stored as a mathematical description of a collection of individual lines, curves and shapes making up the image. Displaying a vector image requires computation to be performed in order to interpret the model and generate an array of pixels to be displayed. For example, the model will represent a line by storing its end points. When the model is rendered for display, the coordinates of all the pixels lying on the straight line between those end points must be computed so the pixels can be set to the appropriate colour. For persistent storage in a disk file, such a model is often implemented as a program in a graphics language, for example SVG or PDF.

There are profound differences between vector and bitmapped graphics. It should be evident that they will make different demands on your computer system: a bitmapped image must record the value of every pixel, but a vector description can be much more compact. For example, consider the extremely simple picture consisting of a red square with a thick blue outline shown in Figure 2.17. The complete picture is a little over 45 mm square; if it was stored so that it could be displayed on a 72 dpi monitor at its natural size without scaling, it would be 128 pixels square, so its bitmap would consist of $128^2 = 16384$ pixels. If we assume that the intended destination is a monitor capable of displaying millions of colours at a time, then we need 24 bits to distinguish the possible colours (see Chapter 5), which means that each pixel occupies three bytes, and the entire image occupies 48 kilobytes of memory.

Figure 2.17. *A simple vector graphic image*

The same picture, on the other hand, could be stored in the form of a description that specified what kind of shape it was and what its size and the colours of its inside and its outline were. One possible format would be a short document in the SVG graphics language, such as the following, which occupies a total of just 284 bytes:

```
<?xml version="1.0" encoding="utf-8"?>
<!DOCTYPE svg PUBLIC "-//W3C//DTD SVG 1.0//EN"
  "http://www.w3.org/TR/2001/REC-SVG-20010904/DTD/svg10.dtd">
<svg  xmlns="http://www.w3.org/2000/svg">
    <path fill="#F8130D" stroke="#1E338B" stroke-width="20"
     d="M118,118H10V10h108V118z"/>
</svg>
```

(SVG is a textual language, designed to be readable by people, so the characters shown here are stored as bit patterns according to some mapping of the sort we described previously.) Most of this document is red tape that identifies the file as SVG and delimits its structure. An entity written between angle brackets is called an ***element*** in SVG and other languages we will meet in later chapters. Only the two lines consisting of the single element:

```
<path fill="#F8130D" stroke="#1E338B" stroke-width="20"
  d="M118,118H10V10h108V118z"/>
```

actually define the square, in just 86 bytes. The element sets the fill colour to a shade of red, the stroke (outline) colour to blue and the stroke width to 20 pixels; it then defines a path for an imaginary pen to follow in order to draw the square.

The sizes of bitmaps and vectors are affected by the content of images in different ways. The memory requirement for any 45 mm-square, 24-bit colour bitmapped image at a resolution of 72 pixels per inch is 48 kilobytes, no matter how simple or complicated the image may be. In a bitmapped image we always store the value of every logical pixel, so the size of the image and the resolution at which it is stored are the only factors determining the amount of memory occupied, unless we apply compression to the data. In a vector representation, we store a description of all the objects making up the image; the more complex the picture, the more objects there will be, and the larger the description that will be required, but since we do not actually store the pixels, the size is independent of the resolution.

At least as important as the technical differences between the two different types of graphics are their different visual characters and the differences in what you can easily do to your images using each approach.

Figure 2.18 shows two flowers: the first is a simplified vector drawing of a Himalayan poppy, made in Illustrator; the other is a bitmapped image, a digital photograph of a real Himalayan poppy. The bitmap captures details of the flower and its background, and provides a good reproduction of the continuous tones and textures in the scene. The vector drawing has a quite different character,

Figure 2.18. *A vector drawing and a digital photograph*

with clearly delineated shapes, made out of a collection of smooth curves, filled in with flat colour. It has a stylized quality that is typical of work in vector form. A good illustrator working with a professional drawing package could produce much more subtle effects, but vector images are always based on the same elements of filled shapes.

Figure 2.19 demonstrates the difference between the two formats in another way. With the vector representation, it is easy to select the individual shapes – petals, stem, stamens – and move, rotate or otherwise transform them independently. Each element of the picture retains its identity and can be edited as an object because the position and attributes of each object are stored in the image model. To achieve a similar effect with the bitmapped image would require a painstaking process of masking out the required pixels and then retouching the gap where the petal had been removed, because this image is just an array of pixels with no underlying model to indicate which belong to the stem and which to the petals. As a result, editing of parts of the image must be performed by selecting areas, either by painstakingly drawing round them by hand or by semi-automatically (and somewhat unreliably) searching for tonal discontinuities or areas of similar colour. On the other hand, applying a special effect, such as distortion or blurring, to the bitmapped image is simple, whereas producing the same distortion on the vector image could only be done by first transforming it to a bitmapped format, since such effects transform each pixel, possibly using the value of its neighbours, but independently of whether they belong to the same object.

Another major difference between vector and bitmapped graphics is the way they behave when they are scaled, particularly when they are made bigger. If a bitmapped image is to be displayed at greater than its natural size, each logical pixel must be mapped to more than one physical pixel

Figure 2.19. *Transforming the vector image and applying effects to the bitmap*

on the final output device. This can be achieved either by multiplying up the logical pixels, effectively increasing their size (for example, to double the linear dimensions, each pixel value in the model should be used to set a block of four pixels on the display), or by interpolating new pixels in between the stored ones. In either case, the effect will usually be a readily perceptible loss of quality. Since a vector image consists of a description of the component shapes of the picture, not the values of pixels, scaling can be performed easily as a simple mathematical operation, before the pixel values are calculated. As a result, curves, for example, will remain smooth, no matter how much a vector image is blown up, whereas they will become jagged or blurred if a bitmapped image is scaled up. Figure 2.20 illustrates this effect, being details of the two flower images scaled up by a factor of 8. The outlines of the drawing remain smooth, whereas the photograph has become coarse, and the blocks of the original pixels are clearly visible. (See also Figure 2.15.)

Memory requirements, the visual characteristics of the image produced and the possibilities for transformations and effects might influence your decision as to which format to work with. Usually, though, the most important factor will be the source of your image. Photographs from a digital camera, screenshots, scanned images and captured video frames are all inherently bitmaps, because of the way the hardware from which they originate works. Accordingly, for the manipulation and retouching of photographs and for most pre-press work, bitmapped images are the only possible choice. Charts, diagrams and other data visualizations generated by a program from data usually, but not invariably, use vector graphics. Artwork made on a computer can be in either form, with the artist's personal preferences, together with the factors mentioned above and the availability of suitable software, determining the choice.

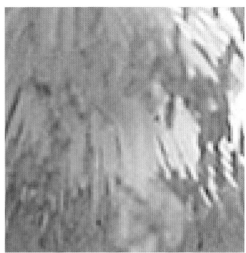

Figure 2.20. *Scaling a vector image (left) and a bitmap (right)*

┌─IN DETAIL──
│
│ Neither of the terms "vector graphics" nor "bitmapped graphics" is entirely
│ accurate. A more accurate term for what we call vector graphics would be
│ "object-oriented graphics", were it not for the potential confusion caused by the
│ meaning of the term "object-oriented" in the field of programming languages.
│
│ Bitmapped graphics does not use bitmaps (except for purely monochrome
│ images), it uses pixel maps, or pixmaps for short, but the term "pixmapped
│ graphics" has never been widely used. You will sometimes see the name
│ "graphics" reserved for vector graphics and "images" used to mean bitmapped
│ images, but this usage tends to cause confusion with the colloquial meaning of
│ these words. Throughout this book we will stick to the terms introduced in the
│ preceding paragraphs, and hope that you will not be misled.
│
└──

Video and Animation

All current methods of displaying moving pictures, whether they are on film or video, broadcast to a television, or stored on a computer system or some digital storage medium, depend on the phenomenon known as *persistence of vision* for their effect. Persistence of vision is a lag in the eye's response to visual stimuli, which results in "after-images" being seen briefly when the stimulus is no longer present. Because of this, if a sequence of still images is presented to our eyes at a sufficiently high rate, above what is called the *fusion frequency*, we experience a continuous visual sensation rather than perceiving the individual images. If consecutive images only differ by a small amount, any changes from one to the next will be perceived as movement of elements within the images. In other words, we see moving pictures. For example, if the pictures making up Figure 2.21 were played back sufficiently rapidly, you would see the left-hand girl jump up and splash her friend with water.

The fusion frequency depends on the brightness of the image relative to the viewing environment, but is around 40 images per second. Below this frequency, a flickering effect will be perceived, which becomes more pronounced as the rate at which successive images are presented is decreased until, eventually, all illusion of motion is lost and we see the sequence of still images for what it really is.

There are two different ways of generating moving pictures. A sequence of frames can be produced by recording actual motion as it is occurring in the real world. Alternatively, we can synthesize the illusion of movement by creating each frame individually. This can be done by photographing single images drawn on paper or painted on acetate sheets, one at a time, by photographing a model, then moving it a little, and photographing it again, by drawing frames within a computer, or by using a program to generate some or all of the frames as they are displayed. We generally use the word *live-action* for sequences recorded from real life, and *animation* for artificially created sequences. Figure 2.21 is an example of live-action; Figure 2.22 is an example of animation.

The word *video* originally referred to systems used for recording television signals to tape (either before or after transmission) and, by extension, to moving pictures recorded using those systems. Digital video was developed to perform the same function by storing the video data using bits. As we have emphasized, once data is stored digitally, it can be manipulated by computers, so digital video is a much more flexible medium than its analogue predecessor and is no longer necessarily connected with television signals or standards, or reserved for professionals and enthusiasts with expensive equipment. It has become the standard means of recording live-action for news-gathering, low-budget film-making and home movies. Digital video cameras are now

Figure 2.21. *Frames from a video sequence*

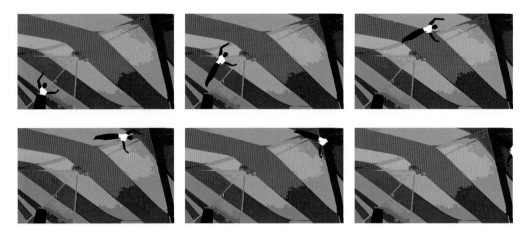

Figure 2.22. *Frames from an animation*

routinely incorporated into mobile phones and laptop computers, and are used for video chatting and creating short ephemeral clips for sharing on the Web and elsewhere.

Video frames are inevitably bitmapped images, because of the way video cameras work – a frame of video is almost the same as a digital photograph. In principle, therefore, video can be represented digitally by extending the representation for still bitmapped images outlined in the preceding section so that a series of images can be stored in a single file and software can play them back one after another at the desired rate. In practice, digital representations of video must be more complex than simple sequences of images combined in a single file, in order to provide a format that can be stored, transmitted and played back efficiently. A major source of complication is the requirement to compress video, which arises because of the size of data that would result if a naïve representation was used.

Each frame of standard-definition video generated by a DV camera is 720 pixels wide. The PAL standard, used for video in most of Europe and Australia, specifies that the frames should be 576 pixels tall and should be displayed at a rate of 25 frames per second. If no compression was applied at all, each pixel would require three bytes, as in a full-colour still image, so each frame would be roughly a megabyte and each second of video would require 25MB, so that a 10-minute clip would occupy just under 15GB. In order to play video in this format over a network, a bandwidth of 200 Mbps is needed. The figures for NTSC video, as used in North America and elsewhere, are the same, since NTSC uses a higher frame rate but smaller frames. Even if the frames are reduced to quarter size, by halving their height and width, the frame rate is lowered, and a standard technique known as chrominance-sub-sampling (to be described in Chapter 6) is applied to reduce the amount of colour information by up to a half, uncompressed digital video inevitably occupies large amounts of storage and requires considerable bandwidth for transmission over networks.

Because of the large quantities of data involved, compression is almost always applied to digital video. Commonly used codecs include **H.264/AVC**, which is part of the **MPEG-4** standard, **On VP6** and **Sorensen Spark**, used by Flash Video, Microsoft's proprietary codec for Windows Media Video, and the Open Source **Ogg Theora** codec. All effective video compression works by not keeping all the data for every frame, but only retaining what is necessary to reconstruct it, as we will explain in Chapter 6. This means that practical video formats are more complicated than a simple sequence of bitmapped images. Since many different codecs are in use, video formats must be flexible enough to accommodate data compressed in different ways. Further complications arise from the need to combine a synchronized soundtrack with video.

Animation may be captured from an external source, such as a series of drawings on paper or cel or a sequence of photographs of a model, or it may be created in a computer. Capturing from an external source will produce a set of bitmapped images. These can be combined in several ways. One useful option is to turn them into video (which is sometimes done automatically at the point of capture), so that they can be played back using the same software and equipment as live-action video. Alternatively, specialized animation formats can be used, which do not have to support all the features demanded by video.

The representation of animation created in a computer offers additional possibilities. For a start, the animation frames can be vector drawings instead of bitmaps. (Simple drawings imported from an external source can also be converted into vector drawings.) This can make for smaller files, and is well suited to the cartoon-style drawing which is used in most popular types of animation. Vector animation is also well suited to interpolation: objects can be drawn in selected key frames, and their motion in the frames in between is calculated by the animation program at the time of creation or by the player program at the time the animation is played back. The animation shown in Figure 2.22 was made in this way – the figure of the human cannonball was drawn once, and his position and angle during the flight was interpolated. The animation format must accommodate both explicitly drawn key frames and the instructions needed to interpolate the frames between them if this approach is employed.

More radically, animation can be generated entirely by a program at the time it is displayed. This way of working is especially suitable for animations that model physical movement: the program can incorporate the appropriate equations and produce motion according to the laws of physics. Alternatively, a program can create animation in response to user input. For such applications there is no explicit representation of the animation. Some or all of the artwork may be created conventionally and stored in a suitable image format, but the motion is implicit in the program. This way, a potentially infinite number of animations can be created from the same artwork.

Sound

Sound is caused by rapid variations of air pressure over time, which are detected by the ears. These variations can be translated into electrical signals, using a microphone, which results in a time-varying waveform, usually called an audio signal. The waveforms for most natural sounds are fairly complex, as Figure 2.23 shows. To convert analogue audio to digital form once it has been turned into an electrical signal, it is only necessary to carry out sampling and quantization as described earlier in the section on *Digitization*.

The Sampling Theorem applies, so it is possible to reconstruct sound accurately from a stream of samples, provided the sampling is done at a high enough rate. The rate of 44,100 samples per second used for CD audio is generally considered to be more than adequate, but higher rates are used in some professional recording formats. Solid state memory card recorders use rates of 48,000, 96,000 or even 192,000 samples per second. Sampling rates are usually expressed in kilo-hertz (kHz), the same units as frequency, so these rates are normally written as 44.1 kHz, 48 kHz, and so on.

Digital audio has been in common use for a long time, first in recording studios, then on CDs. More recently, digital audio files have been made available for download on the Internet and transfer to portable audio players. Digital audio files can be distributed as ***podcasts***, which allow users to subscribe to regularly updated feeds. A podcast is just an RSS feed (described in Chapter 15) with an audio file enclosed.

Almost all audio that is distributed over the Internet is compressed. The best-known form of audio compression is MPEG-2 Layer 3 Audio, universally known as ***MP3***. Although portable music players, such as the iPod, are usually called "MP3 players", MP3 is not the only form of audio compression. In fact, the iPod itself supports a superior compression algorithm called the Advanced Audio Codec, or ***AAC***. The ***Ogg Vorbis*** codec is favoured by the Open Source community.

Because digital audio is nothing more than a stream of numbers, it can be altered using arithmetic operations. This makes applying special effects to digital audio much easier than applying them to analogue audio. Some operations which are difficult or impossible to achieve in the analogue realm are routine with digital audio. In particular, changing the pitch of a note without altering its duration and vice versa are easily achieved by manipulating the number of samples. If a piece of music is slowed down using analogue techniques, the pitch of the notes will drop. If the music has been recorded digitally, it can be slowed down without altering the pitch, just by adding samples. This is somewhat more convenient if it has been slowed down in order to be transcribed, for example. Generally, analogue effects were dependent on the availability of circuits that made desirable modifications to the signal. Digital effects are implemented by programs, and as long as

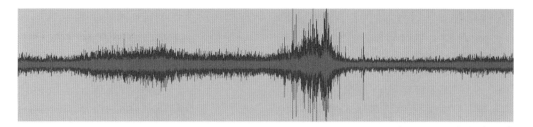

Figure 2.23. *An audio waveform*

it is possible to devise an algorithm that performs the required transformation on the waveform, any effect can be produced digitally.

The ease with which the duration, tempo and pitch of a digitally recorded piece of music can be changed makes it feasible to combine separate pieces into a single composition. The use of samples and loops in this way has opened up many musical possibilities that previously did not exist. Recordings of single notes or parts of notes may be used as samples to allow a single instrument to make the sound of many others. Longer sample loops are combined to build up whole songs.

Text

The basis of the digital representation of text was outlined earlier: for each character we simply choose a number, known as its *code value*, and use that to stand for the character. The realization that text can be represented digitally by mapping characters to numbers is only a first step. For digital text to be useful it is necessary for everybody to agree on the mapping between characters and numbers. That is, we need a standard *character set*, as this mapping is known.

Before we can decide on how to map characters to numbers, we need to decide which characters are going to be mapped. If you live in a predominantly English-speaking country, this may not seem like a particularly difficult decision: the upper and lower-case alphabets, digits and a few punctuations marks and mathematical symbols should suffice for most purposes. For a fairly long time, because of the dominance of English-speaking countries in the computing industries, character sets that worked for these characters were most often used. In particular, the ASCII character set was in almost universal use. However, English (American English, at that) is one of only a small handful of world languages that uses nothing but the 127 characters covered by the ASCII character set.

We will describe the evolution of character sets to accommodate languages that use accented letters and non-Latin scripts in Chapter 9. The result of that evolution is the *Unicode* character set, which is becoming established as the standard for all digital text. In order to allow for all the characters in the alphabets used in China, Korea and Japan, while still remaining efficient for more

ABCDEFGHIJKLMNOP
QRSTUVWXYZ
abcdefghijklmnopqr
stuvwxyz
1234567890

ABCDEFGHIJKLMN
OPQRSTUVWXYZ
abcdefghijklmnopq
rstuvwxyz
1234567890

ABCDEFGHIJKLMN
OPQRSTUVWXYZ
abcdefghijklmnopqrs
tuvwxyz
1234567890

ABCDEFGHIJKLMNOPQRS
TUVWXYZ
abcdefghijklmnopqrst
uvwxyz
1234567890

Figure 2.24. A small selection of fonts

limited applications such as programming languages, practical use of Unicode has introduced an extra level of complexity in the mapping between characters and bytes, but conceptually it remains a simple association between characters and numbers.

The value of characters is not all there is to text, though. When text is printed or displayed on a screen, the precise shape of each character doesn't just depend on which character it is. It is also determined by the *font* that has been used to display it. A font is a set of character shapes, known as *glyphs*, one for each character in an alphabet. Figure 2.24 shows samples of just four of the many thousands of fonts that are available. To display a character – a lower-case letter a, for example – the a-shape from some font must be selected. On modern computer systems, the font is stored as a collection of small vector images in a separate file, and glyphs are displayed to the screen as graphics. This means that a wide selection of fonts can be provided. Much graphic design (and, to a lesser extent, Web design) is concerned with the appropriate choice of fonts to best convey the message in text.

Layout – the way in which text is arranged on the page or screen – is another important aspect of graphic and Web design. Whereas an image can only be displayed in one way, the same words can be arranged in many different ways. As well as the choice of font, the size and weight of the letters and the vertical and horizontal space between words and around blocks of text can vary, making a considerable difference to the appearance of a piece of text and the impression it creates, as Figure 2.25 demonstrates. Notice how the extra space makes the example on the right more readable, while the use of a relatively formal font and straight left and right margins gives an impression of order, while the example on the left, with its typewriter-style font, hyphenation and ragged right

```
MOLOREET VOLOREET EX-
EROS
Etum adionse feuis non
henim ipsusting etum
iriure magna feu feummy
nis augiam, quat.
Minit nibh exer aut au-
gait wisim autpat. Ut
irilit pratisci blam-
conse min ullaorper il
deliquamet, volorer os-
trud te magna at. Upta-
tie dolore doluptat nim
velisci psuscidui tat.
Lum veniatum vel init
lum velit am dolutat,
sissequis numsandreet
at.
```

Moloreet Voloreet Exeros

Etum adionse feuis non henim ipsusting etum iriure magna feu feummy nis augiam, quat.

Minit nibh exer aut augait wisim autpat. Ut irilit pratisci blamconse min ullaorper il deliquamet, volorer ostrud te magna at. Uptatie dolore doluptat nim velisci psuscidui tat. Lum veniatum vel init lum velit am dolutat, sissequis numsandreet at.

Figure 2.25. *Layout and typography*

margin looks comparatively slovenly, while the tight spacing makes it hard to read. (The boxes containing the text for both these examples are exactly the same size.)

The satisfactory display of text thus requires some means of controlling layout. In the simplest case, this is left to the program doing the displaying. Every text file will be laid out in the same way if this arrangement is employed. Any changes to fonts and other aspects of the layout will be made through the program's preferences and will affect every file. Files that do not contain any layout information are called **plain text** files, and the programs used to create and change them are just called text editors. Plain text is invariably used for program source code (see below) but is seldom adequate for text in multimedia.

You are probably familiar with using a word processor to prepare text documents. Word processor documents include special invisible control codes to specify layout and typography. Web pages use a similar approach to layout, but instead of hidden codes they use readable tags (like the ones you saw earlier in our SVG example) to identify the structural elements of the document, and auxiliary stylesheet rules to specify how each element should be laid out. Thus, the text in the source files for a Web page includes not only the textual content that you see when you visit the page, but also additional information that controls how it is displayed.

Tema   Tis   Rolod   Muspi   Merol

DEFT WIDGETS

Lorem ipsum dolor sit amet

Consectetur adipisicing elit

Sed do eiusmod tempor

Incididunt ut labore

Dolore magna aliqua

Lorem ipsum dolor sit amet, consectetur adipisicing elit, sed do eiusmod tempor incididunt ut labore et dolore magna aliqua. Ut enim ad minim veniam, quis nostrud exercitation ullamco laboris nisi ut aliquip ex ea commodo consequat. Duis aute irure dolor in reprehenderit in voluptate velit esse cillum dolore eu fugiat nulla pariatur. Excepteur sint occaecat cupidatat non proident, sunt in culpa qui officia deserunt mollit anim id est laborum.

Lorem ipsum dolor sit amet, consectetur adipisicing elit, sed do eiusmod tempor incididunt ut labore et dolore magna aliqua. Ut enim ad minim veniam, quis nostrud exercitation ullamco laboris nisi ut aliquip ex ea commodo consequat. Duis aute irure dolor in reprehenderit in voluptate velit esse cillum dolore eu fugiat nulla pariatur. Excepteur sint occaecat cupidatat non proident, sunt in culpa qui officia deserunt mollit anim id est laborum.

```
<?xml version="1.0" encoding="UTF-8"?>
<!DOCTYPE html PUBLIC "-//W3C//DTD XHTML 1.1//EN"
    "http://www.w3.org/TR/xhtml11/DTD/xhtml11.dtd">

<html xmlns="http://www.w3.org/1999/xhtml" xml:lang="en">
<head>
    <title>Deft Widgets</title>
    <meta http-equiv="Content-Type"
    content="application/xhtml+xml; charset=utf-8"/>
    <link rel="stylesheet" href="styles.css" type="text/css"
media="screen" title="standard styles" charset="utf-8" />
</head>

<body>
<ul class="navbar">
    <li class="current">Tema</li>
    <li><a href="tis">Tis</a></li>
    <li><a href="rolod">Rolod</a></li>
    <li><a href="muspi">Muspi</a></li>
    <li><a href="merol">Merol</a></li>
</ul>
<div id="content">
    <ul class="sidebar">
        <li>Lorem ipsum dolor sit amet</li>
        <li>Consectetur adipisicing elit</li>
        <li>Sed do eiusmod tempor</li>
        <li>Incididunt ut labore</li>
        <li>Dolore magna aliqua</li>
    </ul>
    <h1>Deft Widgets</h1>
    <p>Lorem ipsum dolor sit amet, consectetur adipisicing elit, sed
do eiusmod tempor incididunt ut labore et dolore magna aliqua. Ut enim
ad minim veniam, quis nostrud exercitation ullamco laboris nisi ut aliquip
ex ea commodo consequat. Duis aute irure dolor in reprehenderit in
voluptate velit esse cillum dolore eu fugiat nulla pariatur. Excepteur sint
occaecat cupidatat non proident, sunt in culpa qui officia deserunt mollit
anim id est laborum.
    </p>
    <p>Lorem ipsum dolor sit amet, consectetur adipisicing elit, sed
do eiusmod tempor incididunt ut labore et dolore magna aliqua. Ut enim
ad minim veniam, quis nostrud exercitation ullamco laboris nisi ut aliquip
ex ea commodo consequat. Duis aute irure dolor in reprehenderit in
voluptate velit esse cillum dolore eu fugiat nulla pariatur. Excepteur sint
occaecat cupidatat non proident, sunt in culpa qui officia deserunt mollit
anim id est laborum.
    </p>
</div>
</body>
</html>
```

```
* {
    margin: 0;
    padding: 0;
    font-size: 100%; }
body {
    font-family: "Lucida Grande", Lucida, Helvetica, sans-serif;
    font-size: medium;
    width: 30em;
    padding: 0 2em;
    border-left: 15em solid #DAB2D5;
    background-color: #DDD;
    margin: auto; }
h1 {
    font-family: Optima, Times, Georgia, serif;
    letter-spacing: 0.5em;
    font-size: 1.1em;
    font-weight: bold;
    text-align: center;
    padding-bottom: 0.8em;
    text-transform: uppercase; }
p {
    text-align: justify;
    padding-bottom: 1em; }
ul.sidebar {
    font-family: Optima, Times, Georgia, serif;
    list-style-type: none;
    float: left;
    margin-left: -15em;
    padding-top: 2.2em;
    width: 12em; }

.sidebar li {
    padding-bottom: 1.2em; }
ul.navbar {
    list-style-type: none;
    padding: 1.5em 0 1em 0;
    margin: 0 0 2em 0;
    border-bottom: 2px dotted #DAB2D5;
    text-align: center; }
.navbar li {
    display: inline;
    padding: 0 1em;
    font-size: 1.2em; }
.navbar li:first-child {
    padding: 0; }
.navbar a {
    text-decoration: none;
    color: inherit; }
.current {
    color: #DAB2D5; }
```

Figure 2.26. *A Web page specified by an HTML document (left) and a stylesheet (right)*

This demonstrates that text can play a dual role in media data. It is not only media data itself, it can also function as a language for describing the structure and appearance of data. On the Web, some version of the markup language HTML defines structure, and the stylesheet language CSS specifies its formatting. Figure 2.26 shows a simple Web page. Below it we have shown the two text files that make up the page's representation. Note that when these are stored on a computer they must be represented by a sequence of character codes, so there are two levels of representation for Web pages.

Text's role as a language does not only apply to text documents. Text-based languages like SVG can be used in the representation of other types of media data too. These languages are usually based on XML, which we describe in Chapter 15. XML itself is stored as plain text. Certain characters, including < and >, are given a special interpretation by programs that process XML, but all the characters themselves are stored as values in some character set (nowadays usually Unicode), so the file can be edited using any text editor.

The **Portable Document Format (PDF)**, developed by Adobe Systems and now an ISO standard, is also often used for text documents. It takes a different approach to representing layout information from that used in Web pages. In a PDF document, the exact position of each glyph is specified. Very little structure is retained: in general, it isn't even possible to tell where words begin and end. Instead, a PDF document contains enough information to be displayed so that it looks exactly as it was originally intended to appear. This makes it an ideal format for distributing electronic books and documents whose layout should be preserved. PDF is primarily a delivery format, therefore: it is not suitable for processing documents, only for displaying them. For this reason, documents are usually created and edited in some other format, such as the proprietary representations used by page layout programs like InDesign, and only turned into PDF when they are finished.

Interactivity

Interactive systems respond to input from their users by doing something. The only way any computer system can do anything is by executing a program, or part of one. As we mentioned previously, programs are ultimately represented as bit patterns, like everything else. These particular bit patterns, called **machine instructions**, cause the computer to execute some operation that is built into its hardware. Each individual instruction only performs a very simple operation, such as adding or comparing two numbers. Useful programs are built out of many such instructions.

Very few people create programs by writing down the bit patterns for each instruction. Instead, they write a description of the computation to be performed using a high-level programming language, which incorporates mathematical and logical notations, in order to be more easily read and written by people, while retaining the precision that is necessary for specifying operations unambiguously.

The processor inside a computer cannot execute programs in their high-level form. The program that is written by a person is often translated into an equivalent sequence of machine instructions, a process known as *compilation*, which is itself carried out by a program known as a *compiler*. An alternative way of executing programs is by *interpretation*. This means that a program called an *interpreter* reads the source version of another program, and carries out the operations it specifies. Interpretation is usually slower than executing compiled code, but it has compensating advantages, notably simplicity of implementation and machine independence.

Interpreters are often used to implement *scripting languages*, which are languages that are used to control the behaviour of some larger program. For example, a scripting language (*JavaScript*) is used on the Web to control the behaviour of a Web browser, making it do things such as change parts of the page it is displaying. A similar language, *ActionScript*, can be used to control the Flash Player. Programs written in these two scripting languages are presently the most important means of providing interactivity in the context of multimedia, but more conventional languages, including ones that are compiled, can be used to manipulate media data and provide multimedia interfaces to any interactive system.

┌─IN DETAIL───

JavaScript and ActionScript look very similar to each other. This is because they are both based on versions of the same language, ECMAScript. ECMAScript only provides a framework for performing computation – doing arithmetic, testing values, repeating loops, calling functions, and so on – but to do its real job of controlling a Web browser or Flash movie, it must be supplemented by a collection of "host objects", which provide an interface to the system being controlled. This collection of objects is called a Document Object Model (DOM). JavaScript is the combination of ECMAScript and the W3C DOM. ActionScript is the combination of ECMAScript and the Flash DOM. (Unfortunately, ActionScript is based on a later version of ECMAScript than that used in JavaScript, so although the two languages are very similar, they are not identical.)

└──

Scripts (as programs written in scripting languages are called) are just text files, whose contents obey the syntactical rules defined by the language in which the script is written. Some scripts may be translated into a more efficient form that is intermediate between the scripting language source and machine code, before being interpreted. These intermediate forms are often called *byte codes*. Like machine instructions, byte codes are bit patterns that cause some operation to be performed. Whereas machine instructions are decoded and executed by hardware, byte codes are decoded and executed by software, in the form of an interpreter. They can therefore be machine-independent, but their execution is more efficient than the interpretation of the source representation of a script.

Metadata

Metadata is data about data. To be practically useful, metadata must be structured, that is, made up of fields each carrying a particular piece of information about the data being described. In fact, most writers define metadata as structured data about data. For example, the metadata about a photograph could include the time and date when it was taken, the GPS coordinates of the place it was taken, the name of the photographer, the exposure time and aperture. Each of these pieces of information could be stored as a separate metadata item or *field*.

Metadata pre-dates computers. Library catalogue cards are a classic example of metadata; the cataloguing in publication information found on the reverse of the title page of most modern books is another. In the latter case, the metadata is carried along with the data it describes, by being allocated a special place in the book and laid out in a standard way. In a similar way, metadata is often included within a file, such as a digital photograph. The file format accommodates metadata items which are structured according to some standard.

Metadata is important for media data because it makes organizing and searching feasible. It isn't really possible for a program to search a collection of images looking for pictures of roses, for instance, because software is not sufficiently good at analysing the content of images, identifying features and relating them to entities in the real world. (People are very good at this, but not so good at dealing with large quantities of data rapidly.) Adding descriptive metadata in a form that can be processed by software makes it possible for programs to search for specific values in certain metadata fields, which allows them to identify the required items.

There are several standards in use defining metadata formats for different kinds of data. *Exif (Exchangeable Image File Format)* files, which are in common use for digital photographs allow extensive metadata to be included. The Exif format supports fields for all of the metadata about photographs mentioned above, as well as many others, which allow almost any technical detail about the camera settings used to take the picture to be recorded. Most digital cameras that create Exif files will attach some metadata to photographs when they are taken.

Another important metadata standard is the *IPTC (International Press Telecommunications Council) Core* specification. The IPTC's main concern is with the exchange of data between news organizations, so the IPTC Core is concerned less with the technical details of the image and more with attribution and rights (who took the picture and who it belongs to); there is therefore little overlap with Exif. Whereas Exif metadata is usually created automatically in the camera, IPTC metadata must usually be added by hand.

Field	Meaning
Title	The name by which the resource is formally known.
Creator	The person, organization or service who made the content of the resource, for instance, the writer of an article or the photographer who took a picture.
Subject	One of the topics of the resource. It is usual to choose keywords from an accepted classification scheme as the value of this field.
Description	This might be an abstract or table of contents, but no special format is required for the description.
Publisher	The publisher is "responsible for making the resource available". This might be a commercial publisher, an academic institution or an individual.
Contributor	A person or organization that has contributed to the content.
Date	This will often be the creation date, but can be used for any date with significance in the resource's life, such as the date of a revised version.
Type	This is not the physical format, but should be a keyword from some controlled vocabulary indicating what sort of resource is being described. Examples from DCMI's vocabulary include "still image", "moving image" or "text".
Format	The media type of the resource. Internet Resource Types ("MIME Types") can be used as the value of this field. Where appropriate, the dimensions will also be included.
Identifier	A unique identifier, such as a URL or ISBN.
Source	If the resource is derived from another, this field is used to identify that source.
Language	The language in which the content is written. The standard ISO language codes should be used for this field.
Relation	The unique identifier for some related resource.
Coverage	An indication of the location, time period, etc. constituting the scope of the resource. For instance, a legal document may only apply in certain locations.
Rights	A statement covering copyright and other rights concerning the resource.

Figure 2.27. *The 15 Dublin Core metadata elements*

The *Dublin Core* metadata standard (ISO 15836:2003) is a very general specification that defines 15 kinds of metadata items, which it calls *elements*. (Generally, we prefer to use the name "field", because "element" has a separate meaning in XML, but here we will follow the standard.) The Dublin Core elements are listed in Figure 2.27. Note that each element is optional, and if present, may appear several times. For example, a document may have more than one subject.

Dublin Core metadata is not tied to any specific concrete representation, and can be used to describe any sort of data, or "resource", as the standard expresses it. The standard is therefore somewhat vague. To make best use of it, some of the elements should only be given values from some controlled vocabulary, that is, a limited set of standard keywords. In some cases, other standards, such as the W3C document defining *Uniform Resource Identifiers* (see Chapter 15), define a suitable format for the values.

Dublin Core metadata is sometimes used on the Web for describing the content of Web pages. In that case, the metadata can be included in HTML documents, using special meta elements. Alternatively, metadata can be held separately from the pages themselves, perhaps in a database. In that case, a more powerful notation can be used: the *Resource Description Framework (RDF)* provides a means of describing relationships using abstract mathematical constructs. RDF metadata may be used written in *RDF/XML*, a metadata language that uses XML as its syntax or embedded in XHTML documents using a collection of attributes known as *RDFa*.

Adobe Systems have defined a subset of RDF/XML, called *XMP (Extensible Metadata Platform)*, which is supported by their widely used Creative Suite programs. The native file formats for these programs permit XMP metadata to be included with the actual data. XMP primarily defines a format for metadata, but the specification includes definitions of "schemas" listing the properties and the allowable types of their values for some important sets of metadata, including Dublin Core and Exif, and several collections for defining metadata related to rights management and workflow, derived from IPTC. (In fact, IPTC is now defined in terms of XMP.)

Tagging represents a less structured approach to metadata. A tag in this context is just a keyword or a short phrase that describes something. (Try not to confuse this sort of tag with the tags used to delimit elements in markup languages.) You might find it helpful to think of adding a tag to something as being like assigning the thing to a category, except that with tags, the same thing can be in many categories. In most tagging systems there is no fixed set of tags – you can just make up your own.

Tagging is popular on Web sites based on social classification of bookmarks, images, video clips, and so on. The theory is that the conglomeration of many different people's tags will provide an intuitively appealing description of the item being tagged.

KEY POINTS

There are established ways of representing images, video, animation, sound and text in bits.

Media data may be represented as a textual description in a suitable language, or as binary data with a specific structural form.

Images are displayed as arrays of pixels and represented using an internal model. Generating the pixels from the model is called rendering.

Images may be modelled as bitmaps or vector graphics.

A bitmap is an array of logical pixels (stored colour values) that can be mapped directly to the physical pixels on the display.

In vector graphics, the image is stored as a mathematical description of a collection of individual lines, curves and shapes making up the image, which requires computation to render it.

Vector graphics are often smaller than bitmaps, are resolution-independent and can be scaled without loss of quality, but they are only suitable for certain sorts of synthetic image, not photographs.

Moving pictures can be created as live-action or animation.

Live-action must be stored as video. Animation may be represented in other more flexible or efficient ways.

Video frames require a lot of storage so video is invariably compressed for delivery.

Sound can be represented as a sequence of samples after digitization.

CD audio is sampled at 44.1 kHz, higher sampling rates are sometimes used.

Audio delivered over the Internet is compressed, often using the MP3 codec.

A character set is a mapping from characters to character codes.

Unicode is a character set capable of representing text in all known languages.

A font is a set of character shapes, called glyphs.

Many aspects of layout must be controlled when text is displayed.

Interactivity is produced by executing a program in response to user input.

In multimedia, programs are often written in a scripting language, such as JavaScript or ActionScript.

Metadata is structured data about data, which may be attached to media files to help with searching and classifying them.

Exercises

Test Questions

1 Identify three phenomena in the natural world that exhibit continuous change. What values would you store to represent each one, and how would digitization affect them?

2 Is the sampling rate of 44.1 kHz used for audio CDs adequate to reproduce musical sounds accurately? Justify your answer.

3 Suppose a piece of film depicting a moving stagecoach is shot at 24 frames per second, and that the wheels are rotating at such a speed that when the film is projected at 24 frames per second the wheels appear to move backwards. What would you expect to see if the same film is projected at (a) 12 frames per second; (b) 30 frames per second; (c) 60 frames per second?

4 Prove (at least to your own satisfaction) that, if the number of bits used to hold a quantized value is doubled, the number of quantization levels is squared.

5 Our argument that no algorithm can achieve compression for all inputs rests on common sense. Produce a more formal proof, by considering the number of different inputs that can be stored in a file of N bytes.

6 Describe three significant differences between vector and bitmapped graphics.

7 For each of the following kinds of image, which would be more suitable, bitmapped images or vector graphics? State the reason for your choice in each case.

(a) Architectural drawings.

(b) Botanical drawings.

(c) Pie charts.

(d) Fingerprints.

(e) A map of the world.

(f) Brain scans.

(g) Illustrations for a children's alphabet book.

(h) A reproduction of the Mona Lisa.

(i) A simple cartoon character, such as Mickey Mouse.

8 Under what circumstances would it be necessary to represent an animation using a video format?

9 How much disk space would be occupied by a 100-minute feature film if it was stored as uncompressed video in PAL or NTSC format? State explicitly any assumptions you make in your calculation.

10 A recent news report about the growth of music download services contrasted "digital music" with CDs. What is wrong with this distinction?

11 Look at a newspaper. Compare and contrast the way fonts and layout are used in news stories and in advertisements.

12 Why are the scripting languages used for interactive multimedia usually interpreted rather than compiled?

13 If you wanted to support tagging and Dublin Core metadata, which Dublin Core element would you use for the tags?

Discussion Topics

1 Digital representations of sounds and images are sometimes accused of being "limited" (e.g. by the number of quantization levels or the sampling rate), and consequently of not being "true" representations. Are analogue representations also limited? Explain your answer and give examples.

2 Unicode can represent nearly a million different characters, but keyboards cannot have that many keys. Discuss ways in which keyboards can be made to accommodate the full range of characters.

3 Suppose Web pages were represented as PDF documents instead of HTML. In what ways would they be different from today's Web pages?

4 For a long time, the Internet Engineering Task Force (IETF) – see the Appendix – stipulated that all standards documents for which they were responsible should be provided online as plain ASCII text files. Why might they have considered this more appropriate than using formatted text?

Practical Tasks

1 A "hex editor" is a program that allows you to open any file and examine the bit patterns it contains. A good one will allow you to display the bytes as numbers or characters. Install a hex editor on your system, if you do not have one already, and look at the contents of some text files and images. In the case of text files, see how the bit patterns correspond to the characters. Pay particular attention to the way characters that are not letters, digits or common punctuation marks are represented.

In the case of image files, can you make any sense of the binary data? Does it help to show the bytes as characters?

2 Investigate the metadata attached to digital photographs and other image files. You can use the Bridge program in the Adobe Creative Suite to look at image metadata.

3 Using a program for processing bitmapped images, such as Photoshop, open a reasonably large digital photograph (several megapixels) that has not previously been processed and experiment with the different JPEG quality settings for export. Determine how much compression of the file size can be achieved without noticeably affecting the quality of the image. If you conclude that the file can be substantially compressed without significant loss of quality, why might you sometimes use a higher quality setting with less compression, or store it in an uncompressed form?

Vector Graphics

■ **Fundamentals**

Coordinates and Vectors. Anti-aliasing.

■ **Vector Objects**

Curves. Paths. Stroke and Fill.

■ **Transformations**

Affine Transformations. Distortion.

■ **3-D Graphics**

3-D Models. Rendering.

Vector graphics provide an elegant way of constructing digital images whose representation is compact, scalable, resolution-independent, and easy to edit. The compact representation permitted by vector graphics has been valued whenever memory, disk space or bandwidth has been limited. These resources are seldom in short supply nowadays, but the simplicity of precise vector drawing still makes it an ideal medium for diagrams, technical illustrations and charts. As we will see in Chapter 7, vectors are also well suited to use in animation.

Although vector graphics has recently been eclipsed by bitmapped representations for two-dimensional images, for three-dimensional work – that is, for images that are constructed as projections of a 3-D model – vector techniques are mandatory, since the use of models made out of the three-dimensional equivalent of pixels ("voxels") is impractical on all but the most powerful equipment.

At the time when most Internet connections were slow, the compactness of vector graphics should have made them particularly attractive for networked multimedia, where the indiscriminate use of bitmapped images can lead to excessive download times because of the large sizes of the image files. Ironically, though, it is only since broadband has become widely available that official and *de facto* standards for vector graphics on the World Wide Web have been produced.

The issue of file formats and languages for vector graphics is a little complicated, because the representations most often used are capable of representing more than just vector graphics. For instance, PDF, developed by Adobe Systems† as a successor to their PostScript language, is primarily a document description language, whose main purpose is to represent documents in such a way that their layout is preserved. To do this, though, PDF must have built-in graphics capabilities that allow it to specify the appearance of pages by describing how to place graphic elements – paths, shapes and fills – on the page. This makes it suitable for use as a vector graphics format. It is, in fact, the native file format of Illustrator - AI files are PDF files with a standard prologue that allows them to be edited in Illustrator.

PDF is not an ideal file format for use on the Web. It attempts to preserve the exact appearance of a document, but Web formats only represent structure, and allow appearance to be defined independently and modified by the browser. It would be possible to use PDF purely for its graphics capabilities, embedding images in HTML documents, but most browsers do not support this. The W3C has defined **SVG (Scaleable Vector Graphics format)** as a standard for Web vector graphics (see Chapter 15). SVG is defined in XML, but in essence, SVG is a derivative of PostScript that

† *Adobe and ISO have been preparing ISO 32000 as an international standard definition of PDF.*

uses the same imaging model but a fixed repertoire of operations and is thus easier to implement, and is more compact for transmission over networks. SVG has been slow to achieve wide acceptance, but browser support for it has been growing steadily.

At the same time, the ***SWF (Flash movie)*** format, originally developed for vector animations using Macromedia's Flash (see Chapter 7), is sometimes also used for still vector images. (After all, a key frame of an animation is a still image.) Although SWF does not have the sanction of the W3C, it has been supported via the Flash Player in the major Web browsers for some years, which gives it *ad hoc* status as a standard. Unlike SVG, which, being XML, is a textual language, SWF is a binary format, so it is highly compact and can be rendered very quickly.

PDF and SVG can be thought of as languages that describe how to draw the shapes that make up a picture. Taking this view further, a vector image can be represented by a program that performs the drawing. Any language can be used for this purpose, provided it can make calls through some API to a library that performs the graphics operations. In particular, in Web browsers that implement the canvas element – an extension that may become part of an HTML standard at some point – scripts in JavaScript can call methods of a graphic object to draw shapes within a Web page. Scripted drawing with the canvas element is another rival to SVG for implementing Web vector graphics.

Fundamentals

In vector graphics, images are built up using shapes that can easily be described mathematically. We expect many readers will be familiar with at least the rudiments of coordinate geometry, the field of mathematics underlying the representation of shapes in vector graphics. For the benefit of readers who may not be used to thinking about shapes and outlines in terms of coordinates and equations, we will begin with a very brief review of the basic concepts.

Coordinates and Vectors

Since an image is stored as a rectangular array of pixels, as we explained in Chapter 2, a natural way of identifying any single pixel is by giving its column and row number in that rectangular array. If we number the columns from left to right, and the rows from the top of the image to the bottom, both starting at zero, then any pixel is uniquely identified by the pair (x,y), called its ***coordinates***, where x is the column number and y the row. In Figure 3.1, the pixel labelled A is at $(3,7)$, while B is at $(7,3)$. The pixel labelled O is at the ***origin*** $(0,0)$.

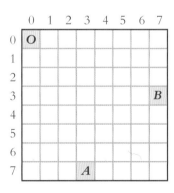

Figure 3.1. *Pixel coordinates*

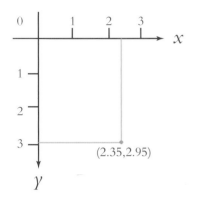

Figure 3.2. *Real coordinates and axes*

The coordinates of pixels in an image must be integer values between zero and the horizontal or vertical dimensions of the image (for x and y coordinates, respectively). For the purposes of modelling shapes in a device-independent way, we need to generalize to a coordinate system where coordinates can have any real value. That is, instead of identifying a finite pixel on a grid, coordinates identify infinitely small geometrical points, so that there are infinitely many of them between, for example, $(0,0)$ and $(1,0)$. Additionally, the values are not restricted to any finite maximum. We also allow negative coordinates: points with negative x coordinates lie to the left of the origin, while those with negative y coordinates lie above it. The vertical line running through the origin, which consists of all the points with an x coordinate of zero, is called the **y-axis**, while the horizontal line through the origin is the **x-axis**. We can label the x- and y-axes with the x and y coordinates of equally spaced points to produce the familiar graph axes, as shown in Figure 3.2, from which coordinates can easily be read off. Vector drawing programs usually allow you to display axes (generally called rulers) along the edges of your drawing.

Although mathematical convention employs a coordinate system where y values increase upwards, graphics languages and formats, such as SVG, SWF and the canvas element, use the opposite convention, with y values increasing downwards. (PDF is an exception: it uses a coordinate system with y increasing upwards.) The same convention is followed by most libraries used for creating two-dimensional (but not three-dimensionsal) vector graphics by programming. The vertical ruler in Illustrator also shows measurements that increase down the document.

IN DETAIL

You should not generally have to concern yourself with the coordinate system used by the output device. Your drawing program will convert from its coordinate system to that of whatever device your drawing is rendered on. This conversion is an example of a coordinate transformation, whereby coordinates in one system (the user space) are transformed into a different one (the device space). Coordinate transformations are inevitable if we are to produce device-independent graphics since, in general, we cannot know the coordinate space of the output device. Another example of a coordinate transformation occurs when an image is rendered in a window on a display. When the image is prepared we cannot know whereabouts on the screen the window will be positioned, so there is no possible way of using absolute screen coordinates to specify the objects in the drawing. Instead, the drawing is prepared in the user coordinate space, and transformed to the device space when it is displayed.

Pairs of coordinates can be used not only to define points, but also to define displacements or movement. For example, to get from A to B in Figure 3.1 we must move 4 units to the right and 4 units up, or, putting it another way, -4 units down (the direction in which values increase). So we can specify the displacement from A to B by the pair $(4, -4)$. In general, for any pair of points $P_1 = (x_1, y_1)$ and $P_2 = (x_2, y_2)$, the displacement from P_1 to P_2 is $(x_2 - x_1, y_2 - y_1)$, which we write as $(P_2 - P_1)$ (see Figure 3.3). When a pair of values is used to specify a displacement in this way, we call it a two-dimensional **vector**. A vector has a direction as well as a magnitude (length). The

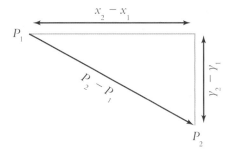

Figure 3.3. *A vector*

vector $P_2 - P_1$ is not the same as $P_1 - P_2$, since moving from P_1 to P_2 is different from moving in the opposite direction from P_2 to P_1. They have the same length but opposite directions.

IN DETAIL

The term "vector graphics" was originally used to refer to the production of images on output devices where the position of the electron beam of a cathode ray tube was controlled directly by setting its (x, y) coordinates, rather than by scanning the screen in a raster pattern. By changing the coordinate values, the beam was made to trace out vectors, hence the name. This type of graphics device only lends itself to the drawing of simple shapes, which is why the name is retained for the shape-based graphics systems we are describing here.

A coordinate system lets us identify points in space. The power of coordinate geometry comes from using letters to represent "unknown" values and using equations in those values to specify relationships between coordinates that characterize geometrical shapes. For example, if (x, y) is any point on a straight line that passes through the origin at an angle of 45° from north-west to south-east, then it must be the case that $x = y$, as you can show using simple geometry. (Remember that we are following the convention that y values increase downwards.) We can use the methods of coordinate geometry to derive equations for arbitrary straight lines, circles, ellipses, and so on. Using such equations we can represent shapes simply by storing the appropriate constants that appear in the equations, since it is these which distinguish between different shapes belonging to the same class.

There is often more than one way of describing the same shape, and practical considerations may lead us to choose one that is not immediately obvious. For example, the equation of a straight line is usually written as $y = mx + c$, where the constants m and c are the slope and intercept, respectively. These two values define the trajectory of the line. However, since we can only use finite segments of lines, it is necessary to store the two end points. The values of m and c can be deduced

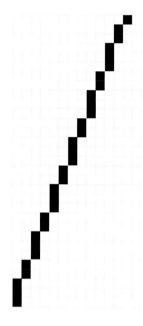

from these. A bit of simple algebraic manipulation, which many readers will have done at school, demonstrates that, if the line passes through (x_1, y_1) and (x_2, y_2), m is equal to $(y_2 - y_1)/(x_2 - x_1)$ and c is equal to $(x_2 y_1 - x_1 y_2)/(x_2 - x_1)$. Hence, the coordinates of the end points are enough on their own to specify both the extent of the line and the constants in its equation, so they alone would be used to represent the line.

When it becomes necessary to render a vector drawing, the stored values are used, in conjunction with the general form of the description of each class of object, to set the values of pixels to form an image of the object described. For example, if a line has end points $(0,31)$ and $(12,1)$, we could compute the y coordinate corresponding to each integer value as x was stepped from 0 to 12. Remember that a pixel's coordinates are always integers (whole numbers), and we cannot set the value of just part of a pixel. This means that the pixel image can only ever approximate the ideal mathematical object which the vector model describes. For example, the line just described has equation $y = 31 - 5x/2$, so for any odd integer value of x, y must be rounded down to get its corresponding integral value. The coordinates of pixels along the line would be $(0,31)$, $(1,28)$, $(2,26)$, $(3,23)$.... To get a continuous line, we set blocks of pixels to the desired colour of the line, but the height of the blocks alternates between 2 and 3 pixels, so that the ideal straight line is approximated by an uneven staircase, as shown in Figure 3.4. This is inevitable, since the output devices we are using are based on a grid of discrete pixels. If the resolution of the output device is low (i.e. the pixels are relatively large) the jaggedness of lines, and other effects due to the same cause, can become offensive. This phenomenon is colloquially known as "staircasing" or, more colourfully, "the jaggies".

Figure 3.4. *Approximating a straight line*

Anti-aliasing

The process of rendering a vector object to produce an image made up of pixels can usefully be considered as a form of sampling and reconstruction. The abstract line that we would like to draw is a continuous signal – the x and y coordinates can vary infinitesimally – which has to be approximated by a sequence of pixel values at fixed finite intervals. Seen in this light, jaggies are a form of aliasing caused by undersampling. This is consistent with the common-sense observation that as the resolution of the output device increases – that is, as we sample at a higher rate – the individual pixels get smaller, so that the jagged effect becomes less noticeable.

You will recall from Chapter 2 that it is necessary to sample at a rate greater than twice the highest frequency in a signal in order to reconstruct it accurately, and that high frequencies are associated with abrupt changes. If an image contains a sharp hard-edged boundary, its brightness or colour will change directly from one value to another crossing the boundary without any intermediate gradation. The representation in the (spatial) frequency domain of such a discontinuity will include infinitely high frequencies. Consequently, no sampling rate will be adequate to ensure perfect reconstruction. In other words, jaggies are always possible, no matter how high the resolution that is used for rendering a vector shape.

In any case, practical and financial considerations impose a limit on the available resolution. In particular, vector graphics that are used in multimedia presentations will usually be rendered on a monitor with a resolution between 72 and 160 dots per inch, and aliasing may be readily visible. To reduce its impact a technique known as anti-aliasing is often employed.

Looking back at Figure 3.4, you will see that the staircase effect is a result of the pronounced contrast between black and white pixels. We can soften the effect by using intermediate grey values for some pixels. In terms of the frequency domain representation, we are removing the spurious high frequencies, and replacing them with lower frequencies. We cannot simply tone down the black pixels to produce a grey line instead of a black one; we want to try to use a range of greys to somehow convey to the eye and brain of someone looking at the displayed line an appearance of smoothness that cannot actually be achieved by the finite pixels.

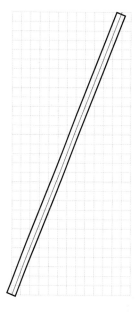

Figure 3.5. *The single pixel approximation to a straight line*

If we did not have to be concerned about the orientation of the pixel grid, at best we could produce a smooth line one pixel wide, as shown in Figure 3.5. Our original attempt at rendering the line on the basis of its defining equation had the effect of setting to black those pixels whose intersection with this one-pixel-wide rectangle was at least half the area of the pixel. Anti-aliasing is achieved by colouring each pixel in a shade of grey whose brightness is proportional to the area of the intersection, as shown in Figure 3.6. The number of pixels that are no longer white is greater than before, but if we take the grey pixels and multiply the area of each one by the value used to colour it, the total amount of greyness, as it were, is the same as that produced by only using a single black level to colour the original collection of pixels. At this magnification the result looks fairly incoherent, but if you hold the book at arm's length it should be apparent that the jaggedness has been subdued somewhat. At normal viewing resolutions anti-aliasing can significantly reduce aliasing effects, albeit at the expense of a certain fuzziness.

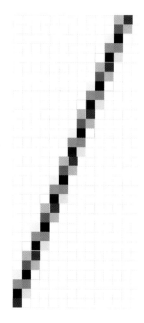

Figure 3.6. *Anti-aliased line*

Vector Objects

When using a drawing program or vector graphics language, you must build up your artwork from the primitive objects it provides, which are generally shapes with a simple mathematical representation that can be stored compactly and rendered efficiently. Usually the repertoire of shapes is restricted to rectangles and squares (possibly with rounded corners), ellipses and circles, straight lines, polygons and a class of smooth curves, called Bézier curves, to be described shortly. Spirals, stars and other more esoteric shapes are sometimes supplied too. Shapes can be drawn with or without outlines, which can be coloured and may be of any width, and they can be filled with colour, patterns or gradients. Because the program works with a description of the shape, not a map of its pixels, it is easy to move, rotate, scale and skew shapes when you are creating and editing vector graphics.

It may sound as if vector programs are very limited in their capabilities, but they can be used to achieve complex and subtle effects, especially once you understand how to work with Bézier curves. The more powerful vector drawing programs support elaborate ways of decorating outlines and filling shapes, which can be used to produce subtle and interesting artwork. Vector drawing programs must be approached in a different way from a freehand drawing medium, though.

Generally, the way in which a drawing program allows you to work with shapes is a reflection of the way in which those shapes are represented in graphics files. For example, in Illustrator you draw a line by selecting a pen tool and clicking the mouse or pressure-sensitive pen at each end of the line: internally, a line can be represented by the coordinates of its end points. In SVG, which might be generated by the drawing program, a line can be represented by a line element, with the end points' coordinates as its attributes, such as `<line x1="300" y1="0" x2="0" y2="300"/>`.

Whereas almost all vector drawing programs provide the same set of tools, which are used in much the same way for drawing shapes, there are different ways of representing most shapes. For instance, a rectangle whose sides are parallel to the axes can be drawn by selecting the rectangle tool, holding down the mouse button where you want one corner, and dragging to the opposite corner. A rectangle can obviously be completely described by the coordinates of its opposite corners, where the mouse button is pressed and where it is released. In SVG, it may be represented as a rect element, which has attributes defining the coordinates of the top left corner, the width and the height – which can easily be computed from the coordinates of the bottom right corner. Alternatively, as the SVG example in Chapter 2 illustrated, a rectangle can be represented as a sequence of four straight line segments. (See Figure 3.7.) As well as being an alternative to the rect element in SVG, this form of representation is used for rectangles in PDF and SWF. Again, it should be clear that the necessary values for drawing each side of the rectangle can be deduced from the coordinates of its corners.

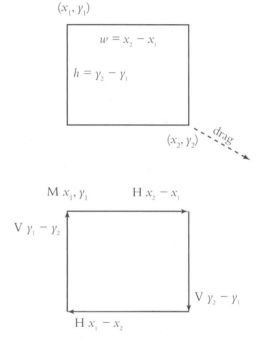

Figure 3.7. *Drawing a rectangle*

Ellipses can be drawn by selecting the appropriate tool and dragging from one point on the perimeter to the opposite point. A pair of points is sufficient to determine the shape and position of the ellipse, and their coordinates can be transformed into one of many convenient representations of the object. For example, in SVG, the ellipse element's attributes record the coordinates of the ellipse's centre and the values of its two radii, for example, `<ellipse cx="70" cy="35" rx="70" ry="35"/>`, which can be deduced from the coordinates of the mouse click and release, as shown in Figure 3.8.

(x_1, y_1)

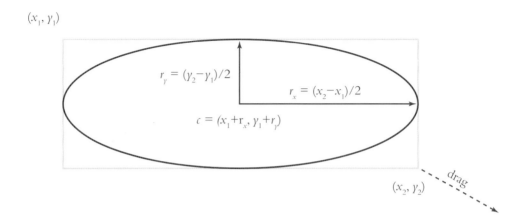

$r_y = (y_2 - y_1)/2$

$r_x = (x_2 - x_1)/2$

$c = (x_1 + r_x, y_1 + r_y)$

(x_2, y_2)

drag

Figure 3.8. *Drawing an ellipse*

Squares and circles are special cases of rectangles and ellipses, respectively, and so do not need any special representation of their own. It is helpful when drawing to be able to ask the program to restrict rectangles and ellipses to squares and circles. In Illustrator this is done by holding down the shift key while using the rectangle or ellipse tool.

Curves

Lines, rectangles and ellipses are sufficient for drawing many sorts of technical diagrams (particularly when your lines can be decorated with arrowheads, as they can be in all professional drawing programs). Less constrained drawing and illustration requires more versatile shapes, which are supplied by *Bézier curves*.

Bézier curves are a class of curve that have several properties which make them especially useful for vector graphics. A Bézier curve is completely specified by an ordered set of points, called its *control points*. The first and last control points are the curve's *end points*, where it starts and finishes. The entire curve will lie within the polygon constructed by joining the control points with straight lines. This polygon is called the curve's *convex hull*. (Foley *et al.*, in their book *Computer Graphics*, suggest helpfully that you think of the convex hull as being the polygon formed by putting a rubber band around the points. The sides do not necessarily connect the control points in order.) The line between the starting end point and the next control point is a tangent to the curve, and so is the line between the final end point and the preceding control point.

The *degree* of the Bézier curve is one less than the number of control points, so a curve with three control points has degree 2, one with four control points has degree 3, and so on. A Bézier curve of degree 1 is a straight line.

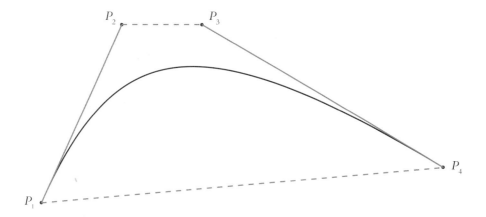

Figure 3.9. *A cubic Bézier curve*

Bézier curves of degree 3, commonly called "cubic Bézier curves", are the type most commonly found in vector graphics. They have just four control points: as always, two are the end points. The other two, which do not usually lie on the curve itself, are called ***direction points***. The name indicates the purpose of these points: being on tangents to the curve, they show the direction in which it sets off from each end point. This is shown in Figure 3.9: P_1 and P_4 are the end points of the curve, P_2 and P_3 are its direction points, and you can see that the curve is accurately described by saying that it begins at P_1, setting off towards P_2, and curving round so that it arrives at P_4 from the direction of P_3, staying within the quadrilateral convex hull $P_1P_2P_3P_4$ throughout.

The lengths of the lines from each end point to its neighbouring direction point determine how wide a sweep the curve makes. You can think of the lengths of these lines as representing the speed with which the curve sets off towards the direction point: the faster it goes, the further out it will curve.

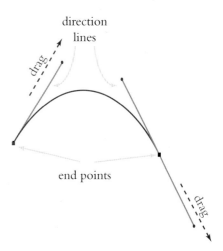

This characterization of the curve is the basis for the way Bézier curves are drawn interactively. After selecting the appropriate tool (usually a pen), you click at the first end point and then drag out towards the first control point, as if you were pulling the curve towards it. You will usually see a ***direction line*** showing you how far you have pulled. In most applications, for reasons that will be explained in the next section, the direction line usually extends away from the end point both in the direction you drag and symmetrically in the opposite direction.

Figure 3.10. *Drawing a curve with the pen tool*

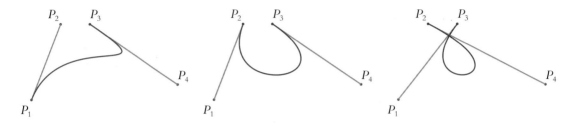

Figure 3.11. P_1, P_2, P_4, P_3 **Figure 3.12.** P_2, P_1, P_4, P_3 **Figure 3.13.** P_3, P_1, P_4, P_2

Once you have the first one right, you click at the point where you want the curve to end, and drag away from the direction point (see Figure 3.10). You will see the curve being formed as you move the cursor. If you do not like the result when you have finished, you can subsequently select any of the control points and drag it around to change the shape and extent of your curve. For more information on drawing Bézier curves, consult our book *Digital Media Tools*.

You can construct a cubic Bézier curve using any set of four control points, but the result is not necessarily going to be useful or lovely. Nor is it always obvious (until you have acquired some experience using these curves) exactly what the curve built from any four control points is going to look like. Figures 3.11 to 3.13 show curves produced from the same set of points as were used in Figure 3.9, but in different orders.

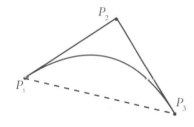

Figure 3.14. *A quadratic Bézier curve*

Bézier curves of degree 2 are called "quadratic Bézier curves". They only use one direction point, so their convex hull is a triangle, as shown in Figure 3.14. Quadratic Bézier curves are less flexible than cubic ones so they are not often used in drawing programs, but having one fewer control point makes them more compact to store, so they are preferred in some graphics formats where small files that are quick to download are wanted. In particular, SWF uses quadratic Bézier curves – even though the Flash program normally used for creating SWF graphics lets you draw cubic curves with a conventional pen tool, these are approximated by quadratic curves in the SWF that it generates. Quadratic Bézier curves are also used in TrueType fonts (see Chapter 9).

SWF is the only major vector format that does not support cubic Bézier curves. SVG supports both cubic and quadratic Bézier curves, while PDF only supports cubic curves. In this respect, PDF is following its predecessor, PostScript. In fact, PostScript has been so influential that the term "Bézier curves" is often understood to refer exclusively to cubic Bézier curves. Curves of higher degree are not often used in two-dimensional graphics. All formats support Bézier "curves" of degree 1 – the use of the pen tool to draw straight lines as well as curves is not coincidental.

Paths

A single Bézier curve on its own is rarely something you want in a drawing. Except in stylized applications for which rectangles, ellipses and straight lines serve adequately, we need to be able to draw a variety of irregular curves and shapes, such as those making up the petals and stamens of the poppy that was illustrated in Figure 2.18. In principle, because the pixels on monitors and printers are finite in size, any shape, no matter how curvaceous, can be approximated as well by a collection of straight lines as by any other method. However, in practice we need to use a lot of very short lines to produce acceptable approximations to curved shapes. We thus lose much of the advantage of vector graphics, inasmuch as our descriptions of shapes become large, unwieldy, inefficient to render and difficult to work with and edit interactively.

What makes Bézier curves useful is the ease with which they can be combined to make more elaborate curves and irregular shapes. Remember that a Bézier curve with control points P_1, P_2, P_3 and P_4 approaches its end point P_4 from the direction of P_3. If we construct a second curve with control points P_4, P_5, P_6 and P_7 (so that it is joined to the original curve at P_4), it will set off from P_4 in the direction of P_5. Provided we ensure that $P_3P_4P_5$ is a straight line, the curve segments will both be travelling in the same direction through P_4, so there will be a smooth join between them, as shown on the left of Figure 3.15. The join on the right is smoother still, because we have made sure that the length of the direction lines is the same on each side of P_4. If you think of the line as a trajectory through space, this ensures that it passes through the shared end point at a constant velocity, whereas, if we only make sure the three points are in a straight line, the direction is constant but the speed changes.

The smoothness of joins when control points line up and direction lines are the same length is the reason behind the display of direction lines in drawing programs. When you drag away from an end point, as we saw earlier in Figure 3.10, direction lines are displayed both to and from it. In other words, you are shown two direction points: one belonging to the curve you are

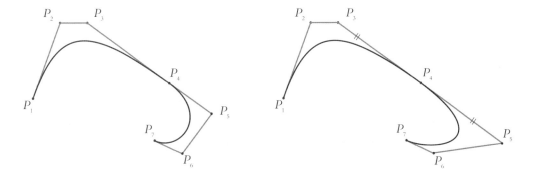

Figure 3.15. *Joining two Bézier curves*

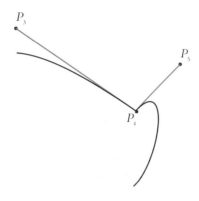

Figure 3.16. *A corner point*

just finishing, the other which could belong to a new curve that joins smoothly on to the end of it. Thus, you can rapidly build up compound curves using a sequence of dragging movements at the points where you want Bézier segments to join.

Sometimes you will want your curve to change direction instead of continuing smoothly. To do this you simply need to arrange that the direction lines of adjacent segments are not lined up (see Figure 3.16). In a vector drawing program, some expedient is required to break out of the default behaviour of smoothly joining curves. In Illustrator, for example, you hold down the **option** (or **alt**) key after creating the direction lines at a point; you can then drag the direction point for the new curve segment round to where you want it, in order to create an abrupt corner. By mixing clicking and dragging it is possible to combine curves and straight lines in arbitrary ways.

Some additional terminology is used to talk about joined curves and lines. A collection of lines and curves is called a ***path***. If a path joins up on itself, it is said to be ***closed***, otherwise it is ***open***. Figure 3.17 shows an open and a closed path. Open paths have end points, closed paths do not. Each individual line or curve is called a ***segment*** of the path; the points where segments join (the original end points of the segments) are called the path's ***anchor points***.

Because cubic Bézier curves can be drawn efficiently and they are so good at approximating other curved shapes, they are frequently used as the only curve-drawing primitive in graphics languages, even though programs generating documents in those languages may provide drawing tools for other shapes. In particular, PDF does not have any primitive operations for drawing anything but line and curve segments. Every object is built as a path made up of such segments. (In contrast, SVG has elements for all of the primitive shapes we described earlier.) This means that it is not

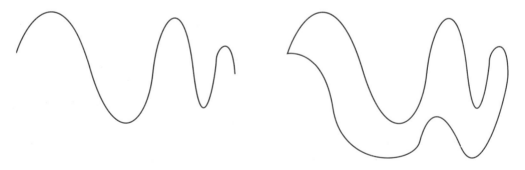

Figure 3.17. *An open path (left) and a closed one (right)*

actually possible to represent a circle precisely in PDF, but four cubic Bézier curve segments can approximate a circle to within less than 0.1%, which is more than accurate enough to look like a perfect circle. Approximating a circle with quadratic Bézier curves requires more segments.

Stroke and Fill

A path, strictly speaking, is an abstract mathematical entity: just as points are infinitesimally small, so a path is infinitesimally thin. Although we have talked about drawing shapes and curves, and shown you pictures of paths, you cannot really see a path. You can, however, use it as a specification of something you can see. You can do this in two different ways. Either you apply a ***stroke*** to the path, making it visible as if you had traced it with ink or some other medium, or you treat the path as the outline of a shape, and ***fill*** it, as if with ink or paint. Or you can do both. Since computer graphics is not bounded by the physical limitations of real art materials, you can stroke or fill paths with more elaborate things than flat colour, such as patterns or gradients.

Practically, you have to be able to see your path while you are drawing it, of course, so drawing programs show you the path as a thin stroke. Once it is complete, each path segment is stroked or filled straight away, so you can see what you are doing. Subsequently, you can select the path and change its stroke at any time.

Consider first applying a stroke to a path. Like physical strokes on paper, the strokes applied by a drawing program have characteristics, such as weight and colour, which determine their appearance. These characteristics can be set and changed by the user of a drawing program. The weight is usually set by specifying the width of strokes numerically, in whatever units are convenient. Specification of colours is more complex, and is described in Chapter 5.

It is customary for drawing programs to support dashed strokes as well as solid ones. Ideally, the length of dashes and of the gaps between them can be specified. Again, this is normally done by the user entering numerical values in appropriate units.

A more subtle feature of strokes is the shape of their ends – the line cap. If a stroke has any appreciable thickness, cutting it off square at the ends with a butt cap may produce an undesirable and ugly effect. It may be preferable to use a round cap, where the line is finished off with a filled-in semicircle built across its end. A third option is to use a projecting cap, with the stroke continued beyond the end point of the path by half the width, so that the weight of the stroke relative to the path is the

Figure 3.18. *Line caps*

same in all directions. Figure 3.18 shows the difference between the three types of cap. The end points of all three fat horizontal lines are on the thin vertical lines. These three line cap options were provided by PostScript, and have been incorporated into PDF and SVG, and are supported by drawing programs like Illustrator.

Combining different line caps with dash patterns provides a range of effects, as shown in Figure 3.19.

Joins at corner points also need consideration, because wide lines can only meet cleanly if they do so at 90°; when they meet at any other angle an unsightly gap or overlap will result. This can be removed in several ways. The three styles of line join provided by Illustrator are a mitre – as in a picture frame, the outside edges of the lines are extended to meet at a point; round – a circular arc is used to produce a rounded corner; and bevel – the segments are finished off square where they join, and the resulting notch is filled in with a triangle to produce a flat ended joint. If mitred joins are used on segments that meet at a very narrow angle, long projecting spikes will result. To avoid this, a limit can be specified, and if the ratio of the spike's length to the stroke width exceeds it, mitres will be replaced by bevels. Figure 3.20 illustrates the different joining styles.

As we noted earlier, some drawing programs can apply strokes that simulate natural media, such as charcoal or painted brush-strokes, or special effects, such as ribbons and Celtic designs. This is done by stretching an image along the line, though, not by applying a stroke to it directly.

Figure 3.19. *Dashed effects*

As well as applying a stroke to a path, you can use it as an outline and fill it. In principle you can only fill a closed path, but most drawing programs also allow you to fill an open path – the filling operation implicitly closes the path with a straight line between its end points.

Mitre

Rounded

Bevel

Figure 3.20. *Joining styles*

The simplest fill is a single colour, and this is often all that is required. When a fill (or, indeed, a stroke) is applied it completely obscures anything underneath it. This applies to a white fill as much as it does to any colour. If you place a shape on a white background and fill it with white, it will seem to be unfilled, but if it overlaps any other shape it will obscure it. To make an unfilled shape, you must explicitly set its fill to none.

Normally, there is no mixing of overlaid colours, as you would expect if you were using watercolour paints for example. This means that, among other possibilities, you can use a shape filled with the background colour to knock out areas of objects underneath it. Recently, the better vector drawing programs have allowed users to set the transparency of an object, allowing anything beneath it to show through partially. When this is done it makes sense to consider combining the colours of the overlapping objects in various different ways, using blending modes – an established technique in bitmapped images, as discussed in Chapter 4. SWF, SVG and PDF all support transparency, with PDF having the most elaborate support for blending modes.

More interesting and sometimes more attractive effects than those permitted by solid or semi-transparent colours can be produced by using **gradient fills** and **patterns**. Figure 3.21 shows some basic examples of gradient fills. This type of fill is characterized by a gradual transition between colours or tones. In the simplest case – a **linear gradient** – the colours at each end of a region are specified, and a smooth blend of intermediate colours is generated in between.

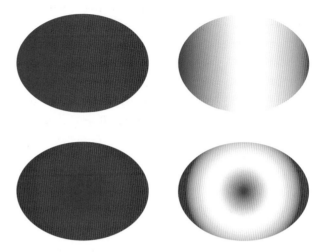

Illustrator provides controls to let you specify intermediate colours, adjust the midpoint of the gradient (where the two colours being

Figure 3.21. *Linear (top) and radial (bottom) gradient fills*

blended are of equal intensity) and the line along which the gradient varies, to get more complicated fills, such as the ones on the right of Figure 3.21. An alternative form of blending, shown at the bottom of Figure 3.21, has the colour varying outwards from a centre point to the outside of the fill. This is called a **radial gradient**.

The more sophisticated gradients used in the picture on the right of Figure 3.22 were created using Illustrator's gradient mesh tool, which allows the designer or artist to set up a two-dimensional mesh of points (shown on the left of the figure), and specify the colours at each mesh point; the colours are blended in the spaces between the mesh points. The shape of the mesh can be adjusted dynamically until the desired effect is achieved. Meshes of this type, which blend in two dimensions, can only be used if the graphics format being generated has adequate support for them. PDF allows the use of very flexible gradient objects, with several different types of blending geometry. SVG and SWF only support linear and radial gradients.

Gradient fills are widely used in artwork created in vector drawing programs, and contribute to the characteristic "air-brushed" look of much of the graphic design that is produced using these programs.

Pattern fills, as the name suggests, allow you to use a repeating pattern to fill in an area, as shown in Figure 3.23. Patterns are built out of elements called tiles. A tile is just a small piece of artwork,

Figure 3.22. *Gradient mesh*

made using the facilities provided by your drawing program (possibly including the facility to import bitmaps as objects, as described later). The name embodies the analogy normally employed for describing how an area is filled with a pattern. Imagine that the artwork is rendered onto a rectangular ceramic tile, such as you might use in your bathroom. Copies of the tile are arranged in rows and columns parallel to the x- and y-axes, butted together as if by a skilled tiler. The resulting pattern is clipped to the area being filled.

Constructing tiles that join seamlessly requires a certain amount of skill – in graphics as in bathroom design. Tiles may be used to produce geometrically patterned areas, such as might be appropriate for drawing textiles or wallpaper (or bathrooms), but they can also be designed so that they produce textured effects. Pattern fills are often used as backgrounds.

Some drawing programs allow you to use patterns to stroke paths – in order to produce a textured outline, for example. This is more difficult than using patterns as fills, because the tiles should be arranged perpendicular to the path, not horizontally. This in turn makes it difficult to get tiles to go round corners, so a pattern intended for tiling a path must include special corner tiles.

If you want to fill a path, you need to know which areas are inside it. For simple shapes, this is a trivial question, but a path may be arbitrarily complex, crossing itself several times. The object at the top left of Figure 3.24 comprises a single path. Which areas are inside it, and which outside?

There is no absolute answer; two different fill rules embodying different interpretations of the concept of "insideness" have equal validity and are supported by PDF and SVG. The top pair of shapes in Figure 3.24 shows one answer to the question, based on the ***non-zero winding number rule***, which may be expressed as an algorithm as follows. To determine whether a point is inside a path, draw a (conceptually infinite) line from the point in any direction. Start by setting the winding number to zero. Follow the constructed line, and every time the path crosses it from left to right, add one to the winding number; every time the path crosses from right to left, subtract one from the winding number. After all the crossings have been counted, if the winding number is zero then the point is outside the path, otherwise it is inside. Note that this algorithm depends on the path's having a direction, which will depend on the order in which anchor points were added to it.

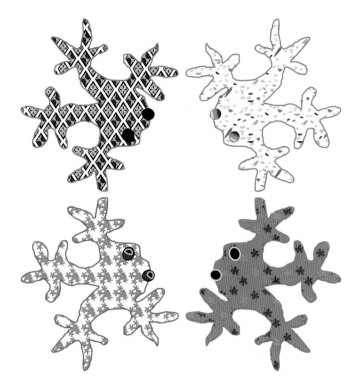

Figure 3.23. *Pattern fills*

An alternative way of distinguishing the inside of a path from its outside is the ***even-odd rule***. Again, to determine whether a point is inside the path, a line is constructed from it, extending in any direction. The number of path segments crossing the line is counted. If it is odd, the point is inside, if it is even, it is outside.

For many shapes, including our example at the top of Figure 3.24, both rules give the same result, but in some cases they will define the inside differently. The lower pair of shapes in Figure 3.24 shows a classic example.

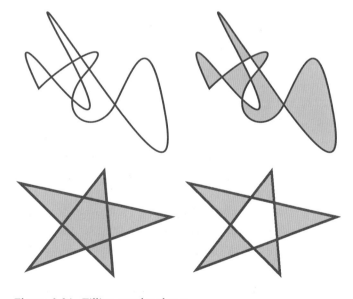

Figure 3.24. *Filling complex shapes*

KEY POINTS

Drawing programs and vector graphics languages provide a basic repertoire of shapes that can easily be represented mathematically.

The commonest shapes are rectangles and squares, ellipses and circles, straight lines and Bézier curves.

Bézier curves are smooth curves that can be specified by an ordered set of control points; the first and last control points are the curve's end points.

A cubic Bézier curve has four control points: two end points and two direction points.

The sweep of a Bézier curve is determined by the length and direction of the direction lines between the end and direction points.

Cubic Bézier curves are drawn by dragging direction lines with a pen tool.

Quadratic Bézier curves only have a single direction point. They are the only Bézier curves supported by SWF. PDF and SVG provide both cubic and quadratic Bézier curves.

Bézier curve segments can be combined to make smooth paths.

A closed path joins up on itself, an open path does not.

If two curves join at a point and their direction lines through that point form a single line, the join will be smooth.

The points where curve segments join are the path's anchor points.

Apply a stroke to a path to make it visible, specifying the width and colour.

Fill closed paths with colours, gradients or patterns.

Use a fill rule to determine which points are inside a path.

Transformations

The objects that make up a vector image are stored in the form of a few values that are sufficient to describe them accurately: a line by its end points, a rectangle by its corners, and so on. The actual pixel values that make up the image need not be computed until it is displayed. It is easy to manipulate objects by changing these stored values. For example, if a line runs parallel to the x-axis from (4,2) to (10,2), all we need do in order to move it up by 5 units is add 5 to the y coordinates of its end points, giving (4,7) and (10,7), the end points of a line running parallel to the x-axis, but higher up. We have transformed the image by editing the model that is stored in the computer.

Affine Transformations

Only certain transformations can be produced by changing the stored values without altering the type of object. For instance, changing the position of just one corner of a rectangle would turn it into an irregular quadrilateral, so the simple representation based on the coordinates of the two corners could no longer be used. Transformations which preserve straight lines (i.e. which don't bend or break them) and keep parallel lines parallel are the only ones that can be used to maintain the fundamental shape of an object. Transformations that behave in this way are called *affine transformations*.

The most important affine transformations are *translation* (moving the object in a straight line), *scaling* (changing its dimensions), *rotation* about a point, *reflection* about a line and *shearing* (a distortion of the angles of the axes of an object). These transformations are illustrated in Figure 3.25. Any modern drawing program will allow you to perform these transformations by direct manipulation of objects on the screen. For example, you would translate an object simply by dragging it to its new position.

Figure 3.25 illustrates another feature of all vector graphics programs. Several objects – in this case, four coloured squares – can be grouped and manipulated as a single entity. Grouping may be implemented entirely within the drawing program, as a convenience to designers; it is also supported within some graphics languages, including SVG. In a related feature, some programs and languages allow an object or a group of objects to be defined as a *symbol*, which is a reusable entity.

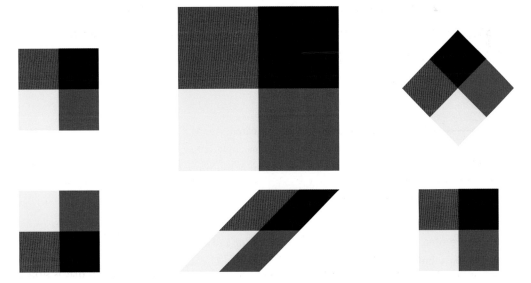

Figure 3.25. *An object being scaled, rotated, reflected, sheared and translated*

Instances of a symbol can be created, all of which refer to the original. If the symbol is edited, all instances of it are updated to reflect the changes. (Symbols behave much like pointers.)

Briefly, the operations which achieve the affine transformations are as follows.

Any translation can be done by adding a displacement to each of the x and y coordinates stored in the model of the object. That is, to move an object Δx to the right and Δy upwards, change each stored point (x,y) to $(x + \Delta x, y + \Delta y)$. Negative Δs move in the opposite direction.

Scaling is performed by multiplying coordinates by appropriate values. Different factors may be used to scale in the x and y directions: to increase lengths in the x direction by a factor of s_x and in the y direction by s_y, (x,y) must be changed to $(s_x x, s_y y)$. (Values of s_x or s_y less than one cause the object to shrink in the corresponding direction.) Thus, to double the size of an object, its stored coordinates must be multiplied by two. However, this has the effect of simultaneously displacing the object. (For example, if a unit square has its corners at $(1,2)$ and $(2,1)$, multiplying by two moves them to $(2,4)$ and $(4,2)$, which are the corners of a square whose side is of length 2, but it is now in the wrong place.) To scale an object in place, the multiplication must be followed by a suitable, easily computed displacement to restore it to its original position.

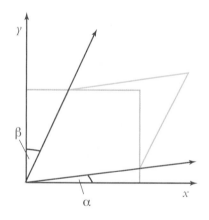

Figure 3.26. *Skewed axes*

Rotation about the origin and reflection about an axis are simple to achieve. To rotate a point (x,y) around the origin in a clockwise direction by an angle θ, you transform it to the point $(x\cos\theta - y\sin\theta, x\sin\theta + y\cos\theta)$ (which you can prove by simple trigonometry if you wish).

To reflect it in the x-axis, simply move it to $(x,-y)$; in the y-axis, to $(-x,y)$.

When an object is sheared, it is as if we took the x-axis and skewed it upwards, through an angle α, say, and skewed the y-axis through an angle β (see Figure 3.26). You can show that the transformation can be achieved by moving (x, y) to $(x + y\tan\beta, y + x\tan\alpha)$.

Applying these operations to all the points of an object will transform the entire object. The more general operations of rotation about an arbitrary point and reflection in an arbitrary line require more complex, but conceptually simple, transformations. The details are left as an exercise.

┌─ IN DETAIL ───┐

Mathematicians will be aware that any combination of translation, scaling, rotation, reflection and skewing can be expressed in the form of a 3×3 transformation matrix

$$T = \begin{bmatrix} a & c & e \\ b & d & f \\ 0 & 0 & 1 \end{bmatrix}$$

To be able to express any transformation, including translation, as a matrix product, a point P = (x, y) is written as the column vector

$$\begin{bmatrix} x \\ y \\ 1 \end{bmatrix}$$

(P is said to be specified using "homogeneous coordinates"), and the effect of applying the transformation is given by the product T·P. Since the bottom row of the transformation matrix is always the same, just six numbers are required to specify any transformation. This compact representation is often used internally by graphics systems to store transformation information, and can be specified explicitly, for example in SVG.

└───┘

Distortion

Other, less structured, alterations to paths can be achieved by moving (i.e. changing the coordinates of) their anchor points and control points. This can be done by interactive manipulation in a drawing program. Anchor points and control points may also be added and deleted from paths, so that a designer or artist can fine-tune the shape of objects.

Some commonly required effects which fall between the highly structured transformations and the free manipulation of control points are provided by way of parameterized commands in Illustrator and similar programs. These are referred to as filters, by analogy with the filters available in bitmapped image manipulation programs. An object is selected and an operation is chosen from a menu of those available. The chosen filter is then applied to the selected object.

Figure 3.27 shows two examples of applying Illustrator's Pucker & Bloat filter to a simple shape. The result is achieved by turning each anchor point into a Bézier corner point, and then extending the direction lines either inwards, to give the puckering effect shown on the left, or outwards, to give

Figure 3.27. *Pucker and bloat*

the bloating effect on the right. The extent of the distortion – the amount by which the direction lines are extended – is controlled by a slider when the filter is applied.

The thin red lines in Figure 3.27 are the direction lines for the two segments to the left and right of the vertex at the top of the original star. There are actually four of them: the two lines at the vertex itself lie on top of each other. (Remember that these are corner points.)

Other filters are available in Illustrator. Zig-zag adds extra anchor points between existing ones in a regular pattern; an option to the filter determines whether the segments of the resulting path should be straight lines, to produce a jagged result, or curves, which produces a smooth version of the effect. Roughening is similar, but adds the new anchor points in a pseudo-random fashion, so that the result is irregular. The tweak filter applies a proportional movement to all the anchor points and control points on a path. These filters are parameterized in values such as the maximum distance an anchor point may be moved. The parameters can be set via various controls presented in a dialogue when the filter is applied.

┌─IN DETAIL────────────────────────────

In Illustrator, distortions are applied as "effects", which do not actually add and modify the anchor points of the path they are applied to. It looks as if they are doing so, but the modification is "live": the actual path is not changed, but the effect is applied when it is displayed or exported to some other format. This means that the parameters can be changed after the initial application, and the effect can eaily be removed or temporarily disabled.

Evidently, these distortions are not affine transformations. By adding anchor points they can turn corner points into smooth points, straight lines into curves and vice versa, so straightness and parallelism are not preserved. The matrix representation cannot be used for such transformations.

The important thing to understand about transformations and distortions is that they are achieved simply by altering the coordinates of the defining points of objects, altering the stored model using nothing but arithmetical operations which can be performed efficiently. Although every pixel of the object must be transformed in the final displayed image, only the relatively few points that are needed to define the object within the model need to be recomputed beforehand. All the pixels will appear in the desired place when the changed model is rendered on the basis of these changed values.

Alterations to objects' appearance of the sort we will describe in Chapter 4, which rely on altering pixels, can only be achieved by rasterizing the objects, which destroys their vector characteristics.

KEY POINTS

Vector objects can be altered by changing the stored values used to represent them.

Affine transformations preserve straight lines and keep parallel lines parallel.

Translation, scaling, rotation, reflection and shearing are affine transformations, which can be performed by direct manipulation in vector drawing programs.

All five of these affine transformations can be defined by simple equations.

An entire object can be transformed by applying an affine transformation to each of its anchor points.

Several objects can be combined into a group, and transformed as a whole.

Less structured alterations to paths can be achieved by moving their anchor points and control points.

Existing anchor points can be moved and direction lines modified.

More structured distortions can be achieved using filters, which modify all a path's anchor points and control points systematically. Some filters add new anchor points.

The modifications implemented by distorting filters are not affine transformations.

3-D Graphics

Pictures on a screen are always two-dimensional, but this doesn't mean that the models from which they are generated need to be restricted to flat two-dimensional shapes. Models of three-dimensional objects correspond more closely to the way we perceive space. They enable us to generate two-dimensional pictures as perspective projections – or perhaps other sorts of projection – onto a plane, as if we were able to photograph the model. Sometimes, this may be easier than constructing the two-dimensional image from scratch, particularly if we can begin with a numerical description of an object's dimensions, as we might if we were designing some mechanical component, for example, or constructing a visualization on the basis of a simulation.

A three-dimensional model allows us to generate many different images of the same objects. For example, if we have a model of a house, we can produce a view of it from the front, from the back, from each side, from close up, far away, overhead, and so on, all using the same model. Figure 3.28 shows an example. If we were working in only two dimensions, each of these images would have to be drawn separately.[†]

† *Frank Lloyd Wright's "Heller House", modelled by Google, from Google 3D Warehouse.*

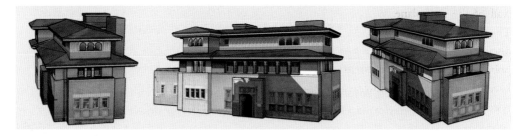

Figure 3.28. *Different two-dimensional views of a three-dimensional model*

3-D graphics – as we call vector graphics based on three-dimensional models – is a complicated subject, though, requiring tools that are hard to master, and it should be left to specialists most of the time. Here, we can only outline the main features of 3-D technology, in order to provide an appreciation of the difficulties it presents and the opportunities it has to offer.

In abstract mathematical terms, generalizing coordinate geometry from two dimensions to three is straightforward. The *x*- and *y*-axes of a two-dimensional coordinate system are perpendicular to each other. If you imagine drawing a set of axes on a flat sheet of paper and pinning it to a vertical wall, you can see that we can place a third axis perpendicular to the other two, coming out of the paper horizontally and projecting from the wall. Just as we can use *x* and *y* coordinates to define a point's horizontal and vertical distance along the wall from the origin, we can use a *z* coordinate, measured along our third axis, to define its distance from the wall. The three coordinates together define a point in three-dimensional space (see Figure 3.29).

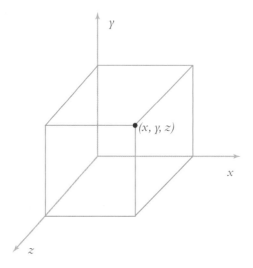

Figure 3.29. *Axes in three dimensions*

The primitive geometrical shapes of 2-D graphics are replaced by 3-D objects: instead of a circle, we have a sphere; instead of a square, a cube, and so on. By an obvious extension, a three-dimensional vector defines a displacement using three components in the same way that the two-dimensional vectors we used earlier define displacements using two components. This allows us to describe translations of objects in three-dimensional space. We certainly have a basis for 3-D vector graphics, but we also have some new problems.

When we introduced a third dimension, we stated that the *z*-axis points out of the imaginary wall of the x–y plane. Why should it not point into it? There is no reason why not. The coordinate system we have discussed is no more than a convention. With the y-axis pointing downwards, as we have assumed until now, we have described what is known as a left-handed coordinate system.

A right-handed coordinate system, with the z-axis pointing into the wall, or equivalently, with the y-axis pointing upwards, as shown in Figure 3.30, is equally valid. This system is more widely used, especially by mathematicians and in 3-D, and we will employ it exclusively in this section. We have also adopted the convention that the vertical axis is labelled y, as it was before, but some systems use the x- and y-axes to define a horizontal ground plane, with the z-axis adding height to it.

Even at this stage it is apparent that three dimensions may be more than one and a half times as complicated as two dimensions. Consider rotation, for example. In two dimensions we rotate about a point; in three dimensions we must rotate about a line. Rotations about an arbitrary line can be built out of rotations about the axes, but that still leaves three distinct rotations to consider, as shown in Figure 3.31, which introduces the names used for each of them – yaw, pitch and roll. (The names of the three rotations are assigned differently to the three variables depending on which convention is used for labelling the axes, but they always retain the same spatial meaning – roll is always a movement around the front-to-back axis, and so on.)

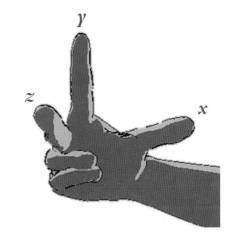

Figure 3.30. *Right-handed coordinate system*

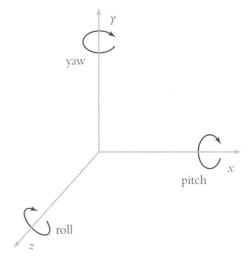

Figure 3.31. *Rotations in three dimensions*

The added complexity of graphics employing the third dimension goes much further than an extra couple of rotations. Instead of defining shapes by paths we must define objects by surfaces, which require more complicated mathematics and are much harder for most people to visualize. The fact that we can only work with two-dimensional representations while building models makes visualization generally difficult. This problem is further exacerbated by the fact that only powerful workstations can provide real-time rendering of 3-D models, so it is usually necessary to work with cruder approximations during the design process.

Once a collection of objects has been modelled, they are arranged in space, usually interactively. Often, a complete scene will be constructed by combining a few objects that are specially modelled with others taken from a library, either developed in earlier projects or brought in as the 3-D equivalent of clip art. For some specialized applications, especially the modelling of human figures, it is common practice to buy high-quality models and customize them instead of attempting to create them from scratch.

As well as the spatial relationships between separate objects, we may also wish to consider the relationships between objects that form part of a larger object. Most complex objects have a hierarchical structure. They can be described as a collection of sub-objects, each of which might be a collection of sub-sub-objects, and so on, until we reach the smallest component objects, which can be modelled in a simple way. For example, a bicycle consists of a frame, two wheels, a saddle, handlebars and front fork. Each wheel is a tyre around a rim, with spokes and a hub. We could model the hub as a cylinder, without decomposing it further. Hierarchical modelling is a well-established way of coping with complexity in many fields. In 3-D it becomes of particular importance when objects are animated, because we can then take advantage of the relationships between components to deduce how the object must move as a whole.

Rendering is no longer a relatively simple matter of generating pixels from a mathematical description. In 3-D we have a mathematical model of objects in space, but we need a flat picture. Assuming that we want to use conventional Renaissance perspective to project the 3-D model onto a plane surface, we will need to consider the viewpoint, or the position of an imaginary camera, and ensure that the rendered picture corresponds to what the camera sees while exhibiting the scaling with distance that we expect from perspective.

We also need to consider lighting — the position of light sources, and the intensity and type of illumination they cast, whether it is a diffuse glow or a concentrated beam, for example. The interaction of the light with the surface of objects, and perhaps — in the case of something like an underwater scene or a smoke-filled room — with the atmosphere, must also be modelled and rendered. If we want to achieve any sort of realism, our models must include not just the geometrical features of objects, but also their surface characteristics — not just the colours, but also the textures — so that the surface's appearance can be rendered convincingly in different positions and under different lighting conditions. Although 3-D systems are reasonably good at using lighting models derived from the underlying physics, they are not perfect, and designers sometimes have to resort to physical impossibilities, such as negative spotlights, for absorbing unwanted light.

These added complications mean that the theory of 3-D graphics is a great deal more elaborate than that of 2-D graphics. It also means that 3-D software is more complex and difficult to use. Finally, it means that rendering 3-D models can be an extremely computationally expensive process, that often requires additional hardware (often in the form of 3-D accelerator PCI cards) to achieve acceptable performance even on today's powerful desktop machines.

2-D images generated from 3-D models may be in any bitmapped format. The 3-D models themselves are usually kept in some proprietary format specific to the program being used to create them, although there are some standard formats, including *3DMF* and *X3D*, which can be used for storing models so that they can be exchanged between different applications. Recent versions of PDF also allow 3-D artwork to be included in a document. When the document is displayed in a program that understands this feature of PDF, 2-D views of the artwork can be generated, or the user can rotate objects and examine them from different angles and orientations.

3-D Models

Broadly speaking, there are three general approaches to modelling 3-D objects, which are often used in conjunction. The simplest approach, **constructive solid geometry**, uses a few primitive geometric solids, such as the cube, cylinder, sphere and pyramid, as elements from which to construct more complex objects. These elements can be distorted, by squashing or stretching, to produce variations on the simple forms. They can also be combined, using operations usually described in terms of the set theoretical operators union, intersection and difference.

These operations only affect two objects that are placed in such a way that they share some of the space that they occupy – normally a physical impossibility, but no problem for a computer model. Their union is a new object made out of the space occupied by the two together. The intersection of two objects is the space that the two have in common. Finally, the difference of two objects is the space occupied by the first but not the second; this operation is useful for knocking holes out of solid objects. Figure 3.32 shows the objects formed by applying these operations to a vertical cylinder and a horizontal ellipsoid. (The shadows and tiled pattern are just cosmetic additions, which should help make it easier to see the third dimension in these illustrations.) The difference operation is not commutative: in Figure 3.32 we have taken the cylinder away from the ellipsoid. You would get a very different object by taking the ellipsoid away from the cylinder.

Figure 3.32. *The union, intersection and difference of two solid objects*

Constructive solid geometry is especially useful for modelling man-made objects and architectural features, which are often built out of the same elementary solids. It is often found in computer-aided design systems. It can take you a long way with modelling camshafts, triumphal arches and toy steam trains. However, as a glance around your immediate environment will show, many objects in the real world are not made out of geometric solids combined by set operations, so they require a different approach.

Free form modelling uses a representation of an object's boundary surface as the basis of its model. This approach is a 3-D generalization of the use of paths to enclose shapes in two dimensions. Instead of building paths out of lines and curves, we must build surfaces out of flat polygons or curved patches. Surfaces constructed as a mesh of polygons can be rendered relatively efficiently, making this a popular representation. (Where fast rendering is required, as in 3-D games, the polygons are often restricted to triangles, which makes rendering more efficient. It also guarantees that the polygons are flat.) However, they suffer from the drawback that, like straight line segments used to approximate a curve, polygons cannot fit together smoothly when they are used to approximate curved surfaces. This is more serious than it may sound, because it affects the way light is reflected off the surface. If reflections are broken up, any irregularities will be readily apparent to the user.

It is possible to generalize Bézier curves to three-dimensional surfaces in order to produce curved patches that can be fitted together smoothly. A cubic Bézier surface patch requires 16 control points, instead of the corresponding curve's four. Just as we could join curves together smoothly by ensuring that they meet at an anchor point with the connected control points in a straight line, we can join patches by ensuring that they meet at a common edge curve and that the connected control points lie in the same plane.

This is easy to say, but Bézier patches are hard to work with in interactive 3-D applications, largely because moving a single control point can affect the geometry of the whole patch in a way that may be hard to predict. A more tractable kind of patch is based on surfaces called *non-rational B-splines* or *NURBs*, which, by using a more complicated construction, ensure that the effect of moving control points is localized. In effect, this makes it possible to sculpt a smooth surface by pulling and pushing it into the desired shape.

The generality and lack of structure of boundary representations can make it hard to get started with a model. To overcome this problem, most 3-D programs provide a means of generating objects with a certain regular structure or symmetry from 2-D shapes. The resulting objects can then either be used directly, or their surface mesh can be altered to produce a less constrained and more convincing object.

The basic idea is to treat a two-dimensional shape as a cross-section, and to define a volume by sweeping the cross-section along a path. The simplest path is a straight line. A shape creates an object with a uniform cross-section as it travels along a straight line. For example, a circle creates a cylinder in this way. Figure 3.33 shows a slightly more elaborate example. This process is known as *extrusion*, since the objects it produces resemble those that can be made by industrial processes in which plastic or metal is forced out through an opening. Extruded text is one application of this technique that has been so widely used in producing corporate logos as to have become a cliché.

Figure 3.33. *Extrusion*

To produce more elaborate objects, a curved path can be used, and the size of the cross-section can be altered as it moves along it. If the path is a conventional Bézier path, organic shapes can be generated.

If the path is a circle, the resulting objects exhibit radial symmetry. This special case is often called *lathing* because of the resemblance of the resulting objects to traditional turned artefacts. If a suitable shape is chosen, circular paths can be used to generate many types of drinking vessel and vase, as well as mechanical components and, as Figure 3.34 shows, some styles of hat.

Figure 3.34. *Lathing*

The third approach to modelling is *procedural modelling*. Here, instead of using models that can be described by equations, and storing only the constants that define a particular instance, we use objects that are described by an algorithm or procedure. Thus, returning to two dimensions for a moment, instead of defining a circle by the equation $x^2+y^2=r^2$, we could define it by some procedure such as "draw a curve that maintains a constant distance r from the origin". In this case, the procedural representation is not very helpful – the equation tells you how to implement the procedure – but for naturally occurring objects with a more complex, less mathematically

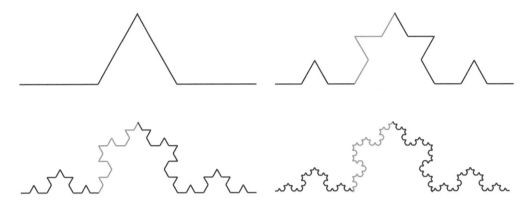

Figure 3.35. *Constructing a well-known fractal curve*

tractable structure, algorithms may provide a description where equations cannot. The best known procedural modelling techniques are based on ***fractals***. These are often described as shapes that exhibit the same structure at all levels of detail. Figure 3.35 shows a famous example of such a shape, and its construction.

IN DETAIL

The structures used in this sort of modelling are not, strictly mathematically speaking, fractals. A mathematician's fractal shows the same structure at all scales, right down to infinity. Fractals are said to be "self-similar". In computer graphics, we cannot do this, nor do we want to: we can't show any detail smaller than a single pixel, and in any case, to model natural features we must introduce a random element. The randomized structures commonly used in modelling are a finite approximation to a class of structures known as "random fractals", which have the property that at any scale the components have the same statistical distribution as the whole structure. This property is a random equivalent of the property of true fractals that at any scale the components are identical to the whole. To ensure such "statistical self-similarity", constraints must be placed on the random factors introduced at each stage of the construction of these objects.

We start with the shape at the top left, consisting of four equal line segments, arranged as a straight line with a bump in the middle. We then replace each segment by a scaled-down copy of the entire shape, as shown at the top right. We continue in the same way, replacing each of the segments of each of the scaled-down copies with a copy of the original shape scaled down further, and so on. The bottom line shows later stages in the procedure.

You can imagine that, if we were able to continue in this way to infinity, we would end up with a crinkly curve, with a bulge in the middle and two lesser crinkly bulges to each side. If you were then to magnify any part of the curve and look at it you would see a crinkly curve, with a bulge in the middle and two lesser crinkly bulges to each side, which, if you were to magnify any part of it …The appearance of certain natural features, such as coastlines, mountains and the edges of clouds, approximates this property: their small-scale structure is the same as their large-scale structure. Figure 3.36 shows that three of the curves we just constructed can be put together to make a snowflake.

Fractals can be extended to three-dimensional structures that exhibit the same sort of similarity at different scales. Whereas this particular sort of structure cannot be described by equations, it is, as we have just demonstrated, easily described by a recursive algorithm.

Where fractal algorithms are used to model natural phenomena, an element of randomness is usually introduced. For example, a very simple fractal might be made by splitting a line into two parts, moving the centre point a certain distance, and then applying the construction recursively to the two halves. If the distance moved is not a constant proportion of the length of the segment but a random distance, the resulting shape will still display a recognizable similarity at different scales, without being exactly internally replicated. Figure 3.37 shows a curve being constructed in the manner just described; it could be said to resemble a mountain slope.

In three dimensions, a similar construction can be applied to construct terrains out of internally subdivided triangular areas. By joining the midpoints of the three sides of a triangle, it can be divided into four smaller triangles. The midpoints can be randomly displaced perpendicularly to the plane of the original triangle, as indicated in Figure 3.38, and then the construction can be applied to each of the small triangles. This process can be applied to arbitrary polygons, and repeated indefinitely to produce

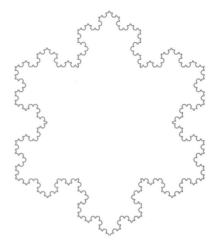

Figure 3.36. *A fractal snowflake*

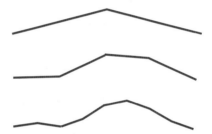

Figure 3.37. *Constructing a fractal mountainside*

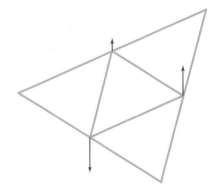

Figure 3.38. *3-D random fractal construction*

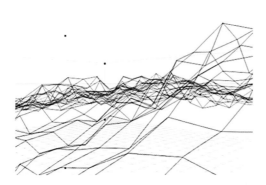 

Figure 3.39. *Fractal terrain*

arbitrarily fine detail with the irregular appearance of natural terrain, as exhibited by the land-scapes in Figures 3.39 and 3.40.

Rendering

3-D models only exist inside computers; all we can see is two-dimensional images generated from them. This is the case both when we wish to produce a final image from a model and when we are working on a model in a 3-D application. In both cases a rendering operation is needed; in the latter case, the rendering must be done rapidly enough to provide visual feedback. As we will shortly see, rendering high-quality images is time-consuming, so it is usually necessary to compromise on quality while a model is being built. Because of the complexity of rendering, and its computational demands, it is common for it to be handled by a specialized module, usually referred to as a **rendering engine**. It may be the case that a rendering engine is optimized for multiprocessing, so that rendering times can be reduced by using a collection of processors operating in parallel.

Almost all contemporary 3-D graphics aspires to the sort of realism associated with photographs. That is, it uses Renaissance perspective conventions (distant objects are smaller than near ones) and attempts to represent the effects of light on different surfaces in a way that is consistent with the laws of optics. Figure 3.40 shows an example of the results that can easily be achieved with mid-range software. There is a definite "computer-generated" quality to most such images, which produces a less than realistic result.

The mathematics of perspective projection has been understood for a long time, so it is relatively easy for a rendering engine to work out which points on an image plane correspond to each of the nodes of a 3-D model. By joining these points to show the edges of objects and of the polygons making up surfaces, it is possible to produce a **wire frame** image of a model, as shown in Figure 3.41.

Figure 3.40. *Photo-realistic rendering*

Wire frames are often used as preview images in modelling programs. They can also be useful in computer-aided design systems, since they contain enough information to provide answers to questions such as "Does the door provide adequate clearance for the piano when it is fully open?". For most purposes, though, they are not acceptable.

The most noticeable feature of wire frames is the absence of any surfaces. This has the obvious disadvantage that no surface detail can be shown, and the less obvious disadvantage that they do not contain enough information to enable us to determine the orientations of objects unambiguously – since a wire frame lets you see through an object, it becomes difficult or impossible to distinguish between front and back. When you look at Figure 3.41, you can probably see the hat as it was in Figure 3.34, with the brim tipped down on the side towards you. If you stare at it for a while, though, and concentrate on the upper curve of the brim, you will probably be able to see it with the near side tipped up.

As the rendering at the left of Figure 3.42 demonstrates, when a wire frame is placed in front of a background, accurate visual interpretation of the object becomes very difficult. For this reason, when wire frame previews are used in interactive 3-D modelling programs, they are usually shown against a plain, neutral background.

Figure 3.41. *Wire frame rendering*

Figure 3.42. *Wire frame, flat, Gouraud and Phong shading*

In order to show the surfaces of objects, it is necessary to determine which of them are visible. The far sides of objects are considered hidden in perspective views, as are surfaces, or parts of surfaces, with other objects in front of them. Determining which surfaces are visible, starting only from a model based on the coordinates of corners of objects, is not a trivial task, but it is one that has received attention almost from the beginning of computer graphics. There are several tried and tested algorithms for performing **hidden surface removal**. Once this has been done the next task is to determine how to render the visible surfaces.

If the outside of an object is simply filled with a flat colour, no sense of the curvature of the surface will be conveyed. The result is an odd mixture of flat surfaces, with edges curved in 3-D, which can be interesting in some contexts but is in no sense realistic, as the second bottle from the left in Figure 3.42 illustrates.

To produce images that resemble photographs we must take account of the way light interacts with surfaces. This means that our models must include sufficient information about lights and surface properties. In most 3-D modelling programs, surface characteristics can be associated with an object by setting the values of some parameters, including its colour and reflectivity. (Some systems allow the designer to paint on the surface of models in order to specify their surface characteristics indirectly.) Lights can be created and positioned in the same way as other objects; the designer merely selects a type of light – spotlight or point source (such as the sun), for example – and specifies its position and intensity. It is up to the rendering engine to produce an image that is consistent with the lights and materials that have been used in the model.

Different algorithms – called **shading algorithms** – are employed for this task, each incorporating different models of how light interacts with surfaces. These models are loosely based on the physics of light transmission, but usually include heuristics that produce a convincing result without being entirely optically accurate. Each shading algorithm uses different approximations to allow rendering to be performed with reasonable efficiency. Rendering engines usually allow you to choose the most appropriate shading algorithm for the needs of a particular model. There is usually a trade-off between the final quality of the image – or at least, of its treatment of light – and the amount of computation required.

The simplest way of shading an object whose surface is made out of polygons is to calculate a colour value for each polygon, based on the light striking it and its own optical properties, and use that value to colour the whole polygon. Adjacent polygons will often have different colours – they may be at a different angle to the light source, for example – and this will make the discontinuities between polygons readily visible.

To disguise this effect, and to produce a more convincing rendering of the polygons, more sophisticated algorithms interpolate the colour across each polygon, on the basis of colour values calculated at the vertices. One such interpolation scheme is **Gouraud shading**. An alternative, which does the interpolation differently, is **Phong shading**. Phong's approach works better when the illumination model being used takes account of specular reflection – the light that bounces off the surface of shiny (or partially shiny) objects. The resulting highlights are rendered by Phong shading in a quite convincing way.

The two bottles on the right of Figure 3.42 have been rendered using Gouraud and Phong shading. Compared to the flat shading, the Gouraud-shaded version (the third bottle from the left) shows more volume, but the Phong-shaded version on the extreme right is the only one that looks reasonably convincing – partly owing to the exaggerated treatment of reflections.

The shading algorithms mentioned so far only deal with each object in isolation, but in reality the appearance of an object may be affected by the presence of others. As an extreme example, the appearance of a glass full of water will depend on what is behind it, while that of a mirror will depend on the objects it reflects. Generally, light may bounce off several objects before reaching the eye, and it will be influenced by their colour and surface.

Ray tracing is a shading algorithm that attempts to take account of this. It works by tracing the path of a ray of light back from each pixel in the rendered image to a light source. On the way, the ray may bounce off several surfaces, and the ray tracer will take account of their effect, using a model of illumination and information about the materials of the objects in the scene to compute the colour and intensity of the starting pixel.

Ray tracing is commonly used to render "realistic" 3-D scenes, such as the landscape in Figure 3.40. The ray tracing computation is quite complex, and it must be repeated for every pixel in the rendered image – very possibly millions of pixels. Until recently, therefore, ray tracing was confined to high-performance workstations, but the extraordinary advance in the speed of personal computers has made it feasible to use ray tracing in desktop 3-D systems. It is now the preferred shading algorithm for photo-realistic graphics.

An alternative approach to the interactions between objects is **radiosity**, which attempts to model the complex reflections that occur between surfaces that are close together. This provides a more accurate representation of scattered and ambient light and is especially useful for interior scenes. Radiosity is more accurately based on the physics of light than other shading algorithms. It also differs from other algorithms in computing the lighting on a model independently of any rendered view of it; essentially, it adds the computed light values to the model. This means that the final rendering of an image can be done very efficiently, although the initial computation of lighting values is slow.

These shading algorithms depend on information about the material of which an object is composed. Where the surface contains a great deal of detail, it may not be feasible to specify this information precisely enough for every small feature to be rendered accurately. A popular way of adding surface details to 3-D models is *texture mapping*. An image, typically a pattern representing some particular sort of surface's appearance, such as fur, bark, sand, marble, and so on, is mathematically wrapped over the surface of the object. That is, mathematical transformations are applied to the pixels of the rendered object, based on those of the image, to produce the appearance of an object with the image wrapped around it.

To see the effect of this, imagine cutting a picture out of a magazine, wrapping it round a physical object, and sticking it down. This works quite well for boxes, producing a box whose surface has the appearance of the picture, but much less well for spherical or irregularly shaped objects. If you imagine that the picture was printed on a very thin sheet of rubber, you can see that it would be possible to glue it to these shapes, but that it would become distorted in the process. Texture mapping is similar to gluing rubber pictures to objects, and may introduce the same sort of distortion, but it can also provide a convenient means of applying detail to a surface. Related operations include *bump mapping*, where, instead of using the picture to form the surface appearance, we use it to apply bumpiness or roughness, and *transparency mapping* and *reflection mapping*, which modify the optical characteristics on the basis of a two-dimensional map in the same way.

Rendering algorithms can do a very good job at producing photo-realistic images, but they are not perfect. It is not uncommon for a rendered image to be imported into an image manipulation program, such as Photoshop, for further processing of the sort we will describe in Chapter 4.

KEY POINTS

3-D is a conceptually simple extension of 2-D with a third axis.

In practice, 3-D graphics is complicated and difficult, requiring 3-D visualization skills and the use of complex tools that are hard to master.

3-D objects must be created and arranged in space, then 2-D images incorporating perspective must be made as if the scene was photographed by a camera, whose viewpoint must be specified.

Lighting and surface textures must be taken into account.

Constructive solid geometry uses the operations of union, intersection and difference to combine primitive geometric solids.

Free form modelling uses a representation of an object's boundary surface as the basis of its model.

Surfaces may be represented as a mesh of polygons, or using more complex surface elements, such as Bézier patches and NURBs.

Extrusion and lathing are methods of generating regular or symmetrical solid objects from 2-D shapes.

Extrusion creates a solid with a uniform cross-section by sweeping a shape along a straight line.

Lathing creates a solid object with radial symmetry by sweeping a shape around a circle.

Procedural modelling defines objects using algorithms.

Fractal algorithms are used to generate models of natural phenomena.

3-D objects may be rendered as wire frames for previewing.

To arrive at a realistic image, hidden surfaces must be removed and visible ones must be rendered using a shading algorithm that models the effect of light on the surface.

Gouraud and Phong shading may be used to colour surfaces. Ray tracing incorporates the interaction between objects on lighting.

Exercises

Test Questions

1 If X is a point with real coordinates $(120.0, 250.0)$, what are the coordinates of the point Y if XY is (a) a horizontal line running to the right, 250 units long; (b) a vertical line running upwards, 120 units long; (c) a diagonal line, running down and to the right at an angle of 45°, 400 units long? How would your answers be different if X and Y were pixels?

2 Anti-aliasing never affects the appearance of vertical and horizontal lines. True or false?

3 What happens if two Bézier curves with control points P_1, P_2, P_3 and P_4, and P_4, P_5, P_6 and P_7 are joined at P_4 so that P_3, P_4 and P_5 are in a straight line and the lengths of P_3P_4 and P_4P_5 are the same, but P_5 and P_3 are on the same side of P_4?

4 In Figure 3.24, which of the two shapes has been filled according to the non-zero winding number rule, and which according to the even–odd rule?

5 Write down equations for the coordinates of the point $P' = (x', y')$ obtained

(a) by rotating $P = (x, y)$ around the point (p, q);

(b) by reflecting $P = (x, y)$ in the vertical line $x = p$;

(c) by reflecting $P = (x, y)$ in the horizontal line $y = q$.

6 Which of the following arrangements of three axes is right-handed and which left-handed?

(a) x pointing right, y pointing up, z pointing towards you;

(b) x pointing up, y pointing left, z pointing towards you;

(c) z pointing right, y pointing up, x pointing towards you;

(d) z pointing right, x pointing up, y pointing towards you.

In terms of transformations, what property relates all left-handed coordinate systems and all right-handed coordinate systems?

Discussion Topics

1 What are the advantages and disadvantages of using primitive shapes, such as rectangles and ellipses, in a graphics language compared with representing every object as a combination of straight lines and Bézier curves, as PDF does?

2 Gradient fills are not directly provided in some low-level graphics languages. Consider how you would implement linear and radial gradients using the other vector graphics primitives described in this chapter.

3 Under what circumstances would you *not* use ray tracing to render a 3-D scene?

Practical Tasks

1 There are 24 possible orders in which the points P_1, P_2, P_3 and P_4 can be used to specify a Bézier curve. Sketch the curves produced by all possible permutations of the points used in the curve shown in Figure 3.9. Their coordinates are (0,0), (4,10), (8,10) and (20,2). Which pairs of curves are identical, and which can be transformed into each other by a geometrical transformation?

2 Using any suitable vector drawing program, draw a large ellipse with the ellipse tool. Using the pen tool, try to draw an identical ellipse (if your program supports layers, draw it on top of the first ellipse to see how closely you can match it) using as few Bézier curves as possible.

3 We remarked that the difference operation in constructive solid geometry is not commutative, that is, if we subtract shape *A* from shape *B* the result is different from what we get by subtracting shape *B* from shape *A*. Figure 3.32 shows the effect of subtracting the cylinder from the ellipsoid. Sketch the object that would be obtained by subtracting the ellipsoid from the cylinder.

4 Which of the following styles of hat could you model using a lathing operation?

(a) Fedora;

(b) Bowler (Derby);

(c) Top hat;

(d) Baseball cap;

(e) Tam o' Shanter;

(f) 42nd Street skimmer.

Sketch the shapes you would use to generate hats in each of the styles which can be lathed. If you have access to a program that can perform lathing, create examples of as many of these hats as you can. (Illustrator's **3D** effect is adequate for this job if you do not want to learn a full-blown 3-D program.)

Bitmapped Images

■ **Resolution**

Device Resolution. Image Resolution. Resampling.

■ **Image Compression**

Lossless Image Compression. JPEG Compression. JPEG2000.

■ **File Formats**

GIF and PNG. JPEG Files. Other Formats. Metadata.

■ **Image Manipulation**

Image Manipulation Software. Layers. Selections, Masks and Alpha Channels. Pixel Point Processing. Pixel Group Processing.

Conceptually, bitmapped images are much simpler than vector graphics. There is no need for any mathematical modelling of shapes; we merely record a value representing the colour of each pixel in the image. Images are not restricted to those that can be constructed from a small repertoire of drawing primitives, so a much broader range of visual possibilities is available. Above all, bitmapped representations can be used to record photographs. The main cost for this simplicity and range is in the potentially large size of image files and the difficulty of identifying objects within an image for the purposes of editing and transformation.

It is rarely necessary to compute and assign the colour value for each pixel explicitly. Many images are created from external sources, such as digital cameras or scanners, which use hardware to sense colours and create the array of values. For creating original digital images, programs such as Painter allow visual artists to use familiar techniques (at least metaphorically) to paint images. Bitmapped images can also be created by rendering vectors.

Resolution

The concept of resolution is a simple one, but the different ways in which the word is used can be confusing. Resolution is a measure of how finely a device approximates continuous images using finite pixels. It is thus closely related to sampling, and some of the ideas about sampling rates introduced in Chapter 2 are relevant to the way resolution affects the appearance of images.

Device Resolution

Originally, a device's resolution was a measure of its ability to distinguish fine detail. In the case of a camera or scanner, this was measured by determining how far apart the lines on a target grid had to be for the device to "see" every one. Resolution can be measured in this fashion for both digital and analogue devices. For a printer or display, the resolution in this sense would be measured by how closely spaced it could reproduce such a grid; its value is quoted as the pitch of the grid, in units of lines per inch (or the metric equivalent). To a first approximation, on digital devices that print or sample individual dots, the number of lines per inch is the same as the number of dots in each inch, since a line one dot wide is the narrowest that can be displayed or sensed.

This accounts for the more modern (if less precise) use of resolution as a measure of the number of dots per unit length that a device can display or sample. In English-speaking countries, resolution in this sense is usually quoted in units of dots per inch (dpi). This value is better called the *pixel density*, and – although use of this term is not as widespread – we will use it where it is important to be clear what sense of resolution we mean.

In the case of scanners, the number of dots per unit length may very well not be the same as the resolution in the original sense, because of the effect of the optical components. Furthermore, it is common for manufacturers to quote very high scanner resolutions in dots per inch by counting interpolated values that are not directly scanned. Occasionally, therefore, you will sometimes see the physical resolution of a scanner – referring to the actual input values recorded by the sensor – quoted in units of samples per inch.

IN DETAIL

There is an extra complication with colour printers. As we will see in Chapter 5, in order to produce a full range of colours using just four or six inks, colour printers arrange dots in groups, using a pattern of different coloured inks within each group to produce the required colour by optical mixing. Hence, the size of the coloured pixel is greater than the size of an individual dot of ink. The resolution of a printer taking account of this way of mixing colours is again quoted in *lines per inch* (or other unit of length), as it is a closer approximation to the resolution in the original sense just described. The number of lines per inch may be as few as one-fifth of the number of dots per inch – the exact ratio depends on how the dots are arranged.

In video, resolution is normally specified in a different way, by giving the width and height of a frame, measured in pixels – its **pixel dimensions**. For example, a PAL frame is 768×576 pixels; an NTSC frame is 640×480. If you know the physical dimensions of your TV set or video monitor, you can translate resolutions specified in this form into dots per inch, but this is not very useful. For video it makes more sense to specify image resolution in the form of the pixel dimensions, because the same pixel grid is used to display the picture on any monitor (using the same video standard) irrespective of its size: a small television will show the same picture as a massive plasma screen, but much smaller. (Digital video has made matters more complicated by using pixels that are not square, as we will explain in Chapter 6, but the same principle still applies.)

Computer monitors are based on the same technology as video monitors, so it is common to see their resolution specified as an image size, such as 1024×768 or 1440×900. However, when preparing images or writing software to display them, it is often necessary to use a value for the resolution of a monitor in the other sense, as a number of dots per inch. At present, this is always taken to be 72 dpi – even though this is almost never the number of dots you would find in each inch if you measured the screen. Assuming that the pixel density will be the same on all monitors ensures that an image will always occupy the same proportion of any screen with the same pixel dimensions, no matter what size the screen is physically. The value of 72 dpi is used for historical reasons, but this convention may change as monitors with much higher resolutions become more common and operating systems start to support "resolution–independent" interfaces.

The introduction of digital cameras has led to another way of specifying resolution – as the total number of pixels in the image. To find the pixel dimensions from such a specification, you need to know the aspect ratio of the image, that is, the ratio of its width to its height. Cameras do not all take photographs with the same aspect ratio, and some cameras offer a choice of aspect ratios. The ratio 4:3, which used to be a standard aspect ratio for TV screens and monitors, is quite common, however, especially in low- to mid-range compact cameras, but higher-range cameras, including many digital SLRs, use the traditional photographic ratio of 3:2 by default. Hence a "5 Megapixel" camera, with roughly five million pixels, might produce images with pixel dimensions of 2584 × 1936 (4:3) or 2736 × 1824 (3:2).

Knowing the number of dots per inch in a camera would only enable you to work out the physical size of the sensor, which is not usually a very interesting piece of information. When a pixel density must be associated with a digital photograph, it is taken to be 72 dpi, to match the assumed resolution of a computer screen. As we will see in a moment, this is not very convenient.

Image Resolution

Now consider bitmapped images. An image is an array of pixel values, so it necessarily has pixel dimensions. Unlike a printed photograph or original artwork on paper, a bitmapped image has no physical dimensions. In the absence of any further information, the physical size of an image when it is displayed will depend on the pixel density of the device it is to be displayed on.

For example, the image in Figure 4.1 is 198 pixels wide and 149 high. If it could be displayed at the nominal screen resolution of 72 dpi it would be 70 mm by 52.5 mm. Displayed without scaling on an actual monitor at 115 dpi, it will only be a little over 43.5 mm wide. If it is printed

72 dpi

115 dpi

600 dpi

Figure 4.1. *Device resolution and image size*

on a 600 dpi printer, it will be about 8.5 mm wide. The height changes proportionally, as shown in Figure 4.1. The image always retains its aspect ratio, but its apparent size may vary considerably.

In general, we have:

$$physical\ dimension = \frac{pixel\ dimension}{pixel\ density}$$

where the pixel density is the device resolution, measured in pixels per unit length. (If the pixel density is specified in pixels per inch, the physical dimension will be in inches, and so on.)

It follows that if two images seem to be the same physical size on devices with different resolutions, the images must have different pixel dimensions. Since the pixels on the two devices are of different sizes, the images will display different amounts of detail. This is illustrated in Figure 4.2.

72 dpi, 198 × 149 px

 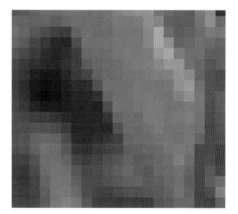

600 dpi, 1654 × 1240 px

Figure 4.2. *Resolution and pixel dimensions*

The top image has been printed at 72 dpi, the bottom one at 600 dpi, at the same size. As the blown-up details on the right show, the low-resolution version is coarse, with the individual pixels clearly discernible at modest magnification. This phenomenon is called *pixellation*. You will probably observe the similarity between the pixellated edges in the image and the jaggies exhibited by lines in vector graphics. Pixellation is a form of aliasing, but bitmapped images do not lend themselves to anti-aliasing of the sort we described in Chapter 3.

Knowing the pixel dimensions, you know how much detail is contained in the image; the number of dots per inch on the output device tells you how big that image will be, and how easy it will be to see the individual pixels.

Many images have a natural size, though – the size of an original before it is scanned, the size of canvas used to create an image in a painting program or a standard print size for photographs, for example. We often want the image to be displayed at its natural size, irrespective of the resolution of the output device.

In order to allow this, most image formats record a resolution with the image data. (Alternatively, we could associate a fixed size in some appropriate units, but this is less convenient.) This resolution is usually quoted in units of pixels per inch (ppi), to distinguish it from the resolution of physical devices in dots per inch.

The stored resolution will be that of the device from which the image originated, where this makes sense. For example, if an image is scanned at 600 dpi, the stored image resolution will be 600 ppi. Since the pixels in the image were generated at this resolution, the original physical dimensions of the image can be calculated from the pixel dimensions and the image resolution. It is then a simple matter for software that displays the image to ensure that it appears at its natural size, by scaling it by a factor of *device resolution/image resolution*.

For example, if a photograph measured 6 inches by 4 inches, and it was scanned at 600 dpi, its bitmap would be 3600 by 2400 pixels in size. Displayed in a simple-minded fashion on a 72 dpi monitor, the image would appear to measure 50 inches by 33.3 inches. To make it appear at the desired size, it must be scaled by $72/600 = 0.12$, which, as you can easily verify, reduces it to its original size. This computation requires that both the image's resolution and that of the output device be known.

This approach breaks down for still photograph and video cameras. As we explained earlier, the pixel density of these devices is arbitrarily assumed to be 72 dpi, to match the nominal resolution of monitors. This means that when the image from a camera is displayed on a monitor, the actual pixels will be displayed. For a video frame, this is quite sensible, since most contemporary monitors are big enough to accommodate a full-sized video frame comfortably. The images from still cameras with 5 Megapixel sensors and higher, though, exceed the size of most monitors at 72 dpi, so these must always be scaled for display. Digital cameras provide the facility to take photographs with very large pixel dimensions on the assumption that the photographs are destined for print on a fairly high-resolution printer. Now that many photographs are taken specifically for display on screen – on a blog or a Web site, for example – much smaller pixel dimensions may be appropriate for many photographs.

Resampling

How is scaling of a bitmapped image to be achieved? We cannot just perform a simple transformation on coordinates, as we could with vector graphics. Scaling changes the pixel dimensions of an image, which means that in the process some pixels must be thrown away, if the image is being scaled down, or inserted, if it is being scaled up.

The process of scaling an image without changing its resolution is essentially the same as that of changing its resolution without changing the size. In both cases, what we are actually doing is altering the pixel dimensions of the stored image, though the altered data will be interpreted differently in the two cases when the image is displayed.

Reducing the pixel dimensions of an image (scaling it down or decreasing the resolution) is called **downsampling**. Increasing the pixel dimensions (scaling up or increasing the resolution) is called **upsampling**. Collectively, the two operations are called **resampling**. Both upsampling and downsampling can lead to a loss of visual quality. If resampling is not performed, changing the resolution will alter the size and vice versa, as we demonstrated previously.

The basic approach to scaling a bitmapped image is essentially the same as the one we used for scaling vectors, but instead of transforming a few coordinates, we must transform every single pixel. That is, for each pixel in the image, we apply the scaling transformation using the same equation as we gave in Chapter 3 to obtain a new pixel in the transformed image. (For simplicity, we will assume we want to use the same factor in both the vertical and horizontal directions.)

However, as Figure 4.3 shows, this transformation runs into trouble because of the finite size of pixels. Attempting to scale up an image by a factor s by taking the value of the pixel at coordinates (x,y) in the original and mapping it to $(x',y') = (sx,sy)$ in the enlargement leads to most pixels being mapped to points that do not lie on the pixel grid of the new image, with gaps appearing between the scaled-up pixels. This is because, unless s is an integer, sx and sy will not in general be integer values. Even if s is an integer only some of the pixels in the new image will receive values. For example, if $s = 2$, only the even-numbered pixels in even-numbered rows of the image correspond to any pixel in the original under this mapping, leaving three-quarters of the pixels in

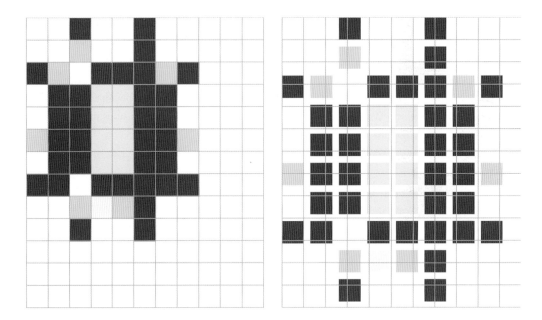

Figure 4.3. *Scaling pixels*

the enlarged image undefined. This emphasizes that, in constructing a scaled-up image, we must use some interpolation method to compute values for some pixels.

An alternative approach to performing the scaling is to compute the transformed image by finding a corresponding pixel in the original image for each pixel in the new image. The advantage of proceeding in this direction is that we compute all the pixel values we need and no more. However, this mapping also has problems because of the finite size of pixels.

Using this inverse mapping, we might try to set the pixel at coordinates (x', y') in the enlarged image to the value at $(x, y) = (x'/s, y'/s)$ in the original. In general, though, x'/s and y'/s will not be integers and hence will not identify a pixel. Figure 4.4 shows how the pixel grid for a scaled-up image would not align with whole pixels when it is mapped back to the original. Many pixels in the enlarged image are made up of fragments of several pixels from the original. A pixel is, by definition, an atomic entity that cannot be broken up in this way, so we cannot simply apply this reverse mapping as we have described it. We can, however, adapt the technique by combining the values of several adjacent pixels.

A useful way of thinking about what is going on is to imagine that we are reconstructing a continuous image, so that we can find the required values in between the pixels of our sampled image, and then resample it. Thus, the general problem is the same as the one we introduced when we discussed digitization in Chapter 2: how to reconstruct a signal from its samples. In practice,

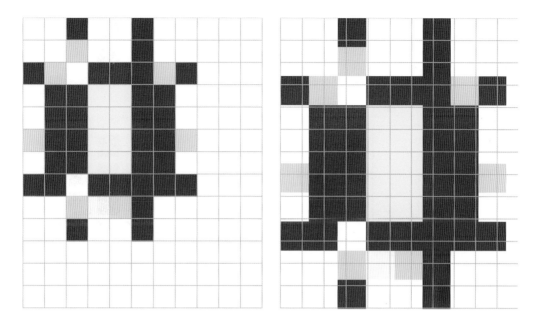

Figure 4.4. *Scaling pixels using a reverse mapping*

of course, we combine the reconstruction and resampling into a single operation, because we can only work with discrete representations.

We know that, for general images which may contain arbitrarily high frequencies because of sharp edges, the reconstruction cannot be done perfectly. We also know from sampling theory that the best possible reconstruction is not feasible. All we can hope to do is approximate the reconstruction to an acceptable degree of accuracy by using some method of interpolation to deduce the intervening values on the basis of the stored pixels. Several interpolation schemes are commonly used; Photoshop provides three, for example, which we will describe next. As is usual in computing, the more elaborate and computationally expensive the algorithm used, the better the approximation that results.

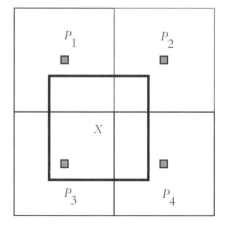

Figure 4.5. *Pixel interpolation*

Suppose that we are scaling an image and we calculate that the pixel with coordinates (x',y') in the resulting image should have the same value as a pixel at some point (x,y) in the original, but x and y are not integers, so no such pixel actually exists. We wish to sample the original image at (x,y), at the same resolution at which it is stored, so we can imagine drawing a pixel-sized square – call it the target pixel – centred at (x,y) which will be the sample we need. As Figure 4.5 shows,

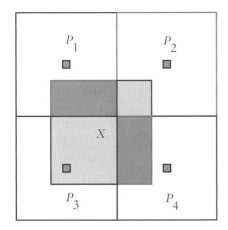

Figure 4.6. *Areas for bilinear interpolation*

in general this area may overlap four pixels in the original image. In the diagram, X marks the centre of the target pixel, which is shown by a red line; P_1, P_2, P_3 and P_4 are the surrounding pixels, whose centres are marked by the small red squares.

The simplest interpolation scheme is to use the **nearest neighbour**, i.e. we use the value of the pixel whose centre is nearest to (x, y), in this case P_3. In general – most obviously in the case of upsampling or enlarging an image – the same pixel will be chosen as the nearest neighbour of several target pixels whose centres, although different, are close enough together to fall within the same pixel. As a result, the transformed image will show the visible blocks of pixels and jagged edges typical of undersampling. An image enlarged using nearest-neighbour interpolation looks as if its original pixels had been magnified.

A better result is obtained by using **bilinear** interpolation, which uses the values of all four adjacent pixels. They are combined in proportion to the area of their intersection with the target pixel. Thus, in Figure 4.6, the value of P_1 will be multiplied by the shaded area within the upper left quadrant, and added to the values of the other three pixels, multiplied by the corresponding shaded areas.

IN DETAIL

If a and b are the fractional parts of x and y, respectively, then some simple mathematics shows that the value of the pixel at (x', y') in the result, whose target pixel is centred at (x, y), will be equal to

$$(1 - a)(1 - b)p_1 + a(1 - b)p_2 + (1 - a)bp_3 + abp_4$$

where p_i is the value of the pixel P_i, for $1 \le i \le 4$.

This simple area calculation is implicitly based on the assumption that the values change linearly in both directions (hence "*bi*linearly") across the region of the four pixels. An alternative way of arriving at the same value is to imagine computing the values vertically above and below (x, y) by combining the values of the two pairs of pixels in proportion to their horizontal distances from x, and then combining those values in proportion to their vertical distances from y.

In practice, the values are unlikely to vary in such a simple way, so that the bilinearly interpolated values will exhibit discontinuities. To obtain a better result, **bicubic** interpolation can be used instead. Here, the interpolation is based on cubic splines – that is, the intermediate values are

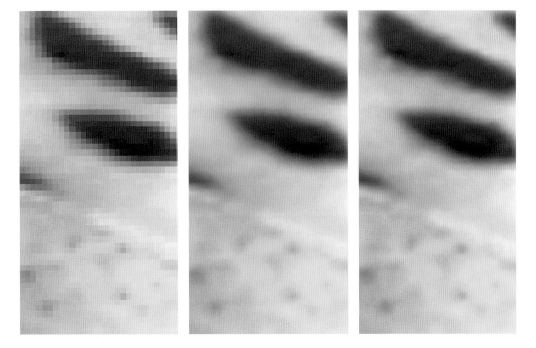

Figure 4.7. *Nearest-neighbour (left), bilinear (middle) and bicubic (right) interpolation*

assumed to lie along a Bézier curve connecting the stored pixels, instead of a straight line. These are used for the same reason they are used for drawing curves: they join together smoothly. As a result, the resampled image is smooth as well.

Bicubic interpolation must take account of 16 pixels of the original image for each pixel of the result, compared with bilinear interpolation's four, and it does take longer than the other two methods to compute. Relatively efficient algorithms have been developed and modern machines are sufficiently fast for this not to be a problem on single images. The only drawback of this interpolation method is that it can cause unwanted blurring of sharp edges.

Figure 4.7 shows a small part of the iris image from Figure 4.1, enlarged using nearest-neighbour, bilinear and bicubic interpolation. At this scale it is not easy to see the subtle differences between the results obtained with the bilinear and bicubic methods, but the characteristic flaws of the nearest-neighbour interpolation are obvious. (Bear in mind that the printing process will have introduced some extra artefacts into the images in this illustration.)

Information can never be regained once it has been discarded. This would seem to imply that one should always keep high-resolution bitmapped images, downsampling only when it is necessary for display purposes or to prepare a version of the image for display software, such as a Web browser, that does not downsample well. However, the disadvantage of high-resolution images soon becomes clear. They contain more pixels and thus occupy more disk space and take longer to transfer over networks. The size of an image increases as the square of the resolution, so, despite the possible gains in quality that might come from using high resolutions, in practice we more often need to use the lowest resolution we can get away with. This must be at least as good as that of an average monitor if the displayed quality is to be acceptable. Even at resolutions as low as 72 or 96 ppi, image files can become unmanageable, especially over networks.

KEY POINTS

Resolution is a measure of how finely a device approximates continuous images using finite pixels.

The resolution of scanners and printers is usually equated with their pixel density (dots per inch).

The resolution of video frames and computer monitors is usually equated with their pixel dimensions (width × height).

The resolution of a digital still camera is often quoted as the total number of pixels in the largest image it can record.

The pixel density of monitors and still cameras is assumed to be 72 dpi ("screen resolution").

A bitmapped image has pixel dimensions but no intrinsic pixel density.

The physical size of an image when it is displayed will depend on the pixel density of the device it is to be displayed on.

Most image formats record a resolution (pixel density) together with the image data; this is usually the resolution of the device on which it originated.

Scaling an image without changing its resolution changes its pixel dimensions in the same way as changing its resolution without changing its size.

Reducing the pixel dimensions is called "downsampling"; increasing them is called "upsampling". Both can lead to a loss of quality.

Scaling can be done either by applying a transformation to each original pixel or by applying the inverse transformation to each pixel in the scaled image.

Interpolation is needed because of the finite size of pixels.

Nearest-neighbour, bilinear or bicubic interpolation may be used.

Nearest-neighbour interpolation is quickest but produces poor-quality results; bicubic is slowest but produces very good results; bilinear is in between.

Interpolation causes a loss of information which can never be recovered.

Image Compression

To reduce the size of bitmapped images without downsampling them we must use techniques of data compression, often called *image coding* in this context. As we explained in Chapter 2, compression may be lossless, in which case decompression of a compressed image will produce an exact copy of the original, or lossy, when some information is discarded during compression, so that decompression only produces an approximation to the original.

Lossless Image Compression

Consider again the simple square design we looked at in Chapter 2. It is shown again in Figure 4.8. We stated on page 36 that its bitmapped representation required 48 kilobytes. This estimate was based on the assumption that the image was stored as an array, with three bytes per pixel. It would have to be represented in this form in order to display the image or manipulate it, but when we only wish to record the values of its pixels, for storage or transmission over a network, we can use a much more compact data representation. Instead of storing the value of each pixel explicitly, we could instead store a value, followed by a count to indicate a number of consecutive pixels of that value. For example, the first row consists of 128 pixels, all of the same colour, so instead of using 384 bytes to store that row, we could use just four: three to store the value corresponding to that colour and a fourth to record the number of occurrences. Indeed, if there was no advantage to be gained from preserving the identity of individual rows, we could go further, since the first 2580 pixels of this particular image are all the same colour. These are followed by a run of 88 pixels of another colour, which again can be stored in four bytes using a count and a colour value, instead of as 264 separate bytes all of the same value.

This simple technique of replacing a run of consecutive pixels of the same colour by a single copy of the colour value and a count of the number of pixels in the run is an example of a compression technique called *run-length encoding (RLE)*. In common with other methods of compression it requires some computation in order to achieve a saving in space. Another feature it shares with other methods of compression is that its effectiveness depends on the image that is being compressed. In this example, a large saving in storage can be achieved, because the image is extremely simple and consists of large areas of the same colour, which give rise to long runs of identical pixel values. If, instead, the image had consisted of alternating pixels of the two colours, applying RLE in a naïve fashion would have led to an increase in the storage requirement, since each "run" would have had a length of one, which would have to be recorded in addition to the pixel value. More realistically, images with continuously blended tones will not give rise to runs that can be efficiently encoded, whereas images with areas of flat colour will.

Figure 4.8. *An easily compressed image*

If we take the 48 kilobyte array representing Figure 4.8 and apply RLE compression to it, we will be able to apply an obvious decompression algorithm to the result in order to get back the original array. RLE is clearly a lossless compression technique, since no information is lost during a compression/decompression cycle.

RLE is the simplest lossless compression algorithm to understand, but it is far from being the most effective. The more sophisticated lossless algorithms you are likely to encounter fall into two classes. Algorithms of the first class work by re-encoding data so that the most frequent values occupy the fewest bits. For example, if an image uses 256 colours, each pixel would normally occupy eight bits (see Chapter 5). If, however, we could assign codes of different lengths to the colours, so that the code for the most common colour was only a single bit long, two-bit codes were used for the next most frequent colours, and so on, a saving in space would be achieved for most images. This approach to encoding, using *variable-length codes*, dates back to the earliest work on data compression and information theory, carried out in the late 1940s. The best known algorithm belonging to this class is *Huffman coding*.

Although Huffman coding and its derivatives are still used as part of other, more complex, compression techniques, since the late 1970s variable-length coding schemes have been super-seded to a large extent by *dictionary-based* compression schemes. Dictionary-based compression works by constructing a table, or dictionary, into which are entered strings of bytes (not necessarily corresponding to characters) that are encountered in the input data; all occurrences of a string are then replaced by a pointer into the dictionary. The process is similar to the tokenization of names carried out by the lexical analyser of a compiler using a symbol table. In contrast to variable-length coding schemes, dictionary-based schemes use fixed-length codes, but these point to variable-length strings in the dictionary. The effectiveness of this type of compression depends on choosing the strings to enter in the dictionary so that a saving of space is produced by replacing them by their codes. Ideally, the dictionary entries should be long strings that occur frequently.

Two techniques for constructing dictionaries and using them for compression were described in papers published in 1977 and 1978 by two researchers called Abraham Lempel and Jacob Ziv, thus the techniques are usually called *LZ77* and *LZ78*. A variation of LZ78, devised by another researcher, Terry Welch, and therefore known as *LZW* compression, is one of the most widely used compression methods, being the basis of the Unix compress utility and of GIF files, which we will describe shortly. The difference between LZ77 and LZ78 lies in the way in which the dictionary is constructed, while LZW is really just an improved implementation for LZ77.

During the 1990s the patent holders of LZW pursued unpopular licencing policies, which led to the development of a new variant of the legally unencumbered LZ77, called *deflate* compression, which combines the basic dictionary-building technique from LZ77 with Huffman encoding of the dictionary entries. Deflate compression is used in PNG files and is the basis of the zlib library, which is used by many programs that perform data compression, including gzip. The patents on LZW have now expired, so the original motivation for replacing it is no longer relevant.

┌─ IN DETAIL ───
Although it must be the case that any compression algorithm will always encounter some input files whose "compressed" version is actually larger than their original size, it is possible to limit the amount of expansion that can occur in the worst cases. For LZW, a file may increase by up to 1.25 times its original size. For deflate compression, though, the worst that can happen is that a file may expand by a total of 11 bytes, or a factor of 1.003, whichever is larger.
└──

JPEG Compression

Lossless compression can be applied to any sort of data. For certain sorts of data, such as binary executable programs, spreadsheet data or text, it is the only sort of compression that can be applied, since corruption of even one bit of such data may invalidate it. Image data, though, can tolerate a certain amount of data loss, so lossy compression can be used effectively for images. The most important lossy image compression technique is **JPEG** compression. JPEG stands for the Joint Photographic Experts Group, which draws attention to a significant feature of JPEG compression: it is best suited to photographs and similar images which are characterized by fine detail and continuous tones – the same characteristics as bitmapped images exhibit in general.

In Chapter 2 we considered the brightness or colour values of an image as a signal, which could be decomposed into its constituent frequencies. One way of envisaging this is to forget that the pixel values stored in an image denote colours, but merely consider them as the values of some variable z. Each pixel provides a z value (its colour) for the point defined by its x and y coordinates, so the image defines a three-dimensional shape. Figure 4.9 shows a greyscale version of the photograph from Figure 4.1, rendered as a 3-D surface in perspective, using its brightness values

Figure 4.9. *Pixel values interpreted as height*

to control the height. Notice how edges with marked brightness transitions, such as the patterning on the petal at the lower left, turn into steep slopes on the 3-D surface.

Such a shape can be considered as a complex 3-D waveform. We also explained (in Chapter 2) that any waveform can be transformed into the frequency domain using the Fourier Transform operation. Finally, we pointed out that the high-frequency components are associated with abrupt changes in intensity – those steep slopes on the surface. An additional fact, based on extensive experimental evidence, is that people do not perceive the effect of high frequencies very accurately, especially not in colour images.

Up until now, we have considered the frequency domain representation only as a way of thinking about the properties of a signal. JPEG compression works by actually transforming an image into its frequency components. This is not done by computing the Fourier Transform, but by using a related operation called the **Discrete Cosine Transform (DCT)**. Although the DCT is defined differently from the Fourier Transform, and has some different properties, it too analyses a signal into its frequency components. In computational terms it takes an array of pixels and produces an array of coefficients, representing the amplitude of the frequency components in the image. Since we start with a two-dimensional image, whose intensity can vary in both the x and y directions, we end up with a two-dimensional array of coefficients, corresponding to spatial frequencies in these two directions. This array will be the same size as the image's array of pixels.

Applying a DCT operation to an image of any size is computationally expensive (the time taken is proportional to the square of the image's size in pixels), so it is only with the widespread availability of powerful processors that it has been practical to perform this sort of compression – and, more importantly, decompression – without the aid of dedicated hardware. When the JPEG standard was devised in the early 1990s, it was considered impractical to apply DCT to an entire image at once. Instead, for JPEG compression, images are divided into 8×8 pixel squares, each of which is transformed separately.

Transforming an image into the frequency domain does not, in itself, perform any compression. It does, however, change the data into a form which can be compressed in a way that minimizes the perceptible effect of discarding information, because the frequency components are now explicitly separated. This allows information about the high frequencies, which do not contribute much to the perceived quality of the image, to be discarded. This is done by distinguishing fewer different possible values for higher-frequency components. If, for example, the value produced by the DCT for each frequency could range from 0 to 255, the lowest-frequency coefficients might be allowed to have any integer value within this range; slightly higher frequencies might only be allowed to take on values divisible by 4, while the highest frequencies might only be allowed to have the value 0 or 128. Putting this another way, the different frequencies are quantized to different numbers of levels, with fewer levels being used for high frequencies. In JPEG compression, the number of quantization levels to be used for each frequency coefficient can be specified separately in a quantization matrix, containing a value for each coefficient.

This quantization process reduces the space needed to store the image in two ways. First, after quantization, many components will end up with zero coefficients. Second, fewer bits are needed to store the non-zero coefficients. To take advantage of the redundancy which has thus been generated in the data representation, two lossless compression methods are applied to the array of quantized coefficients. Zeros are run-length encoded; Huffman coding is applied to the remaining values. In order to maximize the length of the runs of zeros, the coefficients are processed in what is called the *zig-zag sequence*, as shown in Figure 4.10. This is effective because the frequencies increase as we move away from the top left corner of the array in both directions. In other words, the perceptible information in the image is concentrated in the top left part of the array, and the likelihood is that the bottom right part will be full of zeros. The zig-zag sequence is thus likely to encounter long runs of zeros, which would be broken up if the array were traversed more conventionally by rows or columns.

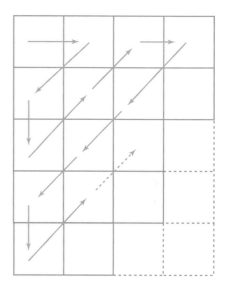

Figure 4.10. *The zig-zag sequence*

Decompressing JPEG data is done by reversing the compression process. The runs are expanded and the Huffman-encoded coefficients are decompressed, then an **Inverse Discrete Cosine Transform** is applied to take the data back from the frequency domain into the spatial domain, where the values can once again be treated as pixels in an image. The inverse DCT is defined very similarly to the DCT itself; the computation of the inverse transform requires the same amount of time as that of the forward transform, so JPEG compression and decompression take roughly the same time (on the same machine). Note that there is no "inverse quantization" step. The information that was lost during quantization is gone forever, which is why the decompressed image only approximates the original. Generally, though, the approximation is a good one.

A useful feature of JPEG compression is that it is possible to control the degree of compression, and thus the quality of the compressed image, by altering the values in the quantization matrix. Programs that implement JPEG compression allow you to choose a quality setting, so that you can compromise between image quality and compression. Even at the highest quality setting, JPEG compression is still lossy: the decompressed image will not be an exact bit-for-bit duplicate of the original. It will often be visually indistinguishable, but that is not what we mean by "lossless".

JPEG compression is highly effective when applied to the sort of images for which it is designed, i.e. photographic and scanned images with continuous tones. Such images can sometimes be compressed to as little as 5% of their original size without apparent loss of quality. Lossless compression techniques are nothing like as effective on this type of image. Still higher levels of compression can be obtained by using a lower quality setting, that is, by using coarser quantization that discards more information. When this is done the boundaries of the 8×8 squares to which the DCT is applied tend to become visible on screen, because the discontinuities between them mean that different frequency components are discarded in each square. At low compression levels (i.e. high quality settings) this does not matter, since enough information is retained for the common features of adjacent squares to produce appropriately similar results, but as more and more information is discarded, the common features become lost and the boundaries show up.

Such unwanted features in a compressed image are called ***compression artefacts***. Other artefacts may arise when an image containing sharp edges is compressed by JPEG. Here, the smoothing that is the essence of JPEG compression is to blame: sharp edges come out blurred. This is rarely a problem with the photographically originated material for which JPEG is intended, but it can be a problem if images created on a computer are compressed. In particular, if text, especially small text, occurs as part of an image, JPEG is likely to blur the edges, often making the text unreadable. For images with many sharp edges, JPEG compression should be avoided. Instead, images should be saved in a format such as PNG, which uses lossless LZ77 compression.

Figure 4.11 shows enlarged views of the same detail from our photograph, in its original form and having been JPEG-compressed using the lowest possible quality setting. The compression reduced its size from 24.3 MB to 160 kB, and even with such severe compression it is not easy to see the difference between the two images at normal size. However, when they are blown up as in Figure 4.11, you can see the edges of the 8×8 blocks – these are not the individual pixels, both images have the same resolution. You should also be able to see that some details, such as the brown specks in the yellow area, have been lost. These symptoms are typical of the way JPEG compression artefacts appear in heavily compressed photographic images.

┌─**IN DETAIL**──
│
│ **Although a single cycle of JPEG compression and decompression at low**
│ **settings may not cause much degradation of the image, repeated compression**
│ **and decompression will do so. In general, therefore, if you are making changes**
│ **to an image you should save working versions in some uncompressed format,**
│ **and not keep saving JPEGs. However, it is possible to rotate an image through**
│ **90° without any loss, providing the image's dimensions are an exact multiple**
│ **of the size of the blocks that are being compressed. This is probably why the**
│ **dimensions of images from digital cameras are always multiples of 8: changing**
│ **from landscape to portrait format and vice versa is such a rotation.**
│
└──

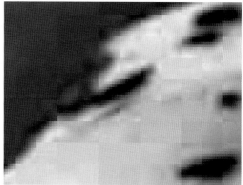

Figure 4.11. *Original (left) and JPEG (right)*

JPEG2000

JPEG compression has been extremely successful: it is used for almost all photographic images on the Web, and by most low- to mid-range digital cameras for storing images. It is, however, by no means the best possible algorithm for performing image compression. Some of its shortcomings are a reflection of the limited processing power that was available on most computers at the time the JPEG standard was devised. Others arise from a failure to anticipate all the potential applications of compressed image files.

A successor to the JPEG standard has been developed in an attempt to overcome these shortcomings. It was adopted as an ISO standard in 2000, hence it is called ***JPEG2000***. Its aim is to improve on the existing DCT-based JPEG in several areas. These include providing better quality at high compression ratios (and thus low bit rates), incorporating lossless compression and alpha channel transparency within the single framework of JPEG2000, "region of interest" coding, where some parts of the image are compressed with greater fidelity than others, better progressive display and increased robustness in the face of transmission errors. Unlike the original JPEG standard, JPEG2000 also specifies a file format.

The basic structure of the compression process is the same. First, the image is divided into rectangular tiles, each of which is compressed separately. JPEG2000 tiles may be any size, up to the size of the entire image, so the artefacts seen in JPEG images at the edges of the 8×8 blocks can be reduced or eliminated by using bigger tiles. Next, a transform is applied to the data, giving a set of frequency coefficients. However, instead of the DCT, a transform based on diffferent principles, known as a ***Discrete Wavelet Transform (DWT)***, is used in JPEG2000.

It's quite easy to get an idea of what the DWT does by considering a simpler sort of wavelet, called the ***Haar wavelet***. (Actually, we are only going to consider a special case, and deal with that informally, because even simple wavelets involve quite complicated mathematics.) To keep things extremely simple, consider a single row of an image with just four pixels, and suppose their values are 12, 56, 8 and 104. We can make a lower-resolution approximation to this row of pixels by taking the average of the first pair and the last pair of pixels, giving two new pixels, whose values are 34 and 56, but in doing so we have lost some information. One way (out of many) to retain that information is by storing the magnitude of the difference between each average and the pixels it was computed from: we can subtract this value from the average to get the first pixel, and add it to get the second. In our example, these *detail coefficients*, as they are called, are 22 and 48. ($34 - 22 = 12$, $34 + 22 = 56$, and so on.)

We can repeat this process, averaging the averages and computing a new detail coefficient. The new average is 45 and the detail coefficient is 11. Finally, we can combine this single average pixel value with all three detail coefficients, as the sequence 45, 11, 22, 48. It should be clear that the original four pixel values can be reconstructed from this sequence by reversing the process we used to arrive at it.

This exercise has not produced any compression, but – as with the DCT – it has rearranged the information about the image into a form where it is possible to isolate detail. You can think of the final sequence, which is the *wavelet decomposition* of the original, as comprising a value that describes the whole image coarsely – it is the average brightness of the whole image – together with a set of coefficients that can be used to add progressively more detail to the image. Using the first detail coefficient we can get a two-pixel image; using the other coefficients gets us back to the full four pixels. Each step in the reconstruction process doubles the resolution. If we want to compress the image by discarding detail, we just have to discard the later coefficients (or quantize them more coarsely than the earlier ones). This is essentially the way in which JPEG2000 compression works.

This transform could be applied to a complete two-dimensional image by first transforming all the rows and then – treating the matrix of values produced by the transform as a new image – transforming all the columns. Alternatively, the same result could be obtained by carrying out the first transform step on all the rows, and then on all the columns, before applying the second step to all the rows, and so on. If the process is carried out in this order, then after a step has been applied to both rows and columns the result will comprise a version of the whole image, at half the horizontal and vertical resolution of the version obtained at the previous step, in the top left quadrant of the matrix, together with detail coefficients in the other quadrants. The process is illustrated schematically in Figure 4.12.

The idea of encoding an image (or any function) at varying levels of resolution, embodied in the example we have just given, can be generalized, but the mathematics involved in doing so is by no

 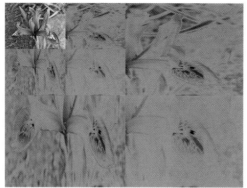

Figure 4.12. *Wavelet decomposition of an image*

means trivial. However, the subject is now well understood and many different ways of obtaining a wavelet decomposition are known. JPEG2000 specifies two: a reversible transform, which does not lose any information, and an irreversible transform, which does. Both of these can be implemented efficiently and relatively simply. The choice of transforms makes it possible for JPEG2000 to perform lossless as well as lossy compression within the context of a single algorithm.

After the wavelet decomposition has been computed, the coefficients are quantized using a quality setting to specify a step size – the difference between quantization levels. If this size is set to 1, no quantization occurs, so this step will also be lossless in that case.

Finally, the quantized coefficients are encoded using ***arithmetic coding***, a lossless compression algorithm that is more effective than Huffman coding.

The structure of the wavelet decomposition makes it easy to define a format for the data which allows an image to be displayed as a sequence of progressively better approximations, since each level of coefficients adds more detail to the image. This was considered a desirable property for images to be transmitted over networks. It also makes it possible to zoom into an image without loss of detail.

It has been estimated that decoders for JPEG2000 are an order of magnitude more complex than those for JPEG. As Figure 4.13 shows, the reward for the added complexity comes in the form of the extremely good quality that JPEG2000 can produce at high compression ratios. Here, the photograph has been compressed to roughly the same size as the JPEG version shown in Figure 4.11. This time, however, there are no block edges to be seen, and although some detail has been lost, the loss takes the form of a general softening of the image, which is more acceptable than the ugly artefacts produced in the JPEG.

Figure 4.13. *Original (left) and JPEG2000 (right)*

JPEG2000 compression is superior to JPEG, and the JPEG2000 file format supports some desirable features that JPEG files lack. However, at the time of writing, there is little or no support for JPEG2000 in digital cameras, Web browsers and graphics programs.

The main obstacle to more widespread support for JPEG2000 lies in the fact that JPEG is so thoroughly entrenched. Many millions of JPEG images are already available on the Web, there are many well-established and popular software tools for creating JPEG images and incorporating them into Web pages, most digital cameras (and even mobile phones) will generate JPEGs, and Web designers are familiar with JPEG.

There is therefore a lack of any perceived need for JPEG2000 and adoption of the new standard has been slow. Some influential institutions, including the Library of Congress and the Smithsonian Institution, do use JPEG2000 as an archival format, so it may be that instead of replacing JPEG as a Web image format, JPEG2000 will find a different niche.

---IN DETAIL---

In 2007, JPEG announced that it would be considering another format for standardization, in addition to the original JPEG and JPEG2000. JPEG XR is the name proposed for a standard version of Microsoft's HD Photo format (formerly Windows Media Photo). This is claimed to possess many of the advantages of JPEG2000, but appears to be better suited to implementation in digital cameras. HD Photo is based on a "lapped biorthogonal transform", which more closely resembles the DCT than DWT.

It is not yet clear whether JPEG XR will become a standard, or whether it will be adopted with any more enthusiasm than JPEG2000.

KEY POINTS

Images can be losslessly compressed using various methods, including run-length encoding (RLE), Huffman encoding and the dictionary-based LZ77, LZ78, LZW and deflate algorithms.

JPEG is the most commonly used lossy compression method for still images.

High-frequency information can be discarded from an image without perceptible loss of quality, because people do not perceive the effects of high frequencies in images very accurately.

The image is mapped into the frequency domain using the Discrete Cosine Transform (DCT).

The Discrete Cosine Transform is applied to 8×8 blocks of pixels.

Applying the DCT does not reduce the size of the data, since the array of frequency coefficients is the same size as the original pixel array.

The coefficients are quantized, according to a quantization matrix which determines the quality. The quantization discards some information.

After quantization there will usually be many zero coefficients. These are RLE-encoded, using a zig-zag sequence to maximize the length of the runs.

The non-zero coefficients are compressed using Huffman encoding.

Decompression is performed by reversing the process, using the Inverse DCT to recover the image from its frequency domain representation.

The decompressed image may exhibit compression artefacts, including blurring and visible edges at the boundaries between the 8×8 pixel blocks, especially at low quality settings.

JPEG2000 improves on JPEG in many areas, including image quality at high compression ratios. It can be used losslessly as well as lossily.

For JPEG2000 compression the image is divided into tiles, but these can be any size, up to the entire image.

A Discrete Wavelet Transform (DWT) is applied to the tiles, generating a wavelet decomposition, comprising a coarse (low resolution) version of the image and a set of detail coefficients that can be used to add progressively more detail to the image.

The DWT may be reversible (lossless) or irreversible (lossy).

The detail coefficients in the wavelet decomposition may be quantized and are then losslessly compressed using arithmetic encoding.

File Formats

There is considerable scope for encoding bitmapped image data in different ways, compressing it and adding supplementary information to it. Consequently, a large number of different graphics file formats have been developed. As is the case with programming languages, most of these are only used by a limited circle of enthusiasts, or for specialized applications, or on particular plat-forms. Even so, there remains a significant number of different formats in wide use, with differing characteristics that make them suitable for different types of image.

The advent of the World Wide Web has had something of a standardizing influence. Although it does not specify any particular graphics file formats, the necessity for cross-platform compatibility has led to the adoption of certain formats as *ad hoc* standards.

GIF and PNG

GIF (Graphics Interchange Format) was originally developed by CompuServe as a common format for exchanging bitmapped images between different platforms. GIF files use LZW compression, so they are lossless. The compression is most effective on simple images, such as cartoon-style drawings and synthetic images produced on computers. It is less successful with scanned and photographic images, which may have wide colour ranges and tonal variations.

GIF files also employ a technique called indexed colour – which we will describe fully in Chapter 5 – to reduce the number of bytes used to store the value of each pixel. As a result of using indexed colour, GIF images are restricted to 256 colours. This also makes them unsuitable for use with colour photographs.

One of the GIF format's most useful features is that one colour can be designated as transparent, so that, if the GIF image is displayed against a coloured background or another image, the back-ground will show through the transparent areas, as illustrated in Figure 4.14.

Figure 4.14. *A GIF with transparent areas*

GIF files are widely used on the Web, especially for simple graphic elements such as logos. Every graphical Web browser is capable of displaying GIF images. They can also be used for animation, as we will see in Chapter 7.

Because the use of LZW compression required the payment of a licence fee while it was patented, an alternative format, called **PNG (Portable Network Graphics)**, was developed for the lossless storage of images to be used on the Web. PNG was intended to supersede GIF. It uses the deflate method of compression, which is free from patent restrictions. Additionally, PNG is not restricted to 256 colours and supports "alpha channels", which allow for partial transparency and special effects based on it, which is impossible in any other Web graphics format.

The PNG format was developed under the aegis of the W3C, and its specification, published in 1996, has the status of a W3C Recommendation and an ISO standard. However, support for PNG has been slow to develop; support for alpha channels in PNG images only became available to most Windows users with the release of Internet Explorer 7. As with JPEG2000 compression, it seems that there is no perceived need for PNG among most Web developers, who are happy to use the older alternatives. PNG files are used in other contexts, though. For instance, icons on Mac OS X are stored as PNG files; PNG is the native file format for the Web graphics editor Fireworks.

JPEG Files

The JPEG standard does not specify a file format, only compression and decompression algorithms and an "interchange format", which specifies how compressed data should be arranged for exchange between programs. Data in this format can be embedded in various sorts of files, including PDF and the Exif files recorded by many digital cameras.

Colloquially, though, the name "JPEG file" is used to refer to what are properly called **JFIF (JPEG File Interchange Format)** files. JFIF is just a wrapper around JPEG interchange format data, subject to some simplifications. There is no standard for JFIF, but it is almost universally used for storing JPEG data in Web graphics.

An official file format called **SPIFF (Still Picture Interchange File Format)** was defined by the JPEG committee (five years after the original JPEG specification) and has become an ISO standard. SPIFF files can contain compressed JPEG data and black and white (but not greyscale) images compressed according to a related standard called JBIG. The SPIFF format is defined in such a way that any program that can read and display JFIF files will be able to read and display SPIFF files, so in practical terms the distinction between the two is irrelevant. SPIFF and JFIF files use the same conventions for file extensions (.jpg, .jpeg) and both are served with the same Internet Media Type (image/jpeg).

JPEG files are the only lossily compressed bitmapped image files that are supported by every graphical Web browser without the use of a plug-in. They are therefore the automatic choice for photographic material to be included on Web pages.

Digital photographs that are compressed using JPEG in the camera are then usually held on the device's removable storage (Flash card, memory stick, etc.) using the *Exif* format, which was devised by the Japan Electronic Industry Development Association (JEIDA). This format can accommodate both JPEG and TIFF (see below) data, and also allows audio to be included. For JPEG data, it can be considered an extension of JFIF, primarily to accommodate metadata, as we mentioned in Chapter 2.

The JPEG2000 standard does include a detailed specification of its own *JP2* file format, and an extension to it, the *JPX* format. These are identified on the Internet by the media types image/jp2 and image/jpx, respectively. However, support for these files in Web browsers is very limited.

As with JPEG, JPEG2000-compressed images can also be embedded in files with other formats, such as PDF.

Other Formats

GIF, PNG and JPEG (JFIF/SPIFF) are the only file formats that can safely be used for bitmapped images on the Web, but other formats are in use in the print-based industries and for storing images for processing. As we noted in Chapter 2, the native Photoshop (PSD) format is in many ways the most important bitmapped image file format, because Photoshop is a *de facto* industry standard for bitmapped image manipulation. Anybody working professionally in this area will be using Photoshop, and will expect other people to be able to read PSD files.

The main rival to PSD as an interchange format is *TIFF (Tag Image File Format)*, an elaborate extensible file format that can store full-colour bitmaps using several different compression schemes, including LZW and JPEG. TIFF files can also be uncompressed, and the format is often used by digital cameras for storing uncompressed images, often supplemented by Exif metadata. It is supported by most bitmapped image manipulation programs on all platforms, although not all programs are equal in the comprehensiveness of their support, so that TIFF files created by one program cannot always be read by another.

BMP, more properly called the *Microsoft Windows Bitmap* format, is another widely used format. As its name indicates, it is platform-dependent, but the near ubiquity of the Windows platforms means that it is widely understood by programs on other systems. Unlike most other bitmapped formats, BMP only supports a simple form of lossless compression, and BMP files are usually stored uncompressed.

As we mentioned in Chapter 3, PDF is a document description language, and although we stressed its use for storing vector graphics, it is capable of representing anything that can appear in a document, including bitmapped images, which are treated as indivisible objects when they are combined with vector paths. Bitmapped images can be embedded in a PDF file as part of a larger document, or they can be the only thing in the document, effectively making PDF into a bitmapped image format.

Image data in PDF can be compressed in many ways: LZW, deflate, RLE, JBIG, JPEG and JPEG2000 are all supported in the current version of PDF.

Normally, we tend to think that a digital camera creates an image in the same way that a film camera takes a photograph, and that the image file is a record of the light entering the camera. This isn't quite true, though. The data from the camera's sensor has to undergo some processing that rearranges it into an image. Sometimes, professional photographers prefer to have access to the original – or "raw" – data, so that they can have complete control over all aspects of its processing.

There is no standard format for camera raw data. Software that processes it must recognize many different variations in order to be able to cope with the raw data from any digital camera that provides it. Programs that can do this do exist, but there is the possibility that some particular camera raw format may cease to be supported one day, making any images that use it inaccessible in their original form.

Adobe's **DNG (Digital Negative)** format is intended to overcome this problem, and serve as an archiving format for camera raw images. It is based on the TIFF format, which is itself an ISO standard, and is fully documented, unlike many manufacturers' raw formats. Hence, it is fairly safe to suppose that images in DNG format will be readable for a long time.

Although few digital cameras produce DNG directly, Adobe have provided a free program that will convert over 150 camera raw formats to DNG. This is frequently updated as new cameras with their own raw formats are introduced.

Metadata

The ability to organize and search collections of images is dependent on metadata, as we explained in Chapter 2. The most convenient place to keep image metadata is in the image file itself. This ensures that the two cannot become separated, and does not tie functions that depend on metadata to the use of any particular piece of software. It is therefore desirable for a file format to provide the ability to store metadata along with the image data itself. (Alternatively, the metadata can be separated from the file and manipulated independently by a program such as Bridge – described in *Digital Media Tools*, Lightroom or Expression Media. The disadvantage of this approach is that it may be difficult to access the metadata without the program.)

All file formats provide a means of recording essential metadata such as the image's height and width, but the file formats we have described so far vary in their support for additional metadata. GIF, for example, has only a general mechanism for adding machine-readable or human-readable data to an image. TIFF provides a more general mechanism for adding metadata fields. Other formats, notably Exif, are specifically designed to accommodate highly structured metadata conforming to some standard.

PSD and DNG files can include XMP metadata, which was described in Chapter 2.

KEY POINTS

GIF files use LZW compression and are restricted to 256 colours. One colour may be used to designate transparency.

They are most suitable for simple images with areas of flat colour.

PNG was developed to supersede GIF. It uses deflate compression, is not restricted to 256 colours and supports alpha channels for partial transparency.

JPEG data can be stored in several different formats.

JFIF and SPIFF are compatible formats for JPEG images and are widely used on the Web.

Exif can hold either JPEG or TIFF data, together with extensive metadata.

JP2 and JPX formats are defined for storing JPEG2000 data.

TIFF is an extensible format, often used for storing uncompressed digital photographs, and for interchange of images.

BMP is a simple bitmapped image format that is native to Windows, but widely supported. BMP files are often uncompressed.

PDF documents can include bitmapped image data, that may be compressed using JPEG, JPEG2000, LZW, deflate, and others.

Camera raw data is used when complete control over image processing is required, but there is no standard format for camera raw data.

Adobe's DNG (Digital Negative) format is a standard, based on the TIFF format, intended for archiving camera raw images.

Image file formats differ in their support for metadata.

Image Manipulation

A bitmapped image explicitly stores a value for every pixel, so we can alter the value of any pixel or group of pixels if we wish to change the image. The sheer number of pixels in most images means that editing them individually is both time-consuming and confusing. How are we to judge the effect that particular changes to certain pixels will have on the appearance of the whole image? Or assess which pixels must be altered and how, in order to sharpen the fuzzy edges in an out-of-focus photograph? In order for image editing to be convenient, it is necessary that operations be provided at a higher level than that of altering a single pixel. Many useful operations can be described by analogy with traditional techniques for altering photographic images for print, in particular the use of filters and masks.

Image Manipulation Software

Many different programs are available for editing bitmapped images, varying from consumer-oriented utilities for carrying out simple tasks with the minimum of effort (and producing correspondingly unsophisticated results) to powerful professional programs that are capable of almost any operation you might think of. Such programs generally supply a kit of tools for making selections and low-level adjustments, and a set of built-in filters and effects, as well as commands for resizing, changing resolution, and so on. They are sometimes called painting programs, to distinguish them from the drawing programs used for vector graphics, but this is misleading. It is much more common for a program to be used for altering an existing image such as a photograph than for it to be used to create a picture from scratch, like a painting.

Adobe Photoshop is, without doubt, the leading application for image manipulation in the professional category, being a *de facto* industry standard. There are other programs though, in particular a powerful package known as ***The Gimp***, which has similar capabilities and a similar set of tools to Photoshop's, and is distributed under an open software licence. Both of these programs include many features concerned with preparing images for print, which are not relevant to multimedia.

Photoshop and The Gimp work interactively through a graphical interface. ***Image Magick*** is a suite of programs that can perform common operations, including format conversions, from a command line. It can also be accessed from within programs written in most languages, by way of an API. This mode of working from inside a program is best suited for generating visualizations of data, or performing repetitive alterations to sets of images. For instance, if you were creating an image gallery for a Web site and you only wanted to keep a full-sized version of each image, you could generate thumbnails on the fly using Image Magick. This way of working requires that all operations be specified numerically, and it provides no visual feedback, so it is effectively useless for those types of image manipulation that require human judgement and intervention. We will therefore concentrate on interactive image manipulations instead.

Before we describe how images can be manipulated, we ought first to examine why one might wish to manipulate them. There are three broad reasons. One is to correct deficiencies in an image, that may have been caused by poor equipment or techniques used in its creation or digitization. The second is retouching the image to change its content; the third is in order to create images that are difficult or impossible to make naturally.

An example of the first type is the removal of "red-eye", the red glow apparently emanating from the eyes of a person whose portrait has been taken face-on with a camera using a flash set too close to the lens. Consumer-oriented image manipulation programs often provide commands that encapsulate a sequence of manipulations to perform common tasks, such as red-eye removal, with a single key stroke. Professional programs allow the correction to be carried out with a greater degree of control, using general-purpose tools for correcting colour. Other defects that can be corrected include poor exposure, colour casts and perspective distortion.

Retouching operations include cropping, which removes extraneous material around the edges to improve the framing and composition, and more subtle alterations, such as removing blemishes and unwanted objects. Unlike the previous class of operations, which are intended to remedy faults in the execution of the image, these changes are concerned with altering the subject. Some people would consider the results of applying retouching operations as fakes; they certainly play a role in the creation of unnaturally glamorous images used for publicity and advertising.

The manipulations performed for the third reason generally fall into the category of special effects, and there is an almost unlimited range of such effects: glows, swirls, distortions and simulated natural media that make photographs look like paintings can all be applied to images. Artificial images are often created by combining elements from several images into collages, either as obviously contrived arrangements of elements, or as a deliberate attempt to create a false impression, for example, by placing a figure from one photograph against the background of another, making it look as if a person was somewhere they were not.

In addition to all these functions, image manipulation software can also be used simply to convert an image from one format to another, which may involve compressing it. The range of formats that each program can read and write varies, but any worthwhile program will be able to convert between PNG, GIF and JPEG, and most will be able to deal with TIFF files. Any program that cannot read PSD files is severely limited in its usefulness.

In the remainder of this section, we will describe the principles behind some of the more important image manipulations, using Photoshop's facilities where concrete examples are needed. For a detailed introduction to the use of Photoshop, consult Chapter 4 of *Digital Media Tools*.

Layers

The ability to organize artwork into *layers* was introduced in Photoshop 3 in 1994. Since then, it has become one of the most significant ways in which digital technology has affected how artists, designers and illustrators work.

A layer is often likened to a digital version of a sheet of clear acetate material, like an overhead projector transparency. You can draw or paint on parts of the layer, leaving some of it transparent. An image can be constructed by stacking layers on top of each other; where a layer is transparent, the layer below it shows through. This may not sound very exciting – you can always draw things on top of other things – but a layer allows you to treat separate parts of an image as separate units, and to blend them together in various different ways.

An immediate consequence of this ability is that it provides a way of distinguishing objects in a bitmapped image. Normally, as we have shown, if you make a picture of a flower as a bitmapped image there is no discrete object corresponding to each petal; there are only areas of pixels. By placing each petal on a different layer, though, the petals can be moved or modified individually, much as the individual shapes making up a vector image can be.

One specific way in which artists take advantage of the separation that layers allow is by using one layer as a background against which objects on other layers are superimposed. These objects can then be moved about over the background until a satisfactory arrangement is found. If they were not on separate layers, whenever an object was moved it would be necessary to touch in the background where it had been before. In a similar way, the use of layers makes it easy to apply effects to parts of an image, since effects can be applied to individual layers. Thus, for example, a background layer might be blurred so that elements on layers placed over it will stand out.

Figure 4.15 is a simple illustration of combining (or *compositing*) layers. The starting point is the two photographs shown at the top, one a flower, the other a butterfly on a wall. These were opened in Photoshop, and the butterfly was extracted from its background (using the magnetic lasso tool, as illustrated in Figure 4.17), scaled up and rotated, to produce the image at the bottom left of Figure 4.15, which was placed on a layer on top of the flower image. (The chequerboard pattern is the conventional way of representing transparent areas.) In the resulting composite image, the butterfly appears to be perched on the flower, which in reality it was not.

A different way of using layers is for experimentation. Layers can be reordered without affecting their contents, so that different stacking arrangements can be tried out. Layers can also be duplicated, and the duplicates altered separately; any layer can be made invisible, so different versions of a layer can be displayed in turn, to see which is better.

Figure 4.15. *Compositing layers*

We have likened layers to transparent sheets of acetate, but they are really data structures inside a computer, so they are not subject to the physical limitations of materials, and can behave in ways that acetate cannot. In particular, the degree of transparency can be varied. By using layers that are only partially transparent, backgrounds or overlays can be dimmed.

The precise way in which separate layers are combined may also be modified. The normal behaviour of layers is for the areas that are not transparent to cover any layers beneath. This is how the layers in Figure 4.15 were combined. Sometimes, it may be preferable for these areas to be blended with lower layers instead, or dissolved into them. Transparency may be made conditional on the brightness of one or other of the layers, so that blending takes place below a threshold value, but above that value the superposed layer conceals what is below it. More complex blending modes and options may be used by graphic designers to create artificial compositions from layers.

The layer metaphor has found such favour as a way of organizing images that it has been extended to incorporate effects as well as image elements. Photoshop's **adjustment layers** are described as being layers through which you can look at the image through a medium that applies one of the effects, such as a tonal adjustment, which we will describe later in this chapter. This makes them a tool for non-destructive editing, i.e. for applying effects without actually changing the pixels on image layers, and a safe means of experimentation. Unlike changes made to image layers, changes made by using settings in adjustment layers can also be altered at a later date, even after a file has been closed and reopened.

Selections, Masks and Alpha Channels

As we have repeatedly stressed, a bitmapped image is not stored as a collection of separate objects; it is just an array of pixels. Even if we can look at the picture and clearly see a square or a circle, for example, we cannot select that shape when we are editing the image with a program, in the way that we could if it were a vector image. In a bitmapped image the shape's identity is not part of the information that is explicitly available to the program; it is something that our eyes and brain have identified. Some other means must therefore be employed in order to select parts of an image when it is being manipulated by a mere computer program.

Some of the tools that are used to make selections from bitmapped images are more or less the same tools that are used to draw shapes in vector graphics. Selections may be made by drawing around an area, much as a traditional paste-up artist would cut out a shape from a printed image using a scalpel. The simplest selection tools are the rectangular and elliptical *marquee tools*, which let you select an area by dragging out a rectangle or ellipse, just as you would draw these shapes in a drawing program. It is important to realize that you are not drawing, though; you are simply defining an area within the image.

More often than not, the area you wish to select will not be a neat rectangle or ellipse. To accommodate irregular shapes, thinly disguised versions of the other standard drawing tools may be used: the *lasso tool* is a less powerful version of Illustrator's pencil tool, which can be used to draw freehand curves around an area to be selected; the polygon lasso is used to select areas bounded by straight lines; a fully-fledged Bézier drawing pen is also available. These tools allow selections to be outlined with considerable precision and flexibility, although their use can be laborious. To ease the task of making selections, other tools are available that make use of pixel values to help define the selected area. These include the *magic wand* and the *magnetic lasso*.

The magic wand is used to select areas on the basis of their colour. With this tool selected, clicking on the image causes all pixels adjacent to the cursor which are similar in colour to the pixel under the cursor to be selected. Figure 4.16 shows an example of the magic wand selecting a highly irregular shape. The wand was clicked in the dark area of foliage in the top image; the selected area is outlined with a moving marquee, as shown in the detail in the middle image; the selected area could then be removed from its background, as shown at the bottom. Because of the uniform

Figure 4.16. *Magic wand selection*

colour of the silhouetted foliage, which is quite distinct from the rest of the image, the selection is extremely clean. The tolerance, that is, the amount by which a colour may differ but still be considered sufficiently similar to be included in the selection, may be specified.

The magnetic lasso works on a different principle. Like the other lasso tools, it is dragged around the area to be selected, but instead of simply following the outline drawn by the user, it adjusts itself so that the outline snaps to edges within a specified distance of the cursor. Any sufficiently large change in contrast is considered to be an edge. Both the distance within which edges are detected and the degree of contrast variation that is considered to constitute an edge may be specified. Where an image has well-defined edges, for example, both of these can be set to a high value, so that drawing roughly round an object will cause it to be selected as the outline snaps to the high-contrast edges. Where the edges are less well defined, it will be necessary to allow a lower contrast level to indicate an edge, and consequently the outline will have to be drawn with more care, using a narrower detection width. Figure 4.17 shows an example. (You may be able to make out the selection indication on the leading edge of the butterfly's wings.) Note how it has been possible to select the fine antennae. This would be quite a demanding task if it was necessary to make the selection by drawing a path with a Bézier pen — although some purists would do it that way.

You should appreciate that these selections, which we describe in terms of colour and colour contrast, are implemented by examining the numerical values that represent colours. The computer is not seeing colours, which means that sometimes selections of this sort don't behave quite as expected. As we will explain in Chapter 5, colour and its perception are complicated topics, which don't always map to numerical computations on stored values in an obvious way.

Figure 4.17. *Magnetic lasso selection and mask*

Once a selection has been made, using any of the tools just described, any changes you make to the image – such as applying filters – are restricted to the pixels within the selected area. Another way of describing this is to say that the selection defines a ***mask***, that is, the area that is not selected, which is protected from any changes. Image manipulation programs allow you to store one or more masks with an image, so that a selection can be remembered and used for more than one operation – an ordinary selection is ephemeral, and is lost as soon as a different one is made.

The technique of masking off parts of an image has long been used by artists and photographers, who use physical masks and stencils to keep out light or paint. A cardboard stencil, for example, either allows paint through completely or stops it completely. We could store a digital mask with similar "all or nothing" behaviour by using a single bit for each pixel in the image, setting it to one for all the masked-out pixels, and to zero for those in the selection. Thus, the mask is itself an array of pixels, and we can think of it as being another image. If just one bit is used for each pixel, this image will be purely monochromatic. By analogy with photographic masks, the white parts of the image are considered transparent, the black ones opaque. The image on the right of Figure 4.17 shows the selection of the butterfly as a one-bit mask.

Digital masks have properties which are difficult to realize with physical media. By using more than one bit, so that the mask becomes a greyscale image, we can specify different degrees of transparency. For reasons which will be explained in Chapter 5, a greyscale mask of this sort is often called an ***alpha channel***. Any painting, filtering or other modifications made to pixels covered by semi-transparent areas of the mask will be applied in a degree proportional to the value stored in the alpha channel. It is common to use eight bits for each pixel of a mask, allowing for 256 different transparency values.

To return to the analogy of a stencil, an alpha channel is like a stencil made out of a material that can allow varying amounts of paint to pass through it, depending on the transparency value at each point. One use for such a stencil would be to produce a soft edge around a cut-out shape.

In a similar way, the edge of a selection can be "feathered", which means that the hard transition from black to white in the alpha channel is replaced by a gradient, passing through intermediate grey values which correspond to partial masking. Any effects that are applied will fade over this transitional zone instead of stopping abruptly at the boundary. A less drastic way of exploiting alpha channels is to apply anti-aliasing to the edge of a mask, reducing the jagged effect that may otherwise occur. Although anti-aliasing resembles feathering over a very narrow region, the intention is quite different. Feathering is supposed to be visible, causing effects to fade out, whereas anti-aliasing is intended to conceal the jagged edges of the selection unobtrusively.

Normally, a layer in a Photoshop image obscures everything underneath it, unless it has some transparent areas which allow everything below to show through. However, every layer may have an associated *layer mask*, which is essentially an alpha channel applied to that layer. When two layers are overlaid, if the upper layer has a mask applied, the lower layer will show through the masked-out parts of the upper layer. In the case of a one-bit mask, this means that the lower layer will show through where the mask is black. (That is, the masked layer itself shows through the white areas of the mask, which denote transparency.) If the layer mask is a greyscale image, the lower layer will partially show through the grey areas of the mask, so the two layers will be blended in those areas.

The value p of a pixel in the resulting composited image is computed as $p = \alpha p_1 + (1 - \alpha)p_2$, where p_1 and p_2 are the values of the corresponding pixels in the two layers, and α is normalized to lie between 0 and 1 – that is, if the α value is stored in 8 bits we divide it by 255.

Layer masks can be used to produce a variety of compositing effects. Figure 4.18 illustrates a popular trick, using a one-bit layer mask to knock out part of one image with another. At the top

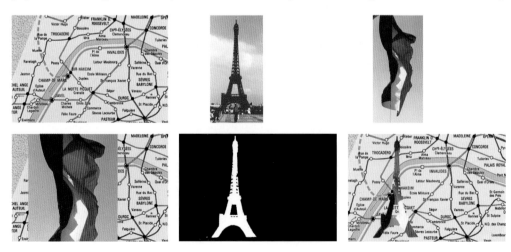

Figure 4.18. *Compositing with a layer mask*

Figure 4.19. *Constructing a vignette with an alpha channel*

of the figure are three original images. The tricolour was resized and pasted into a layer on top of the map of Paris. A mask was constructed by selecting the Eiffel Tower from the photograph (shown top centre) using the magic wand. Photoshop makes it possible to save a selection and then load it into another image, so this cut-out, as shown in the middle of the bottom row of Figure 4.18, was loaded as the layer mask for the tricolour layer, producing the composite shown in the bottom right-hand corner, where the mask has allowed the map to show through except inside the tower. (This is not the only way to achieve this effect.)

A less elaborate example, this time using a greyscale layer mask, is illustrated in Figure 4.19. Here, we started with a single image, and created a mask by drawing an ellipse and feathering its edges to produce the fuzzy shape shown in the middle of Figure 4.19. When this is used as a layer mask, the original image only shows through the black area, but the transition to the white background is softened by the partially transparent edges of the mask. This effect was popular with Victorian photographers (who achieved it without Photoshop).

Pixel Point Processing

Image processing is performed by computing a new value for each pixel in an image. The simplest methods compute a pixel's new value solely on the basis of its old value, without regard to any other pixel. So for a pixel with value p, we compute a new value $p' = f(p)$, where f is called the mapping function. Such functions perform ***pixel point processing***. A simple, if only rarely useful, example of pixel point processing is the construction of a negative from a greyscale image. Here, $f(p) = W - p$, where W is the pixel value representing white.

The most sophisticated pixel point processing is concerned with colour correction and alteration, described more fully in Chapter 5. Here, we will only consider the brightness and contrast alterations that are the typical applications of pixel point processing in greyscale images. Colour processing is an extension – although not a trivial one – of these greyscale adjustments. Once again, we will use Photoshop's tools to provide a concrete example, but any interactive image editing software will offer the same functions, with roughly the same interface.

Figure 4.20. *Brightness (top) and contrast (bottom) adjustments*

The crudest adjustments are made with the brightness and contrast sliders, which work like the corresponding controls on a monitor or television set. These adjustments are illustrated in Figure 4.20. Brightness adjusts the value of each pixel up or down uniformly, so increasing the brightness makes every pixel lighter, as shown in the top right image in Figure 4.20 and decreasing it makes every pixel darker, as shown at top left. Contrast is a little more subtle: it adjusts the range of values, either enhancing or reducing the difference between the lightest and darkest areas of the image. Increasing contrast makes the light areas very light and the dark areas very dark, as shown in the bottom right image in Figure 4.20; decreasing it moves all values towards an intermediate grey, as shown at bottom left. The original photograph, with no adjustments, is shown in the centre.

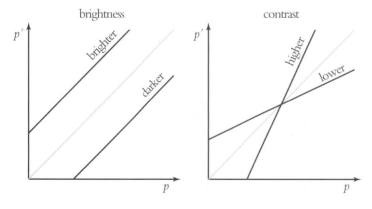

Figure 4.21. *Brightness and contrast mapping functions*

In terms of mapping functions, both of these adjustments produce a linear relationship that would be represented as a straight line on a graph: adjusting the brightness changes the position of the line; adjusting the contrast alters its slope. As Figure 4.21 shows, changing the brightness or decreasing the contrast cuts down the dynamic range – the difference between the lightest and darkest pixel values. Increasing the contrast leads to clipping: any pixel which was originally below a certain value becomes black, any pixel above a certain value becomes white.

More control over the shape of the mapping function can be obtained by making *levels* adjustments. In terms of the mapping functions, this type of adjustment allows you to move the end points of a straight line individually, thereby setting the white and black levels in the image independently. The slope of the line usually changes as a result of these adjustments.

To help with choosing suitable levels, and to help you judge the distribution of light and dark in an image, a display called the *image histogram* is used. This is a histogram showing the distribution of pixel values: the horizontal axis represents the possible values (from 0 to 255 in an 8-bit greyscale image), the bars show the number of pixels set to each value.

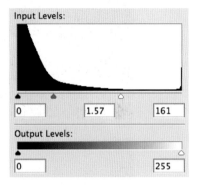

Figure 4.22. *An image histogram in Photoshop's* Levels *dialogue*

The histograms are displayed in Photoshop's levels dialogue with two sets of sliders below them, as shown in Figure 4.22. Looking at the shape of the histogram you might guess that the photograph in question was taken in poor lighting (it is not the image used in Figure 4.20) – it was taken at dusk, and is underexposed. The spike at the extreme right is caused by a bright street light. This is not the only type of image which might have a histogram like this, of course.

The upper set of sliders controls the range of input values. The slider at the left controls the pixel value that will be mapped to black, so, in graphical terms, it moves the bottom end of the mapping function's line along the *x*-axis. The slider at the right controls the pixel value that is mapped to white, so it moves the top end of the line along the horizontal line corresponding to the maximum pixel value. The lower set of slider controls affect the output values in a similar way, i.e. they determine the pixel values that will be used for black and white, so they move the end points of the line up and down.

A rough way of improving the tonal balance of an image is by spreading the range of tonal values evenly. To do this, the input sliders are moved so that they line up with the lowest and highest values that have a non-zero number of pixels shown in the histogram. Moving beyond these points will compress or expand the dynamic range artificially.

So far, all the adjustments discussed have maintained a straight-line relationship between old and new pixel values. The middle (grey) slider on the upper Input Levels control allows you to produce a more flexible correspondence between original and modified pixel values, by adjusting

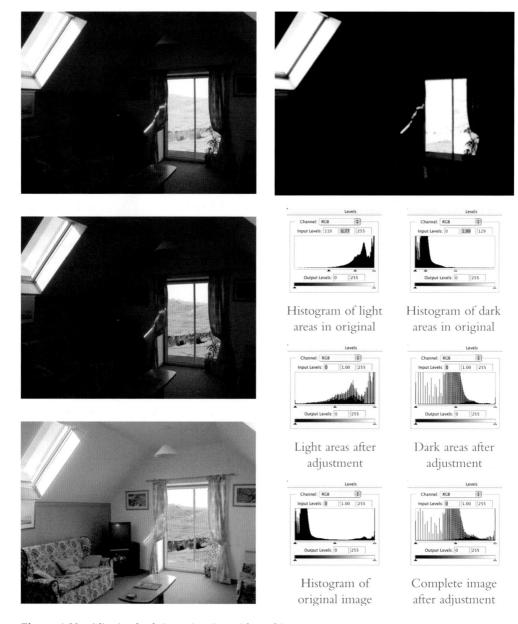

Histogram of light
areas in original

Histogram of dark
areas in original

Light areas after
adjustment

Dark areas after
adjustment

Histogram of
original image

Complete image
after adjustment

Figure 4.23. *Adjusting levels in conjunction with masking*

a third point which corresponds to the mid-tones in the image. If an image's pixel values are concentrated in a particular range, the midpoint slider can be moved underneath the corresponding point on the histogram, so that the values are adjusted to put this range in the centre of the available scale of values.

Figure 4.23 shows the effect that level adjustments can achieve in bringing out detail that has been lost in a very poorly exposed photograph. The original image, shown at the top left, was shot from inside a room, using the auto-exposure feature of a digital camera. Because of the high contrast between the dimly lit interior and the bright light outside the windows, the result is disastrous. The histogram of the original image is shown at the bottom, and the uneven light distribution can be clearly seen. This particular problem cannot be solved by adjusting the levels of the whole photograph; different adjustments are needed for the overexposed exterior and the underexposed interior, so the first step was to create masks to separate the two problems.

The mask used to isolate the light areas is shown at the top right of Figure 4.23. The top left and middle left histograms show the distribution of pixel values in these areas before and after the levels were adjusted. You can also see the slider settings that were used to produce the image in the middle of the left column of images. The inverse of the mask for the light areas was used to isolate the dark areas; before and after histograms for these are shown at the top right and middle right. The final adjusted image is at the bottom left of Figure 4.23; its histogram is shown at the bottom right, beside the histogram of the original image. The final image is quite grainy (hence the spikiness of the adjusted histograms), because of the low light levels, but the amount of detail and colour information that the adjustments have brought out is remarkable.

All of the brightness and contrast adjustment facilities described so far can be considered as making specialized alterations to the graph of the mapping function f to achieve particular commonly required adjustments to the values of individual pixels. In Photoshop it is possible to take detailed control of this graph in the **Curves** dialogue, where it can be reshaped by dragging control points, or completely redrawn with a pencil tool. The almost complete freedom to map grey levels to new values that this provides permits some strange effects, but it also makes it easy to apply subtle corrections to incorrectly exposed photographs, or to compensate for improperly calibrated scanners.

Before any adjustments are made, the curve is a straight line with slope equal to one: the output and input are identical, f is an identity function. Arbitrary reshaping of the curve will cause artificial highlights and shadows, but more often the intention is to bring out detail and to correct poor exposure. Restrained changes to the curve are used to perform tonal adjustments with much more control over the result than the simple contrast and brightness sliders provide. For example, an S-shaped "sigmoid" curve with the general shape illustrated in Figure 4.24 is often used to increase the contrast of an image. The midpoint is fixed and the shadows are darkened by pulling down the quarter-point, while the highlights are lightened by pulling up the

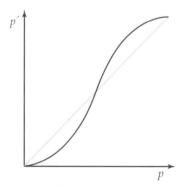

Figure 4.24. *A sigmoid curve for enhancing contrast*

Figure 4.25. *Curve adjustment*

three-quarter-point. The gentle curvature means that, while the overall contrast is increased, the total tonal range is maintained and there are no abrupt changes in brightness.

Figure 4.25 shows another typical application of a curve adjustment applied to a photograph taken under difficult light conditions. Increasing the brightness or adjusting the levels could make the whole picture lighter, but using the curve shown in the inset brings out extra detail and some colour, without losing the overall impression of wintry gloom. The differences between the three approaches can be subtle, but it is always possible to produce the effects achieved by one of the other adjustments using curves.

IN DETAIL

Recent versions of Photoshop include commands that use information in the image to make more intelligent adjustments. In particular, the Shadows/ Highlights adjustment can be used to make separate changes to light and dark areas, of the sort illustrated in Figure 4.23, without the need for explicit masking. At the time of writing this particular adjustment cannot be applied as an adjustment layer, though, and is therefore destructive, producing permanent changes in the image.

Pixel Group Processing

A second class of processing transformations works by computing each pixel's new value as a function not just of its old value, but also of the values of neighbouring pixels. Functions of this sort perform *pixel group processing*, which produces qualitatively different effects from the pixel point processing operations we described in the preceding section.

In terms of the concepts we introduced in Chapter 2, these operations remove or attenuate certain spatial frequencies in an image. Such filtering operations can be implemented as operations that combine the value of a pixel with those of its neighbours, because the relative values of a pixel and its neighbours incorporate some information about the way the brightness or colour is changing in the region of that pixel. A suitably defined operation that combines pixel values will alter these relationships, modifying the frequency make-up of the image. The mathematics behind this sort of processing is complicated, but the outcome is a family of operations with a simple structure.

Instead of transforming our image to the frequency domain (for example, using a DCT) and performing a filtering operation by selecting a range of frequency components, we can perform the filtering in the spatial domain – that is, on the original image data – by computing a weighted average of the pixels and its neighbours. The weights applied to each pixel value determine the particular filtering operation, and thus the effect that is produced on the image's appearance.

A particular filter can be specified in the form of a two-dimensional array of those weights. For example, if we were to apply a filter by taking the value of a pixel and all eight of its immediate neighbours, dividing them each by nine and adding them together to obtain the new value for the pixel, we could write the filter in the form:

$$\begin{array}{ccc} \frac{1}{9} & \frac{1}{9} & \frac{1}{9} \\ \frac{1}{9} & \frac{1}{9} & \frac{1}{9} \\ \frac{1}{9} & \frac{1}{9} & \frac{1}{9} \end{array}$$

The array of weights is called a **convolution mask** and the set of pixels used in the computation is called the **convolution kernel** (because the equivalent of the multiplication operation that performs filtering in the frequency domain is an operation in the spatial domain called convolution).

Generally, if a pixel has coordinates (x, y), so that it has neighbours at $(x-1, y+1), (x, y+1) \dots (x, y-1)$, $(x+1, y-1)$, and we apply a filter with a convolution mask in the form:

$$\begin{array}{ccc} a & b & c \\ d & e & f \\ g & h & i \end{array}$$

the value p' computed for the new pixel at (x, y) is

$$p' = a p_{x-1, y+1} + b p_{x, y+1} + c p_{x+1, y+1}$$
$$+ d p_{x-1, y} + e p_{x, y} + f p_{x+1, y}$$
$$+ g p_{x-1, y-1} + h p_{x, y-1} + i p_{x+1, y-1}$$

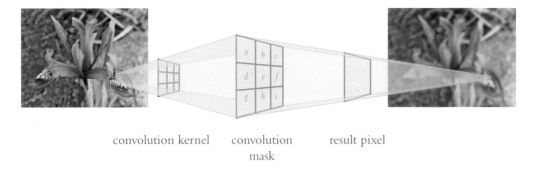

convolution kernel   convolution   result pixel
mask

Figure 4.26. *Filtering with a 3×3 convolution mask*

where $p_{x,y}$ is the value of the pixel at (x,y), and so on. You can think of the pixels of the original image passing through the convolution mask nine at a time as a convolution kernel, picking up their weights as they pass through, and then being added together to produce the value for the pixel at the middle of the 3×3 pixel block. (See Figure 4.26.)

Convolution is a computationally intensive process. With a 3×3 convolution kernel, computing a new value for each pixel requires nine multiplications and eight additions. For an image of 480×320 pixels, the total number of operations will be 1,382,400 multiplications and 1,228,800 additions, i.e. over two and a half million operations in all. Convolution masks need not be only three pixels square, and the larger the mask the more computation is required.

This is all very well, but what are the visible effects of spatial filtering? Consider again the simple convolution mask comprising nine values, each equal to ⅑. If all nine pixels being convolved have the same value, let us say 117, then the filter has no effect: $117/9\times9 = 117$. That is, over regions of constant colour or brightness, this filter leaves pixels alone. However, suppose it is applied at a region including a sharp vertical edge, with pixels whose value is 117 on one side, and 27 on the other. A convolution kernel spanning the edge might have the following values:

117   117   27
117   117   27
117   117   27

The new value computed for the centre pixel will be 105. Moving further into the lighter region, to an area that looks like this:

117   27   27
117   27   27
117   27   27

gives a new pixel value of 57. Beyond this area, assume all the pixels in the kernel have the value 27, so that the result also has this value.

By computing pixel values with this convolution mask, the hard edge from 117 to 27 has been replaced by a more gradual transition via the intermediate values 105 and 57. The effect is seen as a blurring. One way of thinking about what has happened is to imagine that the edges have been softened by rubbing together the colour values of the pixels, in the same way as you can blur edges in a pastel drawing by rubbing them with your finger. An alternative view, based on the concepts of signal processing, is that this operation produces a smoothing effect on the spatial waveform of the image, by filtering out high frequencies. (Engineers would refer to the operation as a "low-pass filter".)

Blurring is often used in retouching scans. It is useful for mitigating the effects of digital artefacts, such as the jagged edges produced by undersampling, Moiré patterns, and the blockiness resulting from excessive JPEG compression.

Although the convolution mask we have just described is a classical blur filter, it produces a noticeably unnatural effect, because of the limited region over which it operates and the all-or-nothing effect caused by the uniform coefficients. The amount of blurring is small and fixed. A more generally useful alternative is **Gaussian blur**, where the coefficients fall off gradually from the centre of the mask, following the Gaussian "bell curve" shown in Figure 4.27, to produce a blurring that is similar to those found in nature.

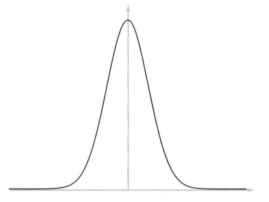

Figure 4.27. *The Gaussian bell curve*

The extent of the blur – that is, the width of the bell curve, and hence the number of pixels included in the convolution calculation – can be controlled. Photoshop's dialogue allows the user to specify a "radius" value, in pixels, for the filter. A radius of 0.1 pixels produces a very subtle effect. Values between 0.2 and 0.8 pixels are good for removing aliasing artefacts. A radius of 100 pixels or more blurs the entire image into incoherence, and one of 250 pixels (the maximum possible) just averages all the pixels in the area the filter is applied to.

Values between the extremes can be used to produce a deliberate effect. For example, Gaussian blur is used in the popular drop shadow effect. An object is selected, copied onto a new layer, filled with black and displaced slightly to produce a shadow. A Gaussian blur with a radius between 4 and 12 pixels is applied to this shadow, softening its edges to produce a more realistic effect.

Figure 4.28. *A drop shadow*

Figure 4.28 shows an example. (Drop shadow is provided as a filter in most bitmapped image manipulation programs, but it is still created in the manner just described, using a Gaussian blur on a displayed copy of a layer.)

Note that the radius specified when using Gaussian blur is not in fact the limit of the blurring effect, but a parameter that specifies the shape of the bell curve. The blurring extends well beyond the radius, but its effect is more concentrated within it, with roughly 70% of the contribution to the value of the centre pixel coming from pixels within the radius.

Blurring is a surprisingly useful effect when applied to digitized images. You might expect blur to be an undesirable feature of an image, but it conceals their characteristic imperfections; in the case of Gaussian blur, it does this in a visually natural way. Sometimes, though, we want to do the opposite, and enhance detail by sharpening the edges in an image. A convolution mask that is often used for this purpose is:

$$
\begin{array}{rrr}
-1 & -1 & -1 \\
-1 & 9 & -1 \\
-1 & -1 & -1
\end{array}
$$

This mask filters out low-frequency components, leaving the higher frequencies that are associated with discontinuities. Like the simple blurring filter that removed high frequencies, this one will have no effect over regions where the pixels all have the same value. In more intuitive terms, by subtracting the values of adjacent pixels, while multiplying the central value by a large coefficient, it eliminates any value that is common to the central pixel and its surroundings, so that it isolates details from their context.

If we apply this mask to a convolution kernel where there is a gradual discontinuity, such as

$$
\begin{array}{rrr}
117 & 51 & 27 \\
117 & 51 & 27 \\
117 & 51 & 27
\end{array}
$$

assuming that this occurs in a context where all the pixels to the left have the value 117 and those to the right 27, the new values computed for the three pixels on the central row will be 317, −75 and −45; since we cannot allow negative pixel values, the last two will be set to 0 (i.e. black). The gradual transition will have been replaced by a hard line, while the regions of constant value to either side will be left alone. A filter such as this will therefore enhance detail.

As you might guess from this example, sharpening with a convolution mask produces harsh edges. It is more appropriate for analysing an image than for enhancing detail in a realistic way. To enhance detail more naturally, it is more usual to use an ***unsharp masking*** operation. This is easiest to understand in terms of filtering operations. A blurring operation filters out high frequencies, so if we could take a blurred image away from its original, we would be left with only the frequencies that had been removed by the blurring – that is, the ones that correspond to sharp edges.

This isn't quite what we usually want to do: we would prefer to accentuate the edges, but retain the other parts of the image as well. Unsharp masking is therefore performed by constructing a copy of the original image, applying a Gaussian blur to it, and then subtracting the pixel values in this blurred mask from the corresponding values in the original multiplied by a suitable scaling factor. As you can easily verify, using a scale factor of 2 leaves areas of constant value alone. In the region of a discontinuity, though, an enhancement occurs.

This is shown graphically in Figure 4.29. The top curve shows the possible change of pixel values across an edge, from a region of low intensity on the left to one of higher intensity on the right. (We have shown a continuous change, to bring out what is happening, but any real image will be made from discrete pixels, of course.) The middle curve illustrates the effect of applying a Gaussian blur: the transition from low intensity to higher intensity is softened, with a gentler slope that extends further into the areas of constant value. At the bottom, we show (not to scale) the result of subtracting this curve from twice the original. The slope of the transition is much steeper, and overshoots at the limits of the original edge, so visually the contrast is increased. The net result is an enhancement of the edge,

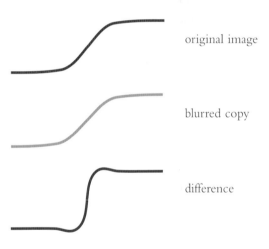

original image

blurred copy

difference

Figure 4.29. *Unsharp masking*

as illustrated in Figure 4.30, where a greyscale photograph (shown on the left) has had an exaggerated amount of unsharp masking applied, giving the result shown on the right.

The amount of blur applied to the mask can be controlled, since it is just a Gaussian blur, and this affects the extent of sharpening. It is also common to allow the user to specify a threshold; where the difference between the original pixel and the mask is less than the threshold value, no sharpening is performed. This prevents the operation from enhancing noise by sharpening the visible artefacts which noise produces. It is a common error to apply too much sharpening, because it appears to improve the picture. The example in Figure 4.30 shows the characteristic result of such over-sharpening; you can see the artefacts which this produces quite clearly.

Figure 4.30. *Unsharp masking, showing over-sharpening*

Although sharpening operations can enhance features of an image, it should be understood that they add no information to it. On the contrary, information is actually lost, although, if the sharpening is successful, the lost information will have been irrelevant or distracting. (It's perhaps more intuitively obvious that information is lost by blurring an image.) It should also be understood that although, in a sense, blurring and sharpening are opposites, they are not true inverses. That is, if you take an image, blur it and then sharpen it, or sharpen it and then blur it, you will not end up with the image you started with. The information that is lost when these operations are applied cannot be restored; each time you apply either blurring or sharpening to an image more information is lost, resulting in increasing degradation of the original.

Nevertheless, applying a small amount of Gaussian blur followed by unsharp masking is often a good way to improve certain images, including over-compressed JPEGs. The blur will remove unwanted artefacts and then the sharpening will restore detail at edges. The procedure is not infallible, however, and you should not apply it indiscriminately to every image.

Less reliably, blurring and sharpening can be used to adjust the focus of an image. The image on the left of Figure 4.31 is incorrectly focussed – a common result of using auto-focus. By careful selection, the out-of-focus flowers were isolated from the background and sharpened, while the foliage in the background was blurred. The combined effect makes it look as if the photograph had been correctly focussed on the flowers – but if you look closely you will see that this is an illusion and the result cannot compare with a properly focussed photograph.

Figure 4.31. *Correcting focus by blurring and sharpening*

Blurring and sharpening are central to the established scientific and military applications of image processing, but now that image manipulation software is also used for more creative purposes some rather different effects are called for as well. Photoshop provides a bewildering variety of filters, and third-party plug-ins add many more. Many of them are based on the type of pixel group processing we have described, with convolution masks chosen to produce effects that resemble different photographic processes or – with varying degrees of success – the appearance of real art materials. These filters usually work by picking out edges or areas of the same colour, and modifying them; they are not too far removed from the more conventional blur and sharpen operations. However, apart from the essential blurring and sharpening operations, filters can easily be over-used and should be approached judiciously.

IN DETAIL

As an example of how image manipulation is done non-interactively, the following command uses the convert program from Image Magick to make a contrast adjustment using an S-curve while resizing a Photoshop file and converting it to a TIFF:

convert sea.psd -sigmoidal-contrast 6x60% -resize 320x24 sea.tiff

Many more options are available, allowing several processing options to be combined into a single command. When operations are performed in this way, you are working blind, and will have no idea what the result will look like until you display the image afterwards. However, if you already know what values to use, programs like this can be used in situations where human interference is not possible, such as on a Web server.

KEY POINTS

Image manipulation software provides high-level operations for systematically altering pixels. Most operations are described by analogy with traditional photographic techniques, such as the use of masks and filters.

Photoshop is the *de facto* industry standard; the Gimp is an Open Source alternative. Image Magick can be used for command-line processing.

Bitmapped images are manipulated to correct technical deficiencies, alter the content or create artificial compositions.

Images are often organized into layers, which are like overlaid sheets that may have transparent areas. Layers are used for compositing or experimenting with different versions of an image.

Areas may be selected by drawing with marquee and lasso tools or a Bézier pen, or selected on the basis of colour similarity or edges using a magic wand or magnetic lasso.

Any selection defines a mask – the area that is not selected. Masked areas of the image are protected from changes.

A greyscale mask, which is partially transparent, is an alpha channel.

An alpha channel can be associated with a layer as a layer mask, and used for effects such as knock-outs and vignettes.

In pixel point processing, each pixel's new value depends only on its old value.

Brightness, contrast and levels are relatively crude pixel point adjustments.

Curves adjustments provide full control over the relationship between original and new values. A sigmoid curve is often used to enhance contrast.

Pixel group processing uses the values of neighbouring pixels as well.

The convolution operation in the frequency domain can be implemented as a weighted average in the spatial domain: for each pixel in the filtered image, the pixels of a convolution kernel are combined using a convolution mask.

Simple blurring uses a 3×3 mask with equal values but produces crude results. Gaussian blur is preferred, as it produces more natural results.

Sharpening with a 3×3 mask is crude. Unsharp masking – combining an image with a Gaussian blurred copy of itself – produces better-looking results. Over-sharpening should always be avoided.

The principle of convolution-based filtering can be used to create many special effects, but such filters should be used judiciously.

Exercises

Test Questions

1   Suppose you want to change both the size of a bitmapped image and its resolution. Will the order in which you perform these two operations make any difference to the result?

2   If you upsample an image to three times its original size and then immediately downsample it again to exactly its original size, will you end up with the same image you started with? Explain the reasons for your answer.

3   An alternative to using bilinear or bicubic pixel interpolation when downsampling an image is to apply a low-pass filter (blur) first, and then use the nearest neighbour. Explain why this works.

4   Explain in detail how JPEG compression works, and how JPEG2000 compression works in comparison. What are the advantages and disadvantages of these two types of compression?

5   Which graphics file formats are currently supported by Web browsers? What are the differences between them, and what purpose would each one be best suited for?

6   How would you put an ornamental frame around a vignette, such as the one shown in Figure 4.19?

7   Why might you want to apply anti-aliasing to a mask? Explain why it is necessary to use an alpha channel to do so.

8   Describe how you would produce the composite image in Figure 4.18 if the map was on a layer on top of the layer containing the flag, instead of the other way round.

9   How would adjusting (a) the brightness and (b) the contrast affect the histogram of an image?

10 Describe the shape of the curve you would use to correct an image with too much contrast. Why would it be better than simply lowering the contrast with the contrast slider?

11 If asked to "sharpen up" a scanned image, most experts would first apply a slight Gaussian blur before using the sharpen or unsharp mask filter. Why?

12 Motion blur is the smearing effect produced when a moving object is photographed using an insufficiently fast shutter speed. It is sometimes deliberately added to images to convey an impression of speed. Devise a convolution mask for a motion blur filter. How would you allow a user to alter the amount of motion blur? What other properties of the blurring should be alterable?

Discussion Topics

1 Why are the screenshots published in tutorial articles in computing magazines often hard to read?

2 It is often claimed that the subjective quality of a high-resolution image that has been down-sampled for display at a low resolution will be better than that of an image whose resolution is equal to the display resolution. For example, when a 600 dpi scan is displayed on screen at 72 dpi, it will often look better than a 72 dpi scan, even though there are no more pixels in the displayed image. Explain why this might be the case.

3 If you are taking photographs with a digital camera for display on Web pages at a standard size of 320×240 pixels, what size do you think the original photographs should be and why? Is it worthwhile using a camera with many megapixels for this kind of work?

4 We showed how scaling of bitmapped images is performed by applying a transform to each pixel, and why this requires resampling. Describe how you would perform each of the other transformations we described in Chapter 3 on bitmapped images instead of vector graphics.

5 Vector graphics can be turned into bitmapped images by rendering; bitmapped images can be turned into vector graphics by automatic "tracing". What use could you make of each of these conversions?

Practical Tasks

1 If you have access to Photoshop, investigate the **Custom** filter (on the **Other** sub-menu of the **Filter** menu). This allows you to construct your own convolution mask, by entering coefficients into a 5×5 matrix. The results are instructive and sometimes surprising.

Alternatively, if you prefer to use Image Magick, investigate the different arguments available to the -filter command-line option.

2 A common piece of "folk wisdom" concerning resampling holds that if you want to reduce the size of an image by a large amount you should do so in several steps. That is, if you have a high-resolution image and you want to reduce its size by one-eighth, you should do so by halving the size three times. Carry out some experiments on different types of image to see whether there is any truth in this claim. Once you have made a judgement one way or the other, see whether you can devise a theory to explain what you have observed.

3 Investigate the facilities for combining bitmapped images and vector graphics that are provided by popular software and graphics languages.

Colour

Colour is an essential element of multimedia. Both vector graphics and bitmapped images can use colour. Video and animation are usually in colour. Even text may be coloured for effect or decoration. For most people, colour is such a commonplace experience that it is somehow surprising to discover that it is actually a rather complex phenomenon, in both its objective and subjective aspects. Representing colour in digital images and reproducing it accurately on output devices are consequently not at all straightforward.

One thing that is worth remembering about colour is that you don't always need it. The long history and continued use of black and white photography and film demonstrates that people are perfectly well able to recognize and understand an image in the absence of colour – variations in brightness are quite adequate. Indeed, the addition of colour is not always an improvement – a fact well understood by advertising agencies, the makers of music videos and lovers of old movies.

Pragmatically as well as aesthetically, there are advantages to using images without colour. As we will see shortly, black and white bitmapped image files can be much smaller than coloured ones. Furthermore, black and white images are largely immune to the variations in colour reproduction of different monitors. You should not forget that some people do not have colour monitors, or prefer to use them in monochrome mode, and that many mobile devices offer only a restricted number of colours. A few people cannot see in colour at all, while many more cannot distinguish between certain colours (see Chapter 13). By working in black and white (or, more accurately, shades of grey) you avoid producing images that may not be seen properly for these reasons.

But people have come to expect colour, and colour can add a great deal to an image, if it is used effectively. Sometimes colour is vital to the purpose for which an image is being used: for example, the colours in a clothing catalogue will influence people's buying decisions, and must be accurate to avoid disappointment and complaints.

The effective use of colour is not something that can be summarized in a few rules. Centuries of experience of artists and designers working in traditional media can be put to good use in digital media, and in large-scale multimedia production it is wise to ensure that there are artistically trained specialists available, and to leave colour decisions to them. However, we discuss some of the fundamental design principles relating to colour in Chapter 11.

As in most of the other areas we will describe, certain constraints associated with the digital nature of the images we can use in our multimedia productions will modify how we approach colour, so artistic sensibility must be augmented with some technical knowledge.

The theory of colour has a muddled history, with mystical ideas and mistaken understandings of how colour is produced and perceived contributing to confused notions about what colour is. There has been a long-standing confusion between colours themselves and the pigments used by artists to create them. Since most people's first encounter with mixing colours comes when they are working with paints in primary school, this confusion often persists. It is essential to remember that when we see colours displayed on a computer monitor, they are produced by the mixing of light, and this behaves in a different way from the mixing of paint.

Colour and Science

Colour is a subjective sensation produced in the brain. In order to reproduce colour electronically, or manipulate it digitally, we need a model of colour which relates that subjective sensation to measurable and reproducible physical phenomena. This turns out to be a surprisingly difficult task to accomplish successfully.

Since light is a form of electromagnetic radiation, we can measure its wavelength – the wavelength of visible light lies roughly between 400 nm and 700 nm – and its intensity. We can combine these measurements into a *spectral power distribution (SPD)*, a description of how the intensity of light from some particular source varies with wavelength. Figure 5.1 shows the SPD of typical daylight. (Notice that it extends beyond the visible spectrum.)

In effect, an SPD is constructed by splitting light into its component wavelengths – much as a prism splits a beam of light into a spectrum when we repeat Isaac Newton's optics experiments in school – and measuring the intensity of each component. (In theory, an SPD ought to be a continuous function, but a satisfactory approximation is obtained by using samples at wavelengths separated by a suitable interval, for example 10 nm, giving an SPD consisting of 31 components.) Subjective experiments show that an SPD corresponds closely to what we mean by "colour", in the sense that observers can successfully match light with a particular SPD to a specific colour. However, SPDs are too cumbersome to work with when we are specifying colours for use in computer graphics, so we need to adopt a different approach.

You may have been told at some point in your education that the human eye contains two different sorts of receptor cells: rods, which provide night-vision and cannot distinguish colour, and cones, of which there are three different sorts, which respond to different wavelengths of light. The fact that our perception of

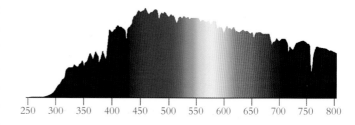

Figure 5.1. *The spectral power distribution of daylight*

colour derives from the eye's response to three different groups of wavelengths leads to the theory – called the **tristimulus theory** – that any colour can be specified by just three values, giving the weights of each of three components.

The tristimulus theory of colour is often summarized (inaccurately) by saying that each type of cone responds to one of red, green or blue light. It follows that the sensation of any colour can be produced by mixing together suitable amounts of red, green and blue light. We call red, green and blue the **additive primary colours**. (These are not the artist's primary colours, usually described as red, yellow and blue, which we will discuss later.)

Putting it another way, we can define a particular colour by giving the proportions of red, green and blue light that it contains. It follows that we can construct television screens and computer monitors using pixels each made up of three dots of different types of phosphor, emitting red, green and blue light, and exciting them using three electron beams, one for each colour. To produce any desired colour we just have to adjust the intensity of each electron beam, and hence the intensity of the light emitted by the corresponding phosphors. Optical mixing of the light emitted by the three component dots of any pixel will make it look like a single pixel of the desired colour.

Since we can construct monitors like that, the simplified tristimulus theory is evidently more or less right, and much of the time we can proceed on the basis of it. However, it *is* a simplified theory, and some subtle problems can arise if we ignore the more complex nature of colour. Fortunately, the worst of these are connected with printing, and do not often occur in digital multimedia work. Reproducing colour on a computer monitor, as we more often need to do, is more straightforward.

RGB Colour

The idea that colours can be constructed out of red, green and blue light leads to the **RGB colour model**, in which a colour is represented by three values, giving the proportions of red (R), green (G) and blue (B) light which must be combined to make up light of the desired colour. The first question that arises is "What do we mean by red, green and blue?". The answer ought to be that these are the names of three colours corresponding to three standard primary SPDs, and in the television and video industries several such standards do exist. (In general, the primary blue is actually better described as "blue-violet", and the red is an orangey shade.) In computing, however, there is no universally accepted standard, although monitors are increasingly being built to use the primaries specified for High Definition TV (HDTV) by the ITU in its Recommendation ITU-R BT.709. However, in the absence of a real standard, the colours produced in response to any particular RGB value can vary substantially between monitors.

It is also important to be aware that – no matter how red, green and blue are defined – it is *not* possible to represent every visible colour as a combination of red, green and blue components. Figure 5.2 shows a pictorial representation of the relationship between the colours that can be represented in that way – the so-called **RGB colour gamut** – and all the visible colours, as determined by some classical experiments on colour perception. The large fin-shaped area is a spatial representation of all the possible colours. (Because the printing process cannot reproduce all colours, the colouring on this diagram should only be considered an indication of the distribution of colours, not an accurate representation of the actual colours themselves. For an explanation of exactly what is being plotted see the detailed comments below.) Shades of

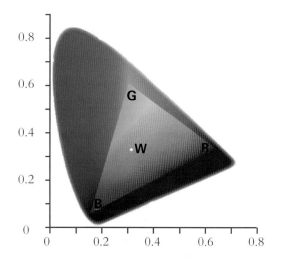

Figure 5.2. *The RGB colour gamut*

green lie towards the tip, with reds at the bottom right and blues at the bottom left. The brighter and much smaller triangular area represents the RGB colour gamut, where R, G and B are the primaries defined in ITU-R BT.709, so this area contains all the colours that can be reproduced on a monitor conforming to that specification.

The triangle of the RGB gamut is entirely enclosed within the fin, showing that there are many colours – roughly half of the total number – that cannot be produced by adding these shades of red, green and blue, and hence cannot be reproduced on a monitor. It should be noted, though, that red, green and blue primaries do produce the largest gamut possible from simple addition of three primaries. Putting that another way, if you were to draw the largest triangle you could fit inside the area of all possible colours, its vertices would correspond to colours you would call red, blue and green.

In practice, however, the RGB model provides a useful, simple and efficient way of representing colours. A colour can be represented by three values. We can write this representation in the form (R,G,B), where R, G and B are the amounts of red, green and blue light making up the colour. By "amount", we mean the proportion of pure ("saturated") light of that primary. For example, if we express the proportions as percentages, $(100,0,0)$ represents pure saturated primary red, and $(50,0,0)$ a darker red, while $(100,50,100)$ represents a rather violent shade of mauve. Since black is an absence of light, its RGB colour value is $(0,0,0)$. White light is produced by mixing equal proportions of saturated light of all three primaries, so white's RGB colour value is $(100,100,100)$. When equal amounts of red, green and blue light are combined, the result is a shade of grey, so any value of the form (x,x,x) represents a grey: the higher the value of x, the lighter the grey.

┌─ IN DETAIL ───

The diagram reproduced in Figure 5.2 is derived from work done under the auspices of the *Commission Internationale de l'Eclairage (CIE)* in 1931. In experiments in which people were asked to mix quantities of red, green and blue lights to produce a colour that matched a displayed sample, it was found that it was necessary to add negative amounts of primaries (by adding them to the displayed sample instead of to the attempted match) in order to match some colours. This is now understood to be because the responses of the three types of cone cell in the eye are not simply used as colour stimuli, in the way that the voltages on the three electron guns of a monitor are, but are combined in a more complex way.

The CIE defined a set of three primaries, known simply as X, Y and Z, whose spectral distributions matched the inferred spectral response of the eye of their "standard observer", and could thus be used to produce any visible colour purely by addition. The Y component is essentially the brightness (or "luminance"). If we put $x = X/(X + Y + Z)$ and $y = Y/(X + Y + Z)$, you should be able to see that any colour can be fully specified by its x, y and Y values, since X and Z can be recovered from the equations. Since Y is the luminance, x and y together specify the colour, independently of its brightness. It is x and y that label the axes in Figure 5.2. (This diagram is called the *CIE chromaticity diagram*, because it plots colour information, independent of brightness.)

The curved area is obtained by plotting the x and y values of an SPD comprising a single wavelength as its value varies from 400 nm to 700 nm. The area is closed by a straight line joining the extreme low and high frequencies – the "line of purples", which corresponds to those colours which do not have a single identifiable wavelength as their dominant spectral component. The RGB gamut is contained inside a triangle with red, green and blue (as defined by the CIE) at its vertices.

The primaries X, Y and Z cannot be realized by physical light sources.

└───

The RGB colour model has a simple geometrical interpetation. As we explained in Chapter 3, a triplet of values can represent the coordinates of a point in three-dimensional space. Because each of our R, G and B values must lie between 0 and some maximum value M – the same maximum for all three – all the possible (R,G,B) points lie within a cube; the length of each side of this cube is M. (If the values are percentages, M will be equal to 100, but as we will explain shortly, other values are usually preferred.)

One corner of this cube is at the origin $(0,0,0)$; it corresponds to black, as we just explained. The diametrically opposite corner (M,M,M) corresponds to white, with the straight line between the two representing all shades of grey, since its equation will be $R = G = B$. Each of the axes corresponds to shades of one of the primaries, since all but one of the components of every point on an axis is zero. The three corners that lie on a single axis correspond to the pure red, green and blue primaries.

Figure 5.3 shows the RGB colour model as the cube just described. The geometrical representation of a colour model is often called a **colour space**. Later in this chapter, we will describe some other colour models, each of which will have a corresponding colour space.

We emphasize once again that the three values in the RGB model represent the amounts of light of the three primary colours which must be mixed in order to produce light of the specified colour. Do not confuse this additive mixing of coloured light with the mixing of coloured pigments, which

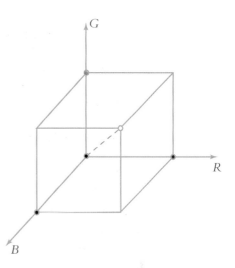

Figure 5.3. *The RGB colour space*

is essentially a subtractive mixing process, as we will explain later on. Computer monitors emit light, so any consideration of how they produce colours must be based on an additive model. Cameras detect incident light (the light that strikes the CCD or the film), and scanners work by detecting light reflected from the scanned document, so they too work with additive colours.

Colour Depth

The three numbers R, G and B used to specify a colour are not absolute values; it is only their relative proportions that matter, so we can choose any convenient range, provided that it allows us to distinguish enough different values. Like many important questions about colour, "How many is enough?" can only be answered subjectively. Different cultures have different ideas about when two colours are different, and people also differ in their ability to distinguish between colours for physiological reasons, but very few people, if any, can distinguish more colours than the nearly 16.8 million combinations which are produced by using 256 different values for each of the red, green and blue component values.

Of course, 256 is a very convenient number to use in a digital representation, since a single 8-bit byte can hold exactly that many different values, usually considered as numbers in the range 0 to 255. Thus, an RGB colour can be represented in three bytes, or 24 bits. The number of bits used to hold a colour value is often referred to as the **colour depth**: when three bytes are used, the colour depth is 24. We often also refer to **24-bit colour**, as a shorthand for colour with a 24-bit colour depth. In 24-bit colour, our mauve shade would be stored as (255,127,255), black is (0,0,0), as always, and white is (255,255,255). (Remember that the values start at zero.)

Any value that can be stored in a byte can be written as a two-digit number in hexadecimal (base-16) notation, as we mentioned in Chapter 2. A 24-bit colour value can therefore be written as a six-digit hexadecimal number. This representation has become popular following its use in CSS and other Web technologies. Usually, hexadecimal numbers are preceded by a # sign to distinguish them from decimal numbers. In this notation, we would write the mauve shade we referred to earlier in the context of the RGB model (255,127,255) as #FF7FFF, and white and black as #FFFFFF and #000000, respectively.

You may well suppose that 24 bits is not the only possible colour depth, and this is indeed the case. One other possibility, less common than it used to be, is 1-bit (bi-level) colour. A single bit allows us to distinguish two different colours. A colour depth of 4 bits allows 16 different colours, which is clearly inadequate for displaying anything but the most simple of colour images; 16 different grey levels, on the other hand, can produce respectable greyscale images. Since greys are represented by RGB colour values (R, G, B), with $R = G = B$, a single value is sufficient to specify a grey level, the other two RGB components being redundant. A single byte permits 256 greys, which is adequate for most greyscale images.

Figure 5.4. *A photograph in 24, 8 (top), 4 and 1 (bottom) bit colour*

Figure 5.5. *24-bit (left) and 8-bit (right) colour*

Most contemporary computers are capable of storing and reproducing 24-bit colour, although older systems were more restricted, often to as few as 8 bits. Phones and other mobile devices do not usually support full 24-bit colour, although they will almost certainly do so in time. At present, 12 and 18 bits (4 and 6 for each primary) are commonly used on these devices. Some mobile phones use 16 bits (2 bytes) to hold colour values. 16 is not divisible by 3, so when RGB values are stored in a 16-bit format, either one bit is left unused, or different numbers of bits are assigned to the three components. Typically, red and blue each use 5 bits, and green is allocated 6 bits, allowing twice as many different green values to be distinguished. This allocation of bits is based on the contention that the human eye is more sensitive to green light than to the other two primaries. (Note the extent of the green area in Figure 5.2.)

The common colour depths are sometimes distinguished by the terms "millions of colours" (24 bits), "thousands of colours" (16 bits) and "256 colours" (8 bits), for obvious reasons, although 16 bits allows 65,536 values, so "tens of thousands of colours" would be a more accurate description for that colour depth.

Figure 5.4 shows four versions of the same photograph at different colour depths. As the number of colours decreases, posterization, as described in Chapter 2, becomes more evident. The effect can be seen clearly in the bottom two versions, where considerable colour shifts are also apparent. The top pair of images look very similar when reproduced at this size, but the magnified details in Figure 5.5 show that posterization and loss of detail are already happening in the 8-bit version.

Although 24 bits are sufficient to represent more colours than the eye can distinguish, higher colour depths, such as 30, 36 or even 48 bits, are increasingly being used, especially by scanners. Support for 48-bit colour is included in the specification of the PNG file format. These very large colour depths serve two purposes. Firstly, the additional information held in the extra bits makes it possible to use more accurate approximations when the image is reduced to a lower colour depth for display (just as images stored at high resolution may look better when displayed on a low-resolution monitor than images stored at the monitor resolution). Secondly, it is possible to make extremely fine distinctions between colours, so that effects such as chroma-key (see Chapter 6) can be applied very accurately.

Colour depth is a crucial factor in determining the size of a bitmapped image: each logical pixel requires 24 bits for 24-bit colour, but only 8 for 8-bit, and just a single bit for 1-bit colour. Hence, if it is possible to reduce the colour depth of an image from 24 bits to 8, the image file size will decrease by a factor of three, and so will the time it takes to send the image over a network (ignoring any fixed-size housekeeping information that is held in addition to the image data). Returning to an earlier point, an image made up of 256 different shades of grey — more than most people can distinguish — will be one-third the size of the same image in millions of colours. Using an arbitrarily chosen set of 256 colours, on the other hand, is unlikely to produce an acceptable result. If the colour depth must be reduced, and greyscale is not desired, then an alternative strategy must be employed.

Indexed Colour

So far, we have implicitly assumed that the stored R, G and B values are used to control the intensity of the monitor's three electron beams, thus determining the colour that is displayed. The relationship between the voltage applied to an electron beam and the intensity of the light emitted by a phosphor when it strikes it is non-linear, as is the response of the eye to the intensity of light which enters it, so the value is not simply used as a voltage, but graphics hardware is built to compensate somewhat for these non-linearities. Often, therefore, the stored values are simply handed over to the graphics hardware and used to control the display, especially in the case of 24-bit colour. This arrangement is called *direct colour*. There is, however, an alternative, known as *indexed colour*, which was once widely used on low-end computer systems and is still employed in the GIF and PNG Web image formats described in Chapter 4.

If — for whatever reason — we are constrained to use only one byte for each pixel, we can use at most 256 different colours in any one image. Using one standard set of 256 colours for all the images we might need, i.e. attempting to use 8-bit direct colour, is unacceptably restrictive. Indexed colour provides a means of associating a *palette* of 256 specific colours with each image. For example, if we wished to produce a pastiche of Picasso's "blue period" paintings, we could use a palette holding 256 shades of blue and obtain a reasonable result. If, on the other hand, we were restricted to using only the blues from a set of 256 colours spread evenly over the spectrum, all of the subtlety and possibly much of the content of the image would be lost.

One way of thinking about indexed colour is as a digital equivalent of painting by numbers. In a painting by numbers kit, areas on the painting are labelled with small numbers, which identify

Figure 5.6. *Images and their palettes*

pots of paint of a particular colour. When we use indexed colour, pixels don't store a 24-bit colour value, but instead store a small number that identifies a 24-bit colour from the palette associated with the image. Just as each painting by numbers outfit includes only those paints that are needed to colour in one picture, so each palette includes only the 24-bit RGB values for the colours used in one particular image. When the image is displayed, the colour from the palette corresponding to each single-byte value stored at each pixel, is used as the colour of that pixel. Figure 5.6 shows two images with different colour characteristics, together with the palettes used when they are stored using indexed colour.

The mapping from stored values to colours can be efficiently implemented using a table. Hence, instead of trying to use 8 bits to hold an RGB value, we use it to hold an index into a table with 256 entries, each of which holds a full 24-bit RGB colour value. For example, if a particular pixel was to be displayed as the colour whose 24-bit RGB value was #A23E1A, instead of storing that value in the image, we could store an index identifying the table location in which it was stored. Supposing #A23E1A was held in the third entry of the table, the pixel would hold the offset 2 (see Figure 5.7). Such an indexed table of colour values is called a ***colour table***. The colours represented in the colour table make up the image's palette, so the colour table itself is often loosely called a palette too.

With indexing, a colour value does not identify a colour absolutely, but only relative to a palette. It may help you to understand what is going on if you consider what would happen if the colour tables for the two images in Figure 5.6 were exchanged, so that the flower image was associated with the seascape palette and vice versa. The seascape palette is mostly made up of shades of blue and brown; the first entry shown on the third line in the illustration is a dark sea-blue. The entry at the corresponding position in the table for the flower is a shade of maroon.

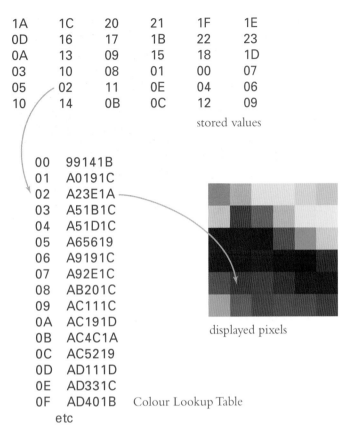

1A	1C	20	21	1F	1E
0D	16	17	1B	22	23
0A	13	09	15	18	1D
03	10	08	01	00	07
05	02	11	0E	04	06
10	14	0B	0C	12	09

stored values

00	99141B
01	A0191C
02	A23E1A
03	A51B1C
04	A51D1C
05	A65619
06	A9191C
07	A92E1C
08	AB201C
09	AC111C
0A	AC191D
0B	AC4C1A
0C	AC5219
0D	AD111D
0E	AD331C
0F	AD401B
	etc

Colour Lookup Table

displayed pixels

Figure 5.7. *Using a colour table*

If the palettes were interchanged, the dark blue of the sea would turn maroon, and the maroon areas of the flower would turn blue. The result of exchanging the entire colour tables between these two images is shown in Figure 5.8. By swapping the two tables we have in effect assigned an arbitrary palette to each image, which produces a visual incoherence more pronounced than you would perhaps have expected. This illustrates just how important colour values are in the representation and interpretation of coloured images. It also shows why it is usually unwise to use an arbitrary colour palette, of course.

If indexed colour is to be used, an image file needs to store the colour table along with the actual image data, but the image data itself can be smaller by a factor of three, since it only needs 8 bits per pixel. For any reasonably sized image there will therefore be a net saving of space. This saving may be increased further if the file format allows tables with fewer than 256 entries to be stored with images that have fewer colours, and uses the minimum number of bits required to index the palette for each colour value.

Of the file formats mentioned in Chapter 4, PNG, BMP and TIFF allow the use of a colour table, although they also support full 24-bit colour. GIF only supports 8-bit indexed colour images, so GIF files must always include a colour table. JFIF and other files used for JPEG images do not support indexed colour.

For created images, a palette of 256 colours will often be acceptable and, since you have control over the colours you use, you can work within the restriction, though subtle variations will be lost. However, with photographic or scanned material, or images that already exist in 24-bit colour, it will be necessary to cut down the number of colours when you prepare a version that uses 8-bit indexed colours.

What can be done with the areas of the image that should be displayed in some colour which is not available in the reduced palette?

Obviously, any missing colour must be replaced by one of those that is in the palette. There are two popular ways of doing this. The first is to replace the colour value of each individual pixel with the colour table index of the colour closest to it. This can have undesirable effects: not only may the colours be distorted, but detail may be lost when two similar colours are

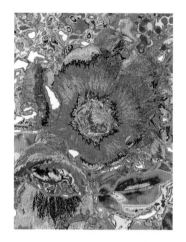

Figure 5.8. *Exchanging the colour tables*

replaced by the same one, and banding and other visible artefacts may appear where gradations of colour are replaced by sharp boundaries. As we noted previously, these effects are collectively known as ***posterization***.

When posterization is unacceptable, the replacement of colours missing from the table can be done another way. Areas of a single colour are replaced by a pattern of dots of several different colours, with the intention that optical mixing in the eye will produce the effect of a colour which is not really present. For example, say our image includes an area of pale pink, but the palette that we must use does not include that colour. We can attempt to simulate it by colouring some of the pixels within that area red and some white. This process is called ***dithering***. It is done by grouping together pixels in the area to be coloured, and applying colour to individual pixels within each group in a suitable pattern. The process is an extension of the use of half-toning, used to print greyscale images on presses that can only produce dots of pure black or white. At low resolutions, dithering may produce poor results, so it is better suited to high-resolution work.

Figure 5.9 shows five distinct ways of distributing black and white among a 2×2 block of pixels. If the pixels were small enough and the image was viewed from a sufficient distance, these patterns would be interpreted as five different shades of grey (including black and white), as the picture of the iris in Figure 5.9 demonstrates. This picture uses only pure black and white pixels. The dithering patterns can be see in the blown-up detail on the right. In general, a block of $n \times n$ pixels can simulate $n^2 + 1$ different grey levels, so you can see that as the size of the block over which we dither is increased, so is the number of grey levels, but at the expense of resolution.

Figure 5.9. *Dithering in black and white*

If each pixel can be one of 256 different colours, instead of just black or white, then the corresponding patterns can simulate millions of colours. However, these simulated colours are, in effect, being applied to pixels four times the area of those actually on the screen. This means that the effective resolution of the image is being halved, resulting in a loss of detail. While this is usually acceptable for printing, where resolutions in excess of 600 dpi are common, it is often intrusive when images are being displayed on 72 dpi monitors. Other artefacts may also be generated when the patterns are superimposed; these can be minimized by clever choice of dot patterns for the generated colours, although this has the effect of cutting down the number of different colours that can be simulated.

This leaves the question of which colours should be used in a palette. Ideally, you will fill the palette with the most important colours in your image. Often, these will be the most common, in which case it is easy for a program like Photoshop to construct the palette automatically by examining the original 24-bit version when it converts it to indexed colour. Sometimes, though, the use of colour will be more complex, and it may be necessary to construct the palette by hand (or, more likely, edit an automatically constructed palette), making subjective judgements to ensure that all the colours considered to be vital are present in the palette.

Figure 5.10. *Dithering and posterization*

Figure 5.10 illustrates the effect of dithering on a colour image. It shows a detail from the top right corner of the flower image from Figure 5.6. The original image is shown at the left; in the middle is a version reduced to indexed colour using an "adaptive" palette of 256 colours, chosen automatically from those in the image, with dithering applied. At this magnification, the effect can be seen quite clearly in this area. On the right, the same palette is used, but without dithering, and posterization can be seen clearly.

┌─ IN DETAIL ──

The main reason for using indexed colour nowadays is to reduce the size of image files without using lossy compression. Previously, though, indexed colour was used on low-end computers as a way of reducing the amount of video memory (VRAM) that was needed on the system's graphics card. By using fewer bits for each pixel, less VRAM is required to drive a monitor of any given resolution. Putting this another way, using lower colour depths meant that the same graphics card could drive a bigger display.

Ideally, in this situation, when an image had a colour table attached to it this table would be loaded into the hardware and used to select the colours for displaying the image. In practice, this was not always done. Instead, the colour table was ignored and the image was displayed using a standard system palette. The system palettes on Windows and Macintosh systems were not identical, so to be sure that your image would display correctly on both platforms it was necessary to restrict it to the set of 216 colours common to both system palettes. Since consistency across platforms is a particular problem for Web pages, this set of colours came to be known as the "Web-safe" palette. This is now obsolete, but you will still see it offered as an option when you save images as GIFs. You can safely ignore it.

└───

> **KEY POINTS**
>
> Colour is an essential element of multimedia, used in vector graphics, bitmapped images, video, animation and text.
>
> Colour science attempts to relate the subjective sensation of colour to measurable and reproducible physical phenomena.
>
> A spectral power distribution (SPD) is a description of how the intensity of light varies with its wavelength. An SPD is a good model of a colour, but is too cumbersome to work with in computer graphics.
>
> The tristimulus theory of colour implies that any colour can be produced by mixing suitable amounts of three additive primary colours.
>
> In RGB colour, the three primaries are standard shades of red, green and blue.
>
> Only colours in the RGB gamut can be represented in this way.
>
> Any colour is specified as three values (R, G, B) giving the relative proportions of the three primaries. This is often written as a 6-digit hexadecimal number, with R, G and B each being between 0 and 255, so a colour value occupies 24 bits.
>
> The number of bits used to store a colour value – the colour depth – determines how many different colours can be represented. The use of lower colour depths leads to posterization and loss of image detail, but reduces file size.
>
> In indexed colour, instead of storing a 24-bit colour value for each pixel, we use an 8-bit value which serves as an index into a colour table. The colour table contains the palette of colours used in the image.
>
> Some colours from the original image may be missing from the palette. Dithering can be used to reduce the resulting posterization.

Other Colour Models

The RGB colour model is the most important means of representing colours used in images for multimedia, because it corresponds to the way in which colour is produced on computer monitors, and it is also how colour is detected by cameras and scanners. Several other colour models are in use, and you should know something about them because you may be required to work with images that have already been prepared for some other medium, especially print, or to use software which is based on a different view of colour from RGB.

CMYK

You have probably seen at some time the experiment, originally devised by Thomas Young in 1801, illustrated in Figure 5.11. Beams of the three additive primaries red, green and blue are shone onto a white surface – which reflects all of the light falling on it – so that they overlap.

Where only one colour lands, we see that colour; where all three overlap, we see white, as we would expect from the previous section. Where two colours overlap, we see a new colour formed by the mixing of the two additive primaries. These new colours are a pale slightly greenish blue, usually called cyan, a slightly bluish red, called magenta, and a bright yellow. Each of these three is formed by adding two of the additive primaries. Since all three additive primaries combine to form white light, we could equally say that cyan, for example, which is the mixture of two of the primaries, blue and green, is produced by subtracting the remaining primary, red, from white light.

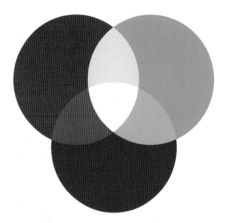

Figure 5.11. *Complementary colours*

We can express this effect pseudo-algebraically. Writing R, G and B for red, green and blue, C, M and Y for cyan, magenta and yellow,[†] and W for white, and using + to mean additive mixing of light, and − to mean subtraction of light, we have

$$C = G + B = W - R$$
$$M = R + B = W - G$$
$$Y = R + G = W - B$$

In each equation, the colour on the left is called the **complementary colour** of the one at the extreme right; for example, magenta is the complementary colour of green.

The relevance of this experiment is two-fold. Firstly, it is the basis for a theory of colour aesthetics which has had a great influence on the use of colour in art and design. Secondly, the idea of forming colours by subtraction of light instead of addition provides a colour model appropriate to ink, paint and other coloured pigments, since these are substances which owe their coloured appearance to the way they absorb light. Neither the aesthetic theory nor the account of mixing stand up to detailed scrutiny, but they are instructive approximations.

An important point to grasp is that the light that is reflected from a coloured surface is not changed in colour by the process of reflection. For example, when you hold a glossy photograph under a bright white light, the light that bounces off it will produce white reflections that interfere with the colour of the photograph. The dyes on a surface such as paper do not supply colour to light reflected off the surface, but to light that penetrates through them and gets reflected or scattered back from beneath it. During the light's journey through the particles of dye, ink or paint, the pigments absorb light at some frequencies. The light that emerges thus appears to be coloured.

---

† The Y that stands for yellow is not to be confused with the Y that stands for luminance elsewhere in this chapter.

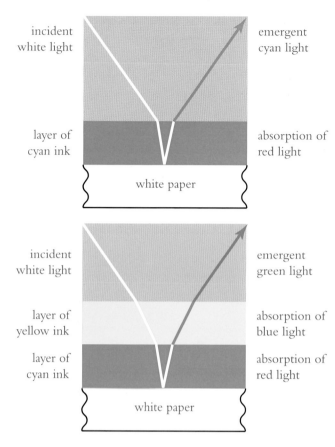

Figure 5.12. *Coloured inks*

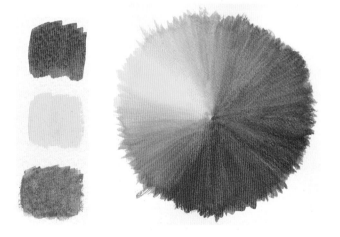

Figure 5.13. *Subtractive colour mixing*

When clear inks or dyes are overlaid, the combination absorbs all the frequencies absorbed by the individual components. When, for example, we talk of "cyan ink", we mean ink that, when it is applied to white paper and illuminated by white light will absorb the red component of the light, allowing the green and blue components, which combine to produce the cyan colour, to be reflected back (see Figure 5.12).

If we apply a thin layer of such an ink to white paper, and then add a layer of yellow, the yellow ink will absorb incident blue light, so the combination of the cyan and yellow inks produces a green colour (the additive primary green, that is), as shown at the bottom of Figure 5.12. Similarly, combining cyan and magenta inks produces blue, while magenta combined with yellow gives red. A combination of all three colours will absorb all incident light, producing black.

Mixtures containing different proportions of cyan, magenta and yellow ink will absorb red, green and blue light in corresponding proportions, thus (in theory) producing the same range of colours as the addition of red, green and blue primary lights. Cyan, magenta and yellow are called the **subtractive primaries** for this reason. Figure 5.13 shows (within the limits of the printing process used for this book) the range of colours that can be produced by mixing paints of the three subtractive primary colours (the three swatches on the left show the only pigments used).

In practice, it is not possible to manufacture inks which absorb only light of precisely the complementary colour. Inevitably, some unwanted colours are absorbed at the same time. As a result, the gamut of colours that can be printed using cyan, magenta and yellow is not the same as the RGB gamut. Furthermore, combining actual inks of all three colours does not produce a very good black. On top of this, applying three different inks is not very good for your paper and leads to longer drying times. For these reasons, in magazine and book printing – the most important applications of subtractive colour mixing – the three primaries are augmented with black. The four colours cyan, magenta, yellow and black, when used in printing, are called process colours, and identified by their initials CMYK.

Figure 5.14 shows the CMYK colour gamut – or to be more precise, *a* CMYK gamut, corresponding to a typical four-colour printer – and compares it with the RGB gamut displayed earlier. (In the interests of clarity we have not attempted to show the colours themselves this time.) You will see that the CMYK gamut is smaller than RGB, but it is not a strict subset – there are CMYK colours that fall outside the RGB gamut, and vice versa. You will also see that, because of the different colour mixing method and the presence of the black, the gamut is not triangular. Black is not a colour on the plot, so there is no point labelled B, but its presence distorts the shape of the gamut.

For print, an understanding of the subtractive CMYK model of colour, and also of the properties of inks and papers, is vital to high-quality colour reproduction. For multimedia, CMYK is of less direct relevance.

If you want people to be able to print accurate copies of the images you use, in colour, then you should ensure that those images only contain colours within the CMYK gamut, otherwise there will be colour shifts on the printed versions. If you are incorporating images that have previously been used in some print medium, you may find they are stored in a format in which colours are specified as C, M, Y and K values, instead of R, G and B. When the images are converted to a suitable file format for multimedia, it may be necessary also to convert the CMYK colour values into RGB. (Programs such as Photoshop can do this.) Having done so, you may be able to apply some colour transformations to improve the appearance by taking advantage of the larger RGB gamut.

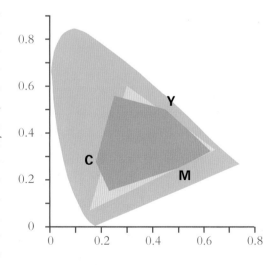

Figure 5.14. *The CMYK gamut*

┌─ IN DETAIL ──┐

The mixing of paints – by stirring them up together in a bucket for painting a house, or combining them on a palette for painting a picture – is more complicated than mixing inks in the manner just described, because it is necessary to take account of the effect of the scattering of light by pigment particles, as well as absorption. The relative importance of scattering and absorption varies with wavelength.

Artists also use other methods of mixing colours, which add further complexity. Sometimes, dots or other small marks of pure colour may be placed close together. Depending on the colours used and the size of the marks, the colours may be optically mixed in the eye, to produce a colour which approximates the additive combination of the colours on the canvas, or one colour may be subjectively modified by the presence of the other, so that it appears brighter. In a similar way, a layer of paint may be scraped back, partially revealing a different colour beneath it, or a thin layer may be painted over dry paint that bears the texture of brush strokes, so that it shows through to a different extent in different places. In either case, the appearance of the paint is modified.

Many artists will use a combination of these and other techniques – such as the over-painting of semi-transparent layers which approximates the subtractive mixing of ink – as well as conventional mixing of paints on a palette.

└──┘

HSL and HSB

Breaking a colour down into its component primaries makes sense when considering the way monitors, cameras and colour printers work, but as a way of describing colour it does not correspond to the way in which we experience colours in the world. Looking at a pale (cyan) blue, you probably don't relate it to a mixture of green and blue-violet light, but probably compare it with other blues, considering how nearly pure blue it is or how greenish or purplish it appears, how bright or dull (greyish) it looks, and how light or dark it is.

Putting this in more formal terms, we can consider a colour's *hue*, its *saturation* and its *lightness*. In physicists' terms, hue is the particular wavelength at which most of the energy of the light is concentrated (the *dominant wavelength*); we could say that hue is the pure colour of light. In less scientific terms, we usually identify hues by names. Isaac Newton identified seven hues in the spectrum, the familiar red, orange, yellow, green, blue, indigo and violet of the rainbow. However, Newton apparently chose seven colours for the rainbow to match the seven notes of a musical scale, not for any scientific reason, and it is more normal to distinguish just four – red, yellow, green and blue – and define hue informally as the extent to which a colour resembles one, or a mixture of two, of these. (But note that here there is no implication that these four hues are any more real or "primary" than any others, except inasmuch as people with normal colour vision will never confuse one of them with any of the others.)

IN DETAIL

> **The equation of hue with the measurable quantity dominant wavelength is appealing, but not quite as simple as one would hope. Some hues cannot be identified with a single wavelength. Most people would consider purple to be a hue, but the SPD for purple has peaks at both short and long wavelengths (red and blue). We know, though, from the discussion of subtractive mixing, that we could consider purple to be made by subtracting light whose dominant wavelength was a shade of green from white light. In other words, the hue purple is associated with a dominant wavelength, but the dominance takes the form of a negative peak.**

A paint of a pure hue can be altered by mixing it with white or black: the dominant hue (wavelength) remains the same, but the appearance is changed. Adding increasing amounts of white creates a sequence of progressively lighter *tints* of the hue; adding black creates a sequence of progressively darker *shades*. Adding different proportions of both creates a range of intermediate *tones* tending to grey, as illustrated in Figure 5.15. (Note that the terms "tone" and "shade" are often used interchangeably and imprecisely, though.) As we move towards the greys, there are more possibilities for different proportions of white and black, so the tones fan out, as shown in the diagram.

A tone's lightness is a measure of how light or dark it is. In Figure 5.15, the height of each swatch above black corresponds to its lightness. The saturation is a measure of the tone's purity or colourfulness, in other words, how much it differs from a neutral grey. In Figure 5.15, the horizontal distance between a swatch and the line of greys corresponds to its saturation. We can thus create a two-dimensional space of all the tones of a given hue, with saturation and lightness labelling the horizontal and vertical axes, as in Figure 5.16. If we can add a third dimension, to incorporate the variation of hue, this would provide an alternative way of specifying any colour.

Since at least the early nineteenth century, painters and other visual artists who like to systematize their thinking about colours have organized them into a "colour wheel". The different hues are organized in a circle, with the subtractive primaries equally spaced around the perimeter, and the additive primaries in between them so that each primary is opposite its complement, as in Figure 5.17. (The additive primaries are only approximate, because this book is printed in CMYK).

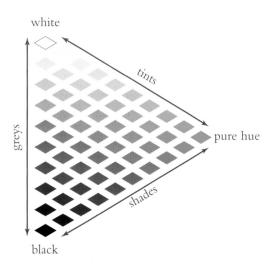

Figure 5.15. *Tints, shades and tones*

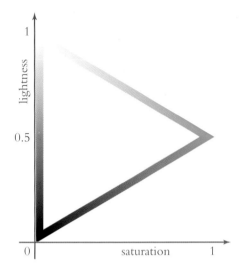

Figure 5.16. *Saturation and lightness*

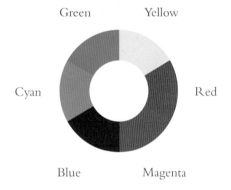

Figure 5.17. *A colour wheel*

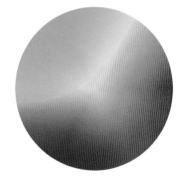

Figure 5.18. *Filling the colour wheel*

In traditional art and design it is the subtractive primaries which are usually referred to as primary colours. Their complements – the additive primaries – are called **secondary colours**, and the colours produced by mixing primaries and secondaries are **tertiary colours**. (The tertiary colours are sometimes added to the colour wheel in between the primaries and secondaries.)

This colour wheel can be combined with a plot of saturation and lightness to produce the desired alternative colour model. First, the distinct primary, secondary and tertiary hues can be augmented to produce a continuum extending all the way round a circle. Any hue can be specified as an angle around the circle, usually measured counter-clockwise, relative to red at 0°. Saturation can be added to the model by filling in the circle, putting 50% grey at the centre of the circle, and then showing a gradation of tints from the saturated hues on the perimeter to the neutral grey at the centre, as shown in Figure 5.18. You can imagine any radial line of the disk thus constructed as being a horizontal line through the centre of a diagram such as Figure 5.16, for tones of the hue that it intersects at the rim.

You can further imagine the colour disk just described as being a horizontal slice through a solid shaped like a double cone, as shown in Figure 5.19, made by rotating the lightness and saturation diagram around the vertical line of greys. Whenever we take a slice through this shape we will get a colour disk whose lightness increases as we move upwards. A particular colour can be identified by its hue (*H*) (how far round the circle from red it is), its saturation (*S*) (how far from the central axis) and its lightness value (*L*) (how far up the axis it is), hence this form of colour description is called the **HSL model**. (Sometimes, you will see it called HLS.) HSL values can be used to specify colours in CSS rules, and for making colour corrections in Photoshop.

There is a well-defined mapping from HSL values to RGB. To see informally how this would work, imagine picking up the RGB cube by its white vertex, and holding it so that it hangs with the black corner immediately below it. The line of greys would be vertical, like the lightness axis of the HSL colour solid. The six vertices apart from white and black would lie in a plane halfway up, defining the positions of the primary and secondary colours. The HSL space would be obtained by "rounding off" the sharp corners of this re-oriented RGB cube, bending its sides in the process. The relationship between individual colours in the two models is therefore not quite the same, but any HSL value can be mapped to an RGB one.

A consequence of the shape of the HSL colour space is that the available range of values for saturation varies with lightness. At the top and bottom, the only possible value is zero. This is correct – how can white or black be more or less saturated? However, it makes implementing colour representations based on HSL problematic, so for practical applications, particularly in colour pickers (see below), it is common to simplify the geometry of the HSL model and use a cylinder, so that each colour disk has the same diameter. This distorts the way the range of colours varies with brightness, but makes it easier to present the colour space on screen.

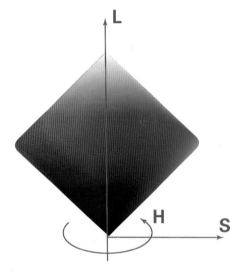

This distortion is considered undesirable by some people. In particular, at the top end of the HSL cylinder, there are pale pastel colours containing a lot of white which nevertheless have a high saturation value, which seems wrong. The **HSB** (hue, saturation and brightness) colour model was developed at roughly the same time as HSL, and shares many of its characteristics, but it uses a different lightness scale, which does not display this phenomenon.

Figure 5.19. *The HSL colour solid*

In HSB, instead of assigning a lightness of 0.5 to pure hues, they are given a brightness value of 1, so that the tones of a single hue are arranged as shown in Figure 5.20. (The name "brightness" is used instead of "lightness" only to allow us to distinguish between the two scales. They both refer to the amount of white. Sometimes, "brightness" is called "value". Apart from this name change, the **HSV** colour model is the same as HSB.) When this arrangement is extended to three dimensions, by rotating it and varying the hue, as before, the result is an inverted cone, with a disk varying from pure hues

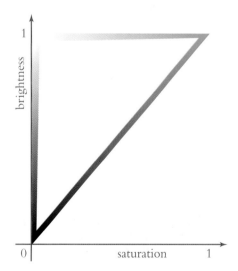

Figure 5.20. *Saturation and brightness*

at the rim to white at the centre on top. When this is distorted into a cylinder, the result is a colour space in which the brightest tones of all colours are on the top, as shown in Figure 5.21. (The bottom slice is still uniformly black, but this is considered less problematic than the uniform white slice on top of the HSL cylinder.)

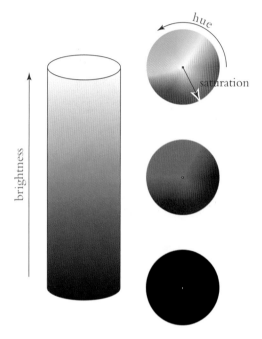

Figure 5.21. *The HSB cylinder*

Although the HSL and HSV models superficially resemble one of the ways in which painters think about colour, it should be remembered that the arrangement of hues around the circle is arbitrary and has no physical basis. In fact, the distortions introduced by the presentation of HSL and HSB as cylinders means that the way in which colours vary with the three components in either model bears little resemblance to the way in which we perceive colour changes. The main advantage of these models, as the *CSS3 Color Module* specification puts it, is that "you can guess at the colors you want, and then tweak. It is also easier to create sets of matching colors (by keeping the hue the same and varying the lightness/darkness, and saturation)". Despite the popularity of "colour schemers", such as Adobe's Kuler (which we describe in Chapter 12), creating sets of colours by keeping the lightness and saturation constant and varying the hue according to geometrical rules of colour harmony is a much less reliable way of creating colour sets.

All colour models provide a way of specifying a colour as a set of numbers, and of visualizing their relationships in a three-dimensional space. This way of describing colour is independent of the many subjective factors which normally play a part in our perception of colour. For computer programs, a numerical, objective colour specification is necessary. For people, it is less so, and most people find that specifying colours by numbers is non-intuitive. Within graphics programs, though, it is normal to choose colours interactively using a **colour picker** dialogue. These may be based on any of the colour models we have discussed, and allow you to choose colours by manipulating controls that affect the values of the components, while seeing a sample of the resulting colour displayed.

Figure 5.22 shows some of the colour pickers provided by the Macintosh system software, as examples of some different styles of picker. The RGB picker on the left simply uses sliders to control the three components. In the HSB colour picker in the middle, a slider is used to control

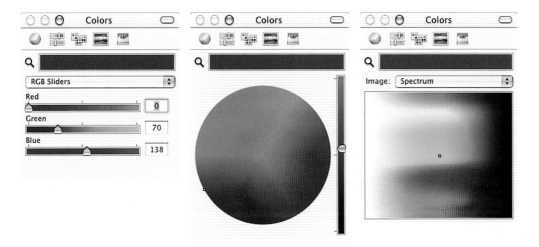

Figure 5.22. *Colour pickers*

the *B* value, while the corresponding slices through the cylinder are displayed; a colour is selected by clicking on a point in the disk, which sets the hue and saturation. The spectrum picker on the right lets you pick a colour directly by clicking.

Windows operating systems and Adobe graphics applications use a slightly different interface to their colour pickers, with RGB and HSV (or HSL in the case of Windows) integrated into a single interface, which is described in Chapter 8 of *Digital Media Tools*.

Industrial designers and graphic artists have long used a different approach to colour specification, based on swatches of standard colours that can be reproduced accurately. A colour is chosen just by looking through an extensive book of sample swatches, arranged in a standard order. The **Pantone** system is widely used for this purpose. A precise colour can be specified by quoting its unique Pantone number. Because the Pantone samples are controlled to high precision, this ensures that the colour which the designer has in mind will be reproduced by the printer. The Pantone system has been adapted for incorporation into computer graphics applications: instead of using a colour picker based on a colour model, it is possible to specify a Pantone number, or look through collections of Pantone swatches on screen. This way of choosing and specifying colours is mainly intended to overcome the difficulties of reproducing colours accurately in print, but choosing a colour from a set of swatches can often be easier and more convenient than another method. Graphics programs therefore include many swatch libraries, including Pantone, the similar Focoltone and HKS systems and the Japanese Toyo system. They also allow users to build their own collections of swatches.

Colour Spaces Based on Colour Differences

For some purposes it is useful to separate the brightness information of an image from its colour. Historically, an important motivation for doing this was to produce a means of transmitting colour television signals that would be compatible with older black and white receivers. By separating brightness and colour, it is possible to transmit a picture in such a way that the colour information is not detected by a black and white receiver, which can treat the brightness as a monochrome signal. Once a means of separating colour and brightness had been devised, it became possible to process the two signals separately in other ways. In particular, it is common practice in analogue broadcasting to use less bandwidth to transmit the colour than the brightness, since the eye is less sensitive to colour than to brightness. There is evidence to suggest that the human visual apparatus processes brightness and colour separately too, so this form of representation also holds some physiological interest.

The basis of the RGB representation of colour is that light can always be broken down into three components. What we consider as brightness – the extent to which a pixel appears to be lighter or darker – is clearly related to the values of the red, green and blue components of the colour, since these tell us how much light of each primary is being emitted. It would be tempting to suppose that the brightness could be modelled simply as $(R+G+B)/3$, but this formula is not quite adequate, because it takes no account of the eye's differing sensitivity to the different primaries. Green contributes far more to the perceived brightness of a colour than red, and blue contributes hardly at all. Hence to produce a measure of brightness from an RGB value, we must weight the three components separately. There are several different formulae in use for performing this computation; the formula recommended for modern cathode ray tubes, as used in older computer monitors and TV sets, is: $Y = 0.2125R + 0.7154G + 0.0721B$. The quantity Y defined here is called *luminance*.

You should be able to see that if you know the values of the luminance and any two of the primaries, you can reconstruct the red, green and blue values. It is normal, though, for technical reasons, to use some variant of a representation consisting of Y together with two colour difference values, usually $B-Y$ and $R-Y$. With these and the relationship between Y, R, G and B just cited, you have four equations in four unknowns, so it is still the case that you can reconstruct R, G and B.

We say "some variant" because different applications require that the three components be manipulated in different ways. For analogue television, a non-linearly scaled version of Y, properly denoted Y', is used together with a pair of weighted colour difference values, denoted U and V. Out of carelessness, the term *YUV colour* is often used to refer to any colour space consisting of a brightness component together with two colour difference components. Digital television and video use a variant called $Y'C_BC_R$, which is like $Y'UV$ but uses different weights for the colour difference computations.

In the digital realm it is possible to take advantage of the greater importance of brightness to perception than colour, by using image and video representations in which fewer colour values are stored than brightness values. This technique of **chrominance sub-sampling** reduces the amount of storage and bandwidth required, without any further compression. Several different sub-sampling regimes are in use in digital video, as we will explain in Chapter 6.

Chrominance sub-sampling is also usually applied to bitmapped images compressed using JPEG. Although the DCT-based compression we described in Chapter 4 can be applied to images using any colour model, the JFIF file specification stipulates that images should be transformed to $Y'C_BC_R$ and then sub-sampled. Normally, the data is reduced by a factor of two by the sub-sampling, although some implementations use less drastic sub-sampling (or none at all) to preserve more information at the highest quality settings. The three components are then compressed independently; different quantization matrices may be used for the brightness and colour values, with finer quantization being applied to the more important brightness data.

Perceptually Uniform Colour Models

As we mentioned earlier in this chapter, the *Commission Internationale de l'Eclairage* (CIE) has carried out work to produce an objective, device-independent definition of colours. Its basic model, the **CIE XYZ colour space**, uses three components X, Y and Z to approximate the three stimuli to which the colour-sensitive parts of our eyes respond. This model is device-independent – it doesn't depend on the characteristics of any particular monitor or printer – but as well as being awkward to work with and impossible to realize with physical light sources, it suffers (as do RGB, CMYK, HSL and most other colour models) from not being **perceptually uniform**.

A perceptually uniform model would be one in which the same change in one of the values produced the same change in appearance, no matter what the original value was. If, for example, RGB was a perceptually uniform model then changing the R component from 1 to 11 would produce the same increase in perceived redness as changing it from 101 to 111. However, this is not what actually happens. This means that computations of the distance between two colours based on their RGB values do not reflect what we consider the degree of difference between them, which in turn makes it difficult to find a closest colour match when reducing an image to a restricted palette.

For many years the CIE tried to produce a colour model that was perceptually uniform, but never quite succeeded. Two models, refined from the original XYZ model to be much more nearly perceptually uniform, were produced in 1976. These are the L*a*b* and L*u*v* models (often written simply Lab and Luv, or CIELAB and CIELUV). In both models, the *L** component is a uniform luminance and the other two components are colour differences. In L*a*b*, they specify colour in a way that combines subtractively, as in CMYK. "Lab colour" is widely used in the pre-press industry as a standard specification of colour difference values for printing. L*u*v* is a similar model, but the colour difference values work additively, as in RGB, so L*u*v* provides a device-independent model of colour suitable for monitors and scanners.

These models do not correspond to any easily understandable way of thinking about colour. However, they do provide a basis for the device-independent treatment of colour, and are used as a reference point for systems that try to guarantee that the colours we specify in our images will look as nearly as possible the same on whatever output device is being used.

KEY POINTS

Cyan, magenta and yellow are the subtractive primaries. They are the complementary colours of red, green and blue, respectively.

Thin layers of ink absorb some components of the incident light, so overlaying ink, as in printing processes, mixes colours subtractively.

The CMYK colour gamut, corresponding to easily printable colours, is smaller than the RGB gamut, but some CMYK colours lie outside the RGB gamut.

A colour can be identified by its hue, saturation and lightness.

Tones of a single hue can be arranged two-dimensionally, with lightness increasing upwards, and saturation increasing from left to right.

Hues can be arranged around the rim of a colour wheel, with complementary colours opposite each other. A hue's value is the angle between its position on the wheel and the position of red.

Hue, saturation and lightness can be combined into a three-dimensional double-cone. Any colour can be specified by its H, S and L components.

HSB is a variant of HSL, where the tones are arranged differently.

Both HSL and HSB are normally distorted into a cylindrical shape, so that they can be presented as colour pickers.

Swatch libraries provide an alternative way of choosing colours.

Colour spaces consisting of a brightness component and two colour differences are used in video. They allow chrominance sub-sampling to be used.

The CIE L*a*b* and L*u*v* colour spaces are perceptually uniform and serve as device-independent reference models.

Channels and Colour Correction

Earlier, we implied that in a 24-bit RGB colour image, a single 24-bit value is stored for each pixel. While this is the way colours are stored in some file formats, there is another possibility: for each pixel, three separate 8-bit values, one for each of red, green and blue, are stored. That is, in terms of data structures, instead of storing an image in a single array of 24-bit values, we store it in three arrays, each consisting of single bytes. This representation has some computational advantages, since 3-byte quantities are awkward to manipulate on most machines. It also provides a useful way of organizing colour images conceptually, irrespective of whether the physical storage layout is actually of this form.

Each of the three arrays can itself be considered as an image. When we consider each colour separately, it only makes sense to consider it as a greyscale image. Each of the three greyscale images making up the colour image is called a ***channel***, so we speak of the red channel, or the green or blue channel. Figure 5.23 shows an RGB colour image and its three channels. In each channel,

Figure 5.23. *An RGB colour image and its red, green and blue channels*

Figure 5.24. *Correcting and over-correcting a colour cast*

the lightness represents the intensity of the corresponding colour, so for example, in the red channel at the top right of Figure 5.23 the bright red berries in the colour image appear almost white, whereas in the green and blue channels at the bottom left and right, respectively, they are black, because there is no green or blue component in their colour at all. (That is, except for the specular highlights, which are white, so they show up in all three channels.)

Each channel can be manipulated separately: since it is an image, the manipulations can be done using the usual image-editing tools provided by Photoshop and similar programs. In particular, levels and curves can be used to alter the brightness and contrast of each channel independently. When the altered channels are recombined, the colour balance of the composite image will have changed. Colour correction operations performed in this way are frequently required to compensate for poor photography or the deficiencies of scanners and other input devices. Figure 5.24 shows an example: the scanned photograph on the left has a marked colour cast. In the middle image this has been corrected; the image on the right shows how colour adjustment can be taken further to produce an artifically coloured image that might be used as a special effect.

It may seem as though adjusting the levels of each channel is just a simple operation. In practice, although some colour adjustments are straightforward – maximizing the contrast in all three channels, for example – producing a desired result can be very time-consuming, calling for considerable experience and fine judgement. Some image manipulation programs for consumers come equipped with "wizards" or "assistants" – software modules to help in some common situations calling for colour correction by walking the user through the required steps. Sometimes, though, a simpler approach is adequate. Just as Photoshop's brightness and contrast controls encapsulate a class of tonal adjustments, so its colour balance and hue and saturation adjustments provide a less refined interface to the adjustment of levels in the three colour channels. (This is described in more detail in *Digital Media Tools*.)

Photoshop's colour balance dialogue provides three sliders – one for each of the pairs of complements cyan and red, magenta and green, and yellow and blue – which allow you to adjust the relative proportions of each pair. The adjustment can be applied to shadows, midtones or highlights separately. The hue and saturation adjustment performs a similar operation – despite its title, it allows you to vary all three of the H, S and L components of colours within specified ranges: reds, greens, blues, and so on. (Notice that although HSB is used on Photoshop's colour picker, the adjustments are made in HSL, because of its symmetry.) This provides a more intuitive way of adjusting the colours. Figure 5.25 shows an example of what can be achieved with these adjustments. The photograph on the left, taken in winter when the grasses were all brown, has been transformed into a spring scene, merely by adjusting the hue and saturation sliders as shown.

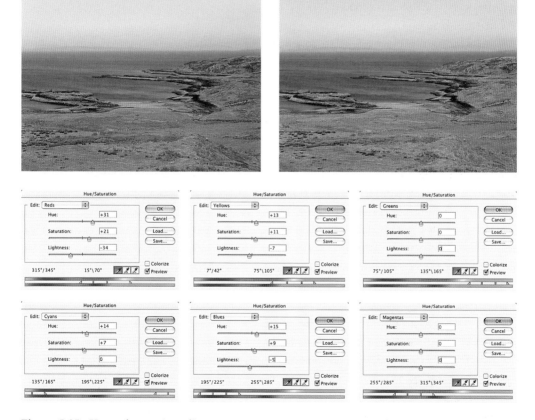

Figure 5.25. *Hue and saturation adjustments*

A different way of making colour changes which, like the two sets of controls just described, works across all the channels at once, is to replace a specified colour wherever it appears with a different one. This is a bit like doing a search and replace operation on a text file using an editor, except that the target and replacement are colours, not text strings. Photoshop's version of this operation is somewhat more sophisticated: you can set a tolerance value, which causes pixels within a certain percentage of the target value (selected by clicking with an eyedropper) to be altered. H, S and L sliders are used to specify a change to those components of pixels that match the target, instead of just specifying an exact replacement colour. Because these changes are relative to the original value, variations in tone are preserved in the replacement.

This is illustrated in Figure 5.26, where we have "repainted" a house door, using the colour replacement settings shown in the inset to turn it from red to blue. A high tolerance was needed to select the entire door successfully. (In fact, we had to extend the initial colour selection, using the eyedropper with a + sign that you can see in the screenshot, to include the darker colour on the weatherboard at the bottom. The colour difference between this area and the flat door panels is maintained in the blue version.)

Although we are only discussing RGB colour, images stored in any colour space can be separated into channels. In particular, the channels of a CMYK image correspond to the colour separations

Figure 5.26. *Colour replacement*

needed by commercial printing processes, while the channels of a $Y'C_BC_R$ image correspond to the components of a video signal. Furthermore, the idea that a greyscale image can be considered to be one channel of a composite image is extended in the concept of alpha channel, which we introduced in Chapter 4. Although alpha channels behave completely differently from the colour channels that make up the displayed image, their common representation has some useful consequences.

One of the most common applications of this duality is in inserting images of people or objects into a separately photographed scene – often one where it is impossible for them to be in reality. This can be done by photographing the person against a blue background (ensuring that none of their clothing is blue). All of the image data for the person will be in the red and green channels; the blue channel will be an image of the area not occupied by the person. An alpha channel constructed as a copy of the blue channel (an operation built in to any software that manipulates image channels) will therefore mask out the background, isolating the figure. It is then a simple matter to copy the figure, using the mask to define it as the selection, and paste it into, for example, an underwater scene. This "blue screen" technique is commonly used in video and film-making, as well as in constructing fake images.

Other sorts of colour image processing can be implemented by applying some greyscale processing to each of the channels separately. An important example is JPEG compression, which, although it is most often applied to colour images, is defined in the standard to operate on 8-bit quantities, so that each channel is compressed individually. One advantage of this is that the compression algorithm is unaffected by the colour space used for the image; it just takes whatever channels are there and compresses them. This offers the freedom to choose a colour space, and apply pre-processing to the channels. For example, as we noted earlier, the JFIF file format demands that images be transformed into $Y'C_BC_R$ so that chrominance sub-sampling can be applied.

KEY POINTS

The R, G and B components of each pixel can be stored as separate values.

The three arrays of values can be treated as greyscale images, called channels.

Making adjustments to the channels alters the colours of the image.

The colour balance, hue and saturation and colour replacement adjustments change the colour of the image as a whole.

Alpha channels can be treated as additional colour channels.

Images using other colour models can also be separated into channels, which can be processed independently.

Consistent Colour

Colour adjustment is messy, and getting it wrong can cause irreparable damage to an image. It would be much better to get things right first time, but the varying colour characteristics of different monitors and scanners make this difficult. Some recent developments in software are aimed at compensating for these differences. They are based on the use of "profiles", describing how devices detect and reproduce colour.

We don't need much information to give a reasonable description of the colour properties of any particular monitor. We need to know exactly which colours the red, green and blue phosphors emit (the R, G and B chromaticities). These can be measured using a suitable scientific instrument, and then expressed in terms of one of the CIE device-independent colour spaces. We also need to know the maximum saturation each component is capable of, i.e. we need to know what happens when each electron beam is full on. We can deduce this if we can characterize the make-up and intensity of white, since this tells us what the (24-bit) RGB value (255,255,255) corresponds to. Again, the value of white – the monitor's **white point** – can be specified in a device-independent colour space.

IN DETAIL

You will sometimes see the white point specified as a "colour temperature", in degrees absolute. This form of specification is based on the observation that the spectral make-up of light emitted by a perfect radiator (a "black body") depends only on its temperature, so a black body temperature provides a concise description of an SPD. Most colour monitors for computers use a white point designed to correspond to a colour temperature of 9300 K. This is far higher than daylight (around 7500 K), or a conventional television monitor (around 6500 K), in order to generate the high light intensity required for a device that will normally be viewed under office lighting conditions. (Televisions are designed on the assumption that they will be watched in dimly lit rooms.) The "white" light emitted by a monitor when all its three colours are at full intensity is actually quite blue.

Computer monitors are not actually black bodies, and so their SPDs deviate from the shape of the black body radiation, which means that colour temperature is only an approximation of the characteristic of the white point, which is better specified using CIE colour values.

Finally, the most complex element in the monitor's behaviour is the relationship between the RGB values presented to it by the graphics controller, and the intensity of the light emitted in response. This relationship is not a simple linear one: the intensity of light emitted in response to an input of 100 is not 10 times that produced by an input of 10, which in turn is not 10 times that produced by an input of 1. The ***transfer characteristic*** of a display – the relationship between the light intensity I emitted by the screen and the voltage V applied to the electron gun is often modelled by the transfer function $I = V^\gamma$, where γ is a constant. Thus, it is common to use the value of γ to characterize the response. Unfortunately, this model is not entirely accurate, and one of the sources of variability between monitors lies in the use of incorrect values for γ which attempt to compensate for errors in the formula. Another is the fact that some display controllers attempt to compensate for the non-linearity by adjusting values according to an inverse transfer function before they are applied to the electron guns, while others do not. In particular, Macintosh and Windows systems deal with the transfer characteristic differently, with the result that colours with the same RGB values look different on the two systems.

However, it is convenient to use a single number to represent the transfer characteristic, and γ serves this purpose reasonably well, and provides the last value normally used to model the behaviour of a monitor. In this context, it is usual to spell out the letter's name, and refer to the display's ***gamma***. Similar collections of values can be used to characterize the colour response of other types of device, including scanners and printers.

Armed with accurate device-independent values for red, green and blue chromaticities, and the white point and gamma of a particular monitor, it is possible to translate any RGB colour value into an absolute, device-independent, colour value in a CIE colour space that exactly describes the colour produced by that monitor in response to that RGB value. This is the principle behind the practice of ***colour management***.

In a typical situation calling for colour management an image is prepared using some input device. For simplicity, assume this is a monitor used as the display by a graphics editor, but the same principles apply to images captured by a digital camera or a scanner. The image will be stored in a file, using RGB values which reflect the way the input device maps colours to colour values – its ***colour space***. Later, the same image may be displayed on a different monitor. Now the RGB values stored in the image file are mapped by the output device, which probably has a different colour space from the input device. The colours which were stored in the input device's colour space are interpreted as if they were in the output device's colour space. In other words, they come out wrong. (See Figure 5.27.)

Figure 5.27. *No colour management*

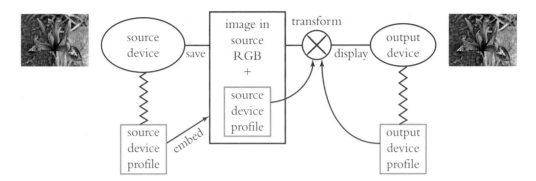

Figure 5.28. *Colour management with embedded profiles*

One way of correcting this, as illustrated in Figure 5.28, is to embed information about the input device's colour space profile in the image file in the form of a **colour profile**. Colour profiles are created by taking accurate measurements of a device's colour response, using standard techniques and colour targets. PSD, PDF, TIFF, JFIF, PNG and other types of file are able to accommodate such information, in varying degrees of detail. At the least, the R, G and B chromaticities, white point and gamma can be included in the file. Software on the machine being used to display the image can, in principle, use this information to map the RGB values it finds in the image file to colour values in a device-independent colour space. Then, using the device profile of the output monitor, it can map those device-independent values to the colour space of the output device, so that the colours are displayed exactly as they were on the input device. In practice, it is more likely that the two profiles would be combined and used to map from the input device colour space to the output device colour space directly.

It is possible, of course, that some of the colours in the input device's colour space are not available in the output device's colour space. For example, as we showed earlier, many colours in RGB lie outside the CMYK gamut, so they cannot be printed correctly. Colour management can only actually guarantee that the colours will be displayed exactly as they were intended within the capabilities of the output device. If software uses colour management consistently, the approximations made to accommodate a restricted colour gamut will be the same, and the output's colour will be predictable, at least.

An alternative way of using colour management software is to modify the colours displayed on a monitor using the profile of a different output device. In this way, colour can be accurately previewed, or "soft proofed". This mode of working is especially useful in pre-press work, where actually producing printed proofs may be expensive or time-consuming. For example, if you were preparing a book to be printed on a phototypesetter, you could use the phototypesetter's colour profile, in combination with the colour profile of your monitor, to make the monitor display the colours in the book as they would be printed on the phototypesetter.

To obtain really accurate colour reproduction across a range of devices, device profiles need to provide more information than simply the RGB chromaticities, white point and a single figure for gamma. In practice, for example, the gammas for the three different colours are not necessarily the same. As already stated, the actual transfer characteristics are not really correctly represented by gamma; a more accurate representation is needed. If, as well as displaying colours on a monitor, we also wished to be able to manage colour reproduction on printers, where it is necessary to take account of a host of issues, including the C, M, Y and K chromaticities of the inks, spreading characteristics of the ink, and absorbency and reflectiveness of the paper, even more information would be required – and different information still for printing to film, or video.

Since the original impetus for colour management software came from the pre-press and printing industries, colour management has already been developed to accommodate these requirements. The **International Colour Consortium (ICC)** has defined a standard device profile which supports extremely elaborate descriptions of the colour characteristics of a wide range of devices. ICC device profiles are used by colour management software such as Apple's ColorSync, the Adobe colour management system built into Photoshop and other Adobe programs, and the Kodak Precision Color Management System, to provide colour management services. Manufacturers of scanners, cameras, monitors and printers routinely produce ICC profiles of their devices.

Colour management is not much use unless accurate profiles are available. In fact, using an inaccurate profile can produce worse results than not using colour management at all. Unfortunately, no two devices are exactly identical and the colour characteristics of an individual device will change over time. Although a generic profile produced by the manufacturer for one line of monitors or scanners is helpful, to take full advantage of colour management it is necessary to calibrate individual devices, at relatively frequent intervals (once a month is often advised). Some high-end monitors are able to calibrate themselves automatically. For others, it is necessary to use a special measuring device in conjunction with software that displays a sequence of colour values and, on the basis of the measured output of the screen, generates an accurate profile.

You may wonder why the profile data is embedded in the file. Why is it not used at the input end to map the colour values to a device-independent form, such as L★a★b★, which can then be mapped to the output colour space when the image is displayed? The work is split between the two ends and no extra data has to be added to the file. The reason for not using this method is that most existing software does not work with device-independent colour values, so it could not display the images at all. If software ignores a device profile, things are no worse than they would have been if it was not there.

Clearly, though, it would be desirable to use a device-independent colour space for stored colour values. The **sRGB (standard RGB)** colour model attempts to provide such a space.

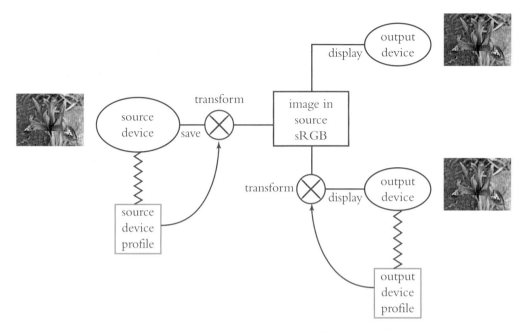

Figure 5.29. *Use of the sRGB colour space*

As you can guess, sRGB is an RGB colour model, and specifies standard values for the R, G and B chromaticities, white point and gamma. The standard values are claimed to be typical of the values found on most monitors (although many people claim that Adobe's standard RGB colour space is more widely applicable). As a result, if the display software is not aware of the sRGB colour space and simply displays the image without any colour transformation, it should still look acceptable. Figure 5.29 illustrates how sRGB can be used in colour management. With the software that transforms the image using the output device profile, colours should be accurately reproduced; if no transformation is applied, some colour shifts may occur, but these should not be as bad as they would have been if the image had been stored using the input device's colour space.

Use of sRGB colour is especially suitable for graphics on the World Wide Web, because there most images are only ever destined to be displayed on a monitor. Colour specifications in CSS are interpreted as sRGB values. Does it really matter if the colours in your image are slightly distorted when the image is displayed on somebody else's monitor? Consider online shopping catalogues or art gallery catalogues. For many images on the Web, accurate colour is important. (To take an extreme example, think about buying paint over the Internet.) One of the factors driving the development of colour management and its incorporation into Web browsers is the desire to facilitate online shopping. As well as the development of the sRGB colour space, this has led to the development of browser plug-ins providing full colour management facilities and increasingly, the incorporation of colour management directly into browsers.

KEY POINTS

The colour properties of a monitor can be roughly summarized by the R, G and B chromaticities, white point and gamma.

Gamma approximately models the relationship between RGB values and light intensity.

If an image is stored in one device's colour space and displayed on a device with a different colour space, colours will not be reproduced accurately.

If a colour profile that models the input device is embedded in the image file, it can be combined with a profile that models the output device to translate between the colour spaces and reproduce colours accurately.

Colours that are out of gamut should be reproduced consistently.

ICC colour profiles provide elaborate descriptions of the colour characteristics of a wide range of devices; they are used as a standard for colour management.

The success of colour management depends on having accurate profiles.

sRGB is intended as a standard device-independent colour space for monitors. It is used on the World Wide Web.

Exercises

Test Questions

1 What advantages are there to using images in greyscale instead of colour? Give some examples of applications for which greyscale is to be preferred, and some for which the use of colour is essential.

2 Is it true that any colour can be produced by mixing red, green and blue light in variable proportions?

3 What colours correspond to the eight corners of the cube in Figure 5.3?

4 Why do RGB colour values (r,g,b), with $r=g=b$ represent shades of grey?

5 Exactly how many distinct colours can be represented in 24-bit colour?

6 Explain carefully why the primary colours used in mixing pigments (paint or ink, for example) are different from those used in producing colours on a monitor.

7 Explain why it is not satisfactory to use just one standard set of 256 colours for all images where saving space is a priority. How does indexed colour avoid the problems inherent in using such a standard palette?

8 If a colour table has 256 entries (so pixels only need a single byte), each 3 bytes wide, how large must an image be before the use of indexed colour provides a net saving of space over the use of direct 24-bit colour?

9 For which of the following images would the use of indexed colour be satisfactory?

(a) A reproduction of your national flag.

(b) A photograph of the surface of Mars.

(c) A photograph of yourself on a beach.

(d) A still from a black and white movie.

For those cases where indexed colour would not be satisfactory, would dithering help?

10 Suppose that a chrominance sub-sampling scheme uses the same number of samples for both colour difference components. What must the ratio of this number to the number of luminance samples be to reduce the space occupied by a sub-sampled image by a factor of two?

11 Explain why the colours of an image prepared using one monitor might appear different on another monitor, even if a colour profile has been embedded in the image file.

Discussion Topics

1 If you give a child a paintbox containing red, green and blue paints only, will they be able to mix an adequate range of colours to paint the ceiling of the Sistine Chapel? Explain why you think they will, or will not.

2 Which colour space should be used for archiving images and why?

3 Give an example of an image whose most important colour is not one of its most commonly occurring colours. When might this cause a problem?

4 The most noticeable effect of the adjustments shown in Figure 5.25 is to turn the dry grasses and bracken bright green, but if you look at the screenshots you will see that no changes were made to the greens. How can this be so?

5 The colour values of pixels in an image are never stored in HSL or HSV. Why not?

6 What can you do to ensure that the colours on a Web site you are developing are seen as accurately as possible by all visitors? What compromises might you have to accept and why?

Practical Tasks

1 Suppose you had an image with too much red in it, perhaps because of poor lighting. Explain what adjustments you would make to its red channel to compensate. What undesirable side-effect would your adjustment have, and what would you do about it?

2 Photoshop's **Save for Web** dialogue can be used (among other things) to convert an image to GIF or PNG format using indexed colour. It provides a range of options for controlling dithering and the size and contents of the colour table. Experiment with the effect of the various available options on a range of images with different colour characteristics. (If you do not have Photoshop, you may be able to find shareware or Open Source utilities that perform the same function with similar options.)

3 Choose a digital photograph with a good range of colours, and display it on as many different devices as you have access to. Disable any colour management while you do so. Try to include a PC and a Mac, CRT and flat-panel displays, and at least one printer. Assess the consistency of the colour reproduction across these devices. Can you improve matters by using colour management? (Don't omit to calibrate the devices.)

Video

■ Video Standards

Analogue Broadcast Standards. Digital Video Standards. DV and MPEG. High Definition Formats.

■ Video Compression

Spatial Compression. Temporal Compression. MPEG-4 and H.264/AVC. Other Video Codecs. Quality.

■ Editing and Post-Production

Traditional Film and Video Editing. Digital Video Editing. Post-Production.

■ Delivery

Streaming. Architectures and Formats.

Video is a medium which has been revolutionized by digital technology in a short period of time. In the late 1990s, video cameras were almost exclusively analogue in nature. Importing video footage into a computer system relied on dedicated capture cards to perform the digitization. Digital video editing placed considerable demands on the hardware of the time – much editing was still done on analogue equipment, by copying back and forth between three recording decks. Less than 10 years later, digital video had become the norm. Affordable digital video camcorders are widely available for the consumer market, and higher-end digital equipment is used for professional applications, from news-gathering to feature film-making. Tiny video cameras are built into mobile phones and computers and it is possible to capture activity on a screen directly to video, without even using a camera. Non-linear digital video editing software that runs on modestly powerful systems is used routinely by both amateurs and professionals.

As a result of this explosive spread of digital video technology, coupled with the higher network speeds of broadband Internet access, video has become a prominent feature of the World Wide Web and the Internet. Web sites dedicated to the presentation and sharing of video have proliferated, but video has also become a common element among other media on many sites. News sites often include embedded video clips among textual news items, and support sites for software increasingly rely on video "screencasts" to demonstrate features of programs by showing them in action. Video is also used for communicating over the Internet: any suitably equipped computer can act as a video phone. As well as showing the participants to each other, video chat applications allow them to show each other images and recorded video clips.

Several factors have made these developments possible. First is the rapid increase in processor speeds and memory, disk capacity and network bandwidth. Second is the development of standards for digital video signals and interfaces, which have largely replaced the earlier confusion of incompatible capture cards and proprietary codecs. Finally, the move to digital video has been driven by its convenience and robustness, and the flexibility and relative simplicity of digital video editing compared to its analogue equivalent.

The high-end professional facilities used for making feature films and top-quality broadcast video lie beyond the scope of this book. For multimedia work, there are two broad classes of hardware and software that are in common use.

Where good quality is required, the most widely used combination of hardware for capturing video comprises a digital camcorder or VTR (video tape recorder) using one of the variants of the *DV* format – mini-DV (often simply called "DV"), DVCAM or DVCPRO – connected to a computer by a *FireWire* interface. (FireWire was formerly known as IEEE 1394, but the more colourful name has now been officially adopted; equipment made by Sony uses the name iLink for the same interface.) These devices capture full-screen video, with frames that are the same size as those used by broadcast TV; they also work at one of the standard television frame rates.

The three DV variants use different tape formats and provide differing degrees of error correction and compatibility with analogue studio equipment, but all send digital video as a data stream to a computer in the same format, so software does not need to distinguish between the three types of equipment. Mini-DV is essentially a consumer format, although it is also used for semi-professional video production. The other two formats are more suited for professional use, being especially widely used for news gathering. All DV equipment supports *device control*, the ability for the tape to be stopped, started and moved to a specific position by signals sent from the computer by software.

IN DETAIL

"DV" stands for "digital video", but that expression is also used in a more general sense, to refer to the storage and manipulation of video data in a digital form, and sometimes it is abbreviated to "DV" when used in this way, too. We will usually use the full term "digital video" in this general sense, and only use "DV" whenever we mean the specific standard we have just introduced.

Some camcorders have an internal hard disk, instead of using tape, while others write directly to DVDs. Such devices may still use the DV format and connect via FireWire, or they may use the MPEG-2 format used on DVDs, and connect via USB. Increasingly, DV equipment employs *High Definition (HD)* standards, which provide higher resolution, but this does not affect the technology in other ways.

Although the subjective quality of DV is very good, it is a compressed format, and as we saw in the case of bitmapped still images in Chapter 4, compression causes artefacts and interferes with subsequent processing and recompression. Figure 6.1 shows a frame of uncompressed video and the same frame compressed as DV. It is hard to see any difference in the full frames, at the top left of each group of images. However, as the blown-up details show, there are visible compression artefacts in the DV. (They are especially noticeable in the water at the bottom of the frame.) As the extreme blow-ups demonstrate, the colour values of the actual pixels have changed considerably in some areas.

The user has no control over the quality of DV. The data stream produced by a digital video camera is required to conform to the appropriate standard, which stipulates the data rate for the

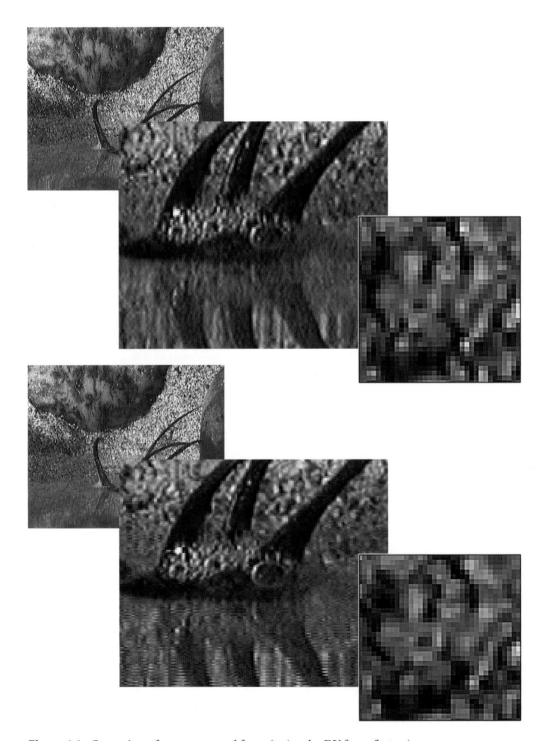

Figure 6.1. *Comparison of an uncompressed frame (top) and a DV frame (bottom)*

data stream, and thus the amount of compression to be applied. If higher quality is required, it will be necessary to use expensive professional equipment conforming to different standards. High-end equipment does allow uncompressed video to be used, but this places great demands on disk space, as we showed in Chapter 2.

Where quality is much less important than cost and convenience, a completely different set of equipment is common. The cheap video cameras built into mobile phones or laptop computers are not generally DV devices. Usually, the compression and storage format are both defined by the MPEG-4 standard, or a simplified version of it designed for mobile phones, known as 3GP. The frame size is usually small enough to fit a mobile device's screen, and the frame rate is often reduced. All of these factors ensure that the size of the video files is very small, but the result is a substantial loss of quality. When video is transferred from a low-end device of this sort to a computer, it is usually through a USB 2.0 connection, not via FireWire. External cameras that connect in this way can also be obtained. They are generally referred to as Webcams, because they are often used for creating live video feeds for Web sites.

Video Standards

Digital video is often captured from video cameras that are also used to record pictures for playing back on television sets — it isn't currently economically practical to manufacture cameras (other than cheap Webcams) purely for connecting to computers. Therefore, in multimedia production we must deal with signals that correspond to the standards governing television. This means that the newer digital devices must still maintain compatability with old analogue equipment in essential features such as the size of frames and the frame rate, so in order to understand digital video we need to start by looking at its analogue heritage. (Although **HDTV** uptake is increasing, the original television standards are still in widespread use around the world, and many areas do not have standard definition digital television yet, although this varies from one country to another and will change over time.)

Analogue Broadcast Standards

There are three sets of standards in use for analogue broadcast colour television. The oldest of these is **NTSC**, named after the (US) National Television Systems Committee, which designed it. It is used in North America, Japan, Taiwan and parts of the Caribbean and of South America. In most of Western Europe, Australia, New Zealand and China a standard known as **PAL**, which stands for Phase Alternating Line (referring to the way the signal is encoded) is used, but in France, Eastern Europe and countries of the former Soviet Union **SECAM** (*Séquential Couleur avec Mémoire*, a similar reference to the signal encoding) is preferred. The standards used in Africa and Asia tend to follow the pattern of European colonial history. The situation in South America is somewhat confused, with NTSC and local variations of PAL being used in different countries there.

The NTSC, PAL and SECAM standards are concerned with technical details of the way colour television pictures are encoded as broadcast signals, but their names are used loosely to refer to other characteristics associated with them, in particular the frame rate and the number of lines in each frame. To appreciate what these figures refer to, it is necessary to understand how television pictures are displayed.

For over half a century, television sets were based on CRTs (cathode ray tubes) – like older computer monitors – which work on a raster scanning principle. Conceptually, the screen is divided into horizontal lines, like the lines of text on a page. In a CRT set, three electron beams, one for each additive primary colour, are emitted and deflected by a magnetic field so that they sweep across the screen, tracing one line, then moving down to trace the next, and so on. Their intensity is modified according to the incoming signal so that the phosphor dots emit an appropriate amount of light when electrons hit them. The picture you see is thus built up from top to bottom as a sequence of horizontal lines. (You can see the lines if you look closely at a large CRT TV screen.) Once again, persistence of vision comes into play, making this series of lines appear as a single unbroken picture.

As we observed in Chapter 2, the screen must be refreshed about 40 times a second if flickering is to be avoided. Transmitting an entire picture that many times a second requires an amount of bandwidth that was considered impractical at the time the standards were being developed in the mid-twentieth century. Instead, each frame is therefore divided into two *fields*, one consisting of the odd-numbered lines of each frame, the other of the even lines. These are transmitted one after the other, so that each frame (still picture) is built up by *interlacing* the fields (Figure 6.2). The fields are variously known as odd and even, upper and lower, and field 1 and field 2.

Interlacing may become evident if the two fields are combined into a single frame. This will happen if a frame is exported as a still image. Since fields are actually separated in time, an object that is moving rapidly will change position between the two fields. When the fields are combined into a single frame, the edges of moving objects will have a comb-like appearance where they are displaced between fields, as shown in Figure 6.3. The effect is particularly evident along the bottom edge of the cloak and in the pale patch in its lining. To prevent this combing effect showing when constructing a single frame, it may be necessary to "de-interlace", by averaging the two fields or discarding one of them and interpolating the missing lines. This, however, is a relatively poor compromise.

odd field
even field

Figure 6.2. *Interlaced fields*

Figure 6.3. *Separated fields and combined frame (right) showing combing*

Originally, the rate at which fields were transmitted was chosen to match the local AC line frequency, so in Western Europe a field rate of 50 per second – and hence a frame rate of 25 per second – is used for PAL. In North America a field rate of 60 per second was used for black and white transmission, but when a colour signal was added for NTSC it was found to cause interference with the sound, so the field rate was multiplied by a factor of 1000/1001, giving 59.94 fields per second. Although the NTSC frame rate is often quoted as 30 frames per second, it is actually 29.97.

When video is played back on a computer monitor, it is not generally interlaced. Instead, the lines of each frame are written to a frame buffer from top to bottom, in the obvious way. This is known as **_progressive scanning_**. Since the whole screen is refreshed from the frame buffer at a high rate, flickering does not occur, and in fact much lower frame rates can be used than those necessary for broadcast. However, if video that originally consisted of interlaced frames is displayed in this way, combing effects may be seen.

Each broadcast standard defines a pattern of signals to indicate the start of each line, and a way of encoding the picture information itself within the line. In addition to the lines we can see on the picture, some extra lines are transmitted in each frame, containing synchronization and other information. An NTSC frame contains 525 lines, of which 480 are picture; PAL and SECAM use 625 lines, of which 576 are picture. It is common to quote the number of lines and the field rate together to characterize a particular scanning standard; what we usually call NTSC, for example, would be written as 525/59.94.

> ┌─IN DETAIL──
>
> **It is possible that you might need to digitize material that was originally made on film and has been transferred to video tape. This would be the case if you were making a multimedia film guide, for example. Most film footage is projected at 24 frames per second so there is a mismatch with all the video standards. In order to fit 24 film frames into (nearly) 30 NTSC video frames, a stratagem known as "3–2 pulldown" is employed. The first film frame is recorded for the first three video fields, the second for two, the third for three again, and so on. If you are starting with material that has already had this conversion applied, it is best to remove the 3–2 pulldown after it has been digitized (a straightforward operation with professional video editing software) and revert to the original frame rate of 24 per second. Using PAL, films are simply shown slightly too fast, so it is sufficient to adjust the frame rate.**

Digital Video Standards

The standards situation for digital video is no less complex than that for analogue video. This is inevitable, because of the need for backward compatibility with existing equipment – the use of a digital data stream instead of an analogue signal is orthogonal to scanning formats and field rates, so digital video formats must be capable of representing both 625/50 and 525/59.94. The emerging HDTV (high-definition television) standards should also be accommodated. Some attempt has been made to unify the two current formats, but unfortunately, different digital standards for consumer use and for professional use and transmission have been adopted. Only cameras intended exclusively for capturing material to be delivered via computer systems and networks can ignore television broadcast standards.

Like any analogue data, video must be sampled to be converted into a digital form. A standard officially entitled *Rec. ITU-R BT.601* but more often referred to as *CCIR 601*[†] defines sampling of digital video. Since a video frame is two-dimensional, it must be sampled in both directions. The scan lines provide an obvious vertical arrangement; only the lines of the actual picture are relevant, so there are 480 of these for NTSC and 576 for PAL. CCIR 601 defines a horizontal sampling picture format consisting of 720 luminance samples and two sets of 360 colour difference samples per line, irrespective of the scanning standard. Thus, ignoring the colour samples and interlacing for a moment, an NTSC frame sampled according to CCIR 601 will consist of 720×480 pixels, while a PAL frame will consist of 720×576 pixels.

† CCIR was the old name of the organization now known as ITU-R.

Observant readers will find this perplexing, in view of our earlier statement that the sizes of PAL and NTSC frames are 768×576 and 640×480 pixels, respectively, so it is necessary to clarify the situation. PAL and NTSC are analogue standards. Frames are divided vertically into lines, but each line is generated by a continuous signal, it is not really broken into pixels in the way that a digital image is. The value for the number of pixels in a line is produced by taking the number of image lines (576 or 480) and multiplying it by the aspect ratio (the ratio of width to height) of the frame. This aspect ratio is 4:3 in both PAL and NTSC systems, which gives the sizes originally quoted. Video capture cards which digitize analogue signals typically produce frames in the form of bitmaps with these dimensions.

The assumption underlying the calculation is that pixels are square. By relaxing this assumption so that there are always 720 pixels in a line, CCIR 601 is able to specify a sampling rate that is identical for both systems. Since there are the same number of pixels in each line for both PAL and NTSC, and 30/25 is equal to 576/480, the number of pixels, and hence bytes, transmitted per second is the same for both standards. CCIR 601 pixels, then, are not square: for 625 line systems, they are slightly wider than they are high, for 525 line systems, they are slightly higher than they are wide. Equipment displaying video that has been sampled according to CCIR 601 must be set up to use pixels of the appropriate shape.

IN DETAIL

Most of the time you don't need to be concerned about the shape of the pixels in a video frame. The exceptions are when you mix live-action video with still images prepared in some other way, or export single frames of video to manipulate as still images. By default, bitmapped image editing programs such as Photoshop assume that pixels are square, so that a video frame with non-square pixels will appear to be squashed when you import it into Photoshop. Similarly, a still image will either be stretched when it is treated as a video frame, or it will have black bars down the sides or along the top.

Recent releases of Photoshop are capable of handling images with non-square pixels correctly, but it is necessary to specify the pixel aspect ratio unless the pixels are square.

Video sampled according to CCIR 601 consists of a luminance component and two colour difference components. The colour space is technically $Y'C_BC_R$ (see Chapter 5). It is usually sufficient to consider the three components to be luminance Y, and the differences $B-Y$ and $R-Y$. The values are non-linearly scaled and offset in practice, but this is just a technical detail. The important point to grasp is that the luminance has been separated from the colour differences. As a first step in reducing the size of digital video, this allows fewer samples to be taken for each of the colour difference values as for luminance, a process known as ***chrominance sub-sampling***.

As we mentioned in Chapter 5, chrominance sub-sampling is justified by the empirical observation that human eyes are less sensitive to variations in colour than to variations in brightness. The arrangement of samples used in CCIR 601 is called *4:2:2 sampling*; it is illustrated in Figure 6.4. In each line there are twice as many Y samples as there are samples of each of $B - Y$ and $R - Y$.

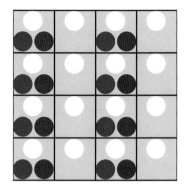

The samples are said to be *co-sited*, because both colour differences are sampled at the same points. The resulting data rate for CCIR 601 video, using 8 bits for each component, is 166 Mbits (just over 20 Mbytes) per second, for both PAL and NTSC.

Other sampling arrangements are possible. In particular, as we will see when we consider DV, some standards for digital video employ either 4:1:1 sampling, where only every fourth pixel on each line is sampled for colour, or 4:2:0,[†] where the colour values are not co-sited and are sub-sampled by a factor of 2 in both the horizontal and vertical directions – a somewhat more complex process than it might at first appear, because of interlacing. (4:2:0 is the sub-sampling regime normally used in JPEG compression of still images.)

Figure 6.4. *4:2:2 chrominance sub-sampling*

DV and MPEG

Sampling produces a digital representation of a video signal. This must be compressed and then formed into a data stream for transmission, or stored in a file. Further standards are needed to specify the compression algorithm and the format of the data stream and file. Two separate sets of standards are in use, DV and the **MPEG** family. Both are based on $Y'C_BC_R$ components, scanned according to CCIR 601, but with further chrominance sub-sampling. However, the standards are only part of the story. As we will describe later, codecs and file formats are commonly used which are not defined by official international standards, but are either proprietary or defined by open standards that lack formal status. To complicate matters further, some non-standardized file formats are capable of holding data that has been compressed with standard codecs.

As we remarked earlier, much of the digital video equipment intended for consumer and semi-professional use (such as corporate training video production) and for news-gathering is based on the DV standard, which is relatively limited in its scope. DV and its main variations – DVCAM and DVPRO – all use the same compression algorithm and data stream as DV, which always has a data rate of 25 Mbits (just over 3 Mbytes) per second, corresponding to a compression ratio of 5:1. There are, however, a high-quality DVPRO and a professional Digital-S format, which use 4:2:2 sampling, unlike DV which uses 4:1:1, and offer better quality at correspondingly higher bit rates. These are for professional use. Finally, HDDV is a high-definition version of DV suitable for low-budget film-making.

† *The notation 4:2:0 is inconsistent; it certainly does not mean that only one of the colour difference values is sampled.*

The term "MPEG" encompasses several ISO standards produced by the ***ISO/IEC Motion Picture Experts Group***. The earliest standard, MPEG-1, was primarily intended for the Video CD format, but it has provided a basis for subsequent MPEG video standards. Its successor, MPEG-2, is used in the first generation of digital studio equipment, digital broadcast TV and DVD. Subsequent improvements, and a widening of the scope of MPEG, has led to MPEG-4, an amibitious standard designed to support a range of multimedia data at bit rates from as low as 10 kbits per second all the way up to 300 Mbits per second or higher. This allows MPEG-4 to be used in applications ranging from mobile phones to HDTV.

MPEG-4 itself is divided into parts. Some parts are concerned with audio compression, some with delivery of data over a network, some with file formats, and so on. At the time of writing there are 23 parts, although not all of them have been finished and ratified. Parts 2 and 10 deal with video compression. ***MPEG-4 Part 2*** is what people usually mean when they simply refer to "MPEG-4 video". It is a refinement of MPEG-2 video, which can achieve better quality at low bit rates (or smaller files of the same quality) by using some extra compression techniques. ***MPEG-4 Part 10*** describes a further refinement, referred to as ***Advanced Video Coding (AVC)***. Because of overlapping areas of responsibility between ISO/IEC and ITU-T, AVC is also an ITU standard, H.264. This has led to a regrettable situation where the same standard is known by four different names: MPEG-4 Part 10, AVC, H.264 and the officially preferred ***H.264/AVC***. It has recently emerged as one of the leading compression techniques for Web video and is also used on second generation, high-definition (Blu-Ray) DVDs.

To accommodate a range of requirements, each of the MPEG standards defines a collection of profiles and levels. Each profile defines a set of algorithms that can be used to generate a data stream. In practice, this means that each profile defines a subset of the complete compression technique defined in the standard. Each level defines certain parameters, notably the maximum frame size and data rate, and chrominance sub-sampling. Each profile may be implemented at one or more of the levels, although not every combination of level and profile is defined. For example, the most common combination in MPEG-2 is ***Main Profile at Main Level (MP@ML)***, which uses CCIR 601 scanning with 4:2:0 chrominance sub-sampling. This supports a data rate of 15 Mbits per second and allows for the most elaborate representation of compressed data provided by MPEG-2. MP@ML is the format used for digital television broadcasts and for DVD video.

H.264/AVC defines a large and growing set of profiles. Some of these are only of interest for studio and professional use. The profiles most likely to be encountered in multimedia are the ***Baseline Profile (BP)***, which is suitable for video-conferencing and mobile devices with limited computing resources; the ***Extended Profile (XP)***, which is intended for streaming video; the ***Main Profile (MP)***, for general use; and the ***High Profile (HIP)***, which is used for HDTV and Blu-Ray. (The Main Profile was originally intended for broadcast use, but has been superseded by HIP.)

The profiles are not subsets of each other: some features supported in the Baseline Profile are not in the Main Profile and vice versa.

For each of these profiles, 16 different levels specify the values of parameters such as frame size and bit rate. For example, BP@L1 (level 1 of the Baseline Profile) specifies a bit rate of 64 kbps, for a frame size of 176×144 pixels and frame rate of 15 fps. At the opposite extreme, HP@L5.1 specifies 300 Mbps at 4096×2048 frames and a rate of 30 fps. (The numbering of the levels is not consistent; each level has two or more additional sub-levels, with the sub-level s of level L being written as $L.s$ but level 1 has an additional 1b.)

Although the main contribution of MPEG-4 to digital video lies in its codecs, it also defines a file format, based on the QuickTime format (see below), which can be used to store compressed video data, together with audio and metadata. **MP4** files in this format can be played by many different devices and programs, including the QuickTime and Flash players. The 3GP format used for mobile phones is a simplified version of the MP4 format, which supports video data compressed according to MPEG-4 Part 2 and H.264/AVC, together with audio data.

High Definition Formats

Domestic televisions have been using the same vertical resolution for decades. The first generation of digital video introduced non-square pixels and fixed the number of horizontal samples, but to the viewer, the picture seemed the same size and contained as much (or as little) detail as ever, just less noise. The long-established resolutions for PAL and NTSC frames are referred to as *Standard Definition (SD)* video. HD video is simply anything with larger frames than SD. It was hoped at one time that a global HD standard for broadcast could be agreed, but there are still several to choose from — sometimes different standards are used in a single country. (You may come across "Enhanced Definition", for example. This generally refers to an SD-sized but progressively scanned frame, written as 480p — see below.)

All the standards agree that the aspect ratio should be 16:9, so the vertical height of the frame is enough to specify the resolution. Two values are in use: 720 and 1080. Each of these might be transmitted at either 25 or (roughly) 30 frames per second, corresponding to the frame rates of the SD standards. Additionally, each HD frame can be transmitted as either a pair of interlaced fields, as we described earlier, or as a single progressively scanned frame. Hence there are eight possible combinations of the different variables. Each one is written as the frame height, followed by the approximate frame rate (for progressive scan) or field rate (for interlaced fields) and a letter i or p, denoting interleaved or progressively scanned, respectively. Thus, for instance, 720 25p would designate a frame size of 1280×720 at a rate of 25 frames per second, progressively scanned, whereas 1080 60i would be a frame size of 1920×1080, interlaced at 60 fields per second — although in actuality, the field rate would really be 59.94, as in SD NTSC.

HD video requires suitable equipment for capture, transmission, reception, recording and displaying, and it has its own tape formats (including HDCAM, DVCPRO-HD) and optical media (Blu-Ray DVD). However, when it comes to digital processing, the only significant difference between SD and HD video is that the latter uses more bits, so it requires more disk space, bandwidth and processing power. MPEG-2, MPEG-4 Part 2 and H.264/AVC can all have levels at which they can be used to compress HD video. For the most part, therefore, in the rest of this chapter, we will not distinguish between SD and HD.

KEY POINTS

DV camcorders or VTRs connected to computers over FireWire are used for reasonable quality digital video capture.

Cheap video cameras are often built into mobile phones and laptop computers or used as Webcams. They usually use MPEG-4 and USB 2.0.

Digital video standards inherit features from analogue broadcast TV.

Each frame is divided into two fields (odd and even lines), transmitted one after the other and interlaced for display. Interlaced frames may display combing when displayed progressively or exported as still images.

PAL: a frame has 625 lines, of which 576 are picture, displayed at 50 fields (25 frames) per second (625/50). NTSC: a frame has 525 lines, of which 480 are picture, displayed at 59.94 fields (29.97 frames) per second (525/59.94, often treated as 525/60).

CCIR 601 (Rec. ITU-R BT.601) defines standard definition digital video sampling, with 720 luminance samples and 2×360 colour difference samples per line. ($Y'C_BC_R$ with 4:2:2 chrominance sub-sampling.)

PAL frames are 720×576 and NTSC are 720×480. The pixels are not square.

DV applies 4:1:1 chrominance sub-sampling and compresses to a constant data rate of 25 Mbits per second, a compression ratio of 5:1.

MPEG defines a series of standards. MPEG-2 is used on DVDs; MPEG-4 supports a range of multimedia data at bit rates from 10 kbps to 300 Mbps or greater.

MPEG-4 is a multi-part standard. Part 2 defines a video codec; Part 10 (H.264/AVC) is an improved version.

MPEG standards all define a set of profiles (features) and levels (parameters). The Baseline, Extended and Main profiles of H.264/AVC are all used in multimedia.

MPEG-4 defines a file format. 3GP is a simpler version, used in mobile phones.

HD video uses higher resolutions and may be progressively scanned. Frames with widths of 720 and 1080 pixels and an aspect ratio of 16:9 are used.

Video Compression

The input to any video compression algorithm consists of a sequence of bitmapped images (the digitized video). There are two ways in which this sequence can be compressed: each individual image can be compressed in isolation, using the techniques introduced in Chapter 4, or sub-sequences of frames can be compressed by only storing the differences between them. These two techniques are usually called **spatial compression** and **temporal compression**, respectively, although the more accurate terms **intra-frame** and **inter-frame** compression are also used, especially in the context of MPEG. Spatial and temporal compression are normally used together.

Since spatial compression is just image compression applied to a sequence of bitmapped images, it could in principle use either lossless or lossy methods. Generally, though, lossless methods do not produce sufficiently high compression ratios to reduce video data to manageable proportions, except on synthetically generated material (such as we will consider in Chapter 7), so lossy methods are usually employed. Lossily compressing and recompressing video usually leads to a deterioration in image quality, and should be avoided if possible, but recompression is often unavoidable, since the compressors used for capture are not the most suitable for delivery for multimedia. Furthermore, for post-production work, such as the creation of special effects, or even fairly basic corrections to the footage, it is usually necessary to decompress the video so that changes can be made to the individual pixels of each frame. For this reason it is wise – if you have sufficient disk space – to work with uncompressed video during the post-production phase. That is, once the footage has been captured and selected, decompress it and use uncompressed data while you edit and apply effects, only recompressing the finished product for delivery. (You may have heard that one of the advantages of digital video is that, unlike analogue video, it suffers no "generational loss" when copied, but this is only true for the making of exact copies.)

The principle underlying temporal compression algorithms is simple to grasp. Certain frames in a sequence are designated as **key frames**. Often, key frames are specified to occur at regular intervals – every sixth frame, for example – which can be chosen when the compressor is invoked. These key frames are either left uncompressed, or more likely, only spatially compressed. Each of the frames between the key frames is replaced by a difference frame, which records only the differences between the frame which was originally in that position and either the most recent key frame or the preceding frame, depending on the sophistication of the decompressor.

For many sequences, the differences will only affect a small part of the frame. For example, Figure 6.5 shows part of two consecutive frames (de-interlaced), and the difference between them, obtained by subtracting corresponding pixel values in each frame. Where the pixels are identical, the result will be zero, which shows as black in the difference frame on the far right. Here, approximately 70% of the frame is black: the land does not move, and although the sea and clouds

Figure 6.5. *Frame difference*

are in motion, they are not moving fast enough to make a difference between two consecutive frames. Notice also that although the girl's white over-skirt is moving, where part of it moves into a region previously occupied by another part of the same colour, there is no difference between the pixels. The cloak, on the other hand, is not only moving rapidly as she turns, but the shot silk material shimmers as the light on it changes, leading to the complex patterns you see in the corresponding area of the difference frame.

Many types of video footage are composed of large relatively static areas, with just a small proportion of the frame in motion. Each difference frame in a sequence of this character will have much less information in it than a complete frame. This information can therefore be stored in much less space than is required for the complete frame.

┌─**IN DETAIL**──
│ **You will notice that we have described these compression techniques in terms**
│ **of frames. This is because we are normally going to be concerned with video**
│ **intended for progressively scanned playback on a computer. However, the**
│ **techniques described can be equally well applied to fields of interlaced video.**
│ **While this is somewhat more complex, it is conceptually no different.**
└──

Compression and decompression of a piece of video need not take the same time. If they do, the codec is said to be **symmetrical**, otherwise it is **asymmetrical**. In theory, this asymmetry could be in either direction, but generally it is taken to mean that compression takes longer – sometimes much longer – than decompression. This is acceptable, except during capture, but since playback must take place at a reasonably fast frame rate, codecs which take much longer to decompress video than to compress it are essentially useless.

Spatial Compression

The spatial element of many video compression schemes is based, like JPEG image compression, on the use of the Discrete Cosine Transform. The most straightforward approach is to apply JPEG compression to each frame, with no temporal compression. JPEG compression is applied to the three components of a colour image separately, and works the same way irrespective of the colour space used to store image data. Video data is usually stored using $Y'C_BC_R$ colour, with chrominance sub-sampling, as we have seen. JPEG compression can be applied directly to this data, taking advantage of the compression already achieved by this sub-sampling.

The technique of compressing video sequences by applying JPEG compression to each frame is referred to as *motion JPEG* or **MJPEG** (not to be confused with MPEG) compression, although you should be aware that, whereas JPEG is a standard, MJPEG is only a loosely defined way of referring to this type of video compression. MJPEG was formerly the most common way of compressing video while capturing it from an analogue source, and used to be popular in digital still image cameras that included primitive facilities for capturing video.

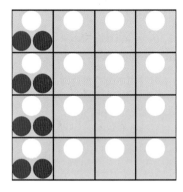

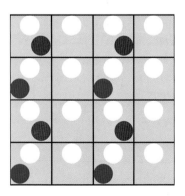

Figure 6.6. *4:1:1 (top) and 4:2:0 chrominance sub-sampling*

Now that analogue video capture is rarely needed, the most important technology that uses spatial compression exclusively is DV. Like MJPEG, DV compression uses the DCT and subsequent quantization to reduce the amount of data in a video stream, but it adds some clever tricks to achieve higher picture quality within a constant data rate of 25 Mbits (3.25 Mbytes) per second than MJPEG would produce at that rate.

DV compression begins with chrominance sub-sampling of a frame with the same dimensions as CCIR 601. Oddly, the sub-sampling regime depends on the video standard (PAL or NTSC) being used. For NTSC (and DVCPRO PAL), 4:1:1 sub-sampling with co-sited sampling is used, but for other PAL DV formats 4:2:0 is used instead. As Figure 6.6 shows, the number of samples of each component in each 4×2 block of pixels is the same. As in still-image JPEG compression, blocks of 8×8 pixels from each frame are transformed using the DCT, and then quantized (with some loss of information) and run-length and Huffman encoded along a zig-zag sequence. There are, however, a couple of additional embellishments to the process.

First, the DCT may be applied to the 64 pixels in each block in one of two ways. If the frame is static, or almost so, with no difference between the picture in each field, the transform is applied to the entire 8×8 block, which comprises alternate lines from the odd and even fields.

However, if there is a lot of motion, so that the fields differ, the block is split into two 8×4 blocks, each of which is transformed independently. This leads to more efficient compression of frames with motion. The compressor may determine whether there is motion between the frames by using motion compensation (described below under MPEG), or it may compute both versions of the DCT and choose the one with the smaller result. The DV standard does not stipulate how the choice is to be made.

Second, an elaborate process of rearrangement is applied to the blocks making up a complete frame, in order to make best use of the space available for storing coefficients. A DV stream must use exactly 25 Mbits for each second of video; 14 bytes are available for each 8×8 pixel block. For some blocks, whose transformed representation has many zero coefficients, this may be too much, while for others it may be insufficient, requiring data to be discarded. In order to allow the available bytes to be shared between parts of the frame, the coefficients are allocated to bytes, not on a block-by-block basis, but within a larger "video segment". Each video segment is constructed by systematically taking 8×8 blocks from five different areas of the frame, a process called **shuffling**. The effect of shuffling is to average the amount of detail in each video segment. Without shuffling, parts of the picture with fine detail would have to be compressed more highly than parts with less detail, in order to maintain the uniform bit rate. With shuffling, the detail is, as it were, spread about among the video segments, making efficient compression over the whole picture easier.

As a result of these additional steps in the compression process, DV is able to achieve better picture quality at 25 Mbits per second than MJPEG can achieve at the same data rate.

Temporal Compression

All modern video codecs use temporal compression to achieve either much higher compression ratios, or better quality at the same ratio, relative to DV or MJPEG. Windows Media 9, the Flash Video codecs and the relevant parts of MPEG-4 all employ the same broad principles, which were first expressed systematically in the MPEG-1 standard. Although MPEG-1 has been largely superseded, it still provides a good starting point for understanding the principles of temporal compression which are used in the later standards that have improved on it, so we will begin by describing MPEG-1 compression in some detail, and then indicate how H.264/AVC and other important codecs have enhanced it.

The MPEG-1 standard[†] doesn't actually define a compression algorithm: it defines a data stream syntax and a decompressor, allowing manufacturers to develop different compressors, thereby leaving scope for "competitive advantage in the marketplace". In practice, the compressor is fairly thoroughly defined implicitly, so we can describe MPEG-1 compression, which combines

---

† *ISO/IEC 11172: "Coding of moving pictures and associated audio for digital storage media at up to about 1.5 Mbit/s."*

temporal compression based on motion compensation with spatial compression based, like JPEG and DV, on quantization and coding of frequency coefficients produced by a discrete cosine transformation of the data.

A naïve approach to temporal compression consists of subtracting the value of each pixel in a frame from the corresponding pixel in the previous frame, producing a difference frame, as we did in Figure 6.5. In areas of the picture where there is no change between frames, the result of this subtraction will be zero. If change is localized, difference frames will contain large numbers of zero pixels, and so they will compress well – much better than a complete frame.

This frame differencing has to start somewhere, with frames that are purely spatially (intra-frame) compressed, so they can be used as the basis for subsequent difference frames. In MPEG terminology, such frames are called *I-pictures*, where I stands for "intra". Difference frames that use previous frames are called *P-pictures*, or "predictive pictures". P-pictures can be based on an earlier I-picture or P-picture – that is, differences can be cumulative.

Often, though, we may be able to do better, because pictures are composed of objects that move as a whole: a person might walk along a street, a football might be kicked, or the camera might pan across a landscape with trees. Figure 6.7 is a schematic illustration of this sort of motion, to demonstrate how it affects compression. In the two frames shown here, the fish swims from left to right. Pixels therefore change in the region originally occupied by the fish – where the back-ground becomes visible in the second frame – and in the region to which the fish moves. The black area in the picture at the bottom left of Figure 6.7 shows the changed area which would have to be stored explicitly in a difference frame.

However, the values for the pixels in the area occupied by the fish in the second frame are all there in the first frame, in the fish's old position. If we could somehow identify the coherent area corresponding to the fish, we would only need to record its displacement together with the changed pixels in the smaller area shown at the bottom right of Figure 6.7. (The bits of weed and background in this region are not present in the first frame anywhere, unlike the fish.) This technique of incorporating a record of the relative displacement of objects in the difference frames is called *motion compensation* (also known as *motion estimation*). Of course, it is now necessary to store the displacement as part of the compressed file. This information can be recorded as a *displacement vector*, giving the number of pixels the object has moved in each direction.

If we were considering some frames of video shot under water showing a real fish swimming among weeds (or a realistic animation of such a scene) instead of these schematic pictures, the objects and their movements would be less simple than they appear in Figure 6.7. The fish's body would change shape as it propelled itself, the lighting would alter, the weeds would not stay still.

Attempting to identify the objects in a real scene and apply motion compensation to them would not work, therefore (even if it were practical to identify objects in such a scene).

MPEG-1 compressors do not attempt to identify discrete objects in the way that a human viewer would. Instead, they divide each frame into blocks of 16×16 pixels known as **macroblocks** (to distinguish them from the smaller blocks used in the DCT phase of compression), and attempt to predict the whereabouts of the corresponding macroblock in the next frame. No high-powered artificial intelligence is used in this prediction: all possible displacements within a limited range are tried, and the best match is chosen. The difference frame is then constructed by subtracting each macroblock from its predicted counterpart, which should result in fewer non-zero pixels, and a smaller difference frame after spatial compression.

The price to be paid for the additional compression resulting from the use of motion compensation is that, in addition to the difference frame, we now have to keep a record of the motion vectors describing the predicted displacement of macroblocks between frames. These can be stored relatively efficiently, however. The motion vector for a macroblock is likely to be similar

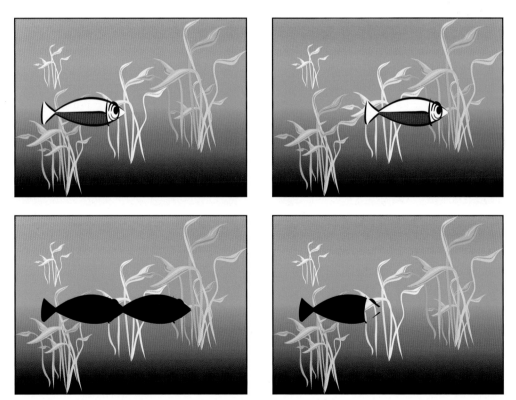

Figure 6.7. *Motion compensation*

or identical to the motion vector for adjoining macroblocks (since these will often be parts of the same object), so, by storing the differences between motion vectors, additional compression, analogous to inter-frame compression, is achieved.

Although basing difference frames on preceding frames probably seems the obvious thing to do, it can be more effective to base them on following frames. Figure 6.8 shows why such backward

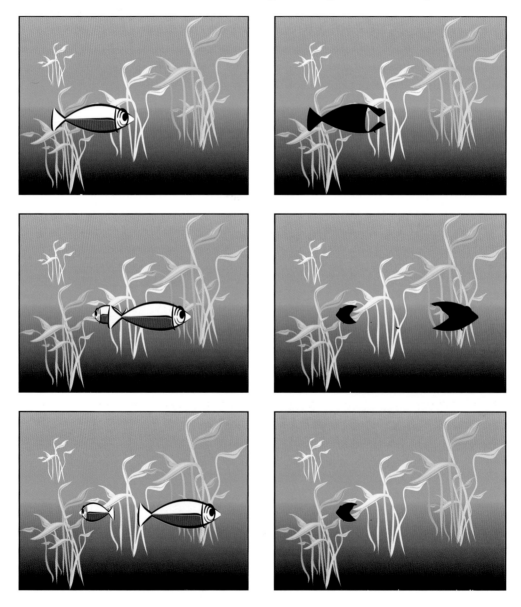

Figure 6.8. *Bi-directional prediction*

prediction can be useful. In the top frame, the smaller fish that is partially revealed in the middle frame is hidden, but it is fully visible in the bottom frame. If we construct an I-picture from the first two frames, it must explicitly record the area covered by the fish in the first frame but not the second, as before. If we construct the I-picture by working backwards from the third frame instead, the area that must be recorded consists of the parts of the frame covered up by either of the fish in the third frame but not in the second. Motion compensation allows us to fill in the bodies of both fish in the I-picture. The resulting area, shown in the middle of the right-hand column of Figure 6.8, is slightly smaller than the one shown at the top right. If we could use information from both the first and third frames in constructing the I-picture for the middle frame, almost no pixels would need to be represented explicitly, as shown at the bottom right. This comprises the small area of background that is covered by the big fish in the first frame and the small fish in the last frame, excluding the small fish in the middle frame, which is represented by motion compensation from the following frame. To take advantage of information in both preceding and following frames, MPEG compression allows for **B-pictures**, which can use motion compensation from the previous or next I- or P-pictures, or both, hence their full name "bi-directionally predictive" pictures.

A video sequence can be encoded in compressed form as a sequence of I-, P- and B-pictures. It is not a requirement that this sequence be regular, but encoders typically use a repeating sequence, known as a **Group of Pictures** or **GOP**, which always begins with an I-picture. Figure 6.9 shows a typical example. (You should read it from left to right.) The GOP sequence is IBBPBB. The diagram shows two such groups: frames 01 to 06 and frames 11 to 16. The arrows indicate the forward and bi-directional prediction. For example, the P-picture 04 depends on the I-picture 01 at the start of its GOP; the B-pictures 05 and 06 depend on the preceding P-picture 04 and the following I-picture 11.

All three types of picture are compressed using the MPEG-1 DCT-based compression method. Published measurements indicate that, typically, P-pictures compress three times as much as I-pictures, and B-pictures one and a half times as much as P-pictures. However, reconstructing B-pictures is more complex than reconstructing the other types, so there is a trade-off to be made between compression and computational complexity when choosing the pattern of a GOP.

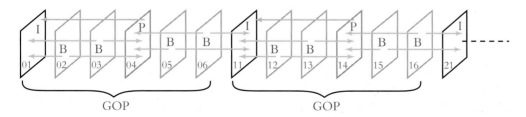

Figure 6.9. *An MPEG sequence in display order*

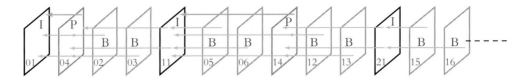

Figure 6.10. *An MPEG sequence in bitstream order*

An additional factor is that random access to frames corresponding to B- and P-pictures is difficult, so it is customary to include I-pictures sufficiently often to allow random access to several frames each second. Popular GOP patterns include IBBPBBPBB and IBBPBBPBBPBB. However, as we remarked, the MPEG-1 specification does not require the sequence of pictures to form a regular pattern, and sophisticated encoders will adjust the frequency of I-pictures in response to the nature of the video stream being compressed.

For the decoder, there is an obvious problem with B-pictures: some of the information required to reconstruct the corresponding frame is contained in an I- or P-picture that comes later in the sequence. This problem is solved by reordering the sequence. The sequence of pictures corresponding to the actual order of frames is said to be in "display order"; it must be rearranged into a suitable "bitstream order" for transmission. Figure 6.10 shows the bitstream order of the sequence shown in display order in Figure 6.9. All the arrows showing prediction now run from right to left, i.e. every predicted frame comes later in the sequence than the pictures it depends on.[†] You will notice that the first GOP is reordered differently from the second; any subsequent groups will extend the pattern established by the second.

Before any of this compression is done, MPEG-1 video data is chroma sub-sampled to 4:2:0. If, in addition to this, the frame size is restricted to 352×240, video at a frame rate of 30 fps can be compressed to a data rate of 1.86 Mbits per second – the data rate specified for compact disc video. 4:2:0 video of this size is said to be in **Source Input Format (SIF)**. SIF is the typical format for MPEG-1 video, although it can be used with larger frame sizes and other frame rates. MPEG-1 cannot, however, handle interlacing or HDTV formats, hence the need for MPEG-2 for broadcasting and studio work.

The preceding description should have made it clear that MPEG compression and decompression are computationally expensive tasks – and there are further complications which we have glossed over. Initially, MPEG video could only be played back using dedicated hardware. Indeed, the parameters used for CD video were chosen largely so that MPEG decoders could be accommodated in VLSI chips at the time the standard was drawn up (1993). Advances in processor speed

---

† For the B-pictures, we have run the arrows to the relevant P- and I-pictures together, with an intermediate arrowhead, in an attempt to keep the diagram less cluttered.

mean that it has since become feasible to play back MPEG-1 video using software only. File sizes are by no means small, however. A 650 Mbyte CD-ROM will only hold just over 40 minutes of video at that rate; an 8.75 Gbyte DVD has room for over nine hours. (You would only use MPEG-1 on DVD if you were just using the disk as a storage medium, though. DVDs employ MPEG-2 when they are Digital *Video* Disks, for playing in domestic DVD players.)

MPEG-4 and H.264/AVC

MPEG-4 is an ambitious standard, which defines an encoding for multimedia streams made up of different types of object – video, still images, animation, textures, 3-D models, and more – and provides a way of composing scenes at the receiving end from separately transmitted representations of objects. The idea is that each type of object will be represented in an optimal fashion, rather than all being composited into a sequence of video frames. Not only should this allow greater compression to be achieved, it also makes interaction with the resulting scene easier, since the objects retain their own identities.

At the time of writing, however, it is the video and audio codecs described in the MPEG-4 standard which have received the most attention, and for which commercial implementations exist. We will look at audio compression in Chapter 8, and only consider video here, beginning with the older MPEG-4 Part 2.

As we remarked earlier, MPEG standards define a collection of profiles for video data. The higher profiles of MPEG-4 Part 2 employ a method of dividing a scene into arbitrarily shaped video objects – for example a singer and the backdrop against which she is performing – which can be compressed separately. The best method of compressing the background may not be the same as the best method of compressing the figure, so by separating the two, the overall compression efficiency can be increased. However, dividing a scene into objects is a non-trivial exercise, so the lower profiles – **Simple Profile** and **Advanced Simple Profile** – are restricted to rectangular objects, in particular complete frames, and it is these profiles which have been implemented in widely used systems such as QuickTime and DivX (see below). For practical purposes, therefore, MPEG-4 Part 2 video compression is a conventional, frame-based codec, which is a refinement of the MPEG-1 codec just described. I-pictures are compressed by quantizing and Huffman coding DCT coefficients, but some improvements to the motion compensation phase used to generate P- and B-pictures provide better picture quality at the same bit rates, or the same quality at lower bit rates, as MPEG-1.

The Simple Profile uses only P-pictures (those that depend only on earlier pictures) for interframe compression. This means that decompression can be more efficient than with the more elaborate schemes that use B-pictures (which may depend on following pictures), so the Simple

Profile is suitable for implementation in devices such as PDAs and portable video players. The Advanced Simple Profile adds B-pictures and a couple of other features.

Global Motion Compensation is an additional technique that is effective for compressing static scenes with conventional camera movements, such as pans and zooms. The movement can be modelled as a vector transformation of the original scene, and represented by the values of just a few parameters. **Sub-pixel motion compensation** means that the displacement vectors record movement to an accuracy finer than a single pixel – in the case of Simple Profile, half a pixel, and for the Advanced Simple Profile, a quarter of a pixel. This prevents errors accumulating, resulting in better picture quality with little additional overhead.

H.264/AVC is an aggressively optimized version of MPEG-4 Part 2. It is one of three codecs which all Blu-Ray players must implement. (The others are MPEG-2, for compatibility with older DVDs, and VC-1, discussed below.) It is routinely claimed that "H.264 can match the best possible MPEG-2 quality at up to half the data rate". Among other refinements contributing to this improved performance, H.264/AVC allows the use of different-sized blocks for motion compensation, so that areas with little change can be encoded efficiently using large blocks (up to 16×16 pixels), but areas that do change can be broken into smaller blocks (down to 4×4 pixels), which is more likely to result in compression, while preserving the picture quality in fast-moving parts of the frame. Additionally, whereas MPEG-4 Part 2, like MPEG-1, only allows difference frames to depend on at most one preceding and one following frame, H.264/AVC allows data from a stack of frames anywhere in a movie to be used. (The whole movie thus becomes a source of blocks of pixels, which can be reused. This is somewhat similar to the dictionary-based approach to compression found in the LZ algorithms we mentioned in Chapter 4.) B-frames may even depend on other B frames.

H.264/AVC takes the same approach as JPEG and the other MPEG video codecs to compressing the individual I-, P- and B-frames – transforming them to the frequency domain, quantizing and compressing the coefficients losslessly – but it improves all three elements of the process. It uses a better transform than DCT, with a choice of 8×8 or 4×4 blocks, logarithmic quantization, and employs a mixture of lossless algorithms for compressing the coefficients, which can take account of context, and between them work more efficiently than Huffman coding. H.264/AVC also incorporates filters for removing some compression artefacts, which result in better picture quality. In particular, a "de-blocking filter" is used to smooth the characteristic discontinuities between the blocks of pixels that are transformed separately.

Some aspects of H.264/AVC compression require more than one pass to be made over the data. This is not practical for live video, and may be too slow for creating rough previews, so codecs typically offer a single-pass mode for occasions when the video has to be compressed as quickly as possible. Single-pass coding is faster but does not produce such good results as the multi-pass mode, which is required if the best results are to be obtained.

Other Video Codecs

Two other video codecs are of considerable practical importance: Windows Media 9 and the On2 V6 codec used for Flash Video.

Windows Media is a proprietary technology, developed by Microsoft. Its video codec has evolved over the years, with the latest version, WMV 9, incorporating many of the same ideas as H.264/AVC, including bi-directional prediction (B-pictures), motion compensation and a de-blocking filter. A significant difference is that WMV 9 supports "differential quantization", which means that different quantization matrices can be used on different parts of a frame. Generally, only two matrices are used, one for simple areas and another for more complex ones. WMV 9 can also apply its DCT to each 8×8 block of pixels as a whole in the conventional way, or break it into two 8×4 blocks, two 4×8 blocks, or four 4×4 transforms. These smaller transform blocks can reduce the visible artefacts at block edges that are typical of DCT-based compression.

A somewhat specialized optimization is that fade transitions (see below) are treated specially. Normally, these transitions are difficult to compress, because every single pixel will change in each frame over the duration of the fade. By detecting fades and treating them as a special case, WMV 9 is able to achieve extra compression. Fades are probably the most common transitions after straight cuts, so this will often be a worthwhile optimization.

The WMV-9 codec has been standardized by the Society of Motion Picture Engineers (SMPTE), under the name **VC-1**. In this guise, it is mandatory for Blu-Ray players. Like the MPEG codecs, VC-1 has several profiles and levels, which cover applications ranging from low bit-rate network video up to 1080p HD video. Subjectively, the quality of VC-1 is at least as good as H.264/AVC, as you would expect given the similarities between the two.

The On2 VP6 codec achieved widespread use when it was adopted for use in Flash Video at the time that format became popular on the Web. Unlike the other codecs we have looked at, On2 VP6 is purely proprietary, and is not defined by an official standard. Instead, it is protected by copyright, and technical details are scarce. It appears to be another DCT-based technique, with inter-frame compression and motion compensation. Unlike the other codecs, it does not support bi-directional prediction: P-pictures can only depend on P- and I-pictures that precede them.

One advantage that is claimed for the On2 VP6 codec is that it is said to be relatively simple to decompress video that has been compressed with it.

On2 VP6 is one of a series of VPx codecs created by On2 Technologies. On2 VP3 has special significance: On2 Technologies granted a licence to an organization called the Xiph Foundation for its free use for any purpose. Xiph Foundation used VP3 as the basis of the Open Source **Ogg Theora** codec, which is free to use for any purpose, unlike all the other codecs described, which are subject to licence fees for some purposes. As a result, Ogg Theora is extensively documented.

Like all the codecs we have described, Theora uses a JPEG-like lossy compression algorithm based on a Discrete Cosine Transform followed by quantization, coupled with inter-frame compression with motion compensation. The DCT is applied to 8×8 blocks of pixels, as usual. Only I- and P-pictures are supported; there is no bi-directional prediction. In other words, Theora lacks most of the refinements present in other popular codecs. The present version cannot handle interlaced video either. Its main interest lies in its Open Source status, not in its technology.

IN DETAIL

Video compression is presently dominated by DCT-based methods. Some work is being done on applying wavelet compression to video. The only standardized wavelet-based format in use is Motion JPEG 2000, which is simply JPEG 2000, as described in Chapter 4, applied to sequences of frames, with no inter-frame compression. It is therefore only suitable for specialized applications, the most important of which is digital cinema. Apple's Pixlet codec is similar: it too does no inter-frame compression and is intended for use by film-makers.

Dirac is an Open Source codec, originally developed by the BBC's R&D department, which does combine wavelet compression with inter-frame compression and motion compensation. It is still at an early stage of development, but it seems likely that it will grow into a significant alternative to H.264/AVC and other DCT-based codecs.

Quality

It is natural to ask "Which codec is best?", but the question does not admit a simple answer. Usually, "best" means producing the best picture quality at a particular bit rate (or the highest compression ratio for the same quality). However, sometimes the speed of compression, the complexity of decompression, or the availability of software capable of playing back video compressed with a particular codec may be of more practical importance than its compression performance.

The parameters which each codec provides for varying the quality are not the same, so it is not easy to compare codecs directly. Some restrict you to particular sets of parameters, others let you specify maximum bit rates, others provide a numerical quality setting, some allow you to select a profile, while others allow you control over all these values. The way in which they interact is not always clear.

Original   H.264/AVC

WMV 9   On2 VP6

Figure 6.11. *Compressed video at high quality*

The quality of compressed video at a particular bit rate produced by each codec will vary with the nature of the source video as well as with the parameters to the compression. In any case, judgements of quality are subjective.

Despite these reservations, Figure 6.11 demonstrates that all of the leading codecs are capable of producing compressed video which is barely distinguishable from a DV original when their parameters are set to produce full-frame video at a bit rate of roughly 2 Mbps. As we showed earlier in the chapter, the DV frame already shows some compression artefacts, but it serves as an appropriate reference point, since it was the format in which the footage was captured, and is thus the best quality attainable in this case. There is a fairly subtle colour shift on the H.264/AVC sample, but otherwise even the inset details, which are considerably blown up, are hard to distinguish from one another. Only the On2 VP6 sample shows any appreciable artefaction.

Figure 6.12. *Over-compression with H.264/AVC (top) and On2 VP6 (bottom)*

For studio-quality source material you would use higher rates, but 2 Mbps will be a reasonable bit rate for multimedia video, so the choice of codec will depend on the other factors just outlined. For instance, despite its excellent quality, WMV 9 can be problematic on systems other than Windows, so to maximize compatibility you might prefer to use H.264/AVC, which can be played on any platform.

It can be instructive to look at what happens if the compression ratio is driven to unreasonable extremes. The top set of illustrations in Figure 6.12 show our example frame as it appears in a version of the clip compressed with H.264/AVC to a rate of only 256 kbps, at its full size and frame rate. The parameters lie outside any level of the standard, so this is not something you would normally do – it should be obvious why not. What is interesting is the way in which the moving figure has broken up very badly, while the relatively static background still retains much of its original quality. In the inset detail of the figure, notice the blurry appearance, presumably caused by the de-blocking filter. In contrast, the version below, compressed to roughly the same size with

On2 VP6, is characterized by a "blocky" over-sharpened appearance, in both the moving figure and the static background. When the movies are actually played, there are more intrusive sudden changes in the background of the On2 VP6 version, but a much greater loss of detail in the H.264/AVC version. Neither is acceptable. If this sort of distortion is occurring you should either increase the target bit rate, if your codec permits it, or reduce the frame size, frame rate or both.

KEY POINTS

Spatial (intra-frame) compression and temporal (inter-frame) compression are used together in most contemporary video codecs.

Chrominance sub-sampling is nearly always applied before any compression.

Spatial compression of individual video frames is usually based on a Discrete Cosine Transformation, like JPEG.

DV compression is purely spatial. It extends the JPEG technique by using a choice of sizes for transform blocks, and by shuffling, to even out change across a frame.

Temporal compression works by computing the difference between frames instead of storing every one in full.

In MPEG terminology, I-pictures are only spatially compressed. P-pictures are computed from a preceding I- or P-picture.

Motion compensation is the technique of incorporating a record of the relative displacement of objects in the difference frames, as a motion vector.

In existing codecs, motion compensation is applied to macroblocks, since coherent objects cannot usually be identified.

B-pictures use following pictures as well as preceding ones as the basis of frame differences and motion compensation.

A video sequence is encoded as a Group of Pictures (GOP). If B-pictures are used, a GOP may have to be reordered into display order for decoding.

MPEG-4 Part 2 uses global motion compensation and sub-pixel motion compensation to improve on the quality of MPEG-1 and MPEG-2.

H.264/AVC adds several extra techniques, including variable-sized transform blocks and macroblocks, and a de-blocking filter, to make further improvements.

Windows Media 9 (standardized as VC-1) incorporates similar improvements.

On2 VP6 and Ogg Theora are less powerful, but widely or freely available.

All modern codecs produce excellent quality at 2 Mbps and higher.

Editing and Post-Production

Any video production must begin with the shooting of some footage. It is not the purpose of this book to teach you how to be a film director, so we won't offer any advice about the shooting, composition, lighting, camera work or any other part of the production. We will assume that you have already shot or acquired some properly lit action taking place in front of a camera, which has been recorded on tape (or even DVD), or on the internal disk of a video camera.

With modern equipment, capturing video from a camera or tape deck is simple. (If you are working from tape it is best to use a tape deck for this process if possible – tape transports in camcorders don't always withstand much winding and rewinding.) Recording to computer disk from a DV device is usually just a matter of connecting the device to the computer using a FireWire cable, starting up some software that can perform capture, selecting the standard to be used (PAL or NTSC) and clicking a button. The software in question can be a simple utility that does nothing but capture video, a consumer-oriented video application which also provides rudimentary editing facilities, such as iMovie or Windows Movie Maker, or a professional or semi-professional program, such as Final Cut Pro or Premiere, which provide capture as part of a comprehensive set of editing and post-production facilities. In each case, the operation is broadly similar. The more sophisticated programs will take advantage of the device control facilities of DV to allow you to start and stop the tape or move to a specific point before beginning the capture.

Shooting and recording video only provides raw material. Creating a finished video movie – whether it is a feature film or a small clip for a Web site – requires additional work. Editing is the process of constructing a whole movie from a collection of parts or clips. It comprises the selection, trimming and organization of the raw footage and – where sound is used – the synchronization of sound with picture. Transitions, such as dissolves, may be applied between shots, but – at the editing stage – no changes are made to the footage itself. We contrast this with post-production, which is concerned with altering or adding to the original material. Many of the changes made at this stage are generalizations of the image manipulation operations we described in Chapter 4, such as colour and contrast corrections, blurring or sharpening, and so on. Compositing – the combination or overlaying of elements from different shots into one composite sequence – is often carried out during post-production. Figures may be inserted into background scenes that were shot separately, for example. Elements may be animated during post-production, and animation may be combined with live action in order to create special effects.

Even if nobody wanted to display it on a computer, send it over a network or broadcast it digitally, video would still be digitized, because the advantages of digital non-linear editing are too compelling to resist. To appreciate this, and to understand the metaphors commonly used by digital editing programs, we have briefly to consider traditional methods of film and video editing.

Traditional Film and Video Editing

Editing film is a physical process. The easiest way to rearrange film is by actually cutting it – that is, physically dividing a strip of film into two clips which may then be spliced together with other clips to compose a scene. When the film is projected, the resulting transition between shots or scenes is the familiar "cut" (the splice itself does not show). A cut produces an abrupt discontinuity in the action on screen, but film audiences have become so accustomed to such jumps that they are accepted as part of the story-telling process in the medium.

Although making straight cuts in film is straightforward, creating other types of transition between clips – such as dissolves and wipes – is much less so, and before the digital era it usually required the use of a device called an **optical printer**. There are several types of optical printer; the simplest to understand comprises a rig that directs the light from a pair of projectors into a camera. Optical filters and masks can be interposed to control the amount of light from each projector reaching the camera. The picture which the camera records can thus be a combination of the pictures on the two original clips, with the filters and so on applied, as shown schematically in Figure 6.13. The result of creating an effect in the optical printer is a new piece of film which can then be spliced into the whole.

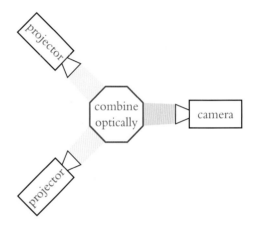

Figure 6.13. *Optical printing*

Despite the apparent simplicity of the set-up, exceptionally sophisticated effects can be achieved using such "opticals", in conjunction with techniques such as matte painting or the use of models. Many famous films of the twentieth century used optical printing to achieve magical special effects. One drawback is that opticals are usually done by a specialist laboratory, so the film editor and director cannot actually see what the transition looks like until the resulting film has been developed. This leaves little room for experimentation. It is no coincidence that the straight cut formed the basis of most films' structure, especially when the budget was limited.

Traditional analogue video editing, although the same as film editing in principle, was quite different in practice. It is virtually impossible to cut video tape accurately, or splice it together, without destroying it. Before digital video, therefore, the only way to rearrange pictures recorded on analogue video tape was to use more than one tape deck and copy selected parts of a tape from one machine onto a new tape on another, in the desired order. It was necessary to wind and rewind the source tape to find the beginning and end points of scenes to be included. Very simple editing could be carried out with just two tape decks, but a more powerful (and more common) arrangement was to use three machines, so that scenes on two separate tapes could be combined onto a third. (This setup was known as a three-machine edit suite.) This arrangement closely resembles an optical printer, but electronic signals are combined instead of light, so only effects that can easily be achieved using electronic circuits can be used. A rich variety of transitions could be produced this way, and – unlike film transitions – they could be reviewed straight away, and parameters such as the speed of a dissolve could be controlled in real time. With this arrangement, straight cuts were not significantly easier to make than any other transition, but they were still the predominant transition because of established film-making convention.

This method of editing required some means of accurately identifying positions on tapes. *Timecode* was devised for this purpose. There are several timecode standards in use, but the only one of any importance is *SMPTE timecode*. A timecode value consists of four pairs of digits separated by colons – such as 01:14:35:06 – representing hours, minutes, seconds and frames, so that the complete value identifies a precise frame. It might seem like a trivially obvious scheme, but the tricky bit was writing the code onto the video tape so that its current frame could be read by a machine. Standards for doing so were developed, and so "frame-accurate" positioning of tape was made possible.

IN DETAIL

Timecode behaves differently depending on the frame rate. For a PAL system, the final component (which identifies the frame number) ranges from 0 to 24, for NTSC it ranges from 0 to 29, but not in the obvious way, because the NTSC frame rate is 29.97.

Since there is not an exact number of NTSC frames in a second, SMPTE timecode, which must use exactly 30, drifts with respect to the elapsed time. The expedient adopted to work round this is called "drop frame timecode", in which frames 00:00 and 00:01 are omitted at the start of every minute except the tenth. (It's a bit like a leap year.) So your count jumps from, say, 00:00:59:29 to 00:01:00:02, but runs smoothly from 00:09:59:29 through 00:10:00:00 to 00:10:00:01. The correct handling of drop frame timecode is one measure of how professional a digital video editing program is.

Digital Video Editing

Now that digital video is widely used, almost all video editing is being done on computers, where the non-linear working mode of film editing can be applied to the digital data representing video sequences. Video editing is therefore now closer in kind to film editing, but without the physically destructive process. An imperfect (but useful) analogy of the difference between linear analogue and non-linear digital video editing is the difference between writing with a typewriter and using a word processor. On a traditional typewriter, words have to be written in their final order, with the potential for corrections limited to what can be achieved with correction fluid. When things go wrong or sections need rewriting, entire sheets of paper have to be thrown away and retyped – which may upset subsequent pagination, in turn requiring even more retyping. Similarly, when analogue video tape was edited, the signals had to be recorded in their final order, and the order could only be changed by rewriting to a new tape. Once the edit was written to the new tape it couldn't be changed – except by over-writing or discarding the tape and starting again.

When you use a word processor instead of a typewriter, however, a potentially infinite number of corrections can be made anywhere in the text at any time, and composition can be written in any order, without regard to pagination or layout – and without throwing anything away and starting again. In the same way, digital video editing software allows scenes to be rearranged and changed just by dragging a representation of the video in an editing window and applying some instructions. Most importantly, it is non-destructive – a huge advantage over pre-digital editing techniques. In film editing the film itself had to be cut up and much of the footage was literally thrown away (some valuable scenes were lost on the cutting room floor), and in analogue video editing the picture had to be copied onto new tape and the original tapes played over and over again. This resulted in degradation of picture quality and eventually of the physical material of the source tape itself. In digital video editing, however, the source clips need never be altered or damaged. It is possible to cut and recut, potentially forever, as the editor changes his or her mind, without any alteration to the original material.

Furthermore – in stark contrast to film – edited digital video can be played back as soon as the hardware on which it is being edited allows. With top-end equipment, playback is instantaneous. On desktop machines there may be some delay, but the delays are measured in minutes – or hours at worst – not the days that it may take for film to be processed. Recent advances in hardware and software mean that now even desktop editing systems often provide instant playback of edited digital video.

Generally, digital video formats are designed to facilitate editing and minimize the need for recompression. For instance, the QuickTime file format (and hence the MPEG-4 file format) separates the media data – the bits representing the actual pictures – from track data – descriptions of how the media data should be played back. Some editing operations can be implemented by changing the track data without altering the media data. For example, a video clip can be "trimmed" by changing the track data to record the point in the clip where it should start to play. In these cases, when the edited video is exported as a complete movie it need not be recompressed (unless it is being exported to a different format, for example for the Web). This means that there will be no loss of picture quality at all.

However, where transitions are used which depend on combining data from two or more video clips, it is necessary to create new frames – in the same way as it is in an optical printer – so that although the source clips themselves are not destroyed, the new frames will not be of quite the same quality as the original source material. Creating composited frames requires decompression before they are combined and recompression when they are exported.

People develop their own methods of working with a particular program, but the facilities provided by different editing applications are basically the same. One simple, idealized procedure for editing with a desktop application would begin with assembling all the clips for a project – capturing them where necessary, and importing them into a library, where they may be arranged for convenient access.

Next, each clip is opened within the application, and roughly trimmed to remove such extraneous matter as the clapper board or obviously excess footage. A frame is designated as the clip's **in point**, that is, the frame where it should begin, and another as its **out point**, the frame where it should end. Trimming digital video does not discard any frames, it merely suppresses those before the in point and after the out point by adjusting track data. If necessary, the in and out points can be readjusted later. If the out point is subsequently moved to a later frame in the clip, or the in point is moved to an earlier one, frames between the old and new points will reappear.

Figure 6.14. *The timeline in Premiere*

The next step is to arrange clips in the desired order on a **timeline**, as shown in Figure 6.14. The timeline provides a convenient spatial representation of the way frames are arranged in time. (The timeline reads from left to right.) Still images can also be placed on the timeline and assigned an arbitrary duration; they will behave as clips with no motion. If the movie is to have a soundtrack, the picture and sound can be combined on the timeline. Often, adjustments will have to be made, particularly if it is necessary to synchronize the sound with the picture. Clips may need to be trimmed again, or more drastic changes may be required, such as the substitution of completely different material when ideas fail to work out. For some basic projects, editing will then be complete at this stage, but more extended or elaborate movies will probably require some more complex transitions, as well as corrections or compositing.

Figure 6.15. *A dissolve*

Using other types of transition changes the style, rhythm and mood of a piece. A dissolve, for example – in which one clip fades into another – is less emphatic than a cut, and tends to convey a sense of gradual change or smooth flow from one thing to another. It may be used to change location between scenes, or in a more imaginative way – for example, extended dissolves are sometimes used to introduce "dream sequences" in movies. In Figure 6.15 the picture dissolves from the shot looking over the outside of a house to the figure standing by the sea, which in the context of the movie also conveys a more subtle change of circumstance. A dissolve to black (a "fade-out") and then back from black into a new scene (a "fade-in") is frequently used to indicate that time has elapsed between the end of the first scene and the beginning of the second.

As most transitions can be described relatively easily in terms of mathematical operations on the two clips involved, digital video editing software usually offers a vast range of possibilities – some video editing applications have well over 50 transitions built in – but many of them are showy gimmicks which are usually best avoided. The more fanciful transitions, such as wipes, spins and page turns, draw attention to themselves and therefore function almost as decoration.

There are two important practical differences between cuts and other transitions. Firstly, in a cut the two clips are butted, whereas in all other transitions they overlap, so that some part of each clip contributes to the resulting picture, as illustrated in Figure 6.16. (Some editing software will display the clips overlapping in this way on the timeline, but other programs will not.) It is therefore necessary to ensure that each clip is shot with enough frames to cover the full duration of the transition in addition to the time it plays on its own.

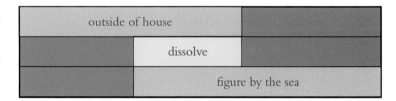

Figure 6.16. *Overlapping clips for a transition*

Secondly, because image processing is required to construct the transitional frames, transitions must be rendered, unlike cuts, which can be implemented simply by copying. Hence, as we mentioned before, there will inevitably be some loss of image quality where dissolves and other transitions are used instead of straight cuts, though in practice this may not be readily perceptible by the viewer.

Post-Production

Most digital video post-production tasks can be seen as applications of the image manipulation operations we described in Chapter 4 to the bitmapped images that make up a video sequence. Contemporary video editing applications which include post-production facilities normally describe them in the same terms as those used when dealing with single bitmapped still images.

As the raw footage of a video sequence is just a series of photographs, it may suffer from the same defects as a single photograph. For example, it may be incorrectly exposed or out of focus, it may have a colour cast, or it may display unacceptable digitization artefacts. Each of these problems can be remedied in the same way as we would correct a bitmapped image in an application such as Photoshop – for example, we may adjust the levels, sharpen the image, or apply a Gaussian blur (see Chapter 4). Post-production systems therefore provide the same set of adjustments as image manipulation programs – some even support the use of Photoshop plug-ins – but they allow these adjustments to be applied to whole sequences of images. Like Photoshop effects, video effects can be used to create artificial images as well as to correct faulty real ones, and the added time dimension also allows some special effects to be created.

Most adjustments have parameters, such as the slider positions for levels controls (see Chapter 4). When adjustments are made to video sequences, it is possible to choose whether to use the same parameter values for each image in the sequence, or to vary the values in order to create adjustments or effects which change over time.

If, for example, a complete sequence has been shot under incorrect lighting, the same correction will probably be needed for every frame, so the levels can be set for the first, and the adjustment will be applied to as many frames as the user specifies. However, if the light fades during a sequence when it was intended to remain constant, it would be necessary to increase the brightness gradually over time to compensate. It is possible to apply a suitable correction to each frame individually, and this may occasionally be necessary, but often it is adequate to specify parameters at a few *key frames* and allow their values at intermediate frames to be interpolated.

Figure 6.17 shows the simplest form of temporal variation being applied to achieve a special effect. Final Cut Pro's colour offset effect is similar to the hue component of Photoshop's hue and saturation adjustment, applied to each colour channel individually. The interface shown at the bottom of the figure is typical of the way in which such effects are applied, though they vary from one application (and version) to another. At the left you can see the controls for the effect – a set of sliders for adjusting the hue in the R, G and B channels. To the right of these are three small timelines, one for each channel. Key frames are added to the timeline, and the desired values of the effect's parameter at the corresponding time are set using the slider. You can add as many key frames as

Figure 6.17. *A colour offset filter applied to video over time*

necessary; the parameters will be interpolated between them. For this simple colour change, a straightforward linear interpolation was used, with all three colours changing in parallel.

Some post-production programs allow you to use Bézier curves to control the interpolation as well as straight lines. Figure 6.18 shows this being done in the creation of a complex special effect that was achieved by varying the parameters of several filters over time (only a few frames of the video sequence are shown here). In this example, abrupt changes in the brightness and colour were used to convey the impression of a sudden intense blast and the disintegration of the scene and figure. The whole sequence is thus created entirely by altering the original bitmapped images of the footage.

Just as some of the image manipulation operations we described in Chapter 4 combined separate layers into a composite result, so some post-production operations combine separate video tracks into a composite. As with still images, some parts of the superimposed tracks must be transparent for superimposition to achieve anything useful. In video, selecting transparent areas is called **keying**. Good video editing and post-production software will offer several different keying methods.

A long-established use of keying in traditional film-making is "blue screening", which is typically used for inserting isolated elements or figures into scenes artificially – for example, to add models to live footage, or to place live actors in seemingly impossible or dangerous situations. Digital post-production systems support both traditional blue screening – where the actor or model is shot in front of a screen that is a particular shade of blue and then the blue channel is removed – and a

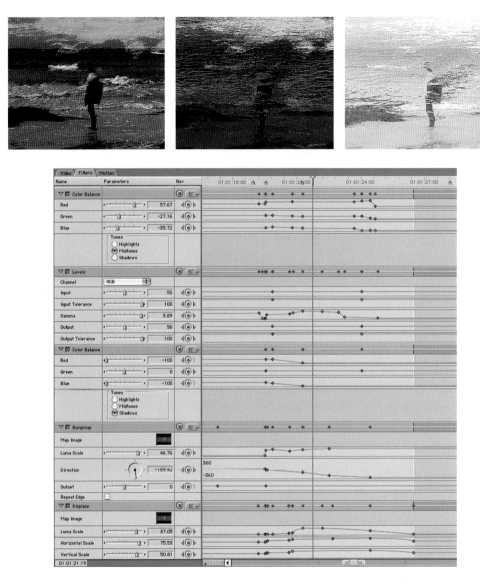

Figure 6.18. *A complex set of filters applied to video over time to achieve a special effect*

more general form of ***chroma keying***, where any colour in a scene can be selected and designated as transparent. Chroma keying is essentially the same as building an alpha channel from a selection made using a magic wand tool. An alternative is ***luma keying***, where a brightness threshold is used to determine which areas are transparent.

In some video editing applications it is possible to use selection tools to create a mask. In film and video, a mask used for compositing is called a ***matte***. Mattes are frequently used for removing unwanted elements (such as microphone booms or lights) from a scene, or for allowing live footage to be combined with a still image to convey a special impression. Throughout the history of film-making, mattes have been used to create the impression of a scene that was not really there (not even as a set). Actors can be filmed on a relatively cheap set containing just a few foreground props, with the set itself constructed to a height not much above their heads. The top of the frame is matted out when the action is being filmed, and subsequently replaced with a painting of a large building, landscape or whatever – designed to blend in with the set itself – in order to create the illusion of a much larger, more elaborate or more fantastic environment for the action. Mattes can also be used for split-screen effects. As with many other editing and post-production operations, digital video applications make matting and keying not only much simpler than they were using traditional techniques, but available at low cost on desktop editing systems.

KEY POINTS

Video editing is the process of constructing a complete movie from a set of video clips or scenes, combining them with sound where required.

Post-production is concerned with making changes or compositing the material, using operations that are similar to bitmapped image manipulations.

SMPTE timecode is used to identify frames by their time coordinates.

During editing, clips are imported, trimmed and assembled on a timeline. Transitions, such as dissolves, may be added between overlapping clips.

In post-production, the values of effects' parameters may vary over time.

Chroma keying, luma keying and mattes are used when combining tracks.

Delivery

The traditional way of delivering video is by way of a dedicated service, usually a broadcast television signal, or on a special medium, for instance a DVD, which is played in a dedicated device, such as a DVD player. However, because digital video can be treated as data by programs, it offers other possibilities.

It is usual to call a self-contained piece of video a "movie", whatever its content may be. A movie can be stored in a file, just as an image can, which raises the usual questions of file formats. It can also be sent over a network, and this raises new issues.

Streaming

A movie stored in a file could be downloaded from a remote server, saved to a local disk and played from there, in much the same way as an image can be downloaded and displayed. Because of the size of video data this would be a slow process, and it would require large files to be stored locally. A better alternative is to deliver a video data stream from the server, to be displayed as it arrives, without storing it on disk first. Such **streamed video** resembles broadcast television, in that the source video is held on the server, which acts like a TV transmitter sending out the signal, which is played back straight away on a client machine. (In contrast, downloading the entire video would be like having the TV company send a courier round with a DVD whenever you wanted to watch a programme.)

Streamed video opens up the possibility of delivering live video, bringing one of the modes of conventional broadcasting to video on computers. It goes beyond conventional broadcast TV in this area, though, because it is not restricted to a single transmitter broadcasting to many consumers. Any suitably equipped computer can act as both receiver and transmitter, so users on several machines can communicate visually, taking part in what is usually called a video conference.

Until recently, a fundamental obstacle to streamed video has been bandwidth. Decent quality streamed video is restricted to broadband connections (or local area networks); dial-up Internet connections cannot handle the required data rate. Even where the bandwidth is available, the network has to be capable of delivering data with the minimum of delay, and without undue "jitter" – a variation in the delay that can cause independently delivered video and audio streams to lose synchronization. We will return to this subject in Chapter 16.

It may help you to understand the nature of what we will sometimes call "true streaming" by contrasting it with alternative methods of video delivery you may meet on the World Wide Web. The simplest method, which we already mentioned, is **embedded video**, where a movie file is transferred from a server to the user's machine, and not played back from the user's disk until the entire file has arrived.

A refinement of this method is called **progressive download** or **HTTP streaming**. With this mode of delivery the file is still transferred to the user's disk, but it starts playing as soon as enough of it has arrived to make further waiting unnecessary. This will be when the time it will take for the remainder to be downloaded is equal to the duration of the entire movie.

For instance, suppose a 30-second movie has been compressed to a data rate of 2 Mbps. The file would take 120 seconds to download over a slow broadband connection operating at 512 kbps – that is, the user would have to wait two minutes before seeing any of the movie. After 90 seconds have elapsed, though, three-quarters of the frames will have been received by the browser. If the movie starts playing at that point, by the time these frames have been used up new ones will have arrived. In fact, since the movie lasts for 30 seconds, and the remaining quarter of it will take that amount of time to arrive, it should be possible to play the entire movie starting from the 90-second point. This is illustrated in Figure 6.19.

There is usually an appreciable delay before playback starts, since progressively downloaded movies are typically made with a data rate that exceeds the bandwidth of the network connection. In such a case, this will be the best that can be achieved if dropped frames are to be avoided. The movie file usually remains on the user's hard disk – at least in their Web browser's cache – after playback is completed. Enough disk space to store the whole movie must be available, so progressive download cannot be used often for huge files, such as complete feature films. Also, since an entire file is downloaded, this method of delivery cannot be used for live video, nor does it allow the user to skip over parts of the file without downloading them.

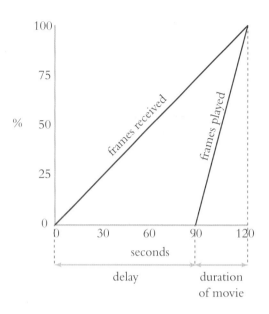

Figure 6.19. *Progressive download*

In contrast, true streaming video is never stored on the user's disk. A small buffer may be used to smooth out jitter, but effectively each frame in the stream is played as soon as it arrives over the network. This means that streams can be open-ended, so true streaming can be used for live video, and the length of a pre-recorded movie that is streamed is limited only by the amount of storage available at the server, not by the disk space on the user's machine. Random access to specific points in a stream is possible, except for live streams. True streaming is thus suitable for "video on demand" applications and video-conferencing. It is also more acceptable to copyright holders, because there is normally no copy of the complete movie left on the user's machine for potential copying and redistribution.

If streaming is to work properly, the network must be able to deliver the data stream fast enough for playback. Looked at from the other side, this means that the movie's data rate, and thus its quality, is restricted to what the network can deliver. With modern codecs and broadband connections, full-frame, full-speed playback can be achieved at acceptable quality, although it is advisable to use smaller frames, to allow for connections at the lower end of the broadband range.

The main drawback of true streaming is that it requires a special server, whereas progressive download can be carried out using an ordinary Web server. (Video podcasts can be delivered in either way, since the podcast is just a wrapper containing metadata, which points to the location of the actual video movie.) We will explain the requirements for streaming in more detail in Chapter 16. Streaming servers often require the payment of licence fees, and are not usually available on shared hosts, so a restricted budget may necessitate the use of progressive download, even where streaming would be technically feasible.

Architectures and Formats

Video formats are more complex than image formats. As we have shown in preceding sections, there are many digital video compression schemes. Each of these schemes requires the information to be encoded in a different way, but does not in itself define a file format. Some standards, such as MPEG-4, define a file format, but the data compressed by the codecs defined in the same standard may be stored in files with other formats, too. Most file formats used for video have been devised to contain data compressed using different codecs. Video is usually accompanied by sound, and as we will see in Chapter 8, audio uses many different codecs and formats too.

To accommodate the multitude of possible combinations of video and audio codecs and formats, the major platforms each provide what is vaguely referred to as a ***multimedia architecture***. The term is not clearly defined, but a multimedia architecture usually features the following:

An API (Application Programming Interface) that provides facilities for media capture, compression and playback, which can be incorporated into multimedia software.
One or more codecs.
A container format for storing media data.
A streaming server (see Chapter 16).
Sofware tools for playback and possibly capture, compression and simple editing. Most multimedia architectures include a Web browser plug-in as well as desktop programs.

Multimedia architectures are component-based, with a mechanism for incorporating additional third-party components. This means, for example, that if some codec is not supported it can be added by way of a component – a new version of the architecture is not required for every new codec.

The container format will usually be able to hold data that has been compressed by many different codecs, not just the native codecs of the architecture. In most cases, the playback functions will be able to cope with many file formats in addition to the architecture's own container. Although this may sound complicated, what it means in practice is that a good multimedia architecture will make it possible to play almost any movie it is presented with, so that users should not have to worry about formats and codecs.

The first multimedia architecture was ***QuickTime***, which was introduced by Apple in 1991 and has been extended through new versions ever since. QuickTime's container format is the movie file, often called a MOV file, as they usually have the extension .mov. QuickTime movies are extremely flexible containers, which can accommodate still images, text and animation as well as many different video and audio formats and compression schemes. Among the video codecs included with current versions of QuickTime are H.264/AVC, MPEG-4 Part 2, Pixlet, and several others developed for specific tasks such as compressing computer-generated animation.

The QuickTime movie file format has been used as the basis of the MPEG-4 file format. To enable application software based on QuickTime to access other types of file, components have been added to make it possible to manipulate files in other formats as if they were native QuickTime. Formats supported in this way include MPEG-1 and MPEG-2, DV, OMF (a high-end professional format), Microsoft's AVI and (using a third-party extension) WMV. As this demonstrates, QuickTime's component architecture makes it easily extensible.

The QuickTime Player is a program that uses the playback components to provide a standard video player that can display movies in any supported format. (Many of its functions have also been incorporated into the popular iTunes program.) A Pro version exists, which adds simple capture, editing and export functions. A fee is charged for activation of the Pro features.

QuickTime is available on both Macintosh and Windows systems. Windows' own multimedia architecture is called *DirectShow*.[†] Although it is organized differently from a programmer's point of view, DirectShow is functionally very similar to QuickTime. It provides a similar set of facilities for creating and manipulating media, including video. Strictly speaking, its container format is *ASF (Advanced Systems Format)* but ASF files containing video data are most often called *Windows Media* or *WMV* files. The Windows Media Video codec which we described earlier can be considered part of DirectShow. Like QuickTime, though, DirectShow allows additional codecs to be added by way of components, so although the number of codecs provided with DirectShow itself is small, many others can be added.

The Windows Media Player is similar to the QuickTime Player. The Windows Media Encoder can be used for capturing and compressing video and converting it between different formats. WMV is the usual format for video data but DirectShow also supports the older AVI format as well as MPEG video and some very early versions of the QuickTime movie format.

The prevalence of the Windows operating system has led to Windows Media and DirectShow being installed on a large proportion of the world's consumer-level computers, but it does not run on any operating system apart from recent versions of Windows.

---

† At least, it is at the time of writing: its name keeps changing.

┌─ IN DETAIL ──┐

Video for Windows was the predecessor of DirectShow; its associated file format was AVI (Audio-Video Interleaved). AVI is generally considered to be an outdated format. In particular, it provides no means of identifying B-pictures in a stream, so data compressed by any codec that uses bi-directional prediction can only be stored in an AVI file by the use of an additional coding hack.

Nevertheless, there are many AVI files in existence, and the format has been adapted to accommodate modern codecs. In particular, the DivX format is a version of AVI that has been adapted to hold video data compressed with MPEG-4 Part 2. When video file-sharing first became popular, DivX was a popular format for distributing movies. Consequently, many domestic DVD players can play movies in DivX format. However, the DivX project has become fragmented, with the appearance of a competing XviD codec, and the development of a new container file format, DivX Media Format. As support for the standard MP4 format becomes more widespread DivX is becoming less relevant.

└──┘

Although QuickTime is available for Windows, it is not installed by default. Similarly, although there is a third-party set of QuickTime components that allow Windows Media files to be played back and created on Mac systems, these are not part of the standard QuickTime distribution. Because of licencing issues, Open Source Linux distributions do not support QuickTime or WMV, so again a third-party program must be installed on such systems to play those formats. (And doing so may be illegal in some countries.) Hence, it is certainly not safe to assume that either WMV or QuickTime movies will be playable on all systems. This becomes a problem when video is distributed through the World Wide Web, since there is no way of predicting which computer system visitors to a site will be using.

A surprising solution to the problem of cross-platform video emerged in the form of Adobe's Flash Player. Although it is not built in to any operating system, the Flash Player is among the most widely installed pieces of software in the world. Originally, it was intended purely for playing vector animations in SWF format, as we will describe in Chapter 7. The only way to incorporate video in a SWF movie was by importing each frame as a bitmapped image. This was often done – and still is, for specialized applications – but it provided no means of applying inter-frame compression, so the resulting movies were large. The ***Flash Video (FLV)*** format was devised to overcome this difficulty.

Flash Video playback in the Flash Player works in a slightly odd way. You can't simply stream an FLV file to the Flash Player. Instead, you must create a SWF (Flash movie) as if you were making an animation. This SWF need only contain a single frame: a script can load and play an FLV movie within that frame. The video can be streamed or progressively downloaded. Typically, the SWF frame holds player controls, which allow the user to start, stop, pause and rewind the video. This way of working is somewhat inconvenient but it makes it simple to customize the appearance of playback controls and other aspects of the player, because they are just part of the SWF you create to load the video. A selection of standard player controls and a "wizard" for importing video are available in Flash, so the process is not onerous. (See Chapter 6 of *Digital Media Tools* for more practical information about creating and playing Flash Video.)

┌─IN DETAIL──
│
│   **There are third-party media players which can simply play a FLV movie the way**
│   **the QuickTime Player plays a QuickTime movie, but these are not installed with**
│   **nearly every Web browser in the way that the Flash Player is.**
│

The near-ubiquity of the Flash Player made FLV into a suitable format for video on the Web. The growth of video-sharing sites – especially YouTube, which used Flash Video – made the format hugely popular in a short period of time. Nevertheless, the quality that could be obtained at suitable bit rates with the original Flash Video codec, or even with the improved On2 VP6 codec that we described earlier, was inferior to what was possible with H.264/AVC. Subsequently, though, Adobe added support for MP4 files using H.264/AVC. It is still necessary to make a SWF to load the video, but instead of generating an FLV file – which can only be done with Flash or the Flash Video Encoder – you can load any MPEG-4 file that uses the H.264/AVC codec, and these can be created with any standard video software. (However, both QuickTime and DirectShow support MP4 playback, so the case for going through the extra step of using Flash is less compelling.)

The file formats most often encountered for video are the container formats associated with the QuickTime and DirectShow frameworks (i.e. MOV and WMV files), Flash Video and the MPEG-4 container format. You may also come across **Ogg** files, Ogg being another container format, associated with the same project as the Theora codec we mentioned earlier. The format is a free open standard so there are no restrictions on its use. It is only normally used with video that has been compressed with open codecs, in particular, Ogg Theora. If you want or need to use purely open technology, Ogg and its associated video and audio codecs are probably the only option. All others are either proprietary or subject to licence fees, in theory if not in practice.

The nearest thing to a multimedia architecture in the Linux/Open Source world is *ffmpeg*, which is a command-line tool for video capture, compression and format conversion. It is supported by a collection of libraries providing codecs and some post-production facilities, which can be used like the APIs in the mainstream architectures to provide these functions in many programs. Various media players have been built on top of these libraries. There is also an associated streaming server. Many codecs are supported, including H.264/AVC and Theora. File formats that can be read and written by ffmpeg include WMV, AVI and FLV.

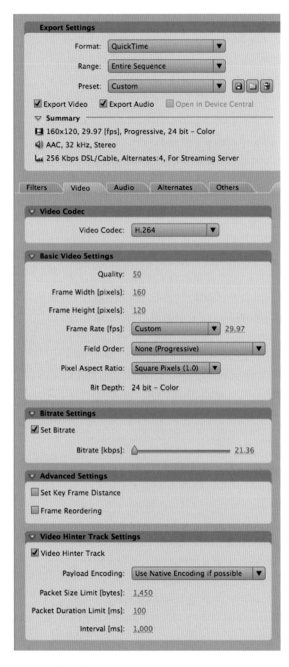

Figure 6.20. *Export settings*

Some platforms demand the use of certain formats and codecs. Video intended for mobile phones must usually be in 3GP format; video for Apple's iPod players must be QuickTime, compressed with H.264/AVC. For playing on computers, there is generally a wider choice, but if you wish to cater for as many people as possible, it is necessary to choose a video format with care.

As we explained earlier, using a format such as WMV or MOV that is tied to a particular multimedia architecture may mean that your video cannot be viewed on all systems. You may decide that this does not matter – if you know for certain that everybody who might watch your video has a recent Windows system, you can safely use WMV and take advantage of the tools for working with that format. For example, this might be the case with a training video that was only intended for distribution over an intranet to employees of a single organization, which had a strict policy concerning the systems that could be attached to the network. More often, though, you will be distributing the video to a heterogeneous collection of systems. This is always the case for video on the Internet. In that case you must use a format that is playable on the largest feasible number of systems.

From our earlier discussion, you should be able to see that MP4 and FLV are the two obvious choices for distribution to heterogeneous systems. MP4 is a standard and playable by DirectShow, QuickTime and the Open Source players available for all platforms. FLV is playable by the Flash Player, which is available for all the major platforms, and is installed on most machines.

Hence, after any resizing and changing of frame rate, video for delivery over networks or for playback on portable devices will usually be exported as MP4, probably using the H.264/AVC codec, or as FLV, using On2 VP6. Almost any video editing software will be able to export MP4. As you can see from Figure 6.20, the format is chosen during export. Usually, the format is the first thing you must choose, as it determines which codecs can be used. For FLV, you will need to use Flash or the Adobe Media Encoder. Additionally, you will have to create the player movie, as we mentioned previously. (If you are dogmatic about only using Open Source, you will have to prepare an Ogg/Theora movie, but don't expect it to be universally playable.)

For video to be streamed over a network it is common practice to produce a range of different versions matched to the speed of users' network connections. QuickTime and Windows Media allow different versions to be combined into a single movie. The server chooses the appropriate version to stream on the basis of information sent by the player about the connection speed.

KEY POINTS

Video may be delivered over a network as a downloaded file, it may be streamed or it may be delivered by progressive download.

Progressive download means that the movie starts playing when the time taken to download the remaining frames is less than the time it will take to play the whole movie.

When video is streamed, each frame is played as it arrives.

Streaming allows live video and does not require a file to be saved on the user's disk, but it does require sufficient bandwidth to deliver frames fast enough to be played.

A multimedia architecture provides an API for capture, playback and compression; a container format; a streaming server; and software tools, such as a player.

QuickTime and DirectShow are the multimedia architectures included with Mac OS X and Windows, respectively. Their file formats are MOV and WMV.

QuickTime and DirectShow are extensible by way of components, which allow them to use many codecs, including H.264/AVC and WMV 9, and to read and write several additional file formats, such as MP4 and AVI.

Flash Video is widely used for Web video. FLV files must be played in the Flash Player with a SWF that controls the video playback (or in a third-party player).

Ogg is an open format, that can be used in conjunction with the Theora codec to produce movies that are not subject to any restrictions or licence fees.

Web video may need its frame size and frame rate reduced before it is compressed and exported to a suitable format (e.g. MP4 or FLV) which can be played back on most systems.

Exercises

Test Questions

1 Why is standard definition broadcast video usually interlaced, but Web video is not?

2 Are the pixels in PAL CCIR 601 frames wider or narrow than NTSC?

3 Verify that the 25 Mbps data rate of DV corresponds to a compression ratio of 5:1.

4 If a 24-bit colour image occupies N bytes, how many bytes would the same image occupy after chrominance sub-sampling using each of the sub-sampling schemes 4:2:2, 4:1:1 and 4:2:0? Explain why 4:2:0 sampling may cause problems with interlaced video.

5 What effect will each of the following common video idioms have on a compression scheme that includes temporal compression?

(a) Cuts

(b) Dissolves

(c) Hand-held camera work

(d) Zooms

(e) Pans

Explain your answers. In which cases does motion compensation help?

6 Explain carefully why a 30-second video clip (containing 25 frames per second) will occupy less disk space than 750 JPEG images of the same size.

7 Suppose an MPEG encoder uses the nine-frame sequence IBBPBBPBB as a GOP. Draw a diagram showing the dependencies between the first 18 frames of a compressed clip produced by this encoder. Show how the pictures would be reordered into bitstream order. Explain carefully why the pattern of I-, P- and B-pictures in the bitstream order of the first nine frames is different from that of the second nine frames.

8 A user starts to download a 905 kilobyte movie of 30 seconds' duration, using progressive download over a connection that provides an average data rate of 2 Mbits per second. How long will it be before the movie starts to play? Why might the user experience jerky playback?

9   List all the factors you should take into account when choosing a format and codec for Web video.

Discussion Topics

1   If it had been possible to formulate new digital video standards without having to worry about compatibility with older analogue ones, how do you think they would differ from the standards we have at present?

2   Would it be feasible or desirable to use indexed colour for video?

3   Suppose you were involved in the design of a software application for domestic use, intended to allow users to create Web pages for domestic events, such as a record of a child's birthday to be uploaded to the Web so that a grandparent on the other side of the world could see it. What assumptions will you make about video for this program, and what facilities will you supply?

Practical Tasks

1   Choose two codecs and carry out a systematic assessment of the quality of video compressed with each at a range of bit rates. Use at least two clips with contrasting visual and dynamic characteristics, and compress them to several different sizes, ranging from DV bit rates down to something suitable for a dial-up connection. Don't change the frame size or frame rate. You may have to experiment with the settings in the two codecs to achieve comparable results. If it is feasible, do A/B comparisons in front of an audience, without telling them which is which, and ask them to assess the relative quality of the corresponding outputs from the two codecs. (If not, assess them yourself trying not to be biased.) Is one rated consistently better than the other, or does the quality depend on the source material or the bit rate?

If you have time, or can work as a group, extend the comparisons to cover all the popular modern codecs.

2   Observant readers will have noticed the shadow of the camera operator's head in the still we used for our examples of codec quality. Look at different ways of removing such undesirable features from video footage.

7

Animation

■ **Image Sequences**

Captured Sequences. Digital Image Sequences. Animated GIFs.

■ **Interpolation**

Interpolating Motion. Motion Paths.

■ **Vector Animation in Flash**

The Timeline and Stage. Symbols and Tweening.

■ **Motion Graphics**

■ **Delivering Animation**

Animation on Video. Comparison of Animation Formats.
The Flash Movie Format. Minor Alternatives.

Animation may be defined as the creation of moving pictures one frame at a time, though the term "pictures" may be interpreted broadly – to include pictures of text, for example. The word is also used to mean the image sequences produced in this way, as in the phrases "a Disney animation" or "Web animation". Throughout the twentieth century, animation was used for entertainment, advertising, instruction, art and propaganda on film, and later on video. As the twenty-first century advances, animation is also widely employed on the World Wide Web and in other forms of multimedia, such as interactive DVD menus.

To see how animation works, consider making a sequence of drawings or paintings on paper, in which those elements or characters intended to change or move during the sequence are altered or repositioned in each drawing. The changes between one drawing and the next may be very subtle, or they may be quite exaggerated. When all the drawings are complete, the sequence is photographed in the correct order, a single drawing at a time. If this resulting image sequence is played back at an appropriate speed, it is perceived in exactly the same way as the sequence of frames exposed when live action has been filmed in real time on a film or video camera. In both cases, persistence of vision causes the succession of still images to be seen as a continuous moving image, despite the fact that in animation this is nothing but an illusion.

"Animate" literally means "to bring to life", which captures the essence of the process. When played back at normal film or video speeds, the static characters, objects, abstract shapes or whatever, that have been photographed in sequence, appear to come to life. Large differences between successive images in the sequence create an illusion of fast movement or change, whereas small differences convey the impression of slow movement or more gradual change.

IN DETAIL

As film is projected at 24 frames per second, drawn animation in traditional media, as we have just described it, technically requires 24 drawings for each second of film, that is, 1440 drawings for every minute – and even more for animation made on video. In practice, animation that does not require seamlessly smooth movement can be shot "on 2s", which means that two frames of each drawing, or whatever, are captured rather than just one. This gives an effective frame rate of 12 frames per second for film, or 15 for NTSC video.

If an animation is made from drawings or paintings on paper, every aspect of the image has to be redrawn for every single frame that is shot. In order to reduce the enormous amount of labour this involves, as well as to allow for new expressive possibilities, many other techniques of animation have been devised. The most widely used – at least until recently – has been *cel animation*.

In cel animation, elements or characters in a scene that were intended to move were drawn on sheets of transparent material known as "cel", and laid over a background which was drawn separately. When producing an animated sequence, only the moving elements on the cels needed to be redrawn for each frame; the fixed parts of each scene were only drawn once. Many cels might be overlaid, with changes being made to different cels between different frames to achieve greater complexity in the scene – interaction between multiple characters moving in different ways, for example. To extend the possibilities for movement in a scene, the background could be drawn on a very long sheet, far wider than any individual frame, and moved slowly along behind the cels between shots, to produce an effect of travelling through a scene. (This effect is borrowed from the theatre and early live-action film, where performers might run on the spot, for example, while scenery was moved behind them to create an illusion of their moving through space.)

The concepts and techniques of traditional cel animation have proved particularly suitable for transfer to the digital realm. Most traditional-looking animated cartoons are now produced entirely digitally, and software has been developed to make it easy to create cel-like animation. The most popular and widely used program is Flash.

Largely because of the huge influence of the Walt Disney studios, cel has dominated the popular perception of animation. It was used in nearly all the major cartoon series from the original *Popeye* in the 1930s onwards, as well as in many full-length feature films, starting with *Snow White and the Seven Dwarfs* in 1937. However, from the very beginnings of moving pictures in the 1890s, animation has been successfully created by employing a variety of other means. Despite the intensive labour involved, many animators do work by drawing each frame separately on paper, while others – even more painstakingly – have painted directly on to film, or scratched the emulsion of blackened film stock. Others work with sand or oil paint on glass, or chalks on paper or card, making changes to the created image between every shot. Some animators have manipulated cut-outs under the camera – Terry Gilliam's distinctive work for the *Monty Python* TV series is a well-known example of cut-out animation. Sometimes animators have invented a completely new way of working for themselves, such as Alexeieff and Parker's pin screen, in which closely spaced pins were selectively pushed through a board and lit so that the shadows they cast form an image, which is changed between each shot. Although the photography and the presentation of animation are now likely to be digital, all of these alternative methods of creating animation remain as valid as they ever were.

A distinct alternative to all of these essentially two-dimensional forms is three-dimensional *stop-motion* animation. This encompasses several techniques, but they all use miniature three-dimensional sets, like stage sets, on which objects are moved carefully between shots. The objects may include articulated figures whose limbs can be repositioned, or solid figures whose parts are replaced, or substituted, between shots, to produce an effect of gestures, walking, and so on.

Malleable modelling material such as Plasticine may be used. Its special qualities allow it to be manipulated between shots, either to produce an effect of natural movement or to create changes and transformations which would be impossible in the real world. This type of animation – often called *clay animation* – has achieved great prominence with the Aardman studios, whose work includes the *Wallace and Gromit* animations.

There is also a long tradition of combining animation with live footage. The most celebrated pre-digital example of this is perhaps *Who Framed Roger Rabbit?* (1988), but a mixture of live action and animation was employed in some of the earliest films ever made, including Georges Méliès' well known "trick films" made at the turn of the twentieth century, and Max Fleischer's *Out of the Inkwell* series of the 1920s, which did much to popularize animation as a form of entertainment. Audiences may often be unaware that much of what they perceive as "special effects" has been achieved by basic animation techniques, whether traditional, as in the 1933 classic *King Kong* and many other monster movies, or digital, as in *The Matrix* and its sequels, for example.

All of the traditional forms of animation have their counterparts in the digital realm, and digital technology has created opportunities for using animation and techniques derived from it in new contexts. It has also brought new ways of creating animation. Animation is now routinely embedded in Web pages or used as a component of "rich media" interfaces to computer programs. When it is presented in these novel ways, animation is freed from the restrictions of film and video. In particular, there is no need to use video frame rates – any rate sufficiently high to create the illusion of appropriate motion for the context can be used – and there is no reason to be restricted to video or film frame sizes and aspect ratios. An animation presented on a Web page, for example, can have any dimensions that fit its place in the layout. Some digital animation formats support transparency, meaning that animations don't even have to be rectangular in appearance.

Animation as we have described it is a sequence of images. Like still images, animations may be represented as bit maps or as vectors, and the properties of these representations, which we described in Chapters 3 and 4, apply to the individual frames of animations. However, animation that is purely digital no longer has to consist of a sequence of explicitly stored images. Frames can be created when the animation is played – for example, by interpolation of elements in key frames, or by the execution of a script or program that draws the frames in real time as the animation proceeds. Digital animations created in this way offer completely new possibilities – they can be created from sets of data, and they can be interactive. As we will explain later, vector representations lend themselves more readily to this kind of dynamically created animation.

You may observe that we have not mentioned computer-generated three-dimensional (CG3D) animation. Following the success of *Toy Story* in 1996, and other films produced by Pixar Animation Studios, CG3D animation achieved great popularity. However, the sophistication that audiences now expect from CG3D animation is not at all easy to achieve. It requires highly specialized skills and software, and considerable computing power. Little can be achieved without these dedicated resources, so we do not cover CG3D in this chapter. The topic requires a whole book of its own, so readers interested in this type of animation should consult the specialized sources.

Image Sequences

An animation is a sequence of frames, each one a still image. Either bitmapped images or vector graphics can be used for the individual frames. Vector graphics offer more possibilities for creating and manipulating frames using computer programs. Bitmapped images are conceptually simpler, though, and correspond more closely to the traditional animations consisting of a sequence of photographed images on film. Like traditional animation, bitmapped animation tends to be labour-intensive: in most cases each frame must be created — at least in part — by hand.

Captured Sequences

Digital technology offers new possibilities for animation and animators, but computers can also be used effectively in conjunction with the older animation techniques discussed above, to produce animation in a digital form. Currently, preparing animation in this way — using digital technology together with a camera and traditional animation methods — offers much richer expressive possibilities to the animator working in digital media than the purely computer-generated methods we will describe later in this chapter.

Instead of recording your animation on film or videotape, a camera can be connected directly to a computer, to capture each frame of animation to disk — no matter whether it is drawn on paper or cel, constructed on a 3-D set, or made using any other technique that does not depend on actually marking the film.

It is common practice to use a video camera for animation capture. Doing so makes most sense if the animation is intended to be delivered as video for cinema projection, television or on a DVD, even if it is also being produced for other delivery media, because the captured data will match video standards, as we explained in Chapter 6. For animation, instead of storing the entire data stream arriving from the camera in real time, as you would if you were capturing live video, you only store the digital version of a single frame each time you have set up a shot correctly. Many small software utilities are available for performing *frame grabbing* of this sort.

Frame grabbers all work in roughly the same way. A recording window is displayed on screen, showing the current view through the camera. You can use this to check the shot, then press a key to capture one frame, either to a still image file, or to be appended to a movie sequence in QuickTime or some other video format. You then change your drawing, alter the position of your models or whatever, and capture the next frame. Frames that are unsatisfactory can be deleted. There may be an option allowing you to see a ghost image of the previously captured frame, to help with alignment and making the appropriate changes. When you have captured a set of frames that forms a complete sequence, you can save it as a movie or as a set of sequentially numbered image files (see below). The latter option is useful if you want to manipulate individual images later on in Photoshop or import them into Flash, for example.

You can also grab frames using a digital still image camera. In many ways, this is a better option. You can use much higher resolutions than a video camera provides, and you don't need to worry about interlacing or non-square pixels (see Chapter 6) unless you are going to prepare a final version for video. However, you can only use a still image camera as a frame grabber if it provides a preview feed and supports the *Picture Transfer Protocol (PTP)*, which enables it to be controlled from a computer. If it satisfies these conditions, it is possible to work with a still image camera in the same manner as we have just described for a video camera. Otherwise, it is necessary to set up each frame through the camera's view finder and capture it to the camera's internal memory, just as if you were taking a snapshot for each frame. The individual photographs can then be transferred to your computer and combined into an animation. This latter way of working is inconvenient and error-prone, though. If you want to make animations by capturing one frame at a time with a still image camera, it is worth investing in one that supports PTP if you can.

Capturing animation to disk in the manner just outlined not only opens up the possibilities of non-linear editing and post-production that we described in Chapter 6, it also allows animation in traditional media to be combined with purely digital animation and motion graphics.

Figure 7.1 shows some frames from a work produced in this hybrid fashion. In this sequence, the animated background of figures and spiral was scratched and painted incrementally on a rock, and captured one frame at a time using a video camera to grab frames direct to disk. The foreground effect of ships sailing towards the viewer on a choppy sea was created digitally, and the chain was photographed and then extracted in Photoshop. These different elements were then composited together in a video editing program, creating a result which combined a completely traditional way of working in physical media with purely digital composition and effects.

For certain types of traditional animation, it is not even necessary to use a camera. If you have made a series of drawings or paintings on paper, you can use a scanner to produce a set of image files from them. You can also manipulate cut-outs on the bed of a scanner, almost as easily as under a camera. A film scanner will even allow you to digitize animation scratched or painted directly onto film stock. As with a still image camera, using a scanner allows you to work at higher resolution, and with a larger colour gamut, than is possible with a video camera.

Figure 7.1. *Stop-frame animation captured to disk and combined with digital animation*

Digital Image Sequences

For drawn or painted animation you can dispense with the physical media and the digitization process entirely by using a graphics program to make your artwork. You can then save your work as a movie or as a sequence of image files. You can use the natural media brushes of recent versions of Photoshop or Painter to produce animation that looks (somewhat) as if it was produced with traditional materials, or you can take advantage of the pixel manipulating facilities of bitmapped image software to produce work with a characteristic digital look. Vector drawing programs can be used to create artwork with the appearance of certain traditional cartoon styles, with areas of flat colour and smooth lines. Frames created in this way may be rendered and saved as bitmapped images, as well as being used in vector animations in ways we will describe later.

Computer programs can provide some assistance with the labour of making image sequences for animation. Photoshop provides animation facilities based on layers (described in Chapter 4), which can be used in ways that mimic our earlier description of cel animation. Layers allow you to create separate parts of a still image – for example, a person and the background of a scene they are walking through – so that each can be altered or moved independently in a way similar to that described for traditional cel animation. The frames of an animated sequence can be made by combining a background layer, which remains static, with one or more animation layers, in which any changes that take place between frames are made.

Thus, to create an animation in a bitmapped image program that supports layers, you could begin by creating the background layer in the image for the first frame. Next, on separate layers, you create the elements that will move. (You may want to use additional static layers in between these moving layers if you need to create an illusion of depth.) After saving the first frame, you might begin the next by pasting the background layer from the first; then, you add the other layers, incorporating the changes that are needed for your animation.

Recent versions of Photoshop streamline this mode of working, by allowing you to maintain a sequence of frames in a single document. Each frame is a "layer comp", which is a configuration of all the layers in the document, recording each layer's position, visibility and transparency, and also any styles that may have been applied to it. An animation could be made by creating the image for each frame on its own layer, making that layer visible and all the others invisible in that frame. More often, though, a background layer and perhaps several other static layers would be made visible in all or some frames.

This identification of frames with layer configurations allows artwork to be reused. If an object appears in several frames, you just need to ensure that its layer is visible in those frames. Even if a layer cannot be reused as it is, it can be duplicated and modified if small changes are needed.

Where the motion in an animation is simple, it may only be necessary to reposition or transform the images on some of the layers. Figure 7.2 shows a few frames from an animation that illustrates this method of working. This particular animation was created from a single still photograph of a sailing boat on the sea. The boat was isolated on its own layer by a painstaking selection operation, and a hand-drawn wake was added to reinforce the impression of movement. Making the boat move across the sea was simply a matter of changing the position of its layer in each frame. The entire animation just consists of the two layers (background and boat), with the only changes recorded in the configurations for each frame being the positions of the layer with the boat. (For a more detailed account of how this animation was made, see Chapter 4 of *Digital Media Tools*.)

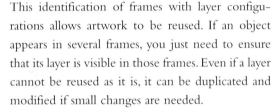

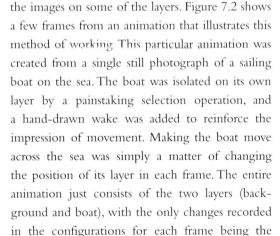

Figure 7.2. *Animation of a layer's position*

Several computer programs, including Photoshop and Flash (which we will describe in more detail later) let you open a movie and modify its individual frames or combine them with other artwork. This offers new possibilities. You can, for example, paint onto or otherwise alter original video material, which is one way of adding animation to live action.

Another option is to trace selected elements from a live-action video clip onto a new layer, one frame at a time, deleting the layers containing the original video images once tracing is complete. This process, whether achieved digitally or by older means, is what is properly referred to as *roto-scoping*, and it has long been used to create animation that accurately reproduces the forms and natural movements of people and animals. Once live-action footage has been traced in this way you can of course add additional animation or drawn backgrounds on additional layers. Rotoscoping by hand is an extremely laborious process, but Flash allows a similar operation to be performed semi-automatically by using its facility for tracing bitmaps.

IN DETAIL

Rotoscoping is named after the rotoscope, a device patented by Max Fleischer (creator of Betty Boop and the original animated Popeye) in 1915. Fleischer's device projected movie footage, one frame at a time, onto a light table, producing a back-projected still image over which the animator could place a sheet of animation paper. When the tracing of one frame was complete, the film was advanced to the next by means of a hand crank. Digital technology allows this same basic technique to be performed much more easily.

In computer graphics the process of painting onto existing video frames is sometimes called "rotoscoping", but this use of the term is inaccurate.

Sequences of image files provide a very flexible representation for working on an animation. Individual files can be opened in a graphics program to be altered. Single files (frames) can be removed from the sequence, replaced or added. The sequence can then be imported into a video editing application or Flash and converted into a movie.

Managing a collection of image files can become complicated, however, especially if you eventually want to import them into a video editing program. In order for this to be possible without tying you to particular software, the files' names must conform to some convention. For example, Premiere can only import a sequence of files if they are all in the same folder, and all the files' names have the same number of digits at the end, for example Animation001.psd, Animation002.psd, ... Animation449.psd. (Failure to provide the necessary leading zeroes will have consequences that you can probably guess at.) If you make any changes to the set of images, you must take care not to disturb the numbering, or to adjust it if necessary.

Flash also requires consistent sequential numbering. If there is a discontinuity in the sequence, only those files before the discontinuity will be imported. Flash will only import a very few image file formats (and it varies between platforms), so if you have saved your files in the wrong format it will be necessary to convert them before they can be imported.

Animated GIFs

Instead of using a set of still image files to hold an animation sequence, it is possible to use a single "image" file to hold many images. While a surprising number of file formats offer this facility (including, but not exclusively, formats intended for use with proprietary animation software), by far the most commonly used is GIF. The images in a GIF file can be displayed in order, so GIF provides a format for animation. In particular, GIF files' ability to store a sequence of images has been used to provide a cheap and cheerful form of animation (especially advertising) for millions of Web pages. Most Web browsers will display each image contained in a GIF file in turn when they load the file. Providing this happens fast enough, the images will be seen as an animation.

The GIF89a version of the format provides for some optional data items that control the behaviour of an *animated GIF*, as these files are called. In particular, a flag can be set to cause the animation to loop – either for a stipulated number of times or indefinitely – and a minimum delay between frames (and hence a frame rate of a sort) can be specified. The delay can be specified for each frame, allowing changes in frame rate. However, animated GIFs do not provide an entirely reliable way of adding animated features to Web pages. As with most aspects of a browser's behaviour, the way in which animated GIFs are displayed can be changed by users. Looping can be turned off, image loading can be disabled – with the result that animated GIFs will not appear – or all types of animation may be prevented. The primary advantage of animated GIFs is that they do not rely on any plug-in, or on the use of scripting (see Chapter 14), so they will be viewable using a wider range of browsers than other animation formats.

Several free or inexpensive utilities are available on the major platforms for combining a set of still images into a single animated GIF. Premiere and Flash allow you to save a movie in this form (though Flash does not always give a satisfactory result when exporting animated GIF), and animations made using Photoshop's layer animation facilities can be exported as animated GIFs direct from Photoshop. Dedicated Web graphics programs, such as Fireworks, can be used to create animated GIFs from scratch or by altering existing images. Potentially, therefore, GIF files can be used to store any form of animation, but in practice they are severely limited in the material for which they are appropriate.

Figure 7.3. *Original (top) and animated GIF (bottom) frames, suitable material*

Just like GIF still images, which we described in Chapter 4, animated GIFs use indexed colour and lossless LZW compression. The effect on image quality and file size depends on the nature of the material. Figure 7.3 shows two frames from a short animation which was originally created as vector graphics. The top pair of images are from the original Flash animation, the lower pair are from an animated GIF made from the vector graphics frames. As you can see, they are more or less indistinguishable. The very limited colour palette means that posterization is not a problem, and the smooth lines and flat coloured areas lend themselves well to lossless compression.

In contrast, Figure 7.4 shows how animation created from bitmapped images may be degraded by being turned into an animated GIF. This simple effect was created by fading the colour from a scanned watercolour painting (intended for the background to an animation) to greyscale over the course of 24 frames. Owing to the use of natural materials and traditional painting techniques, the original image has quite a wide palette (though not as wide as some painted images might have) with continuous colour and fine detail. The reduction to indexed colour therefore causes serious colour shifts over the course of the animation as well as significant posterization. The final frame in the sequence is purely greyscale in the original (shown third from the left on the top row), but in the animated GIF it has many coloured pixels. You can see the comparison in the blown-up details at the far right of Figure 7.4. Sampling of the colour of individual pixels across the image in this final frame of the animated GIF reveals that a large number of them are actually dull shades of many different hues, not shades of grey as they should be. As the coloured image fades over 24 frames, each frame has different colour values. There is no way that the small colour table available in a GIF can cope with the very large number of colours involved in the total animation.

Posterization is also very obvious in the animated GIF. You can see this in the blown-up details of the first frame in the sequence on the left of Figure 7.4. The subtle gradations of the original have been reduced to gross areas of flat colour, with loss of both detail and colour information.

Figure 7.4. *Original (top) and animated GIF (bottom) frames, unsuitable material*

The general problems resulting from the use of indexed colour are considerably exacerbated in the case of animations by the use of a single colour table for a whole set of images. The GIF file format does allow for the possibility of using separate colour tables for each frame, but this is rarely done because the extra space occupied by the additional colour tables adds significantly to the size of the file, which may already be large. Popular tools for creating animated GIFs, including Photoshop and Fireworks, do not offer the option of using individual colour tables at all.

Although lossless compression conserves quality it means large file sizes, and this prevents the use of animated GIF for extended animation sequences or for large-size frames. The actual saving achieved by compression depends on the material. For these two examples, the leaping dolphin of Figure 7.3 had a compression ratio of roughly 12.7, whereas the colour fade of Figure 7.4 had a ratio of 9.3. (Remember that simply converting to indexed colour immediately gives a compression ratio of just under 3.) Not only is GIF compression lossless, and therefore not able to discard redundant information, it does not perform any significant inter-frame compression.

A primitive form of inter-frame compression can be achieved in certain animated GIFs. It is possible to specify a "disposal method" for each frame – these include **Dispose** and **Do Not Dispose**. (These values are represented by a short field in the GIF file.) If the disposal method is **Dispose**, the pixels of each frame are discarded after being displayed, so each frame is shown independently. If the method is **Do Not Dispose**, though, the pixels are left on screen and the next frame is displayed on top of them. If this new frame contains transparent areas the preceding frame will show through them, so this allows a simple form of frame differencing to be employed.

As well as restricting the number of colours and providing poor compression, GIF animation has other drawbacks. You cannot add sound (though for many short animations this may not matter) and the user cannot control the playback, except by globally disabling all GIF animation. There is no way to provide player controls for an animated GIF or to interact with it in any way.

Even more seriously, the playback rate cannot be depended on. Usually, each frame of an animated GIF is displayed by the browser as it arrives. Network speeds mean that there may be excessive, and often irregular, delays between frames. This tends to make any frame rate that may be specified in the file irrelevant, as the animation is rarely actually displayed at that rate. However, if an animation is set to loop, once it has played through the first time it will have been copied into the browser's local cache (unless it is too big), and subsequent loops will play at a speed limited only by the user's processor and disk (which are completely unknown to the animator). In general, there is little chance of an animated GIF consistently playing back at a sufficiently high frame rate to give smooth animation unless it is small. Animated GIFs are not generally used for realistic animation, therefore, but for short, simple and often highly stylized sequences, especially advertising. Despite the popularity of Flash, many Web page advertisements are still in the form of animated GIFs.

> ### KEY POINTS
>
> **Animation is the creation of moving pictures one frame at a time.**
>
> **Traditional animators have developed many techniques, including cel animation, stop motion and claymation.**
>
> **Animation made using these techniques can be captured one frame at a time using a camera connected to a computer, instead of being recorded on film.**
>
> **Animation can be created digitally. Individual frames can be created in a graphics program. Using layer comps to represent the contents of a frame can streamline the animation process.**
>
> **A sequence of images can be stored in consecutively numbered image files, which can be imported into video editing programs or Flash.**
>
> **An animated GIF contains multiple bitmapped images in a single file. The individual images can be displayed in sequence by Web browsers and other programs, without the need for a plug-in.**
>
> **Animated GIFs are only suitable for short simple animations.**
>
> **Animated GIFs use indexed colour and lossless intra-frame compression, whose effectiveness depends on the nature of the images in the animation.**
>
> **Animated GIFs cannot have a soundtrack or player controls.**

Interpolation

During the 1930s and 1940s, the large American cartoon producers, led by Walt Disney, developed a mass production approach to animation. Central to this development was division of labour. Disney's approach to creating animations relied on breaking down the production of a sequence of drawings into sub-tasks, some of which, at least, could be performed by relatively unskilled staff. Disney was not entirely successful at de-skilling animation – character design, concept art, storyboards, tests, and some of the animation, always had to be done by experienced and talented artists. But when it came to the production of the final cels for a film, the role of skilled animators was largely confined to the creation of *key frames*.

We have met this expression already, in Chapter 6. In video compression, key frames are those which are stored in their entirety, while the frames in between them are stored as differences only. In traditional animation, the meaning has a slightly different twist: key frames are typically drawn by a "chief animator" to provide the pose and detailed characteristics of characters at important points in the animation. Usually, key frames occur at the extremes of a movement – the beginning and end of a walk, the top and bottom of a fall, and so on – which determine more or less completely what happens in between, but they may be used for any point which marks a significant change. The intermediate frames can then be drawn almost mechanically by "in-betweeners". Each chief animator could have several in-betweeners working with him[†] to multiply his productivity. (In addition, the tedious task of transferring drawings to cel and colouring them in was also delegated to subordinates.)

Interpolating Motion

In-betweening (which is what in-betweeners do) resembles what mathematicians call *interpolation*: the calculation of values of a function lying between known points. Interpolation is something that computer programs are very good at, providing the values to be computed and the relationship between them can be expressed numerically. Generally, the relationship between two key frames of a hand-drawn animation is too complex to be reduced to numbers in a way that is amenable to computer processing, but for some types of animation, interpolation provides considerable savings of labour.

Interpolation relies on having numerical values to interpolate. In other words, only properties that have a simple numerical representation can be interpolated. The differing characteristics of bitmapped images and vector graphics, which we have described in earlier chapters, mean that although interpolation can be used in animations stored in either form, the properties that can be interpolated will be different.

Since bitmaps do not contain identifiable objects, the use of layers to isolate different elements of an animation is essential if we wish to change them independently. The analogy with cel animations is more or less complete – each layer is like a transparent sheet of acetate with something painted on it. Layers can be moved independently, so an animation can be constructed by placing different elements on different layers, and moving or altering the layers between frames. Where the movement or alteration is easily described algorithmically, it can be interpolated between key frames, just as in-betweeners interpolate between a chief animator's key frames. Typically, between key frames a layer may be moved to a different position, rotated or scaled. These geometrical transformations are easily interpolated, but since we are now concerned with bitmapped images they may require resampling, and consequently cause a loss of image quality, as we explained in Chapter 4. It is also possible to interpolate the values of the parameters of effects that may be applied to layers, so that the intensity of an effect or filter can be made to vary over time. We will demonstrate how time-varying effects may be used later.

In the case of vector animations, we do have identifiable objects, and their properties are represented entirely numerically. This makes interpolating the position, size, colour and other properties of vector objects conceptually and practically easier than interpolating bitmaps. Furthermore,

---

† *This "him" is not a casual slip: the big studios of those days almost always relegated women to mundane work.*

applying transformations to these properties does not necessitate any resampling and consequent loss of image quality.

Although there are many different properties that can be made to vary and interpolated, and these properties and the effects that can be achieved by varying them may be different according to whether we are dealing with vectors or bitmaps, the process of interpolation may be considered in the abstract since it is carried out on numbers, not on the physical properties they represent. To make the description more concrete, though, we will begin by considering interpolating position – which might be the position of a layer in a bitmapped image or of an object in a vector graphic.

The simplest form of interpolation is linear. If we just consider interpolating motion in a straight line, linear interpolation causes an object (or layer) to move an equal distance between each frame, the distance moved per frame being the total distance between the object's positions in the starting and ending key frames, divided by the number of frames in the sequence. Several programs that can be used for animation, including Photoshop, Flash and After Effects, are able to perform such interpolation for you. We have already seen a simple example of this in Figure 7.2.

The sailing boat in Figure 7.2 is an example of linear interpolation applied to the position of a layer. The illustration in the book may misleadingly suggest a small animation, but actually the frames shown are 30 frames apart, because sailing boats move slowly, and the entire animation, during which the boat crosses the picture, is 600 frames long. For each frame, the position of the boat's layer must be changed. The speed of the boat is constant, so the difference is always the same and easily computed: it is one six-hundredth of the complete distance travelled.

Photoshop can interpolate such linear changes. In the simple animation illustrated in Figure 7.2, the boat layer was positioned manually in the first and last frames, and then a single command was used to construct all the intermediate frames. However, only the few layer properties that are stored in a frame can be interpolated by Photoshop, and only simple linear changes are possible. In this example, linear interpolation works well, because the boat is already moving when it comes into the frame, and continues to move out of it. The resulting constant velocity is suitable for a sedate sailing boat. In general, though, linear interpolation is inadequate in two ways.

First, if the motion occurs entirely while the object is within the frame, it begins and ends instantaneously, with objects attaining their full velocity as soon as they start to move, and maintaining full velocity until they stop. Nothing really moves in that way. To produce a more natural movement, programs that implement interpolated motion borrow a technique from traditional handmade animation: the transition from stasis to movement is made more gradual by using smaller, slowly increasing, increments between the first few frames (i.e. the object accelerates from a

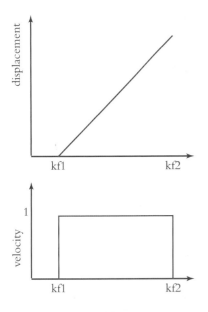

Figure 7.5. *Linearly interpolated motion*

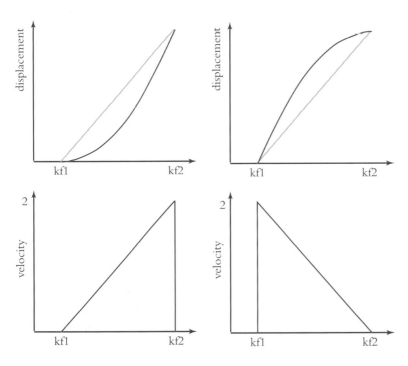

Figure 7.6. *Quadratic easing in (left) and out (right)*

standstill to its final velocity), a process referred to as ***easing in***. The converse process of deceleration is called ***easing out***.

Figure 7.5 illustrates the way in which the horizontal displacement (x coordinate) and horizontal component of the velocity of an object change with time when it is moved from an initial position in key frame 1 (kf1) of (0,0) to a final position in key frame 2 (kf2) of (50,50), using linear interpolation over 50 frames. Figure 7.6 shows how the change might be modified when the motion is eased in or out – we have shown a style of easing that uses quadratic interpolation, that is, the acceleration is constant. More complicated styles are possible and might be preferred.

Flash provides a simple interface for quadratic interpolation. (It also provides a more complex interface for more elaborate styles of interpolation.) When applying easing the animator can set the degree of easing using a slider that moves from maximum easing in, through a constant velocity, to maximum easing out. In effect, this moves the displacement curve from one like that shown at the top of Figure 7.6, via similar curves with less pronounced bulge, through Figure 7.5 and beyond to the lower curve in Figure 7.6 (That is, the acceleration goes from some maximum positive value, through zero, to a maximum negative value.)

The second problem with linear interpolation can be seen in Figure 7.7. This shows how displacement and velocity change if we now append to our original sequence a second one of 50 frames, during which our object moves from its position in kf2 of (50,50) to a new position at (75,75) in kf3. Because each sequence is interpolated separately as a straight line, there is a sharp discontinuity at kf2. As the velocity graph clearly shows, this will appear as a sudden deceleration at that point in the animation. Again, this is an unnatural sort of movement, which will only occasionally be what is desired.

It would be possible to smooth out this abruptness using quadratic easing and some clever manipulation of the easing slider, but a more general solution to the problem is available. In Chapter 3 we stressed that the most attractive property of Bézier curves is that they can be joined together smoothly by aligning their tangent vectors. By using Bézier curves instead of straight lines to interpolate between key frames, smooth motion can be achieved. Note that we do not mean that objects should follow Bézier-shaped paths, but that the rate at which their properties change should be interpolated using a Bézier curve.

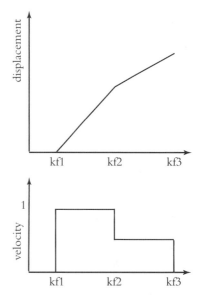

Figure 7.7. *Abrupt change of velocity caused by linear interpolation*

The usual way of providing Bézier interpolation is by way of an interface that presents a graph, similar to the displacement graphs of Figures 7.5 to 7.7, showing how the interpolated value changes over time, and allowing the user to modify the curve by manipulating Bézier control points. By allowing new points to be added, and supporting both smooth points and corner points, this facility can be extended to allow the rate of change of interpolated values to be adjusted in arbitrary ways. Such arbitrary curves may be considered as a generalization of easing in and out. If we use Bézier curves to control the interpolation we can implement easing not only at the beginning and end of interpolated motion, but through any point in between.

Figure 7.8 shows an example. The two graphic objects represent a pair of cogs, moving in interlocked rotation. They can be made to rotate at a uniform rate simply by interpolating their angles of rotation. This creates the impression of a smoothly spinning mechanism, but we wanted something more jerky, suggestive of an old-fashioned complex mechanism. The intention was that the smaller cog should move fairly slowly as the point of the larger one touches it, as if some resistance had to be overcome. It then jerks forward rapidly, and bounces back slightly before settling into position for the next movement. Custom easing was used to modify the interpolation curve of the rotation, in order to produce the desired pattern of motion. The entire sequence loops, so the start and end points are arbitrary. The sequence of frames shown in Figure 7.8 begins with this backward jerk and ends with the rapid forward movement. (You can find a more extended description of how this animation was created, and an explanation of how the motion of the two cogs was matched, in Chapter 6 of *Digital Media Tools*.)

Figure 7.8. *Non-linearly interpolated rotation*

Motion Paths

Objects whose motion is interpolated normally move in straight lines, whether or not you modify the rate of change using easing. Making an object (or a layer) follow a path with a more complex shape by piecing together straight line segments is laborious and inefficient. To make this sort of motion more convenient, programs that support interpolation usually let you create **motion paths**, that is, Bézier paths along which objects or layers can be made to move.

The precise way in which you set up a motion path varies between programs, but the principle is the same no matter what software you use. The path is associated with a sequence of frames during which some motion is interpolated. When the interpolation is performed, the intermediate locations of the moving object are made to lie on the path instead of on a straight line. Usually, there is an option to orient the object to the motion path, as illustrated in Figure 7.9.

Figure 7.9. *Fixed orientation (left) and orientation to the motion path (right)*

Orientation is essential when animating certain types of object whose movements would look totally artifical if they remained oriented in the same direction all the time. Imagine a truck, for example, starting out to climb the hill at the beginning of the path shown in Figure 7.9. The front of the truck would point up the hill, and its wheels would be parallel to the ground. If the truck is not oriented to the path, the front of the truck will still be pointing up in the air to the right and its wheels will be out in mid-air as it descends the hill on the steep downward slope. The way in which any particular object should be oriented of course depends on the nature of the object itself.

Figure 7.10 shows an example of a simple animation that uses a motion path. When the animation plays, the ball shoots into the frame from low down on the left-hand side as though it has been kicked high in the air, rises to a maximum height, then falls and bounces several more times before rolling out of the right-hand edge of the frame.

This was achieved by drawing a motion path, shown overlaid on the image at the top of Figure 7.10. (The drawn path is just a guide, and is not visible when the animation plays, of course.) Notice that the path begins and ends in the grey area which lies outside

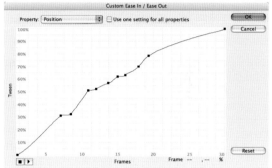

Figure 7.10. *Interpolating motion along a path*

the animation frame. To make the motion seem more convincing, the motion path was combined with custom easing (shown in the lower part of Figure 7.10), which alters the ball's velocity as it bounces. Finally, a rotation was applied to the ball, so that it appears to be rolling as the bounces become small.

When motion paths and custom easing are used in this way, it is usually with the intention of creating an illusion of motion which is sufficient for an animation, but which is not necessarily an accurate representation of how a ball bounces in the real world. The relative heights of the bounces and the variation in velocity in the animation are determined by eye, considering only the appearance of the ball in motion, not the physics of elastic collisions. (In cartoons unnatural or exaggerated effects are often produced deliberately, of course, to enhance comic effect.) It is possible to create much more physically accurate animations of moving objects by applying equations of motion to compute their positions in each frame based on the way the positions vary with time under the influence of gravity, impacts, and so on. This sort of animation must be done by using scripting to compute the positions and control the motion of the objects, but such a specialized application of scripting is beyond the scope of this book.

KEY POINTS

In traditional cel animation, chief animators draw key frames at important points in the animation, and in-betweeners create the intervening frames.

Animation programs perform the equivalent of in-betweening by interpolating the values of properties such as position between key frames.

Interpolation can be applied to layers in bitmapped images or to properties of vector objects.

If motion is interpolated linearly, movement begins and ends instantaneously, and there may be unnatural discontinuities between interpolated sequences.

Easing in and out can be used to cause the motion to increase or decrease gradually.

Custom easing using Bézier curves is used to control the rate of change in arbitrarily complex ways.

Objects or layers can be made to move along motion paths.

When using motion paths, it is usually necessary to orient the moving object to the path to achieve a realistic effect.

Vector Animation in Flash

As we explained earlier, the representation of vector images as numbers is much simpler than that of bitmapped images, making them more amenable to numerical interpolation of more properties. The interpolation can be applied to vector objects, instead of to complete layers as it must be in the case of bitmaps. To be more precise, the transformations that can be applied to vector shapes – translation, rotation, scaling, reflection and shearing – are arithmetical operations that can be interpolated. Thus, movement that consists of a combination of these operations can be efficiently generated by a process of numerical in-betweening starting from a pair of key frames.

The efficiency with which interpolation can be performed on vector objects makes it feasible to carry out the interpolation at the time an animation is displayed. When interpolation is performed on animations made from bitmapped images – as it is in Photoshop or After Effects, for example – the program creates new bitmapped images to serve as the interpolated frames between the key frames. If the animation is then saved in some video format these frames will be compressed, but in essence, the entire image contained in each interpolated frame is stored explicitly in the animation, just as though it had been created by hand.

In contrast, when the motion of a vector object is interpolated in a vector graphics animation program such as Flash, the intermediate frames only contain instructions about how the various parameters defining the properties of the object should be computed in each frame. The representation of the object itself only occurs in the key frames. Thus, vector animations that use interpolation can be extremely compact.

At present, Flash movies – also known as SWF files – are the most popular Web animation format, with Adobe Flash normally being used to create them (although other programs can also export SWF files). Flash is fundamentally a vector-based program, although as we saw in earlier chapters, bitmapped images may be embedded in Flash movies, and video can be streamed by way of the Flash Player. If neither of these facilities is used, though, a Flash movie is a pure vector animation, which has very low bandwidth requirements. It is for this reason that Flash first achieved popularity on the Web, at a time when most Internet access was through slow connections.

Flash is more than an animation program. It supports a powerful scripting language called ActionScript, which makes it possible to add interactivity to animations, create movement by scripting, and build Web applications with user interfaces created in Flash. We will return to these aspects of Flash in Chapter 14. Here we will just give a very short introduction to its animation facilities. More details can be found in Chapter 6 of *Digital Media Tools*.

The Timeline and Stage

When an animation is created in Flash it is organized using a ***timeline***, a graphical representation of a sequence of frames, similar to the timeline in video editing applications. Animations can be built up one frame at a time by inserting key frames into the timeline sequentially. (Note that in Flash CS4 the term "key frame" is not always used in the way we use it here. However, we will continue to refer to any frame in which content is created explicitly, or which forms the start or end point of an interpolated sequence, as a key frame.)

Flash's ***stage*** is a sub-window in which frames are created by drawing or manipulating objects. Objects can be created on the stage using some built-in drawing tools, or they can be imported from Illustrator, which provides a more comprehensive set of drawing tools. Bitmapped images, in formats including PSD (Photoshop), JPEG and PNG, may also be imported and "traced" to make vector objects. Bitmapped images can be embedded in a Flash frame, but they add to the size of the animation and cannot be transformed without potentially degrading the image.

Extensive support is provided for text; characters in outline fonts can be decomposed into their component outline paths, which can be edited or animated separately. Layers can be used to organize the elements of a frame; they also play a key role in interpolating motion. Figure 7.11 shows the stage and timeline. The stage can be larger than the movie's frame size, as it is here (the background image of foliage fills the actual frame), so that objects, such as this creature, can be positioned outside the frame to move into it as the movie plays.

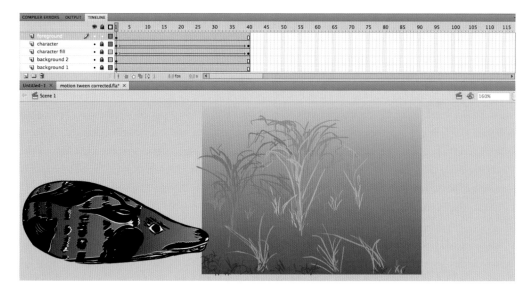

Figure 7.11. *The timeline (top) and stage (below) in a simple Flash movie*

The Flash interface also contains a toolbox containing the vector drawing tools, and a host of panels for colour mixing, alignment, applying transformations, setting typographic options, and so on. These facilities are crude compared with those of a program like Illustrator, however.

When a movie is first created in Flash, it contains a single empty key frame. If a key frame is added to the timeline immediately after an existing key frame, it starts out with a copy of the contents of the preceding key frame. Since most animation sequences only have small changes between frames, an efficient way of working on animations created one frame at a time is by adding key frames incrementally at the end of the current sequence and making changes to their contents. To assist with this, Flash provides an *onion-skinning* facility. When this is turned on, several preceding frames are displayed semi-transparently under the current frame – the number displayed can be chosen to fit the requirements of the work. This makes it easier to see the changes between frames and to align objects correctly. Frames beyond the current one can also be displayed, which is helpful when adjusments are being made to frames that have already been drawn.

As well as key frames, the timeline can also hold simple frames. These contain no objects of their own; when the movie is played back, they continue to display the contents of the most recent key frame. That is, they hold on the key frame. You can add frames and key frames independently to different layers, so one layer may hold a static background image for the duration of the movie, with moving elements on layers above it. The background layer will have just one key frame at the beginning, while the moving layers will have key frames at every point where an object moves. This may be every single frame. In the animation whose timeline is shown in Figure 7.11, the background is built out of two layers which are held, while a third static layer, containing several small plants in the foreground, is placed on top of the layers for the creature, which will therefore appear to move behind the plants (as illustrated in Figure 7.13).

Symbols and Tweening

Graphical objects can be stored in a library in a special form called a *symbol*, which allows them to be reused. Any object (or set of grouped objects) that has been drawn on the stage can be turned into a symbol, using a menu command. Subsequently, multiple instances of a symbol may be placed on the stage. They will all be fundamentally identical, but transformations can be applied, to change the size and orientation of each instance. The transparency and tinting of each instance can also be set independently. Instances remain linked to the symbol, so if the symbol is altered, every instance is automatically altered too, but transformations and so on that may have been applied to each instance are preserved. Figure 7.12 shows how the creature from Figure 7.11 can be multiplied by turning it into a symbol, placing several instances of it on the stage and applying different transformations to each instance.

Since interpolated animations, almost by definition, reuse objects, interpolating (or *tweening*, as Flash calls it) can only be applied to symbols. Although the precise methods of creating a tween in Flash vary between versions of the software, it remains the case that in principle the procedure for creating interpolated motion in Flash consists of creating a symbol, positioning it as required in key frames at the beginning and end of the sequence to be tweened, and instructing Flash to interpolate the motion between those key frames. (The details of how this is done are in *Digital Media Tools*.) Easing can then be applied to the tweened motion.

Flash CS4 distinguishes between "classic tweening" and "motion tweening", but this is simply to accommodate the features of Flash's earlier version of motion tweening ("classic tweening") together with the newer one. In a "classic tween", the tween is indicated on the timeline with an arrow between the two key frames, as you can see in Figure 7.11, where the two character layers have had a very simple tween applied in order to move the creature across the screen in a straight line, as shown in Figure 7.13. (The figure only shows every fifth frame of the animation.)

Figure 7.12. *Instances of a symbol*

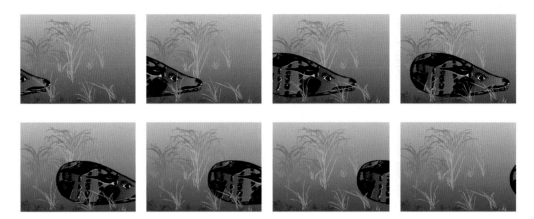

Figure 7.13. *Simple tweened motion of a symbol instance*

Although the process we have described may be referred to as "motion tweening", an object's size, orientation, opacity and colour can also be interpolated in the same way. Tweening can be applied to different layers in Flash, with key frames in different places, allowing the independent animation of many symbols, each of which may be part of a single character. Motion paths may be used, and custom easing can be applied to each tweened layer independently. As well as motion tweening, Flash also supports **shape tweening** – or **morphing**, as it is often known. This is a form of interpolation where the shapes of graphical objects are transformed between key frames – for example, a square could be turned into a circle. Morphing can be used to create a more organic style of animation, but it is much less efficient than motion tweening.

We have referred to "symbols" generically, but there are, in fact, three different sorts of symbol in Flash. **Graphic symbols** are simply reusable vector objects; they are the most suitable type to use for motion tweening, if that is all you need to do with them. **Movie clip symbols** are self-contained animations with their own timelines, that play within the main movie. Instances of movie clip symbols, usually just referred to as movie clips, can be controlled by scripts, as we will describe in Chapter 14. This opens the way to types of interactive animation that cannot be achieved in conventional media. **Button symbols** were a specialized type of symbol, used for adding interactivity to Flash movies, but they have now been superseded by UI components (see Chapters 12 and 14).

Both graphic symbols and movie clip symbols may contain several frames, making either suitable for creating repeated animated elements. The differences are that graphic symbols cannot be controlled by scripts, and always play in synchronization with the main movie, whereas movie clips play asynchronously. For example, a movie clip will carry on playing when the main movie is stopped. This means that animations that use them cannot be exported to video.

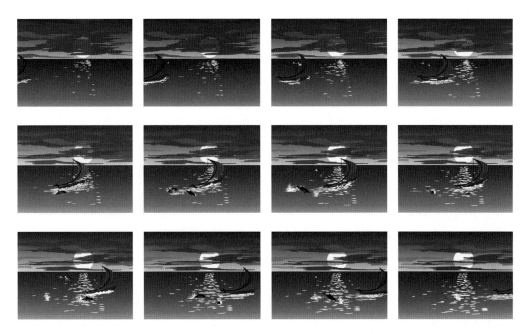

Figure 7.14. *An animation that uses animated symbols*

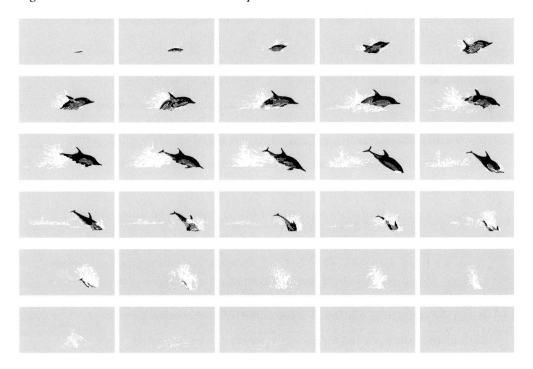

Figure 7.15. *The frames of an animated symbol of a leaping dolphin (superimposed on grey for clarity)*

Figure 7.14 illustrates how animated symbols can be used to create more complex compositions out of simple elements. The dolphins leaping out of the water were added to a basic animation of the boat, sea and clouds by creating a symbol from an animation of a single dolphin jumping, shown in Figure 7.15. Instances of this single dolphin symbol were combined to make two more symbols, comprising schools of two and three dolphins, whose leaps were synchronized differently so that it should not be obvious that the animated elements are repeated. Instances of these symbols were then placed on the stage at different points in the timeline, so that the dolphins leap out of the water at different points in the animation. In order to create the complete animation, the composition had to be built out of many layers, with shape and motion tweening used as well as animated symbols.

KEY POINTS

Flash movies, also known as SWF files, are the most popular Web animation format. They are usually created in Flash, but SWFs may also be exported from other programs.

An animation being created in Flash is organized using a timeline.

The vector objects used in the animation are created on the stage, using conventional vector drawing tools and techniques.

Onion-skinning can be used to help align and change objects in consecutive frames.

Key frames are drawn in their entirety on the stage. Ordinary frames have no content, they just hold the picture from the preceding key frame.

Graphical objects can be stored in a library as symbols. Instances of symbols can be created on the stage, allowing objects to be reused. Instances can be transformed independently and have different visual effects applied to them.

Interpolation ("tweening") is applied to symbol instances.

Easing can be applied to tweened motion.

An object's size, orientation, opacity and colour may also be interpolated.

Shape tweening ("morphing") is used to transform one shape into another.

There are three sorts of symbol in Flash. Graphic symbols are reusable vector objects. Movie clip symbols are self-contained animations with their own timelines, that play within the main movie and can be controlled by scripts. Button symbols have now been superseded by UI components.

Both graphic symbols and movie clip symbols can be animated.

Motion Graphics

The results that can be achieved using tweening and symbols together with interpolated effects that vary over time make this kind of animation particularly well suited to the creation of animated graphic design, or **motion graphics**. Many of the techniques used in motion graphics first appeared in title sequences for feature films, where they frequently involved animation of – or around – text.

After Effects has been the leading desktop application for animation of this kind for some time, although Flash now offers better support for motion graphics than previously, and the animation facilities in recent versions of Photoshop can also be used.

┌─IN DETAIL───┐

Because of their shared provenance, After Effects works well in conjunction with Photoshop and Illustrator. A Photoshop image can be imported into After Effects, with all its layers – including adjustment layers – and alpha channels intact. An Illustrator drawing can be imported and rasterized, again with its layers intact. A common mode of working, therefore, is to use the tools and facilities of Photoshop or Illustrator to prepare the elements of an animation on separate layers, and import the result into After Effects where the layers are animated.

└───┘

The simplest animations are made by repositioning layers, either by dragging them or by entering coordinates, and interpolating motion between key frames. As we showed earlier, this can be used to move objects in a stylized manner. By combining layers and adding effects and filters that also vary over time, moving graphic designs are obtained. The countdown sequence shown in Figure 7.16 was made by importing a set of still images into After Effects and animating them in this way. Apart from the interpolated motion of the complete bitmaps, no moving elements were used.

Interpolation can be applied to other properties of a layer. In particular, its angle can be varied, so that it appears to rotate. Angles may be set by hand in key frames and interpolated, or the rotation may be determined automatically in conjunction with movement, to maintain the orientation of a layer with respect to its motion path. Scaling, which may be used as a perspective effect to convey the impression of approaching or receding movement – or as a zoom in or out – can also be set in key frames and interpolated.

After Effects supports both linear and Bézier interpolation, in both space and time. As we mentioned previously, linear interpolation leads to abrupt changes, whereas with Bézier interpolation the changes are smooth. Both forms of interpolation can be applied to position. This alters

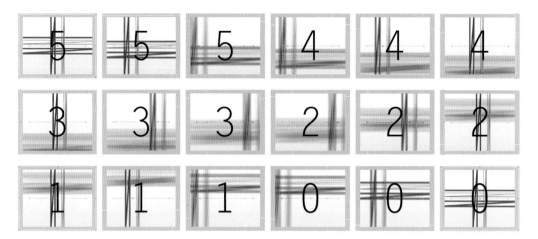

Figure 7.16. *Simple motion graphics*

the path followed by a layer. Layers whose position is linearly interpolated follow a jagged path made up of line segments, while those whose position is calculated using Bézier interpolation will follow smooth curves.

Linear and Bézier interpolation may also be used to affect the rate of change of position with respect to time. Again, this may be linear, with a constant velocity and instantaneous starting and stopping, as discussed earlier in connection with Flash, or Bézier, where the acceleration is smooth. The temporal and spatial interpolation methods are independent – you can use linear temporal interpolation with Bézier motion paths, and vice versa.

The degree of control over the interpolation of these spatial properties offered by After Effects is considerable. Using a conventional Bézier pen tool, the graphs showing how a value varies with time may be redrawn by hand. Key frames are inserted automatically when control points are added to the graph. Absolute values may be entered numerically, allowing complete control over positioning and the rate of movement. Nevertheless, the type of motion that can be produced by interpolating the position, angle and size of a single layer is restricted. Objects appear to move as a whole, with an unrealistic gliding motion. Key frame animation of bitmapped images is there-fore more frequently used for stylized motion. A popular application is the animation of text. Individual characters or words can be placed on layers and animated, just like any other layer, or text may be placed on a path, as in Illustrator, and then moved along that path over time.

As our countdown example shown in Figure 7.16 demonstrates, bitmapped representation allows other properties of the image besides its position, angle and size to be altered over time. So, in addition to geometrical transformations, more radical time-based alterations of the layers can be achieved. As we described in Chapter 4, bitmapped images can be treated with many different

Figure 7.17. *Time-varying colour adjustments*

effects and filters. Most of these filters have parameters, such as the radius of a Gaussian blur, or the brightness of glowing edges. Such parameters can be made to change over time, using the same mechanism of interpolation between key frames which is used for interpolating motion. This allows some unique effects to be generated.

In After Effects, all the controls we have just described for managing interpolation of position and velocity can also be applied to filters and effects. Alternatively, an image can be adjusted by hand in each frame. Figure 7.17 shows some frames from an animation that was produced in Photoshop by making hue and saturation adjustments to a selected part of an image (the flower). As we explained earlier, in Photoshop a frame of animation is stored as a layer comp. In this case, the image was copied onto 30 layers, just one of which was visible in each frame. A saved alpha channel was used to isolate the central flower on each layer, and the adjustment to hue and saturation was then made to the selected area. The result is a looping sequence (it reverses after the frames shown here) during which the flower's colour gently changes and returns to its original state. This animation could not have been produced by interpolation in Photoshop, because only layer properties can be interpolated in that program.

As well as simply varying the parameters of still image filters and effects over time, and applying time-varying adjustments to images, you can also apply new effects which only become possible

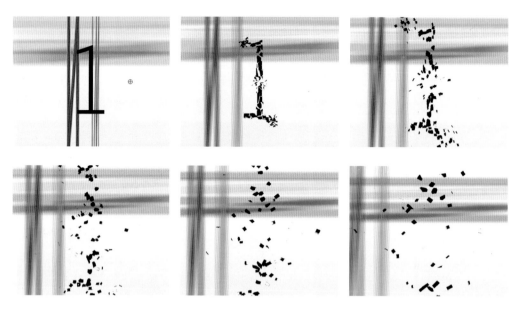

Figure 7.18. *A purely temporal effect*

when a temporal dimension is added to images. Figure 7.18 shows part of an alternative version of the countdown animation, with a shatter effect applied to the numerals.

We have stressed the use of bitmapped images for motion graphics, because they offer the most expressive possibilities as well as a different way of working with bitmaps, but effective motion graphics can of course be created with vector objects too.

KEY POINTS

Motion graphics is animated graphic design.

After Effects is the leading desktop application for creating motion graphics, and offers the most sophisticated controls.

Simple motion graphics can be achieved by repositioning and altering other properties of the layers of a bitmapped image independently.

Layers may be moved along motion paths.

Interpolation may be used to control the rate of change of properties as well as their values.

Parameters of filters and effects may be interpolated.

Purely time-based effects, such as shattering, may be applied.

Delivering Animation

The three predominant formats for delivering digital animation are animated GIF, Flash (SWF) and video. So far in this chapter, we have only described the first two of these, which are specifically animation formats, but for some purposes video may be a better option.

If an animation is destined to be played back on a television, either from a broadcast signal or from DVD, it must be saved as video. The codec, frame rate, frame size, and so on will be determined by the standards of the medium, and there is little scope for choice.

If animation is to be delivered over the Internet or in some medium intended to be played back on a computer, any of the three main formats – GIF, Flash (SWF) or video – could be used, with no intrinsic constraints on their parameters, such as frame rate, aspect ratio, etc. An animation can be delivered in any of these formats, no matter how it was created, although some combinations of creation method and delivery format are more straightforward than others. Each format has its own advantages and drawbacks.

Animation on Video

There is nothing about digital video formats – such as QuickTime, WMV or FLV – that requires the material to originate from a video camera photographing live action. Digital video is just data representing a sequence of images and it doesn't matter how those images were created, as long as there is a route for converting them to a video format. Traditionally, animation could only be presented on film and then on analogue video. Despite the fact that animation is now comprised of digital images, it still often makes sense to deliver it as (digital) video.

Video is made up of bitmapped images. Any animation that takes the form of bitmapped images can be efficiently stored as video. In particular, frame-grabbed animation sequences that are longer than just a few frames lend themselves well to being converted to video. Thus any animation made in a traditional manner – cel, stop-motion, and so on – will often be best delivered as video. If the frames are grabbed using a video camera, the animation will start out in a video format, but even if a still camera or scanner is used, conversion to video is simple.

Video has numerous advantages over animated GIF files. Video allows for millions of colours (24-bit colour), as opposed to the maximum of 256 colours available in an animated GIF, and all video formats allow a synchronized soundtrack to be added to the picture. Video compression using the sophisticated algorithms we described in Chapter 6 is far more effective than the lossless intra-frame compression used in animated GIFs, and video is usually displayed with player controls, enabling the user to stop and start the animation.

In addition, once you have captured an animation sequence and saved it as QuickTime or FLV, for example, what you have is just video, so you can edit it, apply effects, combine it with other clips including live action, and stream it from a server or embed it in a Web page, just like any other video.

However, animation may differ from other types of video in ways which affect how it should be compressed. Certain styles of hand-drawn animation feature simplified shapes and areas of flat colour. (This is not always the case – the characteristics of the images depend on the individual animator's style.) Material of this type will usually be more amenable to lossless compression than other types of video. QuickTime's Animation codec is designed to take advantage of the characteristics of simple cartoon-style drawn animation. Compression is based on run-length encoding (RLE – see Chapter 4), and it is lossless when the codec is used at its highest quality setting. There is also a lossy mode that can be used to achieve higher compression ratios if necessary. Because it is based on RLE, this codec can compress areas of flat colour particularly well.

Photographing drawings, paintings, or models on miniature sets will result in images that have the same characteristics as photographs, with continuous tonal variation. Even though the motion in animation is an illusion, its representation in the sequence of digital images has the same properties as real motion, so inter-frame compression based on motion prediction will be effective. For animation of this type, the same considerations apply to the choice of codec as they do with live-action, so H.264/AVC or WMV 9 would be appropriate.

For animation saved as video – just as with live-action video – playback on a computer requires the use of components of a video architecture, such as QuickTime or Windows Media. Use of a browser plug-in to play it back has the same problems with browser incompatibilities, and the proprietary codecs may have licence restrictions. These problems apply to video in general and are not specific to animation, but the fact that in this case the video contains animation rather than live action does nothing to avoid them.

Comparison of Animation Formats

For vector-based animation there is no real competition to Flash at the present time. It may be that if you insist on using Web standard technology, are a programmer and don't mind that your animation won't play in Internet Explorer, you might prefer SVG or canvas animation, but Flash's only drawback as a delivery medium is the need for a proprietary plug-in. However, it is estimated that the Flash Player plug-in is installed in over 90% of browsers, which is a higher proportion of browsers than correctly implement all the current Web standards. It is thus only when considering delivery of bitmapped animation for some device other than television (or projection in a cinema, which does not concern us here) that there is a real choice to be made.

We described the principal characteristics of the animated GIF format earlier. To recap: animated GIF does not need a plug-in, but it is limited to 256 colours, only compresses well if the subject matter is simple, and it cannot be controlled by the user or have sound. You would not normally use an animated GIF, therefore, unless you did not want to rely on a plug-in or impose its over-head, and your animation had areas of flat colour and simple lines. These visual characteristics are typical of vector drawing, so it is often better to stick with vectors and deliver animations of this sort in Flash.

As we saw in our earlier comparison (see Figures 7.3 and 7.4), animated GIFs do not work well on material with a rich visual texture and a large number of colours. For animations of this sort, Flash or video would be better. The Flash movie format is essentially a vector format (as described below), so although it can handle bitmapped graphics as embedded objects, it is not usually the best choice from a technical point of view. Despite this, however, animators who are used to working with natural media and therefore prefer bitmapped images to vector graphics, often capture animation frames via camera or scanner but then use Flash nevertheless, because it is a convenient and popular way of delivering animation, especially on the Web.

Bitmapped images in Flash movies are usually compressed individually using JPEG, so the considerations we discussed in Chapter 4 apply. The quality and hence the amount of compression can be specified, but because animation may consist of a large number of bitmapped images which are required to play back in rapid succession in a short period of time over relatively low bandwidth, it is necessary to use significantly more compression than would normally be used for a single image to be delivered over the same network. Over-compression will produce visible artefacts and hard lines will tend to be softened. The powerful inter-frame compression of modern video codecs will generally produce better quality and smaller files.

The results obtained by saving the colour-fade animation we showed earlier in the three major formats for bitmapped animation are illustrated in Figure 7.19, which shows magnified details of three frames in each format. We chose H.264/AVC for the video codec because of its perform-ance and because recent versions of the Flash Player plug-in can play video compressed by this codec, so the availability of a plug-in is no more of a problem than it is for actual Flash movies.

General conclusions should not be drawn from a single example, but in this case the results are entirely in line with what one would predict. For this bitmapped image animation, video compressed with H.264/AVC is the best representation – it is smallest, produces the best image quality and can be played by the Flash Player plug-in as well as QuickTime and other video players. However, as you can see from the figure, there is a soft blurriness about the image which is typical of this type of video compression and which is not present in the original bitmapped image (see Figure 7.4).

In comparison, at the quality setting used for this example (medium), the JPEG-compressed Flash movie (SWF) clearly exhibits the blocks typical of JPEG compression. These artefacts would be reduced by increasing the quality, but that would result in a bigger file, which in return might result in jerky playback over some bandwidths. The video version is compressed to a smaller size even than a medium-quality SWF, and such compression artefacts as there are in the video are less intrusive.

We have shown the animated GIF illustrated in Figure 7.4 again at this magnification for comparison with the other formats. The image quality is clearly inferior – not only to the original source material but also to the other animation formats – and you can see obvious posterization and colour shifts, while at the same time the file size is the largest of the three in our example.

If the same animation were stored as a sequence of uncompressed images, it would occupy a little under 5.3 MB, however, so all three formats offer substantial compression.

The Flash representation does have one characteristic, however, that may override all other considerations in some cases. Flash movies are supremely scriptable. The programmatic control offered goes far beyond the simple play, stop, rewind, fast-forward and stepping controls of a video player (and the complete absence of control over an animated GIF). Using scripts, an animation can be presented in novel interactive ways that are not possible with other formats. We will describe some of these possibilities in Chapter 12 and show how they may be implemented in Chapter 14. For interactive animation, the possibilities offered by Flash will often outweigh the relatively poor quality and compression ratios it achieves, even for bitmapped animations.

The Flash Movie Format

The Flash movie file format is designed to be an efficient way to deliver animation over a network. It is a compressed binary representation (see Chapter 2), not intended to be read by people or imported into other graphics programs. The nature of vector drawing and tweening permits a compact representation of most animations in this format.

A Flash movie file begins with a header which defines such things as the frame size and frame rate. This is followed by a sequence of tagged data blocks, each of which begins with a code, called a tag, identifying its purpose. Tags are divided into two broad classes: definition tags and control tags. The former are used in data blocks to represent the objects, including shapes, characters, bitmapped images and symbols, used in an animation. When a data block with a definition tag is encountered by the Flash Player as it reads the movie file, the definition is copied into a dictionary, from which it can be retrieved. Each definition includes a short identifier, which is used to refer to it in other data blocks.

H.264/AVC Video, best
quality: 212 kB

SWF, JPEG, medium quality:
388 kB

Animated GIF: 580 kB

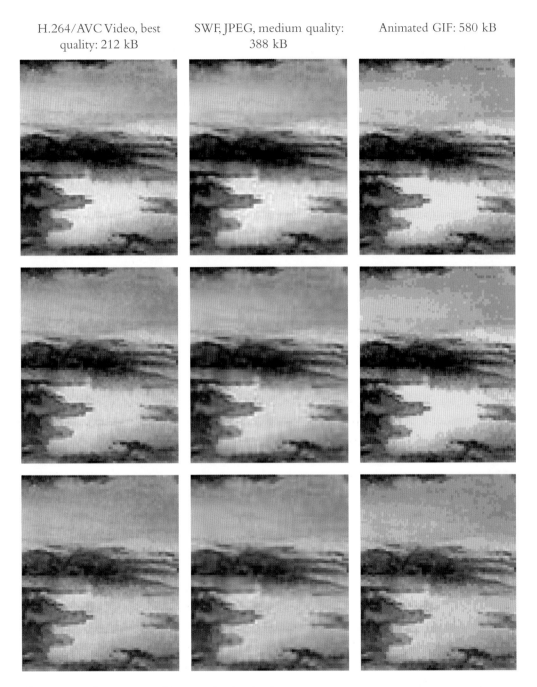

Figure 7.19. *A comparison of bitmapped animation formats*

Control tags are used to place, remove or move an object that has been defined in the movie. Within the control tag, objects are referred to by their identifier in the dictionary. Thus, if a circle was drawn on the stage in Flash in a frame of some animation, the exported movie for that animation would include a definition which stored the parameters used when drawing the circle, such as the stroke and fill colours. This definition would be copied to the dictionary, with its identifier, which we will suppose is 77. The movie would also include a control tag that caused the circle to be placed at the correct position in the frame. The identifier 77 would appear as part of the corresponding data block, to indicate which object to place, and a transformation matrix would be included, to specify where to place it. The use of transformation matrices in the control tags allows the position and any scaling or rotation applied to an object to be specified at the same time. (The instruction for placing an object only causes it to be added to a data structure called the "display list", which holds all the objects for a frame. An additional instruction is used to draw the entire frame by showing all the items on the display list.)

A Flash movie is thus rather like a program, comprising as it does definitions of some objects and instructions that manipulate them. Definitions and control tags can be intermingled freely, as long as a definition always appears before any control tag that refers to it. This allows the movie to be streamed, because all the definitions needed for a frame will have been processed before the frame is drawn.

Although Flash movies may be small, only needing low bandwidth, they can also be very large. Certain styles of drawing and animation lead to vector animations that are of considerable size, and as we remarked earlier, bitmapped images are used in Flash animations more often than its vector nature might lead you to expect. However, each individual bitmapped image becomes a separate definition in the Flash movie, and the images are only compressed using JPEG. If bandwidth considerations are important to you, you need to make a conscious effort to avoid using bitmaps, draw simple vector shapes and use interpolated motion as much as possible in your animations – or deliver it as video.

Minor Alternatives

There are some other possibilities besides animated GIFs, Flash and video for delivering animation, although at present they are not often used. There is an animated PNG format, which is much like animated GIF, but being based on PNG it supports 24-bit colour and alpha channels. (Actually there have been two animated PNG formats, MNG and more recently the less ambitious APNG.) Most other alternatives rely on scripting or programming. JavaScript (see Chapter 14) can be used to create animation in several different ways. It can be used to show a sequence of JPEG or GIF images by repeatedly replacing an image with another, or it can make parts of the page move, creating simple motion graphics, by changing the position of elements on a Web page.

JavaScript can also be used to create and modify SVG graphics dynamically. (SVG is described in Chapter 15.) SVG animation provides an alternative to Flash for vector-based work, but it requires scripting. No software tools are currently available for generating SVG animations in an interactive timeline-based way.

Another scripted alternative for the Web is the canvas element, a non-standard but widely implemented HTML extension. The canvas element itself just allocates some space on the page – it has height and width attributes, like an img or object element, but no other attributes apart from the usual id, class, and so on. All drawing is done by scripts that call functions implementing the conventional vector drawing operations. Because the script can redraw parts of the canvas after a delay, images created in this way can be animated. The canvas element is thus an alternative to SVG that does not require a new markup language but does rely on scripting for all drawing operations. While canvas has a lot of support from browser makers, it too is unlikely to be used much unless tools for animators are developed.

In the early days of the Web, animation was only possible by writing Java applets which used the Java graphics APIs to create and modify images dynamically, using the same approach as SVG and canvas animation. Java animations are rarely seen now, however, except for some scientific visualizations, where the processing of data plays as important a role as the animation.

KEY POINTS

The three predominant formats for delivering digital animation are animated GIF, Flash (SWF) and video.

Video must be used for animation that will be played on a television.

If animation is delivered as video a soundtrack can be added, player controls can be used and high compression can be achieved using modern video codecs.

Flash is superior for vector animations.

For bitmapped animations, animated GIF may be used without a plug-in, but video provides the best quality. Flash should be used for interactive animation requiring scripting.

The Flash movie file format is a compressed binary format that provides an efficient way to deliver animation over a network.

Tags in a Flash movie are of two sorts: definition tags, which identify data blocks containing descriptions of objects, and control tags, which contain instructions for placing and moving those objects.

Alternative formats for animation include APNG, JPEG sequences displayed by JavaScript, scripted SVG and canvas animation. These formats are rarely used.

Exercises

Test Questions

1 What are the advantages and disadvantages of using a scanner or a digital stills camera to capture traditional art work as animation sequences?

2 When would it be appropriate to use an animated GIF for an animation sequence? What shortcomings of animated GIFs limit their usefulness?

3 What problems are associated with using linear methods to interpolate motion between key frames in animations? Explain how Bézier curves are used to overcome these problems.

4 Explain why bitmapped animations that use interpolation are no smaller than those that don't, but vector animations that use interpolation may be much smaller than those that don't.

5 Describe which properties of (a) a bitmapped animation and (b) a vector animation you could expect to be able to interpolate. Explain why there is a difference between the two.

6 Describe the motion of an object whose position is animated in After Effects using Bézier interpolation for the motion path, and linear interpolation for the velocity.

Discussion Topics

1 If an animation sequence is to be saved in a video format, what factors will influence your choice of codec? Under what circumstances would it be appropriate to treat the animated sequence exactly like a live-action video sequence?

2 The term "key frame" is used in connection with both animation and video. What are the similarities and differences between its meanings in the two contexts?

3 Will creating motion one frame at a time always produce a more convincing illusion of movement than using interpolation? Explain the reasons for your answer.

Practical Tasks

1 Create a short animation, similar to the bouncing ball example of Figure 7.8, which uses a motion path. Recreate the same animation, this time without using a motion path. Describe the difference between the two methods and the two results.

2 Flash has a `Trace Bitmap` command, which can be used to convert bitmapped images into vector graphics. Find out how this command works, and use it to convert a short video clip that you import into Flash into a vector animation. Compare the size of the result with the original video. Experiment with changing parameters to the tracing operation, and see what effect they have on the appearance of the traced clip and the size of the final movie.

3 Create a very simple title for a video clip as a single image in a bitmapped graphics application such as Photoshop, and save it as a still image file. Using whatever tools are available (Photoshop Extended, Premiere, After Effects, etc.), create a pleasing 10-second title sequence by simply applying time-varying effects and filters to this single image. (If you want to go for a more sophisticated result, and have the necessary tools, you might create your original image on several layers and animate them separately.)

4 The countdown sequence illustrated in Figure 7.14 was created in After Effects. Create your own countdown that uses similar motion graphics in Flash.

8

Sound

■ **The Nature of Sound**

Waveforms. Perception.

■ **Digitizing Sound**

Sampling. Quantization. Formats.

■ **Processing Sound**

Recording and Importing Sound. Sound Editing and Effects.
Combining Sound and Picture.

■ **Compression**

Speech Compression. Perceptually Based Compression.

■ **MIDI**

MIDI Messages. General MIDI. MIDI Software.

Sound is different in kind from any of the other digital media types we have considered. All other media are primarily visual, being perceived through our eyes, while sound is perceived through the different sense of hearing. Our ears detect vibrations in the air in a completely different way from that in which our eyes detect light, and our brains respond differently to the resulting nerve impulses. Sound does have something in common with one other topic we have considered, though. Although sound is, for most of us, a familiar everyday phenomenon, like colour it is a complex mixture of physical and psychological factors, which is difficult to model accurately.

Another feature that sound has in common with colour is that you may not always need it. Whereas a multimedia encyclopædia of musical instruments will be vastly enriched by the addition of recordings of each instrument, few, if any, Web pages need to play a fanfare every time they are visited. Sounds can be peculiarly irritating. Even one's favourite pieces of music can become a jarring and unwelcome intrusion on the ears when inflicted repeatedly by a neighbour's sound system. Almost everyone has at some time been infuriated by the electronic noises of a portable games console, the cuter varieties of ring tone of a mobile phone, or the rhythmic hiss that leaks out of the headphones of a personal stereo. The thoughtless use of such devices has become a fact of modern life; a similar thoughtlessness in the use of sound in multimedia should be avoided. At the very least, it should always be possible for users to turn the sound off.

There are two types of sound that are special: music and speech. These are also the most commonly used types of sound in multimedia. The cultural status of music and the linguistic content of speech mean that these two varieties of sound function in a different way from other sounds and noises, and play special roles in multimedia. Representations specific to music and speech have been developed, to take advantage of their unique characteristics. In particular, compression algorithms tailored to speech are often employed, while music is sometimes represented not as sound, but as instructions for playing virtual instruments.

The Nature of Sound

If a tuning fork is struck sharply on a hard surface, the tines will vibrate at a precise frequency. As they move backwards and forwards, the air is compressed and rarefied in time with the vibrations. Interactions between adjacent air molecules cause this periodic pressure fluctuation to be propagated as a wave. When the sound wave reaches the ear, it causes the eardrum to vibrate at the same frequency. The vibration is then transmitted through the mechanism of the inner ear, and converted into nerve impulses, which we interpret as the sound of the pure tone produced by the tuning fork.

All sounds are produced by the conversion of energy into vibrations in the air or some other elastic medium. The process may involve several steps, in which the energy may be converted into different forms. For example, if one of the strings of an acoustic guitar is picked with a plectrum, the kinetic energy of the musician's hand is converted to a vibration in the string, which is then transmitted via the bridge of the instrument to the resonant cavity of its body, where it is amplified and enriched by the distinctive resonances of the guitar, and then transmitted through the sound hole. If an electric guitar string is picked instead, the vibration of the string as it passes through the magnetic fields of the pickups induces fluctuations in the current which is sent through the guitar lead to an amplifier, where it is amplified and used to drive a loudspeaker. Variations in the signal sent to the speaker coil cause magnetic variations, which are used to drive the speaker cone, which then behaves as a sound source, compressing and rarefying the adjacent air.

While the tines of a good tuning fork vibrate cleanly at a single frequency, most other sound sources vibrate in more complicated ways, giving rise to the rich variety of sounds and noises we are familiar with. As we mentioned in Chapter 2, a single note – such as that produced by a guitar string – is composed of several components, at frequencies that are multiples of the fundamental pitch of the note. Some percussive sounds and most natural sounds do not even have a single identifiable fundamental frequency, but can still be decomposed into a collection – often a very complex one – of frequency components. As in the general case of representing a signal in the frequency domain, which we described in Chapter 2, we refer to a sound's description in terms of the relative amplitudes of its frequency components as its *frequency spectrum*.

The human ear is capable of detecting frequencies between approximately 20 Hz and 20 kHz, although individuals' frequency responses vary greatly. In particular, the upper limit decreases fairly rapidly with increasing age: few adults can hear sounds as high as 20 kHz, although children can. Frequencies at the top end of the range generally only occur as components of the transient attack of sounds. (The general rule that high frequencies are associated with abrupt transitions applies here.) The highest note on an ordinary piano – which more or less defines the limit of most Western music – has a fundamental frequency of only 4186 Hz when in concert pitch. However, it is the transient behaviour of notes that contributes most to the distinctive timbre of instruments. If the attack portion is removed from recordings of an oboe, violin and soprano, playing or singing the same note, for example, the steady portions are indistinguishable.

Waveforms

Interesting sounds change over time. As we just observed, a single musical note has a distinctive attack, and subsequently it will decay, changing its frequency spectrum first as it grows, and then as it dies away. Sounds that extend over longer periods of time, such as speech or music, exhibit a constantly changing frequency spectrum. We can display the *waveform* of any sound by graphically plotting its amplitude against time.

─IN DETAIL─

The idea of a sound's frequency spectrum changing might be slightly confusing, if you accept that any complex waveform is built out of a collection of frequency components. Strictly, Fourier analysis (as introduced in Chapter 2) can only be applied to periodic signals (i.e. ones that repeat indefinitely). When analysing signals with a finite duration, various expedients must be adopted to fit into the analytic framework.

One approach is to treat the entirety of a signal as one cycle of a periodic waveform; this is roughly what is done when images are broken down into their frequency components.

An alternative is to use a brief section of the signal as if it were a cycle, thus obtaining a snapshot of the frequency make-up at one point. For audio signals, this provides more useful information. A spectrum analysis is typically obtained by sliding a window through the waveform to obtain a sequence of spectra, showing how the signal's frequency components change over time.

Figure 8.1. *"Feisty teenager"*

Figure 8.2. *Didgeridoo*

Examination of waveforms can help us characterize certain types of sound. Figures 8.1 to 8.7 show waveforms for a range of types of sound. Figure 8.1 is a short example of speech: the main speaker repeats the phrase "Feisty teenager" twice, then a more distant voice responds. You can clearly identify the separate syllables, and recognize that the same phrase is repeated, the second time faster and with more emphasis. In between the phrases there is almost silence – the sound was recorded in the open air and there is background noise, which is visible as the thin band running along the axis. You can see that it could be possible to extract individual syllables and recombine them to synthesize new words, and that, if it were necessary to compress speech, a lot could be achieved by removing the silences between phrases. The clearly demarcated syllables also provide a good basis for synchronizing sound with video, as we will see later.

The next four figures show the waveforms of some different types of music. The first three are purely instrumental, and do not exhibit the same character as speech. The first, Figure 8.2, is taken from an Australian aboriginal didgeridoo piece. This is characterized by a continuous drone, which requires the musician to employ a "circular breathing" technique to maintain it. The waveform shows this drone as the thick continuous black region, with its rhythmic modulation.

Figure 8.3. *Boogie-woogie*

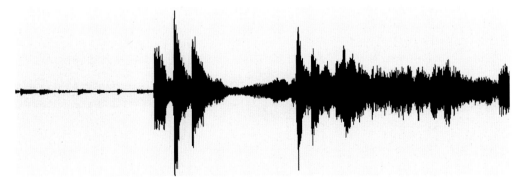

Figure 8.4. *Violin, cello and piano*

Figure 8.3 shows the waveform of a piece of boogie-woogie, played by a pianist accompanied by a small group. The rhythm is clearly visible, but it is not possible to distinguish the melody played by the right hand (unless, perhaps, you are a very experienced audio technician). Figure 8.4 is a completely different waveform, corresponding to a very different piece of music: a contemporary "classical" work arranged for violin, cello and piano. It shows a great dynamic range (difference

Figure 8.5. *"Men grow cold..."*

Figure 8.6. *A trickling stream*

Figure 8.7. *The sea*

between the loudest and quietest sounds). Although the steep attack of the louder phrases tells you something about the likely sound of this music, there is no obvious rhythm, and it is not possible to separate out the different instruments (although they can be very clearly identified when listening to the music).

As you would expect, singing combines characteristics of speech and music. Figure 8.5 is typical: the syllables of each word are easily identifiable, as is the rhythm, but the gaps between sung phrases are filled with the musical accompaniment. It is possible to see the singer's phrasing, but quite impossible to deduce the lyrics,[†] and, although voice prints are unique to each individual, it is unlikely that anyone could identify the singer from this waveform, despite her distinctive voice. (It's Marilyn Monroe.)

Figures 8.6 and 8.7 are both natural water sounds. The first is a recording of the trickling sound of water in a small stream; it is almost continuous and has a small dynamic range. The random spikes do not correspond to any audible clicks or other abrupt sound; they are just slight variations in the water's flow, and some background noise. The second waveform was recorded on the seashore. There is a constant background of surf and two distinct events. The first is a wave breaking fairly close to the microphone, while the second is the water splashing into a nearby rock pool and then receding through a gap in the rocks. This waveform can almost be read as a story.

As these illustrations show, the shape of a waveform can show a certain amount of the gross character and dynamics of a sound, but it does not convey the details, and it is not always easy to correlate against the sound as it is heard. The main advantage of these visual displays is their static nature. A piece of sound can be seen in its entirety at one time, with relationships such as the intervals between syllables or musical beats visible. This makes it relatively simple to analyse the sound's temporal structure – which is especially useful for synchronization purposes – compared with trying to perform the same analysis on the dynamically changing sound itself, which is only heard an instant at a time.

Perception

Waveforms and the physics of sound are only part of the story. Sound only truly exists as a sensation in the mind, and the perception of sound is not a simple registering of the physical characteristics of the waves reaching the ears. Proofs of this abound, both in the literature and in everyday experience. For example, if a pure 200 Hz tone is played, first softly, then louder, most listeners will believe that the louder tone has a lower pitch than the quieter one, although the same illusion is not perceived with higher-frequency tones. Similarly, complex tones sometimes seem to have a lower pitch than pure tones of the same frequency. Most people with good hearing can distinguish the sound of their own name spoken on the opposite side of a noisy room, even if the

† *Men grow cold, as girls grow old, and we all lose our charms in the end.*

rest of what is said is inaudible, or carry on a successful conversation with someone speaking at a volume lower than that of the ambient noise.

One of the most useful illusions in sound perception is stereophony. The brain identifies the source of a sound on the basis of the differences in intensity and phase between the signals received from the left and right ears. If identical signals are sent to both ears, the brain interprets the sound as coming from a non-existent source that lies straight ahead. By extension, if a sound is recorded using a pair of microphones to produce two monophonic channels, which are then fed to two speakers that are a suitable distance apart, the apparent location of the sound will depend on the relative intensity of the two channels. If they are equal it will appear in the middle, if the left channel is louder (because the original sound source was nearer to the left-hand microphone) it will appear to the left, and so on. In this way, the familiar illusion of a sound stage between the speakers is constructed.

Because of the psychological dimension of sound, it is unwise, when considering its digitization and reproduction, to place too much reliance on mathematics and measurable quantities. Pohlmann's comments[†] about the nature of sound and its reproduction should be borne in mind:

> "Given the evident complexity of acoustical signals, it would be naïve to believe that analog or digital technologies are sufficiently advanced to capture fully and convey the complete listening experience. To complicate matters, the precise limits of human perception are not known. One thing is certain: at best, even with the most sophisticated technology, what we hear being reproduced through an audio system is an approximation of the actual sound."

Digitizing Sound

The digitization of sound is a fairly straightforward example of the processes of quantization and sampling described in Chapter 2. Since these operations are carried out in electronic analogue-to-digital converters, the sound information must be converted to an electrical signal before it can be digitized. This can be done by a microphone or other transducer, such as a guitar pickup, just as it is for analogue recording or broadcasting.

Increasingly, digital audio, especially music, is stored in files that can be manipulated like other data. In particular, digital audio files can be stored on servers and downloaded or distributed as "podcasts" (see Chapter 16). Digital audio players, such as Apple's iPod, store such files on their internal hard disks or flash memory. Almost always, audio in this form is compressed.

† *Ken C. Pohlmann, Principles of Digital Audio, p. 5.*

Contemporary formats for digital audio are influenced by the CD format, which dominated audio for over two decades. For instance, the sampling rate and number of quantization levels used for high-quality audio is almost always the same as that used for CD. (Despite the journalistic habit of distinguishing between CD and "digital" music, CD audio is, of course, digital.)

Sampling

If high-fidelity audio reproduction is desired, a sampling rate must be chosen that will preserve at least the full range of audible frequencies. If the limit of hearing is taken to be 20 kHz, a minimum rate of 40 kHz is required by the Sampling Theorem. The sampling rate used for audio CDs is 44.1 kHz – the precise figure being chosen by manufacturers to produce a desired playing time given the size of the medium. Because of the ubiquity of the audio CD, the same rate is commonly used by the sound cards fitted to computers, to provide compatibility. Where a lower sound quality is acceptable, or is demanded by limited bandwidth, sub-multiples of 44.1 kHz are used: 22.05 kHz is commonly used for audio destined for delivery over the Internet, while 11.025 kHz is sometimes used for speech.

Some professional and semi-professional recording devices use sample rates that are multiples of 48 kHz. This was the rate used by DAT (digital audio tape) recorders, which were popular for live recording and low-budget studio work in the late 1990s and early twenty-first century. The solid-state memory card and disk-based recorders that have taken over this function often record at double or even four times this sampling rate (96 kHz or 192 kHz).

CD players and solid state recorders have the advantage that they can generate digital output, which can be read in by a suitably equipped computer without the need for extra digitizing hardware. In this respect, they resemble DV cameras. Digital audio inputs on modern computers usually support sampling rates of 44.1 kHz, 48 kHz and 96 kHz, so it should be possible to read digital audio in most formats to disk without the need to resample it.

IN DETAIL

> The necessity to resample data sampled at 48 or 96 kHz often occurs if the sound is to be combined with video. Some video applications do not yet support the higher sampling rates used by popular recording devices. For multimedia work it may therefore be preferable to sample sound at 44.1 kHz, if this rate is available, since it is supported by all the major desktop video editing programs.

Sampling relies on highly accurate clock pulses to determine the intervals between samples. If the clock drifts, so will the intervals. Such timing variations are called *jitter*. The effect of jitter is to introduce noise into the reconstructed signal. At the high sampling frequencies required by sound, there is little tolerance for jitter: it has been estimated that for CD-quality sound, the jitter in the ADC must be less than 200 picoseconds (200×10^{-12} seconds).

Even though they may be inaudible, frequencies in excess of 20 kHz are present in the spectra of many sounds. If a sampling rate of around 40 kHz is used, these inaudible components will manifest themselves as aliasing when the signal is reconstructed. In order to avoid this, a filter is used to remove any frequencies higher than half the sampling rate before the signal is sampled.

Quantization

We mentioned in Chapter 2 that the number of quantization levels for analogue-to-digital conversion in any medium is usually chosen to fit into a convenient number of bits. For sound, the most common choice of sample size is 16 bits – as used for CD audio – giving 65,536 quantization levels. This is generally sufficient to eliminate quantization noise if the signal is dithered, as we will describe shortly. As with images, smaller samples sizes (lower bit-depths, as we would say in the context of images) are sometimes needed to maintain small file sizes and bit rates. The minimum acceptable is 8-bit sound, and even this has audible quantization noise, so it can only be used for applications such as voice communication, where the distortion can be tolerated. In the search for higher-fidelity reproduction, as many as 24 bits are sometimes used to record audio samples, but this imposes considerable demands on the accuracy of ADC circuitry.

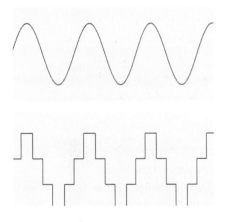

Figure 8.8. *Undersampling a pure sine wave*

Quantization noise will be worst for signals of small amplitude. In the extreme, when the amplitude is comparable to the difference between quantization levels, an analogue signal will be coarsely approximated by samples that jump between just a few quantized values. This is shown in Figure 8.8. The upper waveform is a pure sine wave; below it is a digitized version, where only four levels are available to accommodate the amplitude range of the original signal.[†] Evidently, the sampled waveform is a poor approximation of the original. The approximation could be improved by increasing the number of bits for each sample, but it is usual to employ a more economical technique, which resembles the anti-aliasing applied when rendering vector graphics. Its operation is somewhat counter-intuitive.

Before sampling, a small amount of random noise is added to the analogue signal. The word "dithering" (which we used with a somewhat different meaning in Chapter 5) is used in the audio field to refer to this injection of noise. The effect which this has on sampling is illustrated

---

† *If you want to be scrupulous, since these images were prepared using a digital audio application, the top waveform is a 16-bit sampled sine wave (a very good approximation), the lower is the same waveform downsampled to 2 bits.*

in Figure 8.9. The upper waveform is the original sine wave with added dither. (We have used rather more noise than is normal, in order to illustrate the effect more clearly.) The lower waveform is a sampled version of this dithered signal.

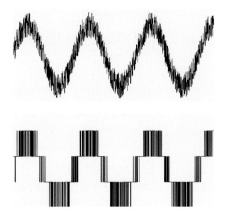

What has happened is that the presence of the noise has caused the samples to alternate rapidly between quantization levels, instead of jumping cleanly and abruptly from one to the next as in Figure 8.8. The sharp transitions have been softened. Putting it another way, the quantization error has been randomized. The price to be paid for the resulting improvement in sound quality is the additional random noise that has been introduced, but this is less intrusive than the quantization noise it has eliminated.

Figure 8.9. *Dithering*

The effect of sampling and dithering on the signal's frequency spectrum is shown in Figure 8.10; the horizontal x-axis represents frequency, the vertical y-axis amplitude (with the colours being used as an extra visual indication of intensity) and the back-to-front z-axis represents time. The first spectrum is the pure sine wave. As you would expect, it is a spike at the wave's frequency, which is constant over time. To its right is the spectrum of the sampled signal: spurious frequencies and noise have been introduced. These correspond to the frequency components of the sharp edges. Below the pure sine wave is the spectrum of the dithered version. The extra noise is randomly distributed across frequencies and over time. In the bottom right is the sampled version of this signal. The pure frequency has re-emerged clearly, but random noise is present where before there was none. However, although this noise will be audible, the ear will be able to discern the signal through it, because the noise is random. Where the undithered signal was sampled, the noise was concentrated near to the signal frequency, in a way that is much less easily ignored.

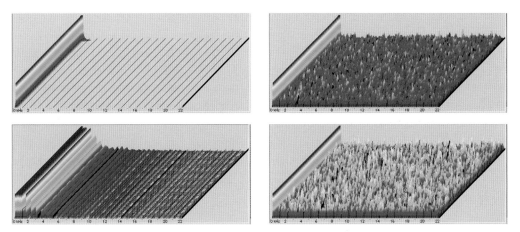

Figure 8.10. *Audio frequency spectra showing the effect of undersampling and dithering*

Formats

Most of the development of digital audio has taken place in the recording and broadcast industries, where the emphasis is on physical data representations and data streams for transmission and playback. There are standards in these areas that are widely adhered to. The use of digital sound on computers is a much less thoroughly regulated area, where a wide range of incompatible proprietary formats and *ad hoc* standards can be found. Each of the three major platforms has its own sound file format: AIFF for MacOS, AU for other varieties of Unix, and WAV (or WAVE) for Windows, but support for all three is common on all platforms.

The standardizing influence of the Internet has been less pronounced in audio than it is in graphics. MP3 files have been widely used for downloading and storing music on computers and mobile music players. "Podcasts" typically use MP3 as the format for the audio that they deliver. The popularity of music-swapping services using MP3 led to its emergence as the leading audio format on the Internet, but QuickTime and Windows Media are used as container formats for audio destined for Apple's iPod music players and various devices that incorporate Windows Media technology. On Web pages, Flash movies are sometimes used for sound, because of the wide deployment of the Flash Player. It is possible to embed sound in PDF documents, but the actual playing of the sound is handled by other software, such as QuickTime, so MP3 is a good choice of format here, too, because it can be played on all the relevant platforms.

MP3 has its own file format, in which the compressed audio stream is split into chunks called "frames", each of which has a header, giving details of the bit rate, sampling frequency and other parameters. The file may also include metadata tags, oriented towards musical content, giving the title of a track, the artist performing it, the album from which it is taken, and so on. As we will describe later in this chapter, MP3 is primarily an encoding, not a file format, and MP3 data may be stored in other types of file. In particular, QuickTime may include audio tracks encoded with MP3, and Flash movies use MP3 to compress any sound they may include.

In Chapter 6, we explained that streamed video resembles broadcast television. Streamed audio resembles broadcast radio – that is, sound is delivered over a network and played as it arrives, without having to be stored on the user's machine first. As with video, this allows live transmission and the playing of files that are too big to be held on an average-sized hard disk. Because of the lower bandwidth required by audio, streaming is more successful for sound than it is for video. Streaming QuickTime can also be used for audio, on its own as well as accompanying video. QuickTime includes an AAC codec for high-quality audio. Windows Media audio can also be streamed. Both of these formats, as well as MP3, are used for broadcasting live concerts and for the Internet equivalent of radio stations.

KEY POINTS

Sounds are produced by the conversion of energy into vibrations in the air or some other elastic medium, which are detected by the ear and converted into nerve impulses which we experience as sound.

A sound's frequency spectrum is a description of the relative amplitudes of its frequency components.

The human ear can detect sound frequencies roughly in the range 20 Hz to 20 kHz, though the ability to hear the higher frequencies is lost as people age.

A sound's waveform shows how its amplitude varies over time.

Perception of sound has a psychological dimension.

CD audio is sampled at 44.1 kHz. Sub-multiples of this value may be used for low-quality digital audio. Some audio recorders use sampling rates that are multiples of 48 kHz.

Audio sampling relies on highly accurate clock pulses to prevent jitter.

Frequencies greater than half the sampling rate are filtered out to avoid aliasing.

CD audio uses 16-bit samples to give 65,536 quantization levels.

Quantization noise can be mitigated by dithering, i.e. adding a small amount of random noise which softens the sharp transitions of quantization noise.

Sound may be stored in AIFF, WAV or AU files, but on the Internet the MP3 format is dominant. MP3 data may be stored in QuickTime and Flash movies.

Processing Sound

With the addition of suitable audio input, output and processing hardware and software, a desktop computer can perform the functions of a modern multi-track recording studio. Such professional facilities are expensive and demanding on resources, as you would expect. They are also as complex as a recording studio, with user interfaces that are as intimidating to the novice as the huge mixing consoles of conventional studios. Fortunately, for multimedia, more modest facilities are usually adequate.

There is presently no single sound application that has the *de facto* status of a cross-platform desktop standard, in the way that Photoshop and Dreamweaver, for example, have in their respective fields. Several different packages are in use, some of which require special hardware support. Most of the well-known ones are biased towards music, with integrated support for MIDI sequencing (as described later in this chapter) and multi-track recording.

Several more modest programs, including some Open Source applications, provide simple recording and effects processing facilities. A specialized type of audio application has recently achieved some popularity among people who are not audio professionals. Apple's GarageBand and Adobe Soundbooth exemplify this type of program. They provide only primitive facilities for recording, importing and editing sound, and only a few of the effects that are found in professional software. Their novelty lies in facilities for creating songs. In the case of GarageBand, this is done by combining loops, which may either be recorded live instruments, or synthesized. In Soundbooth, templates consisting of several musical segments may be customized – for example by changing the orchestration or dynamics, or by rearranging the segments – to produce unique "compositions", which might serve as adequate soundtracks for corporate presentations, home videos and similar undemanding productions.

Video editing packages usually include some integrated sound editing and processing facilities, and some offer basic sound recording. These facilities may be adequate for multimedia production in the absence of special sound software, and are especially convenient when the audio is intended as a soundtrack to accompany picture.

Given the absence of an industry standard sound application for desktop use, we will describe the facilities offered by sound programs in general terms only, without using any specific example.

Recording and Importing Sound

Many desktop computers are fitted with built-in microphones, and it is tempting to think that these are adequate for recording sounds. It is almost impossible to obtain satisfactory results with these, however – not only because the microphones themselves are usually small and cheap, but because they are inevitably close to the machine's fan and disk drives, which means that they will pick up noises from these components. It is much better to plug an external microphone into a sound card, but if possible, you should do the actual recording using a dedicated device, such as a solid-state audio recorder, and a professional microphone, and capture it in a separate operation. Compression should be avoided at this stage. Where sound quality is important, or for recording music to a high standard, it will be necessary to use a properly equipped studio. Although a computer can form the basis of a studio, it must be augmented with microphones and other equipment in a suitable acoustic environment, so it is not really practical for a multimedia producer to set up a studio for one-off recordings. It may be necessary to hire a professional studio, which offers the advantage that professional personnel will generally be available.

Before recording, it is necessary to select a sampling rate and sample size. Where the sound originates in analogue form, the choice will be determined by considerations of file size and bandwidth, which will depend on the final use to which the sound is to be put, and the facilities available for sound processing. As a general rule, the highest possible sampling rate and sample size should be used, to minimize deterioration of the signal when it is processed. If a compromise must be made, the effect on quality of reducing the sample size is more drastic than that of reducing the sampling rate. The same reduction in size can be produced by halving the sampling rate or halving the sample size, but the former is the better option. If the signal is originally a digital one – the digital output from a solid-state recorder, for example – the sample size should be matched to the incoming rate, if possible.

A simple calculation suffices to show the size of digitized audio. The sampling rate is the number of samples generated each second, so if the rate is r Hz and the sample size is s bits, each second of digitized sound will occupy $rs/8$ bytes. Hence, for CD quality, $r = 44.1 \times 10^3$ and $s = 16$, so each second occupies just over 86 kbytes (86×1024 bytes), each minute roughly 5 Mbytes. These calculations are based on a single channel, but audio is almost always recorded in stereo, so the estimates should be doubled. Conversely, where stereo effects are not required, the space occupied can be halved by recording in mono.

The most vexatious aspect of recording is getting the levels right. If the level of the incoming signal is too low, the resulting recording will be quiet, and more susceptible to noise. If the level is too high, *clipping* will occur – that is, at some points, the amplitude of the incoming signal will exceed the maximum value that can be recorded. The value of the corresponding sample will be set to the maximum, so the recorded waveform will apparently be clipped off straight at this threshold. (Figure 8.11 shows the effect on a pure sine wave.) The result is heard as a particularly unpleasant sort of distortion.

Ideally, a signal should be recorded at the highest possible level that avoids clipping. Sound applications usually provide level meters, so that the level can be monitored, with clipping alerts. Where the sound card supports it, a gain control can be used to alter the level. If this is not available, the only option is to adjust the output level of the equipment from which the signal originates.

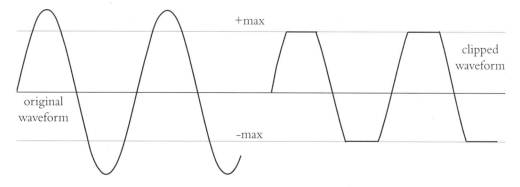

Figure 8.11. *Clipping*

Setting the level correctly is easier said than done, especially where live recordings are being made. To preserve the dynamic range of the recording the same gain must be used throughout, but the optimum can only be determined at the loudest point. When the sound is live, this cannot be known in advance, and only experience can be used to choose gain settings. Where the material already exists (on CD, for example) it is possible – and usually necessary – to make several passes in order to find the best values.

Some software includes automatic gain controls, which vary the gain dynamically according to the amplitude of the signal, in order to prevent clipping. To do this they must reduce the volume of louder passages, so as a side-effect they reduce the dynamic range of the recording. This is generally undesirable, but it may be necessary if suitable levels cannot be maintained throughout the recording.

┌─ **IN DETAIL** ───

It may be obvious, but it seems worth emphasizing that once a signal has been clipped, nothing can be done to restore it. Reducing the amplitude subsequently just produces a smaller clipped signal. There is no way to recover the lost waveform.

Similarly, although sound programs often provide a facility for "normalizing" a sound after recording, by amplifying it as much as possible without causing clipping, this stretches the dynamic range of the original without adding any more detail. In practice it may be necessary to use this facility, or to select and amplify particularly quiet passages within a sound editing application after the recording has been made. In principle, though, the gain should always be set correctly, both when recording to a dedicated device, and when recording or capturing to disk.

A technically simpler alternative to recording sound is to import it from an audio CD. Although audio CDs use a different format from CD-ROM, they are nevertheless a structured collection of digital data, so they can be read by suitable software. QuickTime, for example, includes an audio CD import component that allows any sound application based on QuickTime to open tracks on a CD just like any other file. This is the simplest way of importing sounds, but most recorded music is copyrighted, so it is necessary to obtain permissions first. Copyright-free collections of original music and sound effects can be obtained, much like royalty-free image libraries, although the music tends to the anodyne. Composers and musicians with access to professional recording facilities may supply their work on CD, avoiding the need for the multimedia producer to deal with the sound recording process. However, even when importing sounds from CDs there can be difficulty in getting the levels right.

The Internet is a rich source of ready-made sounds and music. The early music download and file-sharing services of dubious legality have been largely superseded by legitimate downloads through commercial online music stores. While it is legal to download these files, or to listen to them and transfer them to a music player, it remains generally illegal to use them in any published form without obtaining clearance from the copyright holders. Some downloaded music is therefore subject to **Digital Rights Management (DRM)**, which aims to prevent it from being used for any purpose not approved by the copyright owners. However, the efficacy of DRM is limited and it causes considerable resentment among consumers. At the time of writing, its use in connection with music is declining.

In any case, music that is distributed over the Internet is usually compressed using MP3 or AAC (see below). Like JPEG image compression, these compression algorithms discard information, so compressed sound is not an ideal source for subsequent processing.

Sound Editing and Effects

We can identify several classes of operation that we might want to apply to recorded sounds. Most of them have counterparts in video editing, and are performed for similar reasons.

First there is editing, in the sense of trimming, combining and rearranging clips. The essentially time-based nature of sound naturally lends itself to an editing interface based on a timeline. A typical sound editing window is divided into tracks – in imitation of the separate tape tracks used on traditional recording equipment – providing a clear graphic representation of the sound through time. The sound in each track may usually be displayed as a waveform; the time and amplitude axes can be scaled, allowing the sound to be examined in varying degrees of detail. Editing is done by cutting and pasting – or dragging and dropping – selected parts of the track. Each stereo recording will occupy two tracks, one for each channel. During the editing process many tracks may be used to combine sounds from separate recordings. Subsequently, these will be "mixed down" onto one or two tracks, for the final mono or stereo output. When mixing, the relative levels of each of the tracks can be adjusted to produce the desired balance – between different instruments, for example.

A special type of edit has become common in audio: the creation of loops. Very short loops are needed to create voices for the electronic musical instruments known as samplers (whose functions are increasingly performed by software). Here, the idea is to create a section of sound that represents the sustained tone of an instrument, such as a guitar, so that arbitrarily long notes can be produced by interpolating copies of the section between a sample of the instrument's attack and one of its decay. It is vital that the sustained sample loops cleanly. There must not be abrupt discontinuities between its end and beginning, otherwise audible clicks will occur where the copies fit together. Although some software makes such loops automatically, using built-in heuristics such as choosing zero crossings for each end of the loop, the best results require a detailed examination of the waveform by a person. Longer loops are used in certain styles of dance music based on the combination of repeating sections. Again, there is a requirement for clean looping, but this time at the coarser level of rhythmic continuity. Software, such as GarageBand, can be used to put together even longer loops from a pre-recorded library, pitch- and time-shifting them so they are in the same key and tempo. This allows non-composers to produce music of a sort, and musicians to create backing tracks and orchestrations.

As well as editing, audio has its equivalent of post-production – altering sounds to correct defects, enhance quality, or otherwise modify their character. Just as image correction is described in terms of filters, which are a digital equivalent of traditional optical devices, so sound alteration is described in terms of gates and filters, by analogy with the established technology. Whereas analogue gates and filters are based on circuitry whose response produces a desired effect, digital processing is performed by algorithmic manipulation of the samples making up the signal. The range of effects – and the degree of control over them – that can be achieved in this way is much greater than is possible with analogue circuits. Several standard plug-in formats are in use that allow effects to be shared among programs. Although it is not an audio application, Premiere's effects plug-in format is becoming widely used. At a more professional level, the formats associated with Cubase VST and with DigiDesign ProTools are popular.

The most frequently required correction is the removal of unwanted noise. For example, in Figure 8.1, it might be considered desirable to remove the background noises that were unavoidably picked up by the microphone, since the recording was made in the open air. A *noise gate* is a blunt instrument that is used for this purpose. It eliminates all samples whose value falls below a specified threshold, with samples above the threshold left alone. As well as specifying the threshold, it is usual to specify a minimum time that must elapse before a sequence of low-amplitude samples counts as a silence, and a similar limit before a sequence whose values exceed the threshold counts as sound. This prevents the gate being turned on or off by transient glitches. By setting the threshold just above the maximum value of the background noise, the gaps between words in our example will become entirely silent. Since the noise gate has no effect on the speaker's words, the accompanying background noise will cut in and out as he speaks, which may well turn out to be more distracting than the original noise. (You may have heard this phenomenon on the soundtracks of old films that have been restored and reissued on DVD.) This illustrates a general problem with noise removal: the noise is intimately combined with the signal, and although people can discriminate between the two, computer programs generally cannot.

Noise gates can be effective at removing hiss from music, since, in this case, the noise is hidden except in silent passages, where it will be removed by the noise gate. There are more sophisticated ways of reducing noise than the all-or-nothing filtering of the noise gate, though. Filters that remove certain bands of frequencies can be applied to noise that falls within a specific frequency range. *Low pass* filters, which allow low frequencies to pass through them, removing high frequencies, can be used to take out hiss. *High pass* filters, which pass the high frequencies and block the low ones, are used to remove "rumble", that is, low-frequency noise caused by mechanical vibrations. Figures 8.12 and 8.13 show the effect of low and high pass filters on the spectrum and waveform of the sea sound from Figure 8.7. (The upper spectrum and waveform in each figure are the original sound; the lower ones are the sound after filtering.)

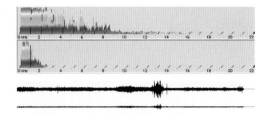

Figure 8.12. *Low pass filtering*

A *notch filter* removes a single narrow frequency band. The commonest use of notch filters is to remove hum picked up from the mains, which will have a frequency of exactly 50 Hz or 60 Hz, depending on the geographical

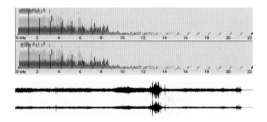

Figure 8.13. *High pass filtering*

location in which the sound was recorded. Some sophisticated programs offer the user the ultimate facility of being able to redraw the waveform, rubbing out the individual spikes that correspond to clicks, and so on. To do this effectively, however, requires considerable experience and the ability to interpret the visual display of a waveform in acoustic terms, which, as the examples shown earlier demonstrate, is not always easy.

┌─ **IN DETAIL** ───

> **Although the noise reduction facilities available in desktop sound applications are fairly crude and ineffectual, more elaborate – and more computationally expensive – approaches have been developed. One approach is based on attempting to analyse the acoustic properties of the original recording apparatus on the basis of the make-up of the noise in quiet passages, and then compensating for it in the music. Sophisticated noise reduction techniques are used to restore old records from the early part of the twentieth century, and also to reconstruct other damaged recordings, such as the tapes from voice recorders of crashed aircraft.**

Specialized filters are available for dealing with certain common recording defects. A *de-esser* is a filter that is intended to remove the sibilance that results from speaking or singing into a microphone placed too close to the performer. *Click repairers* are intended to remove clicks from recordings taken from damaged or dirty vinyl records. (There are also effects plug-ins that attempt to add authentic-sounding vinyl noise to digital recordings.) Although these filters are more discriminating than a noise gate, they are not infallible. The only sure way to get perfect sound is to start with a perfect recording – microphones should be positioned to avoid sibilance, and kept well away from fans and disk drives, cables should be screened to avoid picking up hum, and so on.

When we consider effects that alter the quality of a sound, there is a continuum from those that perform minor embellishments to compensate for poor performance and recording, to those that radically alter the sound, or create new sounds out of the original. A single effect may be used in different ways, at different points in this continuum, depending on the values of parameters that affect its operation. For example, a ***reverb*** effect is produced digitally by adding copies of a signal, delayed in time and attenuated, to the original. These copies model reflections from surrounding surfaces, with the delay corresponding to the size of the enclosing space, and the degree of attenuation modelling surfaces with different acoustic reflectivity. By using small delays and low reflectivity, a recording can be made to sound as if it had been made inside a small room. This degree of reverb is often a necessary enhancement when the output from electric instruments has been recorded directly without going through a speaker and microphone. Although cleaner recordings are produced this way, they are often too dry acoustically to sound convincing. Longer reverb times can produce the illusion of a concert hall or a stadium. Still longer times, with the delayed signals being amplified instead of attenuated, can be used creatively to generate sustained rhythm patterns from a single chord or note. Figure 8.14 shows the effect on the spectrum and waveform of adding an echo to our sea sound.

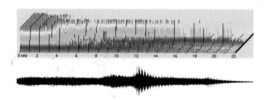

Figure 8.14. *Echo reverb*

Other effects can be put to a variety of uses in a similar way. These include ***graphic equalization***, which transforms the spectrum of a sound using a bank of filters, each controlled by its own slider and each affecting a fairly narrow band of frequencies. These can be used to compensate for recording equipment with idiosyncratic frequency response, or to artificially enhance the bass, for example, to produce a desired frequency balance.

Envelope shaping operations change the outline of a waveform. The most general envelope shapers allow the user to draw a new envelope around the waveform, altering its attack and decay and introducing arbitrary fluctuations of amplitude. Specialized versions of envelope shaping include faders, which allow a sound's volume to be gradually increased or decreased, and tremolo, which causes the amplitude to oscillate periodically from zero to its maximum value.†

---

† *To classical musicians, "tremolo" means the rapid repetition of a single note – this does produce a periodic oscillation of amplitude. The "tremolo arm" fitted to Fender Stratocasters and other electric guitars actually produces a periodic change of pitch, more accurately referred to as "vibrato".*

Time stretching and **pitch alteration** are two closely related effects that are especially well suited to digital sound. With analogue recordings, altering the duration of a sound could only be achieved by altering the speed at which it was played back, and this altered the pitch. With digital sound, the duration can be changed without altering the pitch, by inserting or removing samples. Conversely, the pitch can be altered without affecting the duration.

Time stretching may be required when sound is being synchronized to video or another sound. If, for example, a voice-over is slightly too long to fit over the video scene it describes, the soundtrack can be shrunk in time, without raising the pitch of the speaker's voice, which would happen if the voice track was simply played at a faster speed. Time stretching can also be applied to music, to alter its tempo. This makes it possible to combine loops that were sampled from pieces originally played at different tempos. (Time stretching software is sometimes used to slow down recorded music to make it easier to transcribe.)

Pitch alteration can be used in several ways. It can be applied uniformly to alter the pitch of an instrument, compensating for an out-of-tune guitar, for example. It can be applied periodically to add a vibrato (periodic fluctuation of pitch) to a voice or instrument, or it can be applied gradually, to produce a "bent note", in the same way a blues guitarist changes the tone of a note by bending the string while it sounds. The all-important shape of the bend can be specified by drawing a curve showing how the pitch changes over time. Pitch alteration can also be used to transpose music into a different key – again, this allows samples from disparate sources to be combined harmoniously.

Beyond these effects lie what are euphemistically called "creative" sound effects. Effects such as flanging, phasing, chorus, ring modulation, reversal, Doppler shift and wah-wah, which were originally pioneered in the 1960s on albums such as the Beatles' *Sergeant Pepper's Lonely Hearts Club Band* and Jimi Hendrix's *Electric Ladyland,* have been reproduced digitally, and joined by new extreme effects such as roboticization. These effects, if used judiciously, can enhance a recording, but they are easily over-used, and are generally best enjoyed in private.

Combining Sound and Picture

When sound is used as part of a video or animation production, synchronization between sound and picture becomes a matter of considerable importance. This is seen most clearly where the picture shows a person talking and the soundtrack contains their speech. If synchronization is slightly out, the result will be disconcerting. If it is substantially out, the result will at best be unintentionally funny, but more likely incoherent. Although speech makes the most exacting demands on synchronization, wherever sound and picture are related it is necessary that the temporal relationship between them is maintained. Voice-overs should match the picture they describe, music will often be related to edits, and natural sounds will be associated with events on screen.

In order to establish synchronization, it is necessary to be able to identify specific points in time. Film is divided into physical frames, which provides a natural means of identifying times. Video does not have physical frames, but – as we mentioned in Chapter 6 – it does have timecode, allowing the frames to be identified precisely.

Sound is effectively continuous, though, even in the digital domain. The high sampling rates used for digital sound mean that a single sample defines too short a time interval to be useful. For sound, therefore, the division into frames imposed by timecode is just a useful fiction. This fictional division continues to be used when synching digital audio and video. It enables sound and picture tracks in a video editing application such as Final Cut or Premiere to be arranged on the same timeline.

Unlike the soundtrack on a piece of film or video tape, a sound track in a digital video editing program is physically independent of the video it accompanies, so it is easy to move the sound in time relative to the picture, simply by sliding the sound track along the timeline. This is not something you would normally want to do if the sound and picture had originally been recorded together. In that case, you will usually want to maintain their synchronization during editing. For this purpose, tracks can be locked together, so that, for example, cutting out part of the video track will remove the accompanying part of the sound.

Audio tracks may be displayed as waveforms. When a sound track has been made independently of the picture – a voice-over or musical accompaniment, for example – it will be necessary to fit the sound to the picture. By looking at the waveform to identify the start of syllables in speech, or stressed beats in music, an editor can identify meaningful points in the sound track, which can then be lined up with appropriate picture frames. Performing this matching by eye is difficult, so a method that is often used is to scrub through the sound to identify the precise cue point by ear, and place a marker that can then be lined up on the timeline with the video frame (which can also be marked for identification). Sometimes, it may be necessary to apply a time-stretching filter to adjust the duration of the sound to fit the picture, as described earlier.

Synchronization can thus be established in a video editing program, but it must then be maintained when the video and its soundtrack are played back, possibly over a network. If the sound and video are physically independent – travelling over separate network connections, for example – synchronization will sometimes be lost. This is a fact of life and cannot be avoided. Audio and video data streams must therefore carry the equivalent of timecode, so that their synchronization can be checked and they can be resynched if necessary. Usually, this will require some video frames to be dropped, so that picture can catch up with sound – the greater data rate of the video means that it is video that is more likely to fall behind.

KEY POINTS

For a sampling rate of r Hz and sample size of s bits, each second of digitized sound will occupy $rs/8$ bytes. For CD quality, $r = 44.1 \times 10^3$ and $s = 16$, so each second occupies just over 86 kbytes (for a mono signal).

If the recording level is too high, clipping will occur, causing distortion.

Sound editing programs use a timeline interface, with multiple tracks (usually displayed as waveforms), which are mixed down to produce a stereo or mono output.

Short loops may be used to create voices for samplers; longer loops may be combined (e.g. in GarageBand) to build songs from repeating sections.

Filters and gates are used to correct defects (e.g. remove noise) or to enhance or modify sounds (e.g. reverb).

Time stretching (slowing down and speeding up) and pitch alteration are more easily applied to digital audio than they were to analogue audio. They are used for synchronization and for matching (e.g. when combining separately recorded loops).

Sound can be combined with pictures in a video editing program: sound tracks are displayed on the same timeline as video tracks, where they can be synchronized.

Timecode is just a fiction when working with sound, owing to the high sampling rate, but it is valuable for synchronization.

If sound and video are physically independent in a movie, synchronization may be lost, especially when it is sent over a network.

Compression

While the data rate for CD-quality audio is nothing like as demanding as that for video, lengthy sound recordings rapidly consume disk space. A single three-minute song, recorded in stereo, will occupy over 25 Mbytes. Hence, where audio is used in multimedia, and especially when it is delivered over the Internet, there is a need for compression. The complex and unpredictable nature of sound waveforms makes them difficult to compress using lossless methods. Huffman coding can be effective in cases where the amplitude of the sound mainly falls below the maximum level that can be represented in the sample size being used. In that case, the signal could have been represented in a smaller sample size, and the Huffman algorithm, by assigning short codes to the values it does encounter, will effectively do this automatically. This is a special case, though. In general, some form of lossy compression will be required.

An obvious compression technique that can be applied to speech is the removal of silence. That is, instead of using 44,100 samples with the value of zero for each second of silence (assuming a 44.1 kHz sampling rate) we record the length of the silence. This technique appears to be a special case of run-length encoding, which is lossless (see Chapter 4). However, as Figure 8.1 shows, "silence" is rarely absolute. We would obtain little compression if we simply run-length encoded samples whose value was exactly zero. Instead, we must treat samples falling below a threshold as if they were zero. The effect of doing this is equivalent to applying a noise gate, and is not strictly lossless, since the decompressed signal will not be identical to the original.

The principles behind lossy audio compression are different from those used in lossy image compression, because of the differences in the way we perceive the two media. In particular, whereas the high frequencies associated with rapid changes of colour in an image can safely be discarded, the high frequencies associated with rapid changes of sound are highly significant, so some other principle must be used to decide what data can be discarded.

Speech Compression

Telephone companies have been using digital audio since the early 1960s, and have been forced by the limited bandwidth of telephone lines to develop compression techniques that can be effectively applied to speech. An important contribution of this early work is the technique known as *companding*. The idea is to use non-linear quantization levels, with the higher levels spaced further apart than the low ones, so that quiet sounds are represented in greater detail than louder ones. This matches the way in which we perceive differences in volume.

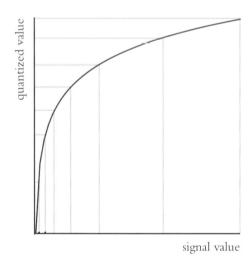

Figure 8.15 shows an example of non-linear quantization. The signal value required to produce an increase of one in the quantized value goes up logarithmically. This produces compression, because fewer bits are needed to represent the full range of possible input values than a linear quantization scheme would require. When the signal is reconstructed an inverse process of expansion is required, hence the name "companding"(itself a compressed version of "compressing/expanding").

Figure 8.15. *Non-linear quantization*

Different non-linear companding functions can be used. The principal important ones are defined by ITU Recommendations for use in telecommunications. Recommendation G.711 defines a function called the μ-*law*, which is used in North America and Japan. This companding method is used in AU files. A different ITU Recommendation is used in the rest of the world, based on a function known as the ***A-law***.

Telephone signals are usually sampled at only 8 kHz. At this rate, μ-law compression is able to squeeze a dynamic range of 12 bits into just 8 bits, giving a one-third reduction in data rate.

┌─IN DETAIL────────────────────────────

The μ-law is defined by the equation:

$$y = \log(1+\mu x)/\log(1+\mu) \text{ for } x \geq 0$$

where μ is a parameter that determines the amount of companding; μ=255 is used for telephony.

The A-law is:

$$y = \begin{cases} Ax/(1+\log A) & \text{for } 0 \leq |x| < 1/A \\ (1+\log Ax)/(1+\log A) & \text{for } 1/A \leq |x| < 1 \end{cases}$$

Another important technique that was originally developed for – and is widely used in – the telecommunications industry is ***Adaptive Differential Pulse Code Modulation (ADPCM)***.[†] This is related to inter-frame compression of video, in that it is based on storing the difference between consecutive samples, instead of the absolute value of each sample. Because of the different nature of audio and video, and its origins in hardware encoding of transmitted signals, ADPCM works somewhat less straightforwardly than a simple scheme based on the difference between samples.

Storing differences will only produce compression if the differences can be stored in fewer bits than the sample. Audio waveforms can change rapidly, so, unlike consecutive video frames, there is no reason to assume that the difference will necessarily be much less than the value. Basic ***Differential Pulse Code Modulation (DPCM)*** therefore computes a predicted value for a sample, based on preceding samples, and stores the difference between the prediction and the actual value. If the prediction is good, the difference will be small.

Adaptive DPCM obtains further compression by dynamically varying the step size used to represent the quantized differences. Large differences are quantized using large steps, small differences using small steps, so the amount of detail that is preserved scales with the size of the difference. The details of how this is done are complicated, but as with companding, the effect is to make efficient use of bits to store information, taking account of its rate of change.

---

† "Pulse Code Modulation" is the term used in audio and communications circles for encoding digital data as a sequence of pulses representing ones and zeros. Whereas this is more or less the only sensible representation for computer use, alternatives, such as "Pulse Width Modulation", exist where the data is to be represented as a stream for transmission, rather than as stored values.

ITU Recommendation G.721 specifies a form of ADPCM representation for use in telephony, with data rates of 16 kbps and 32 kbps. Lower rates can be obtained by a much more radical approach to compression. **Linear Predictive Coding** uses a mathematical model of the state of the vocal tract as its representation of speech. Instead of transmitting the speech as audio samples, it sends parameters describing the corresponding state of the model. At the receiving end, these parameters can be used to construct the speech, by applying them to the model. The details of the model and how the parameters are derived from the speech lie beyond the scope of this book. Speech compressed in this way can be transmitted at speeds as low as 2.4 kbps. Because the sound is reconstructed algorithmically, it has a machine-like quality, so it is only suitable for applications where the content of the speech is more important than a faithful rendition of someone's voice.

Perceptually Based Compression

The secret of effective lossy compression is to identify data that doesn't matter – in the sense of not affecting perception of the signal – and to throw it away. If an audio signal is digitized in a straightforward way, data corresponding to sounds that are inaudible may be included in the digitized version. This is because the signal records all the physical variations in air pressure that cause sound, but the perception of sound is a sensation produced in the brain, via the ear, and the ear and brain do not respond to the sound waves in a simple way.

Two phenomena in particular cause some sounds not to be heard, despite being physically present. Both are familiar experiences: a sound may be too quiet to be heard, or it may be obscured by some other sound. Neither phenomenon is quite as straightforward as it might appear.

The **threshold of hearing** is the minimum level at which a sound can be heard. It varies non-linearly with frequency, as shown in Figure 8.16. A very low- or very high-frequency sound must be much louder than a mid-range tone in order to be heard. It is surely no coincidence that we are most sensitive to sounds in the frequency range that corresponds to human speech. When compressing sound, there is no point in retaining sounds that fall below the threshold of hearing, so a compression algorithm can discard the corresponding data. To do this, the algorithm must use a **psycho-acoustical model** – that is, a mathematical description of aspects

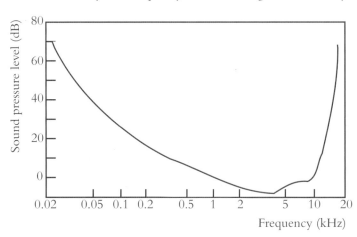

Figure 8.16. *The threshold of hearing*

of the way the ear and brain perceive sounds. In this case, what is needed is a description of the way the threshold of hearing varies with frequency.

Loud tones can obscure softer tones that occur at the same time. In fact, they can also obscure softer tones that occur a little later or – strange as it may seem – slightly earlier. This is not simply a case of the loud tone "drowning out" the softer one; the effect is more complex, and depends on the relative frequencies of the two tones. **Masking**, as this phenomenon is known, can be conveniently described as a modification of the threshold of hearing curve in the region of a loud tone. As Figure 8.17 shows, the threshold is raised in the

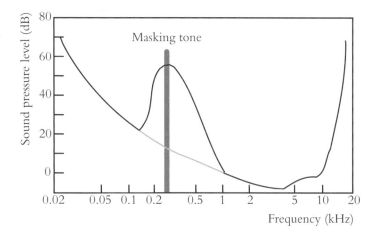

Figure 8.17. *Modification of the threshold of hearing by a masking tone*

neighbourhood of the masking tone. The raised portion, or **masking curve**, is non-linear and asymmetrical, rising faster than it falls. Any sound that lies within the masking curve will be inaudible, even though it rises above the unmodified threshold of hearing. Thus, there is an additional opportunity to discard data. Masking can be used more cleverly, though. Because masking hides noise as well as some components of the signal, quantization noise can be masked. Where a masking sound is present, the signal can be quantized relatively coarsely, using fewer bits than would otherwise be needed, because the resulting quantization noise can be hidden under the masking curve.

It is evident that the phenomena just described offer the potential for additional compression. It is not obvious how a compression algorithm can be implemented to take advantage of this potential. The approach usually adopted is to use a bank of filters to split the signal into bands of frequencies; 32 bands are commonly used. The average signal level in each band is calculated, and using these values and a psycho-acoustical model, a masking level for each band is computed. That is, it is assumed that the masking curve within each band can be approximated by a single value. If the signal in a band falls entirely below its masking level, that band is discarded. Otherwise, the signal is quantized using the least number of bits that causes the quantization noise to be masked.

Turning the preceding sketch into a working algorithm involves many technical details that lie beyond the scope of this book. The best-known algorithms that have been developed are those specified for audio compression in the MPEG standards. MPEG-1 and MPEG-2 are primarily video standards, but, since most video has sound associated with it, they also include audio compression. MPEG audio has been so successful that it is often used on its own purely for compressing sound, especially music.

MPEG-1 specifies three "layers" of audio compression. All three layers are based on the principles just outlined. The encoding process increases in complexity from Layer 1 to Layer 3, while as a result, the data rate of the compressed audio decreases. The quality obtained at 192 kbps for each channel at Layer 1 only needs 128 kbps at Layer 2, and 64 kbps at Layer 3. (These data rates will be doubled for stereo.) MPEG-1 Layer 3 audio, or **MP3** as it is usually called,[†] achieves compression ratios of around 10:1 while maintaining high quality. A typical track from a CD can be compressed to under 3 Mbytes. The sound quality at this rate is sometimes claimed to be "CD quality", but this is something of an exaggeration. Higher bit rates can be used at Layer 3, however, giving correspondingly better quality. Variable bit rate (VBR) coding is also possible, with the bit rate being changed, so that passages which do not compress easily can be encoded at a higher rate than those which do. MP3 can also encode audio at lower bit rates, for example for streaming. At 64 kbps, stereo quality is claimed to be as good as FM radio.

The audio part of the MPEG-2 standard includes an encoding that is essentially identical with MPEG-1 audio, except for some extensions to cope with surround sound. The MPEG-2 standard also defined a new audio codec, **Advanced Audio Coding (AAC)**. AAC is also incorporated in MPEG-4, and is most often considered part of that standard. Unlike MP3, AAC is not backwards compatible with earlier MPEG standards, or lower layers. By abandoning backwards compatibility, AAC was able to achieve higher compression ratios at lower bit rates than MP3. Like MP3, AAC is based on perceptual coding, but it uses additional techniques and a more complicated implementation. Subjective listening tests consistently rate AAC quality as superior to MP3 at the same bit rates, and the same subjective quality is attained by AAC at lower rates than MP3. For instance, AAC audio at 96 kbps is considered to be superior to MP3 at 128 kbps. AAC is the codec used for audio distributed over the Internet from the popular iTunes service.

Lossy compression always sounds like a dubious practice – how can you discard information without affecting the quality? In the case of MPEG audio, the argument is that the information that has been discarded is inaudible. This contention is based on extensive listening tests, and is supported by the rapid acceptance of MP3 and AAC as formats for downloading music. (However, it should be remembered that some people care much more about audio quality than others.) As with any lossy form of compression, though, MPEG audio will deteriorate progressively if it is decompressed and recompressed a number of times. It is therefore only suitable as a delivery format, and should not be used during production, when uncompressed audio should be used whenever possible.

---

† *Despite what you may sometimes read, MP3 does not stand for MPEG-3. There is no MPEG-3.*

> ## KEY POINTS
>
> **Sound is difficult to compress using lossless methods, except for special cases.**
>
> **Some compression of audio can be obtained by run-length encoding samples that fall below a threshold that can be considered to represent silence.**
>
> **Companding uses non-linear quantization to compress speech. μ-law and A-law companding are used for telephony.**
>
> **Adaptive Differential Pulse Code Modulation (ADPCM), which works by storing information about the difference between a sample and a value predicted from the preceding sample, is also used in telephony.**
>
> **Perceptually based compression discards inaudible sounds.**
>
> **A psycho-acoustical model describes how the threshold of hearing varies non-linearly with frequency.**
>
> **Masking is a modification of the threshold of hearing curve in the region of a loud tone. The threshold is raised in the neighbourhood of the masking tone.**
>
> **Filters are used to split a signal into 32 bands, and a masking level for each band is computed. Signals that fall below the level can be discarded.**
>
> **Practical implementations of perceptually based compression are the basis of MP3 and AAC compression.**

MIDI

If we had written a piece of music, there are two ways we could send it to you. We could play it, record the performance, and send you the recording, or we could write it down using some form of notation, indicating the arrangement, and send you the sheet music, so that you could play the piece for yourself. In the first case, we send you the actual sound. In the second, we send you what amounts to a set of instructions telling you how to produce the sound. In either case we are making some assumptions about what you can do. For the recording, we assume you have a machine capable of playing back whichever medium we have recorded our performance on. For the sheet music, we are making the more demanding assumptions that you can read our chosen music notation, have access to the instrument or instruments indicated in the arrangement, and can either play yourself or get musicians to play those instruments. If the music is arranged for a symphony orchestra, this might present some difficulties for you, whereas if we were to send a recording, all the difficulties would lie at our end.

In the digital realm, there is a similar choice of options for delivering music. So far, we have considered ways of delivering digitized sound, that is, the equivalent of recordings. There also exists an equivalent to delivering the sheet music, i.e. a way of delivering instructions about how to produce the music which can be interpreted by suitable software or hardware. Similar assumptions must be made. For sound files, you must have software that can read them – but as we have seen, this is not a demanding requirement. For instructions, you must have software that can interpret the instructions, and some means of producing sounds that correspond to the appropriate instruments.

MIDI (Musical Instruments Digital Interface) provides a basis for satisfying these requirements. Originally, MIDI was devised as a standard protocol for communicating between electronic instruments, such as synthesizers, samplers and drum machines.

By defining a standard hardware interface, and a set of instructions indicating such things as the start and end of a note, it provided a means of controlling a collection of such instruments from a single keyboard. This removed the requirement for huge banks of keyboards, and opened the way for playing traditional keyboard instruments, particularly synthesizers, with other controllers, such as drum pads or wind instruments.

More significantly, perhaps, MIDI allowed instruments to be controlled automatically by devices that could be programmed to send out sequences of MIDI instructions. Originally, ***sequencers***, as these devices are known, were dedicated hardware devices, programmed using their own built-in, relatively clumsy interfaces. It was not long before it was realized that computer programs could offer a more convenient and flexible means of sequencing, provided that a computer could be fitted with a MIDI interface so that it could send the necessary signals to other MIDI devices. Such an interface is a relatively simple and inexpensive device, so computer-based sequencers rapidly became available. A software sequencer provides editing and compositional functions, so it needs to store MIDI sequences in files. This requirement led to the development of a standard file format for MIDI files – that is, a way of storing MIDI on disk. Clearly, such files can be exchanged between computers equipped with MIDI software. They can also be incorporated into multimedia.

Playing back MIDI files requires an instrument that understands MIDI, but a computer, equipped with suitable hardware or software, can be such an instrument itself. Sounds can be either synthe-sized on a sound card, or held on disk in the form of samples, to be played back in response to MIDI instructions. MIDI files are therefore a means of communicating music. Because they do not contain any audio data, they can be much more compact than actual digitized sound files. For the same reason, though, they cannot guarantee the same fidelity. The samples available when the file is produced may be of higher quality than those used to play it back – just as the musi-cian who plays a piece of music from a score may not be sufficiently accomplished to realize the composer's intentions. In both cases, the result is unpredictable.

MIDI Messages

A *MIDI message* is an instruction that controls some aspect of the performance of an instrument. Messages are encoded in much the same way as machine instructions: a status byte indicates the type of the message, and is followed by one or two data bytes giving the values of parameters. Although wind instruments, drum pads and guitars are used as MIDI controllers (as devices that transmit MIDI signals are called), MIDI is markedly biased towards keyboard instruments. Thus, for example, the most commonly used message is "Note On", which takes two parameters. The first is a number between 0 and 127 indicating the note to be sounded, where consecutive numbers represent notes that are a semi-tone apart, like keys on a piano. The second parameter is a key velocity, indicating how fast the key was pressed, and hence the attack of the note. When an actual keyboard is being used to generate MIDI messages, these values will be sensed by the keyboard's hardware as the musician plays the key. When the message is being generated by software, the values are specified by the user.

Other significant MIDI messages include "Note Off", which ends a note, "Key Pressure", which indicates the degree of "aftertouch" to be applied, and "Pitch Bend", which changes note values dynamically, as a guitarist does by bending the string (on MIDI keyboards, a wheel is used for this function).

The status bytes and data bytes in a stream of MIDI instructions are distinguishable by the value of their most significant bit. This makes an optimization possible – where a sequence of messages all have the same status byte, it may be omitted from the second and subsequent messages, for which it will be inferred from the most recent value. This arrangement is called "running status"; it can save an appreciable number of bytes where a sequence of notes is being played with no modifications. Using the convention that the end of a note can be indicated by a "Note On" message with a velocity of zero, the whole sequence can consist of a single "Note On" status byte, followed by a series of data bytes giving the notes to be played and the velocities to be applied to them.

When a MIDI message is interpreted, we say that an event occurs. In a live performance, the timing of events is determined by the player in real time. In a MIDI file, it is necessary to record the time of each event. Each message is preceded by a "delta time", that is, a measure of the time since the preceding event. Near the beginning of the file is a specification of the units to be used for times.

General MIDI

The preceding account indicates how notes are produced, but leaves unanswered the question of how they are to be associated with particular sounds. Typically, the sorts of instruments controlled by MIDI – synthesizers and samplers – provide a variety of "voices". In the case of synthesizers, these are different synthesized sounds, often called "patches" by synthesists. In the case of samplers, they are different instrument samples. A MIDI "Program Change" message selects a new voice, using a value between 0 and 127. The mapping from these values to voices is not specified in the MIDI standard, and may depend on the particular instrument being controlled. There is thus a possibility that a MIDI file intended to specify a piece for piano and violin might end up being played on trombone and kettle drum, for example. To help overcome this unsatisfactory situation, an addendum to the MIDI standard, known as **General MIDI**, was produced, which specifies 128 standard voices to correspond to the values used by "Program Change" messages. The assignments are shown in Figure 8.18. For drum machines and percussion samplers, Program Change values are interpreted differently, as elements of drum kits – cymbals of various sorts, snares, tom-toms, and so on – as shown in Figure 8.19.

General MIDI only associates program numbers with voice names. There is no guarantee that identical sounds will be generated for each name by different instruments. A cheap sound card may attempt to synthesize all of them, while a good sampler may use high-quality samples of the corresponding real instruments. However, adherence to General MIDI offers some guarantee of consistency, which is otherwise entirely missing.

QuickTime incorporates MIDI-like functionality. QuickTime Musical Instruments provides a set of instrument samples, and the QuickTime Music Architecture incorporates a superset of the features of MIDI. QuickTime can read standard MIDI files, so any computer with QuickTime installed can play MIDI music using software alone. QuickTime can also control external MIDI devices. MIDI tracks can be combined with audio, video or any of the other media types supported by QuickTime.

MIDI Software

MIDI sequencing programs, such as Cakewalk Metro and Cubase, perform capture and editing functions equivalent to those of video editing software. They support multiple tracks, which can be allocated to different voices, thus allowing polytimbral music to be constructed. In addition, such packages support composition.

Music can be captured as it is played from MIDI controllers attached to a computer via a MIDI interface. The sequencer can generate metronome ticks to help the player maintain an accurate tempo. Although it is common to use the sequencer simply as if it were a tape recorder, to capture a performance in real time, sometimes MIDI data is entered one note at a time, which allows musicians to "play" music that would otherwise be beyond their competence. Facilities normally found in conventional audio recording software are also available, in particular the ability to "punch in" – the start and end point of a defective passage are marked, the sequencer starts playing before the beginning, and then switches to record mode, allowing a new version of the passage to be recorded to replace the original.

1	Acoustic Grand Piano	44	Contrabass	87	Synth Lead 7
2	Bright Acoustic Piano	45	Tremolo Strings	88	Synth Lead 8
3	Electric Grand Piano	46	Pizzicato Strings	89	Synth Pad 1
4	Honky-tonk Piano	47	Orchestral Harp	90	Synth Pad 2
5	Rhodes Piano	48	Timpani	91	Synth Pad 3
6	Chorused Piano	49	Acoustic String Ensemble 1	92	Synth Pad 4
7	Harpsichord	50	Acoustic String Ensemble 2	93	Synth Pad 5
8	Clavinet	51	Synth Strings 1	94	Synth Pad 6
9	Celesta	52	Synth Strings 2	95	Synth Pad 7
10	Glockenspiel	53	Aah Choir	96	Synth Pad 8
11	Music Box	54	Ooh Choir	97	Ice Rain
12	Vibraphone	55	Synvox	98	Soundtracks
13	Marimba	56	Orchestra Hit	99	Crystal
14	Xylophone	57	Trumpet	100	Atmosphere
15	Tubular bells	58	Trombone	101	Bright
16	Dulcimer	59	Tuba	102	Goblin
17	Draw Organ	60	Muted Trumpet	103	Echoes
18	Percussive Organ	61	French Horn	104	Space
19	Rock Organ	62	Brass Section	105	Sitar
20	Church Organ	63	Synth Brass 1	106	Banjo
21	Reed Organ	64	Synth Brass 2	107	Shamisen
22	Accordion	65	Soprano Sax	108	Koto
23	Harmonica	66	Alto Sax	109	Kalimba
24	Tango Accordion	67	Tenor Sax	110	Bagpipe
25	Acoustic Nylon Guitar	68	Baritone Sax	111	Fiddle
26	Acoustic Steel Guitar	69	Oboe	112	Shanai
27	Electric Jazz Guitar	70	English Horn	113	Tinkle bell
28	Electric clean Guitar	71	Bassoon	114	Agogo
29	Electric Guitar muted	72	Clarinet	115	Steel Drums
30	Overdriven Guitar	73	Piccolo	116	Woodblock
31	Distortion Guitar	74	Flute	117	Taiko Drum
32	Guitar Harmonics	75	Recorder	118	Melodic Tom
33	Wood Bass	76	Pan Flute	119	Synth Tom
34	Electric Bass Fingered	77	Bottle blow	120	Reverse Cymbal
35	Electric Bass Picked	78	Shakuhachi	121	Guitar Fret Noise
36	Fretless Bass	79	Whistle	122	Breath Noise
37	Slap Bass 1	80	Ocarina	123	Seashore
38	Slap Bass 2	81	Square Lead	124	Bird Tweet
39	Synth Bass 1	82	Saw Lead	125	Telephone Ring
40	Synth Bass 2	83	Calliope	126	Helicopter
41	Violin	84	Chiffer	127	Applause
42	Viola	85	Synth Lead 5	128	Gunshot
43	Cello	86	Synth Lead 6		

Figure 8.18. *General MIDI voice numbers*

35	Acoustic Bass Drum	47	Low Mid Tom Tom	59	Ride Cymbal 2
36	Bass Drum 1	48	Hi Mid Tom Tom	60	Hi Bongo
37	Side Stick	49	Crash Cymbal 1	61	Low Bongo
38	Acoustic Snare	50	Hi Tom Tom	62	Mute Hi Conga
39	Hand Clap	51	Ride Cymbal 1	63	Open Hi Conga
40	Electric Snare	52	Chinese Cymbal	64	Low Conga
41	Lo Floor Tom	53	Ride Bell	65	Hi Timbale
42	Closed Hi Hat	54	Tambourine	66	Lo Timbale
43	Hi Floor Tom	55	Splash Cymbal		
44	Pedal Hi Hat	56	Cowbell		
45	Lo Tom Tom	57	Crash Cymbal 2		
46	Open Hi Hat	58	Vibraslap		

Figure 8.19. *General MIDI drum kit numbers*

Sequencers will optionally **quantize** tempo during recording, fitting the length of notes to exact sixteenth notes, or eighth note triplets, or whatever duration is specified. This allows rhythmically loose playing to be brought into strict tempo, which may be felt desirable for certain styles of music, but the result often has an unnatural machine-like quality, since live musicians very rarely play so precisely to the beat.

Most programs allow music to be entered using classical music notation, often by dragging and dropping notes and other symbols onto a stave. Some programs allow printed sheet music to be scanned, and will perform optical character recognition to transform the music into MIDI. The opposite transformation, from MIDI to a printed score, is also often provided, enabling transcriptions of performed music to be made automatically. (In this case, quantization is usually necessary, since otherwise the program will transcribe exactly what was played, even if that involves dotted sixty-fourth notes and rests.) Those who do not read music usually prefer to use the "piano-roll" interface, which allows the duration of notes to be specified graphically, essentially using a timeline. For music which is constructed out of repeating sections, loops can be defined and reused many times.

Once a piece of music has been recorded or entered, it can be edited. Individual notes' pitch and duration can be altered, sections can be cut and pasted, or global changes can be made, such as transposing the entire piece into a different key, or changing the time signature. The parameters of individual MIDI events can be changed – the velocity of a note can be altered, for example. Voices can be changed to assign different instruments to the parts of the arrangement.

Because digital audio is very demanding of computer resources but MIDI is much less so, the two forms of music representation were originally separated, with different software being used for each. Now that computers have become powerful enough to take audio in their stride, the two are commonly integrated in a single application, which allows MIDI tracks to be combined and synchronized with full audio. This arrangement overcomes one of the major limitations of MIDI, namely the impossibility of representing vocals (except for "Oohs" and "Aahs"). MIDI can be transformed into audio, much as vector graphics can be rasterized and transformed into pixels. The reverse transformation is sometimes supported, too, although it is more difficult to implement. MIDI captures the musical structure of sound, since MIDI events correspond to notes. Being able to transform audio into MIDI allows music to be recorded from ordinary instruments instead of MIDI controllers — it can even be recorded from somebody's whistling — and then edited or transcribed in terms of musical notes.

KEY POINTS

MIDI provides a way of representing music as instructions describing how to produce notes, instead of as a record of the actual sounds.

MIDI provides a standard protocol and hardware interface for communicating between electronic instruments, such as synthesizers, samplers and drum machines, allowing instruments to be controlled by hardware or software sequencers.

A computer can control instruments through a MIDI interface, synthesize notes on a sound card or play back samples from disk in response to MIDI instructions.

MIDI messages are instructions that control some aspect of the performance of an instrument.

Each instruction has a status byte, indicating the type of message, and two data bytes, providing the values of its parameters. (e.g. Note On + note number + key velocity.)

Running status allows the status byte to be omitted if it is the same as in the preceding message.

General MIDI is a standard association between 128 Program Change values and voice names. (There is no guarantee that identical sounds will be produced for the same voice names on different instruments.)

QuickTime incorporates MIDI-like functionality. MIDI tracks can be combined with audio, video or any of the other media types supported by QuickTime.

MIDI software allows recording from a MIDI device, input as musical notation or on a "piano roll", and editing, often integrated with sound editing.

Exercises

Test Questions

1 If you had to create an alert sound, to be used to notify users when some important event occurred, would it be sensible to use a pure 18 kHz tone? Explain your answer.

2 Why are the sampling frequencies normally used for "lo-fi" digital sound exact sub-multiples of 44.1 kHz?

3 Explain why a filter is used to remove frequencies greater than half the sampling rate before audio is digitized. Could the filtering be done after sampling had taken place?

4 Why does increasing the sample size reduce the need for dithering of an audio signal?

5 Why is the bit rate of an MP3 file not the same as its sampling rate?

6 What could you do to correct a sound that was digitized with its levels (a) too high; (b) too low? How would you prepare a sound recording with an extremely wide dynamic range for use as a video soundtrack?

7 If you had recorded some music and on playing it back discovered that the recording equipment had picked up hum from the mains, how would you attempt to improve the recording?

8 Why is it important to have an accurate psycho-acoustical model to perform lossy audio compression?

9 Describe the alterations that must be made to a note to raise its pitch by an octave, without changing its duration:

(a) if the sound is represented by a digital recording;

(b) if the sound is represented by a MIDI "Note On" message.

(Raising a note's pitch by an octave is the same as doubling its frequency. There are 12 semi-tones in an octave.)

Discussion Topics

1 What is the point of audio recorders that sample at 192 kHz when the limit of human hearing is around 20 kHz?

2 A problem commonly encountered when recording in the open air is that a microphone will pick up the sounds made by the wind blowing against it. Describe how you would attempt to remove such noise from a digitized recording. How successful would you expect your attempts to be? Suggest an alternative approach to eliminating wind noise.

3 Given that singing has characteristics of both speech and music, which compression algorithms would you expect to be most successful on songs?

4 Is there a limit on how far you can (a) stretch, (b) contract a digitized sound successfully? What aspects of particular kinds of sound might affect the limits?

Practical Tasks

1 Make some recordings of different people reading several different short phrases. Examine the waveforms of these recordings in a program that allows you to do so. Is it possible to identify the phrase being spoken from the waveform? Is it possible to identify the speaker from the waveform?

2 Make an outdoor recording on a windy day, and try to remove the wind noise by applying the solutions you proposed in the first discussion topic.

3 Take the recordings you made for the first practical task and using whatever audio software you think suitable, combine them into a soundtrack that could serve as the background noise to a party scene in a film.

9

Text and Typography

■ **Character Sets**

Standards. Unicode and ISO 10646.

■ **Fonts**

Accessing Fonts. Classification and Choice of Fonts.
Font Terminology. Digital Font Formats.

■ **Layout and Formatting**

Text in Graphics. Layout. Inline and Block Formatting.
Markup and Stylesheets.

Text has a dual nature: it is a visual representation of language, and a graphic element in its own right. Text in digital form must also be a representation of language – that is, we need to relate bit patterns stored in a computer's memory or transmitted over a network to the symbols of a written language (either a natural one or a computer language). When we consider the display of stored text, its visual aspect becomes relevant. We then become concerned with such issues as the precise shape of characters, their spacing, and the layout of lines, paragraphs and larger divisions of text on the screen or page. These issues of display are traditionally the concern of the art of typography. Much of the accumulated typographical practice of the last several centuries can be adapted to the display of the textual elements of multimedia.

In this chapter, we consider how the fundamental units of written languages – characters – can be represented in a digital form, and how the digital representation of characters can be turned into a visual representation for display and laid out on the screen. We will show how digital font technology and markup make it possible to approximate the typographical richness of printed text in the textual components of multimedia.

Character Sets

In keeping with text's dual nature, it is convenient to distinguish between the lexical content of a piece of text and its appearance. By content we mean the characters that make up the words and other units, such as punctuation or mathematical symbols. (At this stage we are not considering "content" in the sense of the meaning or message contained in the text.) The appearance of the text comprises its visual attributes, such as the precise shape of the characters, their size, and the way the content is arranged on the page or screen. For example, the content of the following two sentences from the short story *Jeeves and the Impending Doom* by P.G. Wodehouse is identical, but their appearance is not:

```
The Right Hon was a tubby little chap who looked as if he had
been poured into his clothes and had forgotten to say 'When!'
```

The Right Hon was a tubby little chap who looked as if he had been *poured* into his clothes and had forgotten to say 'When!'

We all readily understand that the first symbol in each version of this sentence is a capital T, even though one is several times as large as the other, is much darker, has some additional strokes, and extends down into the line below. To express their fundamental identity, we distinguish between an abstract character and its graphic representations, of which there is a potentially infinite number. Here, we have two graphic representations of the same abstract character (the letter T).

As a slight over-simplification, we could say that the content is the part of a text that carries its meaning or semantics, while the appearance is a surface attribute that may affect how easy the text is to read, or how pleasant it is to look at, but does not substantially alter its meaning. In the example just given, the fixed-width, typewriter-like font of the first version clearly differs from the more formal book font used for most of the second, but this and the initial dropped capital and use of different fonts do not alter the joke. Note, however, that the italicization of the word "poured" in the second version does imply an emphasis on the word that is missing in the plain version (and also in the original story), although we would normally consider italicization an aspect of the appearance like the use of the small caps for "Right Hon". So the distinction between appearance and content is not quite as clear-cut as one might think, but it is useful because it permits a separation of concerns between these two qualities that text possesses.

Abstract characters are grouped into *alphabets*. Each particular alphabet forms the basis of the written form of a certain language or group of languages. We consider any set of distinct symbols to be an alphabet, but we do not define "symbol". In the abstract, an alphabet can be any set at all, but in practical terms, the only symbols of interest will be those used for writing down some language. This includes the symbols used in an ideographic writing system, such as those used for Chinese and Japanese, where each character represents a whole word or concept, as well as the phonetic letters of Western-style alphabets, and the intermediate syllabic alphabets, such as Korean Hangul. In contrast to colloquial usage, we include punctuation marks, numerals and mathematical symbols in an alphabet, and treat upper- and lower-case versions of the same letter as different symbols. Thus, for our purposes, the English alphabet includes the letters A, B, C, …, Z and a, b, c, … ,z, but also punctuation marks, such as comma and exclamation mark, the digits 0, 1, …, 9, and common symbols such as + and =.

To represent text digitally, it is necessary to define a mapping between (abstract) characters in some alphabet and values that can be stored in a computer system. As we explained in Chapter 2, the only values that we can store are bit patterns, which can be interpreted as integers to base 2, so the problem becomes one of mapping characters to integers. As an abstract problem this is trivial: any mapping will do, provided it associates each character of interest with exactly one number. Such an association is called – with little respect for mathematical usage – a *character set*; its domain (the alphabet for which the mapping is defined) is called the *character repertoire*. For each character in the repertoire, the character set defines a *code value* in its range, which is some-times called the set of *code points*. The character repertoire for a character set intended for written English text would include the 26 letters of the alphabet in both upper- and lower-case forms, as well as the 10 digits and the usual collection of punctuation marks. The character repertoire for a character set intended for Russian would include the letters of the Cyrillic alphabet. Both of these character sets could use the same set of code points; provided that it was not necessary to use both character sets simultaneously (for example, in a bilingual document), a character in the English alphabet could have the same code value as one in the Cyrillic alphabet. The character repertoire for a character set intended for the Japanese Kanji alphabet must contain at least the 1945 ideograms for common use and 166 for names sanctioned by the Japanese Ministry of Education, and could contain over 6000 characters. Consequently, the Japanese Kanji alphabet requires far more distinct code points than an English or Cyrillic character set.

The mere existence of a character set is adequate to support operations such as editing and searching of text, since it allows us to store characters as their code values, and to compare two characters for equality by comparing the corresponding integers; it only requires some means of input and output. In simple terms, this means that it is necessary to arrange that when a key is pressed on a keyboard, or the equivalent operation is performed on some other input device, a command is transmitted to the computer, causing the bit pattern corresponding to the character for that key to be passed to the program currently receiving input. Conversely, when a value is transmitted to a monitor or other output device, a representation of the corresponding character should appear.

There are advantages to using a character set with some structure to it, instead of a completely arbitrary assignment of numbers to abstract characters. In particular, it is useful to use integers within a comparatively small range that can easily be manipulated by a computer. It can be helpful, too, if the code values for consecutive letters are consecutive numbers, since this simplifies some operations on text, such as sorting.

Standards

The most important consideration concerning character sets is standardization. Transferring text between different makes of computer, interfacing peripheral devices from different manufacturers and communicating over networks are everyday activities. Continual translation between different manufacturers' character codes would not be acceptable, so a standard character code is essential. The following description of character code standards is necessarily somewhat dry, but an understanding of them is necessary if you are to avoid the pitfalls of incompatibility and the resulting corruption of texts. Unfortunately, standardization is never a straightforward business, and the situation with respect to character codes remains somewhat unsatisfactory.

ASCII (American Standard Code for Information Interchange) was the dominant character set from the 1970s into the early twenty-first century. It uses 7 bits to store each code value, so there is a total of 128 code points. The character repertoire of ASCII only comprises 95 characters, however. The values 0 to 31 and 127 are assigned to *control characters*, such as form-feed, carriage return and delete, which have traditionally been used to control the operation of output devices. The control characters are a legacy from ASCII's origins in early teletype character sets. Many of them no longer have any useful meaning, and are often appropriated by application programs for their own purposes. Figure 9.1 shows the ASCII character set. (The character with code value 32 is a space.)

American English is one of the few languages in the world for which ASCII provides an adequate character repertoire. Attempts by the standardization bodies to provide better support for a wider range of languages began when ASCII was adopted as an ISO standard (ISO 646) in 1972. ISO 646 incorporates several national variants on the version of ASCII used in the United States, to accommodate, for example, some accented letters and national currency symbols.

A standard with variants is no real solution to the problem of accommodating different languages. If a file prepared in one country is sent to another and read on a computer set up to use a different national variant of ISO 646, some of the characters will be displayed incorrectly. For example, a hash character (#) typed in the United States would be displayed as a pound sign (£) in the UK (and vice versa) if the British user's computer used the UK variant of ISO 646. (More likely, the hash would display correctly, but the Briton would be unable to type a pound sign, because it is more convenient to use US ASCII (ISO 646-US) anyway, to prevent such problems.)

32		33	!	34	"	35	#
36	$	37	%	38	&	39	'
40	(	41	)	42	★	43	+
44	,	45	-	46	.	47	/
48	0	49	1	50	2	51	3
52	4	53	5	54	6	55	7
56	8	57	9	58	:	59	;
60	<	61	=	62	>	63	?
64	@	65	A	66	B	67	C
68	D	69	E	70	F	71	G
72	H	73	I	74	J	75	K
76	L	77	M	78	N	79	O
80	P	81	Q	82	R	83	S
84	T	85	U	86	V	87	W
88	X	89	Y	90	Z	91	[
92	\	93	]	94	^	95	_
96	`	97	a	98	b	99	c
100	d	101	e	102	f	103	g
104	h	105	i	106	j	107	k
108	l	109	m	110	n	111	o
112	p	113	q	114	r	115	s
116	t	117	u	118	v	119	w
120	x	121	y	122	z	123	{
124			125	}	126	~		

Figure 9.1. *The printable ASCII characters*

A better solution than national variants of the 7-bit ISO 646 character set lies in the provision of a character set with more code points, such that the ASCII character repertoire is mapped to the values 0–127, thus assuring compatibility, and additional symbols required outside the USA or for

160		161	¡	162	¢	163	£
164	¤	165	¥	166	¦	167	§
168	¨	169	©	170	ª	171	«
172	¬	173	-	174	®	175	¯
176	°	177	±	178	²	179	³
180	´	181	µ	182	¶	183	·
184	¸	185	¹	186	º	187	»
188	¼	189	½	190	¾	191	¿
192	À	193	Á	194	Â	195	Ã
196	Ä	197	Å	198	Æ	199	Ç
200	È	201	É	202	Ê	203	Ë
204	Ì	205	Í	206	Î	207	Ï
208	Ð	209	Ñ	210	Ò	211	Ó
212	Ô	213	Õ	214	Ö	215	×
216	Ø	217	Ù	218	Ú	219	Û
220	Ü	221	Ý	222	Þ	223	ß
224	à	225	á	226	â	227	ã
228	ä	229	å	230	æ	231	ç
232	è	233	é	234	ê	235	ë
236	ì	237	í	238	î	239	ï
240	ð	241	ñ	242	ò	243	ó
244	ô	245	õ	246	ö	247	÷
248	ø	249	ù	250	ú	251	û
252	ü	253	ý	254	þ	255	ÿ

Figure 9.2. *The top part of the ISO Latin1 character set*

specialized purposes are mapped to other values. Doubling the set of code points was easy: the seven bits of an ASCII character are invariably stored in an 8-bit byte. It was originally envisaged that the remaining bit would be used as a parity bit for error detection. As data transmission became more reliable, and superior error checking was built in to higher-level protocols, this parity bit fell into disuse, effectively becoming available as the high-order bit of an 8-bit character.

Predictably, the different manufacturers each developed their own incompatible 8-bit extensions to ASCII. These all shared some general features: the lower half (code points 0–127) was identical to ASCII; the upper half (code points 128–255) held accented letters and extra punctuation and mathematical symbols. Since a set of 256 values is insufficient to accommodate all the characters required for every alphabet in use, each 8-bit character code had different variants; for example, one for Western European languages, another for languages written using the Cyrillic script, and so on. (Under MS-DOS and Windows, these variants are called "code pages.")

Despite these commonalities, the character repertoires and the code values assigned by the different manufacturers' character sets are different. For example, the character é (e with an acute accent) has the code value 142 in the Macintosh Standard Roman character set, whereas it has the code value 233 in the corresponding Windows character set, in which 142 is not assigned as the value for any character; 233 in Macintosh Standard Roman, on the other hand, is É. Because the repertoires of the character sets are different, it is not even always possible to perform a translation between them, so transfer of text between platforms is problematical.

Clearly, standardization of 8-bit character sets was required. During the 1980s the multi-part standard ISO 8859 was produced. This defines a collection of 8-bit character sets, each designed to accommodate the needs of a group of languages (usually geographically related). The first part of the standard, ISO 8859-1, is usually referred to as **ISO Latin1**, and covers most Western European languages. Like all the ISO 8859 character sets, the lower half of ISO Latin1 is identical to ASCII (i.e. ISO 646-US); the code points 128–159 are mostly unused, although a few are used for various diacritical marks. Figure 9.2 shows the 96 additional code values provided for accented letters and symbols. (The character with code value 160 is a "non-breaking" space.)

IN DETAIL

The Windows Roman character set (Windows 1252) is sometimes claimed to be the same as ISO Latin1, but it uses some of the code points between 128 and 159 for characters which are not present in ISO 8859-1's repertoire.

Other parts of ISO 8859 are designed for use with Eastern European languages, including Czech, Slovak and Croatian (ISO 8859-2 or Latin2), for languages that use the Cyrillic alphabet (ISO 8859-5), for modern Greek (ISO 8859-7), Hebrew (ISO 8859-8), and others – there is a total of 10 parts to ISO 8859 with more projected, notably an ISO Latin0, which includes the Euro currency symbol.

ISO 8859-1 has been used extensively on the World Wide Web for pages written in languages that use the alphabet it supports, but manufacturers' proprietary non-standard character sets have remained in use. There is a fundamental problem with 8-bit character sets, which has prevented ISO 8859's universal adoption: 256 is not enough code points – not enough to represent ideographically based alphabets, and not enough to enable us to work with several languages at a time (unless they all happen to use the same variant of ISO 8859). Newer standards that are not restricted to so few code points are rendering ISO 8859 obsolete.

Unicode and ISO 10646

The only possible solution to the problem of insufficient code points is to use more than one byte for each code value. A 16-bit character set has 65,536 code points – putting it another way, it can accommodate 256 variants of an 8-bit character set simultaneously. Similarly, a 24-bit character set can accommodate 256 16-bit character sets, and a 32-bit character set can accommodate 256 of those. ISO (in conjunction with the IEC) set out to develop a 32-bit **Universal Character Set (UCS)**, designated ISO 10646, structured in this way: a collection of 2^{32} characters can be arranged as a hypercube (a four-dimensional cube) consisting of 256 groups, each of which consists of 256 planes of 256 rows, each comprising 256 characters (which might be the character repertoire of an 8-bit character set). The intention was to organize the immense character repertoire allowed by a 32-bit character set with alphabets distributed among the planes in

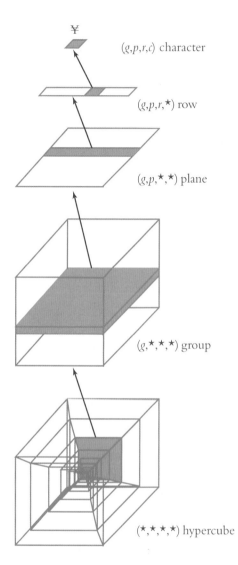

(g,p,r,c) character

(g,p,r,★) row

(g,p,★,★) plane

(g,★,★,★) group

(★,★,★,★) hypercube

Figure 9.3. *The structure of ISO 10646*

a linguistically sensible way, so that the resulting character set would have a clear logical structure. Each character can be identified by specifying its group *g*, its plane *p*, and a row *r* and column *c* (see Figure 9.3). Each of *g*, *p*, *r* and *c* is an 8-bit quantity, which can fit in one byte; four bytes thus identify a unique character, so, inverting our viewpoint, the code value for any character is the 32-bit value which specifies its position within the hypercube.

To make the structure of the character set evident, we usually write code points as quadruples (*g,p,r,c*), which can be considered as the coordinates of a point in a four-dimensional space. By extension, such a quadruple also identifies a subset of the character set using a ★ to denote all values in the range 0–255. Thus (0,0,0,★) is the subset with all but the lowest-order byte zero. In ISO 10646 this subset is identical to ISO Latin1.

At the same time as ISO was developing this elegant framework for its character set, an industry consortium was working on a 16-bit character set, known as *Unicode*. As we noted above, a 16-bit character set has 65,536 code points. This is not sufficient to accommodate all the characters required for Chinese, Japanese and Korean scripts in discrete positions. These three languages and their writing systems share a common ancestry, so there are thousands of identical ideographs in their scripts. The Unicode committee adopted a process they called **CJK consolidation**,[†] whereby characters used in writing Chinese, Japanese and Korean are given the same code value if they look the same, irrespective of which language they belong to, and whether or not they mean the same thing in the different languages. There is clearly a cultural bias involved here, since the same process is not applied to, for example, upper-case A and the Greek capital alpha, which are identical in appearance but have separate Unicode code values. The pragmatic justification is that, with Chinese, Japanese and Korean, thousands of characters are involved, whereas with the European and Cyrillic languages, there are relatively few. Furthermore, consolidation of those languages would interfere with compatibility with existing standards.

† Some documents use the name "Han unification" instead.

Unicode provides code values for all the characters used to write contemporary "major" languages, as well as the classical forms of some languages. The alphabets available include Latin, Greek, Cyrillic, Armenian, Hebrew, Arabic, Devanagari, Bengali, Gurmukhi, Gujarati, Oriya, Tamil, Telugu, Kannada, Malayalam, Thai, Lao, Georgian and Tibetan, as well as the Chinese, Japanese and Korean ideograms and the Japanese and Korean phonetic and syllabic scripts. Unicode also includes punctuation marks, technical and mathematical symbols, arrows and the miscellaneous symbols usually referred to as "dingbats" (pointing hands, stars, and so on). In addition to the accented letters included in many of the alphabets, separate diacritical marks (such as accents and tildes) are available and a mechanism is provided for building composite characters by combining these marks with other symbols. (This not only provides an alternative way of making accented letters, it also allows for the habit mathematicians have of making up new symbols by decorating old ones.)

In Unicode, code values for nearly 39,000 symbols are provided, leaving some code points unused. Others are reserved for the UTF-16 expansion method (described briefly later on), while a set of 6400 code points is reserved for private use, allowing organizations and individuals to define codes for their own use. Even though these codes are not part of the Unicode standard, it is guaranteed that they will never be assigned to any character by the standard, so their use will never conflict with any standard character, although it might conflict with those of other individuals.

Unicode is restricted to characters used in text. It specifically does not attempt to provide symbols for music notation or other symbolic writing systems that do not represent language.

Unicode and ISO 10646 were brought into line in 1991 when the ISO agreed that the plane $(0,0,\star,\star)$, known as the **Basic Multilingual Plane (BMP)**, should be identical to Unicode. ISO 10646 thus utilizes CJK consolidation, even though its 32-bit code space does not require it to do so. The overwhelming advantage of this arrangement is that the two standards are compatible (and the respective committees have pledged that they will remain so). To understand how it is possible to take advantage of this compatibility, we must introduce the concept of a character set *encoding*.

An encoding is another layer of mapping, which transforms a code value into a sequence of bytes for storage and transmission. When each code value occupies exactly one byte it might seem that the only sensible encoding is an identity mapping where each code value is stored or sent as itself in a single byte. Even in this case, though, a more complex encoding may be required. Because 7-bit ASCII was the dominant character code for such a long time, there are network protocols which assume that all character data is ASCII and remove or mangle the top bit of any 8-bit byte. To avoid this it may be necessary to encode 8-bit characters as sequences of 7-bit characters.

One encoding used for this purpose is called Quoted-Printable (QP). This works quite simply – any character with a code in the range 128–255 is encoded as a sequence of three bytes. The first is always the ASCII code for =; the remaining two are the codes for the hexadecimal digits of the code value. For example, é has value 233 in ISO Latin1, which is E9 in hexadecimal, so it is encoded in QP as the ASCII string =E9. Most characters with codes less than 128 are left alone. An important exception is = itself, which has to be encoded, otherwise it would appear to be the first byte of the encoded version of some other character. Hence, = appears as =3D.

For ISO 10646 the obvious encoding scheme, known as **UCS-4**, employs four bytes to hold each code value. Any value on the BMP will have the top two bytes set to zero. Since most values that are currently defined *are* on the BMP, and since economic reality suggests that for the foreseeable future most characters used in computer systems and transmitted over networks will be on the BMP, the UCS-4 encoding wastes space. ISO 10646 therefore supports an alternative encoding, **UCS-2**, which drops the top two bytes. UCS-2 is identical to Unicode.

Unicode encodings go further. There are three **UCS Transformation Formats (UTFs)** which can be applied to Unicode code values. **UTF-8** takes the reasoning we just applied to 32-bit values a step further. ASCII code values are likely to be more common in most text than any other values. Accordingly, UTF-8 encodes UCS-2 values so that if their high-order byte is zero and the low-order byte is less than 128, the value is encoded as the single low-order byte. That is, ASCII characters are represented by the same value in ASCII and UTF-8. Otherwise, the two bytes of the UCS-2 value are encoded using up to six bytes, with the highest bit of each byte set to 1 to indicate it is part of an encoded string and not an ASCII character. (This means that the UTF-8 encoding of characters which are not in the ASCII repertoire is not the same as their encoding in ISO Latin1.)

Text encoded with UTF-8 is thus a string of 8-bit bytes, and is therefore vulnerable to mangling by protocols that can only handle ASCII. **UTF-7** is an alternative encoding which uses a technique similar to that described for QP to turn Unicode characters into streams of pure ASCII text, which can be transmitted safely.

The **UTF-16** encoding has a different emphasis. This encoding allows pairs of 16-bit values to be combined into a single 32-bit value, thus extending the repertoire of Unicode beyond the BMP. Only values in a limited range can be combined this way, with the result that UTF-16 only provides access to an additional 15 planes of the full ISO 10646 character set. These comprise nearly a million characters under UTF-16, which seems to be sufficient for present purposes.

The markup languages used on the Web use UTF-8 Unicode as their character set by default, as do Java and other popular programming languages. Unicode has also been adopted as the native character set in recent versions of the major operating systems, so it is now much easier than it used to be to transfer text that uses characters beyond the US–Anglophone ASCII repertoire.

KEY POINTS

The content of text consists of the characters that make up the words, punctuation, symbols, and so on which convey the meaning or message.

The appearance of text comprises its visual attributes, such as the shape and size of characters, and their layout on the page.

An abstract character may have many different graphic representations.

A character set maps the abstract characters in its character repertoire to their code values in a set of integer code points.

ASCII is a 7-bit character set, providing 95 printable characters and some control characters. It is only adequate for a few languages, including English.

ISO 8859 defines a collection of 8-bit character sets, each one covering a set of related languages.

IS0 8859-1 or ISO Latin1 covers most Western European languages. It is identical to ASCII for code points 0 to 127.

ISO 10646 defines a 32-bit Universal Character Set (UCS), arranged in 256 groups, each of which consists of 256 planes accommodating 65,536 characters each.

The UCS-4 encoding uses four bytes to hold the full 32-bit code value for any character.

The UCS-2 encoding uses just two bytes, to hold 16-bit values for characters on the $(0,0,*,*)$ plane (the Basic Multilingual Plane).

UCS-2 is identical to Unicode, and provides code values for all the characters used to write contemporary major languages.

ISO Latin1 is the 8-bit code equivalent to the $(0,0,0,*)$ row of ISO 10646.

UTF-8 allows any ISO 10646 or Unicode value to be encoded as a sequence of 8-bit bytes, such that ASCII values are left unchanged in a single byte.

UTF-16 is an extension mechanism which provides Unicode with access to an extra 15 planes of the full ISO 10646 character set.

UTF-8 is the default character set used on the World Wide Web.

Fonts

To display a piece of text, each stored character value must be mapped to a visual representation of the character's shape. Such a representation is called a *glyph*. As Figure 9.4 shows, a single character can be represented by a wide range of different glyphs. Many small details can be changed without destroying the fundamental identity of the abstract character being represented. We can recognize all the glyphs in Figure 9.4 as the lower-case letter q. In addition to the variations in shape which the figure illustrates, glyphs can vary in size, from tiny subscripts to banner headlines. If we are to be able to use glyphs systematically, it is necessary to impose some organization on them.

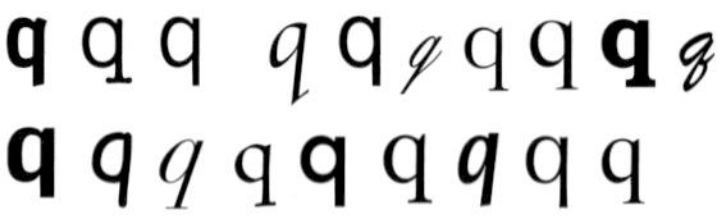

Figure 9.4. *19 glyphs for a single letter*

Glyphs are arranged into collections called *fonts*. The name has been taken from traditional printing. In the traditional letterpress (or "cold metal") technique a page is assembled out of individual pieces of type, each one of which is a metal block, with a mirror image of a letter or other symbol in relief on one end. These blocks are clamped in a frame together with spacers, and pages are printed by inking the faces of the type and pressing the paper against them. In this context, a font is a collection of pieces of type — that is, a collection of actual metal objects. Usually, the typesetter works from a cabinet in which the type is arranged in drawers holding multiple instances of each letter shape at each size that is required. All the shapes in a particular font will have been made from masters produced by a type designer so that they share certain visual characteristics and combine well with each other to make a harmonious and readable page.

Letterpress has been largely superseded, first by mechanical hot metal technologies, such as Monotype and Linotype machines, and now by digital typesetting. However, the concept of a font has been retained through these technological changes, although its realization has evolved — first into a set of moulds into which hot lead is poured to make letters for typesetting machines, and more recently into a computer file that holds a description of the graphic forms of the glyphs. The idea that a font combines a set of glyphs that are visually related and designed to work together has not changed. In fact, many of the fonts available for use on computers today are versions of traditional typesetters' fonts, some of them based on original designs from the fifteenth century.

Accessing Fonts

Text originates as a stream of character codes. To turn it into a form that can be displayed, these must be replaced by glyphs chosen from one or more fonts. Once this replacement has been performed, the content of the text (the character codes) becomes lost and can only be retrieved with difficulty. Essentially, the text turns into graphics, which cannot easily be searched or edited. (A person can still read the text, of course — in fact, they can't read it in any other form — but a program cannot manipulate it in any way.) If you want to recover the characters from text that has been turned into graphics, you need to use special optical character recognition (OCR) software, which uses pattern recognition techniques to analyse the shapes within the bitmapped image and deduce the characters they represent. OCR is a mature technology, but 100% accurate recognition is not often achieved.

Since a stream of character codes is much more compact than an image representing the same text, replacement of character codes by glyphs also increases the storage and bandwidth requirements of the text. The graphical representation of text is inefficient because it takes no advantage of the repetitive nature of text: the same character will typically occur many times, so if glyphs are substituted, many copies of the same glyph will be used, and each will be much larger than the corresponding character code.

Because of these considerations, it is normal to keep text in some character-based form, and only to use glyphs when it is actually displayed or incorporated into a graphic image. The simplest case is that of monostyled text – text that is displayed in a single font. In this case, a text file need only contain the characters of the text itself: it is the familiar "plain ASCII" (or perhaps plain ISO 8859) file. When such a file is displayed, the character codes are used to select glyphs from a font, either a default system font, or a single font selected by the user from within the program being used to display the text.

Monostyled text is rarely adequate for multimedia, where a richer typographic experience is usually required. The principle of selecting glyphs using character codes remains the same, but additional information is needed to control the selection of fonts. We will describe various forms which this information may take later in this chapter. At this point, however, we must consider where these fonts might be found.

There are only three possibilities. Glyphs must be taken either from fonts stored on the system being used to display the text, or from fonts embedded in the text file, or from fonts downloaded from a remote machine. Downloading fonts is a relatively new development, whose success depends on the existence of accessible repositories of fonts. Because of copyright restrictions on the use of fonts, such repositories are rare, so this option is not often possible.

If fonts are embedded in the file that contains the text – as they may be in SWF or PDF files – they must originally have been stored on the system used to prepare the text, and therein lies the most important advantage of this approach. Multimedia designers can use fonts of their own choosing, confident that they will be available when they are needed, because they are embedded in the same file as the text. If they are not embedded in the file, and they cannot be downloaded, only the fonts on the user's system will be available, and there is no reason to suppose that the user's collection of fonts will be the same as the designer's, so it is possible that some font required by the text will not be available. The probability of this occurring is quite high, as designers often have large collections of fonts acquired with specialist software or even purchased individually for design work, whereas many users only have the basic fonts provided with their systems.

Why then might you prefer not to embed fonts in your text files? One compelling reason is that not all text file formats allow you to do so. In particular, HTML has no facility for embedding fonts, although, in conjunction with CSS stylesheets, it does allow you to specify the fonts you wish to be used to display textual elements of Web pages. (CSS also provides a way of specifying downloaded fonts, but not all browsers implement this feature.)

The other reason for preferring to rely on fonts on the user's system is that fonts are fairly large objects – the fonts used for this book, for example, vary in size between about 32 and 50 kilobytes each. It is quite easy to find yourself using half a dozen fonts on a page, so including the fonts with the text can lead to bloated files and consequently to extended download times. PDF and SWF allow you to embed only the characters that are actually used, instead of the whole font, which can reduce the size somewhat.

If a font is not available, various problems can arise. Text in the missing font will not be displayed, or it will be displayed in some other font that has been substituted. The latter case is more common, and is less serious than no display at all, but it is far from ideal. As we will see in the next section, every font has its own distinctive character, so substituting another in its place can seriously impair a carefully thought-out design. Furthermore, the widths of the glyphs in the substituted font will probably be different from those in the intended font, so that the positioning of individual glyphs on the page will be incorrect. Depending on how the layout of text for display is done, this might result in ragged margins where straight ones were intended, uneven gaps between words, or gaps within words. Any of these defects will have a detrimental effect on the appearance of your text, and may make it hard to read.

Classification and Choice of Fonts

There are thousands of fonts available, each with its own special personality. Some broad characteristics are used to help classify them.

A major distinction is that between **monospaced** (or **fixed-width**) and **proportional** fonts. In a monospaced font, every character occupies the same amount of space horizontally, regardless of its shape. This means that some letters have more white space around them than others. For example, the narrow shape of a lower-case l must be surrounded with white to make it the same width as a lower-case m. In contrast, in a proportional font, the space each letter occupies depends on the width of the letter shape. Paradoxically, this produces a more even appearance, which is generally felt to be easier to read in most contexts. It also allows you to fit more words on to a line.

Text in a monospaced font looks as if it was produced on a typewriter or a teletype machine. It can sometimes be used effectively for headings, but monospaced text is especially suitable for typesetting computer program listings. It is also useful for conveying a "low-tech" appearance, for example in contexts where you wish to convey a slightly informal impression. Probably the most widely used monospaced font is Courier, which was originally designed for IBM typewriters in the 1950s, and has achieved wide currency because it is one of the fonts shipped as standard with all PostScript printers.

```
Monospaced Font: Courier
Each letter occupies the
same amount of horizontal
space, so that the text
looks as if it was typed
on a typewriter.
```

Figure 9.5. *A monospaced font*

Proportional Font: Bembo
Each letter occupies an amount of horizontal space proportional to the width of the glyph, so that the text looks as if it was printed in a book.

Figure 9.6. *A proportional font*

Text in a proportional font has the appearance of the printed text in a traditional book, and is usually preferred for setting lengthy texts. It is generally felt to be more readable, since letters appear to be tightly bound together into words. Figures 9.5 and 9.6 illustrate the difference between monospaced and proportional fonts. There are many proportional fonts in common use. As you can see, the font used for the main text in this book, Bembo, is proportionally spaced. Most of the classical book fonts, such as Times, Baskerville and Garamond are proportional, as are many newer fonts, such as Helvetica.

Another broad distinction is between *serifed* and *sans serif* (sometimes "sanserif") fonts. *Serifs* are the little strokes added to the ends of character shapes (see Figure 9.7). These are present in serifed fonts, but omitted in sans serif fonts, which consequently have a plainer look. Serifs originate in marks produced by chisels on Roman stone inscriptions, so serifed fonts are sometimes called Roman fonts. Figure 9.8 shows some text in Univers – a bold version of this sans serif font is used for the section headings in this book.

Figure 9.7. *Serifs*

Sans serif fonts are a comparatively new development, on a typographical time scale, and they only gradually gained acceptance for general use. In some typographical catalogues they are still identified by the alternative name of "grotesques". Sans serif fonts were indeed rather grotesque in the nineteenth century, being crude designs used mostly for advertising and posters. It was only with the development of more elegant and refined designs in the twentieth century that they became accepted for use in books.

Sans Serif Font: Univers
The letters of a sans serif (or sanserif) font lack the tiny strokes known as serifs, hence the name. They have a plain, perhaps utilitarian, appearance.

Figure 9.8. *A sans serif font*

The best known sans serif font is probably Helvetica, which again is one of the standard PostScript fonts. Other commonly used sans serif fonts include Univers and Arial (the latter popularized by Microsoft). Gill Sans, another very popular sans serif font, was based on the font used for the signs on the London Underground, which helped to generate interest in sans serif type.

There is contradictory evidence as to whether serifed or sans serif fonts are more readable, but it seems probable that spacing makes more difference. However, serifs are very small features and therefore difficult to render accurately at low resolutions, which can mean that while text in a serifed font may be easy to read in high-resolution print, it is hard to read on a computer screen simply because the letters are not being accurately reproduced. Sans serif fonts are widely used for such features as window titles and menu entries for this reason.

Spacing and serifs are independent properties: sans serif and serifed fonts can equally well be either monospaced or proportional.

Italic Font: Bembo Italic
The letters of an italic font slope to the right, and are formed as if they were made with an italic pen nib. Italics are conventionally used for emphasis, and for identifying foreign words and expressions.

Figure 9.9. *An italic font*

Slanted Font: Lucida Bright Oblique
The letters of a slanted font share the rightward slope of italic fonts, but lack their calligraphic quality. Slanted fonts are sometimes used when a suitable italic font is not available, but may also be preferred to italics when a more modern look is wanted.

Figure 9.10. *A slanted font*

A third classification of fonts is based on broad categories of shape. In particular, we distinguish between fonts with an **upright** shape, and those with an *italic* shape. Upright fonts, as the name implies, have characters whose vertical strokes (stems) are truly vertical. Italic fonts imitate a certain style of handwriting, and have letters that are slanted to the right. Additionally, the letter shapes in an italic font are formed differently from those in an upright font, so that they share some of the characteristics of italic handwriting. When digital fonts first appeared, "italic" fonts were sometimes produced simply by applying a shear transformation to an upright font. The effect is rather different, since the calligraphic features of true italic fonts are missing. Such fonts are now used in their own right, not as substitutes for italics. They are said to have a *slanted* shape. The difference is illustrated in Figures 9.9 and 9.10, which show italic and slanted versions of two upright fonts.

Most italic fonts are variations on or companions to upright fonts. For example, Bembo Italic is an italic version of Bembo Book. There are, however, some fonts with an italic shape which are designed on their own. These are generally intended to have the character of handwriting, and to be used where something more human than a conventional typeface is desired. Among the best known **calligraphic fonts** are several versions of Chancery, including Zapf Chancery. Specialist fonts based on samples of real handwriting are also available. Figures 9.11 and 9.12 show examples of a relatively formal calligraphic font and a handwriting font.

Digital technology has made it relatively easy to create new fonts, which has led to a great deal of experimentation and whimsy. Fonts which depart radically from convention are sometimes grouped together under the heading of "fantasy fonts". Figure 9.13 shows an example – although, by the very nature of fantasy fonts, there can really be no such thing as a "typical" example. Such fonts should only be used judiciously, if at all.

Some fonts appear somewhat squashed horizontally, compared with the normal proportions of most fonts. They are referred to as **condensed** fonts, and are intended

Calligraphic Font: Apple Chancery
Calligraphic fonts usually resemble 'round hand' or 'copperplate' handwriting, unlike italic fonts.

Figure 9.11. *A calligraphic font*

Handwriting Font: Kidprint
Handwriting fonts are based on samples of real people's handwriting, so they are often quite idiosyncratic.

Figure 9.12. *A handwriting font*

Fantasy Font: Jokerman
Fantasy fonts defy characterization, and often break all the rules. They are easily over-used.

Figure 9.13. *A fantasy font*

for applications such as marginal notes or narrow newspaper columns, where it is desirable to be able to fit text in as tightly as possible. In contrast, some fonts, described as **extended**, are stretched out horizontally, making them more suitable for headings and other isolated text elements.

Finally, fonts can be classified according to their **weight**, that is, the thickness of the strokes making up the letters. Thicker strokes make text look darker and more solid. Conventionally, we call fonts with a heavy weight (thick strokes) **boldface** or simply **bold**. Like italics, bold fonts are usually versions of other fonts. As a result, boldness is not an absolute property – a bold version of a font whose normal weight is particularly light may be lighter than the normal version of a heavy font, whose own bold version will be even heavier. Some fonts may exist in several versions, exhibiting varying degrees of boldness. Under these circumstances, individual styles are described by terms such as ultra-bold, semi-bold, light and ultra-light.

Because of the limitations of computer displays, boldface may be used more widely for text to be displayed on screen than would be appropriate in printed text, where it is traditionally considered intrusive. For example, conventionally you never use boldface for emphasis, but always italics. However, italic text often renders badly at low resolutions because of its slant, making it hard to read on a computer monitor, so the use of bold text for emphasis may be justified. Bold fonts are also used quite widely for window titles and menu items, because they show up well.

> ┌─IN DETAIL───
> **Word processors often treat underlining as a styling option similar to italicization and emboldening, so you might suppose that there would be underlined versions of fonts, too. However, underlined fonts are extremely rare. Underlining is scorned in traditional typography, where it is considered to be a poor substitute for italicization, only suitable for use on typewriters which lack italics. On the World Wide Web, underlining is conventionally used to designate hyperlinks. This convention is so well established that it is likely to be confusing to use underlines for any other purpose.**
>
> **More flexible effects than a simple underline can be produced by combining ordinary fonts with lines of various thicknesses and styles, such as dots and wavy lines, so underlined fonts would not be very useful anyway.**

Because it makes sense to talk about an italic version or a bold version of an upright font, fonts can be grouped into families. A *font family* corresponds closely to what is traditionally called a typeface. A font is a particular style of some typeface. In pre-digital typography each different size would be regarded as a separate font, but when working digitally it is more useful to consider that the same font can be rendered at different sizes.

Usually, an upright serifed font is assumed to be the normal form, which is augmented by versions in different weights, perhaps an italic form or a sans serif form. Variations are often combined to produce additional versions, such as bold italics, or slanted sans serif.

The Lucida Bright family is an extreme example, consisting of 20 fonts. Lucida Bright is an upright serifed font which is also available in bold, italic and bold italic. Lucida Sans is the sans serif version, which comes in the same four versions, as do Lucida Typewriter, a fixed width Lucida font, and Lucida Fax, a variant form designed to be especially readable at low resolution. Three calligraphic fonts and a slanted font complete the family. All 20 fonts share a similar feel so that they can be combined without any obtrusive visual discontinuities.

Text that is set in Bembo goes well with *Bembo italic* and ***Bembo bold italic*** but it looks **quite wrong mixed with Cheltenham and** *Cheltenham italic.* (All this text is 12 pt.)

Figure 9.14. *Combining fonts from different families*

In contrast, when fonts from different font families are combined, their differences can be very noticeable, as Figure 9.14 shows. Traditionally, such discontinuities have been carefully avoided, but in recent years designers have taken advantage of the ease with which desktop publishing software allows them to combine fonts in order to explore new combinations that defy the established conventions. As a general rule of thumb, if you want to combine fonts, they should be either from the same family, or from families with completely different character-istics (a serif with a bold sans serif, for example). Fonts that look similar but not quite the same will look worst of all together.

In the days of letterpress and hot metal typesetting, different sets of type were required in order to produce text at different sizes, so each set qualified as a separate font. Only a limited number of different sizes could easily be made available. With digital fonts, arbitrary scaling can be applied to glyphs, so that fonts can be printed at any size. Purists maintain that simple scaling is not adequate, and that letter shapes should be designed to look their best at one particular size, and should only be used at that size. However, contemporary font technology supports the idea that a font should exist at only one size and should be scaled to produce any other size that is needed. Special infor-mation contained in the font is used to help maintain a pleasing appearance at all sizes, as we will describe in a later section.

As well as the objective factors of spacing, serifs, shape, weight and size that can be used to classify type, there is a more subjective classification based on the sort of jobs for which a font is most suitable. The basic distinction is between *text fonts* and *display fonts*. This terminology is rather silly, since all fonts are used for text. The distinction is between fonts suitable for continuous text, such as the body of a book or article, and those fonts suitable for short pieces of isolated text, such as headings, signs or advertising slogans on posters.

IN DETAIL

Sometimes, a finer distinction is drawn within the class of display fonts. "Decorative fonts" are those for which appearance is the primary design consideration. They often incorporate ornaments and other features that make them unsuitable for extended use. "Headline fonts", as the name implies, are designed for use in headlines and other situations where it is important to attract the reader's attention. This leaves a category to which the name "display fonts" is often attached, consisting of fonts intended especially for use at large sizes, with other features designed to take advantage of the possibilities offered by large characters; for example the serifs might be especially fine.

Text fonts must be unobtrusive, so that they do not distract the reader's attention and interfere with the primary message of the text. They must also be easy to read, so that they do not cause fatigue when they are read for hours at a time. To some extent, whether or not a font is intru-sive depends on whether it is familiar; at the same time, the criteria for selecting text fonts have not changed over the years. The combination of these factors means that text fonts tend to be conservative. They are always upright, more often serifed than not, and of a medium weight.

Display fonts are another matter. Here, the intention is to get across a short message. Garish design that would be offensive in a text font becomes eye-catching in a display font; innovation attracts attention. Fantasy fonts that would be completely useless for continuous text can often serve very well for display. Nevertheless, the choice of appropriate fonts – and the combination of display fonts with each other and with text fonts – calls for considerable judgement. There is a far greater diversity of design among display fonts than among text fonts, and whereas the same text fonts continue to be used year after year, display fonts are subject to fashion.

Conventional ideas about font usage are based on centuries of experience of making books, pamphlets, posters, packaging, road signs, shop fronts and other familiar forms of printed text. While much of this experience can be applied to the textual components of multimedia, some aspects of the new media demand a fresh approach. Generally, display fonts can be used on a computer monitor in much the same way as they can on paper, so where text is combined with images, fonts can be used as they would be on a poster – for example, attention-grabbing headings can effectively use the same display fonts as you might find in a book. Continuous text is more problematic. The low resolution of most monitors can lead to distortion of letter shapes, making fonts that work well on paper hard to read, especially at small sizes. The obvious solution is to use fonts at larger sizes than is customary in books, and this is often done; text for electronic display is often set as much as 60% larger than text in ordinary books. An alternative is to look for a font that has been designed to be readable at low resolution – Verdana and Arial are examples of such fonts. Sans serif fonts tend to survive better at low resolutions, which makes them more suitable for this purpose, and explains why they are so often used on Web pages.

The way in which text in multimedia is arranged gives rise to some less technical questions concerning fonts. Long continuous passages covering many pages are cumbersome and tiring to read on a screen, and do not integrate well with other media. It is common, therefore, to find multimedia text elements constructed as small pieces that fit onto one or two screenfuls. These pieces will often resemble – in form and style – the short explanatory placards attached to museum displays and zoo exhibits. This sort of text partakes of the character of both continuous text for which we would use a text font (it has a non-trivial extent and content) and the shorter texts normally set in a display font (it is succinct and usually has a message to get across). A restrained display font will often work well in this situation, as will some quite unconventional solutions, such as a text font in a large bold version, or coloured text on a contrasting background. Even for short passages of text, however, readability must be paramount.

Text for multimedia is often prepared using the same tools that are used in "desktop publishing" (DTP). It is important to remember that the output from many conventional DTP programs is intended for printing on paper. We reiterate that text that will look excellent when printed on paper may well be unreadable when viewed on a computer monitor. It is necessary to adapt the way you use these tools, bearing in mind the actual medium for which your output is destined, or to use tools that have support for output to alternative media.

One final consideration which is unique to digital text is that, in many cases, the multimedia designer has no control over the fonts that will be used when text is finally displayed. This is especially true in the case of Web pages. As we explained previously, it may be necessary for completely different fonts to be substituted on different computer systems. In some cases, the software used for display may let users override the original fonts with those of their own choosing. Consequently, unless you are certain that neither of these circumstances will arise, there is no point in carefully exploiting the features of a particular font to achieve some special effect – the effect may never be seen by anyone except you.

Most of the preceding description of fonts has concentrated on letters, implicitly in the Latin alphabet. However, as the discussion of character sets in the previous section indicated, we use far more characters than these letters, and just as we need character sets to provide code values for a large character repertoire, so we need fonts to provide glyphs for them.

In fact, you can think of a font as a mapping from abstract characters to glyphs, in much the same way as a character set is a mapping from abstract characters to code points. Like a character set, a font is only defined for a specific character repertoire. Most fonts' repertoires consist of the letters from some alphabet, together with additional symbols, such as punctuation marks. You might be forgiven for hoping that fonts would be structured around one of the character set standards, such as ISO Latin1, but this is not usually the case. It is generally possible to access the individual glyphs in a font using a numerical index, but, although the printable ASCII characters are usually in their expected positions, other symbols may well be in positions quite different from that corresponding to their code values in any ISO character set.

The way in which glyphs are grouped into fonts owes more to printing tradition than to the influence of character code standards, with the alphabet being the focus of design. Even then, some fonts may not include lower-case letters – if the designer intended the font only to be used for headlines, for example. Specialized non-alphabetic symbols, such as mathematical symbols, are usually grouped into their own fonts, known as *symbol fonts* or *pi fonts*. Some fonts consist entirely of graphic images (you may encounter fonts of arrows, or fonts of pointing hands, for example). Some images are considered to be symbols and are included in character sets – fonts containing these symbols are called *dingbat fonts* – but others are put together by font designers for special applications, and do not fit into any character set framework.

As a result of all this, another level of encoding is required in order to map stored character codes in some character set to glyphs. Additionally, some mechanism may be needed to combine separate fonts for example, an alphabetic font and a symbol font, to provide glyphs for all the characters used in a document – a problem which will become acute as the larger range of characters provided by Unicode comes into wider use. Fortunately, the mechanisms for accessing glyphs are usually handled transparently by text layout software.

Font Terminology

Typography has its own specialized vocabulary, some of which it is necessary to understand if you are to find your way around among fonts and their descriptions.

Much of the description of a font's characteristics consists of measurements. These are usually given in units of *points (pt)*. In digital typography, one point is $\frac{1}{72}$ of an inch, which makes 1 pt equal to just under 0.3528 mm. A point is thus a very small unit, suitable for measuring the dimensions of such small objects as typeset characters. For larger quantities, such as the distance between lines of text, we often use a *pica (pc)*, which is equal to 12 pt ($\frac{1}{6}$ inch or 4.2333 mm).

IN DETAIL

Unlike other units of measurement, such as the metre or the foot, the point does not have an internationally agreed standard magnitude. The value of exactly $\frac{1}{72}$ of an inch is a comparatively recent innovation, pioneered by PostScript. In English-speaking countries the traditional printer's point is $\frac{1}{72.27}$ of an inch, and some software, such as TeX, still uses this value by default. In France, the Didot point, which is about 7% larger than the printer's point, is preferred.

A font's size is quoted in points, as in "12 pt Times Roman" or "10 pt Helvetica". The value specified is the font's *body size*. In the days of letterpress, the body size was the height of the individual pieces of metal type, each of which were the same size so that they could be fitted together. Hence, the body size was the smallest height that could accommodate every symbol in the font. This remains the case today. The size is not necessarily equal to the height of any character in the font (although parentheses are often as tall as the body size), but it is usually the height between the top of the highest character and the bottom of the lowest. However, the body height is actually an arbitrary distance, chosen to provide a suitable vertical space for the letters to sit in when they are set in lines. A font with a particularly open character might have a body size somewhat larger than is necessary just to accommodate all its characters, so that there is always some extra space around them when text is set in that font on conventional baselines.

In normal text, characters are arranged so that they all sit on the same horizontal line. This line is called the baseline; the space between successive baselines is called the *leading* (pronounced so as to rhyme with "heading"). The term originally referred to the thin strips of lead inserted between lines of print in letterpress printing.

An important dimension which helps determine a font's distinctive characteristics is the height between the baseline and the top of a lower-case letter x. This value is the font's *x-height*; the bodies of most lower-case letters fit in between the baseline and the x-height. Some letters, such as h, have strokes that rise above the x-height; these strokes are called *ascenders*. Similarly, some letters,

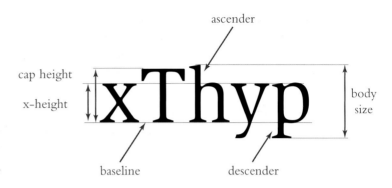

Figure 9.15. *Some font terminology*

such as y and p, extend below the baseline. The extending strokes are called *descenders*. These terms are illustrated in Figure 9.15. Sometimes, the size of the largest ascender (measured as the distance between the x-height and the top of the body) is called the *ascent*, and the corresponding descending dimension is called the *descent* of the font.

Ascenders are not the only things that extend above the x-height – capital letters do so as well. In many fonts, though, the capitals do not extend to the full height of ascenders, so we need another quantity, the *cap height*, also shown in Figure 9.15, to characterize the vertical extent of capitals. (In English text, the difference between cap height and ascent is most obvious when the combination "Th" occurs at the beginning of a sentence.)

The ratio of the x-height to the body size is one of the most important visual characteristics of a font. Since the bulk of the text lies between the baseline and the x-height, a font with a relatively high x-height will look bigger than a font with a lower x-height at the same size. If you look carefully at Figure 9.14, you will be able to see that one of the things that prevents the text in Cheltenham merging happily with that in Bembo is that Bembo has a slightly lower x-height. This feature is common to the entire Bembo family, so the Bembo Italic mixes easily with the upright Bembo. Similarly, the two fonts in the Cheltenham family have the same x-height.

If you look closely at Figure 9.15 you will see that the curved tops of the h and p actually extend through the x-height. This phenomenon is called *overshoot*, and helps make the letters look more uniform in size. The extent of the overshoot in a font is another factor that helps to determine its distinctive appearance.

The x-height of a font is used as a unit of measurement, usually written ex. It has the useful property of not being an absolute unit, like a point, but a relative one. It changes with the font's size, and is different for different fonts, but it always stands in the same relation to the height of lower-case letters, so it provides a convenient way of expressing vertical measurements that we might want to change in proportion to this quantity.

A similar unit of horizontal distance is the em. Traditionally, 1 em is the width of a capital letter M. In many fonts, M is as wide as the body size, so the meaning of 1 em has altered over the years, and is now usually taken as a unit of length equal to the font size. For a 10 pt font, 1 em is equal to 10 pt, for a 12 pt font it is equal to 12 pt, and so on. Long dashes — like these — which are sometimes used for parenthetic phrases, especially in books published in the United States, are 1 em long, so they are called em-dashes. You will sometimes see another relative unit, the en, which is the width of a capital N, and usually defined as 0.5 em. An en-dash is 1 en long; en-dashes are used for page or date ranges, such as 1998–99, or instead of em-dashes (as in this book).

Other features which characterize the look of a font include the size and shape of serifs, and the ratio of the thickness of thick and thin strokes. For example, so-called "modern" fonts (actually based on designs about 200 years old) are characterized by high contrast between the thick and thin strokes, and the use of serifs without brackets (the curves that join the serif to its stem). Fans of these fonts claim that these features produce a brilliant, sophisticated appearance on the page, while their detractors find them affected and illegible, compared to the "old-style" fonts with their more uniform solid appearance, or the cleaner lines of twentieth-century sans serif fonts. The implications for display at low resolution should by now be clear.

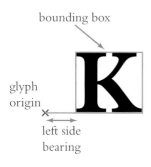

Figure 9.16. *Side bearing*

The features of individual letters are not all that we need to consider in a font. We also have to look at how the letters are combined. As we stated earlier, most text fonts are proportionally spaced, with each letter occupying as much horizontal space as it needs. As Figure 9.16 shows, each letter has a bounding box, which is the smallest box that can enclose it. Normally, a slight gap is left between the bounding boxes of adjacent characters. In other words, when drawing a glyph immediately following another one, it is drawn relative to a glyph origin, which lies outside the bounding box – usually to its left – by a distance known as the character's ***left side bearing***, as shown in Figure 9.16 (where the magnitude of the side bearing is considerably exaggerated).

Sometimes, when two particular letters are placed next to each other, the total amount of space between them looks too great or too small. Typographers normally adjust the spacing to make it look more uniform. (Once again, you will notice an apparent contradiction. It is necessary to deliberately introduce non-uniformity in order to achieve the subjective appearance of uniformity.) This process of adjustment is called ***kerning***, and is illustrated in Figure 9.17. (You may need to look closely at the figure – kerning is subtle.) The kerning pairs for a font are defined by its designer. Carefully produced fonts may have hundreds of kerning pairs for different combinations, each with its own spacing. The information about which pairs of letters are to be kerned, and by how much, is stored as part of the font. Advanced typesetting software will allow you to adjust the kerning between individual pairs of letters by hand.

kerned   not kerned

AV AV
Ta Ta

Figure 9.17. *Kerning*

The measurements which describe the size of individual characters and the spacing between them are collectively known as ***font metrics***. Programs that perform typesetting need access to font metric information, in order to determine where to place each glyph as they build up lines, paragraphs and pages. The organization of this information depends on the font format, computer system and typesetting software being used.

Two operations related to kerning are ***letter spacing*** and ***tracking***. Letter spacing is the process of changing the space between all the letters in a font, with the effect of stretching or squeezing the text. This may be done either to change the appearance of the font, or to fit an awkward line of text on to a page. (The latter operation is severely frowned on in the best typesetting circles.) Tracking is a systematic application of letter spacing depending on the font size: large letters need proportionally less space between them to look right.

Certain letter combinations just will not look right, no matter how you space them. Printers traditionally replace occurrences of such troublesome sequences by single composite characters, known as ***ligatures***. In English text, commonly used ligatures in traditional printing include ff, fl, fi and ffl. There is no standard set of ligatures, and some fonts provide more of them than others. Monospaced fonts do not usually provide any. The extent of support for ligatures also depends on the font format. Most PostScript and TrueType fonts only offer ff and fi ligatures, but OpenType fonts may provide a full set. (Font formats are described in the next section.) Figure 9.18 shows why we need ligatures, and the improvement achieved by using them. Ligatures are stored as extra characters in the font.

without fine fluffy soufflés
with   fine fluffy soufflés

Figure 9.18. *Ligatures*

High-quality text layout software will automatically deal with kerning and ligatures, making the appropriate spacing corrections and character substitutions when it encounters the codes for combinations of letters that require such treatment. Word processors and Web browsers, however, cannot generally do this, which means that the text they produce or display has a different appearance.

Digital Font Formats

Glyphs are just small images, which can be stored in a font using either bitmaps or vector graphics. This leads to two different sorts of fonts, **bitmapped fonts** and **outline fonts**, based on these two graphics technologies.

Glyphs in bitmapped fonts exhibit the same characteristics as bitmapped images – in particular, they cannot be scaled without loss of quality – while outline glyphs share the characteristics of vector graphics, and can be resized arbitrarily. Since character shapes are usually built out of simple curves and strokes, and lack any subtle texture, there is little advantage in using bitmapped fonts on the grounds of expressiveness. The main advantage of bitmapped fonts is that glyphs can be rendered on-screen simply and rapidly, using a bit copying operation. This advantage is being eroded by the wider availability of efficient graphics hardware and faster processors. Bitmapped fonts remain available, but are likely to disappear soon. Each platform has its own native bitmapped font format, usually optimized in some way to work efficiently with the system software routines responsible for text display.

In contrast, outline fonts are usually stored in a format that can be used on any platform, although the actual font files may be platform-dependent. The three most widely used formats are Adobe *Type 1* (often simply referred to as ***PostScript fonts***, although there are other types of PostScript fonts), *TrueType* and *OpenType*. Outline fonts are more widely used than bitmaps for elaborately formatted text.

Outline fonts in either Type 1 or TrueType formats can contain up to 256 glyphs. The glyphs in a Type 1 font are simply small programs, written in a restricted subset of the PostScript language. The restrictions are intended to make it possible for the glyphs to be rendered efficiently on-screen at sufficient quality to be acceptable at screen resolution. TrueType is an alternative format, based on quadratic curves instead of the cubic Bézier curves used by PostScript. A character outline in a TrueType font is stored as a series of points which define the lines and curves making up its shape.

OpenType is a more recently developed format, which extends the TrueType format in several ways. It allows either TrueType or Type 1 outlines to be stored, and provides a cross-platform font format. (OpenType fonts supplied by Adobe contain Type 1 data, while those from Microsoft use TrueType, but the difference should not be evident to somebody using the font.) OpenType fonts are superior to the older formats in many ways. Their encoding is based on Unicode, and they can accommodate many more than 256 characters – up to 65,536 glyphs are allowed. This allows a single font to include glyphs for more than one alphabet – Latin and Cyrillic, for example – which would otherwise have to be kept in separate fonts. OpenType fonts are the only fonts which are truly platform-independent: the same font file can be installed on any platform.

A compact representation of the glyphs is used, so that OpenType fonts can be smaller than their Type 1 equivalents. OpenType also has better support for the niceties of fine typography, such as an extended range of ligatures, old-style numerals, small capitals and glyphs for some fractions.

As well as descriptions of the glyph shapes, both Type 1 and TrueType fonts (and therefore OpenType fonts, too) include extra information that can be used by a rendering program to improve the appearance of text at low resolutions. This information concerns rather subtle features, which tend to lose their subtlety when only a few pixels can be used for each stroke. In Type 1 fonts, it takes the form of declarative "hints", which provide the values of parameters that can be used to direct glyph rendering at low resolutions. For example, some hint information is intended to cause overshoots to be suppressed. As we stated previously, overshoots normally help improve the regular appearance of a font. However, at low resolutions, when the amount of overshoot is rounded to the nearest pixel, the effect will be exaggerated and text will appear to be more irregular than it would if all the lower-case letters were exactly as high as the x-height. The point at which overshoot suppression is effective depends on the design of the font, so it cannot be applied without information from the font designer. The Type 1 hints allow this information to be supplied. Other hints similarly suppress variations in stem width, which while aesthetically pleasing at high resolutions, merely look uneven at low resolutions.

Another example of the use of hints concerns bold fonts. It is quite conceivable that the rounding effect of rendering at low resolution will cause the strokes of a normal font to thicken to such an extent that it becomes indistinguishable from the boldface version of the same font. A hint allows rendering software to add additional width to boldface fonts to ensure that they do always appear bold.

TrueType fonts achieve the same sort of improvements using a more procedural approach, allowing the font designer to write instructions that specify how features of a character should be mapped to points on a pixel grid at any resolution.

As with other sorts of vector graphics, the appearance of outline fonts can sometimes be improved by anti-aliasing (see Chapter 3) – that is, softening a hard, and inevitably jagged, edge between those pixels that are on and off by using a pattern of grey pixels over a wider area. The smoothing effect thereby achieved is illustrated in Figure 9.19. In the figure the upper letter A is not anti-aliased, but the lower one is. As you can see, anti-aliasing is very effective with large characters; it also works well at medium resolutions, such as that of a laser printer. At low resolutions, however, small type (below about 12 pt), although noticeably smoother, also begins to look blurred, which may leave it harder to read than it would be if it had been left jagged. Anti-aliasing should therefore be applied to fonts judiciously.

Figure 9.19. *Anti-aliased text*

A technique called ***sub-pixel anti-aliasing*** is becoming common, which takes advantage of the way pixels on LCD screens are arranged to produce a finer anti-aliased effect by adjusting the relative intensities of the individual colour components. Sub-pixel anti-aliasing was implemented under the name ClearType in Windows XP, although the technique is older.

KEY POINTS

A glyph is a graphic representation of a character's shape. A character may be represented by many different glyphs.

A font is a collection of glyphs.

Fonts may be embedded in SWF or PDF files. Web browsers usually access fonts on the user's system, but may download them from a remote server.

Fonts may be classified by their spacing (monospaced or proportional); the presence or absence of serifs (serifed or sans serif); their shape (upright, italic or slant); stretch (extended or condensed); and weight (bold, normal or light).

Fonts are grouped into families, consisting of related versions of a typeface.

Text fonts are intended for extended passages of text, so they must be readable and unobtrusive. Usually they are upright and serifed.

Display fonts are intended for short pieces of isolated text, such as headlines and slogans. They should be eye-catching and are often unconventional.

Text fonts designed for print may not work well on screen.

1 pt (point) is $\frac{1}{72}$ of an inch. 1 pc (pica) is 12 pt.

The body size is the nominal size of a font, but is not usually equal to the height of any glyph in the font.

The leading is the distance between baselines.

The x-height is the height between the baseline and the top of a lower-case letter x. Strokes that rise above the x-height are ascenders; those that extend below the baseline are descenders.

Relative units are useful for measurement. 1 em is equal to the body size; 1 en is 0.5 em; 1 ex is equal to the x-height.

Kerning is the adjustment of the space between letter pairs (e.g. AV) to make them look more uniform. Ligatures are composite single glyphs used to replace combinations of letters (e.g. fi) that don't look right next to each other.

Type 1 (PostScript), TrueType or OpenType are outline font formats.

Anti-aliasing is often applied to type to make it appear smoother.

Layout and Formatting

When characters are combined into words, sentences and extended passages of text, we need to think about how they should be arranged on the screen. How are paragraphs to be broken into lines? How are headings, lists and other textual structures to be identified and laid out? How are different fonts to be used?

As we explained in Chapter 2, layout commands and visual characteristics can all be specified using a text-based markup language. In later chapters we will show how links to other documents, the location of images and video clips, interaction with users, and synchronization of time-based media can also be specified textually in a markup language. The best known such language is HTML. We will introduce XHTML, its newer reformulation in XML, in the next chapter. Layout information can also be represented using invisible characters embedded in the text, and for a long time this was the way that word processors dealt with layout and formatting, but XML-based markup languages, such as **ODF (OpenDocument file format)** and **Microsoft's OOXML (Office Open XML)** are now taking over.

Text in Graphics

Markup languages are ideal for Web pages and conventionally formatted text, but the greatest flexibility in the layout of text can be obtained by treating text as graphics and manipulating it with a graphics program. Text can then be placed at will – possibly using layers to overlay it – and treated with effects and transformations. The integration of text and graphics occurs naturally, so this approach to text is ideally suited to graphic design incorporating text, such as posters, packaging, company logos and letterheads, book jackets and CD covers. Text prepared in this way becomes part of an image, so it can then be used in any situation where an image can be used – on a Web page, for instance.

If text items are created from outline fonts, they can be treated as objects in a vector graphics program. They can be arranged on the page arbitrarily, and all the transformations and effects that can be applied to other graphical objects can be applied to them. Words and letters can be scaled, rotated, reflected and sheared. They can be stroked with colours, gradients, or even patterns. The leading drawing programs provide extra facilities for laying out text, which take account of its sequential nature. Tools allow you to fill areas with text, arranged either horizontally or vertically. (Vertical text is intended for languages that are normally written that way, but can be applied to horizontal languages for a special effect.) The text flows automatically to stay within the area, with line breaks being created automatically as required. Text can also be placed along a path.

Figure 9.20 shows some ways of treating text in a vector graphics program. The design down the left was made by setting the name Shakespeare vertically, using a mid-blue to colour the text,

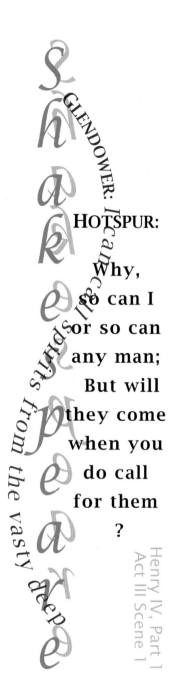

Figure 9.20. *Text as vector graphics*

taking a copy and reflecting it about the vertical axis. The mirrored copy was then filled with a lighter shade of blue and displaced slightly vertically and horizontally. Glendower's speech is set in red on a Bézier path, while Hotspur's reply is centred within an oval. Again, slightly different shades have been used to distinguish the components. The attribution has been rotated, and all the elements were scaled to fit their spaces. The text remains editable: spelling mistakes can be corrected – you can even use a spelling checker – and the fonts and type size can be changed. The shapes into which the text has flowed, and the paths along which it is placed, can be changed using the normal vector editing tools, and the text will move to accommodate the changes.

By treating text as bitmapped graphics, quite different results can be obtained. Any text can be rendered – that is, converted into pixels. Once this has been done, it becomes susceptible to all the retouching and filtering that painting programs provide. (However, unless the text is set in a large font, many effects either do not show up, or obliterate it entirely.) Text can be warped and distorted, embossed and bevelled, set in burning metal, or weathered and distressed. Figure 9.21 provides some examples, with various filters and effects applied to different textual elements. In order to apply the bitmapped effects the text must be rendered – it can then no longer be edited as text, but must be retouched like any other part of the image. Using the terminology from earlier in this chapter, text in vector graphics form retains its lexical content, whereas in a bitmapped image it is reduced entirely to appearance.

Both approaches to text in graphics have their uses, and they can be profitably combined. Vector text can be created in both Photoshop and Illustrator, and both programs allow you to apply vector effects or rasterize the text and apply bitmapped effects, though as you might expect, Illustrator has better vector support and Photoshop has better bitmapped support. In either program, text can be combined with a bitmapped image, though Photoshop provides better facilities for working with the pixels. The distinction between the two approaches to graphics and text remains. Programs are increasingly combining the two, but the underlying representations remain distinct.

Graphics programs offer complete control over the appearance and placement of text, but this is not always what is required. Quite the contrary, in fact. If you are preparing some conventional text, such as a letter or an article, you want to be able to just type the words and have a program do as much of the layout as possible for you. For this, we have to turn to a different class of programs, and consider some new questions – in particular, how do we exercise control over layout without having to place everything explicitly? Before we can do that, though, we need to have a clearer idea of the layout and formatting that are conventionally applied to text.

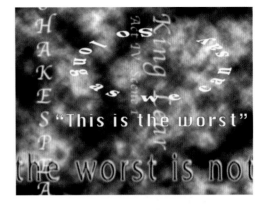

Figure 9.21. *Bitmapped effects applied to text*

Layout

Advertisements, posters, logos and CD and DVD covers may use graphic text effects such as the ones illustrated in the preceding section, but most text is laid out according to conventions developed over many years and familiar to us all from books and magazines. The book you are reading now illustrates most of these conventions. The text is arranged on lines, which are combined into paragraphs, and these are placed on the page. Formatting may be applied to characters within a paragraph – the font may be changed, for instance – and to entire paragraphs – space may be added within lines so that all the lines in a paragraph, except the last, are the same length, or the lines may be allowed to be of different lengths. These are fundamentally different types of formatting operation, and it is usual to distinguish between *inline* or *character formatting*, and *block-level* or *paragraph formatting*.

At a still higher level, there are questions of how blocks should be positioned relative to each other. Usually, paragraphs are placed one after the other vertically, with approximately even space between them, to be read in sequence, but – as you will see if you look at any magazine – blocks of text may be positioned in other ways. Captions are placed under or beside illustrations, for example, and supplementary material is often set off in sidebars, sometimes with distinctive background shading. Blocks are also set in a special style for headings, and they may be arranged to form lists of items.

The sophistication and elegance with which formatting is applied to text varies widely, depending on the program being used. Word processors provide a basic set of facilities suitable for business documents, and produce results that are adequate but lack many of the typographical niceties offered by page layout applications such as InDesign, which can generate output comparable to the best typography achieved by traditional means. Typography for Web pages is restricted by the facilities of the markup languages employed, and by the capabilities of Web browsers, which tend to be limited in this respect. We will look at this special case in the next chapter, after describing layout and formatting in more general terms in the remainder of this.

Text layout for print has to deal with issues of page make-up. These include how blocks are placed within the fixed area of the page, how text is broken between pages, and the placement of fixed elements – such as running headers and page numbers – on each page. In multimedia work intended for display on-screen these issues do not arise, since text is not usually systematically broken into pages, but arranged within a window, using scroll bars to deal with overflowing text. On Web sites, each Web page may have a similar layout, however, and page templates are commonly used to ensure consistency. However, the allocation of text to pages is usually performed manually by the Web author.

Inline and Block Formatting

Inline formatting is applied to sequences of characters, often called *spans*, within a block. Inline formatting specifies the font properties described earlier. The font family and variant and size of the characters within each span can be set. For example, a span may be set in an italic font for emphasis. (In this book, we apply boldface italics to spans containing words that appear in the glossary.) Where text is destined for an output medium that supports colour, characters may be set in different colours. For subscripts and superscripts, a baseline offset may be set, so that the characters (which will usually be set at a smaller size) will be moved vertically into an appropriate position. Note that this will increase the height of the span, as will setting characters in a larger size, which may necessitate increasing the leading for affected lines.

Most modern word processors and page layout applications allow you to define named *character styles*, which collect together a set of properties used for a particular purpose, and allow you to apply them by name, instead of setting the individual properties separately. For instance, you might define a character style called emphasized, which set the font style to italic. You would apply this style to emphasized text instead of setting the font style explicitly. This ensures consistency and makes modifying styles easier. If you wanted to use boldface for emphasis instead of italics, you would only have to change the style definition, and all text to which it had been applied would be changed to bold.

The use of character styles is an application of the principle of separating the specification of appearance from structure. Applying the style marks the span to which it has been applied as being emphasized. You specify how that should be expressed visually by defining the style, which is independent of any specific span of emphasized text.

In conventional documents, each block will be treated as a paragraph, even though some blocks, such as headings, will just be single lines. Each paragraph will have default settings for the formatting properties of characters – in the absence of any explicit inline formatting, the text of the paragraph will be set in the default font, using a default value for the leading. The block treated as a whole has additional formatting properties concerned with the way space is added to the lines within the block, and the way the block is placed relative to its surroundings and other blocks.

Figure 9.22 demonstrates the four common ways of dealing with the spacing of words within lines.[†] If the inter-word spacing is kept uniform, text may be *left-aligned*, so that the left margin is straight, but the right margin is ragged; *right-aligned*, with a straight right and ragged left margin; or *centred*, with both margins ragged but equal. Left alignment is the norm (for languages that are read from left to right), with right-aligned and centred text normally reserved for headings and other displayed items. For more formal publications, such as most books, text is *justified*. This means that extra space is added between words, where necessary, to make each line (except the last in a paragraph) the same length. This may be done in different ways. The crudest is to add words to a line until no more will fit, then insert equal amounts of space between every word to fill up the line. This can produce badly stretched-out lines. Usually, words may be broken and

> Dolore et praesto odit, susciduipit lore feum delis acil dolore conulput utet vel in ut lobortie magna feugait autat lum vullaortio od mod et irit exer sed er aliquismodip esent landreet nim erat et luptate tat.

> Dolore et praesto odit, susciduipit lore feum delis acil dolore conulput utet vel in ut lobortie magna feugait autat lum vullaortio od mod et irit exer sed er aliquismodip esent landreet nim erat et luptate tat.

> Dolore et praesto odit, susciduipit lore feum delis acil dolore conulput utet vel in ut lobortie magna feugait autat lum vullaortio od mod et irit exer sed er aliquismodip esent landreet nim erat et luptate tat.

> Dolore et praesto odit, susciduipit lore feum delis acil dolore conulput utet vel in ut lobortie magna feugait autat lum vullaortio od mod et irit exer sed er aliquismodip esent landreet nim erat et luptate tat.

Figure 9.22. *Left-aligned, right-aligned, centred and justified paragraphs*

[†] *It also illustrates the typographer's use of garbled Latin text to demonstrate layout features, so that the text's meaning does not intrude on the layout.*

hyphenated at the ends of lines, to reduce the need for inter-word space. The rules and conventions governing how words may be hyphenated are complex and somewhat arbitrary, and differ among languages, so automatic hyphenation is not always very successful. To obtain more even text, and to avoid "rivers of white" when spaces line up on consecutive lines, more elaborate algorithms, which consider the entire paragraphs instead of individual lines, may be employed.

┌─**IN DETAIL**───

For justified text, the last line of each paragraph is usually set left-aligned, but for some sorts of document, every line is justified. Occasionally, the last line of a justified paragraph is centred, which can look elegant for isolated blocks of text, but is not very readable for long passages consisting of many paragraphs.

└───

Fully justified text has a neat and orderly appearance, whereas ragged right is less formal – some say that it looks more restless. However, even if you wish to present a formal appearance, justification should be used with caution for text to be displayed on a monitor. Because of the low resolution of monitors, text is usually set in relatively large sizes, which means that fewer words can be fitted on to a line of reasonable length. This in turn provides fewer gaps between which to distribute the extra space needed for justification, with the result that the text may acquire large or uneven gaps, "rivers of white", and other undesirable artefacts that interfere with readability.

Every block of text may be surrounded by space on all four sides. Setting space above and below a block marks it off from its neighbours. The space between the left edge of the block and the edge of the page or window is usually called the *indent*. Sometimes, the first line of a paragraph is indented differently from the other lines. One convention for indicating the start of a paragraph is to indent the first line relative to the others. First lines may also be *exdented*, that is, indented a negative amount relative to the rest of the paragraph. This form of layout is often used for lists. (See, for example, the way that exercises are laid out at the end of each chapter of this book.) The items in a list may be numbered, or introduced by bullets or other dingbat characters.

Sometimes frames are put around blocks. This gives rise to extra places to insert space – between the text and the frame, and between the frame and its surroundings. All of these spaces must be controlled when text is laid out. It is also fairly common to allow blocks to have a background colour; frames too may be coloured.

Just as named character styles are used to abstract inline formatting, so a collection of values for a block's formatting – its default font settings, alignment, indentation and spacing – may be given a name as a paragraph style, and used to set multiple paragraphs in a consistent fashion.

Blocks of text are sometimes arranged in rows and columns as tables. Generally, the cells of a table can contain images as well as text. Although tables are intended for the tabular display of data and other information, the regular grid that a table imposes may be found convenient for other formatting tasks, such as attaching a caption to an image, or setting text in two columns. (As we will explain in Chapter 10, the use of tables for this purpose should be avoided.) The formatting of tables can be complicated: the height of rows and the width of columns must be specified, or determined automatically. The text inside each cell of the table must be formatted and arranged within the space of the cell, and the vertical alignment of cells with respect to each other must be set. Adjacent cells may be merged in some of the rows so that they span more than one column, or merged in columns to span more than one row. Columns may have headings set in a different style from the contents of the cells. Rules (lines) may be used to separate some or all of the rows and columns.

Finally, at the highest level of organization of text, blocks must be positioned and combined into a page. Normally, paragraph and heading blocks are arranged one after the other vertically, with the surrounding space as specified for each. Where less conventional layouts are used, each block may need to be placed at a specific point, either relative to the origin of the page, or relative to another block. Some systems allow you to embed a block within another block. Within the enclosing block, the embedded block is treated as if it was a single character, although most inline formatting does not then make sense.

Markup and Stylesheets

In the days before desktop publishing and word processors, authors' manuscripts were usually produced on a typewriter. Consequently, they could not be laid out in exactly the same form as the final published book or paper. The author, the publisher's copy editor and possibly a book designer would annotate the manuscript, using a variety of different coloured pens and a vocabulary of special symbols, to indicate how the text should be formatted by the typesetter when it was eventually printed. This process of annotation was called "marking up" and the instructions themselves were often referred to as *markup*. With the transition to computer-based methods of publication, the function of markup was transferred to annotations inserted (often by the author) into the digital text file that now corresponds to the manuscript. At first, markup was used to specify the detailed appearance of the text, as it had been before computer programs were used, but markup is now generally used to indicate the structure of a document, with its appearance being specified separately.

Many text documents are prepared using *WYSIWYG* formatting systems and word processors. WYSIWYG stands for "What you see is what you get", a phrase which succinctly captures the essence of such systems. As you type, text appears on the screen laid out just as it will be when it is printed or displayed. Font and size changes, indentation, tabulation and other layout features are controlled by menus, command keys or toolbar icons, and their effect is seen immediately. The markup, although present, is invisible. Only its effect can be seen, presenting the illusion that the formatting commands do not insert markup, but actually perform the formatting before your very eyes, as it were.

An alternative way of working it to prepare the document using a plain text editor. In this case the text is interspersed with the markup, which takes the form of special layout commands, often known as *tags*. Tags are lexically distinguished from the text proper – by being enclosed in angle brackets or beginning with a backslash character, for example. (Text editors often have modes for common markup languages, in which the tags can be inserted using a single keystroke or menu selection, so inserting tag-based markup is no more arduous than applying WYSIWYG formatting.) Tags do the same job as the commands in a WYSIWYG system, but their effect is not immediately visible. A separate processing phase is usually required, during which the formatting described by the tags is applied to the text, which is displayed (in a Web browser, for instance) or converted into a form that can be displayed or printed, such as PDF.

Although the subjective experience of preparing text using these two different types of system is very different, calling for different skills and appealing to different personalities, their differences are mostly superficial and concern the interface much more than the way in which layout is actually controlled. Underneath any WYSIWYG system is a tag-based text formatter; sometimes the tags may be binary control codes which are inaccessible to the user of the WYSIWYG editor, but they may be text tags which can be accessed using a different mode or by opening the file in a text editor.

For the most part, we will concentrate on layout using textual tags, partly because it is easier to see what is going on, and partly because, after years in the shade of layout based on hidden control codes, it has acquired a new importance because of the World Wide Web. An advantage of using textual markup, instead of binary codes or some data structure, is that the marked up document is plain text, which can be read on any computer system and can be transmitted unscathed over a network. This is particularly important for the Internet, with its heterogeneous architectures. Here, HTML brought tagging into wide use. XML, and a clutch of languages developed from it, promised to extend the use of this sort of markup into other areas of multimedia, but so far there has been no widespread acceptance of XML as a broad basis for markup. In Chapter 15 we will look at XML and describe how its tagging mechanism has been applied to vector graphics in SVG.

The difference between tag-based text editing and WYSIWYG layout is merely a cosmetic difference between interfaces. A more profound distinction is that between *visual markup* and *structural markup*, which we touched on when describing character styles. In visual markup, tags or commands are used to specify aspects of the appearance of the text, such as fonts and type sizes.

In structural markup, tags identify logical elements of a document, such as headings, lists or tables, and the visual appearance of each type of element is specified separately.

The distinction between visual and structural markup exists in a crude form in any word processor that supports the use of paragraph and character styles. For instance, if you were writing a paper divided into sections, you would almost certainly want to distinguish the section headings from the body text – let's say by setting them in a large boldface sans serif font and inserting some extra space above the heading. A purely visual approach to markup would lead you to select each heading, insert space above it and set the font, its size and shape, using the appropriate menu commands or controls on the formatting palette. You would have to apply the correct settings to each section heading.

However, if you were to adopt a more structural approach, you would define a paragraph style – **sectionheading**, for example – which abstracted the correct font and spacing settings for section headings. Whenever you added a new section, you would just apply the **sectionheading** style to its heading. If you were adopting this approach, you would probably also define styles for the body text, sub-headings, paper title, and so on, for all the textual elements in your paper. You could go further and create a document template containing all these style definitions, which you could use to produce papers with a consistent layout.

Structural markup has distinct advantages over visual markup. Perhaps most obviously, it allows us to change the appearance of a document globally by changing the definitions of the styles just once. If, for example, we wanted to use a more imaginative layout for our section headings – right-aligned in upper-case boldface italics, for example – we would only have to edit the definition of the **sectionheading** paragraph style and every section would be reformatted in the new style. Consistency is ensured. In contrast, if we had marked up each section heading individually, we would have had to find and change the markup of each one.

A sufficiently powerful system based on structural markup allows you to re-define the effect of your markup tags for different output media. For example, if you wished to produce a version of your document to be read to blind people by a speech synthesizer, you might re-define a section heading so that the words of the heading were read with increased emphasis. This sort of application is best suited to tag-based structural markup, in which the structural tags themselves need not specify any form of processing but just identify different sorts of textual element. Hence, they can be used as the basis for presentation of the document in any medium, including media which had not yet been invented when the document was written.

A related advantage of structural markup is that it permits a separation of concerns, and a division of labour, between the appearance of a document and its structure. The writer need only concentrate on identifying the logical divisions within the document while he or she is writing. The question of which typographical features should be used to identify those divisions in a perspicuous and pleasing way can be dealt with separately, ideally by a specialist designer. If visual markup is used, the processes of writing and layout become intertwined, and control over appearance is left to the whim of the author.

The final advantage of structural markup is that identifying the structural elements by name makes it easy for a computer program to analyse the structure of the document. Although people can identify the structural elements from their appearance, this depends on knowledge and understanding – things which it is notoriously difficult to incorporate into computer programs. Programs are extremely good at searching text for strings with a specific form, such as XML tags, or word processor control codes, however. This makes it relatively easy to write programs to extract tables of contents or other tagged pieces of information. It also makes it easier to translate between different forms of a document. For instance, both Word and InDesign use paragraph and character styles. An import filter allows Word documents to be placed into InDesign, while mapping named styles from the former program to styles with the same name in the latter. Thus, an author can type a manuscript in Word, and apply styles, whose names are specified by a designer, but whose appearance in Word is irrelevant. When the document is placed into InDesign, each of the author's placeholder styles is replaced by the book designer's styles for the same element, so that section headers which were merely boldfaced in Word can be set in a more elaborate, carefully spaced way in InDesign, without any new markup being applied explicitly.

If you take the idea of structural markup to its logical conclusion, it leads to the complete separation of appearance from structure and content. Markup tags should only indicate structure. However, when documents are displayed or printed they have some appearance and it is natural to want to specify this. Where pure structural markup is used, the specification of appearance must be left to a separate mechanism. On the World Wide Web, for instance, the CSS language can be used to write rules which specify how each type of element should be formatted.

Commonly, many documents will share a similar appearance. For instance, the headings on each page in a Web site should all be styled in the same way, to give an appearance of unity to the site. This can be done by putting a set of rules in a separate document, called a *stylesheet*, which is attached to every page in the site.

For each tag being used, a stylesheet provides one or more rules describing the way in which elements with that tag should be laid out. As we will describe in Chapter 10, rules may specify styling in a context-dependent way, so that, for instance, a list element may be formatted differently when it occurs in the header of a page and when it occurs in the main body.

There may be more than one stylesheet for a particular document or collection of documents, providing a different appearance to the same structure – as, for example, a fancy style with extravagant graphic design and a plain style intended for people with poor eyesight. Stylesheets can also be used to specify the equivalent of formatting for screen reading devices. Stylesheets can be altered or substituted without any need to alter the markup of the document itself.

KEY POINTS

Markup consists of annotations that control a text document's layout and formatting or indicate its structure.

In WYSIWYG systems, markup is invisible and the effects of formatting commands are displayed immediately.

Markup may take the form of readable tags, which can be inserted using any text editor.

In visual markup, tags specify aspects of the text's appearance. In structural markup, they identify logical elements, such as paragraphs, lists or headings.

Structural markup allows global formatting changes to be made easily, permits the same markup to be used for different output media, allows a separation of concerns between content creation and design, and makes it easier for computer programs to analyse and process marked-up documents.

A set of styles can be collected into a stylesheet, which may be attached to many documents to ensure a consistent and unified appearance.

Exercises

Test Questions

1 Give two examples of ways in which ASCII control codes are used on modern computer systems.

2 Why do you think programming languages usually require you to write the multiplication operator as an asterisk (*)?

3 Explain why 8-bit characters sets are not adequate for modern computer applications.

4 Naïve commentators sometimes claim that using Unicode or ISO 10646 is wasteful of space for documents whose textual content can be adequately represented in ASCII. Explain why this is not so.

5 What is the difference between a character and a glyph?

6 If you were preparing a paper and wanted to be sure that it was displayed with the fonts you had chosen on any machine, what format would you choose to save it in?

7 Is the combination of a font family name, shape, weight and size sufficient to identify any font?

8 Arrange the following quantities in increasing order: body size, cap height, leading, x-height. State clearly any assumptions you make.

9 Why is justified text less common on Web pages than in printed books?

10 What are the advantages of using structural markup, as opposed to visual markup?

Discussion Topics

1 Although Unicode can represent nearly a million different characters, keyboards cannot have that many keys. Discuss ways in which keyboards can be made to accommodate the full range of characters.

2 Is there a meaningful distinction to be made between fonts that are readable and those that are legible? If so, what is it?

3 Although a distinction is usually drawn between italic and upright fonts, there are other differences between italic and roman fonts, besides their slant. What would an "upright italic" font look like? Would it be useful for anything?

4 Is the traditional distinction between text fonts and display fonts a helpful one when considering fonts to use when displaying text on a computer screen?

5 Discuss the relative merits of implementing markup with invisible control sequences, as in older word processors, and with readable tags, as in Web pages.

Practical Tasks

1 Look at a newspaper both in printed form and online. Compare and contrast the way fonts are used in news stories and in advertisements in the two cases.

2 Find out which fonts are available on your computer, and print samples of each. Which would you consider to be suitable for display purposes and which for text?

Which of the fonts available on your system would you use for each of the following jobs?

(a) The opening credits of a science fiction movie.

(b) Your *curriculum vitae*.

(c) The body copy of a community newsletter.

(d) A wedding invitation.

(e) The body text of a Web page about your college course.

(f) The list of ingredients on the back of a jar of jam.

Explain each of your choices.

3 Design a font for Scrabble® tiles. You only need the upper-case letters. You will have to ensure that your letter forms fit harmoniously and legibly into the square tile (and don't forget the little number for the letter's value). If you don't have access to font design software, such as FontForge or FontLab, you should design the character shapes on squared paper in sufficient detail to be mapped to pixels; otherwise, use the software available to you to generate a font in a suitable format and use it to typeset some sample words.

4 Choose a bitmapped image with a simple composition and add text to it to create a poster for a forthcoming event. Experiment with the different text effects available in whichever graphics program you use to make the poster, but don't let the effects obscure the content and message.

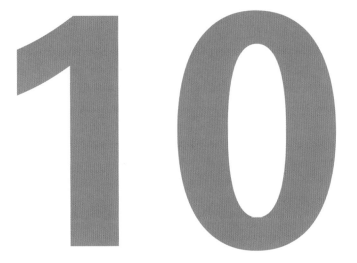

10

Hypermedia

■ **Text Layout Using XHTML and CSS**

Elements, Tags, Attributes and Rules. XHTML Elements and Attributes. CSS Properties. Advanced Selectors.

■ **Links**

URLs. Anchors.

■ **The Web and Hypermedia**

Internet Media Types. Embedded Media. Links and Images.

In Chapter 9 we described the character of digital text, one of the most important components of multimedia. As well as being an important and long-established medium in its own right, text forms the basis of hypertext and hypermedia. Hypertext is text augmented with links – pointers to other pieces of text, which may be elsewhere in the same document or, more often, in another document, perhaps stored at a different location. Hypertext thus allows us to store a collection of related texts and browse among them. Hypermedia goes a step further, by allowing pages to have images, sounds, video and animation embedded in them, and scripts associated with them to perform interaction with the user.

The description in the preceding paragraph will probably sound familiar. The **World Wide Web** (more commonly, simply the Web) is just such a network of media elements connected by links. It has become the defining example of hypermedia.

IN DETAIL

Although popular perceptions of hypermedia focus on the World Wide Web, the concept has a long history. Its origin is generally traced to an article entitled "As We May Think" written in 1945 by Vannevar Bush, a scientific advisor to President Roosevelt, in which Bush described a machine for browsing and annotating a large collection of documents.

The Memex, as Bush's device was known, included a mechanism for creating links between documents, allowing documents related to the one currently being read to be retrieved, in much the same way as Web pages related to the current one can be accessed by following a link. The Memex was a mechanical device, based on photosensors and microdots, and it is hardly surprising that it was never built – digital computer technology provides a much more suitable mechanism for linked data retrieval.

The title of Bush's article refers to his contention that association of ideas is fundamental to the way people think, and that document storage systems should work in a way that reflects these associations, hence the need for links.

Unlike earlier hypermedia systems, which used proprietary formats and were largely closed and self-sufficient, the Web uses publicly available technology, and plug-ins and helper applications which allow browsers to handle arbitrary media types. In particular, Web pages are constructed from documents marked up with a textual language, so anyone can create a Web page with a text editor. The languages used for marking up and formatting Web pages provide an insight into the implementation of hypermedia.

Hypertext is basically text, and must be laid out and displayed typographically in the manner we described in Chapter 9. Hence, as well as being an example of hypermedia, the Web is also an example of the use of structural markup and stylesheets. We will begin by describing the layout of individual Web pages, before explaining how links and embedded media can be added to them.

Text Layout Using XHTML and CSS

Originally, the World Wide Web was intended as a means of dissemination of scientific research, so the markup language for Web pages, **HTML (Hypertext Markup Language)**, contained tags corresponding to the main elements of a scientific paper – headings that can be nested several levels deep to introduce sections, sub-sections, sub-sub-sections and so on, and lists of various types such as enumerations and bullet points, and paragraphs of text. Additionally, HTML allows you to mark text as emphasized or strongly emphasized, and to identify abbreviations, quotations and sections of code. (Early versions of the language provided some explicit typographical tags too, for choosing fonts and so on, but these tags are now deprecated.†) Later revisions of HTML added tables and interactive forms to its repertoire. As well as these layout tags, HTML crucially includes tags for hypertext linkage and for inclusion of images and other media elements, as we will describe later in this chapter. Stylesheets written in **CSS (Cascading Style Sheets)** are used for typographic styling and layout specification, in accordance with the principles of structural markup, which we discussed in Chapter 9.

Our main interest in describing HTML is to introduce you to hypermedia and the syntax of markup on the Web, and to illustrate structural markup. Similarly, with CSS we intend to show how stylesheets can provide sophisticated layout control to complement the markup. We assume that most readers will have some knowledge of HTML, but will not necessarily be acquainted with CSS. Those readers needing additional detailed information should consult the references given on this book's supporting Web site.

The current version of HTML is known as **XHTML**. The X ostensibly stands for "Extensible", but is actually a reference to XML (see Chapter 15), since XHTML is a reformulation of HTML in XML. The XHTML 1.0 specification was adopted as a W3C Recommendation in January 2000. Provided that a few simple conventions are observed, XHTML is compatible with the earlier HTML 4.0 Recommendation, in the sense that legal XHTML is also legal HTML 4.0. The reverse is not true, however, since XHTML is stricter than HTML in some respects. (In fact, the XHTML 1.0 Recommendation consists of a reference to the HTML 4.0 Recommendation, supplemented by a few pages describing the differences between XHTML and HTML.)

---

† *"Deprecated" does not just mean "disapproved of" in the context of Web standards. It means that the features are likely to be removed from later revisions of the language. Their use should therefore be avoided.*

Although most people are familiar with Web pages being displayed by a Web browser, such as Firefox, Safari or Internet Explorer, the structural markup of XHTML can also be interpreted by other programs, such as a text-to-speech converter. In the following pages, we will adopt the name *user agent*, used in W3C specifications, to mean any program that interprets XHTML markup. A user agent, such as a conventional Web browser, that formats XHTML documents and displays them on a monitor, is an example of a *visual user agent*. A text-to-speech converter is an example of a *non-visual user agent*.

┌─IN DETAIL───────────────────────────────────────

XHTML 1.0 is not the most recent HTML specification, but its successors, XHTML 1.1 and the draft XHTML 2, are problematic. The difficulties arise because of the way in which user agents determine what type of data is contained in a document. We will go into this further in Chapter 16, but for now it is sufficient to know that the way a user agent treats the content of a file it is trying to display is ultimately determined by information sent by the Web server, which overrules any specification found inside the document. (This may sound strange, but it is the way the Internet works.) Few Web servers are set up to send the correct information to indicate that a document is XHTML, so user agents end up treating XHTML documents as HTML, which is why the conventions we mentioned earlier must be observed in XHTML documents.

XHTML 1.1 defines a "purified" version of XHTML which cannot be treated this way: it must be parsed as XML. Some user agents simply cannot handle this correctly, so if XHTML is served in the proper way, it will not be displayed. Since XHTML 1.1 cannot be served any other way, using it runs a considerable risk that Web pages will not be displayed in some popular browsers. As a result, XHTML 1.1 has struggled to achieve any adoption.

XHTML 2 was intended to build on XHTML 1.1 and to abandon backward-compatibility with HTML. In view of the failure of XHTML 1.1, and of "HTML as XML" generally, the future of XHTML 2 looks bleak. In response, a W3C Working Group has been set up to define HTML 5, an alternative successor to XHTML 1.0 and HTML 4, which is intended to avoid the problems. HTML 5 is mostly a consolidation of the existing Web technologies, whereas XHTML 2 was intended as a forward-looking development that could better accommodate the Semantic Web. At present, neither is fully implemented, and it is not clear how Web markup will develop, but it is certainly the case that HTML 5 is preferred by the browser implementors.

At the time of writing, though, XHTML 1.0 and HTML 4 remain the two versions in common use. We prefer XHTML because of its compatibility with other XML-based languages, but the choice makes little difference in practice.

Elements, Tags, Attributes and Rules

XHTML markup divides a document into *elements* corresponding to its logical divisions, such as paragraphs and lists. Some elements may contain other elements. A list typically contains several list items, for example, and this containment is reflected in the markup. On the other hand, some elements may not appear within certain others – a paragraph can't contain a list or another paragraph, for instance. Rules concerning which elements an element may contain or appear within are part of the definition of XHTML.

Each element is introduced by a *start tag* and ends with an *end tag*. Between these two tags is the element's *content*, which, as we just observed, may include other elements with their own start and end tags. Elements must be properly nested – that is, if an element starts inside another, it must end inside it, too. This means that each element forms part of the content of a unique parent element that immediately encloses it.

Every type of element available in XHTML has a name. Its start tag consists of its name enclosed in angle brackets – for example, `<p>`, which is the start tag of the element used for paragraphs, the name of which is **p**. In XHTML the names of tags consist of lower-case letters and numbers. (In earlier versions of HTML, the case was irrelevant, with `<p>` and `<P>` being considered the same; in XHTML they are different.) The end tag is similar, except that the element's name is preceded by a slash - for example, `</p>`. So every paragraph in an XHTML document has the form:

```
<p>
content of the paragraph element
</p>
```

All other elements have the same structural form – start tag, content, end tag – but with their own identifying tags.

White space consists of space, tab and formfeed characters, and line breaks, which may be of the form used on any of the major platforms: carriage return, linefeed or both. In text, white space separates words in the usual way. Visual user agents will format the text in accordance with the conventions of the writing system being used. In English this will usually mean that runs of spaces are replaced by a single space. (In **pre** elements, which we describe later, white space is left exactly as it is typed.) White space immediately following a start tag or preceding an end tag is ignored, so that the following two examples will be displayed identically.

```
<p>
Shall I compare thee to a summer's day?
</p>

<p>Shall I compare thee to a summer's day?</p>
```

Some elements have no content; these are called ***empty elements***. An example is the hr element, which produces a horizontal rule (a line). There is no sensible content that can be supplied to such an element – it is just a horizontal rule – so there is nothing for an end tag to do. You can put an end tag anyway, but it is more customary to run the start and end tags together into a single tag, where the fact that the element is empty is indicated by putting a / before the closing >, as in <hr />. (The space before the / would not be required if the XHTML was being treated as XML, but putting it in makes it possible for browsers to treat XHTML as HTML.)

Most elements, whether or not they have any content, have certain properties. For instance, the img element, which is used to include images in a document, has as one of its properties the location of the file containing the image data; another property is a short textual alternative to the image, for the benefit of non-visual user agents. In XHTML such properties are called ***attributes***. The attributes which may be associated with a particular element are specified as part of its definition in the language.

Values for each attribute may be assigned within the start tag of an element. For example, to set the source file of an img to pm-asparagus.jpg, specify its dimensions and provide a suitable textual alternative, we would use the following tag:

```
<img src = "pm-asparagus.jpg" width="240" height="180"
  alt="The Prime Minister eating asparagus" />
```

The img element is empty. The attributes src and alt are used for specifying the image source and its textual alternative, respectively.

Attributes' names must be in lower case. Values are assigned using an = sign. The values assigned to attributes must be enclosed in double or single quotes (even if they are numbers). Where there is more than one attribute, they are separated by white space.

An inevitable problem arises if tags and attributes are written in the same character set as the text proper: we must lexically distinguish tags from text, and delimit the values assigned to attributes. This is done using some special characters (in XHTML the angle brackets that surround the element name in a tag and the quotes that surround attribute values). We therefore need some mechanism for representing those special characters when they appear in the text or in attribute values as themselves. In XHTML, a < symbol can be represented by the ***character entity reference*** < (the terminating semi-colon is part of the entity reference). Similarly, a > symbol is represented by the character entity reference >, " by " and ' by '. This now leaves us with the problem of representing an & so as not to cause confusion. Again, a character entity reference is used; this time it is &.

The default character encoding for XHTML is UTF-8. Any esoteric characters that you can type on your keyboard will be displayed correctly if (but only if) your XHTML file is saved using UTF-8 as its character encoding. If it is not, some characters may be incorrectly displayed unless you explicitly designate a different character set or encoding. As you may have guessed, character entity references provide a general mechanism for inserting characters that are hard to type or are not available in the chosen character encoding. References are available for all the characters in the top half of ISO 8859-1 (see Chapter 9), as well as for mathematical symbols and Greek letters, and for layout characters, such as an em-dash. Some examples are given in Figure 10.1; for the full list, consult section 24 of the HTML 4.0 specification.

There are many Unicode characters without character entity references. For these you can use a **numeric character reference**, which specifies a character using its ISO 10646 character code. A character with Unicode value D (in decimal) is written as &#D; so, for example, < is an alternative to <. If you are more comfortable with base 16 numbers, you can write your numeric entity references in hexadecimal, putting an x after the # to indicate that you are doing so. Another alternative to < is thus <. Whichever notation you use, don't omit the ; at the end, which is part of the reference. (Specialized HTML editors or Web authoring programs will usually allow you to select entity and character references from a palette or menu, and insert the correct characters for you.)

&iexcl;	¡
&pound;	£
&euro;	€
&sect;	§
&Aring;	Å
&aring;	å
&piv;	ϖ
&forall;	∀
&exist;	∃
&isin;	∈
&ni;	∌
&ndash;	–
&mdash;	—
&dagger;	†
&Dagger;	‡

Figure 10.1. *A few examples of character entity references*

Attributes should not be used for specifying the appearance of a document, although there are some deprecated attributes in XHTML 1.0 which perform this function. Instead, as we explained in Chapter 9, appearance should be specified separately, in a stylesheet. In principle, since stylesheet information is separate from markup, any stylesheet language can be used with XHTML. In practice, most Web browsers only support CSS, a simple stylesheet language which works well with XHTML, and can be easily mastered.

Let's return to paragraphs to demonstrate how a stylesheet can be used to control layout. For now, don't worry about how the stylesheet and XHTML document are combined.

A paragraph element is a logical division of the text of a document. In the absence of any stylesheet, a user agent is free to express this division in whatever way it chooses. In English text, several different conventions are employed for laying out paragraphs. The simplest convention from a visual point of view relies only on the insertion of additional vertical space between paragraphs.It is also common to use a slightly more sophisticated form where the vertical space is augmented or replaced by applying an indentation to the first line of each paragraph. Most, if not all, visual user agents use the simplest convention by default. Suppose we want to use the more elaborate form, with indentation.

CSS allows us to specify various visual properties of each document element. One of these properties is the indentation of the first line. We specify that the first line of each paragraph should be indented by 4 pc with a CSS *rule* like this:

```
p {
    text-indent: 4pc;
}
```

The rule has two parts: a *selector* (here p) which indicates which elements the rule applies to, and some *declarations* (here there is only one) which provide values for some visual properties. Here the declaration specifies a text-indent (the name of the property controlling the amount of indentation applied to the first line) of 4 pc. The declaration part of a rule is enclosed in curly brackets, as you can see. Each declaration (there may be several in a rule) is terminated by a semicolon.

Whenever the rule just given is in force, every paragraph will be displayed with its first line indented by any user agent that implements CSS stylesheets (and is configured to do so). Suppose now that we did not wish to apply this indentation to every paragraph. Many manuals of style suggest that the first paragraph of a section should not be indented, for example. In order to be more selective about which paragraphs a rule applies to, we need some way of distinguishing between different classes of paragraph, such as those that are indented and those that are not. The XHTML attribute class provides one way of doing so. This attribute is a property of virtually every XHTML element; its value is a distinguishing name that identifies a subset of that element. For example, we might use a class noindent for paragraphs we wished to be displayed with no indentation.

In a CSS rule, a selector can consist of an element name followed by a dot and a class name. To specify that paragraphs of class noindent should not be indented, we would add the following rule to the previous one (note that when a length is zero, the units can be omitted):

```
p.noindent {
    text-indent: 0;
}
```

As you would probably expect, when there is a general rule for some element (like our first example) and a more specific rule for some class of that element (like our second example), the more specific rule is applied to elements of that class, and the general rule is only applied to elements belonging to no class, or to some class for which no specific rule is available. If, for example, we had some paragraphs of class unindent, they would be displayed with a 4 pc first line indent, since the only rule that applies to them is the general one with selector p.

Rules can be used to control a range of properties. Even a simple rule with only a couple of declarations can produce useful effects. For example, the following rule causes paragraphs to be displayed with a hanging indent.

```
p.hang {
    text-indent: -4pc;
    margin-left: 4pc;
}
```

The margin-left property applies a left margin to the paragraph. By setting the text-indent to a negative value, we make the first line stick out into the margin, so that the paragraph has a hanging indent. The effect of these three rules is shown in Figure 10.2, which shows the display of the following XHTML document by a user agent that understands stylesheets.

```
<!DOCTYPE html PUBLIC "-//W3C//DTD XHTML 1.0 Strict//EN"
    "http://www.w3.org/TR/xhtml1/DTD/xhtml1-strict.dtd">
<html xmlns="http://www.w3.org/1999/xhtml" xml:lang="en" lang="en">
<head>
    <meta http-equiv="content-type" content="text/html;charset=utf-8" />
    <title>Paragraphs</title>
    <style type="text/css">
    p {
        text-indent: 4pc;
    }
    p.noindent {
        text-indent: 0pc;
    }
    p.hang {
        text-indent: -4pc;
        margin-left: 4pc;
    }
    </style>
</head>

<body>
    <p class="noindent">
```

```
Lore veraessissit ulla alit dolorero od do dolorem etc.
</p>
<p class="unindent">
Lore veraessissit ulla alit dolorero ...
</p>
<p class="hang">
Lore veraessissit ulla alit dolorero ...
</p>
</body>
</html>
```

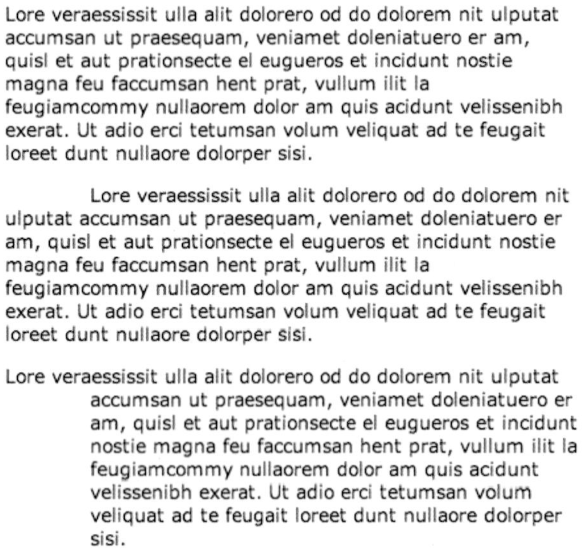

Lore veraessissit ulla alit dolorero od do dolorem nit ulputat accumsan ut praesequam, veniamet doleniatuero er am, quisl et aut prationsecte el eugueros et incidunt nostie magna feu faccumsan hent prat, vullum ilit la feugiamcommy nullaorem dolor am quis acidunt velissenibh exerat. Ut adio erci tetumsan volum veliquat ad te feugait loreet dunt nullaore dolorper sisi.

Lore veraessissit ulla alit dolorero od do dolorem nit ulputat accumsan ut praesequam, veniamet doleniatuero er am, quisl et aut prationsecte el eugueros et incidunt nostie magna feu faccumsan hent prat, vullum ilit la feugiamcommy nullaorem dolor am quis acidunt velissenibh exerat. Ut adio erci tetumsan volum veliquat ad te feugait loreet dunt nullaore dolorper sisi.

Lore veraessissit ulla alit dolorero od do dolorem nit ulputat accumsan ut praesequam, veniamet doleniatuero er am, quisl et aut prationsecte el eugueros et incidunt nostie magna feu faccumsan hent prat, vullum ilit la feugiamcommy nullaorem dolor am quis acidunt velissenibh exerat. Ut adio erci tetumsan volum veliquat ad te feugait loreet dunt nullaore dolorper sisi.

Figure 10.2. *Browser display of paragraphs with different indents*

This document also illustrates some features of XHTML that we have not yet described. The first two lines make up the *document type declaration*, also known as the DOCTYPE declaration, which identifies the version of HTML being used, in this case XHTML 1.0. The enigmatic form of the specification can just be treated as red tape; Chapter 15 provides an explanation of what is going on and why it is needed.

Next comes the start tag for the html element. This is the root of the entire document structure; all the elements of the document proper are contained within it. There are only two document elements that can come immediately inside the html element: head followed by body. The head of the document contains information about the document, which is not actually displayed within it. The body of the document contains the real text, images and other content.

There are three elements contained in the head of this document. The meta element should also be treated as red tape: it is used as a way of specifying that the character set is UTF-8. This is the default, but it is good practice to specify the character set explicitly in this way. If you do so, the meta element should be the first thing in the head. The title element contains a short title, which is usually displayed in the title bar of the browser's window. It is not displayed within the window, because it is not part of the text contained in the body. Every document's head element must include a title, though.

The next element in the head is a style, which is where the stylesheet rules governing the layout of this page are to be found. The start tag has an attribute type whose value is the media type of the stylesheet. For CSS rules, this is always text/css. Where a stylesheet is to be applied to more than one document, duplicating it in every one is wasteful and leads to maintenance problems. Under these circumstances, a stylesheet is usually stored in its own file, and incorporated into every XHTML document that needs it, by way of a link element in the document's head, which for this purpose has the form:

```
<link href="stylesheet's URL" rel="stylesheet" type="text/css" />
```

The body of the document contains the paragraphs themselves, with their class attributes. The stylesheet rules in the head are applied to them to produce the desired display.

Most XHTML documents contain more content than this one, so the impression that the content is overwhelmed by red tape and markup which our example may give is exaggerated, although it is still valid to some extent.

KEY POINTS

Text in an XHTML document is marked up with tags that delineate the document elements corresponding to the logical divisions of the text.

Each element consists of a start tag, followed by its content and an end tag.

A start tag consists of the element name written in angle brackets. An end tag is the same except that a slash precedes the name, e.g. <p>...</p>.

Empty elements have no content. Their start and end tags may be combined, e.g.
.

Elements may have attributes, whose values are assigned in the start tag.

Character entity references and numeric character references may be used to represent characters that are used as part of the markup or which are not available on a conventional keyboard.

Stylesheet rules written in CSS may be used to control the layout of elements.

The selector of each rule determines which elements it applies to, and the corresponding declarations set properties that control their appearance.

The class attribute is used to distinguish between different subsets of an element type, so that finer control can be exerted over their layout.

An XHTML document begins with a document type declaration. Its root is the html element, which contains the head and body elements. Stylesheet rules may appear in a style element in the head.

XHTML Elements and Attributes

We are now in a position to describe the XHTML tags that can be used to mark up text, and the CSS properties that can be used to control its layout. Although we are describing these particular languages, you should appreciate that the underlying principles of markup and layout apply to any system of text preparation.

Please note that the account which follows is not exhaustive. The scope of this book does not allow us to provide a full tutorial on XHTML and CSS, or a definitive reference guide. More details can be found in *Web Design: A Complete Introduction*, or in the detailed reference material listed on the supporting Web site.

The HTML 4.0 specification – and thus the XHTML 1.0 specification – defines 91 elements, of which 10 are deprecated, since there are now preferred ways of achieving the same effect. (Many attributes are also deprecated, even for elements which are not.) Only a few of these elements are concerned purely with text layout. Those that are can conveniently be divided into **block-level** and **inline** elements. Block-level elements are those which are normally formatted as discrete blocks, such as paragraphs – i.e. their start and end are marked by line breaks. Inline elements do not cause such breaks; they are run in to the surrounding text. Thus, the distinction corresponds to the general distinction between block and inline formatting described in Chapter 9.

IN DETAIL

There are three DTDs for XHTML 1.0: Strict, Transitional and Frameset. The Strict DTD excludes the deprecated elements and attributes, whereas the Transitional DTD, which is intended as a temporary expedient to make it easier to transform older HTML documents to XHTML, permits the deprecated features to be used.

The Frameset DTD includes an additional feature that allows a Web page to be created from a set of independent documents. The page is divided into "frames", one for each document, which can be updated independently. Frames cause usability problems, and their use has declined as CSS features can be used to achieve the most common layouts that frames were formerly used for.

The Strict DTD should always be used unless there are compelling reasons to use one of the others.

The most frequently used block-level textual element is the paragraph (p) element, which we have looked at already. Other block-level elements concerned purely with text layout include level 1 to level 6 headers, with element names h1, h2, ..., h6, br which causes a line break, and hr the horizontal rule (straight line) element, which is sometimes used as a visual separator. The blockquote element is used for long quotations, which are normally displayed as indented paragraphs. Note, though, that using blockquote as a way of producing an indented paragraph is an example of the sort of structural markup abuse that should be avoided: markup is not intended to control layout. This being so, the pre element, which is used for "pre-formatted" text and causes its content to be displayed exactly as it is laid out, is something of an anomaly, yet may be useful when the other available elements do not serve and elaborate stylesheet formatting is not worthwhile.

The only elaborate structures that XHTML supports as block-level elements are lists and tables. Tables are relatively complex constructions (as they must be, to accommodate the range of layouts commonly used for tabulation), but since their use is somewhat specialized we omit any detailed description. Lists, in contrast, are quite simple. XHTML provides three types: "ordered" lists, in the form of ol elements, "unordered" lists, ul elements, and "definition" lists, dl elements. Both ol and ul elements contain a sequence of list items (li elements), which are laid out appropriately, usually as separate blocks with hanging indentation. The difference is that, by default, user agents will automatically number the items in an ordered list. The items in an unordered list are marked by some suitable character, often a bullet. The distinction is somewhat arbitrary: all lists are ordered, in the sense that the items appear in a definite order. CSS rules can be used to number items automatically or insert bullets in front of them in either kind of list, but lists are often laid out and styled in a completely different way. If the list is being used structurally as a container for a sequence of items, it is conventional to use a ul element, with ol being reserved for lists where numbering is part of the semantics, such as a list of the 10 best-selling books on multimedia.

The items of a dl element are somewhat different, in that each consists of two elements – a term (dt) and a definition (dd). The intended use of a dl is, as its name suggests, to set lists of definitions. Typically each item consists of a term being defined, which will often be exdented, followed by its definition. Figure 10.3 shows the default appearance of lists produced by the following XHTML fragment. Note that a list item element can contain a list, giving nested lists.

- first item, but not numbered 1;
- second item, but not numbered 2;
- the third item contains a list, this time a numbered one:
  1. first numbered sub-item;
  2. second numbered sub-item;
  3. third numbered sub-item;
- fourth item, but not numbered 4;

ONE
    the first cardinal number;
TWO
    the second cardinal number;
THREE
    the third cardinal number

Figure 10.3. *Default display of XHTML lists in a browser*

```
<ul>
    <li>first item, but not numbered 1;</li>
    <li>second item, but not numbered 2;</li>
    <li>the third item contains a list, this time a numbered one:
    <ol>
        <li>first numbered sub-item;</li>
        <li>second numbered sub-item;</li>
```

```
        <li>third numbered sub-item;</li>
    </ol></li>
    <li>fourth item, but not numbered 4;</li>
</ul>
<dl>
    <dt>ONE</dt><dd>the first cardinal number;</dd>
    <dt>TWO</dt><dd>the second cardinal number;</dd>
    <dt>THREE</dt><dd>the third cardinal number</dd>
</dl>
```

The most abstract block-level element is **div**, which simply identifies a division within a document that is to be treated as a unit. Usually, a division is to be formatted in some special way. The **class** attribute is used to identify types of division, and a stylesheet can be used to apply formatting to everything that falls within any division belonging to that class. We will see some examples in the following sections. Even in the absence of a stylesheet, classes of divisions can be used to express the organizational structure of a document. However, **div** elements should not be over-used; applying rules to other elements using contextual selectors (which we will describe later) is often more efficient.

Inline elements are used to specify formatting of phrases within a block-level element. It might seem that they are therefore in conflict with the intention of structural markup. However, it is possible to identify certain phrases as having special significance that should be expressed typographically without compromising the principle of separating structure from appearance. Examples of elements that work in this way are **em** for emphasis, and **strong** for strong emphasis. Often the content of these elements will be displayed by a visual user agent as italicized and bold text, respectively, but they need not be. In contrast, the i and b elements explicitly specify italic and bold text. These two elements are incompatible with structural markup and should be avoided (especially since a stylesheet can be used to change their effect).

There is an inline equivalent to **div**: a **span** element identifies a sequence of inline text that should be treated in some special way. In conjunction with the **class** attribute, **span** can be used to apply arbitrary formatting to text.

All the elements we have described can possess a **class** attribute, which permits subsetting. Additionally, each may have an **id** attribute, which is used to specify an identifier for a particular occurrence of the element. For example,

```
<ul id="navigation">
```

is the start tag of a list identified as **navigation**. The values of **id** attributes must be unique within a single document, so that each value identifies exactly one element. This identifier can be used in various ways, one of which is in a CSS selector, where it must be prefixed by a # symbol instead of the dot used for classes. For example,

#navigation { text-indent: 6pc; }

will cause the list with its id set to navigation to be displayed with a special indent.

One important collection of elements, which we will not consider in detail here, is concerned with the construction of forms for data entry. XHTML provides a form element, within which you can use several special elements for creating controls, such as check boxes, radio buttons and text fields. We will look at how the data entered in such a form may be used as the input to a program running on a server in Chapter 16. For a more thorough description, consult *Web Design: A Complete Introduction*.

KEY POINTS

Block-level elements are normally formatted as discrete blocks; inline elements are run in to the surrounding text.

The block-level elements in XHTML include p (paragraph), h1–h6 (headings), br (line break), hr (horizontal rule), blockquote and pre (pre-formatted).

Unordered, ordered and definition lists are marked up as ul, ol or dl elements, which contain li elements (ul or ol) or pairs of dt (term) and dd (definition) elements.

Divisions of a document that should be treated as a unit are identified by div elements.

Inline elements include em (emphasis) and strong; span is used to identify arbitrary inline divisions.

Any element may have a class attribute, and/or an id attribute with a unique identifying value.

CSS Properties

CSS can be used to transform the sparse text markup provided in XHTML into an expressive and flexible formatting system. Again, note that the principles of layout – the values that can be changed and the ways they can be combined, for example – apply to many text preparation systems. Paragraph and character styles in a word processor or a DTP system such as InDesign perform a very similar function to that of stylesheets and are applied to the text of a document via its markup in a similar way. In turn, these formatting operations closely resemble the tasks that have been performed in setting type by hand for hundreds of years.

The properties we will describe are defined in the CSS 2.1 specification. For reasons to do with the standardization process, this document is not a W3C Recommendation, only a Candidate Recommendation, but it is, in effect, the standard defining CSS.

CSS allows you to control the typography of your document, by choosing fonts and setting the type size. Five properties control the font characteristics described in Chapter 9. Several of them display some ingenuity in coping with the inevitable uncertainty about the capabilities of user agents and the availability of fonts. This is most evident in the **font-family** property: its value may be a list of font names (separated by commas) in decreasing order of preference. For example:

```
p.elegant { font-family: "The Sans",Verdana,Arial,sans-serif }
```

says, in effect, that we would ideally like text in paragraphs of class **elegant** to be set in a font called "The Sans". (Note that we must surround the name by double quotes in the CSS declaration because it contains a space.) Should that font not be available, we will settle for the more common Verdana, failing which Arial will do. If even Arial is not possible, any sans serif font should be used. Our fallback choices are based on pragmatic considerations. Verdana is similar to the preferred font, and is distributed with Internet Explorer, so there is a good chance that it will be available. Next we try for a sans serif, which, although not as good a match, is almost certain to be on any user's system, being the Windows system font and distributed with MacOS X. Finally, we have used a generic font family, in the expectation that a user agent will substitute an appropriate font that falls into that family. CSS provides five such generic families: **serif, sans-serif, monospace, cursive** and **fantasy**, which correspond to the font styles introduced in Chapter 9. The actual font selected when a generic font must be used will depend on the configuration of the browser. There is no actual guarantee that it will fall into the class identified by the name.

The two properties **font-style** and **font-variant** are used to select different font shapes. The **font-style** property can have the values **normal, italic** or **oblique** (normal being upright, and **oblique** what we have termed "slanted"). The value of **font-variant** may be **normal** or **small-caps**. CSS considers **small-caps** a variant form rather than a different style, in theory allowing for small caps italic fonts, and so on. The effect of declarations for these properties is to select an appropriate member of the font family chosen on the basis of the value of **font-family**. A slanted font is considered to be an appropriate choice for the font style **italic** if no real italic font is available.

The **font-weight** property has to deal with the fact that the terms used for font weights only make sense within a font family – as we remarked in Chapter 9, the bold version of one typeface may well be lighter than the medium version of another. For simple situations, CSS lets you use the values **normal** and **bold** for this property, with the expected effect. However, many font families provide more than two different weights, but with no universal naming convention to distinguish between them. Instead of imposing a single naming scheme, CSS uses numbers to identify different weights.

You can set font-weight to any of the nine values 100, 200, ..., 900, which represent an ordered sequence of fonts, such that, as the font-weight value increases (numerically), the font's weight will not decrease, and may increase. Thus, if there are nine different weights (TrueType fonts always have nine different weights), each value will select a different one, but if the font has fewer than nine weights, some values will be mapped to the same weight of font. Finally, you can use the values bolder and lighter. This requires some consideration of inheritance.

The formatting described by a CSS rule's declaration is applied to any document element that matches the rule's selector. Each element, except html, has a parent element – the element immediately enclosing it. Any properties that are not explicitly changed by a rule for an element are left with the values they had in the parent – the properties' values are inherited. This is almost certainly what you would expect: it means that the font you set for the body element is used by default throughout the document, for example. It introduces the possibility of specifying property values not in absolute terms, but relative to the inherited values. Values for font-weight of bolder and lighter are the first example of this that we have seen so far. Their effect is to set the font weight to the next larger or smaller numerical value that corresponds to a different font from the inherited one, if such a font exists. (You cannot, for example, make a font any bolder than 900.)

Thus, if the following rules were applied to the example illustrated in Figure 10.3, the inner numbered list would be set in a font weight that was lighter than the enclosing bulleted list. For most fonts, this would mean that it was set at the normal weight.

```
ul { font-weight: bold; }
ol { font-weight: lighter; }
```

A similar option is available for the font-size property. This may take on the values smaller or larger, which cause a relative size change. Font sizes can also be specified as a percentage of the parent element's font size, or as a multiple of the em or ex of the inherited font. Sizes can also be specified independently of the parent font. Here the range of values can be chosen from xx-small, x-small, small, medium, large, x-large and xx-large; it is suggested that these values correspond to sizes forming a geometric progression, with a ratio of 1.5. The absolute values will be determined by the choice of size for medium, which will be the "natural" size of the font, as determined by the user agent or set as a preference by the user.

There is no guarantee that all user agents will produce the same set of sizes, even for the same font. Sizes can also be specified as absolute lengths, in any unit, although points will usually be preferred. However, this practice is discouraged – users may choose to set their default font size large or small, depending on their eyesight or the resolution of their screen. Web designers should respect such settings and design pages so that they work at any (reasonable) font size.

Normally, when we select a type size, we also specify the leading (see Chapter 9). In CSS, the line-height property is used for this purpose. The default value, normal, allows the user agent to select a "reasonable" size. This is invariably too small. Most user agents (following the advice in the CSS specification) choose a value between 1.0 and 1.2 times the font size. This follows convention for printed matter, which is partly dictated by economic considerations – if the lines are closer together, it is possible to fit more words on a page. This consideration is irrelevant for screen display, where the more open appearance lent to text by more widely spaced lines can compensate for the physical strain most people experience when reading from a screen. A line height of about 1.5 times the font size is therefore more suitable. This can be set with any of the following declarations, which illustrate some of the different units available for this property.

```
line-height: 150%;
line-height: 1.5;
line-height: 1.5em;
```

Line heights may be expressed as a percentage, a ratio or in units of ems, all of which are relative to the font in use in the current element. Heights may also be specified as absolute values in any units.

All of the font properties may be combined in a shorthand declaration for the font property. Its value is a list comprising the values for the five font properties style, variant, weight, size, family. The first three may appear in any order, but the size must come next, with a list of font families separated by commas coming at the end. Any properties which you don't want to set can be omitted. The individual property values are separated by spaces.

In a font declaration – but not elsewhere – a value for line-height can be combined with the font-size, separating the two with a slash. This closely follows printers' conventions: 12 pt/14 pt is the way a printer specifies a 12 pt font on 14 pt baselines. A typical font declaration would look like this:

```
p { font: italic bold 14pt/21pt "The Sans",Verdana,Arial, sans-serif }
```

Where no attribute is supplied for a font property (such as font-variant here) the default is used. This is usually the value inherited from the parent element.

One of the important differences between printing and displaying text on screen is that printing in colour is an expensive process, but displaying in colour is free – although you cannot guarantee that colour will be reproduced accurately on every monitor. Therefore, using coloured text and text on coloured backgrounds is an option which should be considered and is often to be preferred to imitating ink on paper by using black text on a white background. This is because the white areas of a screen are actually emitting light, which is usually quite bright and – as we noted in Chapter 5 – has a very high colour temperature. It can therefore be a strain to look at a large area of white on a screen for a long time. Furthermore, the high contrast between black text and a white background can result in an optical illusion, whereby the type appears thinner, as if the background had spread over it. The same effect occurs in reverse if white text is placed on a black background. Provided adequate tonal contrast is maintained, and you avoid combinations that may cause problems for people with defective colour vision, many combinations of colours can work more effectively than black and white on a screen.

The two CSS properties **background-color** and **color** control the colour of the background and the text, respectively. (CSS uses North American spelling for all properties.) Their values specify colours in the sRGB colour space (see Chapter 5), although user agents are given considerable latitude in how faithfully they approximate sRGB colours. Several formats are provided for colour specifications. The most intuitive takes the form **rgb(r%,g%,b%)**, where **r**, **g** and **b** are the percentages of red, green and blue in the desired colour. Instead of percentages, you may use numbers in the range 0–255 if you prefer, as we did in Chapter 5. The most commonly used form of colour specification in CSS is the least readable: the three components are expressed in hexadecimal (base 16), and combined into a single, six-digit number, preceded by a #. The following specifications all describe the same shade of mauve: **rgb(80%,40%,80%)**, **rgb(204,102,204)** and **#CC66CC**. You can also use names for some colours, but the only ones sanctioned by the standard are the 16 belonging to the VGA colour palette, so this option is of limited use.

Applying colour, fonts and line spacing to different document elements, such as the body text, headers, emphasized passages and general **div**s and **span**s, goes a long way to producing attractive and expressive text for use in multimedia. CSS – and DTP packages – provide control over several more aspects of a document's appearance. We will briefly describe some of the more useful of these, leaving the details to the references given on the supporting Web site.

Control over alignment in CSS is provided by the **text-align** property, which takes values **left**, **right**, **center** or **justify**, corresponding to the four styles of paragraph alignment we introduced in Chapter 9 and illustrated in Figure 9.22. For example, to justify the body text of a document with the exception of any paragraphs of class **display**, which should be centred, the following rules could be used:

```
body { text-align: justify }
p.display { text-align: center }
```

The value of **text-align** is inherited, so setting it to **justify** in the rule for **body** means that every element in the body, including headings and lists, will be justified unless a rule with a more specific selector applies to them. If we had used **p** as the selector, only paragraph elements would have been justified; others would have the default value (usually left-alignment) applied to them.

Text layout for multimedia and the Web has more in common with magazine and advertising layout than with mainstream book design. Rather than trying to construct a layout for extended reading of flowing text, the designer is concerned with arranging text on a screen so that each screenful stands on its own and communicates its message or makes its impact as effectively as possible. An established approach to such layout is to place individual blocks of text on a grid. Designers have been known to use HTML tables as grids, positioning each block in a table cell, but CSS provides several ways of controlling the positioning of document elements, which make such misuse of the table elements unnecessary.

To understand positioning in CSS you need to know about CSS's model of text rendering, which is typical of the models employed by layout programs. The model is fundamentally simple, although the fine detail (which we will gloss over) gets quite involved in places.

You will recall that XHTML document elements can be classified as either block-level or inline. The layout algorithm reflects this classification. Each element is notionally placed into a box. Text that is not contained in any inline element is placed into an anonymous box. These anonymous boxes and the boxes containing inline elements are placed next to each other horizontally, and then this line of boxes is, as it were, folded up to fit into the available width – i.e. the width of the browser window, or of the enclosing element if that has had its width set explicitly, as we will describe shortly. The alignment specified for the parent element is used to control the distribution of space between the boxes. In this folding process, some boxes may be split between adjacent lines – for example, an em element may need to be broken across lines.

When the inline elements and text contained in a block-level element have been arranged as described, they are placed in a box corresponding to the whole block. The boxes for blocks are placed vertically, one below another, as shown in Figure 10.4. For computer displays, there is no notion of "available height" – windows scroll – so no further adjustment or selection of page breaks is necessary.

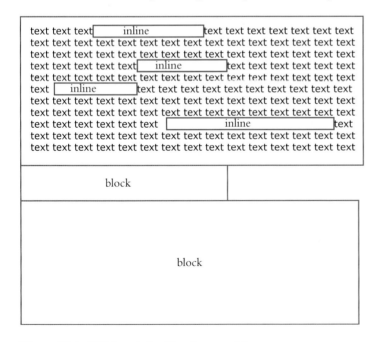

Figure 10.4. *CSS layout algorithm for normal flow*

In the absence of any further stylesheet information, this algorithm produces the familiar sequence of uniformly spaced blocks of text, all fitted into lines of the same width. CSS lets you exert some control over the disposition of text, to produce more interesting and effective layouts. Since a box corresponds to an element, which may have a **class** or **id** attribute (or both), it is possible to create CSS rules that affect the appearance of boxes.

IN DETAIL

Lists are treated slightly differently, since we usually want to display the label or marker for each list element outside the block containing the element itself. The modification to the basic algorithm is simple. A somewhat more complicated algorithm is used to lay out tables, although in all cases layout is performed by arranging boxes next to each other horizontally and vertically. Full details can be found in the CSS specification.

Each box can be surrounded by a *border*, which is separated from the box's contents by some *padding*. Beyond the border, *margins* can be used to separate the box from its neighbours, or from the edges of its enclosing box. (See Figure 10.5.) Borders, margins and padding are controlled by a multitude of CSS properties, which provide control over each of them on each of the four sides of the box. For example, margin-top, margin-right, margin-bottom and margin-left are used to set the margins on the respective sides, and the margin property allows all four to be set at once. Similar properties – named in the same way – are available for padding and border, though the border properties must set the colour and style (solid, dotted, and so on) as well as the width.

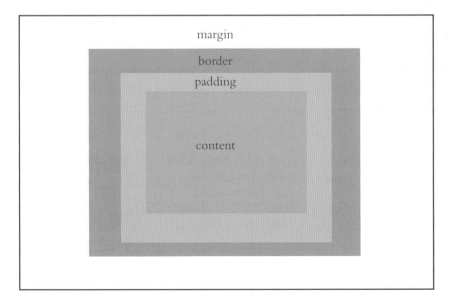

Figure 10.5. *CSS box model*

The width and height of each box's content area can be specified explicitly, subject to certain constraints, using the **width** and **height** properties. The value may use absolute units, such as **px**, units relative to the font size – usually **em** – or it may be a percentage, which is calculated relative to the box's parent. The choice of units affects how the box behaves when the browser window is resized or the font size is changed. This is one of the more important differences between designing for the Web and designing for print: you cannot fix the layout of a page, and you must be careful to ensure that the layout does not become unreadable or unusable when it changes.

For instance, if you set the width of a box to a value in **px** units, when a user makes the font size bigger the text will expand and reflow, line breaks will change, and the text may become hard to read if the box is narrow. If the height of the box has also been fixed, the text will overflow it, with undesirable results. On the other hand, if the dimensions are specified in **em** units, the box will expand or contract with the font size, so that the line breaks will stay in the same place. (And don't forget that named font sizes, such as **medium**, refer to a value that the user can alter, so you don't ever know how big any user's default font will be.) However, increasing the size will often cause the box to grow wider than the browser window, so that horizontal scrolling will be needed to read each line. This is always a bad thing. Percentage units were popular for a while as a means of avoiding horizontal scrolling, but they suffer from the same problems as **px** units when the font size is changed.

The text colour and background can be specified separately for each box as well as for the whole page, using the **color** and **background-color** properties in rules with suitable selectors. (You can also set background images, but we won't go into the details here.) This provides one way of distinguishing different areas of a page, such as the navigation links or a side bar.

It is possible to break out of the normal flow of layout and make boxes float to the left or right margin, while text flows around them. This facility is often used for embedding images into paragraphs of text, but it can also be used – in conjunction with margin settings – to float text past text, as shown in Figure 10.6. The **float** property can take the values **left** or **right**, with the

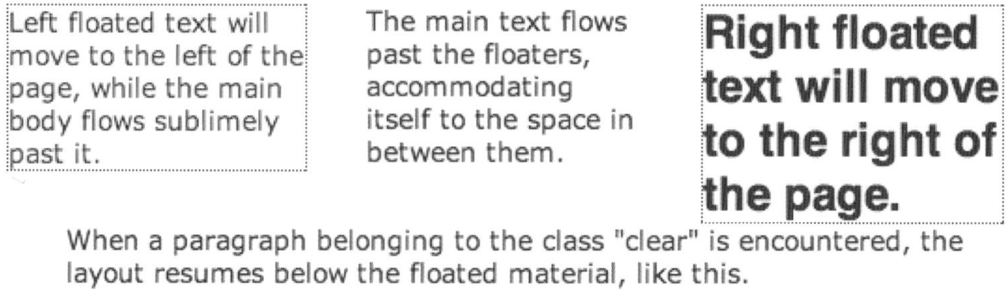

Left floated text will move to the left of the page, while the main body flows sublimely past it.

The main text flows past the floaters, accommodating itself to the space in between them.

Right floated text will move to the right of the page.

When a paragraph belonging to the class "clear" is encountered, the layout resumes below the floated material, like this.

Figure 10.6. *Floated elements*

expected effect. A complementary property **clear** is used to control the placement of text that might be flowing past a floated box. It takes values **left**, **right**, **both** or **none**, indicating which sides of the box may not be adjacent to a floating box. Putting it another way, a value of **left** for **clear** forces a box to go below the bottom of any left-floating element, and so on.

The body of the XHTML document that produced Figure 10.6 looks like this:

```
<body>
<p class="leftfloater">
Left floated text will move to the left ...
</p>
<p class="rightfloater">
Right floated text will move to the right...
</p>
<p>
The main text flows past ...
</p>
<p class="clear">
When a paragraph belonging to the class "clear" is encountered...
</p>
</body>
```

and the relevant stylesheet rules (omitting the rules that add the margins and the dotted box outlines and different fonts and colours) were as follows.

```
p.leftfloater {
    margin-left: 0;
    float: left;
    width: 30%;
}

p.rightfloater {
    margin-right: 0;
    float: right;
    width: 30%;
}

p.clear {
    clear: both;
    width: 90%;
}
```

A popular technique for making pages with two or three columns makes use of the **float** property in conjunction with negative margins. Figure 10.7 shows how this works. The structure of the XHTML document is simply as follows:

```
<body>
<div id="main">
    <div id="left">
        Lorem ipsum ...
    </div>
    <p>Lorem ipsum...</p>
    <p>Lorem ipsum...</p>
</div>
```

In the version of the page shown at the top of Figure 10.7, we have set the width of the text box with id equal to **left** to a relatively narrow value and floated it to the left. As before, it pushes the main text out of its way, and the text resumes below it. If we apply a margin equal to the width of the floated box to the **div** element containing the main text, the entire page simply moves to the right, as shown in the middle of the figure. If, however, we apply a negative left margin to the floated box, equal in magnitude to the left margin of the main **div** (and thus to its own width), it moves back to the edge of the page, while the main text stays over to the right, so that there seem to be two columns of text, as shown at the bottom of Figure 10.7. That is:

```
#main {
    margin-left: 180px;
}
#left {
    width: 180px;
    float: left;
    margin-left: -180px;
}
```

The dotted borders are again only there to show where the edges of the boxes are. Normally, you would also apply some padding, to separate the text boxes. The technique can easily be extended to three columns.

Earlier, we said that XHTML elements can be classified as either block-level or inline. The default classification, which usually conforms to the semantics of the element, can be changed using the **display** property in a rule. Probably the most common case in which this is done concerns list elements. An **li** element is a block-level element, so that lists are laid out with each item in a separate block, as we illustrated in Figure 10.3. Sometimes, though, you may want list elements to be laid out horizontally. This may be the case if you have used a list for the main navigation bar in a site. Setting display to inline causes list items to be treated like spans, and laid out within lines. By adjusting other properties as well it is possible to lay out horizontal navigation bars in a variety of different styles. In particular, setting list-style-type to none removes the bullet or number from any list item.

The ultimate in layout control comes from using *absolute positioning* of elements. If an element is formatted according to a rule that sets the position property to absolute, then you can assign lengths to the top and left properties, thus determining the position of the top left-hand corner of the box. In conjunction with width and height these properties

Figure 10.7. *Using floats to make two columns*

allow you to place boxes arbitrarily on the screen. This, of course, allows you to place boxes on top of each other, which raises the question of their stacking order. The z-order property can be used to control this. Its value is a number; elements with higher z-order values are placed in front of those with lower values.

Use of the absolute positioning properties apparently allows you to lay out text with the same degree of control over its positioning as you could achieve using a graphics program, but without having to convert to a graphics format. Sadly, because of the differences between Web pages and print, absolute positioning can cause problems unless it is used carefully. Absolutely positioned elements are most often generated by software that allows designers to draw out text boxes inter-actively on their screens, and generates the markup and stylesheet automatically. Almost always, the coordinates and dimensions of the generated boxes will be specified in absolute units, which means that changing the text size will spoil the layout. If the generated values use relative units, changing the font size will make boxes move and change size, often causing them to overlap in unwanted ways.

You should never forget that user agents may ignore stylesheets (or fail to interpret them correctly). It can be quite difficult to ensure that a document which is laid out using absolute positioning remains comprehensible when it is laid out using a user agent's default interpretation of the structural markup alone. You should also remember that your documents may be rendered by a non-visual user agent, perhaps for the benefit of people with impaired vision. Here again you should avoid producing documents whose comprehensibility depends on their layout. Because of these considerations, many experienced Web designers avoid absolutely positioned elements.

IN DETAIL

Neither the use of floated elements with negative margins nor absolute positioning is entirely satisfactory. To provide facilities for multiple columns and grid-based layouts, comparable to those available in page layout software for print, CSS3 will define new properties for defining the number and width of columns within a box, so that text can flow from one to the next, as it does in a typical magazine layout, and a method for defining page templates, with content areas arranged in a grid.

CSS3 is still at an early stage of development and implementation of its features has been slow, so Web designers will almost certainly have to go on using less elegant means for achieving layouts for some time.

Advanced Selectors

We have shown three types of selector: an element name (e.g. h1), which selects every element of the corresponding type, an element followed by a class name prefixed by a . (e.g. p.indented), which selects every element of the corresponding type with a matching class attribute, and an identifier prefixed by a # (e.g. #navigation), which selects the unique element with a matching id attribute. Some more complex selectors can be used to apply styling selectively, which often has the result of simplifying the XHTML markup that is needed. In particular, many div elements and class attributes can be omitted if selectors are written more carefully.

One selector that is often overlooked is *, which matches any element. One reason for applying a rule to every element is to override the defaults which most browsers apply to some elements, such as headings and links (see below). For example, most browsers set level 1 headings in a large bold font, with some additional spacing. By using the following rule:

```
* {
    font-size: 1em;
    padding: 0;
    margin: 0;
    border: none;
}
```

you can reset all the values that are applied by the browser, giving yourself a clean start for your own formatting.

The * selector can be used like any element name, so selectors such as *.fancy are used for rules that apply to any element of a particular class (fancy in this case). This is such a common requirement that the * may be omitted. That is, a selector consisting of a . followed by a name matches all elements of any type whose class attribute's value matches the name in the selector.

Context-sensitive selectors allow you to stipulate that a declaration should only be applied to elements that occur within an element which matches some selector. For example, you might wish to apply a special sort of formatting to em elements that occur within other em elements, or within a list whose id was navigation. This is done by writing two or more selectors of the types we have described, separated by spaces. The second selector is only applied to elements that match the first.

As a simple example, suppose that you are the sort of writer who uses emphasis within emphasis. By convention, emphasis is indicated by italics, which could be expressed using the following rule:

```
em { font-style: italic; }
```

If you had a piece of text marked up as follows:

```
Lorem <em>ipsum dolor sit amet, <em>consectetur adipisicing elit</em>, sed do eiusmod
tempor incididunt</em> ut labore et dolore magna aliqua.
```

all the words from *ipsum* to *incididunt* would be italicized and the internal emphasis would be lost. To make the nested emphasis appear in boldface italics, the following rule could be added to the stylesheet:

```
em em { font-weight: bold;}
```

This rule only matches em elements that appear within the content of another em element. There is no need to identify the inner elements with a special class, and the italic font style is inherited – it doesn't need to be specified explicitly in the second rule.

The example just given is a little contrived. Generally, you should avoid nesting emphasis. A more realistic example concerns the use of ul elements to represent a navigation bar (a list of site-wide links). Typically, a navigation bar is marked up in the following way:

```
<ul id="navigation">
    <li>First link</li>
```

```
        <li>Second link</li>
        <li>Third link</li>
        <li>Fourth link</li>
</ul>
```

(The content of each li element is normally more elaborate, as we will describe later.) As we mentioned earlier, navigation bars are often laid out horizontally, without item bullets. This can be achieved without adding class attributes to the li elements in the following way:

```
#navigation li {
        list-style-type: none;
        display: inline;
        padding: 0 1em;
}
```

The properties in this rule are applied only to li elements that occur in the body of the ul whose id is navigation – that is, they are only applied to the elements of the navigation bar, which is accordingly laid out horizontally.

In this rule, we have added some padding to the left and right of each item, to space them out and make them easier to read. (This illustrates one form of the **padding** shorthand property: the first length is applied to the top and bottom, the second to the left and right.) This padding is applied to every item, which means there is a 1em space to the left of the first item and to the right of the last, which is not usually desirable. To avoid this happening, we need to be able to apply special styling to the first and last items in the list. CSS provides a pair of *pseudo-classes*, first-child and last-child. These are used in rules in the same way as class names, except that they are preceded by a : instead of a .. For example, to suppress the spacing in front of the first item in our navbar, we would use the following rule:

```
#navigation li:first-child {
        padding-left: 0;
}
```

The rule is applied to any li element that is the first child of the element with id equal to navigation (i.e. the first element contained in the ul – not the first child of the li). The last-child pseudo-class works in a similar way.[†]

CSS provides a number of extra pseudo-classes and additional operators for combining selectors. In particular, if two selectors are separated by a > sign instead of a space, the rule is only applied to elements that match the second and occur immediately inside an element that matches the first.

---

† *The last-child pseudo-class is a CSS3 feature, so it is not universally implemented.*

This sort of discrimination is most often needed where lists are nested within other lists, and the styling to be applied to items depends upon which list they appear in. The selectors we have described suffice for most tasks you are likely to come across, though – and you can usually work around awkward cases by using extra class attributes. If you want to know about the more elaborate possibilities, consult the CSS specification.

With all the possibilities available for writing selectors, it is quite possible that you will end up writing several rules with different selectors but the same declarations. These can be combined: several selectors, separated by commas may appear in a rule. The single rule behaves as if it was a sequence of rules – one for each of the selectors – with identical declarations. Thus, if you wanted to set headings at all levels in a document in blue, instead of writing six rules for each of the heading element types, you could write a single rule:

```
h1,h2,h3,h4,h5,h6 { color: blue; }
```

Our intention in presenting this description of CSS has been to illustrate the sort of control over text layout that is available to designers, by examining in some detail one particularly easy to understand means of achieving it. We have by no means described all its features, and have simplified some of those which we have discussed. Readers whose main interest is in Web design should look at *Web Design: A Complete Introduction* for more details.

IN DETAIL

Although matters have improved considerably in recent years, for a long time some of the leading Web browsers implemented CSS partially and incorrectly. In particular, no version of Internet Explorer (IE) prior to IE 8 implemented all of CSS, XHTML or HTML correctly.

Because of the dominant position of Microsoft Windows, which installs IE as the default browser, the majority of visitors to Web sites have thus spent years using a browser that does not conform to the standards. As a result, many professional Web designers have had to learn a compendium of hacks and work-rounds to cope with IE's deficiencies while still making pages that work in browsers (present and future) which do follow standards.

Pressure from the Web design community eventually led to all browser vendors, including Microsoft, committing themselves to standards, so this situation should improve in the future, though at present many users around the world are still using older versions of browsers.

Font characteristics are controlled by the font-family, font-style, font-variant, font-weight and font-size properties in CSS.

The font-family property's value is a list of font names in decreasing order of preference. Generic font families (serif, sans-serif, monospace, cursive and fantasy) may be used as fallback values.

The font-style property can have the values normal, italic, or oblique.

The font-weight property can have the values normal or bold, or 100, 200, ..., 900. The values bolder or lighter may be used to set the weight relative to the inherited value.

The font-size property can have the values xx-small, x-small, small, medium, large, x-large, xx-large, larger or smaller. Font sizes can also be set numerically in absolute units (usually px), relative units (em), or as a percentage of the inherited value.

Leading is specified using the line-height property.

All of the font properties may be set at once using the font property.

The colour of text is set using the color property; a background colour may be set using background-color. Colours in the sRGB colour space may be specified as percentages, numbers or a hexadecimal value. A few named colours may also be used.

The text-align property controls alignment (left, right, center or justify).

Each element is placed in a box. Inline elements are wrapped inside the enclosing block's box. Block element boxes are arranged vertically.

Each box may have a border, separated from the box's contents by some padding. Margins separate the box from its neighbours.

Padding and margin widths, and border width, colour and style can all be set with collections of properties that set the top, right, bottom and left values independently, or a single property that sets them all at once.

Boxes can be floated to the left or right margin using the float property.

Setting the position property to absolute allows the coordinates of a box's corners to be set explicitly so it can be positioned anywhere on the page.

The * selector matches any element. It is omitted if followed by a class name.

Context-sensitive selectors are used to apply rules to elements that occur within an element that matches some selector.

Pseudo-classes can be used to select first and last child elements.

Links

As we remarked at the beginning of this chapter, the World Wide Web is the defining example of hypertext and hypermedia and it can be used to illustrate the fundamental concepts. If we confine ourselves for the moment to pages consisting purely of text, these are self-contained passages, which may be of any length, but usually fit on a few screens. Within a page, the normal sequential structure of text is exhibited. You can sensibly read a page from beginning to end (although you don't have to), and elements such as headings and paragraphs are used to structure the content of the page, as we have seen. Familiar typographic and layout conventions are used to make this structure apparent.

Connections are made between pages through *links*. Within the text of a Web page, a link is usually a short sequence of text (often only one or two words) that a user can click on to cause a different page to be displayed. Links can also be attached to images and other elements. Within text, links are distinguished in some way. They are often shown in a different colour from other text and they may be underlined. It is also usual to have some effect – such as a change of background colour – occur when the cursor moves over a link.

On the Web, links are the only connections between pages. Even though a link may be labelled "next" or "previous", such sequential connections between pages must be made with explicit links. There is no concept of intrinsic page order, such as you find in a book or magazine.

The Web is not the only hypertext system in existence, and some experimental systems include features that may find their way into the Web in the future. In general, hypertext systems are constructed out of self-contained elements, analogous to Web pages, that hold textual content. These elements are called nodes. Some systems impose restrictions on their size and format – many early hypertext systems were built on the analogy of 3 by 5 index cards, for example – whereas others allow arbitrarily large or complex nodes.

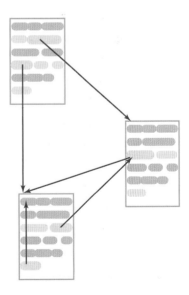

Hypertext links are connections between nodes, but since a node has content and structure, links need not simply associate two entire nodes – usually the source of a link is embedded somewhere within the node's content. To return to the World Wide Web, when a page is displayed, the presence of a link is indicated by highlighted text somewhere on the page, and not, for example, by a pop-up menu of links from that page. Furthermore, a link may point either to another page, or to a different point on the same page, or to a

Figure 10.8. *Simple uni-directional links*

specific point on another page. Hence, Web links should be considered as relating specific locations within pages, and links generally connect parts of nodes (see Figure 10.8).

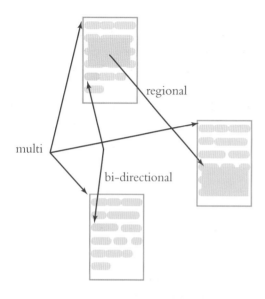

regional

multi

bi-directional

Figure 10.9. *Extended links*

In XHTML, each link connects a single point in one page with a point (often implicitly the start) in another, and can be followed from its source in the first page to its destination in the other. We call links of this type *simple uni-directional links*. Other, more elaborate, hypertext systems provide a more general notion of linking, allowing the ends of a link to be regions within a page (*regional links*), links that can be followed in either direction (*bi-directional links*), and links that have more than just two ends (*multi-links*). Figure 10.9 illustrates these generalized forms of link, collectively known as *extended links*. As you can see, a bi-directional link is just a special case of a multi-link.

Regional links can be added to PDF documents, but the regions most often coincide with a short piece of text or an image, just as if the link was a simple one. The other forms of extended link have been described in the academic literature, but they are not often encountered in practice either. Extended links present implementation problems and lack the intuitive appeal of straightforward hyperlinks, so they are not widely implemented. A W3C Recommendation defining a linking language for XML called *XLink* – which provided facilities for multi-links   attracted relatively little attention. For the present, it seems that simple uni-directional links are considered adequate, but increasing attention is being paid to adding metadata to links, so that their purpose can be determined.

URLs

The links that can be embedded in a Web page marked up in XHTML are simple and uni-directional. What distinguishes them from links in hypertext systems that pre-dated the Web is the use of *Uniform Resource Locators (URLs)* to identify destinations.

As the name suggests, a URL uniformly locates a resource, but the concept of "resource" is quite hard to pin down. The specifications are not very helpful here. They say "A resource can be anything that has identity […] The resource is the conceptual mapping to an entity or set of entities, not necessarily the entity which corresponds to that mapping at any particular instance in time." (IETF RFC 2396 *Uniform Resource Identifiers (URI): Generic Syntax*). "[R]esource: A network data object or service that can be identified by a URI, …" (IETF RFC 2068 *Hypertext Transfer Protocol -- HTTP/1.1*). In practice, a resource is anything that can be accessed by one of the higher-level Internet protocols such as HTTP, FTP or SMTP.

Often – but by no means always – a resource is a file or some data, but the way in which you can access that data is constrained by the protocol you use. For example, a mailto resource identifies a user's mailbox, but only allows you to access the mailbox by sending a message to it. An ftp resource identifies a file, and might even be used to identify a user's mailbox on systems where mailboxes are stored as files, but an ftp resource can be fetched over the network from its remote location. A resource is thus something like an abstract data type, identifying some data and providing a set of operations that can be performed on it. Web pages are resources that can be retrieved using the HTTP protocol (see Chapter 16).

IN DETAIL

All recent W3C Recommendations, including XHTML 1.0, stipulate the use of Uniform Resource *Identifiers* (URIs) rather than URLs. URIs are a superset of URLs, which also include Uniform Resource Names (URNs). URNs are intended to provide a location-independent way of referring to a network resource, unlike URLs which pin a resource down to a specific location for all time. Web pages invariably use URLs, so we will stick to the more familiar term and concept.

The URL syntax provides a general mechanism for specifying the information required to access a resource over a network. For Web pages, three pieces of information are required: the **protocol** to use when transferring the data, which is always HTTP, a **domain name** identifying a network host running a server using that protocol, and a **path** describing the whereabouts on the host of the page or a script that can be run to generate it dynamically.

The basic syntax will be familiar. Every Web page URL begins with the prefix http://, identifying the HTTP protocol. Next comes the domain name, a sequence of sub-names separated by dots, for example www.macavonminiatures.co.uk, which usually identifies a machine within an organization, within a sector, within a country. (Occasionally, the numerical IP address is used instead of a readable domain name, but the practice is discouraged.) Many domain names use **generic top-level domains (gTLDs)**, where the country is omitted and the last component of the domain is a sector – commercial, educational, government, etc. Some gTLDS, such as .edu, are reserved for institutions in the USA, but others, especially .com, are used throughout the world. (Some countries' domain names are available in all parts of the world, allowing companies to register memorable domain names that are not available in their own country, while others are restricted to organizations based in the corresponding country.)

There may be more intermediate domains in a domain name than we have shown in this example. Universities, for instance, typically assign sub-domains to departments, as in www.cs.ucl.ac.uk, a Web server in the computer science (CS) department of University College London, an academic institution in the United Kingdom. Domain names are registered with a central agency for a small fee.

After the domain name in a URL comes the path, giving the location of the page on the host identified by the preceding domain name. A path looks very much like a Unix pathname. It consists of a /, followed by an arbitrary number of segments separated by / characters. These segments identify components within some hierarchical naming scheme. In practice, they will often be the names of directories in a hierarchical directory tree, but this does not mean that the path part of a URL is the same as the pathname of a file on the host – not even after the minor cosmetic transformations necessary for operating systems that use a character other than / to separate pathname components. For security and other reasons, URL paths are usually resolved relative to some directory other than the root of the entire directory tree. However, there is no reason for the path to refer to directories at all. It might be some access path within a document database, for example, or data that is used by a program to create the document.

IN DETAIL

In advertisements and other material you will frequently see the URLs of Web pages given with the leading http:// omitted, and most Web browsers allow you to omit the protocol when typing URLs, making intelligent guesses on the basis of the rest. Although such usage in these contexts is sanctioned in the relevant standards, within an XHTML document you must always use a complete URL, or a partial URL, of the form and with the meaning described below.

The only characters that can be used in a URL belong to the ASCII character set, because it is important that URL data can be transmitted safely over networks, and only ASCII characters can be considered safe for this purpose – and not even all ASCII characters. Certain characters that may get corrupted, removed or misinterpreted must be represented by *escape sequences*, consisting of a % followed by the character's ASCII code in hexadecimal. In particular, spaces must be written in a URL as %20.

A URL with the components described so far can identify a Web page in one of three ways. In all cases, the domain name identifies the host running an HTTP server. The path might be a complete specification of the location on the host machine of a file containing XHTML, as in http://www.webdesignbook.org/info/index.html. If it ends in a / character, the path specifies the location of a directory. At the cost of some inefficiency, a trailing / may be omitted: http://www.digitalmultimedia.org/ and http://www.digitalmultimedia.org both identify the root directory of the support site for this book, for instance. Where a path identifies a directory, the configuration of the Web server determines what resource the URL specifies, and thus what is retrieved when the URL is used in a request. Most often, it is a file within that directory with a standard name, such as index.html.

The third way in which a URL identifies a Web page is via a program that generates the content dynamically. Again, the precise mechanism depends on the server's configuration. The oldest convention for communicating between a Web server and a program that generates content is called the **Common Gateway Interface**, which provides a means for a server to pass information to and receive it from other programs, known as **CGI scripts**. CGI scripts were commonly used to provide an interface – or "gateway" – between the Web server and databases or other facilities. Several mechanisms are provided to pass parameters to CGI scripts, including appending a query string to the end of the URL used to invoke the script. The query string is separated from the path by a ? as in http://uk.search.yahoo.com/search?p=macavon. (We will describe other ways of passing such information, which do not affect the URL, in Chapter 16.)

Although the Common Gateway Interface was intended to provide a standard for interaction between a Web server and other resources, many Web server programs and database systems provide their own methods for performing the same function. The widely used Apache server has its own system of modules, while Microsoft servers support the use of Active Server Pages (ASP). Other non-proprietary mechanisms include Java servlets and PHP. These solutions are often more efficient or easier to write than CGI scripts, and have been widely adopted in commercial Web sites. Their approach to URLs varies. In many cases, the URL is mapped to functions within the script in such a way that there is no longer a simple relationship between the path component of the URL and the directory structure on the server.

We have described a hypertext network as consisting of nodes connected by links, but the nodes (i.e. pages) of the World Wide Web are grouped into **Web sites**, each comprising a relatively small number of pages, usually held on the same machine, maintained by the same organization or individual, and dealing with related topics. Within a site, links pointing to other pages on the same site are common. **Relative URLs** provide a convenient shorthand for such local links.

Informally, a relative URL is a URL with some of its leading components (the protocol, domain name, or initial segments of the path) missing. In contrast, a complete URL, where all the components are present, is called an **absolute URL**. When a relative URL is used to retrieve a resource, the missing components are filled in from the **base URL** of the document in which the partial URL occurs. This base URL is usually the URL that was used to retrieve the document, although sometimes it might be specified explicitly (see below). The way in which base and relative URLs are combined is very similar to the way in which a current directory and a relative path are combined in hierarchical file systems – the syntax is identical to that used in Unix pathnames. For example, suppose some Web page can be retrieved using the absolute URL http://www.digitalmultimedia.org/chapters/index.html. If the relative URL videoindex.html occurs anywhere within this document, it will be equivalent to the absolute URL http://www.digitalmultimedia.org/chapters/videoindex.html. In particular, if the domain name is omitted, a relative URL is treated as a path on the same machine.

The special segments . and .. are used within a path to denote the current level in the hierarchy described by the path (i.e. the directory containing the file in which the relative URL occurs) and its immediate parent. Within the document referred to above . would be the chapters directory, which contains the file index.html and .. would be the root directory / which contains that chapters directory. The relative URL ../links/index.html would therefore be the same as http://www.digitalmultimedia.org/links/index.html. Generally, if a relative URL begins with a / the corresponding absolute URL is constructed by removing the path from the base URL and replacing it with the relative URL, so – still within the same document – /links would refer to the same directory as http://www.digitalmultimedia.org/links. Otherwise, just the last segment of the path (which will usually be the document's file name) is replaced, and then . and .. are interpreted as described.

IN DETAIL

If relative URLs are resolved using the URL of the document in which they occur as the base URL, it is possible to move an entire hierarchy of Web pages to a new location without invalidating any of its internal links. This is usually something you want to be able to do, but occasionally you may need the base URL to be independent of the location of the document containing relative URLs.

Suppose, for example, that you have constructed a table of contents for some Web site. You will want to use relative URLs, because all your links point to pages on the same server. If, however, you wish to be able to duplicate the table of contents (but not the site itself) on several sites, you will not want to use each copy's own location as the base URL for these relative URLs. Instead, you will always want to use a URL that points to the site you are indexing. To achieve this, you can explicitly set the base URL in a document using the XHTML base element. This is an empty element, with one attribute href, whose value is a URL to be used as a base for resolving relative URLs inside the document. The base element can only appear within a document's head. Base URLs specified in this way take precedence over the document's own URL. Hence, if a document included the element <base href="http://www.digitalmultimedia.org" />, then, no matter where the document itself was stored, the relative URL links/index. html would be resolved as http://www.digitalmultimedia.org/links/index.html.

One more refinement of URLs is needed before they can be used to implement simple uni-directional links as we have described them. We emphasized that links connect parts of nodes, but a URL specifies a complete page. To identify a location within a page – a particular heading, or the beginning of a specific paragraph, for example – the URL needs to be extended with a *fragment identifier*, consisting of a # character followed by a sequence of ASCII characters. The fragment identifier will match an identifier attached to a particular location within a document (we will see how shortly) which will then be used as the destination for the link.

A fragment identifier is not really part of a URL – it is not used by HTTP requests, but is stripped off by the user agent making the request, which retains it. When the requested document is returned, the user agent will find the location designated by the fragment identifier, and display the document so that the designated part of it is in the window.

Anchors

We have glossed over some of the fine detail of HTTP URLs – if you need to know everything about URLs consult the specifications – but the description just given should suffice to show that URLs provide the information required to access a Web page from anywhere on the Internet. The HTTP protocol, described in Chapter 16, provides a means of retrieving a Web page, given its URL. The combination of URLs and HTTP can therefore be used to implement hypertext links in the World Wide Web, providing we have a means of embedding URLs as links in XHTML documents. This is provided by the **a** (anchor) element.

The **href** attribute is what enables an anchor to serve as the source of a link. Its value is a URL, which may be absolute, if the link points to a document elsewhere on the World Wide Web, or relative, if it points to a document within the same hierarchy. The URL may have a fragment identifier appended to designate a specific location within the destination document, or it may consist solely of a fragment identifier, for links within the same document. The **a** element has content, which is displayed by user agents in some special way to indicate that it is serving as the source of a hypertext link. For example, most popular browsers by default show the content of anchor elements in blue and underlined. When a link's destination has been visited, a different colour (often purple) is used to display the visited link whenever the document containing the source is displayed again within a designated period of time.

A CSS stylesheet can provide rules for formatting **a** elements, just like any other element. To cope with the desire to change the appearance of a link when it is visited, CSS provides special pseudo-classes **link**, **visited**, **hover** and **active**. These are used like the **first-child** and **last-child** pseudo-classes we mentioned earlier to identify subsets of some class of elements matching a selector: they are separated from an element name in selectors by a colon. Whether an element belongs to the subset matched by one of these pseudo-classes depends on its condition in the browser.

The link and visited pseudo-classes are used in selectors to identify hypertext links (which will be a elements in XHTML) and visited links, respectively. Formatting specified for the active pseudo-class is applied to a link when the user has clicked on it, and that for hover is applied when the cursor is over the link. These pseudo-classes can therefore be used to identify links and their states by special formatting. Most commonly, the hover pseudo-class is used to implement simple rollovers on links, which provide visual feedback to indicate that something will happen if the link is clicked.

The following rules stipulate that links should be set in a shade of blue with a dotted underline (made by adding a border to the bottom – omitting the colour in the border-bottom property causes it to be the same as the text). Links that have been visited turn a paler shade of the same blue. When the cursor rolls over a link, it will be highlighted by turning the background grey, and when the user clicks on the link, the underline will briefly turn solid and red.

```
a:link {
    color: #88C5E3;
    border-bottom: 1px dotted;
}
a:visited {
    color: #93D9FA;
    border-bottom: 1px dotted;
}
a:hover {
    background-color: #E3E3E3;
}
a:active {
    border-bottom: 1px solid red;
}
```

As we explained earlier, any element in a document may have a unique identifier as the value of its id attribute. This identifier can be used as a fragment identifier attached to a URL, so that any element within a document may be the destination of a link.

The following XHTML code shows examples of the use of fragment identifiers in links, both within a document and to a section of a separate document.

```
<h1>Links and URLs</h1>
<h2 id="links">Links</h2>
<p>Hypertext links are implemented in HTML using the &lt;a&gt; element and
<a href="#urls">URLs</a>.</p>
```

```
[etc, etc.]
</p>
<h2 id="urls">URLs</h2>
<p>An introduction to the use of URLs in HTML and XHTML can be found in
<a href= "http://www.w3.org/TR/REC-html40/intro/intro.html#h-2.1.1"> the HTML4.0
specification</a>. They are the basis of <a href="#links">links</a> in Web pages. </p>
```

Colloquially, we say that when a user clicks on a highlighted a element in a Web page, the browser "goes to" the page that is the destination of the link. By extension, we talk about "visiting" Web sites and pages. This metaphor of visiting has achieved almost universal currency, despite the fact that, in reality, the opposite takes place. We do not visit Web pages, they come to us. Clicking on a link that references a separate document causes the resource identified by the URL that is the value of the href attribute of the anchor to be retrieved via HTTP. Assuming that the resource is a Web page, the browser interprets the XHTML and any associated stylesheet and displays the page. If a fragment identifier is appended to the URL, the browser will find the corresponding anchor (assuming it is there) and scroll the display to it. Usually, the newly retrieved page replaces any page being currently displayed by the browser, hence the idea of "going to" the new page.

As well as the href attribute itself, an a element may have attributes hreflang and charset which indicate the natural language and character set of the document to which the link points. In theory, these can be used to prevent following links to documents that a user would not understand. The title attribute should also be used to add some information about the link that can be presented to users to help them decide whether the link is worth following. Web browsers often display the title as a "tooltip" when the cursor moves over the link. However, the title attribute is of more use to people who access the Web with non-visual user agents, such as screen readers, for whom the effort of following a link and discovering what the linked page is about may be considerable. Poor implementation of title in browsers has meant that the attribute is not used as often as it should be, though.

There is nothing – apart from the link text itself and perhaps a title attribute – to suggest why a link has been established using an a element. Good choice of link text can help to make the purpose of a link explicit to users, but information expressed in natural language cannot easily be extracted by programs, which cannot therefore analyse the semantics of a site's link structure – for example, to improve the accuracy of search results or to provide automatic navigational hints. The rel (relationship) attribute is an attempt to capture more of links' semantics. Unlike the title, which can be any text, the value of the rel attribute is a *link type*, which is a string designating a type of relationship. For example, an occurrence of a technical word in a document may be linked to an entry in a glossary; the rel attribute of the source anchor for this link could have the value glossary:

```
... by means of a <a href="../terms.html#url" rel="glossary">URL </a> ...
```

Link types may be taken from a controlled vocabulary defined by the XHTML standard. The collection of standard link types is defined to designate common relationships between documents, such as next, prev and start, which can be used to connect together a sequence of documents, or chapter, section, subsection and contents, which can be used to organize a collection of documents in the form of a conventional book.

Although only a small number of link types are defined in the standard, it is permitted for new types to be defined by a "profile", which should be referred to from a document's head element using the profile attribute. In practice, profiles are usually defined in an informal document using natural language and are adopted by convention. Informal profiles of this sort are used to define "microformats", which are a systematic means of annotating Web pages to make common structures and relationships – such as events or contact details – recognizable by computer programs. Each microformat defines a limited set of strings that can be used as the values of rel and class attributes for this purpose. For example, the rel-tag microformat is used for adding tags to blog posts for ad hoc classification purposes. The text of the tag is enclosed in an a element, with its rel attribute set to tag, and the destination set to a URL with a specific structure that allows the tag name to be extracted easily. (The link should point to a "tag repository" containing a collection of tag definitions.)

An important non-standard value for the rel attribute is nofollow, which is used to direct search engines not to follow a link when carrying out indexing operations. This is most often used to frustrate the intentions of spammers who plant links in blogs' comment pages.

Hyperlinks are one way of connecting documents, but some kinds of relationship between entire documents, such as one document being a translation of another into a different language, are not expressed naturally by hypertext links between anchors within documents. The link element is provided to express such relationships. This element can only appear in a document's head. It has an href attribute, whose value is a URL identifying the linked document, and may also have a rel attribute. Since they are in the document's head, link elements are not displayed by browsers – they have no content. It is envisaged that they might be used to construct special-purpose menus or toolbars to assist with navigation among a set of related documents.

You have already seen an example of the use of link elements. When a document references an external stylesheet in a separate file, the reference is a link, with the rel attribute being used to indicate that the link relates a document to its stylesheet, as we showed earlier:

```
<link href="stylesheet's URL" rel="stylesheet" type="text/css" />
```

Links are used to make connections between nodes in a hypertext system.

Simple uni-directional links point from a single source to a destination.

More complex extended links (regional, bi-directional and multi-links) are possible, but are rarely used in practice.

URLs are used to identify destinations on the World Wide Web.

A Web page URL consists of the prefix http://, followed by a domain name identifying a host machine and a path which gives the location of the resource on the host.

Certain characters, including spaces, must be represented by a % followed by their ASCII code in hexadecimal when they appear in URLs.

An absolute URL has all three components. In a relative URL some may be omitted, and resolved with reference to the URL used to retrieve the document.

A URL may have a fragment identifier appended, consisting of a # and a name that identifies a location within a page.

The a element is used in XHTML as the source of a link. Its href attribute's value is the URL of the link's destination.

Special CSS pseudo-classes (:link, :visited, :active, :hover) are used to apply styling to links in different states.

The id attribute of any element can be used to give it a unique identifier that can be used in a fragment identifier.

The hreflang, charset and title attributes can be used to add extra information to a link. The rel attribute may be used to indicate its purpose.

The link element is used to create links between entire documents.

The Web and Hypermedia

The World Wide Web is not a hypertext system, it is a hypermedia system, which means that the resources identified by URLs are not all XHTML documents. Some of them may be JPEG or GIF images, Flash movies, video clips or other types of media file. If it is to be possible to incorporate such disparate types of media into the same system, there must first of all be a means of identifying the type of a resource, so that a browser or other user agent will know what sort of data it has received.

Internet Media Types

Individual operating systems have their own methods of identifying the type of a file. Generally, the extension of a file's name distinguishes the type – a file whose name ends .JPG on a Windows system is assumed to contain a JPEG image, one whose name ends in .MOV a QuickTime movie, and so on. There is nothing standard about the mapping from content type to extension, though – another system may use .jpeg and .qt – and not all media data is stored in a file. A live video stream may be transmitted without ever being saved to disk, for example. Some other means of identifying content types is required in a networked environment.

MIME (Multipurpose Internet Mail Extension) was an extension to the Internet mail protocols to support the inclusion of data other than plain ASCII text in mail messages. It provides a simple and convenient way of specifying the type of data transmitted over a network, which has been adopted by HTTP, the protocol used to transfer Web pages over the Internet. Although you will still often see references to "MIME types", now that they are used more widely the correct name for these specifications is ***Internet media types***.

An Internet media type takes the form *type*/*subtype* where *type* provides a broad indication of the sort of data, such as text, image or sound, and *subtype* specifies a more precise format, such as HTML, GIF or AIFF. For example, GIF images have the type image/gif, CSS stylesheets have the type text/css, while MP3 audio has the type audio/mpeg. This last type is used for any MPEG-1 or MPEG-2 audio data, irrespective of level. The media type only provides enough information for the program receiving the data to know how to begin dealing with it. It is not a full specification of all the data's characteristics.

The available types are text, image, audio and video, which have the obvious meanings; model for 3-D model data, which has seen little use; message, which indicates an email message; and application, which means binary data that must be processed in some way. For example, a GNU Zip (gzip) archive would have the Internet media type application/gzip, since it must be passed to an unzipping utility for processing. Notice that, despite its name, the application type does not generally refer to executable programs (applications). The most general subtype of application is application/octet-stream, which is a catch-all type for any binary data. There is also a multipart type, which is used for data steams containing more than one sort of media.

The range of subtypes is extensive (none more so than the subtypes of application) and supports most multimedia file formats, although some use "experimental" subtypes, identified by the prefix x- . While these are not included in the list of supported media types maintained by the ***Internet Assigned Numbers Authority (IANA)***, they are widely recognized by Web browsers.

We will decribe how Internet media types are used by Web servers and browsers in more detail in Chapter 16. For the present, you need only know that when a browser receives a document it also receives information about the type of data it contains, in the form of an Internet media type, and that the browser will use that type to determine how to treat the data.

IN DETAIL

This point is worth emphasizing. You might think that an XHTML document is identified as such by the presence of an appropriate DTD, but this is not the case. If a text file containing an XHTML 1.0 Strict DTD and valid XHTML markup were to be received by a Web browser with the media type image/jpeg attached to it, then as far as the browser is concerned it would have received a (badly corrupted) JPEG image. This has turned out to have an unfortunate consequence for XHTML.

The media type for HTML documents is text/html; that for XML documents is either text/xml or application/xml, depending on how the document is intended to be used. XHTML is technically just XML, but practically it is more like HTML, so what media type is appropriate? The official answer is application/xhtml+xml, but this is rarely used, because certain Web browsers fail to process pages correctly if they are sent with this media type. Instead, most XHTML is sent with the text/html type, which means that user agents treat XHTML documents as HTML. This is why it is necessary to add a space in front of the closing / of an empty element's tag, and so on, as we mentioned earlier. A vicious circle has thus developed, whereby Web designers write XHTML that is compatible with HTML because Web servers set the media type to text/html because Web browsers don't display the correct media type properly, so Web designers go on writing XHTML that is compatible with HTML, and so on.

This description begs a question. How does an HTTP server know what Internet media type to specify when it sends some data to a browser? It would be unrealistic to expect the server to analyse the data and deduce its type, so a more prosaic solution is adopted. The server has access to a configuration database, maintained by whoever looks after the server, which provides a mapping from filename extensions to media types. Where data is generated dynamically, the program generating it must take responsibility for attaching the correct media type before it is sent from the server.

Embedded Media

Up to now, we have implicitly assumed that all data has the media type text/html, so that Web browsers treat it as text with HTML markup. However, a URL can identify any resource on the Internet, so clicking on a link might cause any kind of data to be retrieved. What does the browser do if the content type is not text/html? Either it will be intelligent enough to deal with it anyway, or it will have to get another program to do so.

Consider the second option first. Web browsers can be configured so that, for each Internet media type, a program is nominated to deal with documents of that type. The nominated programs are usually called *helper applications*. If a document arrives which the browser cannot display itself, it starts up the appropriate helper application to do so instead. For example, suppose your browser is configured so that the Adobe Reader was the helper application for data of type application/pdf (PDF documents). If you click on an anchor whose href attribute's URL points to a PDF file, the data will be retrieved as usual. When it arrives, the browser will use the operating system's facilities to start up another process to run Adobe Reader, handing it the retrieved data. The PDF document will be displayed in a new window belonging to Adobe Reader, with that program's interface, independent of the Web browser. Thus, although you read the PDF after retrieving it via a Web page, it is not integrated with any other Web data – we have not really achieved hyper-media, although we can link together different media using hyperlinks.

In order to properly integrate the display of media besides formatted text into a Web browser, we must first extend the capabilities of the browser so that it can render other media. It is not realistic to expect a Web browser to be able to cope with absolutely any imaginable type of data; for some obscure types a helper application will always be the best option. On the other hand, some types – especially image types and plain text – are so common that it is reasonable to expect browsers to have code to display them built in. Other types, such as video and audio, fall in between. It would be nice to handle them in the browser, but there is a range of formats – some of them proprietary – so the necessary implementation effort on the part of the browser manufacturers to support all of them is not justified, and not all users will be happy with the resulting increased resource requirements of their browsers.

The solution to this dilemma is *plug-ins* – software modules that can be installed independently by users who need them. Plug-ins are loaded by a browser when it starts up and add functionality to it, specifically the ability to deal with additional media types. There are two different types of plug-in. The most widely used conforms to an interface originally defined for the now-defunct Netscape Navigator browser. "Netscape plug-ins" are used by all conventional browsers, except for Internet Explorer. This uses modules called *ActiveX controls*, which are specific to Windows. ActiveX controls perform the same function as plug-ins – they extend the capabilities of the browser – but they work in a different way, which has an effect on the way markup is used to embed media in Web pages, as we will explain shortly. Where there is no ambiguity we will use the term "plug-in" to include ActiveX controls.

One of the most widely used examples of this technology is Adobe's Flash Player plug-in and ActiveX control, which add the capacity to play Flash movies to any browser. Users only need to install the plug-in or ActiveX control if they want to view Flash movies within their browsers. This way, users with no interest in Flash and Web animation do not incur the associated overhead. Installation is usually automatic. If a browser encounters some markup which indicates that the Flash Player is required, it will offer to download and install it. This process usually only takes a short amount of time.

Once a browser becomes capable of rendering non-textual data without the aid of a helper, the possibility exists of integrating the display of such data with the other elements of Web pages. This leads to a mode of multimedia presentation based on a page layout model. This model is derived from long-established practice in print-based media for combining text and graphics. It can be fairly naturally extended to incorporate video and animation, by treating them as if they were pictures to be placed on the page, but with the added property that they can be made to move. Sound sits much less comfortably on a page, being purely non-visual.

An expedient which is often employed is to represent a sound by an icon or a set of controls, which can be treated as a graphic element and then activated to play the sound in the same way as a video element is acti-

Figure 10.10. *Embedded audio*

vated. Figure 10.10 shows an example.

Special markup is required for embedding these new elements in Web pages. Early versions of HTML only provided support for bitmapped images, in the form of the img element. In XHTML, the object element is provided for embedded media of all types – it is flexible enough to accommodate new media types that have not yet been implemented or invented. However, the img element is still available in XHTML and its use has become so well established that, for the bitmapped image formats supported by most browsers – JPEG, GIF and PNG – it is unlikely to be superseded by object.

Part of the enduring attraction of img is its simplicity. It is an empty element. In the simplest case it has just two attributes – src, whose value is a URL pointing to an image file, and alt, which is used to provide a textual alternative for non-visual user agents. img is an inline element, so the image is displayed where the tag occurs. This enables you to run images in with text, use them as headings or labels on list items, and so on. Alternatively, you can isolate an image by enclosing it in its own paragraph or some other block element.

To understand the necessity for **img**, consider the following two fragments of HTML:

```
<p>Let us show you a <a href="cows.jpeg">picture of some cows</a>.</p>
```

and

```
<p>These cows have more presence:</p>
<p><img src="cows.jpeg" alt="Highland cattle" /></p>
```

Let us show you a <u>picture of some cows</u>.

These cows have more presence:

Figure 10.11. *Linking to (top) and embedding (below) an image*

In the first case, the word "picture" would be highlighted as a link, just as if it pointed to another page. When the highlighted text is clicked, the image is displayed alone in the browser window, replacing the current page. In the second case, the image is displayed as part of the page, like a picture in a newspaper or magazine. Figure 10.11 illustrates the difference between the two cases.

Like any other XHTML element, an **img** can be laid out using CSS rules. Images can be aligned and floated, using the properties introduced earlier in this chapter. Margins and padding can be used to add space around images, and the method we described earlier for creating multiple columns using negative margins can be used to create a grid layout for combining images with text.

The **img** element may have **width** and **height** attributes, which specify the dimensions in pixels at which the image is to be displayed. (These attributes' values are just numbers – there is no need to specify the units, which are always pixels.) It is generally not a good idea to set these to any values other than the actual dimensions of the image. If you do, the browser will resize the image to match the values you specify, but browsers usually make a poor job of this, with a resulting loss of image quality. (If the image is not the right size for your purposes, it should be resized in advance, using an image manipulation program such as Photoshop.) The attributes are not entirely redundant, though, because they allow the browser to reserve space for the image before it has been downloaded. This can speed up page rendering. Certain layout tricks only work if the size of the image is known, so you should supply these attributes if you can.

You can override the **width** and **height** attributes by using the CSS properties with the same names to set the image dimensions in a stylesheet, but again this is usually not a good idea. You should always try to prepare images to their final size before adding them to a Web page. Occasionally you may need to set the width in **em** units in a CSS rule, if you wish to have images scale up along with a page that has been laid out using relative units. It is better to design a layout in which the images can remain the same size, though. For example, you can put all the images in a fixed-width column down one side of the page.

The **object** element is the officially preferred way of embedding multimedia in Web pages. (It can also be used to embed executable content in the form of Java "applets", but this is rarely done these days, so we will not describe the relevant attributes.)

Unlike **img**, which it resembles in some ways, **object** is not an empty element. Its content is displayed if, for some reason, the object itself cannot be. Thus, the content serves an analogous purpose to the **alt** attribute of **img**, but allows for richer alternatives – for example, an image as an alternative to a video clip, or styled text as an alternative to an image. The element's content is available to search engines, unlike the value of the **alt** attribute of an **img**.

The **object** element has several attributes, which must be used in different combinations to cover different types of media content and the two different browser extensions – plug-ins and ActiveX controls.

The simplest possibility is a browser that uses plug-ins and a media type for which a plug-in exists. In that case, specifying the media type as the value of the **type** attribute is sufficient for the browser to identify the required plug-in. The location of the data is given by the **data** attribute, which functions in the same way as the **src** attribute of the **img** element: its value is a URL.

Since the browser must reserve space to display the object, it needs to know its dimensions. This is done using the **width** and **height** attributes, whose values are the corresponding lengths, in pixels.

As an illustration of the simple use of **object**, consider embedding a Flash movie in a page. The Internet media type for Flash movies is **application/x-shockwave-flash**. Hence, to include a Flash movie with the relative URL **human-cannonball.swf** in an XHTML document, for the benefit of browsers that use the Flash plug-in to play them, the following markup could be used:

```
<object data="human-cannonball.swf" type="application/x-shockwave-flash" height="400"
  width="550">
  content of the object element
</object>
```

As well as elements to be displayed in case the Flash movie cannot be, the content of the **object** element can include **param** elements, which are used to pass additional information to the plug-in. Since there is no way of knowing what parameters might be required by any plug-in that may be written in the future, the mechanism for passing information must be as general as possible. Accordingly, the **param** element has two attributes, **name** and **value**, which are used to specify the name of a parameter which the plug-in understands, and its value. The possible parameter names should be listed in the documentation for any plug-in. For instance, the Flash plug-in has a parameter called **quality**, which may be used to specify how much anti-aliasing is applied to vector objects, and thus how smoothly drawn they will appear. This parameter can be set to **high** with the following element, to force all vector artwork in the movie to be anti-aliased:

```
<param name="quality" value="high" />
```

If there are any **param** elements, they must be the first things in the content of the **object** element.

It may not be possible for a browser to show the specified Flash movie for several reasons – the absence of the plug-in, network or server errors preventing the data being received, or a typographical error in the URL used in the tag, for example. In any of these cases, the browser will display the content of the **object** element. In the case of a Flash movie, a sensible fallback would be to display a still image from the movie. Normally, you would probably use an **img** element to do this, but it is possible to use **object** here too, at least in theory. Doing so allows you to specify a second-level fallback, in the form of some text. Taking this approach, the complete markup for embedding our Flash movie would be as follows:

```
<div>
<object data="human-cannonball.swf" type="application/x-shockwave-flash" height="400"
width="550">
  <param name="quality" value="high" />
  <object data="human-cannonball.jpeg" type="image/jpeg" height="400" width="550" >
        <p>The human cannonball flies!</p>
    </object>
</object>
</div>
```

This markup will not work as intended with Internet Explorer: a blank area will be displayed on the page where the movie should be. For that browser only, **object** must be used with different attributes in order to invoke the Flash ActiveX control to play the movie.

The required information is an identifier for the ActiveX control. This takes the form of a pseudo-URL, beginning with **clsid:**, which serves the same function as **http:** in Web URLs of identifying the sort of information contained in the rest of the URL. In this case, this information consists of a string of apparent gibberish, known as a *Globally Unique Identifier*, which is simply a codename for the plug-in, which is guaranteed to be unique. This entire pseudo-URL is the value of the **classid** attribute. As before, the height and width must be specified, so that space for displaying the movie can be reserved on the page. To embed a Flash movie, the following markup is required:

```
<object classid="clsid:D27CDB6E-AE6D-11cf-96B8-444553540000" width="550"
  height="400">
  content of the object element
</object>
```

Most people do not remember the identifier. Markup such as this is usually generated automatically by Flash or by Web authoring programs.

You will notice that there is no mention here of the location of the Flash movie itself. This is because ActiveX controls work in a conceptually different way from plug-ins. A plug-in is loaded by the browser to extend its capability to deal with embedded content – it can be considered as a dynamically loaded part of the browser. An ActiveX control, on the other hand, is considered to be embedded (executable) content, which can load data – such as a Flash movie – and display it. Thus, the markup does not really embed the movie, it embeds the ActiveX control, which needs to be told where the movie is. This is done using a **param** element, with its **name** attribute set to **movie** and its **value** set to the movie's URL. As before, an image could be used as a fallback in case the movie cannot be displayed. This time we will use an **img** element for this purpose.

```
<div>
<object classid="clsid:D27CDB6E-AE6D-11cf-96B8-444553540000" width="550"
  height="400">
    <param name="movie" value="human-cannonball.swf" />
    <param name="quality" value="high" />
    <img src="human-cannonball.jpeg" alt="The human cannonball flies." />

</object>
```

This is all very well, but what is required is markup that will embed the Flash movie so that it can be played in any browser. Based on our account of how the content of an **object** element is displayed if the element itself cannot be, you might think that it would be possible to put the **object** element for a browser that uses plug-ins inside that for ActiveX. Since the browser using a plug-in will not be able to find an ActiveX control, it should display the content of the outer **object** – that is, the inner **object** – which will cause it to show the movie using its plug-in.

The reasoning is sound, but it doesn't work, because no version of Internet Explorer earlier than IE 8 implements nested **object** elements correctly. It always tries to display both. (This is why we used an **img** as the fallback content in our ActiveX **object** markup.) Several solutions are available to work round this defect. The best is the use of "conditional comments", which are an informal extension to XHTML, allowing content to be recognized by Internet Explorer but ignored by other browsers. An alternative is the use of JavaScript to construct the appropriate markup for the browser while the page is being displayed. Finally, many Web designers and Web authoring programs make use of a different element – the embed element – as an alternative to object. This element was introduced at the time the plug-in mechanism was developed, as a way of including content for plug-ins to display. It is understood by all browsers that use plug-ins, but has never been part of any official HTML or XHTML standard. Its use cannot therefore be recommended and one of the other solutions should be used for as long as defective versions of Internet Explorer must be catered for.

Similar markup to that we have shown for displaying a Flash movie can be used to display video or to include audio in a page, with appropriate changes to the type and classid attributes' values.

As we mentioned in Chapter 3, SVG is a language for representing vector graphics, which was developed for use on the Web. SVG images in a file can be embedded in an XHTML page using object with the type attribute set to image/svg, provided that the browser implements SVG. Since SVG is an XML-based language, it should also be possible to include an svg element within an XHTML document, providing a suitable namespace declaration is provided (see Chapter 15). However, browser implementations of SVG are patchy and incomplete, and the latter option, in particular, may not always work. At present, the vast majority of vector graphics on the Web is in the form of Flash. If anything, interest in SVG is declining, so this seems likely to continue to be the case. A still image in Flash is just a movie with only one frame, so embedding it is done using object, as we have described.

IN DETAIL

The object element should have been sufficient to embed any type of media object in a Web page, but its implementation has been poor. In practice, it has been abducted as a way of embedding ActiveX controls for Internet Explorer, with other browsers being forced to rely on the non-standard embed element most of the time. Although techniques of using object markup that work in all browsers are becoming better known, the damage has been done.

In an effort to simplify matters, the draft HTML5 standard has introduced two new elements, video and audio, intended to provide a standard way of embedding these media and presenting playback controls. It isn't clear whether video is supposed to be used for Flash. The draft standard has also sanctioned the use of embed, and retains object. This only seems to be adding to the confusion, but the standard is at a very early stage at the time of writing, and will no doubt be improved by the time it is adopted.

Links and Images

One of the places you can use images is between the start and end tags of an **a** element with an **href** attribute. The effect is to produce a clickable image that serves as the source of a link. This may be indicated by outlining it in a special colour. A common use of this facility is to create clickable icons or buttons; another is to produce image catalogues consisting of small "thumbnail" pictures. Clicking on a thumbnail causes a full-sized version of the picture to be displayed. Alternatively, it may just be considered more appropriate to use an image as the linking element, if it somehow captures the semantics of what it links to. For example, an image of a book's cover may be used as the source of a link to a page of an online book store from which it can be purchased. (It is, however, more difficult to convey a link's meaning unambiguously using an image than it is using words.) When images are used as links it is especially important to supply a textual alternative, as the value of the **alt** attribute, for the benefit of people using non-visual user agents.

There is a slightly more elaborate way of adding links to images: an ***image map*** is an image containing "hot spots", which are areas of the image that are associated with URLs. Clicking on such an area causes the resource identified by its associated URL to be retrieved.

For example, a floorplan of a museum or art gallery could have hot spots for each of the rooms, linked to pages describing the objects that are on display in that room. Clicking in a room on the plan would cause the corresponding page of exhibits to be displayed. Figure 10.12 shows such an image map. Normally, the hot spots are not visible – the image is displayed as it is shown on the left. On the right, we have indicated the hot spots' borders in orange, for the sake of clarity. As you can see, hot spots may be rectangular, polygonal or circular. There is no requirement that they correspond to any features of the image itself, although normally – as in this case – they will.

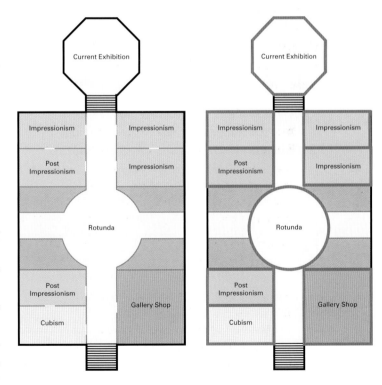

Figure 10.12. *An image map*

To make an image into an image map it must be associated with a **map** element, by giving it a **usemap** attribute whose value is a fragment identifier. This must match the value of the **name** attribute of a **map**. (According to the standard, it may also be identified by its **id** attribute, but this is less reliable, since not all browsers use **id** correctly in this context.) Thus, for example,

```
<img src="images/floorplan.gif" alt="Gallery plan" usemap="#floorplan_Map" />
```

associates the image in **images/floorplan.gif** with a map whose start tag looks like:

```
<map name="floorplan_Map">
```

The content of a **map** is a series of empty **area** elements, each having an **href** attribute whose value is a URL in the usual way, together with two attributes **shape** and **coords**, which together describe a region within the image which is to be linked to the specified URL. The options for **shape** and the corresponding interpretation of **coords** are listed in Figure 10.13. Each **area** should have an **alt** attribute, giving a textual alternative, so that non-visual user agents can display the image map's links in a textual form.

The **map** element associated with the floor plan looks like this:

```
<map name="floorplan_Map">
    <area shape="poly"
    coords-"85,94, 58,67, 58,29, 85,2, 122,2, 149,29,
    149,67, 122,94, 85,94" alt="Current exhibition"  href="current.html" />
    <area shape="circle" coords="104, 254, 50"
    alt="Sculpture gallery" href="sculpture.html" />
    <area shape="rect" coords="122,158,206,203"
    alt="Impressionists I" href="impressionists1.html" />
    area elements for the other hot spots
</map>
```

Shape	Coordinates	Interpretation
rect	*left-x, top-y, right-x, bottom-y*	coordinates of top left and bottom right corners of the rectangle
circle	*centre-x, centre-y, radius*	coordinates of the centre and radius of the circle
poly	$x_1, y_1, x_2, y_2, \ldots, x_n, y_n$	coordinates of the polygon's vertices

Figure 10.13. *Image map areas*

It is not usually necessary to measure the coordinates by hand. Most graphics programs that include some Web facilities allow you to draw the hot spot areas on top of an image, and will generate the markup – including the coordinates – automatically. There also exist small utilities dedicated to the same job.

KEY POINTS

Internet media types (also known as MIME types) provide a means of identifying the type of a resource.

An Internet media type takes the form type/subtype where type provides a broad indication of the sort of data and subtype specifies a more precise format. Common examples include image/jpeg, text/css, audio/mpeg and application/octet-stream.

Plug-ins and ActiveX controls are used to extend the capabilities of browsers, allowing them to display additional types of media.

The img element is used to embed bitmapped images in Web pages. Its src attribute is a URL pointing to the image data; its alt attribute provides a textual alternative. The width and height attributes allow the browser to speed up page display by reserving space for the image before it has been downloaded.

The object element is the officially preferred way of embedding multimedia, including video and Flash movies, in Web pages. If the media object cannot be displayed, the content of the object is used as a substitute.

For plug-ins, the data attribute points to the media data and the type attribute gives its media type. The width and height attributes are used to reserve space on the page. Within the object's content, param elements, with name and value attributes, are used to pass parameters to the plug-in.

For ActiveX controls, the value of the classid attribute provides a Globally Unique Identifier for the control. For video and Flash movies, a param element whose name is movie and whose value is a URL points to the movie.

Conditional comments or JavaScript must be used to combine both types of object so that media will display in any browser.

An image placed within an a element can act as a graphic link.

Where an image is used as a link it is essential to provide a textual alternative, as the value of the alt attribute, for the benefit of people using non-visual user agents.

Hot spots (active regions) can be added to an image with the map element and usemap attribute to create image maps. The map element contains area elements defining the geometry of the hot spots.

Exercises

Do not worry too much about getting all the CSS in your answers to these exercises working in any version of Internet Explorer earlier than IE 8, unless it is the only browser to which you have access.

Test Questions

1 What is the difference between an element and a tag in XHTML?

2 What errors are there in the following XHTML markup?

```
<p>XY&Z Corporation today announced a merger with <em>Desperate Software.
<p>Desperate Software</em> denied rumours that the merger would lead to the
abandonment of <span class=product name>TextFridge<span />.</ p>
```

3 By default, **em** elements in XHTML documents are displayed in italics. As we stated in the previous chapter, for display on-screen it may be preferable to use boldface for emphasis. Write a CSS rule to specify this appearance for **em** elements.

4 Show how you would specify that an entire XHTML document should be displayed with one and a half times the normal leading.

5 Write a CSS rule to set level 1 headings (**h1** elements) as "call outs" – that is, the heading text should be set entirely in the margin with its top on a level with the top of the first paragraph of the following text. (You will need to specify a wide margin.)

6 Can a single resource be identified by more than one URL? Can a single URL identify more than one resource (at the same time)?

7 In regional links, the source and destination of a link are arbitrary rectangular areas that may contain some text. Why can't HTML use this model for anchors?

8 Explain why an **object** element that uses the **classid** attribute to identify an ActiveX control does not use the **type** attribute to identify the type of the media object being embedded.

Discussion Topics

1 There are three approaches in use for creating and editing Web pages. They are (a) use a text editor to edit XHTML tags and CSS rules by hand; (b) use an "almost-WYSIWYG" visual editor, such as Dreamweaver, to edit XHTML and CSS indirectly by changing the layout on screen; (c) create a layout visually in Photoshop or some other graphics or page layout program, and use a plug-in such as SiteGrinder to generate equivalent XHTML and CSS from it. Discuss the relative advantages and disadvantages of these three approaches.

2 Wikipedia, the *Encyclopædia Britannica* and several good dictionaries are now available online, so – in principle – every term used in any Web page could be linked to its definition in one of these reference works. Would this be (a) practical and (b) useful?

3 An **area** element may have an attribute **nohref**, which, if true (**nohref="nohref"**), specifies that the designated area has no URL associated with it. Since no part of the image is associated with a URL unless it is within the shape defined by some **area**, what possible use could you make of this attribute?

Practical Tasks

1 Construct a CSS stylesheet in which all the block-level and inline XHTML elements described in this chapter are distinguished purely by colour. That is, every element should be set in the same font at the same size and weight, but the combination of text and background colour should be unique for each element. Choose a colour scheme that is visually appealing, and ensures that people with defective colour vision can still distinguish the different elements (refer to Chapter 13). Create a page that uses these elements with your styling and evaluate its readability and aesthetics.

2 Find a Web page that uses visual layout tags, such as **font** and **center**, and attributes, such as **align**. (You will have to view the HTML source to discover this.) Take a copy of the page, remove all the visual layout and replace it with a CSS stylesheet that produces an identical layout on a suitably equipped browser.

3 Rewrite your CSS stylesheet from the previous exercise to change every aspect of the page's layout without altering the tags.

4 Design a Web page to display a short video clip (QuickTime, WMV or FLV), together with a title and some brief details about the clip. Use appropriate markup and a stylesheet to create a page that enhances the experience of viewing the clip without detracting from it.

Visual Design

- **Visual Communication**

  Semiotics.

- **Gestalt Principles**

  Grouping. Visual Hierarchy.

- **Colour and Tone**

  Colour in Multimedia Design. Combining Colours.
  Contrast and Tonal Values.

- **Layout Grids**

  Alignment. Grids.

No multimedia or interface designer can afford to ignore the basic principles of visual design and visual communication, because every multimedia application and every Web page is necessarily an expression of those principles, whether the creator of that page or application has given the design careful thought or not.

Clear layout and structured visual organization, careful use of contrast, tone and colour, a well-informed but practical approach to typography, an appropriate choice and presentation of images and well-designed video and animation should all work together to make multimedia both easy and pleasant to use. The basic principles of visual design have been developed through hundreds of years' accumulated experience in traditional media. Digital multimedia presents both new opportunities and new problems, especially where it is interactive. However, the fundamental principles of visual design apply in all contexts where content is being conveyed visually. With the exception of people who cannot see at all, every multimedia user will benefit from good visual design.

Neglect of visual design (or inept visual design) is one of the main factors that lead to multimedia applications and Web sites being difficult to use. As a result, this neglect can lead to failure as surely as a neglect of technical principles, resulting in commercial failure of a multimedia application, lack of returning visitors to a Web site, or poor sales on an e-commerce site, for example. If a Web site visitor cannot see how to complete a purchase and check out, a sale will be lost, even if all the technical functions of the site work perfectly. If the potential user of a multimedia application cannot see how to make it work, they will not use that application.

Figure 11.1 shows the interface of a geological slides player application (see Chapters 12 and 14) on the left, and a completely different "design" for the same interface on the right. Both examples have exactly the same function and the same controls and readouts (even the inclined slider works as it should do). The only difference between the two is the visual design of the interface. One seems fairly "normal" and is reasonably usable, whereas the other is so chaotic that it simply seems ridiculous, and it is almost impossible to see how to use it even though it is actually fully functional in all respects.

We are so used to design that often we don't even notice it, and don't realize what is involved in creating a new design until we face that challenge ourselves. This lack of awareness of the role of visual design has sometimes led to the view that it is just ornamentation – or "eye candy" as it is disparagingly referred to – but as you can see from the examples in Figure 11.1, such a view is entirely mistaken. For sighted people, interaction with a computer screen is governed primarily by visual data received by the brain. The visual appearance and organization of the material the user is looking at – whether it is text, images, moving pictures or a combination of these – is therefore

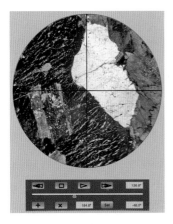
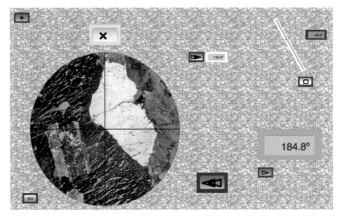

CHAPTER 11

Figure 11.1. *Interface design: order (left) and chaos (right)*

of primary importance in allowing sighted users to interact easily and effectively. (We discuss the different considerations applicable to users who cannot see in Chapter 13.)

We do not have space in this book to cover interface design or graphic design in detail. These are both specialist subjects that require whole books or courses to themselves. We therefore limit our discussion in this chapter to a brief introduction to some of the most valuable principles of visual design, which all multimedia and Web designers need to understand.

IN DETAIL

If you are working on a Web site, remember that structure and content should be separated from presentation. Graphic designers working in print media are accustomed to developing a structure visually. On the Web structure is already explicitly present in markup, and so – in addition to ensuring usability and the effective communication of content – it is also the job of visual design to express that inherent structure clearly, through CSS rules that control the layout and appearance of the elements of the page.

The hierarchy which is already defined by the page's markup should be expressed through the appearance and position of elements on the page, by the use of such attributes as size, colour and spacing. Ideally, this visual presentation and the explicit structure will work hand-in-hand.

This ideal situation falls down in the face of the limited repertoire of elements provided by XHTML, which are not always adequate to express the appropriate structure of a page. The use of class and id attributes to provide hooks for styling is a way of getting round this shortcoming and, at the same time, creating *ad hoc* markup to express the true structure, so in a sense, the visual design does contribute to the development of the structure.

Visual Communication

Visual communication is exactly what it sounds like – communication by visual means. This often happens in a way which the user or viewer does not consciously reflect on. Visual communication depends upon a range of factors which cannot easily be quantified or systematized. It is determined by the individual's response to colours, shapes, symbols, patterns and representational images – a response which may be highly subjective – as well as by physical and cultural factors.

Figure 11.2 shows two advertisements intended to attract visitors to a fictional tourist location, Glenfingal. They might be displayed on a Web site. The example on the left conveys some very specific information about the place, presented as text in simple fonts, with inline links. The one on the right provides much less concrete information, but uses photographs, a more elaborate layout, a coloured background, a mixture of fonts and a conventional navbar for the links.

Despite its relative lack of information, most people would agree that the right-hand example provides more incentive to visit the place. It uses strong, warm colours, a casual font and photographic images to convey an immediate sense of beauty and romance which is lacking in the other example. For many people, these visual elements will evoke a positive response which is not necessarily logical. Not everyone reacts in the same way, however. Some viewers may remain unmoved, or even experience a strong negative response rather than a positive one. (Some people fear the sea or wide open spaces, or dislike rural environments, for example.) The immediacy of visual elements conveys things – positive and negative – in a direct way which text cannot. These elements provoke a response in an instant, whereas it takes time to read through a textual description, no matter how effective it may be. Visual communication thus works with the seemingly illogical in order to convey impressions which cannot necessarily be adequately described in words. To some extent, this can be deliberately controlled and manipulated by the designer.

Figure 11.2. *Which of these pages would make you want to visit Glenfingal?*

Figure 11.3. *Interaction of textual and visual communication*

For example, it is common for the use of an image – or simply the use of certain colours – to alter the meaning of what is being communicated, either in a subtle way (as we saw in Figure 11.2) or in a gross way. Figure 11.3 shows six versions of a newsflash. Each of the six contains exactly the same text, but with a different visual presentation. Only the example in the centre of the top row is "neutral" – that is, only this example conveys nothing more than what can be inferred from the words themselves. Every other example uses visual communication to deliberately alter or manipulate the way in which the viewer will interpret the news.

The highly coloured version at top left conveys a bright and cheerful impression. The use of the rainbow palette together with an informal font suggests that it might be intended for a children's news site, or for a Web site with a casual approach to design. This is contrasted with the example immediately below it, at bottom left. People in some cultures – though not all – will immediately associate the use of a black border on an announcement with death. It might be inferred from this example, therefore, that either the princess or some or all of the quintuplets did not survive the birth. However, this interpretation – and therefore this use of the black border device – is highly culturally sensitive.

The other three examples in Figure 11.3 all make use of photographic images. At the top right, the addition of pretty flowers in conjunction with coloured text conveys a subtle and imprecise but positive impression, leaving the interpretation to the imagination of the viewer. They might think of the new mother being presented with beautiful flowers, or associate the image with spring and regeneration, or just feel a generally positive response. Although the image adds nothing specific to the information conveyed, it does not seem inappropriate. In the example beneath this, however (at the bottom right of Figure 11.3) an image is used which – in this context – is likely to puzzle the viewer, having no apparent connection with the words. It therefore establishes a conflict with the message communicated by the text. An enigmatic image which the viewer cannot readily connect with the rest of the communication is disruptive.

Finally, the example in the centre of the bottom row of Figure 11.3 combines a single image with the same text used in the other examples, but in doing so completely alters the way in which the newsflash is likely to be interpreted. This example of visual communication is so clear that few viewers could be left in any doubt that the "princess" is in fact a cow (or is being likened to one satirically). Most will even go a step further than this and infer that "Princess" is therefore probably the cow's name, rather than a description of her pedigree. The message conveyed by the words is irretrievably altered by the use of a particular image.

The examples we have discussed so far provide a very brief and limited introduction to some of the ways in which appearance can communicate non-verbally. However, it is one thing to observe effects, and another to learn how to produce or control them. In order to design visual communication we need some understanding of general principles, and a broader grasp of visual organization. The subject is complex and depends on individual background, culture, tempera-ment, perception, psychology and other influences. Few of these factors are amenable to precise description and quantification, so any hopes you might have of being taught a set of precise rules which you can follow to ensure effective visual communication are doomed to disappointment. (If you do come upon such a set of rules presented elsewhere you should treat them with caution.) It should also be said that, just as not everyone finds they are suited to computer programming, not everyone is able to produce effective visual communication, even if they wish to.

That is not to say that no useful principles exist, however, only that their application is subtle and indirect and does not translate into quick hints and guidelines that can be applied mechanically. Effective visual communication comes from good visual design, which comes from a combination of a good innate visual sense with practice, experience and exposure to many examples. Even for people with "a good eye" it takes time, and cannot be achieved in a day.

We do not have space in this book to cover all the principles which are applicable to visual design. Later in the chapter we look again at colour, this time in the context of visual communication, and discuss layout. To start with, however, we will consider some important theories developed from other areas of study which provide valuable insights into certain aspects of the ways in which visual communication works – and explain how and why it may fail.

Semiotics

Semiotics (or semiology, as it is known in Europe) was originally concerned with the way in which natural language is built up out of meaningless phonemes – that is, the distinguishable units of speech – into whole words that have meaning. In semiotics we distinguish between the ***signifier***, which is the form which the ***sign*** takes (a word, when we are considering natural language), and the ***signified***, which is the meaning or concept which the sign refers to. For example, the word "elephant" is understood to refer to the animal "elephant" by all who know English and are familiar with the relevant creature. When we hear or read the word "elephant" we think of an elephant. The word "elephant" is the signifier and the elephant itself is the signified.

It is essential to grasp that the relationship between the signifier and the signified is arbitrary. We can only understand any particular sign through knowledge of the specific system of signs within which it operates – in the case of our example, the English language. (You may understand this better if you consider that the word for "elephant" in languages other than English is quite different, and yet the same animal is signified.)

This approach to the understanding of how meaning is created was extended to cover visual language and the way that we understand images and graphic signs. Although the analysis of the content of images is of considerable importance in graphic design, it is not directly relevant to the work of most interface and Web designers, although it is useful to have some familiarity with this when designing anything which includes images. (Those who are interested in this field of study will find suggestions for further reading on the book's supporting Web site.) However, the meaning of symbols and simple graphic signs such as icons is of major importance to interface designers.

One of the simplest examples of signification in user interfaces is the use of underlining to indicate hypertext links. As we observe in Chapter 12, the association between the underline and the function of linking to another document (or another part of the page, perhaps) is entirely arbitrary, and has been established only by convention. In semiotic terms the underline is the signifier and the fact that we will reach a different page (or perhaps a different part of the same page) if we click on that underlined term is what is signified. If we know what a link is, the underline signifies "link". In this case, however, the situation is slightly complicated by the text that is involved. The text that is underlined should tell us something about what we are likely to find if we click, so the text acts in conjunction with the underlining signifier.

The problem with underlining links, though, it that it uses an existing sign – the underline – in a new context. Underlining in hand-written and printed media had long been used to signify emphasis, and in the early years of the Web some designers continued to use it for this same purpose, carrying on the established convention. However, it soon became clear that using the same signifier to signify two completely separate things just could not work. Users were

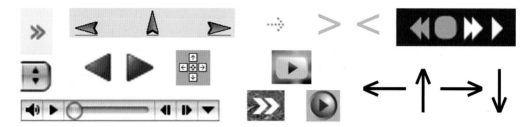

Figure 11.4. *Arrows*

understandably confused. So usability experts started to prescribe that underlining must only be used for links, in order to avoid confusion, and this has now become standard practice. We might say that in the system of signs that is used on the Web, underlining signifies a link, but in the system of signs used in marking up paper documents, an underline signifies emphasis.

Not all of the uses of signifiers in interface design have become so well defined, however. Consider the simple arrow. Arrows of various designs are often used in interfaces, most frequently in the vestigial form of arrowheads. We have used them ourselves in the example of the interface for the geological slides player, illustrated in Figure 11.1 and elsewhere in this book. Figure 11.4 illustrates some of the many versions of this symbol that may be seen in different interfaces. In this case, in the same way that we are able to recognize the same letter in the different-looking glyphs of different fonts (see Chapter 9), we can recognize the arrow in its many forms.

It is not enough that the user recognizes the sign. If an interface is to be usable it has to be absolutely clear what is being signified. It is confusing to the user if the same signifier, such as an arrowhead, relates to several different signifieds – that is, if it has several different meanings. Nevertheless, this is quite often seen in practice. For example, the use of arrowheads pointing to the right and left at the bottom of a Web page probably means "go to next page" and "go to previous page" in a sequence of pages, and clicking on the arrow will perform that function. Arrowheads used to separate breadcrumbs indicate a page's place in the site's hierarchical structure, and in this case clicking on an arrow will achieve nothing at all as it (usually) serves only as a sign, not as a link. Arrowheads used in the context of a time-based media player are conventionally connected with player controls (as in Figure 11.1 and the standard players illustrated in Chapter 12), but the symbols for these differ. It is not always obvious what clicking on each sign using an arrowhead in this context will achieve, but it is very unlikely to link to another document. In a quite different context, arrowheads are frequently used for pop-down menus, in which case the user is expected to click on the arrowhead beside a menu item to reveal the sub-menu. Sometimes, arrowheads are used in menus simply to point to each of the menu items, or in a navbar to indicate the current page, and these have no interactive function at all. In each of these cases the same signifier has a different signified. So how is the user to know what is being signified in any particular case?

The designer of the interface or Web page relies upon a combination of convention, context and users' experience to convey signification accurately to the user. But all three of these factors require that the user has some pre-existing knowledge to draw on, which might not always be the case. It is important to remember that the connection between visual symbols (signifiers) and what they signify is arbitrary – just like the connection between the word "elephant" and the animal. We cannot expect a user to intuit or guess what is being signified, except on the basis of experience. An arrow may signify many things, and at any time it could come to be associated with a new meaning.

The use of symbols in interface and Web design is therefore both contentious and subject to fluctuation. For example, a few years ago it used to be common to see a simple graphic of an envelope used on a Web site's navbar as a link for "contact us", and a crude graphic of a house for "home". Fashions changed, and for a while these symbols were abandoned for plain text links. Recently, however, some resurgence of the use of these icons has occurred.

Some graphic signifiers have become well established. Simplified drawings of shopping carts or baskets are still widely used on e-commerce sites to signify "show the contents of my shopping basket", and many variations on this theme can be found, from an almost indecipherable graphic of a large, pink bag to an elegantly simplified line drawing of a wire basket of the kind commonly used in supermarkets. When a designer uses one of these icons they are relying upon the user's recognizing what it is and what it means. Once again it is vital to remember that the connection between the signifier and what is signified is arbitrary. After all, in almost every case the graphic shows the basket or shopping cart empty, whereas in fact it is a link to view the contents. (This serves to illustrate the arbitrary relationship between signifier and signified, as the image represented in the graphic symbol is not to be interpreted literally.)

Although there are obvious reasons for avoiding signs which may be potentially confusing, there are at least two good reasons for retaining some graphic symbols in interface design.

First, multimedia applications and Web pages are generally aimed at a global community of people who speak many different language. It follows that there are always bound to be some users who will have difficulty understanding any links which are only in text form. The use of a symbol such as a shopping cart – if sufficiently widely established as a convention – transcends language barriers. For example, for anyone who cannot read Japanese, the shopping cart graphic is the only understandable link on the navbar of the Japanese version of a well-known online bookstore's site. This signifier alone transcends the language barrier in this case.

Second, there are some circumstances where it is virtually impossible to think of an adequate alternative for a symbol. The underlining of hypertext links is one example. It would be possible to think of an alternative signifier – such as putting a circle around each link, perhaps – but that is simply to change to the use of a different symbol, not to abandon the use of symbols altogether. The use of arrowheads for pop-down menus is another example. It is difficult to see how to indicate that a menu can be popped down without the use of some symbol, and an arrowhead pointing downwards can be understood to signify that there is something "below", although this meaning is not intuitively obvious. Both these examples also serve to transcend barriers of language as well, of course. The only apparent alternative to using graphic symbols is the use of written text, which would be extremely clumsy and repetitive. (Imagine every pop-down menu bearing some label such as "Menu below".)

In practice, therefore, although icons and symbols should always be used cautiously and with due thought, they should not necessarily be avoided, as in many cases there is no better alternative.

KEY POINTS

Poor visual design is one of the main factors that lead to multimedia applications and Web sites being difficult to use.

Visual communication depends upon a range of psychological, cultural and physical factors which cannot easily be quantified or systematized.

Images and colours immediately convey impressions which cannot necessarily be adequately described in words.

Visual communication may alter the meaning of what is being communicated by words, in a gross or subtle way.

Semiotics is the study of systems of signs and the relationship between signifier and signified within them.

The signifier is a sign's form – for example, a word or a graphic symbol.

The signified is the specific meaning or concept which a sign refers to.

The relationship between the signifier and the signified is arbitrary and can only be understood within a particular system of signs.

Convention, context and users' experience determine whether a user will understand a sign correctly.

Graphic symbols transcend language barriers, so – within an established system of signs – they can be understood more widely than written text.

Graphic symbols are capable of conveying complex meanings succinctly and there may sometimes be no sensible alternative to using them.

Gestalt Principles

Gestalt principles of visual design are derived from the theories of ***gestalt psychology***, which were applied to the study of visual perception in the 1930s and 1940s in order to investigate how the human brain tends to organize the visual information that reaches the eyes.

It was found that although humans are able to identify the parts of a visual image separately – for example, we can see that each of the four images in Figure 11.5 is actually composed from individual dots – we nevertheless tend to organize visual information into patterns and structures, rather than concentrate on each piece of discrete information (each object) in the visual field.

Grouping

Perception of patterns and structures is determined by various factors, but especially by the ***grouping*** of objects in a visual field. Our recognition of grouping is in turn determined by a number of specific features – the proximity of elements, similarity between elements, symmetry, the distinction between figure and ground, and closure (that is, the brain's ability to infer a complete visual pattern or image from incomplete information). The theories of how perception works in this way are often referred to as the "gestalt laws of perceptual organization". You may sometimes see these gestalt principles summed up by the adage that the whole is greater than and different from the sum of the parts.

In Figure 11.5 the image on the far right immediately stands out, because we quickly perceive that the arrangement of dots forms a crude drawing of a human figure, a symbol which is likely to be recognizable by almost all people and cultures. This universal recognition of the human figure is so strong that it is almost impossible to see this image simply as a collection of dots. In the image on the far left of Figure 11.5, however, we can discern no symbolic pattern or sign. Here we just see a field of dots, but we do notice that they are aligned into a regular grid. If you stare at this

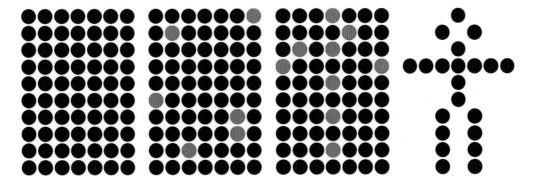

Figure 11.5. *Gestalt principles of visual perception*

image for a while you may perhaps be able to see the regular lattice pattern formed by the nega-tive white space between the dots, rather than the pattern formed by the black dots. However, if you do manage to make the white pattern dominant in this way, you can no longer perceive the black pattern of dots at the same time. This is known as the figure–ground phenomenon. ("Rubin's vase" is a particularly famous example of a figure–ground illusion, in which you can either see two black faces or one white vase, but not both at the same time.)

In the field of black dots on the left of Figure 11.5, we perceive grouping as a result of similarity (all the dots are identical), proximity (the dots are close to one another, and the whole group is set apart from its surroundings by some white space), and a distinction between figure (black dots) and ground (white background), which with some effort we can reverse to make the white lattice pattern (the ground) seem dominant. We can organize this particular image no further, but this sort of non-symbolic ordering is the foundation of structure in visual design.

In the two middle images in Figure 11.5, some of the dots have been coloured red. When we look at these two fields of dots the red ones stand out, and we attempt to organize them into some kind of visual structure or pattern. In the second image from the left, however, there is no pattern to be found – there is neither any meaningful symbol nor any discernible abstract pattern to be seen in this particular arrangement. The human brain works in such a way that this can make the image seem the most frustrating of the four – we try in vain to find a visual structure, and may be annoyed that we have expended time and effort on this fruitless attempt.

The third image from the left is more satisfying, however. With a little effort we can see a symbol in this image, composed from the arrangement of the red dots. This demonstrates one of the most interesting principles of gestalt theory: closure. Almost half of the dots that form the arrow shape (not counting all the other dots in the field) are black and not red. In other words, nearly half of the visual information that says "arrow" to us is missing from this symbol. In addition, the red dots are contained within a larger field of black dots, and the whole is organized into a regular grid once again. Despite this, however, we pick out the arrow shape without much difficulty, and do not try to arrange the red dots (or the black ones) into another visual pattern. The brain completes or "closes" the pattern implied by the dots that are coloured red so that we can almost see a complete red arrow if we stare at the image.

The gestalt principle of closure is illustrated in a different way in the illustration at the bottom of Figure 11.6. Here, a photographic image is disrupted by a series of random jagged white marks across it. A significant proportion of the original image is missing, and yet we have no trouble in recognizing the iris (providing we have seen an iris before). Once again the brain completes the missing part of the image.

The other images in Figure 11.6 demonstrate (reading from the top down) the gestalt principles of proximity, similarity, figure–ground and symmetry.

In the top image we perceive three distinct groups of flowers. Because the flowers in each group are close to one another, and the three groups are clearly separated by white ground, proximity dominates our perception and seems more important than the fact that some of the flowers in different groups are similar to each other.

The second image works in a different way however. The flowers here are fairly evenly dispersed and are not divided into distinct groups by proximity. In this case similarity is dominant – that is, we mentally group the instances of flowers of the same kind and look for the visual patterns which those groupings make. Where proximity occurs as well, grouping is particularly striking. The combination of similarity and proximity is stronger than the grouping perceived as a result of one of those elements alone.

The middle image in Figure 11.6 illustrates another example of the figure–ground phenomenon. In the field of dots on the far left of Figure 11.5 we observed that it was possible to see a white lattice pattern instead of a grid of black dots. In the image in Figure 11.6 it is possible to see either a matrix of roses, or the capital letter M. Images that exploit the figure–ground phenomenon may be used to convey two visual ideas at the same time.

Finally, the image one up from the bottom in Figure 11.6 demonstrates symmetry. When we see two visual elements that are symmetrical, we integrate them into one whole object, or link them together in our minds, even if they are physically separated. This can be important in interface design. For example, the backwards- and forwards-pointing arrows in a media player interface (as in Figure 11.1) make use of this symmetry. We don't conceive of the arrows as a single object, but we do link them together conceptually when they are presented symmetrically within a group.

Gestalt visual principles are of great importance to multimedia interface and Web designers. We need to understand that the user's brain is going

Figure 11.6. *Proximity, similarity, figure–ground, symmetry and closure (reading from top to bottom)*

to be looking for patterns, whether or not they are consciously aware of this process. This means that a user will find an interface easy to use if its elements are arranged in accordance with gestalt principles, and difficult or frustrating to use if no visual structure or order can be perceived (as we saw in the interface illustrated on the right of Figure 11.1).

Ignoring gestalt principles frequently results in confusion for the user. Consider, for example, a weather forecasting site which offers a set of predictions for temperature, precipitation, wind speed, etc., using graphic symbols to indicate the different weather types. We expect these symbols to be used in a consistent way – so that the same graphic (signifier) is always used for bright sunshine (signified), for instance – and organized on the page in a way that is visually coherent. This may be so intuitively obvious that few people will stop to think about it, but imagine how confusing it would be if the symbol for bright sunshine was a different size, a different colour, or even of a different design each time it was used on the site. As we discussed in the section on semiotics, the user would probably infer that each different symbol was intended to convey a different meaning, and would try to work out what the meaning of each symbol was.

Monday	**Heavy Rain**
Tuesday	Heavy Rain
Wednesday	HEAVY RAIN
Thursday	Heavy Rain
Friday	**Heavy Rain**
Saturday	*Heavy Rain*
Sunday	*Heavy Rain*

Figure 11.7. *A confusing absence of similarity*

To simplify matters further, suppose the forecast was provided in text only, set out in a table with a row for each of the next seven days (which we assume will be very wet), but that the font used for the forecast "Heavy Rain" was different almost every time it appeared, as in Figure 11.7. Many users would assume that there was some reason for the difference – that the heavy rain set in one font was going to be somehow different from the heavy rain set in a different font, and – conversely – that the two occurrences of the same font signified similarity. (In other words, they would interpret the same text in different fonts as different signifiers.) They might guess, for example, that the days for which "Heavy Rain" was forecast in the largest and boldest font were going to experience particularly torrential downpours. However, if every occurence of "Heavy Rain" is in the same font, size and colour, they would simply recognize the similarity without giving it any thought, and assume that the actual conditions on each day would be similar.

It follows that the component parts of an interface or Web page should usually be organized according to gestalt principles. On a Web page this is particularly necessary in the case of the navbar. The convention has become so well established that users are unlikely to stop to think about how this works, which is as it should be. However, there is no underlying structural reason why a navbar should appear as a visually coherent whole. The types of menu and navbar that we

Figure 11.8. *Using gestalt principles in Web page design*

are used to seeing and constructing owe their concept to gestalt principles of visual perception. In a contemporary navbar, links are usually all presented in the same font, in the same size and colour, in close proximity to one another, and organized into an ordered structure. In the Web page illustrated in Figure 11.8, for example, there are two immediately recognizable navbars. We understand that they are navbars as a result of a combination of two factors. We see grouping in accordance with gestalt principles – that is, we see two collections of short pieces of text or words, which by virtue of their similarity in font, colour and size, and their proximity to one another, we recognize as two distinct groups. At the same time, we know from experience what kinds of words appear in navbars, so we combine this semantic recognition with the visual perception, and immediately infer "navbar".

The organization of the page according to gestalt principles goes much further than this, however. It is not sufficient just to group the navbar elements together and let everything else take care of itself. In the example shown in Figure 11.8 we can see gestalt principles working in a number of other areas. Underlines make use of similarity (as well as semiotic principles) to indicate links. The body text of the page is presented in one coherent "group" because the text is all in the same font, size and colour (similarity), the paragraphs are in close proximity and they are all left-aligned.

Headings stand out and are noticed because of a lack of similarity with the body text, but at the same time they are visually linked with it by their colour and proximity. In the gallery section towards the bottom of the page, symmetry is used for the arrows linking to the previous and next pages, and similarity of colour is used to indicate which is (and is not) the current page. (This is further reinforced by the use of a box around the current page number – an absence of similarity makes this stand out, as we will discuss shortly.) Finally, the images themselves appear as a group, reinforcing the idea of a gallery, because of their proximity and similarity of size and labelling.

It is necessary to ensure that any of the visual components of an interface or Web page which are linked conceptually will also seem linked visually, in the sort of way just described. Groupings will depend upon the nature of each case, but they will always be required. In the case of our geological slides application for example, illustrated in Figure 11.1 (and elsewhere in the book), it is essential to group the player controls together in the manner familiar from physical media players in order for the user to be able to find and use them quickly. The chaotic version of the interface illustrated in Figure 11.1 shows that it is not sufficient simply to have the controls available somewhere in the interface.

Gestalt principles should also be applied when designing the presentation of information or feedback to the user. Again, we saw in the chaotic version of the interface illustrated on the right of Figure 11.1 that presenting the readouts for angle of rotation and so on in different styles, sizes and colours would tend to mislead the user, suggesting importance or distinction for particular elements where none existed. We will discuss this phenomenon shortly.

IN DETAIL

The navbar is an excellent example of gestalt principles in operation which also illustrates the relationship between document structure and visual structure.

The very earliest Web sites had no navbars; HTML had (and XHTML 1.0 has) no element type suitable for grouping together a set of links. But designers seeking to make the links that define the top-level structure of a site conspicuous and easy to find soon came up with the idea of grouping them together in a distinctive style and a consistent position. This is a classic application of the gestalt principles of visual design.

This purely visual grouping led to the emergence of the navbar as a concept, which then led Web designers to use ad hoc markup to delimit navbars: first, a table, then a div element, finally a consensus has emerged that navbars should be marked up as unordered lists. They aren't, though. It is only with the inclusion of the nl (navigation list) and nav elements in the XHTML 2 and HTML 5 proposals, respectively, that markup has been provided to specify navbars as structural elements.

Visual Hierarchy

Visual hierarchy is concerned with the way in which particular elements may dominate a visual field. Having considered how the gestalt principles of visual perception explain perceived grouping, it is not difficult to understand that if we partially disrupt that grouping we will alter how a design is perceived and interpreted. Effective visual communication often depends upon inverting the gestalt principles so as to deliberately destroy grouping in order to make something stand out or to overturn an inherent dominance in a visual field. It is usually the anomalies in a design that create visual hierarchy. However, this principle can only be applied successfully within a structured whole. As we have already seen (in the example on the right of Figure 11.1), without structure there is simply chaos.

The simplest kind of visual hierarchy to understand is concerned with size, but it is important to realize that although size may be used, visual hierarchy does not always depend upon it. In any visual hierarchy there may be a range of different levels of prominence – a hierarchy is a structure which may contain many levels, although it does not necessarily have to contain more than two.

Figure 11.9 shows two simple examples using text alone. The text is identical in each case, so if we could not see the difference in presentation we would not realize that there was any distinction between the two. When we see the examples laid out in this way, however, we do not interpret them in the same way. In the left-hand example there is no visual guide to interpretation – all the words are similar in size (as well as font and colour) so we perceive them as a group in which each has equal importance, and interpretation is dependent upon the meaning of the words alone. In the right-hand example, though, we infer an emphasis on certain words (and the meaning of those words) from the fact that they are written in a larger (or smaller) size than the others. Certain words stand out and others recede precisely because of a lack of similarity. In this case visual hierarchy is established through the use of size alone, but the hierarchy is complex. For example, it would seem that tigers may be scarier than bears, perhaps, and both of them scarier than lions,

Figure 11.9. *Expressing hierarchical emphasis through type size*

Figure 11.10. *Visual hierarchy is not necessarily determined by size*

but at the same time the phrase "Oh my!" also stands out because it is so tiny. (We might infer from this that it is therefore spoken in a tiny, scared voice.)

Figure 11.10 takes the concept a little further, although it is still based only on text. Here, visual hierarchy is altered in the different examples simply by changing the colour of the text and background. On the far left, where all the text is black and the background uniformly white, size alone determines visual hierarchy – although even here the setting apart of the word "Hierarchy" helps it be noticed (by avoiding proximity and therefore avoiding grouping). In the second example from the left, changing the colour of the word "Hierarchy" to red immediately draws attention to it, so that it now challenges the dominance of the heading "Visual Design". This is achieved by emphasizing dissimilarity (inverting similarity), as well as by using a colour which tends to stand out. (We discuss colour in visual design in more depth in the next section.)

In the next example, the uniformly grey background and the use of greys for the text undermines hierarchy by blurring the distinction between figure and ground (which is very marked in the other examples) and by re-asserting similarity. The result is a much less striking design, in which there is no clear dominance. Finally, in the example on the far right, the background is divided into two areas of unequal size, with very high tonal contrast between each other and the text written upon them. This makes the strongest design of all (if a little lacking in subtlety), in which there is a more complex relationship between the visual elements. In this case, the figure–ground distinction is particularly prominent. The large area of black ground behind the small white text helps to compensate for the text's lack of size, whereas the small area of white ground around

Figure 11.11. *Visual hierarchy in an image*

the large black text helps to focus attention on that text. The result is a closer balance and a less obvious visual hierarchy.

Visual hierarchy of course applies to all visual fields, not just to designs using text. Analysis of all the ways in which hierarchy may be achieved in images and graphic design would require far more space than is available here, but one simple example of visual hierarchy in an image is shown in Figure 11.11. The image on the left is a simple, unaltered greyscale photograph. Nothing has been done to it to change any hierarchy inherent in the original. In this case, therefore, the foghorn tends to be visually dominant, as it is so clearly distinguished from its ground (the sky) and lacks proximity to the other elements. In the example on the right, however, we have undermined this "natural" hierarchy simply by colouring one element in the image bright red. As a result this element becomes visually dominant – going to the top of the visual hierarchy – by virtue of its extreme dissimilarity from the rest of the elements in the image.

KEY POINTS

Gestalt principles of visual perception are derived from the theories of gestalt psychology. They are concerned with how the human brain tends to organize the visual information that reaches it through the eyes.

Perception of patterns and structures may be determined by the grouping of objects in a visual field.

The gestalt principles of proximity, similarity, symmetry, figure/ground and closure determine our recognition of grouping.

Non-symbolic ordering based on the gestalt principles is the foundation of structure in visual design.

The precise appearance and arrangement of objects may lead to one principle dominating the others.

Ignoring gestalt principles frequently results in a confusing design.

The component parts of an interface or Web page should usually be organized according to gestalt principles.

Navbars on Web pages, and the conventional arrangement of controls on media players illustrate the application of gestalt principles to multimedia design.

Visual hierarchy describes the dominance of one or more elements in the visual field. Like other hierarchies, it may have many levels.

Visual hierarchy may be achieved by applying gestalt principles "inversely", in order to disrupt grouping and make one or more elements appear dominant.

Visual hierarchy is not necessarily determined by size.

Colour and Tone

We discussed the technical aspects of colour in Chapter 5, and we consider the accessibility issues relating to the use of colour in Chapter 13, so we will not discuss those aspects of colour again here. However, colour also plays an important role in visual communication and design. Every element in an interface or on a Web page will be assigned some colour, even if it is only black or white; there can be no such thing as a visual element which is colourless. Even when transparency is used, there will always be some coloured area underneath.

Colour plays many roles in visual design. It may be used to establish visual hierarchies, as we have just discussed. It may be used to help create structured designs, for example by colouring several elements in the same way (grouping through similarity). Sometimes it may also be a signifier, as certain colours are associated with specific aspects of life (death, marriage, gender, and so on) in different cultures. The use of colour in visual design is therefore highly complex, and this is not made simpler by the fact that colour is not particularly easy to work with.

Colour in Multimedia Design

As we saw in Chapter 5, computer displays use an RGB colour space which includes millions of different colours. In reality, however, it is unlikely that anyone can perceive the subtle distinctions between all these possible colours. Even in the much more limited table of just a few thousand colours shown in Figure 11.12 it is difficult to distinguish many of the colour samples from one another, although in fact no two are identical. When we consider that it is also impossible to know how any colour we might specify will appear on a user's monitor, we realize that it is not worthwhile being too particular about choosing one subtle shade of a colour in preference to another. This can be very frustrating to graphic designers who are used to having much tighter control over colour in print media, but in multimedia this problem is unavoidable.

In practice this means that although we need to think carefully about colour, we should do so in fairly broad terms, and not worry too much about minor distinctions between hues or tones. Even then, however, it can be difficult to choose colours, and it is necessary to consider the target audience for your multimedia application or Web page as responses to colour are not only physiological but can be personal and emotional.

Various theories about subjective responses to colour have been put forward, but many are contentious or culturally insensitive. For example, when it is suggested that black is a funeral colour it exhibits ignorance of the fact that in many cultures black does not play this role, whereas other colours do. It is impossible to discuss people's response to colour without reference to personal taste, aesthetics, cultural differences and fashion, and these are imprecise factors upon which to base colour decisions. Cultural conventions also play a role. (Why do some cultures roll

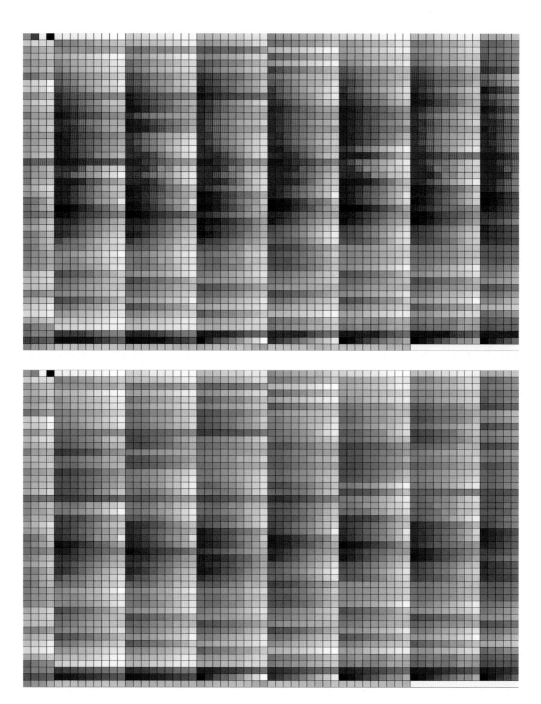

Figure 11.12. *Colours and tones*

out a red carpet for VIPs to walk on and not a white one? Why do bankers typically wear dark grey suits and not yellow ones?) People also develop surprisingly strong personal feelings about specific colours which may be idiosyncratic and sometimes emotional in origin. This necessarily conditions their response to the display of colours in multimedia. Although the factors which determine people's response to colour may be imprecise and changeable, they are nevertheless real and cannot simply be ignored.

The one thing you can be certain of is that – given a large enough sample of people around the world – there will be a wide range of different opinions about which colours work best, or which colours and colour combinations they like or hate, and this will tend to vary between cultures as well as between individuals. Despite what anyone might claim to the contrary, there is no right answer when it comes to colour (apart from issues affecting accessibility). As there is so much variation both culturally and personally in response to colours it is impossible to arrive at any general guidelines for the choice of colours in multimedia, and any that are proposed must be liable to change as fashions and conventions change.

---IN DETAIL---

It is prudent to be wary of people or services which claim to tell you right answers about colour choices. For example, there are a number of "colour schemers" available online or even to purchase. You may find some helpful, but the colour schemes they provide are of very variable quality, often being created by mechanical application of colour harmony "rules" giving no consideration to cultural or personal feelings about colour, and usually ignoring the necessity for the use of good tonal contrast.

Adobe's Kuler, whose interface we describe in Chapter 12, adds an interesting twist. It is "community-based", meaning that designers can post colour schemes they have devised using Kuler's tools, and visitors to the site can rate and comment on them. Thus, the service provides a collection of colour schemes – many of them produced by experienced professional designers, – which have been subject to scrutiny by an extended community. As with any community-based service, there is no guarantee that the ratings and comments are worth anything, but the addition of an element of human judgement is an improvement over a purely algorithmic approach to colour schemes.

Combining Colours

A single colour is seldom used in isolation. In almost all cases, it will be placed next to one or more other colours. When this happens, the perceived colour is modified. This is a consequence of the way colour perception works in the eye and brain, in contrast to the way colours are modified by being mixed as light or pigment, which is a consequence of the physics of light.

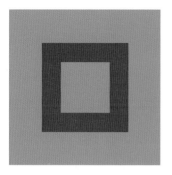

Figure 11.13. *The effect of colour combinations on perception of colour*

In Chapter 5 we mentioned the artists' technique – pioneered by the Impressionists – of placing different-coloured small dabs of paint close to each other to enhance their brightness. Optical mixing – that is, new colours mixed in the brain rather than on the canvas – may occur whether this effect is intended or not. In the same way that you will get green if you actually mix blue and yellow paint together, you will see green, not separate spots of blue and yellow, if there are sufficient small dabs of pure blue and pure yellow paint on a canvas – or dots of ink on a page – in very close proximity.

While larger areas of colour placed in close proximity will not produce the same effect of optical mixing, the colours will interact in a way that alters perception. The colour of the red frame shape in Figure 11.13 is identical in all three cases, and yet it not only seems to have a different hue when superimposed upon different-coloured backgrounds, it also seems to be brighter or duller and more or less lifeless, according to the colour upon which it is superimposed. You may also find that the size of the red shape seems to vary too.

Conversely, taking a colour away from its surroundings can also alter the way it appears. In the example shown in Figure 11.14 we sampled the colour from four pixels in the photograph on the left and used them to fill the four rectangles. All the areas of a single colour look flat and dull compared with their vibrance in the context of the image of the flower from which they are taken. Furthermore, you may not recognize these colours as being components of the photograph.

Figure 11.14. *Colours removed from their pictorial context*

Figure 11.15. *The effect of colour combinations on perception of size*

In particular, it is hard to believe that the two colours on the far right were taken from one of the stamens of the flower, as in fact they were. It is often tempting to try sampling colours from an image when you are devising a colour scheme for a background on which the image is to appear, but the result is often disappointing or worse. In many cases, it is best to avoid flat coloured areas if possible, and use gradients or textured patterns instead.

Juxtaposing colours can alter our perception in other ways. Figure 11.15 shows how it can affect the apparent size of coloured objects. The yellow and red squares are all of exactly the same size, but they don't look it. (The black and white frames are of identical sizes too.) We say that a colour seems to "advance" or "recede" according to whether it appears nearer and larger, or further away and smaller. Most people will find that the colours on the black backgrounds advance, but some people will see them receding. While most people experience this phenomenon to some extent, there does not seem to be universal agreement on which colours advance and which recede in particular circumstances. (There is some evidence that it depends on the physiology of an individual's eyes.) Thus, although we can be aware that such changes occur, it is hard to use them as a basis for a set of guidelines on combining colour.

You are probably also familiar with the concept of the afterimage – if you stare at an area of pure colour for a while and then look away you will "see" an area of the same shape but in the complementary colour, superimposed upon whatever is actually in your field of view. For example, if you stare hard at a yellow patch you will see a violet one, or if you stare at something light blue you will see an orange afterimage, and so on. If you place small grey squares on strong plain-coloured backgrounds (of equal brightness to the grey) and look at them for a while each grey square will seem to take on a tinge of the colour which is complementary to the background, although of course they do not change in fact.

One obvious way in which juxtaposition alters perception is through contrast – the difference in tonal values. As we have seen, perception of contrast also affects visual hierarchy and the ability to distinguish between figure and ground (which is why it is so important for accessibility).

Contrast and Tonal Values

Two colours are said to have high contrast if there is a great difference between their brightness. The greatest contrast, therefore, is between black and white. Colours will have low contrast if their brightness is very similar, regardless of their hue. It is conventional to refer to colours with the highest levels of brightness as "light", and colours with the lowest levels as "dark". (In the RGB representation the darkest tones in each colour component have the lowest numerical values, and the lightest have the highest values.) High contrast results when light colours are combined with dark ones. As we will explain when we discuss the implications of colour choices for accessibility in Chapter 13, to make multimedia more accessible for people with any kind of vision problems – and more usable for all – good tonal contrast should be used. While it is certainly not always necessary to use maximum contrast on a page, it is advisable to use high contrast between text and background (figure and ground) and at least medium contrast between any other elements which need to be readily distinguished from one another.

Contrast affects how easy it is to distinguish details. In particular, the contrast between text and its background affects its legibility. However, it isn't always easy to judge the tonal values of colours when their hues are different, and some people naturally find this much more difficult than others. In the lower part of Figure 11.12 we showed an approximation of the tonal values of the several thousand colours above, by converting the colour chart to greyscale. You will notice that most of the colours converted to a grey which is neither very light nor very dark. Just as we cannot perceive the subtle nuances of hue that distinguish one colour in the upper chart from another, we cannot always see differences in tonal value either, and can even completely misjudge the relative brightness of colours.

IN DETAIL

One of the effects of aging is an increase in the opacity of the lens of the eye, so that less light enters it. Older people therefore perceive a reduced range of tonal values. If you are still young you may need to boost contrast of critical elements beyond what you perceive as necessary, in order to cater for older users. Testing the response of users in the appropriate age group may be necessary.

As we explain in Chapter 13, tonal contrast in interface or Web page design is of particular importance for users who cannot perceive colour differences well, as well as for people with poor sight. Although the term "colour blindness" is often used to describe vision defects that lead to difficulties in perceiving colour, it is misleading. Very few people are unable to see colours at all. It is much more common for people to be unable to distinguish between certain pairs of colours. For example, a person who cannot distinguish green from red (this may apply to as many as one in eight males in some parts of the world) will see an image such as the one shown on the left of Figure 11.16 more or less in the way shown on the right. It is easy for people with full colour

Figure 11.16. *Different colours with similar tonal values (red–green confusability)*

vision to distinguish the red berries from the other parts of the image on the left. If the same people try to identify the berries in the image on the right, however, it becomes much harder.

Figure 11.17. *Testing tonal contrast in greyscale*

It is always prudent to test the tonal contrast of a colour scheme by temporarily converting either your display or your colour space (in Photoshop or a similar program) to greyscale. If, having done this, you can still read or distinguish the different textual and graphic elements without difficulty then your tonal contrast is probably adequate for good usability and accessibility. Figure 11.17 shows the same image as Figure 11.16, reduced to greyscale. You should be able to see that the contrast exhibited in this version allows you to distinguish only the features that are distinguishable by a person who confuses red and green. There is no way to predict the actual colours.

The principle illustrated in these images is of vital importance in interface design. If different colours with similar tonal values are used to distinguish functional or other important elements in a design, people with imperfect colour vision may fail to perceive those elements. For them the interface will be unusable. For example, messages such as "Fields marked in red are compulsory" on a form may fail to indicate which fields are compulsory to some people, especially if other fields are marked in green. Taking an extreme example, text that is the same red as the berries in the image on the left of Figure 11.16 would be invisible if it was placed on a background the same colour as the leaves. However, it is not the colours themselves that are of primary importance in this case. Red text on a red background will be legible if there is sufficient contrast, just as dark grey text would be legible on a light grey background. High tonal contrast must therefore always be used to ensure that important interface elements can be distinguished.

KEY POINTS

Colour plays many roles in visual design, affecting visual hierarchy, perception of structure, and even meaning.

Individuals' responses to colour may be emotive, or determined by fashion or culture.

When colours are juxtaposed, their perceived appearance is modified.

Hue and brightness may appear to be modified when the same colour is placed against different backgrounds.

Large flat areas of a single colour look quite different from pixels of the same colour within an image.

Colours may seem to advance or recede when placed on different-coloured backgrounds.

Tonal contrast affects perception of the distinction between figure and ground. Contrast therefore affects the legibility of text.

It can be difficult to judge the contrast between colours of different hues.

As people age, less light enters the eye, so a smaller range of tonal values is perceived.

A significant number of people suffer from defective colour vision, most commonly an inability to distinguish between red and green.

The tonal contrast of coloured designs should be tested by converting to greyscale.

Colour should not be used as the sole means of conveying information.

Layout Grids

We have already seen how gestalt principles of visual perception can be used to create grouping and visual hierarchy. We must look at one more principle before we can consider the organization of multimedia elements into the contents of an entire window. Although digital multimedia is invariably destined to be looked at on a screen, the principles we will discuss in this section are derived from print media, so we will refer to the contents of a window as a "page", to avoid any clumsy circumlocution.

Alignment

If objects are placed so that they lie on a clear vertical or horizontal line, they will appear to be connected in some way, even if they are not particularly close together. (You might consider alignment a form of similarity, based on spatial position.) We almost always make use of alignment when displaying text, as we described in Chapter 9. By aligning the left or right margins of paragraphs – or both – we supply them with a visual coherence and uniformity which is pleasing to the eye and makes reading easier. The idea is naturally extended to images or other graphic elements that are included with text on a page.

A valuable guideline to use when considering alignment is that objects should either appear to be aligned perfectly or it should be obvious that they are not aligned. The tendency to perceive alignment is a strong one, so if objects are almost aligned but not quite, they will just look untidy.

Volummol esequis sectet lametum vulla faci ea adit iureet, sim dolore commodiam, quis, "nostrud tissed miniam" estio dolenisl irilit ilit iriuscip essenis accum dolor iurer sit adio od ting ea consequipsum dolobore "tat ut at" conse tat iure magna conum in erin in venit.

Volummol esequis sectet lametum vulla faci ea adit iureet, sim dolore commodiam, quis, "nostrud tissed miniam" estio dolenisl irilit ilit iriuscip essenis accum dolor iurer sit adio od ting ea consequipsum dolobore "tat ut at" conse tat iure magna conum in erin in venit.

Figure 11.18. *Hanging punctuation*

Figure 11.19. *Aligned irregular shapes*

As always where perception is concerned, matters are not entirely simple. It may be that the best way to make objects appear to be aligned perfectly is by not aligning them. This has long been understood in connection with typography. Traditionally, lines of text that begin or end with a punctuation mark are extended slightly so that the punctuation moves outwards into the margin, a technique known as *hanging punctuation* or *optical margin alignment*. This effect is illustrated in Figure 11.18.

The term "optical marginal alignment" explains its purpose. Because the punctuation marks are smaller than glyphs for letters and have a relatively large amount of white space around them, margins will not appear straight when one of these punctuation characters appears next to them. Hanging the punctuation restores the appearance of alignment. In the upper version of the paragraph in Figure 11.18, the margins seem indented where the commas and quotation marks appear next to them, producing apparently ragged edges. When these punctuation markes are nudged outwards into the margins in the lower version, the margins seem straighter, even though they are not, because the eye is led down the edges of the letters.

Similar adjustments may be necessary when aligning images that are not rectangular As the simple shapes in Figure 11.19 illustrate, there may be no hard straight edge to the content, and an image's bounding box may not provide a suitable substitute for the purposes of alignment. In this case it looks as though the ellipse and rounded rectangle are indented slightly, but actually all the shapes are left-aligned.

Centred alignments are less likely to be successful than left or right alignment. Figure 11.20 shows a popular way of using centred alignment. The pink boxes represent images, the blue ones paragraphs of text. Placing a single image centrally above the text produces an impression of symmetry and balance. When the same approach is taken to the group of three images, however, the eye groups the three into one "unit" on the basis of similarity (see the section on gestalt principles), and recognizes that the width of this unit is similar to the width of the paragraph below (though not quite identical to it). This means that what is most striking – and disconcerting – about their placement is the near-alignment of the left and right edges with the margins of the block below. Many people (though not all) would find this layout more pleasing and natural if the three images were spaced slightly further apart, so that the margins were aligned. The problems caused by aligning images centrally are worse if the practice is used in conjunction with blocks of text that are not justified. If the right margin is ragged there is no visual reference for the centre.

Figure 11.20. *Centred alignment*

The same thing happens if headings are centred. If the heading is not significantly narrower than the paragraph below, it will appear to be misaligned, although in fact it is centred. If the paragraph is not justified, the heading's position will appear to be arbitrary.

Grids

Graphic designers frequently align objects on a ***layout grid*** to help organize the elements of a page in a way which is visually structured and coherent. A layout grid is a geometrical division of the page that can be used to control the placement of text blocks and images. Figure 11.21 shows some examples. Simple grids – such as the two on the left of the figure – divide the page into areas, such as text blocks and margins. More complex grids – such as the one on the right – define a framework, into which different-sized blocks can be placed so that their edges are aligned.

A grid does more than define alignments. As the example on the left of Figure 11.22 shows, elements can be aligned but still look untidy and not clearly grouped. For example, we cannot tell by a quick glance whether the text between the images belongs with the image above or below it – to discover this we either need to read the text or check how the text is placed with respect to the top or bottom image. The way in which the images appear on the right-hand side but the text is aligned to the left interferes further with our ability to recognize grouping. The eye also has to move repeatedly backwards and forwards across the page from image to text.

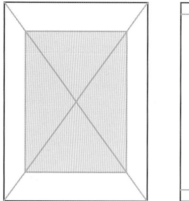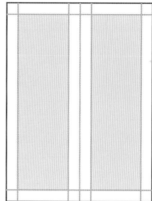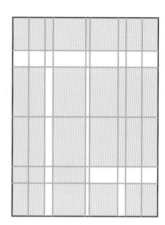

Figure 11.21. *Layout grids*

Contrast this with the example on the right of Figure 11.22. Even though the images are not all of the same width, the strict left-alignment of the images and text blocks in two columns is sufficient to make the page look ordered, while the top-alignment of each block of text with the relevant image, combined with their proximity, makes it possible for us to recognize without difficulty how the blocks of text and images are grouped – that is, we can see at a glance which bit of text belongs with which image. The two pages in fact present the same information and have the same function; the only difference lies in their appearance, which makes one more usable (and more satisfactory to look at) than the other. You will note that the more usable page also allows more information to be seen without scrolling. A good layout grid often helps make the most efficient use of space.

Although alignment is of great importance in creating visual coherence, the grid's additional func tion of defining regions is what makes it such a powerful tool for visual organization. As long as the same grid is used throughout a set of connected pages, such as an entire Web site, different combinations of text blocks, images and embedded time-based media objects can be used on different pages, while preserving a feeling of uniformity throughout. Users will recognize the same overall pattern and groupings, even though the individual elements change, and this helps establish an identity (branding) for a site. It also makes a Web site or a multimedia application easier to use, as we remember where particular types of elements were placed on previous pages or frames and look for them in the same place again.

Although the grid is a powerful design element, the grid itself normally remains invisible – we see only the resulting visual structure that it imposes on layout, and not the supporting structure itself. The grid is exceptional, therefore, in that it is an abstraction – unlike visual design elements such as typography or colour.

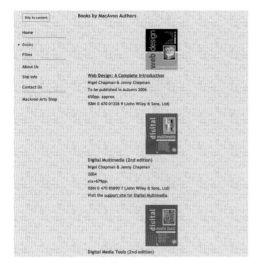

Figure 11.22. *Alignment and a grid*

The simplest grids, such as the first two in Figure 11.21, divide a page into columns of equal height. (The very simplest "grid" consists of a single column.) Two- and three-column layouts are popular both on the Web and in print. If each column holds text, and especially if the text flows from one column to the next, it is usual to make them all the same width. When one or more holds images, it is more common to use different widths for the columns.

Grids are often based on ratios, such as $\sqrt{2}$ or the Golden Ratio, to create elements with pleasing proportions. Many books have been written on the subject of creating layout grids to make harmonious pages. However, there is a serious problem in applying established guidelines for layout grids to design intended for a screen – we never know how tall or wide a page will be, because users have screens of different sizes and they can resize their windows. The geometrical principles behind many traditional grids, as used in book and magazine design, rely on the grid's being imposed on a rectangle with fixed bounds. Where this rectangle cannot be fixed, grids must be designed less rigidly.

For Web pages, there are extra problems. We do not necessarily know how big any element on a page will be, because sizes might be defined in relative units, which depend on the font size or window dimensions. Trying to create a fixed grid layout based on the geometry of a page is not going to work for the Web. (This hasn't stopped designers trying – the result has been pages that force some users to scroll horizontally, others to see vast areas of blank space, and others to see a mess of overlapping text and images.)

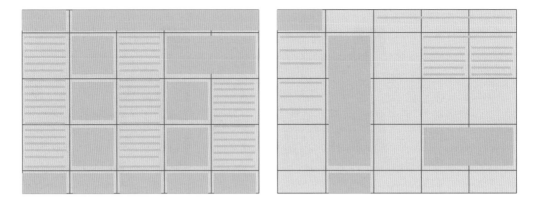

Figure 11.23. *Dense and sparse grid layouts*

However, grids aren't an end in themselves, they are simply an aid to creating alignment and grouping, and enforcing uniformity. If you abandon rigid geometrical constraints, it is possible to employ a modified type of grid that accommodates the dynamic dimensions of Web pages, while maintaining a framework for vertical and horizontal alignments. Specifying the grid dimensions in *em units* leads to *elastic layouts*, in which all the elements maintain their relative sizes at any font size. Using percentages for the grid leads to *liquid layouts*, where the proportions between the elements and the window's width always stay the same. An extensive account of how layouts of this type may be implemented for Web pages using CSS can be found in *Web Design: A Complete Introduction*. In Flash, scripting must be used to make layouts elastic or liquid. Recent developments in Web browsers, which allow them to alter the page layout dynamically when either the font or window size changes, may soon make these layouts obsolete for the Web.

Grids with more than three columns are best treated as a framework which can be used to align elements on the page, horizontally as well as vertically. Broadly speaking, there are two ways of using a grid for layout of this sort, which we will call "dense" and "sparse". These possibilities are illustrated in Figure 11.23. (The pink rectangles are images, the grey bars represent text and the pale blue areas are empty.)

In a dense layout, most of the grid cells are filled with text or images (or embedded time-based media objects). The widths of these elements are chosen so that they occupy one or more grid cells, with standard margins around them. The result is similar to some newspaper layouts. Using a dense layout will tend to create a cluttered effect, but it does allow you to pack a lot of information into a small space, which may sometimes be required.

A sparse layout leaves many of the cells empty, creating negative spaces around the elements in the filled cells. By placing those elements on the grid, though, related elements can be connected visually by their alignment and proximity. For example, in the sparse layout on the right of Figure 11.23, the tall narrow image (indicated by an orange rectangle) naturally leads downwards to the small image at the bottom below it.

Notice that – in all cases – it is not necessary that every element on the page is exactly the width of one of the grid's divisions. It is only necessary that they align on the edges of the grid. It is common for images to span both columns of a two-column grid, for example. As we mentioned earlier, precise geometrical alignment may not always be the best way of positioning objects with respect to the grid. It may be necessary to nudge them to make them appear aligned. It may also be advantageous to move objects slightly off the grid to create a less mechanical appearance, but doing this without producing a sloppy result requires skill and experience.

Arbitrary grid layouts are easily created in Flash by drawing out text areas and then aligning them. For Web pages, if you don't care about what happens when users resize their browser window or increase the font size, grid layouts can be implemented very easily using absolute positioning, some simple arithmetic and a bit of trial and error. Web authoring programs, such as Dreamweaver, allow you to lay out blocks on a grid just by dragging out rectangles on the screen. They then generate stylesheet rules that set the position and size of div elements that correspond to each box you have drawn in px units.

> ### KEY POINTS
>
> **Alignment can give an appearance of coherence and visual order to a Web page or multimedia interface.**
>
> **It is sometimes necessary to misalign irregular objects slightly to make them look as if they are perfectly aligned.**
>
> **Hanging punctuation is used to prevent punctuation marks at the ends of lines of text appearing misaligned.**
>
> **Centred layouts may be problematic – images and headings may look untidy unless one of the aligned elements is significantly narrower than the other.**
>
> **A layout grid is a geometrical division of the page that can be used to structure the placement of text blocks and images.**
>
> **The grid itself is simply an aid to layout and remains invisible.**
>
> **Modified grids may be used to accommodate the dynamic dimensions of Web pages while maintaining a framework for vertical and horizontal alignments.**
>
> **Arbitrary grid layouts may be created in Flash.**

Exercises

Test Questions

1 According to gestalt principles of visual perception, how do we recognize grouping in a visual field?

2 For what purposes would you use gestalt principles when designing the layout and appearance of a Web page?

3 Explain what is meant by the signifier and the signified in semiotic terminology. List all the examples of signifiers you can identify in the geological slides player interface illustrated on the left of Figure 11.1.

4 What is meant by the term "visual hierarchy"? What use would you commonly make of visual hierarchy in the design of a Web page?

5 What problems might be caused by inappropriate choice of colours in an interface, and how can they be avoided?

6 Does using a grid layout for a design that includes text and pictures mean that every picture must (a) be the same size, (b) have the same aspect ratio, or (c) be one of a limited number of sizes? Explain.

Discussion Topics

1 What is the relationship between visual design and usability?

2 To what extent do the gestalt principles of visual perception account for the way that visual communication works? What other factors are involved in communicating visually, and how can the designer exploit them?

3 List at least six different things you could do to make one interface element stand out from all the rest in your interface design.

4 How important is colour in the design of a multimedia interface? What roles might it play?

5 Is it appropriate or necessary to use a layout grid when designing a multimedia interface? Justify your answer and provide concrete examples.

Practical Tasks

1   Study the Web site of a large organization or commercial venture. Identify all the ways in which the design of the site makes use of (a) the gestalt principles of visual perception and (b) signs (in the semiotic sense). Note any ways in which the design of the site could be improved in these respects.

2   Open a photograph in an image manipulation program such as Photoshop. Experiment with selecting different small areas of the photo to remain in colour, and convert the rest of the image to greyscale (desaturate). Observe how you can create different visual hierarchies in the same image.

3   In a vector drawing application such as Illustrator, draw four rectangles, all filled with the same colour, in the following sizes (width $\times$ height): 300 px $\times$ 200 px, 200 px $\times$ 100 px, 100 px $\times$ 200 px and 200 px $\times$ 200 px. Using the program's alignment facilities, arrange these shapes so that they are aligned along (a) their right edges, (b) their left edges, (c) their vertical centre lines, (d) their top edges, (e) their bottom edges, (f) their horizontal centre lines. Which arrangements best convey an impression of order? Do any of them tend to impose grouping or a visual hierarchy on the rectangles? Experiment by adding further rectangles with different aspect ratios and see how well they can be made to align on a grid.

Interactivity

■ **Interacting With Multimedia**

Media Players. Hyperlinks. Scripted Interaction.
Slide Shows and Presentations.

■ **Interacting Through Multimedia**

XHTML Forms. Flash UI Components. Multimedia Interfaces.

Interactive computer systems, including Web applications, provide services to their users by way of processes that require interaction with the system and the presentation of information. Until fairly recently, users could only interact with programs by means of a limited repertoire of controls. Most programmers took advantage of the standard controls provided by Windows or the Mac OS, so that buttons, pop-up menus, text input fields, dialogue boxes and so on, all looked the same and worked in the same way in most programs on each of those platforms. Modal and modeless dialogues incorporating the standard controls were the main way of providing interactivity. Specialized tools and mouse gestures were used in different classes of program, such as word processors and graphic editors, but most programs in a particular class shared many tools and conventions with each other. Thus, familiarity was assured and many programs could be used by experienced computer users without ever consulting a manual or help file.

The arrival of the World Wide Web and new technologies such as Flash have permitted a greater variety of interaction. They have also allowed a much larger group of people to design and create interactive systems. Whereas designing the user interface to an application program or an operating system is usually done by experienced specialists, designing the user interface to a Web application is normally done by Web designers (or perhaps the site owner's notorious 15-year-old nephew). Technologies such as "widgets" and Adobe AIR, which allow Web technologies to be used to create desktop applications, mean that non-specialists are designing and implementing many types of user interface.

The discipline of interaction design is concerned with designing interface elements and processes that allow users to perform tasks efficiently in a pleasant way. Much interaction design deals with household products, such as DVD players, mobile phones and coffee machines. In these cases, the purpose of interaction design is to ensure that the process of using the product is simple, effective and hopefully enjoyable, or at least stress-free. Similar ideas are applied to the design of interactions with computer programs. Among the factors contributing to good interaction design are preventing confusion, minimizing effort, making learning easy and providing feedback. These factors are maximized by using elements and processes that are familiar to users. Where interaction is through a graphical user interface it is necessary to apply the general principles of good design already discussed in Chapter 11. It is also essential to take account of a range of accessibility issues, which we discuss in detail in Chapter 13.

When we consider interaction and multimedia, we can distinguish two possibilities: interacting *with* multimedia and interacting *through* multimedia.

Interacting With Multimedia

There are limited opportunities for interacting with images and text, and established ways of doing so that are familiar to almost all computer users. Time-based media and hypermedia require new forms of interaction.

Media Players

It makes sense to start, stop, pause and rewind video, animation and sound. All three media extend through time at a fixed rate, so these operations make equal sense for all of them, even though they are created in different ways. In the case of sound, there is also a need to control the volume. Since video and animation are often accompanied by sound, volume controls are appropriate to all three time-based media.

Many user interfaces are based on metaphors: making controls look and behave in a similar manner to something familiar in the physical world. There is a ready source of metaphor for controlling time-based media in the shape of media players. Audio tape recorders established the conventional set of buttons — play, stop, pause, rewind, fast forward — which were adopted unchanged by Walkmen and other cassette players, VHS decks and DVD players. Where appropriate, a record button is added to the set. Even the "click-wheel" on a classic iPod contains the same collection of buttons, although they are arranged in an innovative way.

Because of the success of this *de facto* standard for controlling time-based media, these five buttons are the basis for the controls of most video, animation and audio playing software. Figure 12.1 shows the controls provided by the QuickTime Player: you will recognize the buttons as being the same as the corresponding buttons on a physical media player; they use the same icons for the various functions. (The **Next** and **Previous** buttons here serve a dual purpose: a single click advances or goes back a single frame, clicking and holding fast-forwards or reverses.)

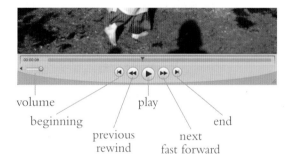

Figure 12.1. *QuickTime Player controls*

However, there is a significant difference between the QuickTime Player and a physical device. Because it is a program, not a piece of hardware, the QuickTime Player can change its appearance easily. Figure 12.2 shows the player controls when a movie is actually playing. The **Play** button in the centre has turned into

Figure 12.2. *QuickTime Player controls while playing*

a **Pause** button. This not only saves space, it means that only those functions that can be meaningfully applied are available. It doesn't make sense to start a movie that is already playing, but it does make sense to pause it. By changing the control, the design makes the player easier to operate. It isn't necessary to identify and choose the right button, because the wrong one isn't there.

The QuickTime Player's controls are adapted to the virtual nature of the software in other ways. Volume is controlled by a slider. Both sliders and rotating knobs are used to control volume on physical devices, but turning a virtual knob using a mouse is awkward, so sliders are almost invariably used for this purpose. A slider is also provided above the buttons for "scrubbing" the movie, that is for moving rapidly backward and forward by dragging the control. Where this function is provided on physical devices, it too is usually controlled by a rotating knob. By using a slider here, which moves as the movie plays, an indicator of the position of the current frame within the whole movie is provided without using any extra space.

Figure 12.3. *Player controls for an embedded movie*

As Figure 12.3 shows, the set of controls displayed for playing a QuickTime movie when it is embedded in a Web page is a smaller simplified version of the stand-alone Player's controls. They are less intrusive, which is more appropriate for the context, but they still follow the same conventions. So do the controls on the Windows Media Player, which are shown in Figure 12.4. The arrangement of the controls is different, with the fast-forward and rewind buttons moved out to the ends of the scrubbing slider, but the basic design is the same, and like the QuickTime Player's it is solidly based on the design of the controls on a physical player.

Figure 12.4. *Windows Media Player controls*

Flash Video is slightly different. You will remember from Chapter 6 that an FLV movie is usually loaded into a single-frame SWF that is played by the Flash Player. The Flash Player has no playback controls, just a primitive contextual menu. Controls for playing the FLV movie can be provided using Flash and ActionScript within the containing SWF movie. Usually, one of several standard sets of controls is chosen from a library. Not surprisingly, the standard sets of controls are based on the conventional media player buttons. Figure 12.5 shows one of the standard options for player controls. Again, the conventional icons have been used. Flash allows you to choose which of the controls to display; here we have used the full available set, which includes a button for toggling full-screen playback and another for displaying captions. Most combinations of the available

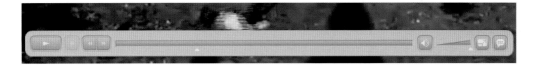

Figure 12.5. *Flash video playing controls*

buttons are provided and you can choose whether to place the controls on top of the video, as we have done here, or below it, as in the standard media players.

It is possible to create your own Flash video controls, which can have any kind of appearance that you like. In the case of Flash animations, you must create your own controls if you want to provide any, although there are library items for making buttons with the standard icons.

All the media player controls use semiotic and gestalt design principles (see Chapter 11). Some versions of the intrinsically meaningless signs that have been established to denote Play, Pause, Rewind and so on, are always used. In particular, the Play and Pause buttons always use the conventional icons. The buttons are always grouped and set apart in some way, so that they can be perceived as a unit – the controller – which is clearly not part of the content. This is true even in the case of the Flash controls that are superposed over the movie.

Interestingly, iPod music/video players that have a multi-touch screen use controls that are almost the same as those used by software media players, as Figure 12.6 illustrates. The virtual controls based on the metaphor of buttons on physical players have found their way back into physical devices. Here again, though, the absence of physical constraints has allowed some extra refinements.

The set of controls normally available has been reduced to the essentials. (The slider is the volume control.) Additional controls can be displayed at the top of the screen; these include a slider for scrubbing, and buttons for making the current song play repeatedly and for shuffling the current "playlist" – often the tracks of an album. The elements of the playlist itself can also be displayed instead of the album cover, as shown in Figure 12.6. None of these operations is particularly easy to provide on a device for playing cassette tapes or CDs. The nature of the player has made new ways of listening possible, and the controls have had to evolve to accommodate them. There is, though, a clear line of development from the controls of earlier devices with physical buttons.

Figure 12.6. *iPod touch controls*

Hyperlinks

In the case of hypermedia, there is no such precedent in physical media. The nearest thing to a hyperlink in print is a cross-reference, which is usually expressed by the form of words, such as "see page 148". Some special typographic treatment is often applied, such as italicizing the word *see*, but it is not universal practice to do so. The meaning of the words is usually considered sufficient.

In hypertext, some additional means of indicating that a link can be followed by clicking is required, because links are attached to arbitrary pieces of text, not just to a small set of stock phrases. Thus, the first generation of Web browsers indicated links by underlining and displaying them in blue. When CSS became available, it brought the possibility of distinguishing links by applying arbitrary styling to them. This was a desirable development, because blue underlined text cannot always be happily integrated with colour schemes and typographical designs. However, it leads to a new problem – or rather, it brings back the original problem – how are links to be made evident to users, when there is no standard appearance for them?

The theories of visual design, which we introduced in Chapter 11, suggest ways of distinguishing links from surrounding text, but on its own that is not sufficient. We may want to distinguish text for other reasons – to emphasize it, or because it is a heading, or an attribution, or for other reasons that have nothing to do with links. The Web design community has therefore developed conventions for indicating links.

Underlining, which pre-dates CSS, is still the most common signifier for links. The underlining may be done in a stylesheet by setting the **text-decoration** property to **underline**, or by applying a border to the bottom of every link. There are differences in the appearance resulting from these two methods. The underline text decoration is applied to the characters as part of the text styling, but the border is applied to the element as a whole. The immediately visible result is that borders always hang below any descenders in the link text, whereas an underline will go through them. Figure 12.7 shows the appearance of text with an underline (top) and with a bottom border. The positioning is evident in the relationship between the underlined text and the line below it, as well as in the descenders on the p and g. If you wanted to use a bottom border to underline links, it would be advisable to increase the leading. (Recall from Chapter 10 that the space between the border and the box's contents is the padding. Unlike margins, padding cannot be negative, so there is no way of pulling the border up to the position occupied by an underline.)

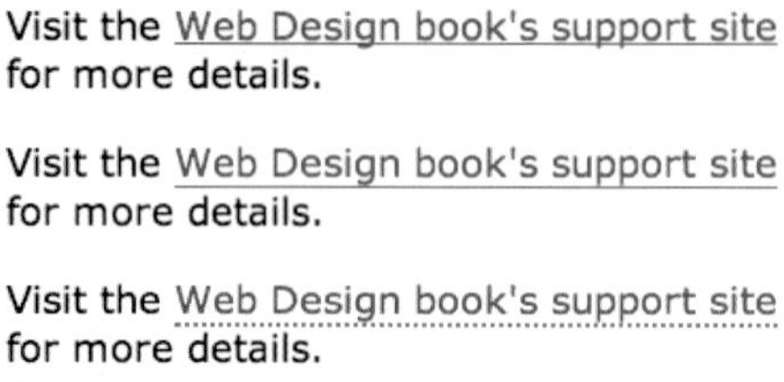

Visit the Web Design book's support site for more details.

Visit the Web Design book's support site for more details.

Visit the Web Design book's support site for more details.

Figure 12.7. *Different ways of underlining links*

In compensation for its incorrect positioning, the border can be styled in different ways. Its colour can be specified independently of the link text's colour, while an underline decoration always matches it. Borders can be drawn in different styles: solid, dotted, dashed, double, grooved or ridged, and in any width. The example at the bottom of Figure 12.7 shows one possibility, a 2 px dotted red border.

What distinguishes link text from other text is the fact that something will happen when you click on it. To help make this clear, it has become common to make the appearance of link text change when the cursor moves over it. This shows that the area is receptive to events, because it reacts to the mouseover, and the change draws attention, as movement or change on the screen always will. In Chapter 10 we showed how the :hover pseudo-class could be used in CSS selectors to add a background highlight to links when the cursor moves over them.

Any relevant CSS property could be changed on rollover, there is no universal convention and the mere occurrence of a change acts to signify that the link is active. Changes that alter the size of the link text should be avoided, though, since they can cause the entire text of a paragraph to jump. This includes changing the weight: boldface text usually occupies more space than the normal weight of the same font.

---IN DETAIL---

The methods for distinguishing links that we have described are all visual, so they only convey information to people who can see. As we explain in more detail later, multimedia – the Web in particular – should be accessible to everybody, irrespective of any disabilities, including blindness. Programs such as screen readers used by people who cannot see can distinguish links in Web pages by the markup and will be able to indicate the presence of a link by some means appropriate to the medium they use to communicate with them.

Adding a rollover effect to links helps offset an undesirable side-effect of the range of possibilities for link styling offered by CSS. Because Web designers have used many different styles to indicate links, users have become accustomed to clicking on any text that looks different from its surroundings. However, they are less likely to click if no rollover effect occurs.

In the early Web, links were usually contained within the body text of the page, and there was a tendency to assume that this was an essential property of hypertext. That is, hypertext was considered to be normal text, parts of which were active links. The difficulties of writing text in such a way that links can be embedded in it naturally led to the widespread habit of including links reading Click Here, or just Here. In Chapter 13 we explain why this is bad practice from the perspective of people with disabilities, but links of this sort are obviously awkward and clumsy.

Modern Web pages often move the links out of the text into separate areas of the page. The most common example of this is seen in the use of navigation bars. As we described in Chapter 10, these are lists of links to the main pages on a site, which appear on every page. The principles of gestalt are routinely applied (whether consciously or not) to distinguish a page's navigation bar (or *navbar*) from its contents. Navbars are positioned in a consistent place on every page, usually separated from other elements of the page by negative space, often in a larger or heavier font. This way, there is no need to underline links or apply rollover effects to them; experienced Web users will recognize the links by the visual character of the navbar as a whole.

In a similar way, sets of links are often collected into a separate sidebar on a page. This is a common device on blog pages, where links to previous posts or other blogs are usually placed in a separate column. The use of sidebars to present subsidiary material does have a precedent in print. It is a common device for providing background information in magazine articles, for instance. Various devices are used to mark off the sidebar from the main page, including the use of space, tinted backgrounds, borders and the use of different fonts in the body and sidebar. These devices are easily implemented in CSS.

Signifying links when they are attached to images is more problematic and no satisfactory solution is available. The default stylesheets of most browsers apply a blue border to images that have links. The shade of blue used is usually the bright colour denoted by the value **blue** in CSS, which does not go well with many colour schemes. Choosing a border colour that will work with arbitrary photographs is virtually impossible, and in many cases a designer will prefer to leave images without borders for aesthetic reasons. "Underlining" images always looks odd, as does changing background colours on rollover.

Because no convention for indicating linked images is in general use, but images do often have links attached, users often try clicking on any image to see whether anything happens. This is not efficient. One way of dealing with this is by ensuring that something always does happen when an image is clicked on, but it is prudent to avoid relying on a linked image as the only link to a destination, unless the accompanying text makes the situation clear. For instance, any logo on a page should always be linked to the site's home page, but that should not be the only link home.

Scripted Interaction

So far, we have only considered the essential forms of interaction with time-based media and hypermedia and established types of control. For these, standards and conventions exist, which you should always follow unless there is a good reason for doing otherwise. It is possible to create arbitrary types of programmed interaction with multimedia by adding scripts which perform some computation and alter the display or playback when events such as mouse clicks and key presses occur. There may be no precedent or convention that is relevant in such cases.

An important class of interactions that can be enabled through scripting is the direct manipulation of media elements. The most familiar example of direct manipulation is "drag and drop", which is used in many contexts to allow users to move objects on the screen with the mouse. This technique is often used with images. If you use Photoshop or some other image editing program, you are probably familiar with being able to drag a layer to reposition it, or drag the whole image so you can see a different part of it when it is zoomed in.

In a similar way, when an image is being displayed users can move around it by dragging, if the necessary script is provided. Image dragging is most easily implemented in Flash, at present. For example, Figure 12.8 shows an interface to a display of a thin-section geological microscope slide (petrological slide), of the kind geologists use to study the minerals present in a rock sample. An image at sufficiently high resolution to display all the details in a slide would be too big to fit on most screens. By masking part of the image so that it looks like it is being seen through a microscope, and making it possible to drag the image with a mouse while the virtual eyepiece stays in the same place, an interface to the image can be supplied that corresponds roughly to the experience of viewing a real slide and moving it under the microscope. However, with a digital image we are not restricted to any particular size, but can move around an arbitrarily large picture.

Dragging an image can be used in many different ways. For instance, a popular device, especially on tourism sites, is the "draggable panorama". A single long image is constructed by stitching together photographs taken at intervals while a camera is rotated through 360°. Part of this panoramic image is displayed with a conventional aspect ratio, as if it was the view in one direction from the camera's viewpoint. By dragging the image with the mouse, the user can scroll it horizontally,

Figure 12.8. *Image dragging*

revealing new parts of the panorama, as if they are turning round on one spot and looking at the view in a different direction. A similar effect can be achieved by taking a set of photographs of an object, rotating it on a turntable between each picture. If these images are stitched together and made draggable, the object will appear to rotate when it is dragged. Online maps provide a particularly successful application of image dragging. It is possible to zoom in on a selected point on a large-scale map to see more detail, and to drag the map to see adjacent areas. This application is more difficult to implement than the other examples we have mentioned, because maps can extend an arbitrary distance in every direction. It may be necessary to download new data as a map is dragged, effectively creating the image from pieces on the fly.

As we explained in Chapter 7, a Flash movie can contain elements known as movie clips, which are self-contained movies-within-a-movie, each with its own timeline. A movie may contain many movie clips, which play back in parallel. In the absence of scripting, this is merely a convenient way of organizing a complicated movie. However, movie clips can be controlled by scripting, just as whole movies can. A clip can be started, stopped, sent to a particular frame of its own timeline, or made to disappear, independently of any other clip or the main movie. Since scripts can perform arbitrary computation as well as controlling movie clips, this permits essentially infinite variations of behaviour, particularly as the computation can take account of variables such as the position of the cursor.

A simple example illustrates how novel forms of presentation can be implemented in such a fashion. A Flash movie can be constructed that consists of a single frame, in which the playback head is stopped by a script. In this frame are placed two movie clips, both of the same size as the frame, positioned with their top left corners at the top left of the frame. The foremost clip must have some transparent areas, so when the movie is played the user will see a composite frame made up of a frame from one clip overlaid on a frame from the other. Even if the two clips just loop – unless they are the same length – as the movie plays a sequence of different composite frames much longer than either of the individual clips will be seen. For example, if one clip has 13 frames and the other 11, there will be 143 frames before the movie repeats.

To make the movie more engaging, scripting can be used to arrange that the particular frame displayed from each clip at any moment is controlled by the position of the cursor. The clip at the front can be sent to a frame which is a function of the horizontal mouse coordinate; the clip at the back to a frame which is a function of the vertical coordinate. (For instance, when the cursor was half-way across the window, the front clip would go to its middle frame, when the cursor was at the extreme left, it would go to its first frame, and so on. Similarly, if the cursor was at the top of the window, the rear clip would be in its first frame, and so on.) If this is done, as the user moves the mouse, the two movies will interact in unpredictable (at least to the user) ways.

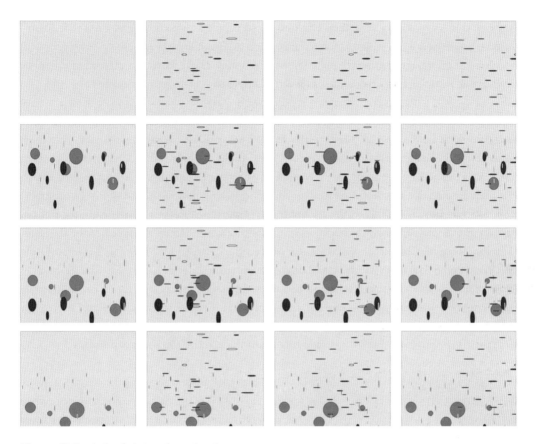

Figure 12.9. *A simple interactive animation*

Figure 12.9 shows a simple animation responding to mouse movements in this way. Across the top, we have shown the effect of moving the cursor along the top of the window: the small red objects in the front movie clip move from left to right. The leftmost column shows how the other movie responds to vertical movements down the left-hand side of the window. The other images show some of the ways in which frames will be combined when the cursor is in the middle of the window. Remember, though, that this is an animation, so the objects move when the cursor moves, and the recombination of frames is dynamic. (There are actually 60 frames in each of the two movies, so there are many more possible combined frames.) This example is purely a schematic illustration of the principle. By using more complicated movies, it is possible to tell non-linear stories in this way, as well as producing unpredictable patterns and pictures.

The idea of using mouse movements to control the timeline instead of controlling the physical position of an object can be used in more practical ways. Returning to the presentation of images of thin-section geological slides, we might want to simulate viewing a slide under polarized light. When this is done, the colours of the minerals will change as the slide is rotated. One way of showing this is by taking a succession of photographs through a microscope of a real slide illuminated by polarized light, which is rotated through a small angle between each photograph. This sequence of still images can be combined into a Flash movie, and when it is played back the slide will appear to rotate. (This technique is just an example of stop-motion animation.)

By adding extra controls, this simple animation can be transformed into a valuable interactive simulation that can be used by people without access to a real microscope and slides, to help them learn about the composition of rocks. Figure 12.10 shows a crude interface for this purpose. At the top of the panel of controls are conventional video player buttons. These are used to display the rotating slide as a movie, for passive viewing. The slider below them functions as a scrubbing control: its position is used to set the current frame of the movie, so as it is dragged to the right or left, the movie plays forwards or backwards, at a speed determined by the speed of the dragging. This is nothing new, but because of the linear relationship between the slide's angle of rotation and the frame number, it looks and feels as though dragging the slider pulls the slide round, almost as if the slider was attached to a mechanism that rotated the slide. Because of this linear relationship (which follows from the way the animation was created by rotating the slide through a fixed angle between taking each photograph), it is trivial to compute the angle of rotation, relative to the slide's starting point, and display it, as you can see to the right of the player controls.

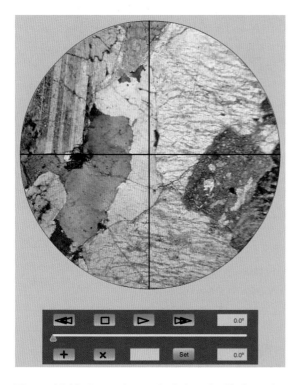

We can take advantage of this linear relationship to add other useful features. For instance, when minerals with a certain crystal structure are rotated under polarized light, they will go black at a certain point, which tells the geologist something about the orientation of the crystals. It is necessary to know the angular difference between the point where the crystal goes black and a reference orientation. In our example application, cross-hairs can be displayed by superimposing a static movie over the slide. This allows the reference to be set by dragging the slide until the crystal of interest is aligned with the cross-hairs. By clicking the **Set** button, this angle is recorded internally, and as the slide is dragged further, the angular difference is displayed below the absolute value of the current angle. Thus, when the crystal goes black, the angle can be read off the display.

Figure 12.10. *Interactive manipulation of a Flash movie*

A further refinement allows the user to compare the slide as it appears under single polarized light and "cross-polarized" light, which uses a pair of polarizing filters. Two movies can be prepared – one of the slide as it rotates under plain polarized light, the other under cross-polarized light. A button can be used to switch between the two. What this does is change the z-order of the movies, that is, it moves one movie to the front, hiding the other. At the same time, the current frame of the new frontmost movie is set to the same point as the other, so that the orientation of the slide is not changed. It therefore appears simply as if the cross-polarizing filter had been turned on or off; it is not evident to the user that they are actually switching between two different movies.

In this application, the scripts are really just moving the playhead and doing a little calculation, but the presentation conveys the impression of directly manipulating the object.

Dragging isn't the only form of interaction that is possible, but it is particularly effective in conveying the impression of being able to manipulate objects directly. A different impression is given by scripts that respond to cursor movements that are made without the mouse button being held down to perform a drag. We have already seen responses of this kind, in the form of rollovers, used to highlight links. Rollovers on Web pages are best implemented using CSS, as we showed in earlier chapters, but scripts can be used to achieve a similar effect. As we will see in Chapter 14, a script can easily change the source URL of an img element, which has the effect of swapping one image for another. Triggering such a script when the cursor moves over an image has the effect of making the image change on rollover. Formerly, it was common practice to create navbars out of small images of text, and to use a script to make rollovers for the navbar links by swapping the image of the link in its normal state for an image with some highlighting applied. Using images in this way instead of altering the CSS styling is superficially attractive, because it offers more control over the appearance of the links and the rollover effect. However, the practice suffers from accessibility problems and is discouraged.

A script can be used to alter the styling applied to an element (for instance, by changing the value of its class attribute). In this way, the principle behind CSS rollovers can be extended. In particular, a script can be used to change the appearance of an element when the cursor moves over some other element on the page. When this happens, we say that a **remote rollover** occurs. Remote rollovers triggered by hot spots on an image map can be an effective way of presenting supplementary information dynamically. For example, Figure 12.11 shows yet another way of displaying a geological slide. In this version, an image map is superimposed over the slide, with hot spots around the areas of interesting minerals. When the cursor moves over one of these hot spots, an arrow appears beside the name of the mineral. Here, for example, the cursor is over the black area near the bottom right, which is a piece of magnetite, as the arrow against its name in the list on the left of the page indicates. This effect was achieved using a script, activated by the

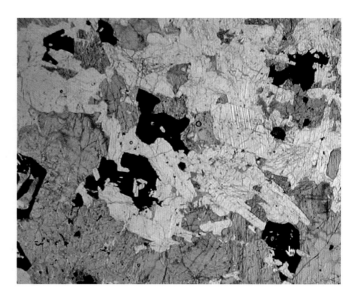

Minerals

Plagioclase
feldspar

Augite

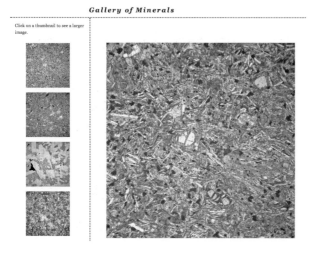Magnetite

Chlorite

Figure 12.11. *Displaying supplementary information using a remote rollover*

cursor moving over a hot spot, which changes the background of the corresponding item in the list of minerals on the left from a plain colour to an image with the arrow.

Similar techniques can be used in many other ways. For example, instead of changing the background, a script may be used to change the visibility of an element. This can be used to make "tool tips" appear only when the cursor is over a particular object or piece of text on the page. A similar method can be used to create drop-down menus.

Gallery of Minerals

Click on a thumbnail to see a larger image.

Although the term "remote rollover" is widely used, it is not only rollovers that may be used to trigger "remote" changes. Clicks on one element can trigger scripts that cause changes to other elements. A popular approach to constructing image galleries, such as the one shown in Figure 12.12, makes use of remote image swaps. When a click occurs on one of the small images on the left, a full-sized version is shown in the main area to the right. The substitution is implemented by changing the source URL of the img element for the main image, as we will describe in Chapter 14.

Figure 12.12. *An image gallery*

Figure 12.13. *Tabbed panels*

More complicated scripts are used to display images and text in various space-saving layouts, such as sets of collapsible and tabbed panels like the one illustrated in Figure 12.13. (Adobe's Spry framework, which is included with Dreamweaver, provides several easy-to-use "widgets" of this sort, as we describe in Chapter 7 of *Digital Media Tools*.)

There is another important use of scripting in interfaces: creating controls only when they are needed. This is a good way of reducing clutter. For instance, in our little application for viewing geological slides, the controls for setting a base value and displaying the angular difference are only shown when the cross-hairs are displayed, so when the angular difference is not being measured, the controls are not in the way.

Creating and altering controls dynamically in this way can improve usability too. Consider the example shown at the top of Figure 12.14, which might appear on a DVD movie menu. Does the red highlighting indicate that subtitles are already on, or that clicking on the highlighted word will turn them on? Either interpretation makes sense; both are used. As it stands, this is frustratingly ambiguous. On the other hand, the display in the middle of Figure 12.14 is quite unambiguous. Using a script, it is easy to arrange that when somebody selects ON, not only are the subtitles turned on, but the controls are rewritten as shown at the bottom of Figure 12.14. By making the controls sensitive to the state of the subtitles, we have avoided the possibility of their being misinterpreted. Any control which toggles the state of some parameter is subject to the same risk of ambiguity as this example. Where scripting is available, the ambiguity can and should be resolved in this way.

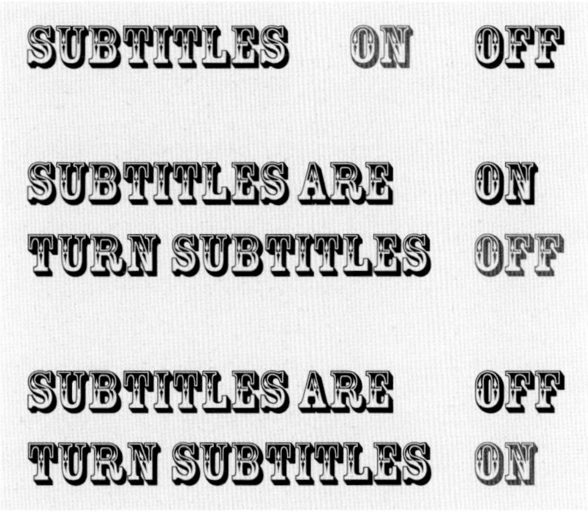

SUBTITLES   ON   OFF

SUBTITLES ARE   ON
TURN SUBTITLES   OFF

SUBTITLES ARE   OFF
TURN SUBTITLES   ON

Figure 12.14. *Resolving ambiguity in controls*

This technique of creating and altering controls dynamically is used on the Web (less often than it ought to be) to allow pages to use JavaScript but still to be usable by people whose browsers do not support it, or who have disabled it. If controls are provided whose operation is dependent on JavaScript, use a script to create the controls. If scripting is not supported, the controls will never appear, so users will not be presented with something that doesn't work. It is necessary to create the page so that there are fallback mechanisms for performing its essential functions in the absence of scripting. If necessary, parts of the page can be removed by a script and replaced with elements that provide an improved experience through scripting.

Slide Shows and Presentations

Although our illustrations of remote rollovers and image swaps are taken from Web pages, they can equally well be used in Flash movies. The time dimension that is available in Flash permits another way of interacting with the display of images: the slide show.

In its most basic form, a slide show is just a sequence of still images, to be shown one after another at a speed much slower than a movie, so that there is no illusion of motion. Slide shows can play automatically, with a designated interval between the slides, or under manual control with the next slide being displayed in response to mouse click or key press. The only controls required are **Next Slide** and **Previous Slide** buttons. Sometimes an extra button is provided for showing thumbnails of all the slides, turning the slide show into an image gallery. Despite the minimal controls and limited interactivity, slide shows can be the best means of presenting a set of images.

Slide shows are also a popular way of presenting information – in lectures, conference keynotes or sales presentations, for instance. In this case the images may be replaced by pages containing short pieces of text, each of which presents a single idea or key point. There is no need to limit the content of the slides to text; diagrams, charts, photographs and drawings are often interspersed to illustrate the text. Time-based media can also be used in slide shows. Movies or animations may be embedded in a single slide and will play while that slide is being displayed.

Slide shows may be created in Flash, or even in XHTML, using JavaScript to control the display of slides, but programs dedicated to the task are often used. The best known program of this sort is Microsoft's PowerPoint, which has become synonymous with presentation software, although there are alternatives, including Apple's Keynote and the Open Source Impress. These programs extend the slide show paradigm by adding transitions between slides and animations within slides, which allow the content to be built up or rearranged incrementally. Figure 12.15 shows some examples of transitions and animation. (As most readers of this book are probably aware from experience, these effects are easily abused, and often the simplest presentations are the best. We have shown these transitions here purely for purposes of illustration.) More justifiable uses of these sorts of effect include charts which build up over a series of slides, or a list of points displayed

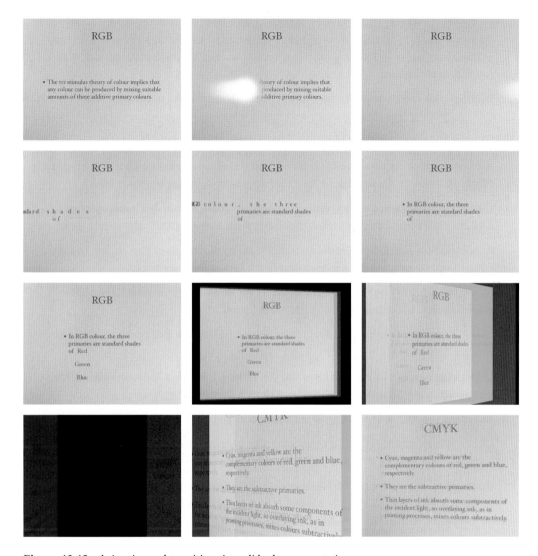

Figure 12.15. *Animation and transitions in a slide show presentation*

cumulatively. Presentations of this kind are created by allocating each part of the complete chart or list to a stage in a "build" – a sequence of slides that are displayed cumulatively.

Although PowerPoint and similar programs seem crude compared to Flash and modern Web applications they are nevertheless among the most widely used multimedia applications in the world. Much of their attraction lies precisely in their lack of sophistication. It takes little effort to learn the use of these programs, and even their most advanced features (such as they are) require no programming knowledge.

KEY POINTS

Controls used by software for playing time-based media are derived from an established set of buttons used by physical media players: play, pause, stop, rewind, fast forward.

Software allows controls to be more flexible than their physical equivalents.

Media player controls use semiotic and gestalt principles: a set of standard icons are arranged so that they are perceived as a unit.

In hypertext, some means of indicating that a link can be followed by clicking is required; there is no precedent for this requirement in traditional media.

Underlining is the most common signifier for links. It may be implemented in CSS as a text decoration or a bottom border on a elements.

It is common practice to add some highlight to links when the cursor moves over them, to indicate that something will happen if a user clicks.

Navbars and other collections of links may be moved to a separate area, where their function is evident without additional decoration.

Signifying the presence of links on images is problematic and no convention for this has yet been developed.

Users often expect images to have links on them. Provide a link where possible, but avoid using an image as the only link to a destination.

Scripting permits the creation of arbitrary controls and types of interaction.

Direct manipulation by dragging is used to move around panoramas, maps and other large images.

Controlling the timeline of Flash movie clips using mouse movements can present the illusion of directly manipulating objects on the screen, for example, by causing them to rotate when a slider is dragged.

Scripts can be used to implement remote rollovers, to display supplementary information, make image galleries and to display images and text in various space-saving layouts, such as tabbed panels.

Using scripts to display different controls according to context can reduce screen clutter and eliminate ambiguity in the user interface.

Using a script to create controls for operations that depend on scripting ensures that the controls will not be visible if they cannot be operated successfully.

Slide shows and presentations incorporating transitions, animated effects and time-based media can be created as Flash movies or using specialized software, such as PowerPoint.

Interacting Through Multimedia

The distinction between interacting with and through multimedia is not a precise one, but loosely speaking, controllers, hyperlinks and direct manipulation only allow you to control the display of the media content of Web pages and time-based media. By embedding controls in the content, we can provide means of interacting with some underlying data or computational process instead.

The most straightforward, if dull, way of providing an interface for this kind of interaction is by using standard dialogue controls, such as pop-up menus, check boxes, text input fields and buttons. Every computer user is accustomed to dialogues using controls of this sort, so it may be hard to consider them as examples of multimedia, but a typical dialogue box contains a mixture of text and graphics, along with moving elements, such as pop-up menus, which fall within the definition of animation.

XHTML has fairly extensive facilities for including controls for data entry in Web pages. Forms built out of these controls are used on the Web for entering address and credit card details in e-commerce sites, for entering search terms, for gathering data in surveys, for typing messages to be sent to help desks, and for a host of other purposes when a user has to submit some input.

Most often, controls are used to elicit input from users, which is then sent to a program running remotely on a Web server for processing. We will briefly describe the way the data is transferred in Chapter 16. For more details, consult *Web Design: A Complete Introduction*. Data which is entered into form controls can also be processed by scripts running in the browser. This is rarely useful on its own, but is often used in conjunction with processing on the server to provide extra convenience, for example by checking the validity of data before it is submitted, or by providing auto-completion in text fields (i.e. suggesting a set of possible values on the basis of the first few characters typed).

XHTML Forms

Figure 12.16 shows a simple survey form. (A stylesheet could be used to improve its appearance.) Most of the available types of interface elements used to enter data are illustrated in this form. In the "Course Details" section at the top of the form are three single-line *text input fields*, into which site visitors can type short pieces of text. The next section of the form uses *pop-up menus*, from which a single answer to the question can be chosen. The "Upgrading" question uses *radio buttons*; again, only one option can be chosen, this time by clicking on the button. The next section uses *check boxes*, which are similar to radio buttons, except that more than one box in the group can be checked. The "Other Comments" section provides a *text area*, which allows longer pieces of text occupying more than one line to be typed in. Finally, at the bottom of the form,

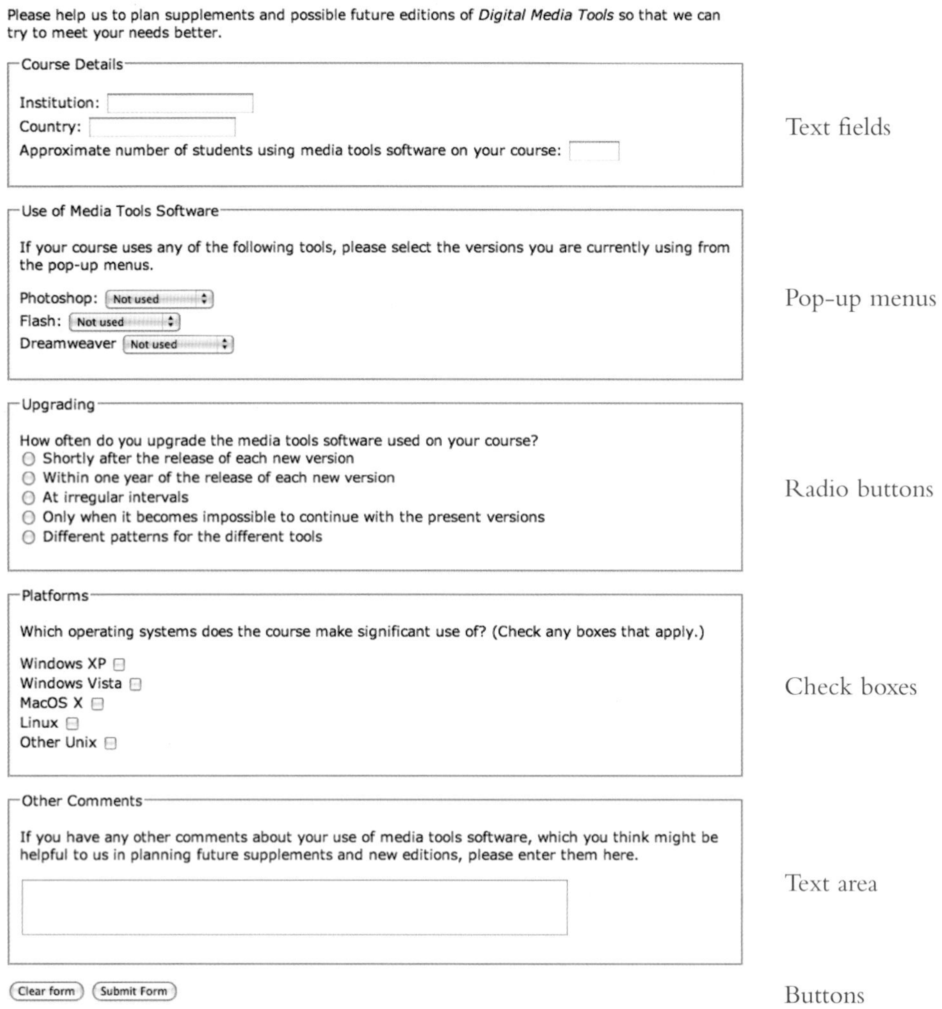

Please help us to plan supplements and possible future editions of *Digital Media Tools* so that we can try to meet your needs better.

Course Details

Institution: [   ]

Country: [   ]

Approximate number of students using media tools software on your course: [   ]

Text fields

Use of Media Tools Software

If your course uses any of the following tools, please select the versions you are currently using from the pop-up menus.

Photoshop: [Not used ⬍]

Flash: [Not used ⬍]

Dreamweaver [Not used ⬍]

Pop-up menus

Upgrading

How often do you upgrade the media tools software used on your course?
○ Shortly after the release of each new version
○ Within one year of the release of each new version
○ At irregular intervals
○ Only when it becomes impossible to continue with the present versions
○ Different patterns for the different tools

Radio buttons

Platforms

Which operating systems does the course make significant use of? (Check any boxes that apply.)

Windows XP ☐
Windows Vista ☐
MacOS X ☐
Linux ☐
Other Unix ☐

Check boxes

Other Comments

If you have any other comments about your use of media tools software, which you think might be helpful to us in planning future supplements and new editions, please enter them here.

[   ]

Text area

(Clear form) (Submit Form)

Buttons

Figure 12.16. *An XHTML form*

there are two ***buttons***, one for submitting the form, the other for resetting it to its original state. We will refer to all these types of element collectively as ***controls***.

Controls can appear anywhere in a document, but if they are being used in the conventional way, for accepting input to be passed to a program on the server, they must appear among the content of a `form` element. This element has two attributes which determine what happens to the data when the form is submitted. The value of the `action` attribute is the URL of a program on the server which will process the data. The `method` attribute determines how the data is sent to the server. We will explain this attribute in Chapter 16, when we describe how form data is sent to the server and processed there. For now, it is sufficient to note that the value of the method attribute is either "get" or "post".

The survey form has the following skeleton structure:

```
<form action="survey-script.php" method="post">
  controls and other elements appearing in the form
</form>
```

Controls can be intermixed with ordinary text elements, including headers and paragraphs, in the body of the form element. Some special elements for organizing forms are also provided.

Each of the controls is implemented as an XHTML element. All control elements have a name attribute. The name attribute's main purpose is to identify each value that is sent to the server. Again, we will explain how this works in Chapter 16.

Many of the kinds of control available in XHTML are implemented as input elements, whose type attribute is used to distinguish different sorts of control. For example, the tag `<input type="text" name="Country"/>` produces a text input field, whereas `<input type="submit" name="Submit" value="Submit Form"/>` produces a submit button. Figure 12.17 lists the principal values for the type attribute, and the kind of control which each produces. If the type attribute is omitted, its value is assumed to be text, so an input element defaults to being a text input field.

type Attribute	Control	Type-specific Attributes
text	text input field	maxlength
checkbox	check box	checked, value
radio	radio button	checked, value
submit	submit button	
reset	reset button	
button	push button	
file	file selector	

Figure 12.17. *Principal types of* input *element*

In our survey form, the set of text fields at the top was created using the following markup.

```
<fieldset>
    <legend>Course Details</legend>
    <p>
        <label for="inst"> Institution: </label>
        <input name="Institution" type="text" id="inst" /><br />
        <label for="cntry"> Country: </label>
        <input name="Country" type="text" id="cntry" /><br />
```

```
                  <label for="nos"> Approximate number of students ...: </label>
                  <input name="NumberOfStudents" type="text" size="6" id="nos" />
              </p>
          </fieldset>
```

The fieldset element is used to group controls together, and legend provides a field set with a title. These elements are responsible for the annotated boxes around the sections of our form.

Every input element may have a size attribute, which determines the width of the displayed control. Normally, you would use a stylesheet to set the size of form controls, but it is worth using the size attribute too, because styling of form elements is one of the areas in which browsers' stylesheet support is least satisfactory. The width is given in pixels, except for text fields, for which it is given as a number of characters.

Most form controls have some text near them, which serves as a label, indicating to the person filling in the form what each choice or field represents. The principle of structural markup, introduced in Chapter 10, suggests that the labels ought to be marked as such, according to their logical function in the document. The label element type is provided for just this purpose. It has an attribute called for, whose value is the id of the form control element to which the label is logically attached. Hence, if label elements are to be used, every control element that is to be labelled must have a defined id attribute. We have used label elements and id attributes in this way throughout the survey form.

Both radio buttons and check boxes are usually organized in groups, as in our survey example. In this case, all of the controls in the group have the same name. In the case of radio buttons, the browser will ensure that only one button in a group can be selected at a time. For check boxes and radio buttons, a value attribute must be provided. Every input element may have a value attribute, but it is compulsory for check boxes and radio buttons. For these, the attribute is used to provide the value sent to the server if the control is selected when the form is submitted. (The user never enters this value explicitly.) For all other types of input element, it provides a default value, which is displayed initially and whenever the form is reset.

These types of control may also use the Boolean attribute checked. The control will be initially selected if this is set (checked="checked"), otherwise it will not. For a group of radio buttons, this attribute should be set for one of the buttons, because the behaviour of the browser if none of the radio buttons is checked is undefined.

The radio buttons and check boxes in the survey form are marked up as follows. (Only the essential tags are shown here.)

```
<p>How often ...? <br />
    <input type="radio" name="Frequency" value="ShortlyAfter" id="shortly" />
    <label for="shortly"> Shortly after ... </label><br />
    <input type="radio" name="Frequency" value="OneYear" id="oney" />
    <label for="oney"> Within one year ... </label><br />
    <input type="radio" name="Frequency" value="Irregular" id="irreg" />
    <label for="irreg"> At irregular intervals </label><br />
    <input type="radio" name="Frequency" value="OnlyWhen" id="only" />
    <label for="only"> Only when ... </label><br />
    <input type="radio" name="Frequency" value="Differs" id="diff" />
    <label for="diff"> Different patterns ... </label>
</p>

<p>Which operating ...? (Check any boxes that apply.)</p>
<p>
    <label for="winxp"> Windows XP</label>
    <input type="checkbox" name="WindowsXP" id="winxp" /><br />
    <label for="winvista"> Windows Vista</label>
    <input type="checkbox" name="WindowsVista" id="winvista" /><br />
    <label for="osx"> MacOS X </label>
    <input type="checkbox" name="MacOSX" id="osx" /><br />
    <label for="lnx"> Linux </label>
    <input type="checkbox" name="Linux" id="lnx" /><br />
    <label for="unx"> Other Unix </label>
    <input type="checkbox" name="Unix" id="unx" />
</p>
```

Notice that we put the labels for the radio buttons after the input elements, not before them as we did with the text fields and check boxes. This produces a more readable layout for the form.

The implementation of buttons as **input** elements is a little messy. If the **type** is **submit**, then clicking the button will always cause the form data to be sent to the server; similarly if the **type** is **reset**, clicking will always cause the fields to be cleared and reset to their default values. By default, these buttons are labelled **Submit** or **Reset**, respectively, when they are displayed by the browser. If you want to use a more specific label, as in our example, you can assign it to the **value** attribute. This value will also be sent as part of the form data, in the usual way, which allows the server script to determine which of several buttons has been pressed, provided each has a different value. It doesn't usually make sense to attach a label to a button, because buttons label themselves.

Our buttons' markup is simple:

```
<input type="reset" name="Reset" value="Clear form" />
<input type="submit" name="Submit" value="Submit Form" />
```

If the **type** is set to **button**, a push-button control with a label provided by the **value** attribute is created. It doesn't do anything. That is, it doesn't do anything unless a script activated by mouse clicks is attached to it. (See Chapter 14.) This means that the button will not do anything on a browser that does not support scripting, or for which the user has disabled scripting. The use of such buttons cannot therefore be encouraged.

The final option we will consider for the **type** attribute of an **input** element is **file**. This causes the browser to display a control that can be used to select a file on the user's computer. This control usually takes the form of a button that opens a system file navigation dialogue. The contents of the chosen file will be sent with the data from the other controls when the form is submitted. This facility might be used on a software manufacturer's bug-reporting page, for example, to allow users to upload a system log file when reporting a bug.

The remaining kinds of form control are implemented using two other element types. A **textarea** element, not surprisingly, is used to create a text area. Besides the common attributes for all elements, and those for controls, it has two attributes which define the size of the box displayed on the page for text entry. These are **cols** (columns) and **rows**, which define the width and height in units of characters and lines respectively. For example, the comments box on the survey form uses the following tag:

```
<textarea cols="75" rows="4" name="Remarks" />
```

Since users may need to enter text that exceeds the bounds of this box, browsers are expected to provide scroll bars and to wrap overlong lines.

The remaining element type we will describe, **select**, is somewhat more complex. It is used for any control that presents several options to the user, from which one or more may be chosen. The presentation of a **select** element may take the form of a pop-up menu or a list. The user agent is free to choose the form of presentation, and different browsers may present the same **select** element in different ways. Some will use the operating system's normal pop-up menus and lists, others prefer their own variations. The **size** attribute of a **select** element specifies the number of lines of a list that should be displayed, if the element is presented in that form. The Boolean attribute **multiple**, if set, specifies that more than one item may be chosen. (This almost certainly means that the element will be displayed as a list.)

Where do the individual items to be selected come from? A select element must contain at least one option element. Usually, of course, it contains more than one. Each option element has a value attribute; if that option is selected, this attribute provides the value to be sent with the name of the select element in the form data. The content of each option may be used as the text for the corresponding menu entry. Finally, the Boolean selected attribute is used to indicate a default selection. If it is true (selected="selected"), the option will be shown as the selection when the menu is first displayed and chosen if the user makes no explicit selection

The XHTML code for the first menu in the *Use of Media Tools* section of the form in Figure 12.16 is as follows:

```
<label for="psver"> Photoshop: </label>
<select name="PhotoshopVersion" size="1" id="psver">
    <option value="No" selected="selected">Not used</option>
    <option value="LessThanCS">Earlier than CS</option>
    <option value="CS">CS</option>
    <option value="CS2">CS 2</option>
    <option value="CS3">CS 3</option>
    <option value="CS4">CS 4</option>
</select>
```

The code for the other menus follows the same pattern.

All of these controls are inline elements, so they must appear within some block element, usually a paragraph. CSS provides various means of positioning and aligning them, which are more elegant and powerful than the simple line breaks we have used here.

IN DETAIL

The elements we have described have been used successfully in Web forms for a long time. They do have some deficiencies, though, which new standards are trying to rectify. The draft HTML 5 specification adds some new types of input element, including URL and email, and extra attributes that can be used for checking the validity of data entered into fields and for pre-populating a form with data, without using scripting. XForms is a separate specification, intended for integrating form features with any XML-based language. As well as providing for data validation, it offers a means of describing the format of the data to be sent to the server when the form is submitted. This means that form data can be sent as structured XML instead of the *ad hoc* name/value pairs, which we will describe in Chapter 16.

Flash UI Components

It has always been possible to implement data entry controls in Flash by drawing something that looks like a conventional control, turning it into a movie clip and using some scripts to make its behaviour match its appearance. There are two drawbacks to creating controls in this way. One is that much of the scripting must be repeated for every control; the other is that it offers unbounded scope for designing the appearance of controls. This may sound like an advantage, but as we mentioned at the beginning of this chapter, one of the keys to usability is familiarity. Users need to be able to look at a control and know with reasonable certainty what it does. This was not the case with some of the controls created by imaginative designers in the early days of Flash.

Recent versions of Flash support the use of reusable *components*, which are described in the documentation as "movie clips with parameters that allow you to modify their appearance and behavior". In particular, a collection of user interface (UI) components is distributed with the Flash program. In effect, they are ready-made interface elements which have a standard appearance and behaviour. Individual instances of a component will differ in some respects: for instance, each time a "combo box" component is used to create a pop-up menu, it will have its own set of menu items.

Figure 12.18 shows how some UI components could be used to recreate part of the survey form we implemented in XHTML in the preceding section. (The dropped-down Flash menu is obscuring the Dreamweaver menu.) It is possible to customize the appearance of the components, but if the defaults are used the appearance will be identical on all platforms and in all browsers. While consistency may be considered desirable in many ways, it means that Flash-based user interfaces never look quite right on any platform.

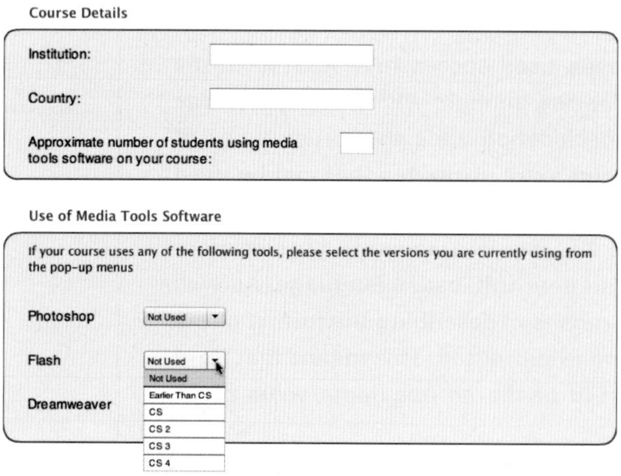

There are Flash UI components equivalent to all the XHTML control elements, except that every button must be created from the **Button** component, with its behaviour determined by the script that is attached to it. There are no distinct submit, reset and file upload buttons. Pop-up menus are provided by the **ComboBox** component, which is slightly more general than XHTML's **select** element. If the component is made editable, which is done by setting a property in the Flash environment, a text box is displayed above the menu. A user can either select an item from the menu or type something else into the text box, as shown

Figure 12.18. *Flash text field, label and combo box components*

in Figure 12.19, where the user has typed the value FreeBSD instead of choosing one of the menu items. Radio buttons, check boxes, text fields and text areas all have their own components, and there is a component that can be used to attach labels to controls. (Flash only has extremely primitive support for styling text: deprecated HTML appearance tags, such as <font> can be included in the label text, otherwise a script must be used to apply the styling.)

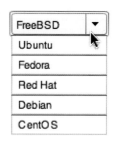

Figure 12.19. *A* ComboBox

The repertoire of Flash UI components extends beyond the set of standard XHTML input elements. Components are available for creating progress bars and sliders. A ColorPicker component can be used to create a primitive swatch selector with a field for entering hexadecimal colour codes and the **NumericStepper** component is available for creating fields for entering numbers: the small arrows at the right add one to, or subtract one from, the number shown in the field. As well as these components, which are illustrated in Figure 12.20, there are several others for displaying and editing data in various ways. There are also video player components, as we mentioned earlier.

┌─**IN DETAIL**──
│ **The Draft HTML 5 specification includes new types of input element and**
│ **other elements and attributes which will add much of the functionality of the**
│ **standard Flash UI components to HTML. The standard is under development**
│ **and is unlikely to be finalized or implemented universally before 2010.**
└──

There are significant differences between the way Flash UI components and XHTML control elements are used. Trivially, XHTML tags can be written by hand and styled explicitly with CSS rules, whereas Flash interfaces are usually built visually on the stage. This is a somewhat illusory distinction, though, because XHTML is often created in visual authoring programs, like

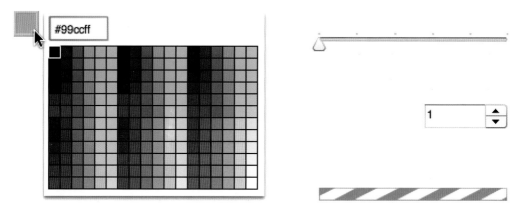

Figure 12.20. ColorPicker, Slider, NumericStepper *and* ProgressBar *components*

Dreamweaver, and Flash movies can be created outside the Flash authoring environment, using ActionScript and an XML-based layout language. However, there is a real distinction between the two in the way in which they are displayed. A Flash movie's appearance is fixed: components will always be the same size and occupy the same positions. As we explained in Chapter 10, text on a Web page can reflow, or change its size, which may radically change the layout and appearance of the page. Forms are always difficult to lay out well, but accommodating the dynamic appearance of Web pages makes them harder still.

More significantly, Flash UI components don't do anything useful without some scripting. Of course, a Web form on its own is useless, too, but it will always submit its data – any processing can be confined to a script on the server, which will often be designed and written almost independently of the form. A form built from Flash UI components must be supplemented by some ActionScript, even to make it send its data to a server. Often, data derived from the components is used by scripts within the Flash movie to perform non-trivial computation, the results of which are displayed in the form itself.

XHTML forms are created using markup. Flash UI components are more akin to the user interface widgets provided by the APIs of an operating system. They can be laid out in a visual design environment, but they need programming before they will do anything. In both cases, there may be additional programs running on a server that process data sent from a form.

Multimedia Interfaces

Despite our earlier remarks about familiarity, there are occasions when the standard controls are not adequate or appropriate, and some special device for interaction is needed. In such cases, it is necessary to strike a balance between convention and innovation. A new application may call for a new interface. If it does something that nothing else does, this will be inevitable. However, people are rarely willing to read a manual or watch a video to find out how to operate the controls. If they can't at least work out the basics straight away, they won't use the application.

In trying to use a new program or Web site, people will rely on their past experience of physical objects and of other programs and Web sites as their main guides. Almost nobody in the developed world needs to read a manual to find out how to operate the QuickTime Player, because almost everybody has used a video player, DVD or CD player. In fact the controls are different – they are not physical buttons at all. However, by using recognizable elements and symbols, with a familiar purpose, and by making sure the relationships between them are clear and understandable, interfaces can be built that, when taken as a whole, are new.

Flash can be used as a means of creating interfaces that are not constrained to a set of standard controls. Any movie clip may have scripts which respond to events attached to it, as we will

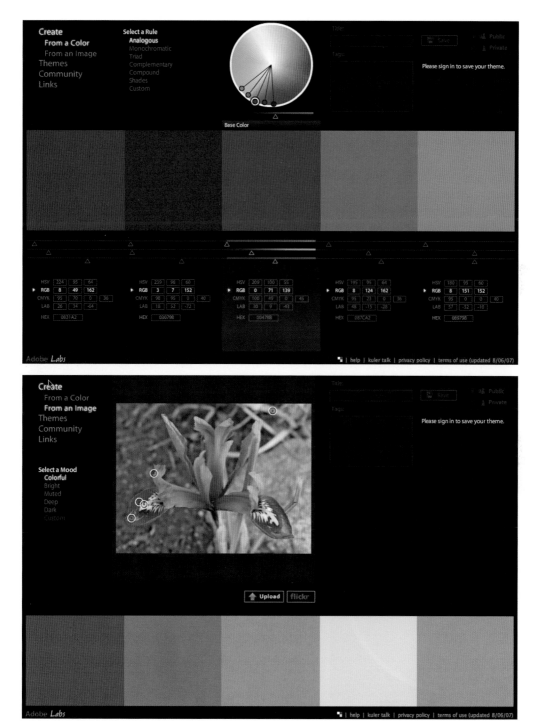

Reproduced with permission from Adobe Systems.

Figure 12.21. *Kuler*

demonstrate in Chapter 14, so it is possible to create "controls" with any appearance whatsoever. Movie clips have a timeline, so controls can easily be animated. Objects can be created or modified by scripts, so interface elements created in this way can change dynamically. Completely innovative user interfaces can be made relatively easily.

A pioneering example of the use of Flash to create a multimedia interface is Adobe's **Kuler** application. Kuler is an online application for creating and sharing colour schemes – that is, sets of colours which will go well together in a design. Figure 12.21 shows the interfaces it provides for creating colour schemes. (Unfortunately, the greyscale background used on the Kuler site, while good for providing a neutral context for the colour schemes, makes the text on the screenshots hard to read.)

At the top left of the page, under the heading **Create**, you can choose between the options **From a Color** and **From an Image**. The top screenshot shows the interface for creating a scheme from a colour. You begin by choosing a base colour, which is the starting point for the colour scheme. This can be done using the slider controls or by entering values in one of several colour spaces in the fields below the central colour swatch. These controls are Flash components, customized for this application. They resemble controls used in the standard interface to Adobe Creative Suite applications, so their operation is clear to anybody who has worked with those programs (which most people using Kuler probably will have done).

Above the base colour swatch is a colour wheel, with circles attached to radial lines on it that correspond to the five colours in the colour scheme. (Figure 12.22 shows the colour wheel in more detail.) To the left of the colour wheel is a menu headed **Select a Rule**. By choosing a colour harmony rule from this menu, you can generate a set of colours based on the rule. You can adjust the colours in the scheme by dragging the circles in the colour wheel. When you do so, the harmonic relationships between the components are preserved. As we suggested in Chapter 5, the mechanical application of rules may not always yield the best results when choosing colours, so you can also choose the **Custom** rule and adjust each colour by hand, either by dragging in the colour wheel or by using the controls below each swatch.

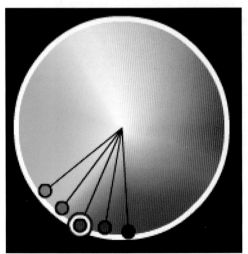

Reproduced with permission from Adobe Systems.

Figure 12.22. Colour wheel controls in Kuler

It should be clear that some complex computation of colour values is occurring behind this interface. The use of a specialized multimedia interface is entirely appropriate here, as it allows direct manipulation of visual objects corresponding to the colour data that is being calculated. The use of non-standard controls, specifically the colour dots on the wheel, is justified, because the operations being carried out are themselves non-standard. However, the use of single dots on a colour wheel to select HSB colours is well established, so it is easy for users familiar with colour wheels in image processing applications to appreciate how Kuler's grouped controls work as an extension of the more familiar colour picker.

Reproduced with permission from Adobe Systems.

Figure 12.23. *Selecting colour from an image in Kuler*

The lower screenshot in Figure 12.21 shows Kuler's alternative way of creating colour schemes, starting with an uploaded image. In this case, instead of choosing a colour rule, you can choose a "mood": Colorful, Bright, Muted, Deep or Dark, and Kuler will pick colours from the image that its algorithm considers to have the quality appropriate to the chosen mood. The pixels from which the colours are taken are shown with circles around them, as the detail in Figure 12.23 shows. In this case, it is not possible to adjust the colour scheme, except by moving individual colour selectors to a different place on the image by hand. The resemblance between these circles and the ones used on the colour wheel suggests that such movements are possible. The colour scheme's swatches change as the circles are moved, to provide feedback that this is happening.

We have stressed the use of Flash for creating multimedia interfaces because it is presently the only means of doing so relatively easily, in a platform-independent way, which can be embedded in Web pages to provide the interface to Web applications. For desktop applications, the Adobe Integrated Runtime (AIR) may be used to run programs with Flash-based interfaces on any platform.

However, Flash is not the only possibility for creating multimedia interfaces. The major desktop operating systems provide extensive APIs for creating, displaying and manipulating images and time-based media. Using a system programming language like C++ or Objective-C, a programmer can create interfaces every bit as media-rich as anything made in Flash. The result will probably be more efficient and is more likely to match other interfaces on the system, but programming at this level is harder and more time-consuming than writing ActionScript.

The technology defined by Web standards should provide an alternative means of creating interfaces to Web applications. Scripts triggered by events can be attached to any document element, and they can dynamically rewrite the page or alter stylesheets to hide or reveal elements, change their appearance or move them. JavaScript is not as powerful a language as ActionScript, though, and Web browsers have many inconsistencies in how they implement it, which makes JavaScript programming more difficult and less reliable than using ActionScript. Furthermore, the Document Object Model (DOM), which defines how JavaScript can interact with page elements, does not provide as much control over document elements as ActionScript does over movie clips. New Web technologies, such as SVG and HTML 5, promise more opportunities, but their development and adoption so far has been very slow.

JavaScript libraries, including Prototype, script.aculo.us, jQuery, SproutCore, Adobe's Spry, the Yahoo! Interface Library and a growing list of others, are available to make it easy to use the existing capabilities of JavaScript and the DOM to implement dynamic interfaces. These libraries do not enable you to do anything that you couldn't do otherwise, using your own scripts, but they remove the need for repetitive programming of common tasks, particularly in respect of ensuring compatibility with all browsers. Their facilities are usually packaged in code that makes them easy to reuse – some of the libraries we have mentioned could be described as frameworks. Many of the effects they enable depend on a technique known as AJAX, in which data is retrieved from the server by a script, instead of by loading a new page into the browser in the usual way. The retrieved data is typically used to rewrite the current page. We will describe AJAX in a little more detail in Chapter 16; for a detailed example, see *Web Design: A Complete Introduction*.

KEY POINTS

By embedding controls in multimedia, we can provide ways of interacting with data or computation.

Standard dialogue controls can often be used for such purposes.

XHTML provides input elements, for text fields, check boxes, radio buttons, etc., textarea for multiple lines of text and select and option elements for pop-up menus and lists. These elements are used within a form to send data to a script on the server.

Flash UI components provide the same controls, plus a few others. They must be combined with some ActionScript to do anything useful.

Flash movie clips and ActionScript can be used to create interfaces that are not restricted to using standard controls. Flash-based interfaces can be used in a Web browser or in desktop applications using AIR.

Multimedia applications which do something new may require innovative interface design. Users will draw on existing experience when trying to use new interfaces, so familiar features and ideas should be used where possible.

JavaScript and other Web-standard technology can be used to program multimedia interfaces, but the possibilities are less extensive than those which Flash offers. JavaScript libraries are used to make the task simpler.

Exercises

Test Questions

1 What controls would you provide for the user if you were designing a video player program? Are any of them redundant? If so, should they be omitted?

2 What are the two ways of underlining a link with CSS? What are the relative advantages and disadvantages of each method?

3 Why would it usually be inadvisable to change the font size of link text when the cursor moves over it? Are there any circumstances in which changing the font size would be an acceptable form of rollover effect?

4 Give three examples of the use of dragging to interact with images.

5 Are there any rollover effects that can be implemented on a Web page using JavaScript but not using CSS alone? Consider only cases where the effect is applied to the element that the cursor rolls over, not remote rollovers.

6 In an XHTML form, which type of control would you use for each of the following questions?

    (a) What is your email address?

    (b) What is your country of residence?

    (c) How many people live at your present address?

    (d) What sex are you (male or female)?

    (e) What party did you vote for at the last general election?

Which Flash UI components would you use for the same questions?

7 Give three reasons why Flash UI components should be used in preference to purpose-built movie clips for implementing controls. What factors might make you choose to implement your own Flash controls instead of using UI components?

Discussion Topics

1 If a program is available for several platforms (e.g. Photoshop on Mac and Windows), is it better for all versions to present an identical platform-independent interface or for each to use the native controls and conventions of the platform it is running on? Justify your answer.

2 A commonly cited rule in interface design is Fitts's Law, which is usually expressed as: "The time to acquire a target is a function of the distance to and size of the target." In the context of computer interfaces, "acquiring a target" means moving the cursor over something, such as a button or menu item, so that it can be clicked on. Compare the layout of the controls for the QuickTime Player and Windows Media Player shown in Figures 12.1 and 12.4. Which operations does Fitts's Law predict will be quicker in each player? Experiment with using both players. Does your experience confirm the prediction? If not, why not?

3 The relationship between the position of a slider and the value it controls is usually linear. For instance, when the scrubbing slider in a video player is dragged half way along its length, the movie will be at the middle frame, and so on. Are there cases where a non-linear relationship would be more useful?

4 Flash's UI components provide a standard set of interface elements, but it is still possible to create custom controls with unique behaviour and appearance in Flash, by drawing the controls and writing scripts from scratch. Why is this rarely done? Are there any circumstances under which the use of such unique controls would be justified?

Practical Tasks

1 Create a set of video player controls for Flash using the standard buttons arranged vertically down one side of the frame instead of horizontally at the bottom. Carry out some experiments with volunteers to assess whether this arrangement of buttons is significantly less usable than the standard arrangement. If your experiments suggest it is, explain why this might be so. If not, why do you think controllers are always arranged horizontally?

2 Experiment with using CSS to style links attached to images in different ways. Try just styling the rollover state – does this provide an adequate indication that a link is present? Can you devise a convention for links of this sort which could be used universally? If not, for a given page, can you devise a convention which would fit in with the design and be recognized by users as indicating the presence of a link?

3 Design a control for toggling some parameter between two states, which always shows unambiguously which state the parameter is currently in.

4 Create a short presentation on some topic that interests you, using PowerPoint, Keynote or Impress. Do not use any transitions or animated effects. Create a second presentation on a related topic, using any transitions and effects that appeal to you. Give the two presentations to an audience, and assess their reactions.

5 Experiment with creating colour schemes from colours and images at kuler.adobe.com. What different interfaces can you suggest for creating colour schemes from the same starting points?

13

Accessibility

■ **Background**

Problems with Access. Assistive Technology. WAI Content Accessibility Guidelines. Structural Markup. PDF and Flash.

■ **Textual Alternatives**

Still Images. Time-Based Media.

■ **Accessible Multimedia Content**

Colour. Motion. Text.

■ **Interactivity**

Keyboard Access. AJAX. Timing and Error Recovery.

People who have good vision, hearing and motor control, and have no cognitive disabilities, tend to take these faculties for granted and often forget that not everybody shares their good fortune. They also often fail to realize that their present condition is not likely to last forever. In Chapter 1, we mentioned that most media are visual in nature, and we have made an implicit assumption when describing interactivity that a mouse or other pointing device is used for input in conjunction with a keyboard. But for many people, seeing, hearing and using a mouse and keyboard are difficult or impossible, because they suffer from some congenital condition or have had an illness or accident, or are simply suffering from the common effects of advancing age.

It may be tempting to think that – although this may be unfortunate for those concerned – there is nothing to be done about it. This is not true. As we will describe shortly, technology is available to allow people with disabilities to perceive and operate computers, even if the normal means of doing so are denied them. However, the creator of a Web page or an application with a multi-media interface may have to make some extra effort to ensure that people who depend on such technology to use computers are not excluded.

Background

If a program or Web page is equally usable by everybody, irrespective of any physical or mental limitations they may suffer from at the time, it is said to be *accessible*. Accessibility has received most attention in the context of the World Wide Web. W3C's *Web Accessibility Initiative (WAI)* has produced sets of guidelines to help Web designers produce accessible pages. Recognizing that the Web is not restricted to the standard technologies, such as XHTML and JavaScript, but may include Flash, PDF and other media, WAI has tried in the most recent version of the guidelines to incorporate principles that apply to all multimedia. We will therefore base our description of accessibility on the Web and WAI's guidelines, but we will concentrate on the broad concepts which are more widely applicable. If you only need specific guidance on creating accessible Web pages, consult Chapter 9 of *Web Design: A Complete Introduction* or some of the specialized works listed on this book's support site.

Problems with Access

Figure 13.1 summarizes some of the problems that people may experience when using the Web and multimedia. The range is broad, and each may create different barriers. However, none of these problems makes it impossible to use a computer. This is fortunate, as many conditions can be mitigated by using computers and the Internet. For example, people who cannot see may not be able to go out shopping alone, but they ought to be able to shop using e-commerce Web sites.

	Typical Conditions	Problems with Multimedia	Assistive Technology
Vision	Blindness	Inability to perceive graphical interface	Screen readers, Braille displays
	Low vision	Difficulty seeing and reading	Screen magnifiers
	Colour defects	Inability to perceive information represented by colour	Browser option to set stylesheets
Hearing	Deafness	Inability to perceive information in sound	Signing avatars
	Tinnitus		
Movement	Repetive Strain Injuries	Inability to use pointing device and/or conventional keyboard	Alternative devices simulating keyboard input, voice input
	Limb injuries		
	Effects of stroke		
	Cerebral palsey		
Cognition	Dyslexia	Difficulty perceiving information conveyed in text	Screen readers
	Attention deficit disorders	Difficulty concentrating	
	Lack of sleep		
	Autism	Difficulty understanding content, problems with orientation and navigation	
	Down's syndrome		
	Effects of stroke		
	Alzheimer's disease		
Age-related	Presbyopia	Difficulty reading small text	Controls to increase text sizes
	Loss of coordination	Difficulty using pointing device	
	Short-term memory loss	Loss of orientation	

Figure 13.1. *Some conditions affecting accessibility*

They will have to rely on the aid of assistive technology such as screen readers, so Web designers must ensure that they do nothing to erect additional barriers to accessibility.

Making Web sites and programs with multimedia interfaces accessible can assist a wide range of people, but it most obviously and effectively helps people with physical and mental disabilities. If this doesn't make you feel a social obligation to maximize accessibility, you should be aware that in many countries there are legal requirements to do so. Legislation forbidding discrimination against people with disabilities is increasingly common around the world. Although there is considerable variation among the laws in different countries, generally, where disability legislation is in force, it is considered to apply to digital services and sources of information, including Web sites.

It is not possible to arrive at an accurate value for the number of people in the world who have difficulties that interfere with their use of computers. Not all problems are reported; the only figures that are readily available are those for people who are officially registered as disabled, but definitions of what qualifies as a disability vary from country to country. A broad picture can be obtained for some conditions, though.

There were, for instance, 364,615 people in the UK who were registered as "severely sight impaired" (blind) or "sight impaired" (partially sighted) at the end of March 2006. RNIB (the Royal National Institute for the Blind) estimated that about two million people in the UK have significant sight loss. In the United States, according to the latest census statistics, 1.5 million people over the age of 15 suffered from blindness.

An often-cited statistic is that 1 in 12 men and 1 in 200 women suffer from some defect in their colour vision, usually an inability to distinguish clearly between reds and greens. We will discuss how this may interfere with the perception of user interface elements later in this chapter. Since colour defects are largely genetically determined, their prevalence varies among different populations, and the figures quoted only apply to people of European origin. People originating from other parts of the world do not suffer as commonly from colour defects: among Asians the figure is estimated at 1 in 20 males, and among people of African origin it is as low as 3%, and the common form of deficiency is different from that found among Europeans.

Determining how many people suffer from repetitive strain injuries (more accurately known as cumulative stress disorders) is problematical, because of the difficulty in diagnosing the condition accurately — or even defining it. The US Bureau of Labor Statistics has reported that 60% of all reported occupational illnesses are RSIs; in 2001, a study reported that 10% of Canadians (an estimated 2.3 million people) had suffered some form of RSI "serious enough to limit their normal activities" in the preceding year. Both these studies concluded that the incidence of RSI was increasing.

The developed world presently has an aging population. That is, the proportion of people over the age of 60 is increasing steadily. With increasing longevity comes an increase in age-related problems, such as deteriorating vision, arthritis, loss of muscular strength and coordination and lapses in short-term memory.

The problems people with disabilities experience when accessing multimedia are related to problems potentially experienced by people using mobile devices. A mobile phone user may disable the loading of images when using the phone to access the Web. They are therefore in the same position with respect to those images as a blind person: if information is conveyed solely by images, they won't see it. Mobile phones may be used in bright sunlight, so that colours are hard to see on the screen: the user is temporarily colour-blind, as other people are permanently. It may be hard to hear when a device is used in a crowded place, so the phone user shares the problems of somebody who is hard of hearing. The absence of a mouse and proper keyboard on most mobile devices may make selecting objects on the screen as difficult for the phone user as it is for somebody with restricted mobility using a conventional computer. It follows that measures to enhance accessibility for people with disabilities often provide benefits for users of mobile devices too.

Such measures may also be appreciated by people with no actual problems. A survey carried out on behalf of Microsoft in 2003 estimated that 40% of computer users of working age used some of the built-in accessibility options or utilities on their computers. Interestingly, not all of these people absolutely needed to do so; many suffered no difficulties, or only slight ones that did not prevent their using the standard interface. However, they found it more convenient or comfortable to use options for changing the display or mouse behaviour. Accessibility will enhance their experience, allowing them to use their computers in ways that they prefer.

Hence, even if we add together all of the people who might possibly be suffering from some permanent or temporary condition that interferes with their use of computers, we still underestimate the potential benefits of accessibility.

Assistive Technology

To understand what is required to enhance accessibility, you need to know something about the devices that people use to help them overcome their limitations. *Assistive technologies* are software or hardware products that provide alternative forms of input and output for people who cannot use the conventional mouse, keyboard and screen. These products allow some users to interact with computers in ways that they would otherwise find difficult or impossible.

Among assistive technologies, the devices used by people who are blind or have very limited vision probably present the biggest challenge in connection with multimedia. These devices alter what psychologists call the "modality" of the interaction with the computer. This means that the information is transmitted via a different sense – hearing or touch instead of sight – and processed in the manner appropriate to that sense.

Screen readers are programs that use speech synthesis to speak text. Simple screen readers in effect scan a window, reading whatever they encounter in the order it appears. Simple programs of this type are sometimes called "screen scrapers", since they just take the text off the screen. More sophisticated programs work at a deeper level, rendering actual data as spoken text. These work particularly well in the context of the Web, where they are able to interpret the structural information contained in XHTML documents and use it to create a more meaningful verbal rendering of the page. For instance, if a page is laid out in two columns, using absolutely positioned div elements, a screen scraper might read straight across the columns, whereas a screen reader that could interpret the markup would distinguish the contents of the two div elements correctly.

As well as their obvious benefits to blind people, screen readers are also of use to people who are dyslexic or illiterate.

┌─IN DETAIL───

Screen readers may be independent programs, they may be built in to the operating system, or, for the Web, they may be implemented as browser extensions. The leading screen reader program, which is often taken as a *de facto* standard of screen readers' behaviour, is called JAWS. Both JAWS and its leading competitor, Window Eyes, only run under Microsoft Windows. (And both are very expensive.) Less powerful screen reading capabilities are built into Mac OS X in the form of VoiceOver, while FireVox is a free extension that adds screen reading to the Firefox browser on Windows, MacOS X and Linux.

Braille is a system of representing text as patterns of raised dots that blind people can learn to read with their fingers. *Refreshable Braille displays* use pins that can be dynamically raised or lowered to present a changing Braille representation of the text on a computer screen. Such displays are particularly useful to people who are both blind and deaf, and cannot therefore use a screen reader.

Both screen readers and refreshable Braille displays alter their users' perception of multimedia in two ways. First, they reduce it entirely to text, so that any information that is conveyed by images alone is lost. Second, they make everything into a time-based experience; when the elements of a Web page are read out or translated into Braille in order over time, for example, it makes sense to talk about the page's duration. This can be not only time-consuming but tedious; if every page of a Web site has a navbar across the top, a blind person using a screen reader might have to wait to hear all the navbar's links on each page before getting to that page's main content.

People with poor eyesight who can nevertheless see to some extent may need to increase the size of text on their screens in order to read it. The huge numbers of middle-aged and elderly people who suffer – as almost everybody over a certain age does – from the hardening of their eyes' lenses known as presbyopia find it difficult to focus at short distances, so they cannot read small print or text in a small font on a screen. For them, increasing the font size in their browser by a factor of up to two is usually sufficient to make text readable without the use of reading glasses (which are not very satisfactory for use with a computer screen). Almost all Web browsers now provide a means of doing this. The effect on the layout of pages not designed to accommodate changes in font size may be highly disruptive. As an alternative to increasing the size of text, most browsers allow the entire page to be magnified. This avoids any problems with layout, but means that horizontal scroll bars will often be needed, which interferes with usability.

People with more severely impaired vision may need to magnify the contents of their screen to a much greater extent. Screen magnifiers perform this function. As Figure 13.2 shows, extreme magnification may lead to an almost complete loss of context, especially on pages with a lot of empty space. (Both shots in this figure show the same area of the screen, at normal magnification on the left, zoomed to the maximum amount available by way of the Mac OS X Universal Access Zoom feature on the right.) A certain amount of trial and error will be needed for the person viewing this page to get back to the top navbar, for example.

Mice, trackballs and trackpads are among the main causes of RSI in computer users, so there are many people who must avoid using these devices. In that case – and if the injury does not prevent it – RSI sufferers use the keyboard for all input. Blind people cannot use a pointing device, since they are unable to see what they are pointing at, so they also rely on keyboard input. Many physical and cognitive disorders can make it difficult for people to point accurately with a mouse.

Figure 13.2. *Zooming in with a screen magnifier can lead to a loss of context*

Anybody who cannot use a mouse or an equivalent pointing device must use keys to move around the screen: sometimes the arrow keys can be used as a direct substitute for a mouse to control the cursor. More often in Web browsers some designated key or combination of keys is used to move from one element of a page to the next. Normally, the tab key is used to move between form elements, as it is in spreadsheets. A browser option is often available to include all elements, including links, among those that can be reached by tabbing, although some browsers require a modifier key to be held down, or use a different key for this purpose. Flash provides a similar way of moving between controls in a movie using the keyboard.

People who are unable to use conventional keyboards may need to use a variety of alternative devices. If they can use the mouse or an equivalent device, they can select keys by pointing at a virtual keyboard on the screen. If the use of a pointing device is impossible, a keypad consisting only of over-sized arrow keys can be used to move the cursor to make selections from the virtual keyboard or other controls, such as input elements. (Interaction with these devices is rather like using the arrow keys on a remote control to select options from a DVD menu.) In cases of severely impaired movement, switches controlled by blowing and sucking through a tube, or by eye movements, can be used in a similar way.

The common property of all these alternative input methods is that they generate the same input as a keyboard. That is, a program receives keystrokes, even though they were not generated by pressing keys. In most cases, the function of a pointing device cannot be simulated, so the fundamental action of pointing at something such as a link and clicking, or dragging a control of the sort we described in Chapter 12, is not possible.

WAI Content Accessibility Guidelines

The Web Accessibility Initiative (WAI) of the World Wide Web Consortium takes responsibility for ensuring that W3C technologies support accessibility, and for developing guidelines to be followed in order to maximize accessibility. The *Web Content Accessibility Guidelines (WCAG)* provide the most fully developed advice available on making Web sites accessible.

There have been two versions of WCAG. Version 1.0 provides the most widely recognized set of guidelines for making Web pages accessible. Legislation in many countries explicitly or implicitly requires some level of conformance to WCAG 1.0, which consists of 14 pieces of advice that should be followed by Web designers. Under each of these 14 guidelines, several checkpoints which may apply to a Web page are listed. If a page satisfies certain sets of checkpoints, it conforms to WCAG 1.0 at a corresponding level, so accessibility requirements can be expressed in concrete terms, as for example, level AA conformance. The checkpoints were mostly concerned with ways of using HTML to enhance accessibility. (WCAG 1.0 pre-dates XHTML.)

WCAG 2.0 is a more ambitious set of guidelines, which attempt to take account of developments in Web technology since WCAG 1.0 was published in 1999. In particular, the authors of the guidelines have tried to produce general advice that applies to content in different formats, not just HTML. It was intended that WCAG 2.0 should be applicable to future technologies.

WCAG 2.0 states that a page is accessible if and only if its content is *perceivable* by every user, any interface components it contains are *operable* by every user, the content and controls are *understandable* by every user and the content is *robust* enough to work with current and future technologies. These four principles of accessibility are sometimes collectively referred to by the acronym **POUR**. These principles are general enough to apply to any multimedia interface, not just the Web, so we can take them as a starting point for multimedia accessibility.

You should appreciate, as you read the rest of this chapter, that accessibility is not a property that can be checked completely automatically, in the way that validity of XHTML markup can. For instance, one of the features that is required of accessible Web sites is that all non-textual content should have a meaningful textual alternative. (We discuss this requirement more fully later on.) It is simple for a program to check that all non-textual content has a textual alternative, but only a human being can determine whether the alternative is meaningful.

Structural Markup

It isn't just accessibility guidelines that are more fully developed for the Web than for other types of multimedia. The technology itself provides more support for accessibility. That is, XHTML includes features that can be used to enhance Web pages' accessibility. By using these features correctly and avoiding others which may have the opposite effect, Web pages can be made accessible to everybody, not just to able-bodied people with good eyesight and hearing, perfect colour vision and no cognitive impairments who are able to make full use of a conventional keyboard and mouse. Alternatives to XHTML, particularly Flash, have less support for accessibility.

When you are making Web pages, the most important steps towards accessibility are the use of valid markup and the separation of structure from presentation. Assistive technology is not always as forgiving as a graphical Web browser when presented with invalid documents, so validators should be used to ensure that your markup conforms to the relevant standards. A document type declaration should, therefore, be included, and all the compulsory page elements, such as title, should be provided.

Using valid markup is the key to the robustness component of POUR. We have Web standards to ensure that pages will work with any browser or other user agent, including those that do not yet exist. If you write code that does not conform to the standards, new user agents will not be able to display your pages correctly unless they have been written to emulate non-standard behaviour.

Standards are supposed to prevent that necessity. The standards provide a stable specification, which applies to assistive technology for the Web as much as it does to graphical Web browsers.

Validators can be used to determine automatically whether documents conform to the rules specifying which elements may appear where. They cannot tell whether elements are being used for their intended purpose, but if a page is to be accessible they always must be. Don't, for example, use **blockquote** elements to make indented paragraphs, but do use them for lengthy quotations. Put a meaningful title in the content of the **title** element. (Almost all Web creation software will put the default "title" **Untitled**; don't just leave it like that.) Using elements suitably in this way will make it easier for assistive software to determine the meaning of the document and present it in an appropriate way.

It is particularly important to use heading elements (**h1**, **h2**,…) correctly to mark the main divisions of a page. Screen readers usually include a means of presenting all the headings on a page, which provides their users with a quick summary of the page's contents and structure similar to the overview that sighted users obtain by scanning the page quickly for distinctively styled headings. Screen readers can only create their list from correctly marked up headings. If you just set a single-line paragraph in large bold type with some extra space above it, sighted readers may recognize a heading, but screen readers won't. It is also important to nest headings properly, and not, for example, to jump from a level 1 heading (**h1**) to a level 3 heading (**h3**), with no intervening level 2 heading, since the heading levels convey the hierarchical structure, and an omitted level may lead users to think that they have missed something.

Another important special case is the use of the **label** element in conjunction with form controls. As we explained in Chapter 12, this element is used to associate labelling text explicitly with a control. By using a **label** instead of just placing the text in the vicinity of the control, you make it possible for programs to discern the relationship between label and control. Some screen readers have a special form-filling mode, which depends on being able to do this in order to tell their users about each control. In the absence of proper **label** elements with correct **for** attributes, screen reader users may hear nothing except the words "Text field", with no indication of what the field is for. You should therefore always use **label** elements in the way we described, and never rely on proximity alone for labelling the controls in a form.

By using CSS for controlling presentation you can provide layout and typography that is as rich and sophisticated as you like for the benefit of visitors who can see, without interfering with the information about structure which is embodied in the XHTML markup. Users who find it difficult to see the page displayed using your stylesheets can use their own to present it in a way that is suited to their needs. For instance, an aural stylesheet which describes how a screen reader should speak the page can be used by blind people. People with poor eyesight can specify a stylesheet that uses large easy-to-read fonts, and provides high contrast between foreground text and the page's background. People with defective colour vision can use a stylesheet to specify a colour scheme that does not use combinations of colours that they find confusing. You should do nothing to interfere with this capability, such as using deprecated HTML attributes to specify presentation in the markup.

This list of accessibility techniques for Web designers is by no means complete, but it should serve to demonstrate that using XHTML correctly in itelf helps make Web pages accessible. In contrast, when you are using Flash or PDF, you must make positive efforts for the sake of accessibility.

PDF and Flash

There is a common misconception that Web pages constructed from pure XHTML and styled with CSS are the only form of accessible multimedia, and that PDF and Flash cannot be made accessible. The idea was probably encouraged by one of the guidelines in WCAG 1.0, which reads "Use W3C technologies and guidelines". However, this does not mean that W3C technologies are the only accessible ones. This is even more true now than it was when WCAG 1.0 was published, because of improvements in the accessibility of some other technologies.

PDF, in particular, can be highly accessible. This may sound unlikely, because PDF is best known as a format that preserves the layout and appearance of documents, the antithesis of separating structure and content from appearance. However, recent versions of the PDF specification include support for a system of tags, similar to XML tags, which can be inserted into a PDF document to describe its structure by identifying elements such as headings, paragraphs, lists and figures. The tags have no effect on the appearance of the document when it is displayed in the normal way, but programs that read PDF can use the tags to identify the logical components of the document and present them in a way suited to any assistive technology that is being used.

The accessibility of PDF depends on the program that reads it, as well as the document itself. Adobe Reader can read text out loud (without the need for a separate screen reader) and reflow the text so that it is more readable. The program has other accessibility features built in to it, including the ability to scroll documents automatically, so that people with motor difficulties do not need to drag scroll bars or click a **Next Page** button repeatedly. Other programs used to display PDF may not provide all these features.

The main accessibility problems with PDF arise from the difficulty of creating tagged PDF in the first place. Adobe's own professional applications, such as InDesign, will export tagged PDF. Creating tagged PDF from other programs relies on Acrobat, or some utility derived from it. Simply saving a document as PDF, as you can in any program on Mac OS X, for example, will not generate tags. Adobe Reader will try to infer a tagged structure from an untagged PDF, but the result may not be accurate. In any case, it is recommended that Acrobat be used to fine-tune the tagging of documents or to change the reading order, if the default is not appropriate.

Flash is more problematic. There is no systematic structure that is shared by all Flash movies and any structure that a movie does have is hidden in the relationships between the objects and symbols it is made from. In addition, Flash is inherently graphical, unlike text-based formats such as XHTML.

There are two routes to making a Flash movie more accessible. The first makes use of accessibility features built into the Flash Player and authoring environment. Recent versions of the Player have support for a technology called *Microsoft Active Accessibility (MSAA)*. MSAA can act as a bridge between the Flash Player and screen readers such as JAWS, so that the contents of a Flash movie can be made available in spoken form. The Flash program itself has an accessibility panel, in which descriptions of elements of the movie and text alternatives to them can be set. It is possible to have any text associated with an object made available to MSAA. Parts of the movie can be designated to be ignored by screen readers, allowing purely decorative elements to be hidden. For controls, a tab order can be defined, to optimize the way people who cannot use a mouse navigate through a set of controls. Flash provides a set of accessible components, which can be used to add accessible controls to a movie with little extra effort. As its name may suggest, MSAA is a technology that only works on Microsoft Windows, so this route is not available if you want your Flash movies to be accessible on all platforms.

The second route to accessible Flash movies is by way of ActionScript. Flash movies are entirely scriptable: it is possible to make them respond to keyboard input so that the use of a mouse is not needed. If the standard UI components described in Chapter 12 are used, tab and arrow keys will automatically work as required for keyboard access to controls. Scripts can be used to enlarge text and other objects (Flash is vector-based so this can be done without loss of quality), scripts can be attached to controls to stop playback for users who find moving elements disturbing or hard to follow, and so on. ActionScript can be used to play a synchronized commentary. Using scripting in these ways does not depend on MSAA, but it cannot duplicate the function of MSAA and pass text on to a screen reader.

Where MSAA is available, scripts can also be used to set the accessibility properties that would otherwise be set in the accessibility panel, so even fully dynamic Flash movies, parts of which are created by scripts as the movie runs, can be accessible. It is possible for a script to determine whether a screen reader is being used when a movie is played, so the movie can behave differently for users with screen readers. Making a movie adapt itself dynamically for accessibility in this way demands extra work from the Flash programmer.

Textual Alternatives

Screen readers can only read text. If non-textual multimedia elements – images, sound, animation and video – are to be perceivable by all users, as required by the POUR principles, some way of making them evident to screen readers and similar technology is required. Text is also a way of making audio perceivable by deaf people. Providing alternatives that are purely textual is therefore one of the most important steps in making multimedia accessible.

Still Images

The mechanism by which textual alternatives are attached to images depends on the multimedia technology being used. In XHTML, as we explained in Chapter 10, the img element has an alt attribute, which allows a short textual alternative (often abbreviated to *alt-text*) to be provided for images. If no alt attribute is provided, screen readers will normally speak the entire URL of an image. This usually conveys no useful information, and is exceedingly tiresome to listen to. In XHTML the alt attribute is compulsory, so checking the validity of a document will verify that every img has its alt. It cannot, however, determine whether the alt-text is a proper alternative to the image. A document will validate even if the values of all the alt attributes it contains are empty strings or pure gibberish, like "dkfgdhjag". Some Web page creation programs set the alt-text of images to their URLs by default. This is entirely pointless and does not constitute an alternative to the image.

In tagged PDF, the `<Figure>` tag serves roughly the same purpose as img in XHTML. It too can have alt-text attached to it, though you must use Acrobat Pro to do so. There are two options: the "alternate text" is a general textual alternative; the "actual text" is used for the special case where the image is a picture of some text, as might be the case in a scanned document for example.

In Flash, any movie clip may be given a textual alternative by selecting it and entering the text in the **Accessibility** panel. Each clip may have either a short name, a longer description or both. Screen readers read both by default, so the distinction is just one of convenience. Still images included in a Flash movie can be given text alternatives by converting them to movie clip symbols. This does not affect their appearance or behaviour, but makes it possible to add the alt-text (and to control them with scripts). A useful feature in Flash is the ability to group several images or other objects together and provide a single textual alternative to the whole group. (We stress again that these textual alternatives are only available to screen readers on Windows, via MSAA.)

Irrespective of how it is associated with an image, the alt-text must be chosen to provide a suitable textual alternative. What constitutes a suitable textual alternative depends on how the image is being used. An image might convey information, as in the case of a pie chart, it might be functional, as in a graphical button, it might be there simply to be looked at, as in a reproduction of a painting or a photograph of scenery, or it might not be any of these, as in a small image used as a marker for unordered lists or a textured background. Each of these cases must be treated differently.

To start with the easiest case, images such as list markers, which are largely decorative in nature, should be given alt values of "" (the empty string) in XHTML, left untagged in PDF or not made accessible in Flash. These measures will cause screen readers to ignore the image entirely. Since the image provides no information or functionality, this is the best thing to do. It allows the screen reader to get on to the meaningful content, without distracting, or possibly confusing, the person listening to it. Note that in XHTML it is necessary to add the attribute with its empty string value explicitly. Simply leaving it out will cause the screen reader to read the image file's URL, as well as invalidating the markup.

If an image is there to be looked at, the experience it evokes is not going to be provided for people using screen readers (or text-only browsers). The standard advice for such images is to provide alt-text with a short description of the image, so that such users can understand what is being shown. Without this minimum of information, they might become confused. Hence, alt-text should provide a clear indication of what the image shows. For example, a news photograph might be given the alt-text "The Prime Minister eating asparagus". Remember also that people using screen readers will hear this text spoken. While it should be short, so that it does not take too long to convey its meaning, it should not be so short that it may be missed or misunderstood. "PM pic" would not be a good alt-text for the example just given.

Some images convey information. An example would be a pie chart showing, for instance, the distribution of browsers among the visitors to a Web site. Such information can usually be presented in an alternative, purely textual, way. In this example, a list of browsers, with the percentage values for each could be given. However, this list would be too long to be used as alt-text for the image, and could benefit from some markup, which cannot be applied within the value of the alt attribute.

Many pictures can be described at greater length for the benefit of people who cannot see. This may be tricky with something like a reproduction of a painting, or even a scenic photograph, but some attempt to describe it in a way meaningful to those who cannot see should still be made.

Various techniques are used to hide such extended descriptions from users who can see the image, but you might well ask yourself why you should hide the long description from most users. If you have gone to the trouble of writing a description, why not let everyone read it if they want to? Redundant information is not a bad thing in itself; people often benefit from being told the same thing in different ways. If space allows, there is much to be said for putting the long description right next to the image it describes. If this is impossible or undesirable, a link or its equivalent that points to a long description can be provided, with a suitable label.

┌─IN DETAIL───

XHTML provides the longdesc attribute of the img element as an intended means of providing lengthy textual alternatives. Its value is a URL which points to a separate document containing the alternative descriptive text. Although this attribute has been provided in versions of HTML for a long time, it has not proven to be a very successful mechanism. Almost all graphical browsers simply ignore it, even if image loading is turned off. Only the high-end screen readers implement longdesc in such a way that a user can access the long description of an image. Neither of the putative successors to XHTML (XHTML 2.0 and HTML 5) includes the longdesc attribute in their latest draft specifications.

Images that provide functions, such as graphical buttons and links, should have alt-text that clearly describes their function not their appearance. For instance, the popular icon used for links to the home page of a site should have alt-text Go to the Home Page, not A drawing of a little house. However, the use of images as the only source for links should generally be avoided; if clearly labelled textual links are used instead, their meaning will be clear to everybody.

Time-Based Media

Time-based media require textual alternatives at least as much as still images do. Since video and animation often include soundtracks, and sound is sometimes used alone on Web pages, when considering time-based media we must take account of the needs of people who cannot hear, either because they are deaf or hard of hearing, or because they are using devices that do not support audio. These people require written text alternatives to the audio content. For video and animation, as for still images, we need to consider people who cannot see. Their needs may be met by an audio equivalent to the visual content, such as a spoken commentary track.

Any controls for starting and pausing playback, and so on, should not require the use of a pointing device. This is usually a property of the plug-in being used, which cannot be controlled by the designer, but Flash movies with embedded controls must take account of the needs of people who cannot use a mouse.

Ideally, time-based media should be provided with a synchronized textual alternative, in the form of captions or sub-titles, comprising a transcript of any dialogue or commentary and representations of any significant sounds that occur, interspersed with a description of what is happening in the scene being displayed. This is a tall order, especially for live video, and a lesser compromise may be required. On the other hand, even providing synchronized captions does not satisfy the needs of all users. Some people who are deaf, especially those who were born deaf, are more fluent in sign language than they are in written language, so to provide the best experience for such people, a sign language interpretation should be supplied (as it often is for televised transmissions of important political events, for instance). Since the sign languages used in different countries are different, this presents considerable problems, and is a task that would usually require the services of a specialist agency.

XHTML provides no means for attaching synchronized text tracks to video, but all the major Web video formats do. Hence, adding these tracks is part of the video post-production process. Plug-ins do not always make it possible to turn captions on and off, so it may be necessary to provide two versions of a video clip, and allow users to choose which one to play.

Software tools for creating caption text and adding timecode to it in order to synchronize it with video are available. Advice on how to write captions so that they convey their information most efficiently can be obtained from various organizations concerned with captioning; a considerable body of experience has grown up from the use of captions in television. To augment the synchronized captions, a complete transcript should also be supplied. Whereas captions that are part of the embedded video may not be accessible to screen readers, a transcript of this sort always would be, so it can serve as an alternative for blind users. Transcripts can also benefit people with cognitive difficulties who may have trouble following what is going on in a video, and people who are learning the language used on the soundtrack. As with captions, the transcript should include a description of significant actions and sounds, as well as any spoken content.

If it is not feasible to supply a synchronized textual alternative or a full transcript for embedded time-based media, you must at least provide a short alternative, as you do for images. Ideally, the description should give some indication of what happens, but if this is not possible in a few words the text should state the subject of the video or animation. Before falling back on this option, you should consider the implications. If a video screencast is the only form of documentation you have provided for a computer program and you do not provide a synchronized textual alternative or a transcript, you have denied your program to anybody who cannot access information presented as video.

KEY POINTS

Providing textual alternatives to images and time-based media is one of the most important steps in making multimedia accessible.

Alt-text can be attached to images in XHTML, PDF and Flash.

Alt-text should provide a suitable alternative to the image, so its form will depend on how the image is being used.

Purely decorative images should have empty alt-text so that screen readers will ignore them.

Alt-text for images intended to be looked at should provide a short description of the image.

Images that convey information should be accompanied by text that provides the same information.

Images that provide functions should have alt-text that clearly describes their function, not their appearance.

Audio and video should have a synchronized textual alternative, in the form of captions or subtitles.

Synchronized textual alternatives to time-based media should be supplemented with a complete transcript.

If a synchronized textual alternative and transcript cannot be provided, static alternatives to the time-based media should be made available as for images.

Accessible Multimedia Content

Certain types of multimedia content can present special difficulties to certain groups of people. Usually, a little care and thought is all that is needed to avoid problems, but you need to be aware of the issues involved if you are to avoid creating accessibility problems unintentionally.

Colour

If colour is used unwisely, people with defective colour vision may be unable to distinguish some material displayed on a screen. To take an extreme – and, we hope, unlikely – example, if you use green text on a red background of the same brightness (or vice versa), people who are red/green colour-blind will be completely unable to read it – indeed they may not even realize that there is text on the page. The top row of images in Figure 13.3 shows such an example, together with the way it is likely to appear to someone who is red/green colour-blind (centre image), and the version they would see if they switched their screen to greyscale in an attempt to avoid the problem. In situations where colour is used to convey information, as when red is used to highlight compulsory fields in a data entry form, people who cannot distinguish the colours used may fail to perceive the necessary information.

You can use programs that simulate what people with various colour defects see, in order to find out whether a particular combination is likely to cause problems. More simply, you can just switch your display to greyscale. Although few people are unable to distinguish any colours at all, this will show you the tonal contrast present in your colour scheme. As the lower row of images in Figure 13.3 illustrates, tonal contrast can compensate effectively for an inability to distinguish between different hues. Somebody who is red/green colour-blind will be able to read red text on a green background, provided the red and green differ enough in tone. (Just as anybody can read red text on a red background, if one red is light and the other dark.) Maintaining high tonal contrast between text and its background will ensure that information can be perceived by the

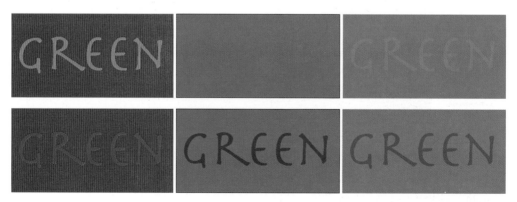

Figure 13.3. *Green text on a red background may not be visible at all*

maximum number of sighted users, and is generally to be recommended in all cases. WCAG 2.0 stipulates specific values for minimum contrast in different contexts.

As Figure 13.4 demonstrates, it is not always immediately obvious which precise colour combinations in the red and green areas of the spectrum will work and which will not. The apparently bold contrasts in the plain version of the page on the left disappear almost completely, leaving the links invisible to somebody with a red/green vision defect, even if they switch to greyscale. Notice that it isn't the red in itself that is a problem – the red-coloured text can easily be read against the white background on the left, even though the actual hue cannot be perceived. You might think that the version of the page on the right would be altogether less readable, because the background is fussy and there is a green cast over it all which might cause problems with the dark red text. But in fact, because of the high tonal contrast, this page is perfectly readable without its full colour, or indeed any colour.

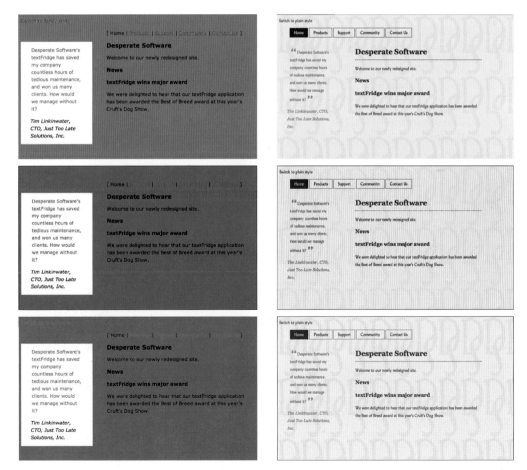

Figure 13.4. *Red/green confusibility and the effect of tonal contrast*

Where diagrams or other created graphics are used, colour schemes should also be chosen to maintain good tonal contrast. For instance, in a pie chart, the colours of adjacent slices should contrast in tone. High contrast is, in itself, of great benefit to anybody with low vision, so maintaining it wherever possible contributes to accessibility for a much larger group of people than those who have problems distinguishing different colours.

If a page uses a patterned or textured background, you should make sure that there is even more tonal contrast between it and any text that is superimposed on it. Your own eyes should tell you if a background texture is interfering with the legibility of text, but if in doubt, avoid the use of textured backgrounds.

The WCAG guidelines also require you to ensure that all information conveyed with colour is also available without colour. Context or additional styling should be used to supplement any colour coding. For instance, where a colour is used to denote which of the fields in a form the user is required to complete, an asterisk, or the word "required", can be placed next to the field's label, or the label can be set in bold or italic. The classic example is the default style of displaying links on Web pages. They are shown in blue and underlined, so anyone who cannot perceive the colour will see the underlining.

Using tonal contrast and alternative signifiers does not only benefit people with classical colour vision defects. Anybody with poor eyesight will have difficulty distinguishing text from its background if there is little contrast between them. Many older people find it hard to distinguish between close colours and tones, because the amount of light entering the eye decreases as the lens becomes less transparent with age.

Motion

In individuals with what is known as a "photosensitive seizure disorder", epileptic-like seizures may be triggered by flashes at certain frequencies. These seizures are serious and can lead to hospitalization; potentially they can lead to injury or death. Flashes of a saturated red colour are most likely to trigger photosensitive seizures.

There are detailed technical definitions of flash thresholds that must be avoided to prevent the possibility of seizures being triggered, but there is a simple and safe way of guaranteeing that you will never be responsible for them: never use blinking or flashing content. On the Web, this means avoiding the value blink for the text-decoration property in CSS. Generally, it means never creating animations that use strobe-like effects or other rapid alternations of images.

Another, less dramatic, reason for avoiding blinking is that it has a distracting effect. Most people can cope with this, but people suffering from certain cognitive problems, including attention deficit disorders, may find blinking elements so distracting that they are unable to use an interface that blinks. If you are certain that your blinking will not be dangerous and you are convinced that its function of attracting attention is really necessary, you should arrange that nothing blinks for more than about three seconds.

Moving elements of all kinds can be difficult for people with various sorts of cognitive problems. In particular, people who have difficulty reading will find it even harder, or impossible, to read moving text. If you have found a compelling use for crawling or rolling text, you should, in the interests of accessibility, provide a way for users to pause the movement of the text to give themselves a chance to read it. This will be of general benefit, in fact, as people read at a wide range of different speeds, especially if the text is not in their first language.

Text

Although text is accessible to screen readers and can be read by people who have trouble hearing, the textual content of Web pages may nevertheless present accessibility problems to some people.

In the first place, text that is an integral part of an image is not accessible to screen readers. There are several circumstances under which this sort of text may be used. The image may originate in some other medium – for example, it may be derived from a poster – so that the text cannot be isolated. The image may be a scan of a document containing text, which has not been processed by optical character recognition (OCR) software. On the Web, some designers who cannot learn to live with the way in which Web browsers may substitute fonts for those they have carefully chosen set type in a graphics program and export it as a GIF image, which is then embedded in the page in an **img** element. This last possibility is explicitly forbidden by WCAG 2.0, except for "decorative text" and logos, but it still happens.

Providing alt-text for any textual image makes the text available to screen readers again (use the "actual text" option for tagged PDF), but users cannot change the font size. As a general rule, you should assume that at least some visitors to your site will want to use a type size bigger than the one you originally selected, whether it is because they are not young enough to read small type easily or because they are using a high screen resolution. If you must use an image as text, don't use small type in the image.

A quite different kind of barrier to accessibility lies in the natural language used on a page. If a screen reader cannot identify whether the text, or part of it, is in Finnish, say, or in Japanese, it will have trouble reading it out. Software is not usually intelligent enough to determine the language of a piece of text automatically, so some annotation is required to communicate this information.

In XHTML the natural language used on a page is indicated by the lang and xml:lang attributes of its html element. (It is advisable to use both of these attributes in XHTML documents, to allow them to be served as either HTML or XML.) These attributes can be used with almost any element to indicate a change of natural language, such as a French word or phrase embedded in a paragraph of English:

```
<p>Creating successful Web applications requires business <span lang="fr"
xml:lang="fr">savoir faire</span> as well as technical skill.</p>
```

In a similar way, the language property can be set for any tag in a tagged PDF.

Flash takes a different, more elaborate approach to supporting different languages. All the strings used in a movie can be stored in an XML file, and it is possible to create alternative versions of this file for different languages. ActionScript can be used to select a language for the movie, or the Flash Player can detect the system language on the user's computer and match it in the movie. This mechanism means that a screen reader will encounter the same language in the Flash movie as in the operating system user interface. However, it does not provide a simple way of mixing languages.

Like phrases in foreign languages, abbreviations may cause problems to screen readers, since they may not be able to pronounce a string of letters that does not make a word in their dictionary, and the pronunciation of abbreviations is inconsistent — some are spelled out as letters, others pronounced as if they were words. Abbreviations may also cause problems to people who do not understand their significance — this may be because the person has difficulties with reading, or because the abbreviation itself is obscure. In any case, it is good practice to mark abbreviations as such, if possible. In XHTML, the abbr element is available for this purpose. It is recommended that its title attribute be used to provide the full form of the abbreviation. Where other technologies are being used, it may be necessary to provide a separate key to abbreviations.

Text that is used as the anchor for a link requires special treatment. Because pointing and clicking is central to the idea of following links, people who use screen readers and those who cannot use a pointing device have particular problems with navigation.

The links on a Web page will normally be obvious to a sighted person — they can be found in navbars or else they are distinctively styled. A person who cannot see is not able to obtain this stylistic and positional information. Screen reader software almost always provides a facility for constructing a list of all the links on a page, though, and screen reader users can take advantage of this list to obtain an overview of the structure of a site and to go directly to pages which look interesting. Figure 13.5 shows a Web page that utilizes a common style for the text of its links.

The inset panel shows what a screen reader user would hear read to them as the list of links on that page. A similar situation would occur on a typical blog front page, where the abstract of each article was followed by a link labelled More.... The user has no clue what any of these links mean or what they might point to. To make pages accessible, this lazy approach to link text must be abandoned and the page must be rewritten so that the links make sense out of context. Usually, this results in a more natural and readable page as well as making the lists of links useful. Figure 13.6 shows how this example page might be rewritten, and the list of links that results.

Figure 13.5. *Poorly written link text*

Figure 13.6. *Improved link text*

While it is essential that link text works out of context, it is also desirable to keep it short. Remember that screen reader users have to listen to everything being read out to them. Notice in this example that we have not included the words "Download the" in the text of the first link. It will be clear to most users that activating the link will cause the update to be downloaded. In XHTML, additional information about the link can be added using the title attribute of the a element. Some screen readers will read this extra information on request. We could usefully clarify the slightly obscure second link on this page as follows:

```
<a href="http://downloads2.desperatesw.co.uk/textfridge/tf412.tar.gz" title="Download the update from our mirror site">mirror download site</a>
```

Not all screen reading software understands title attributes, though, so you cannot rely on this mechanism to make up for meaningless link text.

Although PDF can include hyperlinks, Adobe Reader does not provide a way of extracting a list of links. In Flash, there is no concept of a link as such, but URLs can be associated with objects that respond to clicks. If you wish to make a list of such "links" in Flash movies available to screen readers, it will be necessary to write special scripts to do so.

The issue of writing style and content is a tricky one. Forcing everybody to write in a simplified style with a limited vocabulary, as if they were writing for tabloid newspapers, is not acceptable. It is therefore inevitable that some content will be beyond the understanding of some readers. This is not necessarily a bad thing – consider the large number of medical articles online, for example, which use highly technical but essential specialized terms beyond the understanding of the lay person. As with any form of writing, it is always best to use language as simple as the material you are presenting allows, so that you get your message across to as many people as possible. Providing summaries of factual content never does any harm, and can be of great assistance to people who find it hard to follow complex written material. A glossary can also be provided if a document uses obscure technical terms.

Use headings and lists to make the structure of your text explicit. The signposts that headings provide may help people to get a general idea of the topic and the way the material has been organized. Remember that screen readers turn text into a time-based medium, so that it takes up users' time. Experienced sighted readers often skim a page of text, in order to obtain a quick idea of what the page is about. Screen reader users are not able to do this normally, but screen readers do often provide a means of extracting the headings from a page. If you use headings meaningfully, this list can provide a similar quick summary of the page's contents.

KEY POINTS

People with defective colour vision and some elderly people may have trouble distinguishing colours that only differ in hue.

Maintaining high tonal contrast between text and its background will make the text easier to read for everyone.

Any information conveyed with colour should also be available without colour.

Avoid the risk of triggering photosensitive seizures: never use blinking elements.

Provide a means of stopping or pausing moving elements, especially text.

Only use images of text when absolutely necessary (e.g. logos) and never use them for small type.

Use available methods for indicating the natural language of text and identifying abbreviations.

Make sure that link text makes sense out of context. Use simple language wherever it is appropriate and provide summaries of complex material and glossaries of obscure terms.

Use headings to make a document's structure explicit and to provide a quick view of its contents.

Interactivity

Unless the controls in a multimedia interface are operable by all users, the underlying application is inaccessible – some people will not be able to use it at all. This is perhaps more serious than when content is not perceivable. Being able to use a Web site for shopping, for example, may make a blind person independent in a way that is otherwise denied to them. It is therefore especially frustrating if Web sites or multimedia applications cannot be operated because they are not accessible to people who are unable to point to something on the screen.

Keyboard Access

As we explained earlier, input devices which are used as a substitute for mice and trackballs produce input which is equivalent to key strokes, so we can make controls accessible by making them respond to the keyboard as well as to the mouse. A control is said to "have focus" when it can receive input. For example, a text field has focus when the cursor is in it. Controls usually receive the focus when they are clicked with the mouse, but people who cannot use a pointing device need some other method of setting the focus – they must be able to activate elements such as links and radio buttons using the keyboard, instead of by clicking.

To begin with, consider how this applies to Web pages. All graphical browsers support the use of the tab key to move between controls on a form, but the extent of further support for keyboard navigation varies. In some cases, an option is provided to change the behaviour of the tab key so that it causes the cursor to move between links as well as form controls (as shown in Figure 13.7); in some browsers, this is the default behaviour. Others require a modifier key, and some require the use of the arrow keys, possibly with a modifier key, instead of tab. There are also browsers that provide no means at all of navigating to links using the keyboard. At the operating system level,

Figure 13.7. *Tab key options in a browser*

there may be options for using keyboard keys to control the movement of the cursor. Typically, once a user has tabbed to a link, pressing return or enter has the same effect as clicking on it.

All of a site's visitors benefit from the presence of navbars on its pages. Normally, the navbar appears at the top or the left, which usually means that it is the first thing in the XHTML source document for the page. This means that screen reader users must listen to all the links in the navbar being read on every page before they hear any of its main content. It is possible to reorder the source and use CSS absolute positioning to move the navbar to the top of the page, but there is empirical evidence that a substantial number of screen reader users value having the navigation links read out at the beginning of a page sometimes, and they just want a way of skipping past them when they choose.

The problem is that the current version of XHTML does not provide an element to be used for navbars. (The proposals for both XHTML 2.0 and HTML 5 do, but it will be a long time before either of these languages becomes the standard for Web page markup.) It is therefore up to the Web designer to provide a means of skipping navbars. This is usually done by placing a link, often referred to as a ***skip link***, at the beginning of the page, whose destination is an anchor at the beginning of the main content, like this:

```
<a href="#content" title="Go directly to the main content" accesskey="S">Skip to main
content</a>
```

If the page's main content were enclosed in a div element, it could be marked up with the following start tag so that activating this link will cause a jump to the beginning of the main part of the page.

```
<div id="content">
```

---IN DETAIL---

To be more precise, when a link is activated, the display focus – the part of the page at the top of the window, or the part that will be read next by a screen reader – is transferred to its destination. At the same time, the tab focus – the notional point from which the tab key moves forward – should also be moved to the same place, so that the next time a user presses the tab key, the first link within the main content should be activated. In practice, some commonly used browsers do not transfer the tab focus, which makes skip links almost useless to people using those browsers. Nevertheless, since screen readers usually do follow skip links correctly, they should be included if there is a substantial number of links on a page before its main content.

Integrating skip links into a page design is not easy, especially since it is essential that the skip link be the first thing in the reading order. Sighted readers using a mouse are likely to be confused by a skip link, which to them appears to serve no purpose. Various CSS tricks are commonly employed to hide the skip link while still making it apparent to screen readers, but this does not serve users who can see but rely on the keyboard for input. Some accessibility experts consider skip links unnecessary, because screen readers and other assistive technology usually provide a way of skipping directly to headings, so ensuring that each page's main content begins with a level 1 heading should be adequate to allow users to skip over the navbar. Other experts consider them essential. WCAG 2.0 requires that "A mechanism is available to bypass blocks of content that are repeated on multiple Web pages", but the accompanying list of techniques for satisfying this guideline describes skip links. In the future, successors to XHTML 1.0 may provide a way of specifying a skip link using a special attribute, with user agents being left to interpret it correctly.

XHTML already provides a little-used feature to allow users to activate links and move the cursor directly to form controls by pressing a key, thereby avoiding the need to tab through every preceding link or control and, in the case of screen reader users, avoiding the need to listen to them all. Any a element, form control or label element may have an **accesskey** attribute, whose value is a single letter. For example,

```
<a href="support.html" title="product support" accesskey="2">
```

The idea is that by pressing the 2 key, a user can follow the link to support.html. In practice, browsers usually require a modifier key to be pressed at the same time, which is not helpful to RSI sufferers and other people who have trouble using their hands. An additional problem with using this feature is that few, if any, browsers provide a means of finding out which access keys have been defined on a page, and what they do. (It is possible to write scripts to provide this facility.) It is therefore advised that such information should be provided explicitly somewhere on the page or site. If access keys are used consistently across a site, for instance, to activate the links on a site-wide navbar, an accessibility statement can include a list of available keys and their function.

Since some users will activate elements using the keyboard and not by pointing with a mouse, the concept of mouse or cursor coordinates will not always make sense. Any operation that depends on sensing the current position of the mouse may behave unpredictably if the cursor is not being used in the conventional way. The recent interest in using client-side scripting to provide dynamic user interfaces to Web applications means that scripts may use mouse coordinates, for example, to implement drag and drop. You should provide an alternative to such features. For instance, if your interface supports drag and drop editing, you should make sure that it also supports cut and paste, and that selection is possible using the keyboard as well as the mouse.

Keyboard access in Flash depends on scripting. As we will explain in Chapter 14, scripts can be made to run when a particular key is pressed. Key presses can therefore be made to transfer the cursor to a text field, or activate some other control. It is up to the person writing the script to decide which keys will perform these operations, but it is sensible to use the tab and arrow keys conventionally to move between controls. Most of the standard Flash UI components provide the necessary behaviour, although it needs to be enabled explicitly by a script. The **Accessibility** panel can be used to pass information to screen readers about which keys are being used to operate controls.

Acrobat can be used for creating PDF forms that can be filled in on a screen. Unlike forms in Web pages or Flash movies, the data from PDF forms is not sent to a server for processing; it is added to the PDF document, just as if you had filled in a form on paper with a pen. The form is then typically printed out or emailed to somebody. These forms need to be accessible in the same way as Web forms, and this is achieved in a similar way using the tools in Acrobat. When form fields are created, they can be given a description, which can be read by screen readers. A tabbing order between the fields can be defined. Like any other PDF document, a PDF form can be tagged to make its structure evident. As with other aspects of PDF accessibility, the facilities of the format are adequate, but depend on the user agent (Adobe Reader and so on) to present them to users.

AJAX

Recent fashions in Web design have brought with them new accessibility problems specific to Web pages. In Chapter 12 we mentioned the AJAX technique, which is becoming increasingly popular on the Web. Its defining feature is the dynamic retrieval of data from a server using a script, which usually rewrites part of the page to display the data. AJAX usually goes hand-in-hand with the use of special interface elements, often called "widgets", which rely on scripts instead of the standard XHTML input controls. They therefore lack the built-in accessibility features we described earlier.

A Web designer who creates custom controls is in the same position with respect to accessibility as a Flash developer. They must take on the responsibility for ensuring that their controls are accessible, by writing scripts that permit them to be operated by the keyboard alone, by making it possible to tab between controls and by making sure that descriptive text is associated with each control in a way that is evident to screen readers.

More seriously, the dynamic redrawing of the screen can compromise accessibility in itself. It is possible that a user agent may not be aware that the redrawing has occurred, or the redrawing may interrupt the order in which the page is being processed. For instance, whenever part of the page is refreshed, some screen readers go back to the start, others to the beginning of the changed area. It seems that there is no reliable way for a script to inform a current screen reader that part of the page has been updated and force it to read the updated contents, or not as appropriate in the circumstances.

The root cause of this problem is that the markup does not contain enough information for scripts and screen readers to determine whether areas of the page are dynamically updated and how updates are to be interpreted. The **WAI-ARIA (Accessible Rich Internet Applications Suite)** is a W3C standard presently under development, which defines the necessary extensions to the relevant Web technologies for this to happen. Until WAI-ARIA is implemented, though, the use of AJAX on the Web should be considered potentially inaccessible.

In 1997, the authors of WCAG 1.0 considered JavaScript support in assistive technology to be so unreliable that they effectively banned its use. This advice is outdated, though, and in fact JavaScript may profitably be used to enhance accessibility. For instance, a script may allow a user with poor eyesight to switch from an elaborately decorated layout to a more basic readable one, with a plain background, high contrast and larger text. (We will show how this can be done in Chapter 14.) However, it is necessary to take account of the possibility that the page is being accessed by a user agent that does not implement JavaScript. (This is actually more likely to be the case with mobile phones than with modern screen readers.) The best way to do so is by creating a page that works without JavaScript and then adding scripts to make it better. The trick here is to use scripts to create any controls that depend on scripting support and to override the default behaviour of links and input elements. The technique is sometimes referred to as *Hijax*.

For example, in Chapter 12 we illustrated an image gallery (Figure 12.12). Clicking on a small image causes the main image to be replaced; this effect is achieved using JavaScript. If the image gallery is implemented in a naïve way, clicking on the small images would achieve nothing when the gallery is displayed by a user agent that does not implement JavaScript. This behaviour would leave the user frustrated and possibly confused.

The Hijax technique could easily be applied to this situation. Each thumbnail image could be provided with a link that pointed to a page on which the corresponding large image was displayed in the main area on the right. That is, we achieve exactly the same visual effect as the scripted image gallery, but instead of swapping the images *in situ*, we load a new page whenever a thumbnail image is clicked. This will cause extra requests to be sent to the server and the screen may be refreshed when a new image is selected, so we might prefer to use the script to change a single page, as we originally described. We can do this safely if we have added links to the images because the links will still work in user agents without JavaScript. All we have to do is make sure that the script prevents the links being followed when they are clicked. This is easily done – the requirement is such a common one that a means of doing so is provided by JavaScript.

This example does reveal an alternative way of avoiding problems with user agents that do not support JavaScript: simply avoid using JavaScript. If you have created separate pages for each image in the gallery, why not just rely on the links? The usual answer is that using scripting and changing pages dynamically allows Web pages to provide a more reponsive and "fluid" user interface. In some cases, where complex scripting is used to implement elaborate interfaces that mimic desktop applications, this may be the case, but in a simple case such as an image gallery the use of scripting is harder to justify. Most Web browsers will cache images, so loading a new page of an image gallery will only cause the main image to be fetched; it will not require the thumbnails to be retrieved again. That is, there is very little extra network traffic caused by fetching separate pages for the gallery. Furthermore, most browsers will be written so that they only update areas of the screen that change when a new page is loaded. If all the pages in a gallery are identical except for the main image, only the area occupied by that image will be refreshed when a new page is loaded. What the user sees happening will be no different from what they would see if the image was swapped using a script.

Hence, when you are considering using AJAX or any other effects that rely on scripting, you should first implement your pages without scripting. You should then consider carefully whether scripts are actually required. Only if the version without scripting has serious deficiencies should you go on to add scripts, while ensuring that the page still works on user agents that do not support JavaScript. For the benefit of users who may find dynamic scripted interaction confusing, such as people with certain cognitive difficulties, an option to disable the scripted effects and fall back on the standard behaviour provided for users without JavaScript should be offered.

Timing and Error Recovery

Sometimes it is considered necessary to set a time limit, within which some interaction must be completed. An important example is to be found in online banking sites, where time limits are imposed on security grounds. If a customer fails to provide a password within a specified time, or if they are logged in to the site but no activity takes place for a certain time, it is assumed that something suspicious is going on and the customer will usually be logged out or have their access disabled. This is a reasonable security measure for able people, but users with motor disabilities may find it difficult or impossible to complete a task within the time limit.

In less critical contexts it may be possible to provide an option to disable the time limit. In controlled environments, such as a university's internal network, administrators may be able to set more generous limits for individuals. For instance, if a test or survey is being conducted online, students with disabilities may be able to ask for extra time to complete each question.

For banks and other security-conscious organizations, time limits may be considered necessary. In such a case, WCAG 2.0 makes the suggestion that an option to extend the time limit for an additional period be offered, to be triggered by a very simple action, such as pressing the space bar. Some such mechanism should be considered wherever time limits are imposed. It is acknowledged, though, that sometimes time limits that cannot be extended must be considered essential.

Everybody makes mistakes sometimes. Users with disabilities may be more prone to make mistakes than others. For example, somebody with poor control over their movements may accidentally click a **Submit** button when they meant to click **Cancel** if the two buttons are close together. The consequences could be quite serious: some Web sites implement "One Click" purchases, which may perhaps improve accessibility by reducing the number of inputs needed to buy something, but can also make it too easy to buy something by mistake. Not providing any means of recovering from such errors may legitimately be considered a barrier to accessibility; being afraid of making irrecoverable mistakes may be as effective at preventing somebody from using a Web site or application as being unable to operate the controls.

If possible, some means should be provided for undoing actions. Unlimited undoing is now normal in conventional desktop applications, but is less common in Web applications. Where undoing is not feasible, it may be helpful to require confirmation of critical operations, such as committing yourself to a purchase. Confirmations must be used judiciously, though. If every action has to be confirmed, users will tend to ignore the confirmation dialogue and agree to everything automatically.

In this case, accessible design is the same as good design. The accessibility requirements just add weight to the need for a means of recovering from errors and preventing them in the first place.

KEY POINTS

Controls must be operable by the keyboard alone and not depend on the ability to use a mouse or other pointing device.

It should be possible to move between form controls and links using a key.

Provide a skip link or some other means of bypassing navbars on Web pages.

Access keys may be used to provide direct navigation to some elements.

Keyboard access in Flash depends on scripting.

Until WAI-ARIA is implemented, the use of AJAX on the Web should be considered potentially inaccessible.

Use Hijax to provide fallback behaviour when JavaScript doesn't work.

Wherever possible, avoid using time limits that cannot be disabled or extended.

If possible, provide ways of recovering from errors and try to prevent them occurring.

Exercises

Test Questions

1 If you suffered a repetitive strain injury in your wrist, how would it affect the way you used your computer? What features of Web sites and multimedia interfaces might present difficulties that you had not encountered before you suffered the injury?

2 Usability experts recommend testing using small groups of users, often as few as five. Is testing on this scale likely to identify accessibility problems?

3 Explain how using structural markup for Web pages contributes to each of the four POUR principles.

4 Write suitable alt-text for the photograph on the left of Figure 2.12 in Chapter 2 and the diagram of Figure 6.2 in Chapter 6.

5 What is the best way to ensure that a Web site will not cause problems for people with defective colour vision? How can you test whether a Web page will be readable by someone with defective colour vision?

6 How would you explain to a client who wanted to include blinking buttons on the home page of their site that it was not a good idea?

7 On the Web, it is quite common to see small images used as the items on a navbar, to ensure that the navbar links will always appear in the desired font and to allow styling to be applied to them which is not possible with CSS. What potential accessibility problems result from this practice, and what could you do to minimize them?

8 Suppose a blog site's front page consists of the opening paragraphs of the 12 most recent entries, each with a link to the full entry. What would you use as the text of the links, and why?

9 Explain why some Web sites have a link labelled **Skip to Content** at the top of each page.

Discussion Topics

1 "Adobe Flash […] offers the most complete set of tools for authoring accessible rich media applications" [From *Adobe Flash CS3 Professional Accessibility Overview*, at **www.adobe.com**.] Assess this claim by comparing Flash's accessibility support with that of Web pages incorporating multimedia and AJAX. (Refer to whichever version of Flash you are using.)

2 It is unreasonable to expect everybody who uploads a home-made video clip to a video-sharing site such as YouTube to add captions and provide a transcript. Does it matter that their video clips will therefore not be accessible?

3 A screen reader user who is also a Web developer and programmer is quoted on the Royal National Institute of Blind People's Web site as follows: "For me being online is everything. It's my source of income, my supermarket, my telephone. It's my way in." Assess the potential barriers and difficulties which this user may encounter in their life online and identify ways in which as many of these problems as possible could be avoided.

Practical Tasks

1 Choose a fairly prominent Web site, such as a medium-sized online retailer or your college's site, and write a report on its accessibility. Begin by checking how many WCAG guidelines it follows and then try to carry out some typical tasks at the site, such as finding some information and contacting the site's owners using or simulating assistive technology. (You can approximate the effect of using a screen reader by visiting the site with a text-only browser, and simulate a colour-blind person's experience either by using a simulator or by switching your screen to greyscale. To appreciate the problems of people who cannot use a pointing device, disconnect or deactivate yours.) Finally, if the site is unsatisfactory in any way, produce a set of recommendations for improving its accessibility.

2 Design a computer game that will be completely accessible while still being exciting to play for people who do not suffer from disabilities.

14

Scripting

■ **Objects and Events**

The Object Metaphor. Objects and Multimedia. Events.

■ **ECMAScript**

Names, Variables and Assignment. Flow of Control. Containers.
Functions and Methods.

■ **JavaScript and the DOM**

DOM Objects, Properties and Methods. Adding Scripts to Pages.
Events and Listeners.

■ **ActionScript**

The Document Class. Implementing Interactivity Using ActionScript.

In Chapter 12 we described how users could interact with and through multimedia. Apart from some passing references to the use of scripts, we did not explain how this could be achieved. We don't want to leave you with the impression that scripting is magical or mysterious, but we do not have space in this book to teach it in any detail. Although it is usual to refer to "scripts" and "scripting", what we are doing when we create interactivity is programming, even though the languages typically used for the purpose have some characteristics that differ from those of languages used for more conventional programming tasks. Programming is a skilled job, requiring experience and knowledge of specialized techniques as well as a facility for abstract symbolic thinking. Without teaching you programming, it would be futile to teach much about the scripting languages used in interactive multimedia.

It may be hard for anyone without a programming background to learn how to design and write scripts. However, it should not be difficult to understand the mechanism that allows interaction to occur, at least informally. We suggest that readers who have never done any programming read the following section on objects and events to get an idea of the mechanisms that allow interactivity to occur, and something of the process by which it is implemented. If you find that material easy, or are familiar with it already, you can go on to look at the subsequent examples of some simple scripts. (If you have trouble reading the notation, just read the accompanying description.)

Objects and Events

Interactive systems are event-driven — that is, the user does something, such as clicking a button, and something happens as a result. A familiar example of an event-driven system is the graphical user interface provided by modern operating systems. You will be used to double-clicking an icon and having an application program start up. The double-click is an event; the starting of the program is the response to it. Almost all the programs you are likely to use on a modern operating system with a graphical user interface are event-driven. In some cases, events only occur rarely and the response to them takes a long time. For instance, to install a program, you might click an installer's Install button, and then wait for 20 minutes or so while it copies the components of a complicated application to your hard disk. In other cases, such as when you are playing certain games or working with an interactive graphics editor, events occur almost continuously, as you click and drag. (But what seems rapid on a human time scale is still very slow compared with the speed at which computers perform their operations in response to those events.)

Most modern computer programs are organized as a collection of *objects*, which interact with each other to perform some computation or provide some service. Event-driven systems are particularly well suited to being built in this way, and the scripting languages used for multimedia programming are based on the concept of objects.

Readers who are already experienced programmers and familiar with object-oriented concepts may safely omit the next section and move on to the description of ECMAScript.

The Object Metaphor

There are several ways of describing the use of objects in programming, but the most popular is by way of a metaphor. Objects in a program are considered to be like objects in the real world, in that each object has certain properties that describe its current state and can perform certain actions. To see how this works, let's start by considering an imaginary interaction between people in a branch of a large international chain of coffee houses.

A customer, Theophilus, walks up to the counter, behind which sits the assistant Stanislaus. On seeing Theophilus approach, Stanislaus asks "What can I get you today?", to which Theophilus replies "Double espresso". Stanislaus picks up a paper cup and scribbles a 2 in the box labelled E and puts the cup on the counter next to Erica, the barista. Turning back to Theophilus, Stanislaus asks "Anything else?" Theophilus thinks about pastries for a moment but then answers "No, thanks". Stanislaus asks for £1.35. Theophilus hands over £1.50. "Your drink will be ready in a minute", Stanislaus says as he hands back the change.

It's rather more than a minute before Theophilus's coffee is ready. Erica is busy preparing various beverages for other customers. Whenever she finishes one customer's order, she calls out the names the company uses for the drinks she has just made. In response, people come and claim their drinks. Eventually, she picks up Theophilus's cup, measures out coffee and does things with the large shiny machine behind the counter. When the last drop has fallen into the cup, Erica puts it on the counter and calls out "*Espresso dopio!*" Theophilus picks up the cup and goes to sit down by a window, where we must leave him.

If we look at this story as if we were considering writing a computer program to simulate the coffee-ordering procedure, perhaps for some business game or to study ways of making it more efficient, we could safely ignore the superficial aspects of the situation. We would need to simulate a barista and a counter assistant, but now that we are not dealing with real people, we feel justified in calling these two things objects, which, as we explained, have certain properties and can perform certain actions.

As far as the simulation is concerned, the barista Erica can only do two things: make drinks and call them out to customers. These are the actions this object can perform. During the making of a drink, Erica must remember what she is making: the type of drink is part of her state of mind, so it is one of the properties of the object.

Erica is not the only barista in the world. When she finishes her shift, Ming will take over, and he will also be able to make drinks and call them out. That is, there is a *class* of baristas, all of whom can do the same things and have the same properties. The actual values of the properties will be specific to the object and may change over time.

Stanislaus belongs to a different class, so he can do some different things. (In practice, he might well be a barista too, but we'll suppose for now that the roles in our fictional coffee house are distinct – the management believes in specialization.) He can greet customers, take orders and money, calculate and give change and pass orders on to a barista. His state of mind is made up of a different set of properties, such as the price of the drink that has just been ordered, or the amount of money the customer has handed over.

In our simulation, we thus have two classes. Using a convention we will describe more fully later, we would call these two classes Barista and CounterAssistant. Each of the two objects in the simulation can be referred to by its name: stanislaus and erica. (Most programmers use names consisting only of lower-case letters for the objects in their scripts.) The way names are attached to objects in scripts is not as straightforward as you might expect, so for now we will just take it to be the case that objects can be referred to by names. The object called stanislaus belongs to the class CounterAssistant. We would usually say that stanislaus is a CounterAssistant. Similarly, erica is a Barista.

Both Erica and Stanislaus are employees of the coffee chain, so both the class of baristas and the class of counter assistants are *sub-classes* of the class of employees. Looking at this from the other side, the class of employees is the *parent class* (sometimes called the super-class) of the two sub-classes. A class is said to be *derived* from its parent class. Some properties make sense for all employees. For instance, both Erica and Stanislaus can tell you how long it is until the end of their shift. This information is not affected by whether they are a counter assistant or a barista. So baristas have some properties which belong to all employees. These properties are said to be *inherited*. Some actions can also be inherited. For instance, any employee can take a lunch break.

When you analyse an existing situation, inheritance is a way of modelling specialization. A barista is a special sort of employee, because a barista does some things that other sorts of employee don't do. When you synthesize systems, inheritance becomes a way of extending classes by creating sub-classes which do the same things as their parent class, plus some extra things. These two views of inheritance are just different ways of looking at the additional behaviour in sub-classes.

┌─ IN DETAIL ───┐

Inheritance is sometimes more complex than our simple outline suggests. An action may be common to every member of a class, but it may work differently depending on the sub-class. For instance, every employee can start work, but what they do when they start work will depend on the type of employee they are. A barista may need to check the levels in the coffee machine, a counter assistant may need to unlock the till, and so on. In such a case, we say that the interface – essentially the name of the operation – is inherited, but the implementation – how the operation is carried out – is determined by the sub-class. It's even possible that some operation might be the same for most sub-classes, but different for one or two. In that case, its implementation would be defined in the parent class and inherited by most sub-classes, but would be redefined in the sub-classes where different behaviour was required. These refinements are important in the construction of large programs, but can be overlooked for now.

└──┘

Any of the actions that workers of either of the two types we have described can perform may be broken down into simpler sub-actions. For instance, the barista's routine for making a drink consists of determining which drink is required – as we described earlier – followed by making the drink, placing it to one side, determining whether the same customer has ordered more drinks and either making those as well or, if they are all done, calling out the order. There is a separate procedure for making each drink, which can itself be broken down into steps. Making an espresso begins with measuring and grinding the beans, then tamping them into the filter, inserting the filter into the coffee machine and pressing the button, and so on. This process requires the barista to interact with the coffee machine, which is also something that can perform a limited repertoire of actions. It is an object that belongs to the class of coffee machines.

Each action that an object can perform is a sequence of more simple operations. Such a sequence is called a ***method***, since it defines a way of doing something. Each method has a name, such as call_order, and when we want an object to perform a method, we write the object's name, then a dot followed by the method's name. This has the effect of "calling" the method, so to get the object named erica to call out an order we might write erica.call_order().

You probably wonder why the empty brackets appear at the end of the method call. Remember that when Erica (the person) starts to make a drink, she picks up the cup and reads the specification off its side. The specified values are then used to determine which drink to make. If we had a method make_drink, which was invoked to simulate the making of a drink, we would need some way of handing information received from a CounterAssistant object to the method, so that it could choose which drink to make. Values which are passed to a method are called ***arguments***. When a method is called, the values of any arguments are written in brackets after the method name, as in erica.make_drink("espresso"). When there are no arguments, the brackets are left empty, as in the example at the end of the previous paragraph.

The reason no arguments are passed to call_order is that the names of the drinks are remembered in one of the object's properties. It is usually good practice to keep properties internal to the object and only set their values indirectly, by passing arguments to some method, and to use them only in methods. Sometimes, though, it is convenient to be able to get at the value of a property directly. A reference to the value of a property looks like a method call, except that there are no brackets after the name, so if Barista objects had a current_drink property, you could obtain its value in the object called erica by writing erica.current_drink.

We have been using a familiar example to show how it is possible to use objects to model systems made up of interacting components. Objects with their methods and properties are a feature of programming, but as we have shown, they are an analogy of one of the ways we can describe some aspects of the real world. Many people have found that this analogy provides a helpful way of organizing and thinking about the structure of a program or script. Do bear in mind, though, that when we describe objects as "knowing how to perform some operation" and so on, we are only using an analogy. Objects are really constructs provided by a programming language for organizing the computation performed by a program, and they don't "know" anything – the programmer has to specify everything that they do. Not all the objects in a real program correspond to physical objects or people. Objects are often highly abstract.

Objects and Multimedia

Perhaps you can already see how the object metaphor might be applied to multimedia. You will recall that the elements of an XHTML document have attributes, which resemble properties. By adding some methods that allow the values of attributes to be changed, we can turn the elements into objects and alter them by scripts. Including extra properties that model the structure of the page, by connecting each element's object to the objects corresponding to its content, allows a script to move from one element to another.

This is essentially how Web scripting works. The browser maps the elements of the page to objects. These objects have properties corresponding to the elements' attributes and relationships, and a collection of methods is provided not only for changing attributes, but also for finding, inserting, deleting and rearranging objects – and thus elements – within the document. In this way, scripts can make changes that have the same effect as rewriting the document.

An object called document is created when an XHTML document is loaded into a browser. It corresponds to the entire document. Among the document object's methods is one called getElementById, which takes a string as its argument and returns an object corresponding to the element within the document that has that string as the value of its id attribute. For example, if a document included the following markup:

`<p><img id="view" src="front-view.jpg" alt="the view from the front of the house" /></p>`

the method call `document.getElementById("view")` would return an object corresponding to the img element. That object would have properties called `src` and `alt`, whose values were the values of the attributes with the same names. That is, `document.getElementById("view").alt` would be the string `"the view from the front of the house"`. As we will explain later, it is possible for a script to change the values of properties. Here, we might change the value of the `src` property to a different URL. This change to the object would be reflected in the browser window: a different image would be displayed after the change.

A Flash movie is even more like a collection of objects. In Chapter 7 we described symbols as re-usable objects. There we were not using "object" in the technical sense we have introduced in this chapter, but the underlying concept is similar. We can create instances of a symbol, just as we can create objects belonging to a class. All the instances share the same appearance, but each one has its own properties. It is not, therefore, a large step from instances to objects, and ActionScript – the language used for writing scripts to work in Flash movies – provides a collection of classes that correspond to the types of element that can appear in a Flash movie. These classes enable symbol instances and other objects on the stage to be controlled and altered by scripts. In particular, movie clip objects (objects belonging to the class **MovieClip**, or some class derived from it) allow movie clips in the movie to be manipulated in many different ways, and UI component objects provide a means of interacting with users.

The interface shown in Figure 14.1 illustrates how a Flash movie can be viewed as a collection of objects. As we described in Chapter 12, the movie is a "player" for thin-section geological slides which allows a user to rotate the slides as though they were viewing them through a microscope. The labels attached to the screenshot show the class to which each object belongs. The slide itself is an instance of a movie clip symbol, so it is an object belonging to the **MovieClip** class. This means that it has methods that can be used to start and stop it playing

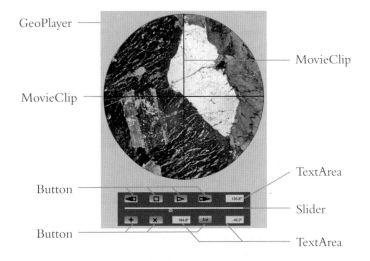

Figure 14.1. *Objects in a Flash movie*

(which makes it look as if the slide is turning round, because of the way the movie was created), and move it to a specific frame, among many other methods provided by this class. These methods are used in our player to make the slide rotate continuously or to move it round by a small amount.

The MovieClip object also has a collection of properties, including totalFrames, which holds the total number of frames in the movie clip, and currentFrame, which is the number of the frame which is currently being displayed. These properties are "read-only" – their values can be used but they cannot be changed. Other properties of MovieClip objects can be changed. For example, the alpha property, which controls the clip's transparency, may be altered by a script. Setting it to zero is one way of making a clip disappear.

The controls below the image of the slide are also objects, belonging to classes that correspond to various types of UI component: buttons, sliders and text areas. These also have methods and properties that allow them to perform their functions. In particular, the TextArea object has a property text, which holds the string it contains. By setting the value of this property, a script can cause a string to be displayed in the text field. Another property of this object is editable. If this were true (which it isn't in this movie), a user could enter text in the field, and that text could be read by a script.

One useful method that is shared by all the component objects (because it is inherited from their common parent class UIComponent) is setStyle. This takes two arguments. The first is a string that identifies some aspect of the object's appearance, such as "textformat", which refers to the formatting of any text associated with the component. The second is an object that has a collection of properties which are values of different components of that aspect. A TextFormat object, for example, has properties controlling font family, style, weight and size, among others. By building a TextFormat object and handing it to an object's setStyle method, a programmer can control the appearance of text in that object. This technique was used to arrange for the numbers displayed in the text fields in our example movie to be right-aligned.

The entire Flash movie is an object. By default, movies belong to the MovieClip class, which makes sense because movie clip symbols are movies within the movie, so both clips and movies ought to belong to the same class. Because a movie is a MovieClip object, a script can start and stop it, and control it in the same way as any other movie clip. Flash makes it easy to define a special class for each movie, though, in order to provide special behaviour for it. Usually, the document class, as the movie's class is called, is derived from MovieClip, but the programmer adds methods to it which provide the movie with its characteristic interactivity. In this case, we derived the GeoPlayer class from MovieClip and defined a collection of methods that are used to control the slide movie in response to user input, as we will describe fully later in the chapter.

Events

Programs can be constructed by defining some classes, creating objects belonging to those classes and calling methods through those objects. Normally, a method is called from within some other method, often belonging to a different object. For instance, if we were simulating the coffee shop, as we described earlier, we might use an object belonging to the class Till, to model the till. It would be used to record the amount of money taken in and to calculate change. In the real world, when Stanislaus has taken some money from a customer, he can ring up the price and the amount proferred in the till and it will show him how much change to give. (We assume that coffee shop managers do not put much faith in their employees' abilities at arithmetic.) In the simulation, the object corresponding to Stanislaus would call a method of the object corresponding to the till to compute the change.

Some methods must be invoked differently, though, because they depend on something happening that is external to the system of objects. For instance, one of the things that a counter assistant can do is greet a customer. This action should only occur when a customer arrives at the head of the queue at the counter, but it should occur every time that happens. Similarly, Stanislaus should only take money from a customer when it is offered. These actions must be triggered by some external event, not called from some other object. Nevertheless, when we model our system with objects, these actions must still be methods. Methods that are triggered by external events are called *event listeners*, or just *listeners*, because they behave as if they are listening for notification of an event, and only do something when they hear about the event happening.

In multimedia scripts, many events correspond to input from the user. For instance, a listener may be notified when a mouse click occurs, when the cursor is moved or when a key is pressed on the keyboard. Other events occur when data has been received, for example when a Web browser has finished loading a page. In Flash, an event occurs whenever a new frame of a movie is displayed.

Event listeners may need to use information about the event to deal with it. When a mouse click occurs, for instance, it is sometimes useful to know whether any modifier keys were held down at the time. Information about events is passed to listeners in the form of an object, whose properties are the values relevant to the type of event that has occurred. Usually, this object belongs to a sub-class of the Event class, such as MouseEvent or KeyboardEvent, for events caused by pointing devices or keyboards, respectively. (Although these objects are referred to as events, they would be better called "event descriptions".)

Adding an event listener for some event to an object doesn't necessarily mean that the object will be notified every time an event of that type occurs. Mouse events happen in a specific place – the current location of the cursor – and normally only objects at that location should be notified. It would be odd – and not at all useful – if every button on a page was notified whenever a mouse click occurred anywhere on the page. Only the button that was actually clicked should be notified, and this is what happens. The object under the cursor is notified of mouse events; it is said to be the *event target*. If an object is to be the target of a mouse event, it must have a graphical representation with a well-defined extent.

> ─IN DETAIL─────────────────────────────────
>
> **If the button is on a Web page, it might be within a paragraph, which is within a div, which is part of the body of the document. Strictly speaking, all of these elements could be notified of the event, though normally you would only want the button to respond to it. It is possible, using the event-handling model in ActionScript and modern Web browsers, to arrange for some or all of the elements containing the button to respond to the event as well as, or instead of, the button. Sophisticated event handling of this sort is very flexible but rarely needed, so we will ignore the possibility.**

Other events, such as keyboard events, do not have a physical location, so they do not have a single target. All objects with a listener for the keyPress event will be notified when a key is pressed for instance. The listener may have to inspect the Event object it is passed to determine whether it should do anything.

Event listeners often need to be dynamically turned on and off. For instance, if a button acts as a play control for a movie, it should be disabled when the movie is playing. Often, the easiest way of making sure that key presses are handled by text fields is to turn the field's listener for those events on only when the cursor is in the field. A button can be made to ignore clicks by removing the event listener that deals with clicks on the button. A text field's listeners can be added or removed whenever the field receives or loses the input focus – which causes an event to occur.

In Flash and modern Web browsers, any object that is capable of responding to events (which means almost any object) will belong to some class derived from a class that provides the interface for event handling. On the Web, this class is called EventTarget; for Flash it is EventDispatcher. Any object belonging to a sub-class of this class will have a method addEventListener, which can be called to set up an event listener for that object. It is passed the name of an event and a method as its arguments. (We will explain shortly how methods can be passed as arguments.) The complementary method removeEventListener can be used to remove a listener that has been added previously. Older Web browsers use an ad hoc mechanism for adding listeners to objects corresponding to document elements, which we describe in *Web Design: A Complete Introduction*. Although this mechanism is more widely supported at present, we will not describe it here, because it should eventually become obsolete and it is not our purpose in this book to teach practical Web scripting.

ECMAScript

One definition of a scripting language, taken from the ECMAScript specification, is

"…a programming language that is used to manipulate, customize, and automate the facilities of an existing system."

The authors of the specification go on:

"In such systems, useful functionality is already available through a user interface, and the scripting language is a mechanism for exposing that functionality to program control. In this way, the existing system is said to provide a host environment of objects and facilities which completes the capabilities of the scripting language."

A scripting language that conforms to this definition provides some control structures which allow scripts to make decisions and repeat operations, a few basic types and a means of defining classes and creating objects. These facilities are sufficient to write simple programs, but a scripting language also includes objects and classes, which provide access to and control over some "existing system". For example, a scripting language for the Web must provide objects corresponding to elements of XHTML documents, as we explained earlier. In programming jargon, these objects are said to constitute an *Application Programming Interface (API)* between the scripting language and the host system.

The first scripting language for the World Wide Web was a proprietary product called LiveScript, which was embedded in Netscape's Navigator Web browser. LiveScript changed its name to JavaScript shortly after its release, even though its actual relationship to the Java programming language is slight; the resemblance between the names has been a source of some confusion ever since. Microsoft, in its role as the other major browser manufacturer, produced its own version of JavaScript, known as JScript, which was not quite identical to Netscape's. To avoid yet another source of browser incompatibility, the industry association ECMA International† was called upon to produce a standard based on JavaScript and JScript. This standard gave the name *ECMAScript* to the language it defined.

It was always the case that JavaScript comprised a "core language", providing general-purpose programming facilities and some rudimentary object-oriented features, and a set of built-in objects that allowed JavaScript programs to interact with some other system. In the most familiar case, the other system is a Web browser, and the built-in objects correspond to elements of Web pages and browser windows. By providing a different set of built-in objects, the same language could be used to interact with other systems. Server-side JavaScript, for instance, allowed scripts to interact with Netscape Web servers and with files and databases.

ECMAScript only started out as a formally defined version of the JavaScript core language, but it has slowly been revised and is now treated as the definition of the JavaScript core language, although the version of the language implemented in browsers lags behind the latest ECMAScript standard. The standard explicitly concedes that ECMAScript is not "computationally self-sufficient": it has to be combined with host objects that allow scripts to manipulate a host system, such as a Web browser.

Scripting of a sort was available in early versions of Flash, using an ad hoc system of "actions". This system was limited, and it was apparent that the full potential of scripting in Flash could only be realized with a full-blown scripting language. Macromedia (who owned Flash at that time) chose to adopt ECMAScript as the basis of such a language when Flash 5 was released in 2000.

† *Formerly known as the European Computer Manufacturers' Association.*

Thus, scripting for the Web and scripting in Flash share a basic syntax. However, ActionScript, being under the control of a single company, has been able to develop faster than JavaScript, which is controlled by standards committees and implemented independently by several browser makers. The current version of ActionScript[†] is based on a more recent version of the ECMAScript standard than JavaScript is, and it has a much improved mechanism for defining classes and inheritance. However, at the level of detail we need here, ActionScript is close enough to ECMAScript and ECMAScript is close enough to JavaScript for the syntax and core semantics of ActionScript to be comprehensible to anyone who already knows JavaScript, and vice versa. We will therefore begin by considering ECMAScript without reference to any particular host environment.

IN DETAIL

Web browsers and Flash movies are not the only host environments which ECMAScript is used with. ECMAScript is commonly used to provide scripting control over application programs, in particular Adobe's Creative Suite applications. The language is invariably referred to as "JavaScript" in this context, even though only the core language, which is identical to ECMAScript, is being used.

Some contemporary programming and scripting languages are based entirely on objects and classes. Everything is an object belonging to some class, all classes are derived from the Object class, and everything is done by calling methods, although sometimes the syntactical form of the method calls is unusual.

ECMAScript belongs to an older tradition, though, where some basic operations and primitive values are not treated as objects and basic control flow is implemented using special syntax instead of method calls. The language provides a framework of basic operations, into which any collection of objects can be fitted. We must begin by looking at some of these basic operations.

In the interests of simplicity we will only introduce the minimum of syntax necessary for understanding the examples later in this chapter. You should not suppose that what we describe is anything like the complete syntax of ECMAScript.

Even the minimum for understanding simple example scripts is quite a lot of syntax, however. If you are not comfortable with the ideas we have introduced so far, you may find the notation in the remainder of this chapter hard going and prefer to skip it. However, you may still benefit from skimming through the rest of this chapter, just to get a feeling for what can be achieved with scripts.

---

† All references to ActionScript in this chapter refer to ActionScript 3.

Names, Variables and Assignment

Our informal description of objects showed that it is necessary to give names to objects if we are to work with them. The host objects provided in JavaScript and ActionScript are given names by the host system. For example, we already mentioned that a script running in a Web browser has access to an object called document. There is no need for a programmer to do anything to create this object or give it its name. In Flash, symbol instances can be given names in the Properties panel when they are placed on the stage, and the names can be used to refer to the corresponding objects within a script.

As we explained earlier, these objects belong to classes. Their classes also need names, and the names of the built-in classes (such as MovieClip) are also provided by the system.

The names that can be used for objects and classes – and other names that you can use in a program – are subject to some restrictions. They must consist only of letters (upper- or lower-case), digits, underscore (_) or $ symbols, and they cannot begin with a digit. Note that this does not allow names to contain spaces.

Certain conventions are used to restrict the form of names further. Names beginning with under-scores and $ symbols are usually only used by libraries and machine-generated code. Names of methods and properties defined in scripts are usually written in lower-case, with underscores being used to separate multiple words. Class names, and the methods in classes defined by APIs, are conventionally written in "camel-case". That is, when the name consists of more than one word there are no spaces between words, but each word starts with a capital letter. Class names consisting of just a single word begin with an initial capital letter (which means they are just a degenerate case of the general rule).

---IN DETAIL---

> **The ECMAScript standard's rules that define the allowable forms for names are more complicated than we have stated, because they allow the use of Unicode characters beyond the ASCII subset. However, it would be unwise to rely on any implementation supporting any non-ASCII characters in names.**

Some names which look as if they ought to be legal are not allowed to be used to name objects and so on, because they are *reserved words*, which are used by the language as part of its syntax. We will mention some reserved words as we go along.

Various sorts of entity which need names can appear in a program besides classes, objects, methods and properties. *Variables* are the most common of these.

Variables are containers – or "locations", in the jargon of programming languages – that have a name (often called an identifier) and can hold a value. The value stored in a location can be changed by the operation of **assignment**. Storing a value in a location allows it to be referred to using the variable's name. Variable names follow the same convention as method names.

Values can be stored in variables using the assignment operator, written as =. (This is a potential pitfall if you are not used to programming and expect the = sign to mean equality, as it does in mathematics. In ECMAScript – and many other programming languages – equality is written ==.) So, if the_amount is a variable

```
the_amount = 149
```

will store the number 149 in it.

A single number is not the only thing that can be assigned. Strings, written between " signs, like attribute values in XHTML, can also be assigned, and so can Booleans (which may be true or false). As well as values of these "primitive" types, objects belonging to any host class or class you have defined yourself can be stored in variables.

Expressions of any of these types may be constructed using operators. For numbers, the conventional arithmetic operations are provided (+, –, *, /, %, where * is multiplication and % is remainder after division); for strings, the only operator is concatenation, written as +, which sticks two strings together; for numbers, the logical and, or and not operations are available, written **&&**, **||** and **!**.

Variables can be used in expressions. When the name of a variable appears in an expression, its current value is substituted. For example, after the assignment just shown, the expression the_amount + 1 has the value 150. In most scripts, method calls and references to objects' properties are commonly used in expressions, as you will see later.

Expressions can be assigned to variables. We might write

```
the_amount = the_amount + 1
```

which would store 150 in the variable. That is, we can change the value stored in a variable as a program's execution proceeds.

The names of objects' properties can be used in the same way as variables, but they must be accessed through an object using the dot notation we described earlier. For instance, if **tf** is a TextFormat object, we can set its **align** property using an assignment such as

```
tf.align = "right"
```

Assignments are one of the sorts of *statement* that ECMAScript provides. Statements are the primitive pieces of executable code from which programs are constructed.

In early versions of ECMAScript and in current versions of JavaScript, if you want to introduce a variable into your program you just use it. Generally, it's a good idea to assign something to it as the first thing you do, because otherwise it holds the special value undefined, and trying to use it will always be a mistake.

In JavaScript, you can, if you like, explicitly declare a variable, by using the reserved word var in front of the initial assignment, as in

var the_start_angle = 0

This makes it clear that you are using a new variable, but doesn't do anything else. In ActionScript, though, things are different. You must declare all your variables before you use them. Furthermore, when you do so you must specify what type of value will be stored in them, by adding a colon followed by a class name after the variable's name, as in

var the_start_angle:Number = 0

The class names Number, String and Boolean are used for the primitive types of value. The name of any class can be used instead, if you are storing objects in your variable.

As we mentioned earlier, some properties of host objects are "read-only" and cannot be changed. Sometimes you want to create a variable whose value cannot be changed. This can be done in ActionScript (but not JavaScript) by declaring variables using the word const instead of var:

const MAUVE:Number = 0xFF7FFF

By convention, the names of constants are written entirely in upper case, as we have done here. You are most likely to see constants as properties of certain host objects. This example also demonstrates that numerical values can be written in hexadecimal notation by prefixing them with 0x.

Flow of Control

If you write a series of assignments one after the other on separate lines, they will be executed in order when your script runs. (If you like, you can add a semi-colon after each assignment to terminate the statement, but it is not necessary. You only need to use semi-colons to terminate statements if you want to place two statements on the same line.)

Most useful computation demands that statements be executed in a more elaborate order than a straight sequence. The first requirement is to be able to execute a statement if and only if some condition is true. You use a ***conditional statement*** for this purpose. It takes the form

```
if ( E )
    S₁
else
    S₂
```

where if and else are reserved words, E is an expression and S_1 and S_2 are statements – either single statements, such as an assignment, or blocks, consisting of a sequence of statements enclosed between curly brackets { and }. The indentation is used to show the structure of the conditional; this is a convention not a requirement. The effect of the conditional statement is as you might expect: if E is true, S_1 is executed, otherwise S_2 is executed. This implies that E should be something whose value is either true or false – that is, a Boolean expression.

Boolean values are most commonly created by comparing variables with other values. For example, x > 0 has the value true when (the value stored in) x is positive but false otherwise. ECMAScript has a full range of comparison operators, but owing to the restricted character set available on keyboards, the operators only approximate the conventional mathematical symbols. They are <, <= (for ≤, less than or equal), == (equal, as noted earlier), != (not equal), >= (for ≥, greater than or equal) and >. These operators can be applied to numerical values with the expected meaning, but also to strings, when a dictionary-order comparison is performed. "digital" >= "multimedia" is false, for example, because "digital" comes before "multimedia".

You can combine conditions using the Boolean operators we listed earlier. It is advisable to use brackets in complicated cases. You can also assign the result of a comparison to a variable, as a way of remembering it. Subsequently, the variable name can be used on its own in any context where you could use a comparison.

IN DETAIL

It is not necessary to put curly brackets round a single statement when you use it as an alternative in a conditional (or most other contexts where you can use a single statement or a block), but it does no harm to put them, and a lot of people prefer to do so. We prefer to omit them unless they are needed, but there is no special virtue in this.

As an example of using a conditional statement, suppose that you wish to compute a payment, perhaps a commission. Say the payment is 10% of some total amount, except that if the amount is less than 10 (euros, dollars, zlotys, or whatever), no payment is made. Assume that the total is held in a variable called **amount**, declared elsewhere, and we want to compute the payment and store it in a variable called **payment**. This can be achieved in JavaScript in the following way:

```
var commission = amount * 0.1    // 10% = 0.1
if (commission < 10)
     payment = 0
else
     payment = commission
```

(In ActionScript, we would have had to add :**Number** after **commission** on the first line.)

The characters from // to the end of the first line are a **comment** – that is, text which has no effect on the computation, but serves as an annotation for the benefit of people reading the script. You won't see many comments of this sort in this chapter, because the accompanying text does the job of explanation here. However, large or subtle scripts benefit from the use of meaningful comments, and you should develop the habit of adding them, if only to help you remember what you have done when you come back to it after an interruption.

If there isn't anything to be done when E is false you can leave out the **else** S_2 clause from a conditional statement. For example, you may have realized we could have assigned the commission provisionally to **payment** and then reset it if it was too small. This would use a single-branched conditional, like this:

```
var commission = amount * 0.1
var payment = commission
if (payment < 10) payment = 0
```

As well as saving a bit of code, this allows us to declare **payment** only when we have a meaningful value to assign to it. (If you like to keep your code short, you can eliminate the variable **commission**, too. We leave that to you for now.)

You use a conditional statement when you need to make a choice, as in the example just given. **Loops** are used when you need to repeat an operation. As a simple example, suppose you wished to replicate a string a certain number of times, and that variables s and **repetitions** held the string and the replication count, respectively. So, if the value of s was "ECMA" and that of **repetitions** was 4, you would want to produce "ECMAECMAECMAECMA". You could accomplish this operation by setting a variable **ss** to the empty string, and then sticking s onto the end of it four times. You could just write four assignment statements, but if you wanted to change the value of **repetitions**, you would need to change the number of assignments. If the value of **repetitions** depended on a user's input, you could not do this.

Loops allow you to use the value of a variable (or any expression) to control the number of times something is done. ECMAScript has several sorts of loop. We will only describe one – the *for loop* – which captures a common pattern, where the loop is controlled by a counter whose value is increased every time the loop is executed.

The form of a for loop is illustrated by the following JavaScript code to replicate a string:

```
ss = ""
for (i = 0; i < repetitions; i = i + 1)
    ss = ss + s
```

The loop is introduced by the reserved word **for**. All the book-keeping concerned with iteration is kept together at the top of the loop inside the brackets. First comes the initialization, which is performed once before the loop. Next comes the condition which determines how many times the loop is executed: the condition is evaluated every time round the loop and the loop is only repeated again if it is true. The third component is the increment, which is performed at the end of each iteration.

After all these components comes the loop's body, which is executed repeatedly as long as the condition remains true. Note that in this case the condition depends on the value of i, which is changed in the increment, so there is reason to suppose that the value of the condition will eventually become **false**. If the condition depended only on values that were not changed in the increment or the loop's body, the loop would run on forever.

┌─IN DETAIL────────────────────────────────

The increment in a for loop does not have to consist of adding one to a variable but it often does. JavaScript has a special shorthand for this operation: **++i** is equivalent to **i = i + 1**. This shorthand is itself a contraction of a more general shorthand. We could have written the same operation as **i += 1**. In general, any assignment statement where a variable is combined with some value using a single operator and immediately assigned back to the same variable can be contracted: **x = x @ v** can be written **x @= v**, where **@** stands for any binary operator. We would normally have written the example loop as:

```
ss = ""
for (i = 0; i < repetitions; ++i)
    ss += s
```

These shorthands are very useful and are used by most experienced programmers, but they may be confusing to newcomers, so we will avoid them in our examples. You are likely to encounter them if you read many actual programs, though.

It is safest to use the variable that controls a for loop only in the loop, so it is convenient to declare it in the initialization clause of the loop's header, which is done in the same way as variables are declared elsewhere. In JavaScript, it is sufficient to prefix the assignment with var. In ActionScript the type (Number for conventional loops) must also be declared, like this:

for (var i:Number = 0; i < repetitions; i = i + 1)

Containers

Often, we need to work with a collection of related values or objects. For instance, in JavaScript document.getElementsByTagName("a") will return a collection containing objects for all the a elements in the document. This collection is ordered — it makes sense to talk about the first, second, …, last a element in the document. Ordered collections like this are frequently required. ECMAScript uses *arrays* to hold them.

An array is a sequence of values, each of which can be identified by a numerical *index*, which is its position in the sequence. The individual values are the array's *elements*. (Not to be confused with XHTML elements, although the elements of arrays in JavaScript are often objects corresponding to elements in the document.) The process of extracting an individual element using a number is called *indexing*, written by putting the index in square brackets after the array's name: a[0], a[1], a[2], … are the first, second, third, … elements of the array a.

In general, if a is the name of an array, and E is an expression that evaluates to a number greater than or equal to zero, a[E] gives the value of the element stored in the array at the corresponding position. Notice that the index values start at zero, not one, even though we invariably refer to the first element, and so on. This can be confusing and it frequently leads to programming errors, especially as some other programming languages do use one as the first index.

Arrays are often returned by calls of methods in an API, as we will see later, but sometimes you will need to create them explicitly. The expression new Array() can be used for this purpose — it returns a new array, which can be assigned to a variable. ECMAScript does not require you to specify how many elements there are in the array when you create it; it will grow as necessary as soon as you assign a value to an element. Note that if an array a has n elements, the highest element is at a[n-1]. The number of elements in a is given by the expression a.length, so a[a.length] is always the first free element beyond those that are occupied.

You should have observed the use of the same dot notation for obtaining the length of an array as we use for accessing the properties of an object. This is because arrays are objects and length is one of their properties. Arrays also have some methods, which are often useful, but we will confine ourselves to simpler operations which do not use the method-calling syntax.

It is often the case that you need to access the value of each element of an array in turn. This is best done using a for loop in which the loop variable ranges from 0 to the highest element. The length property of the array can be used as the upper limit of the loop variable, like this:

```
for (var i:Number = 0; i < a.length; i = i + 1)
```

Loops with headers of this form can be used for any task that computes some function of every array element or applies some operation to every element – for example, adding them all up, computing their average, setting them all to zero, adding one to them all, and so on.

The following JavaScript code could be used to determine the width of the widest image on a Web page.

```
var max_width = 0
var all_images = document.getElementsByTagName("img")
for (var i = 0; i < all_images.length; i = i+1)
    if (all_images[i].width > max_width)
        max_width = all_images[i].width
```

The code works like this: the variable max_width will be used to hold the maximum value of the width attribute of the document's img elements. To begin with, its value is set to zero, because no img elements have been examined yet. The call to the method document.getElementsByTagName with the string "img" as its argument returns an array of objects, one for each img element in the document.

The main work is done in a loop, which has the form we just described. The loop variable i takes on values from zero to one less than the number of elements in the array in turn. Thus, inside the loop's body, the value of the expression all_images[i] is the object corresponding to the first, second, … image on the page, running through the whole collection of img objects. Each time the loop's body is executed, we compare the width property of the current img object – which holds the value of the corresponding img element's width attribute – with the current maximum, as remembered in max_width. If it is greater, we update the value of max_width. You should be able to see that when the loop terminates, every img object has been inspected and max_width holds the required maximum value.

As this example demonstrates, you can use conditional statements within the body of a loop. You can also do the reverse and put a loop in one of the clauses of a conditional statement, or use loops within loops, conditionals within conditionals, and so on. If you find you are nesting these constructs to any great depth, though, the chances are that your code could be simplified.

Note also that a conditional statement counts as a single statement, so when you use it as the entire body of a loop, you don't need curly brackets round it.

IN DETAIL

Arrays are potentially large complicated things, so they are manipulated via "references" – things that point to the whole array. This means that if you assign an array to a variable, only the reference gets copied, not the array elements. So if a is an array (or, strictly speaking, a variable containing a reference to an array), an assignment like b = a creates a synonym for a, not a copy of the array it refers to. This means that writing ++b[7] will increment a[7] too. If you do want to copy an array, you must use a loop to assign a copy of each element explicitly, like this:

for (var i = 0; i < a.length; ++i) b[i] = a[i]

ECMAScript goes beyond the traditional concept of arrays as numerically indexed sequences, by providing *associative arrays*, which are indexed by strings instead of numbers. Associative arrays are sometimes called "lookup tables", which conveys a better idea of how they work: a string is associated with some other value, and the indexing operation lets you look up the value, given the string. For example, you might use an associative array to store the meaning of certain abbreviations – that is, to associate the abbreviations with their expansions. The abbreviation could be used as an array index, with its expansion being the value. Such an array could be set up like this:

```
var abbreviations = new Array()
abbreviations["DMM"] = "Digital Multimedia"
abbreviations["DMT"] = "Digital Media Tools"
```

and so on. Later, if we had stored an abbreviated string in a variable **abbr**, we could obtain its expanded form just by using the expression **abbreviations[abbr]**.

Like numerically indexed arrays, the associative arrays we will encounter in this chapter are properties of host objects, so we will not go into any more detail about creating your own arrays.

When strings are used as array indexes, they are often referred to as *keys*, and we say that the array maps keys to values.

Functions and Methods

Object-oriented programs, especially those that use extensive APIs like those provided by Web browsers and Flash, often consist of almost nothing except method calls. In event-driven programs, much of the code is contained in event listeners, which are methods. An understanding of methods is thus essential.

The object-oriented concept of a method is closely related to an older concept, that of a *function*. Functions pre-date programming; they are used by mathematicians for describing operations which map values, known as the function's arguments, to some new value. An example which will probably be familiar is the sine function, sin(x). This maps angles to numbers between 0 and $1 - \sin(0°)$ is equal to 0, sin(90°) is 1, sin(45°) is $\frac{1}{2}\sqrt{2}$, and so on. In mathematics, this relationship between the argument and the value produced by the function just exists, but in computing functions perform some calculations to turn their arguments into results. In order to make a function perform its computation it must be explicitly called, and the value it computes is said to be "returned" from the call.

You can think of a function in a program as a sort of black box, into which argument values are placed when it is called. Generally, functions may take several arguments and combine them into a result. Some computation goes on inside the box, but when we use a function we do not need to worry about how it happens. A result comes out of the box and it can then be used.

In almost all programming languages, functions are called using the classical mathematical notation: the function name is followed by the values being supplied as arguments in brackets. For example, average(312, 68) is a function call. If the function average was defined to compute the arithmetic mean of its two arguments, this call would produce the value 190.

A method is like a function, in that it takes argument values, does some computation using them, and may generate a result. The difference is that methods are associated with, and must be called through, objects and can use the properties of the object they are associated with, as well as the arguments they are passed explicitly, in order to perform their computation. Methods often have side-effects: as well as (or instead of) computing a result, they change the values of some of their object's properties.

"Pure" object-oriented languages only allow you to define methods, there is no such thing as a function that is not part of some object, even if it is some global object that holds your entire program. In ECMAScript, though, you can define functions independently of any object. (At least, you can define functions as if they were independent of any object, although the language standard goes through some semantic contortions to explain how this works.) Functions of this kind are often found in JavaScript programs. In particular, event listeners in JavaScript are usually defined as functions. In ActionScript nowadays it is more common to define methods that belong to the object representing the movie. There isn't much difference in practice. We will explain how methods are defined when we look at ActionScript towards the end of this chapter. For now we will only consider defining functions.

Earlier, we wrote some code to compute the commission on a payment. If you frequently needed to perform this computation, you would have to cut and paste this piece of script wherever it was needed. If, however, it was turned into a function – called rake_off, say – you could just use its name wherever you needed to compute a commission – as rake_off(11450) or rake_off(the_price), for example.

A suitable definition in JavaScript of such a function based on our earlier code would look like this:

```
function rake_off(amount)
{
    var payment = amount * 0.1
    if (payment < 10)
        payment = 0
    return payment
}
```

The definition is introduced by the reserved word **function**, which identifies what follows as a function definition. Next comes the name of the function, in this case rake_off. Following this, in brackets, is an identifier, which is sometimes called a ***formal parameter*** of the function. When the function is called, the value supplied as its argument is assigned to the formal parameter. Inside the function it is used just like any other variable.

The code enclosed between curly brackets (which are required even for functions that only have a single statement in the body) specifies the computation that the function performs. It is called the ***function body***. As you can see, it is quite like the original code fragment, except that we have eliminated a superfluous variable. One significant difference is that the value for the formal parameter **amount** is supplied by the argument when the function is called, whereas before we had to assume that a value had been assigned to it somewhere else. The other difference between the function body and the original script is that the variable **payment** is used in the ***return statement***, consisting of the reserved word **return** followed by a value – in this case, just the variable – at the end of the function body. This value will be the result of the function (the value that comes out of the output slot of the black box).

When this function is called, by writing an expression such as rake_off(11450), the code in the function body is executed, with the formal parameter **amount** set to 11450. At the end of the computation, **payment** will hold the value 1145, which is returned as the value of the function call. A function call can be used as part of an expression, wherever any other value can be used. For example, var annual_total = 12*rake_off(11450)

assigns 12 (presumably monthly) commissions on an amount of 11450 to annual_total.

A function in ECMAScript is itself an object, although it is rarely treated as one in simple scripts. However, one important consequence of this fact is that you can assign functions to variables and, most important of all, pass them as arguments to other functions and methods. We will show why this is so significant in the next section.

When you need to store a function or pass it as an argument, you just use its name, like any other object. You don't put any brackets: doing so will call the function. It is also possible to create anonymous functions, when all you need to do is pass the function as an argument. This technique is commonly used in scripts, but we will continue to define functions with names in the interests of clarity.

KEY POINTS

A scripting language uses the objects of an API to control and manipulate a host system, such as a Web browser or a Flash movie.

ECMAScript is the standardized version of the core JavaScript language, which is also (in a later version) the basis of ActionScript.

Variables are named containers that can hold values, including objects. A variable's value is changed by the operation of assignment (e.g. x = x + 1).

The primitive values in ECMAScript are numbers, strings and Booleans. Standard operators are provided so you can create expressions of all three types.

In JavaScript variables may be declared; in ActionScript they must be declared.

A conditional statement is used to execute one of two statements or blocks, depending on the value of some Boolean expression, often a comparison.

For loops are used for repeating statements while a specified condition remains true. The loop header combines initialization, testing and increment.

An array is an ordered sequence of values. Individual array elements can be accessed using the indexing notation a[x].

Associative arrays are indexed by strings; they can be used as lookup tables.

A function combines its argument values and produces a result. Methods are functions that are called through an object and have access to its properties.

In ECMAScript, functions can be assigned to variables and passed as arguments.

JavaScript and the DOM

As we explained earlier, ECMAScript is an abstraction of the core of JavaScript. In other words, JavaScript consists of ECMAScript combined with host objects that allow scripts to manipulate Web pages in a browser. (The JavaScript implementations of most contemporary browsers are based on ECMAScript 3.) Historically, different browsers have provided different sets of host objects, making it difficult to write scripts that work correctly on all browsers. The W3C *Document Object Model (DOM)* is a standard set of host objects for modelling XML and HTML documents, which should now be supported by all browsers. The DOM does not provide all the facilities that are needed for Web scripting, though, and sometimes it is necessary to use non-standard objects. New standards are being developed to fill these gaps, but for now it is still sometimes necessary to work round incompatibilities between browsers.

As with our description of ECMAScript, we will not attempt an exhaustive description but only describe the DOM in sufficient detail for you to understand some fairly simple examples.

> **IN DETAIL**
>
> The documents making up the W3C DOM Recommendations actually define two object models. The "Core DOM" is suitable for modelling any XML document, including XHTML documents. The "HTML DOM" adds additional objects, properties and methods, which are specific to HTML and XHTML documents, taking advantage of the fixed set of element types in those languages. Although it is possible to manipulate any XHTML document using the Core DOM objects only, it is often more convenient to use the HTML DOM.

DOM Objects, Properties and Methods

The structure of XML and XHTML documents is hierarchical: elements contain other elements. The DOM models this hierarchy: objects contain other objects. We say that the objects modelling a document form a tree. Figure 14.2 shows how the element hierarchy of a simple XHTML document can be displayed as a tree. We are using "tree" in a technical sense here, to mean a collection of *nodes* connected by *edges*, which connect a node with its children. In the diagram, nodes are indicated by the text in blue or red, and edges by the connecting lines — edges run down and to the right. The node at the top left, which corresponds to the html element of the document, is also the root of the tree. With the exception of the root, each node has exactly one parent node. You should be able to see how the tree diagram captures the hierarchy of elements in the XHTML document, and how the relationship between nodes and their children mirrors the relationship between elements and their children.

```
html [ xmlns: "http://...", xml:lang: "en", lang: "en" ]
├ head
│   └─sub-tree for head contents
└ body
    ├─text [ \n ]
    ├─img [ src: "gradient.gif", ... ]
    ├─text [ \n ]
    ├─h1
    │   └ text [ Desperate Software ]
    ├─text [ \n ]
    ├─ p
    │   └─text node for p contents
    ├─text [ \n ]
    ├─h2
    │   └ text [ Our Products ]
    ├─text [ \n ]
    ├─ p
    │   └─text node for p contents
    ├─text [ \n ]
    ├─ ul
    │   ├─text [ \n ]
    │   ├─ li
    │   │   └ a [ href: "fridge.html" ]
    │   │      └─text [ textFridge ]
    │   ├─text [ \n ]
    │   ├─ li
    │   │   └─sub-tree for 2nd list item
    │   ├─text [ \n ]
    │   └─ li
    │       └─sub-tree for 3rd list item
    ├─text [ \n ]
    ├─h2
    │   └─sub-tree for h2
    │  and so on...
```

```html
<html xmlns="http://www.w3.org/1999/xhtml"
xml:lang="en" lang="en">
<head>
        ...
</head>
<body>
<img src="gradient.gif" alt="sunburst logo" width="87"
height="222" />
<h1>Desperate Software</h1>
<p>
Purveyors of fine computer programs to the gentry.
</p>
<h2>Our Products</h2>
<p>
Click on a link below for feature lists, download links, and
more.
</p>
<ul>
        <li><a href="fridge.html">textFridge</a></li>
        <li><a href="magnet/index.html">
            ScreenMagnet</a></li>
        <li><a href="freezer/index.html">
            Widget Freezer X</a></li>
</ul>
<h2>Contact Us</h2>
...
</body>
</html>
```

Figure 14.2. *A document tree*

Two types of node appear in the tree in Figure 14.2. **Element nodes**, in blue, correspond to the XHTML elements in the document. Their attributes' values are shown in square brackets where there are any. **Text nodes**, in red, correspond to the text that appears in the content of some elements. Here the square brackets contain the actual text. (The trees for XML documents may include several other types of node, but we will not be concerned with those.) A noticeable feature of the tree is the large number of text nodes containing a single newline character (written as \n in the diagram). Although white space in the document does not affect the appearance in a browser, it does appear in the DOM tree.

Element objects have properties for accessing the objects corresponding to nearby element and text nodes. These include firstChild, lastChild and parentNode, for accessing the nodes below and above, and previousSibling and nextSibling for accessing those on the same level. For instance, if li1 was the object corresponding to the first li element in the tree shown in Figure 14.2, whose content is the link for the textFridge product, then li1.firstChild is an Element object corresponding to the enclosed a element, and so is li1.lastChild (because li1 only has one child). The li element is contained in the ul element, so li1.parentNode is an object corresponding to the ul. Since these properties are themselves Element objects, we can use their properties to access the parent's parent, or the first child's last child, and so on.

In the HTML DOM, as we have mentioned already, each Element object has properties for each attribute. For instance, li1.firstchild.href returns the URL attached to the link. Usually, the attribute properties have the same name as the attribute, as you would expect, but there is one important exception. The property whose value is taken from the element's class attribute is called className, not class, because in almost every modern programming language, class is a reserved word. (Ironically, it is only reserved "for future use" in JavaScript.)

All the properties we have mentioned so far each have a single object or a string as their value. The childNodes property of an Element object is different: it returns an array of objects corresponding to all the element's children. These can then be examined in turn, using a for loop as we demonstrated earlier.

As well as passively traversing the tree, the DOM provides Element objects with methods for changing it. The most useful of these is appendChild, which takes an Element or Text object and inserts it as a new child, following any existing children. For instance, if tn is a text object, containing an exclamation mark, li1.appendChild(tn) would add it after the node for the textFridge link, causing it to be displayed as textFridge! (though the ! would not be part of the link). Shortly, we will explain how such a text node would be created. By appending nodes to its tree it is possible to add new elements to the document, which will be displayed in the browser window. In other words, new content will be added to the page by the script.

The **document** object represents the entire document, as we explained before. It has properties corresponding to the DTD and the **html** element, among others. As we demonstrated in previous examples, it also has the methods **getElementById** and **getElementsByTagName**. The former can be used to obtain the object corresponding to any element in the document which has an **id** attribute. The **getElementsByTagName** method takes a string, such as **"h1"**, which is the name of an element type, and returns an array containing objects for all the elements of that type in the document – all the **h1** elements, in this particular case.

The **document** object is also where the methods for creating new nodes are found. The **createElement** method takes an element type name and returns a brand new object corresponding to an element of that type. For example, **document.createElement("h1")** would be used to create a new **h1** object. Similarly, the **createTextNode** method is used to wrap up a string as a text node – **document.createTextNode("Notes")** turns the string **"Notes"** into a text node. The result of either of these methods would be suitable for appending to the children of some other **Element** object. For instance, the following code would have the effect of adding a new heading at the end of the page:

```
var h1 = document.createElement("h1")
h1.appendChild(document.createTextNode("Notes"))
var body = document.getElementsByTagName("body").[0]
body.appendChild(h1)
```

First, we ask **document** to create the node, and store it in a variable called **h1**. Next, we tell the newly created node object to add a text node – which **document** creates from the string – to its children. We then ask **document** to get all the body objects; there is only one, but we can't access it easily any other way, so we take the first item from the list that is returned, and store that in a variable, too. (Remember, the first item has index zero.) Finally, we ask the **body** object to add the node we created and populated with text to its children.

This pattern of creating nodes using the **document** methods and then appending them to **Element** nodes is a common one used in scripts that create parts of documents dynamically. Another common pattern consists of assigning new values to properties representing attributes to change the appearance of elements on the page. One example of this pattern, which has been popular for a long time, is the assignment of a new value to the **src** attribute of an image, so that a new image is displayed. Triggering such an assignment by an event that occurs when the cursor rolls over the image was the traditional way of implementing rollovers before CSS rollovers became possible. Triggering it with a mouse click is the usual way of implementing Web image galleries, such as the one shown in Figure 12.12.

Many sweeping changes to the appearance of a page can be achieved by altering the value of the class attribute of one or more elements, by assigning to the **className** property of the corresponding DOM objects. Suppose, for example, that a stylesheet includes the following rules:

```
body.plain {
    background-color: white;
    color: black;
    font-family: Verdana, sans-serif;
    font-size: 110%;
    text-align: left;
}

body.fancy {
    background-color: #D6D6D6;
    color: #561A1A;
    font-family: "Trajan Pro", serif;
    font-size: 12px;
    text-align: justify;
}

.plain #navbar {
    list-style-type: disc;
}
.plain #navbar li {
    display: list-item;
}

.fancy #navbar {
    list-style-type: none;
}
.fancy #navbar li {
    display: inline;
    padding: 0 10px;
}
```

If the class of the body element was set to "fancy", a page with a navbar (marked up as a list) would look like the screenshot at the top of Figure 14.3. Executing the following code would change it so that it looked like the lower screenshot in Figure 14.3.

```
var body = document.getElementsByTagName("body")[0]
body.className = "plain"
```

As before, an object representing the body element of the document is obtained, and then its className property is changed. The browser will then show the page as if the class attribute had been set to "fancy" in the body element's opening tag. Any contextual selectors in the stylesheet for elements contained within .fancy, such as those we have provided for #navbar, will be matched. Thus, in conjunction with a stylesheet that uses contextual selectors, these two lines of JavaScript (which could be condensed into one, at the cost of a little readability) can completely change the appearance of the entire page.

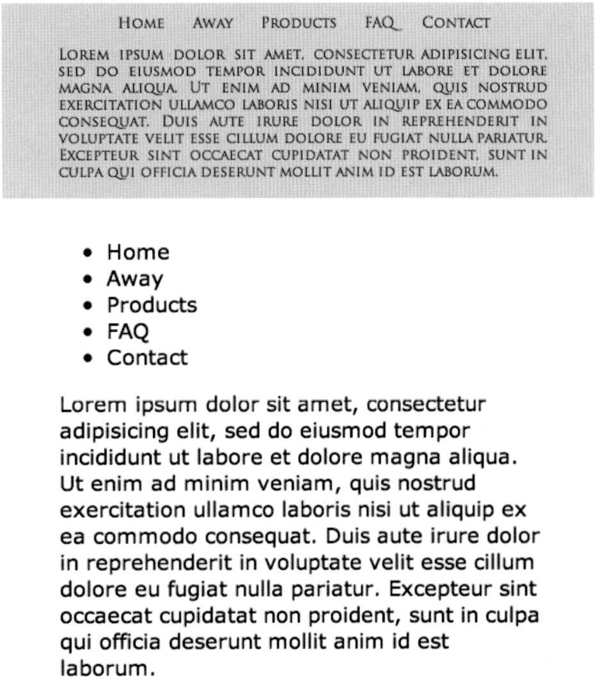

This is not just a whimsical exercise. By providing a "stylesheet switcher" of this sort, a Web designer can make it possible for people with vision problems to change a page to a more readable layout, with bigger type and more contrast, as we have done in

HOME   AWAY   PRODUCTS   FAQ   CONTACT

LOREM IPSUM DOLOR SIT AMET, CONSECTETUR ADIPISICING ELIT, SED DO EIUSMOD TEMPOR INCIDIDUNT UT LABORE ET DOLORE MAGNA ALIQUA. UT ENIM AD MINIM VENIAM, QUIS NOSTRUD EXERCITATION ULLAMCO LABORIS NISI UT ALIQUIP EX EA COMMODO CONSEQUAT. DUIS AUTE IRURE DOLOR IN REPREHENDERIT IN VOLUPTATE VELIT ESSE CILLUM DOLORE EU FUGIAT NULLA PARIATUR. EXCEPTEUR SINT OCCAECAT CUPIDATAT NON PROIDENT, SUNT IN CULPA QUI OFFICIA DESERUNT MOLLIT ANIM ID EST LABORUM.

- Home
- Away
- Products
- FAQ
- Contact

Lorem ipsum dolor sit amet, consectetur adipisicing elit, sed do eiusmod tempor incididunt ut labore et dolore magna aliqua. Ut enim ad minim veniam, quis nostrud exercitation ullamco laboris nisi ut aliquip ex ea commodo consequat. Duis aute irure dolor in reprehenderit in voluptate velit esse cillum dolore eu fugiat nulla pariatur. Excepteur sint occaecat cupidatat non proident, sunt in culpa qui officia deserunt mollit anim id est laborum.

Figure 14.3. *Switching styles from fancy (above) to plain (below)*

this example, while still providing a more stylish layout as an alternative. This will only be useful if we provide a way for the user to cause the style switching code to be executed. As you may have deduced from our remarks earlier in the chapter, this is done using events.

Before we can demonstrate how a style switcher can be activated by an event, we must describe how scripts are attached to Web pages and how event listeners are defined in JavaScript.

Adding Scripts to Pages

Scripts are added to XHTML documents using the script element. This can be used either to point to a script contained in a file external to the document or to embed a script in the document itself. The former option is usually to be preferred, since it avoids unpleasant problems with & and < characters (which have special meanings in both JavaScript and XHTML) in the script, and encourages a clean separation between scripts and the page's content. The script element's src attribute is used to hold the URL of an external script; its type attribute must also be used to specify the scripting language it uses. (Although JavaScript is the most common language, there is nothing in the XHTML specification to prevent other languages being used.) The value application/javascript is the correct type for JavaScript scripts (but more browsers recognize the officially obsolete type text/javascript.) A typical script element being used in this way would look like:

```
<script type="application/javascript" src="script.js"></script>
```

(Although a script element with a src attribute is normally empty, it is best to use an explicit end tag, as we have done here, since some browsers do not deal correctly with empty script elements written with a combined start and end tag.)

If you prefer to keep the script within the document, it can be placed in the content of a script element. There are expedients for preventing XHTML's interpretation of & and < within the script, but they are ugly and may be unreliable in the future, so it is always safest to use an external script file.

Whichever method you use for including your scripts, they are executed when the browser encounters the script element. A script cannot use properties or methods of any objects that have not been created at that point. Since the most convenient place for script elements is the document's head, this is something of a problem – the objects for the body and everything it contains will not have been set up when the script is encountered. We will show how this problem can be overcome shortly.

Events and Listeners

The method addEventListener is an example of a method that takes a function as one of its arguments. For simple cases, addEventListener takes two arguments. The first is a string, whose value is the name of an event; the second is a function which will act as the listener for events of that type. We use the function's name only, because we are passing the function object, not calling it.

For instance, if switch1 was an object corresponding to an element of a document, which was required to respond to mouse clicks by changing the class of the body element to "plain", and plainify was a function that performed that change, in the way we showed earlier, the object could be made to respond using the following call:

```
switch1.addEventListener("click", plainify)
```

Figure 14.4 lists the names of the principle events that can be used in JavaScript. The ones marked "not a DOM event" are not part of the official DOM Events standard, but are supported by the major browsers. The focus and blur events refer to form controls. A control is said to "have the focus" when it is about to receive input. This might happen when a user clicks on the control, or uses the tab key to move to it.

Event Name	Meaning	Restrictions
load	All the content of a page has been loaded.	body only
unload	The document has been removed from the window.	
click	The mouse was clicked with the cursor over the element.	
dblclick	The mouse was double-clicked with the cursor over the element.	not a DOM event
mousedown	The mouse button was pressed with the cursor over the element.	
mouseup	The mouse button was released with the cursor over the element.	
mouseover	The cursor was moved onto the element.	
mousemove	The cursor was moved while it was over the element.	
mouseout	The cursor was moved away from the element.	
focus	The element has received the focus.	a, area and form control elements
blur	The element has lost the focus.	
keypress	A key was pressed and released while the cursor was over the element.	not a DOM event
keydown	A key was pressed while the cursor was over the element.	
keyup	A key was released while the cursor was over the element.	
submit	The form was submitted.	form only
reset	The form was reset.	
select	The user selected some text in a text field.	input and textarea only
change	The element has lost the focus and its value has been modified since it received the focus.	input, select and textarea only

Figure 14.4. *Principal HTML events*

Any function that is to be used as an event listener should be defined to take a single argument, which will be the Event object corresponding to the event that caused the listener to be executed. Often this argument is simply ignored, but sometimes the values stored in it are needed. In particular, its target property holds the object that received the event.

IN DETAIL

Some elements on a Web page already respond to events. In particular, links respond to clicks. If you add a listener for click events to a link, you usually want to override the default behaviour.

For example, if you were creating an image gallery, such as the one in Figure 12.12, you might put links on each thumbnail pointing to a page displaying the full-sized image, so that users who had disabled JavaScript would still be able to see the image, though not within the gallery page. The event listener that you attach to these links would load the image into the page, and you would not then want the link to be followed. In order to suppress the default response to an event, an event listener should call the preventDefault method of the event object passed to it as an argument.

We can now define and add event listeners for switching styles. We must provide some way for the user to choose one of the two styles. For now, we will simply add the following at the end of the document body.

```
<p class="switches"><span id="switch1">plain</span>
<span id="switch2">fancy</span></p>
```

The words plain and fancy will appear on the page; we can use the switches class as the basis of CSS selectors to style them in a suitable fashion.

We need to define a pair of functions, one to set the body's class to "plain", the other to set it to "fancy". These will be almost identical, so to avoid duplicating code we will define a third function, switch_style, that takes the class name as its argument.

```
function switch_style(s) {
    var body = document.getElementsByTagName("body")[0]
    body.className = s
}
```

The event listeners are then trivial. We will declare them with an event as their parameter, even though we are not going to use it.

```
function fancify(e) {
    switch_style("fancy")
}

function plainify(e) {
    switch_style("plain")
}
```

Now we have a problem. We want to add these functions as listeners for the click event to the two elements with id values switch1 and switch2. We know how to find these elements, using document.getElementById and we know how to add event listeners to them. However, as we explained earlier, the script is executed when the browser encounters it. If the script is in the document head, those elements don't exist yet.

Some Web designers respond to this problem by placing their scripts at the end of the document, but there is a much more elegant solution. Although it is not part of the DOM, all browsers implement the window object, which models the browser window. As well as having some useful properties and methods, the window object is an EventTarget so we can add listeners to it. In particular, the window receives a load event when all the elements of the page have been loaded. At that time, it is safe to add listeners to any element.

We therefore proceed in two steps. First, we define the following function that adds the event listeners to our switches.

```
function prepare(e) {
    var switch1 = document.getElementById("switch1")
    var switch2 = document.getElementById("switch2")
    switch1.addEventListener("click", plainify)
    switch2.addEventListener("click", fancify)
}
```

Then we add prepare itself to the window object as a listener for the load event:

```
window.addEventListener("load", prepare)
```

As a result, when the window loads, prepare is called and adds the listeners to the switches, so that if a user clicks on one of them, it will set the class of the body element appropriately.

We have now presented the user with two working controls for changing the page's style, but no indication of which style is currently applied. We could easily manipulate the class of the span elements so that one or other of them was distinguished, but no matter how we chose to highlight one of the controls, we would be in exactly the situation we criticized in connection with Figure 12.14 in Chapter 12. The user would not be sure whether the highlight indicated the style that was currently in effect, or the style that could be changed to. We can avoid this problem by modifying our script so that it doesn't just change the style, it also alters the control so that there is only ever one on the page, which clearly causes a change to a different style.

To begin with, we'll define a function that creates some text inside a **span** element with an **id** attribute. It takes the text and the **id** value as arguments, so it can be used to create either of the **span** elements we originally placed in the document explicitly.

```
function make_switch(the_text, the_id) {
    var text = document.createTextNode("change to " + the_text + " style")
    var span = document.createElement("span")
    span.id = the_id
    span.appendChild(text)
    return span
}
```

This is a fiddly business, because we must first create a text node. We add some standard text to the argument while doing so — since this will always be the same, this is the appropriate place to do so. Next, we create a **span** element and set its **id** to the value passed as an argument. Finally, we make the text node into a child of the **span**, effectively inserting the text as the contents of the **span** element. We return the **span** as the result of the function. You should be able to see that a call of this function

```
make_switch("plain", "switch1")
```

will create an object corresponding to the XHTML

```
<span id="switch1">change to plain style</span>
```

For now, we are going to cheat a little, and assume that there is an empty paragraph somewhere in the document, just waiting to contain such a **span** element. To make it easy to find, we will give it an **id**.

```
<p id="sw" class="switches"> </p>
```

With this assumption in place, we can write another function which will take some text and an **id** value and put a **span** element built by **make_switch** into this paragraph. But the whole point of this exercise is to create a control for switching between styles, so this **span** needs an event listener. We will pass a listener as an extra argument, and add it once we have put the switch into the paragraph.

```
function do_switch(the_text, the_id, the_listener) {
    var the_switch = make_switch(the_text, the_id)
    var switch_p = document.getElementById("sw")
    switch_p.replaceChild(the_switch, switch_p.firstChild)
    the_switch.addEventListener("click", the_listener)
}
```

Now the modifications to our previous functions to make sure that only the applicable control is visible are trivial:

```
function fancify(e) {
    switch_style("fancy")
    do_switch("plain", "switch1", plainify)
}

function plainify(e) {
    switch_style("plain")
    do_switch("fancy", "switch2", fancify)
}
```

The **prepare** function, which we call to set everything up when the window loads, just has to create the control for the initial state, in which we assume the fancy style is being used to display the page:

```
function prepare(e){
    do_switch("plain", "switch1", plainify)
}
```

Creating the controls dynamically like this has a significant extra advantage. If a user has disabled JavaScript, they will never see any controls, because none will be created. If the controls had been added to the page statically instead, just using markup, such a user would have seen the style-switching control, but it would not have done anything for them.

There is just one loose end left, and that is the empty paragraph we put at the end of our document to hold the control. It doesn't really do any harm, even for users who have disabled JavaScript, but since we know how to create page elements dynamically there seems no reason not to build this paragraph the same way, so we can be sure it is only created if it is going to be used. All we need to do is extend the **prepare** function with some more node-building method calls.

```
function prepare(e){
    var para = document.createElement("p")
    para.id = "sw"
```

```
    para.className = "switches"
    para.appendChild(document.createTextNode(" "))
    get_body().appendChild(para)
    do_switch("plain", "switch1", plainify)
}
```

We have used a function **get_body** here, which simply returns the object for the **body** element, using the expression we had before. The function can also be used in **switch_style**, whose function body can be simplified to **get_body().className = s**. The new function only serves to avoid repeating the same code.

IN DETAIL

Building up page elements a node at a time like this is so tedious that many Web developers prefer an alternative. In most browsers, objects have a property called innerHTML. A string can be assigned to this property, and it becomes the new content of the corresponding element. The string may contain HTML markup, which is interpreted when the modified element is displayed, so instead of creating nodes from the inside out and assigning them it is possible to assign an HTML string. Our make_switch function would be redundant, because we could assign a string of HTML to the innerHTML property of the paragraph containing the switch.

The innerHTML property is not part of any relevant standard, though, so it should be avoided. It may be defined in some future standard, when you will have to decide whether the convenience of assigning to innerHTML outweighs the inelegance of mixing markup with operations on the tree structure.

As this example demonstrates, adding event listeners to objects associated with page elements and using them to change attribute values and add new elements to the page is not very difficult. The potential for adding interactivity to Web pages in this way is considerable. With the addition of the **XMLHttpRequest** object to load data from a remote server, which we describe briefly in Chapter 16 and in more detail in *Web Design: A Complete Introduction*, many forms of interactivity that are familiar from desktop applications may be added to Web applications.

More complicated scripts are required to achieve more elaborate effects, of course, but the basic approach is the same as that we have demonstrated here. Despite recent improvements in support for the relevant standards in browsers, practical scripts still need to be written to take account of incompatibilities between different browsers. Most Web sites that use a lot of JavaScript rely on libraries and frameworks, such as prototype and jQuery, to take care of such details and provide general-purpose functions that can be reused for many applications.

KEY POINTS

The W3C Document Object Model (DOM) is a standard set of objects for modelling XML and HTML documents.

A document is represented by a tree of nodes representing elements connected by edges that model the hierarchical relationships between elements.

Nodes may be text nodes or element nodes.

Element objects have properties for accessing nearby nodes.

In the HTML DOM each Element object has properties for each attribute. Most of these properties have the same name as the attribute, but the class attribute is accessed through the className property.

Methods of the document object, including getElementById and getElementsByTagName (which returns an array) can be used to retrieve nodes.

The methods document.createElement and document.createTextNode can be used to create new nodes, which can be inserted into the tree to add new elements to the page.

Many changes to the appearance of a page can be achieved by altering the value of the properties corresponding to attributes of one or more elements.

Changing the value of the className property of the body object can change the appearance of the entire page.

Scripts are added to XHTML documents using the script element, either to point to an external script file or to embed JavaScript code in the document.

The addEventListener method takes two arguments: the name of an event and a function which will act as the listener for events of that type.

The listener function receives an Event object as its argument.

Add a listener for the load event to the window object to perform any set-up and add listeners to elements within the body of the document.

Create controls for changes that are implemented in JavaScript using a script, to ensure that only applicable controls are visible and that users who have disabled scripts will never see the controls.

Powerful JavaScript libraries and frameworks are used to create elaborate interactivity with event listeners and DOM objects.

ActionScript

ActionScript is based on ECMAScript 4, a later version of ECMAScript than that which forms the basis of JavaScript. The main difference from the subset of JavaScript which we used in the preceding section is that ActionScript requires all variables to be declared, together with the type of value they may hold. A bigger difference between JavaScript and ActionScript is the way in which classes are defined and inheritance is specified. We quietly avoided this topic in our description of JavaScript, because the mechanism used is unconventional and rarely needed in simple scripts, which usually just make use of the host objects without creating any objects of their own. ActionScript uses a more conventional and easily understood mechanism, which plays a more prominent role, as we will describe.

The most significant difference between ActionScript and JavaScript lies in the host objects each supplies, because they are used to "manipulate, customize and automate" two completely different host systems. ActionScript's repertoire of objects is considerably more extensive than the DOM, so in this chapter we can do no more than scratch the surface of what can be achieved with some of them.

Formerly, Flash movies could only be created within the interactive "authoring environment" of the Flash program. Scripts were added to frames, to be executed when the frame was displayed, and to symbols, to react to events. This was done using the timeline and stage. There are now alternative ways of creating Flash movies. It is possible to use the *Flex* framework to build movies which act as small applications with an interactive multimedia interface. Components may be arranged using a markup language called *MXML*, or created dynamically by scripts, without the need for Flash itself. Even if you work in Flash — as we shall in our example — it is both simple and beneficial to separate all the ActionScript code into an external file, so that the scripts do not need to be entangled with the elements of the movie.

The Document Class

When we were demonstrating the use of JavaScript to create interactivity on the Web we described how scripts are added to a page using the script element. We were able to separate the script code from the XHTML markup in the document's body by using a listener for the window's load event to add listeners to elements on the page. With ActionScript, a script may be added to a movie using a different mechanism, which allows the preparatory addition of event listeners to be done in a more elegant way.

You will recall that a Flash movie is, by default, an object belonging to the MovieClip class, but that its class can be changed. This is done in Flash by typing a class name into the Document class field in the Properties panel with nothing selected (so the movie properties are showing), as shown in Figure 14.5. The class name does not have to match the name of the Flash document, although it often does. It must, however, match the name of a text file, with extension .as, containing the definition of the class. That is, if the document class is set to GeoPlayer, there must be a file called GeoPlayer.as, somewhere Flash can find it – usually in the same folder as the Flash document. This file can contain all the ActionScript code for event listeners and any other methods that are needed to provide the required interactive operations. When a Flash movie is exported from the document, the code will be combined with the animation to produce the working application.

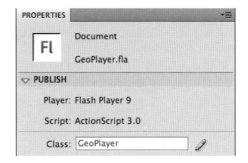

Figure 14.5. *Setting the document class in Flash*

The definition of the class consists for the most part of definitions of its methods, which are syntactically the same as the function definitions we have seen (except that, because we are now writing ActionScript, types must be declared, as we will show, and we need to specify whether each method is available outside the class, a detail we will explain shortly).

One method is special. It is called the class's **constructor**, and it is called automatically whenever an object belonging to the class is created. Every class can have a constructor, which usually performs some initialization, such as assigning values to the newly created object's properties. The constructor's definition looks like that of any other method, but its name must be the same as the class's name. For our example, the constructor is a method called GeoPlayer. The constructor for the document class is called when the movie object is created. This makes it the ideal place to add any event listeners that will be needed when the movie runs.

As well as the definitions of the constructor and other methods, some additional rubric is needed in the file containing the document class's definition. It may appear quite intimidating, though it does make sense in the larger context of the ActionScript language. You can treat it as a pure formality, similar to the DTD and so on that must appear in every XHTML document.

Here is the outline of GeoPlayer.as.

```
package {
    import flash.display.MovieClip;
    import flash.events.*;
    import fl.events.*;
    import flash.display.DisplayObject;
```

```
import fl.controls.Button;
import flash.text.*;

public class GeoPlayer extends MovieClip {
    declarations of properties

    public function GeoPlayer()
    {
      body of the constructor
    }

    declarations of other methods

  }
}
```

In ActionScript, *packages* are collections of classes. Their purpose is to organize large programs and libraries, but even in a small program like our example, every class must belong to some package. There is an anonymous default package, which is appropriate for holding document classes. To add a class to the default package, the class definition is enclosed in curly brackets and preceded by the reserved word **package**. This is what the first and last lines of the outline do.

The classes for the Flash host objects are all defined in packages. To use a class from some named package, it is necessary to import it explicitly – you cannot just use a host object, the way that you can in JavaScript. The six lines each beginning with the reserved word **import** make the classes that are needed by our script available within the class definition. You may consider all this as just being necessary housekeeping for now. If you go on to write your own scripts you will have to become familiar with the way the Flash API is organized into packages.

Inside a package, classes can be public, which means they can be used from outside the package, or private, meaning they can only be used by other classes inside the same package. A document class must be public, so its definition begins with the reserved words **public class**, followed by its name, **GeoPlayer**. As we said earlier, this class must be a sub-class of **MovieClip**, because the movie is itself a movie clip and we need to be able to call **MovieClip** methods through it. This relationship is indicated by the clause **extends MovieClip**. The body of the class is enclosed in curly brackets, hence the whole definition has the form shown above.

Like classes, methods can be public or private, so the definition of the constructor (the method called **GeoPlayer**) is preceded by **public**.

The definition of any document class would have the same form as this one: an enclosing package declaration containing some import statements and the public class definition for the document class itself. This will consist of declarations of any properties and methods of the document class and normally the definition of a public constructor. What distinguishes each class is the methods and properties declared within the class. The methods are what define the behaviour of the particular movie. A typical pattern for the document class comprises definitions of several private methods, which are added to objects in the movie as event listeners in the constructor. Extra private methods may be used to break up the program into more manageable pieces. We will use this pattern to implement the thin-section geological slide viewer which we have been using as an example in several chapters.

Implementing Interactivity Using ActionScript

The movie was created in Flash, but as it consists only of a single key frame it could have been made in Flex. Looking back at Figure 14.1, you can see that the controls are instances of UI components, mostly **Button** and **TextArea** components. In the version of the player we are going to analyse here, the image of the slide itself is a Flash movie that was prepared independently from a sequence of photographs taken through a real microscope, and imported into the library as a movie clip symbol, an instance of which was created on the stage. A more useful viewer would load the movie from an external file, so it could be used to view different slides. We will not describe the complications that are caused by this enhancement here, however.

Figure 14.6. *Naming a symbol instance*

All the component and symbol instances were given names in Flash. This makes the corresponding object available to scripts by that name, without requiring the name to be declared or the object created explicitly. For instance, the movie clip of the slide was given the name geo_slide (see Figure 14.6), so within our script we can call methods such as geo_slide.play() to control it. The object called geo_slide belongs to the class **MovieClip**, because we created it from a movie clip symbol. We imported all the classes from a package called flash.display.MovieClip so all the relevant methods are available.

It is easy to make the top row of buttons that control the playback of the slide movie work. Any movie clip object has methods **play**, **stop**, **prevFrame** and **nextFrame**, which provide the basic operations required by these buttons. It is not quite adequate just to create simple event listeners that call these **MovieClip** methods, and add the appropriate listener to each button. In the first place, the buttons for stepping forwards and backwards must work even at the beginning or end of the movie. In the second place, as we are aiming for good interaction design, only those buttons that can usefully be pressed should be active at any time. For instance, it should not be possible to step back while the movie is playing, so this button should be disabled at that time.

Clicking either of the step forward or step backward buttons does not alter which controls should be enabled, so we will start by writing a click listener for stepping forward. The basic operation is performed by calling the relevant **MovieClip** method, **nextFrame**. We will handle the end conditions in an obvious way, by checking whether we are at the end of the movie, and, if we are, going back to the beginning. Two very useful properties of **MovieClip** objects are **currentFrame**, which holds the number of the frame being displayed, and **totalFrames**, which holds a count of the number of frames in the clip. So, if **geo_slide** is at its final frame, the expression **geo_slide.currentFrame == geo_slide.totalFrames** will have the value **true**.

MovieClip objects also have methods called **gotoAndStop** and **gotoAndPlay**. These take a frame number as their argument, and display the corresponding frame. If **gotoAndStop** is called, the movie then stops, whereas if **gotoAndPlay** is called instead, it plays on from that frame. In the present case we want to stop, because we are only stepping through the movie.

The listener for a click event on the button to step forward is defined as follows:

```
private function step_forward(e: MouseEvent): void {
    if (geo_slide.currentFrame == geo_slide.totalFrames)
        geo_slide.gotoAndStop(1)
    else
        geo_slide.nextFrame()
}
```

Notice the small additions to the function declaration compared with JavaScript. We have preceded the declaration with the reserved word **private**, because we don't want the function to be called explicitly from outside the class. (We will shortly add it to the relevant button as an event listener, and that is the only way in which it should be called.) The formal parameter has its type appended. In ActionScript, events are divided into sub-classes: clicks belong to the **MouseEvent** class. We also have to declare a return type for the function. This function doesn't actually return a value, so its return type is set to **void** – a common device in programming languages for denoting the absence of any type.

The click listener for the step backward button is similar, except that it moves to the previous frame and tests for the beginning of the movie.

```
private function step_backward(e: MouseEvent): void {
    if (geo_slide.currentFrame == 1)
```

```
        geo_slide.gotoAndStop(geo_slide.totalFrames)
    else
        geo_slide.prevFrame()
}
```

The play and stop buttons' click listeners present a different problem. Their operations can both be implemented with a call to a **MovieClip** method, without having to consider any special cases, because movie clips play in a loop, automatically going back to the beginning when they reach the end. The complication here is ensuring that an appropriate set of buttons is enabled. When the movie is playing, only the stop button should be enabled. When it is stopped, the others should be enabled instead. As well as the buttons that control playback, the slider which is used to scrub through the movie should be disabled while the movie is playing. Its name is **rotator**; the names of the other buttons should be self-explanatory.

Each instance of the **Button** component has a property called **enabled**, which can be set to **true** or **false**, to enable or disable the button. When a **Button** component is disabled, it is automatically dimmed – it is not necessary to change its colour explicitly as the dimming is part of the behaviour built in to **Button** components.

These click listeners are defined in the following way:

```
private function play_it(e: MouseEvent): void {
    play_button.enabled = forward_button.enabled = back_button.enabled = false
    rotator.enabled = false
    stop_button.enabled = true
    geo_slide.play()
}

private function stop_it(e:MouseEvent): void {
    play_button.enabled = forward_button.enabled = back_button.enabled = true
    rotator.enabled = true
    stop_button.enabled = false
    geo_slide.stop()
}
```

We have used a neat shorthand here. Although an assignment may be used on its own as a statement, assignments are actually expressions, which have a value – the value that was assigned. You can make use of this fact to "chain together" assignments when you want to set several variables to the same value, as we have done here. (Using the value of an assignment expression in any more elaborate ways is a common source of errors and is not advisable.)

None of what we have done so far will be any use unless the listeners are added to the appropriate objects. As we explained earlier, this is best done in the constructor. The **addEventListener** method in ActionScript works in just the same way as its counterpart in JavaScript.

```
public function GeoPlayer() {
    stop()
    stop_it(null)
    forward_button.addEventListener(MouseEvent.CLICK, step_forward)
    back_button.addEventListener(MouseEvent.CLICK, step_backward)
    stop_button.addEventListener(MouseEvent.CLICK, stop_it)
    play_button.addEventListener(MouseEvent.CLICK, play_it)
}
```

Notice first that the name of the event is **MouseEvent.CLICK**, because of the way events are defined within classes in ActionScript. Notice also that we have done a bit more than add the event listeners. First, we have called the **MovieClip** method **stop**. Since we have not specified any object, it is called using the object being constructed – that is, the movie itself. The result is to stop it playing – otherwise it loops on the single frame, with distressing results. After that, we have called the **stop_it** method explicitly, to stop the slide movie rotating and to enable the appropriate set of buttons. We have passed **null** as an argument, because there is no event to pass, but in ActionScript a method that has been defined with a formal parameter must be passed something as the corresponding argument.

We have now implemented a basic movie player, with play, stop, step forward and step backward controls. Adding code to make the slider work to scrub through the movie introduces some extra events.

The slider – which we called **rotator** – is an instance of the standard **Slider** UI component. **Slider** components can respond to some events defined specifically for them in the **SliderEvent** class. In particular, a slider may respond to the **SliderEvent.THUMB_DRAG** event, which occurs when the slider's control (its "thumb") is dragged by a user. When this happens, we want the geological slide to appear to rotate, which means moving it to a new frame.

Every **Slider** object has a **value** property. When the slider is created in Flash, some parameters can be specified. In particular, you can set a maximum and a minimum, which will be the **Slider** object's values when the thumb is at the right and left ends, respectively. The value at any intermediate point is interpolated linearly. When we created this slider, we set the maximum to 150 and the minimum to 1, because we knew that our movie had 150 frames. As a result, mapping the value directly to a frame number means that the movie's current frame always bears the same relation to the duration of the whole movie as the slider's position does to the length of the slider. When the thumb is in the middle of the slider, the middle frame is displayed, and so on.

Hence, making the movie follow the slider is simple. First we define a one-line method:

```
private function follow_rotator_drag(e: SliderEvent):void {
    geo_slide.gotoAndStop(rotator.value)
}
```

Then we add it to the slider as an event listener, by adding the following code to the movie's constructor:

```
rotator.addEventListener(SliderEvent.THUMB_DRAG, follow_rotator_drag)
```

This is not all, though. The relationship between the thumb's position and the geological slide movie's frame will be disrupted if a user clicks the play button or one of the step buttons: the slider will be left where it is. We need to ensure not only that the movie follows the slider, as we have, but also that the slider follows the movie. As a nice side-effect, if we do this, the slider will provide a visual indication of the position of the geological slide.

It's trivially easy to write a method to move the slider to the right position.

```
private function move_rotator(e: Event) {
    rotator.value = geo_slide.currentFrame
}
```

But how do we ensure that this method is called whenever it should be?

Frame events are used for purposes such as this. Flash started out as an animation program, displaying a sequence of graphic frames. It continues to behave in roughly the same way, but frames are now more complicated things than just images. They can include movie clip symbols, which progress independently, and may require the execution of scripts. It may be more helpful to imagine that each movie clip, including the main movie, is processed by some sort of device, which includes an instrument called a **playhead**. The playhead is placed over the frames one at a time, and the device processes the frame under the playhead before moving it on to the next frame, which may be the next frame on the timeline, or may be determined by a script. Every time the playhead looks at a new frame, an event occurs. It is identified by the constant Event.ENTER_FRAME.

We want the **move_rotator** method to be called every time the geological slide rotates to a new position, which is every time the movie clip **geo_slide** enters a new frame. This will happen if we add the method to the clip object as a listener for the ENTER_FRAME event, so we just need to add this line to the constructor:

```
geo_slide.addEventListener(Event.ENTER_FRAME, move_rotator)
```

The slider's position will now stay in sync with the geological slide's angle of rotation. This would be a good way of showing how far through a movie we were, if these controls were being used as a simple movie player, but it would be more useful to a geologist if the angle of rotation was displayed numerically.

Back in Figure 14.1, you can see there is a TextArea component to the right of the player controls. Its name was set in Flash to angle_display, and its purpose is to display the current angle of rotation.

The first thing we need to do is find out what the angle of rotation is. At any time, we know what the current frame number is, and we know that there are 150 frames in the movie, which takes the geological slide all the way round through 360°. It shouldn't be hard to see how to calculate the number of degrees of rotation that correspond to advancing the movie by one frame, and hence the angle corresponding to the current frame. We will make this a separate method, because we will need the computation again later.

```
private function find_angle(): Number {
    const degrees_per_frame: Number = 360/geo_slide.totalFrames;
    return ((geo_slide.currentFrame - 1) * degrees_per_frame)
}
```

This method isn't going to be an event listener, so it doesn't have to take an Event object as its argument. It is going to return a value, though, so we declare the return type. The calculation is carried out in a straightforward way, which you should be able to understand without further explanation.

Most of the values returned by find_angle will not be whole numbers. (It might have been better if there had been 180 frames in the slide movie, but the number was determined by the hardware used to take the original sequence of photographs.) If a value that is not an integer is displayed, many decimal places will be shown by default. This is not appropriate: it will be hard to read, and implies a degree of accuracy that is not consistent with the material. We need to round the angle to a small number of decimal places. One place seems suitable. The Number class has a method called toFixed, which returns a string representing the number. It takes an argument indicating the required number of digits after the decimal point. Hence, find_angle().toFixed(1) gives us the angle to one decimal place of accuracy.

What are we going to do with this string? We want to display it in the TextField component angle_display. TextField components have a property called text. Assigning a string to this property causes it to be shown in the field, which is what we want to do. We'll append a degree sign in the process:

```
private function show_angle(e: Event): void {
    angle_display.text = find_angle().toFixed(1) + "°"
}
```

This time, we have declared the method with an Event as its parameter, because we want to make it into an event listener. The angular display should be updated every time the slide moves, just as the slider control was, so we also add show_angle to geo_slide as a listener for the ENTER_FRAME event. You can add any number of listeners for an event to an object. They will all be executed when the event occurs. (If you need to know what order they are executed in, your program is probably too complicated.) Again, we just need to add one line to the constructor:

```
geo_slide.addEventListener(Event.ENTER_FRAME, show_angle)
```

That completes the code for the top row of controls and the slider. The controls on the bottom row introduce some more features, but we will describe them more rapidly, because the basic mechanism should be familiar by now.

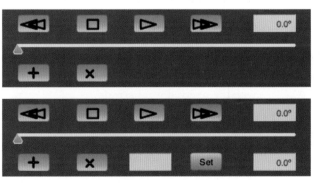

These lower controls are dynamic – they are not all displayed all the time. To begin with, only the two buttons at the left are shown. The first of these (called cross_hair_toggle) causes the cross-hairs to be displayed over the geological slide, for setting up a measurement, and also brings up the remaining button and two text fields. (See Figure 14.7.) Clicking the button again causes the cross-hairs and extra controls to vanish.

Figure 14.7. *Toggling the read-out*

In JavaScript, the only way to make an element disappear is by changing its display property to none, either indirectly by changing the className property as we did previously, or directly by manipulating the element's style property. In ActionScript, though, we can add objects to the frame and remove them from it using methods of the stage property of the movie. The addChild method adds an object to the stage, so it becomes visible, the removeChild method removes it so that it disappears. In Flash, we combined the text fields and Set button into a single movie clip, which we called delta_readout. The cross-hairs are also a movie clip, called cross_hair. Hence, the following pair of statements displays the cross-hairs and controls:

```
stage.addChild(cross_hair)
stage.addChild(delta_readout)
```

and the following pair hides them:

```
stage.removeChild(cross_hair)
stage.removeChild(delta_readout)
```

(These calls occur inside the document class, so the **stage** property belongs to the movie.)

We don't just want to make these objects appear or disappear, though. They are controls, so they need event listeners in order to operate. We must step back a little to see what these must do before we can see how to add them.

The idea is that, with the geological slide stopped in some position, clicking the **Set** button will record the current angle of rotation — it will be shown in the text field to the left of the button — and thereafter the text field to the right of the button will show the difference between the current angle and the remembered value. (Typically, a geologist would want to record the angle at which some crystal in the sample was aligned with the direction of polarization of the light being used to illuminate the slide, and then rotate the slide until the sample went dark. Knowledge of the angular difference can be used to help identify the minerals in the sample.)

It is clear that some way of remembering the start angle is needed. We will declare a property in the document class for this purpose. This is done just like declaring a variable, but within the class definition. We don't want the value to be used from outside the class, so we prefix the declaration with the reserved word **private**.

```
private var the_start_angle:Number = 0
```

We know that at some point we will want to display the value of this property in the text field, so we might as well write a little method to do so. The field was given the name **start_display** in Flash, but you will recall that we combined it with the other read-out controls into a movie clip called **delta_readout**. Components or movie clips within other movie clips can be accessed as if they were properties of the movie clip containing them, so the text field for showing the start angle is **delta_readout.start_display**, and our method can be defined as follows:

```
private function set_start_angle(e:MouseEvent): void {
    the_start_angle = find_angle()
    delta_readout.start_display.text = the_start_angle.toFixed(1) + "°"
}
```

Because the_start_angle is not declared inside the method, the assignment will store the value in the document class property we just declared. We can reuse the find_angle method we defined earlier.

We also know that we are going to display the difference between the current angle and the stored angle in the other text field (delta_display) inside delta_readout. This is easily done, too.

```
private function find_delta(): Number {
    return find_angle() - the_start_angle
}

private function show_delta(e:Event): void {
    delta_readout.delta_display.text = find_delta().toFixed(1) + "°"
}
```

All that remains to be done is to set and remove event listeners at appropriate times. Obviously, set_start_angle should be attached to the Set button as a listener for click events. Since the angular difference changes every time the slide is moved, show_delta needs to be a listener for ENTER_FRAME events on the slide, just as show_angle was. These listeners should only operate while the read-out is visible, so they are added when the cross-hairs are displayed, and removed again when they are hidden – so the relevant calls to addEventListener are made within a pair of methods called show_cross_hairs and hide_cross_hairs. These are going to listen for click events on the button for toggling the cross-hairs. This means that when one of them is called, it should remove itself as a listener and add the other, so that the button always switches between the two states.

Putting these ideas together gives the following definitions.

```
private function show_cross_hairs(e:MouseEvent): void {
    stage.addChild(cross_hair)
    stage.addChild(delta_readout)

    cross_hair_toggle.removeEventListener(MouseEvent.CLICK, show_cross_hairs)
    cross_hair_toggle.addEventListener(MouseEvent.CLICK, hide_cross_hairs)

    delta_readout.start_angle_set.addEventListener(MouseEvent.CLICK, set_start_angle)

    geo_slide.addEventListener(Event.ENTER_FRAME, show_delta)
}

private function hide_cross_hairs(e:MouseEvent): void {
    stage.removeChild(cross_hair)
    stage.removeChild(delta_readout)
```

```
        cross_hair_toggle.removeEventListener(MouseEvent.CLICK, hide_cross_hairs)
        cross_hair_toggle.addEventListener(MouseEvent.CLICK, show_cross_hairs)

        delta_readout.start_angle_set.removeEventListener(MouseEvent.CLICK, set_start_angle)

        geo_slide.removeEventListener(Event.ENTER_FRAME, show_delta)
    }
```

The read-out is visible when the movie first loads, because of the way it was created in Flash, so it is necessary to hide it and add the correct event listener to the cross-hair toggle control in the constructor. To consolidate this account, we will show the complete constructor.

```
public function GeoPlayer() {
    stop()
    stop_it(null)

    /* Add all the event listeners */
    forward_button.addEventListener(MouseEvent.CLICK, step_forward)
    back_button.addEventListener(MouseEvent.CLICK, step_backward)
    stop_button.addEventListener(MouseEvent.CLICK, stop_it)
    play_button.addEventListener(MouseEvent.CLICK, play_it)
    geo_slide.addEventListener(Event.ENTER_FRAME, show_angle)
    geo_slide.addEventListener(Event.ENTER_FRAME, move_rotator)
    rotator.addEventListener(SliderEvent.THUMB_DRAG, follow_rotator_drag)
    cross_hair_toggle.addEventListener(MouseEvent.CLICK, show_cross_hairs)

    /* hide the cross-hairs etc */
    removeChild(cross_hair)
    removeChild(delta_readout)
}
```

┌─ IN DETAIL ───┐

If you download the working version of this example from the supporting Web site, you will find some extra lines of code in the constructor, which we have not described here. Their purpose is just to set the icons on the buttons and the formatting options for the text fields. It adds little to the understanding of scripting for interactivity, so we have omitted it in the interests of brevity.

└───┘

The only thing missing from this script is some code to switch between two different views of the geological slide (typically under polarized and cross-polarized light) by clicking on the second button on the bottom row. We leave this as an exercise.

If you have not previously looked at any scripts or done any programming yourself, you may be surprised at how much code is needed to achieve a relatively simple task. Although a lot of small pieces have to be fitted together, we hope that it is evident that all we are doing is making objects respond to events.

We have tried to make the code shown here as easy to follow as possible, instead of striving for elegance and efficiency. We invite you to remedy some of its defects in the exercises.

KEY POINTS

ActionScript is based on ECMAScript 4, and requires all variables to be declared, together with their types.

Unlike JavaScript, ActionScript provides a conventional mechanism for defining classes and inheritance.

Code to be used in a Flash movie can be defined in methods of the document class, which is usually derived from the MovieClip class.

Event listeners can be set up in the document class's constructor, which is called before the movie starts playing, when the movie object is created.

Document classes are defined within the default package. The class and constructor must both be public.

The methods play, stop, gotoAndPlay and gotoAndStop can be used to control playback of objects belonging to the MovieClip class.

UI components have methods and properties that implement the expected behaviour and appearance of controls such as buttons, sliders and text fields.

The ENTER_FRAME event can be used to cause a listener to be executed every time the playhead enters a new frame.

A string can be displayed by assigning it to the text property of a TextField component.

Objects can be made to appear and vanish by adding them to and removing them from the frame using the addChild and removeChild methods of the movie's stage property.

Properties of the movie, declared in the document class, can be used to store values that can be used by its methods.

Complex interactivity is created by making objects respond to events.

Exercises

When you need to test Web pages containing JavaScript, use a Web browser that supports all the relevant standards. Do not try to use any version of Internet Explorer earlier than 8.

Test Questions

1 Rewrite the code fragment on page 546 to eliminate the variable **commission**. Write your code in both JavaScript and ActionScript.

2 Any loop can be replaced by a sequence of statements made by replicating the loop's body, provided you know how many times the loop will be executed. Give an example of a situation where this would be impossible.

3 If **a** is an array, explain carefully why its last element is **a[a.length−1]**. Assuming that **a** contains a sequence of numbers, write a loop to add together all the elements in **a**.

4 In the example on page 549 for computing the width of the widest image on a Web page, what will happen if there are no images on the page? How would you modify the program to compute the width of the narrowest image on a Web page?

5 Define a JavaScript function called **average2** that computes the arithmetic mean of two numbers. Define another function, called **average**, that takes an array of numbers and computes their arithmetic mean.

6 Write a JavaScript function that takes a string as its argument and adds a paragraph containing that string to the end of the document.

Discussion Topics

1 We described how ActionScript requires variables to be declared together with the type of value they may hold, but JavaScript does not. Which do you consider the better way of declaring variables and why?

2 What approaches could be adopted to enable designers to add interactivity to multimedia without having to rely on the assistance of programmers? Do you consider it desirable for them to be able to do so?

3 What scripting features that you might want to use on your Web pages are not part of the W3C DOM?

Practical Tasks

1 Create a Web page containing a single image. Create another image the same size, and add a script to your page so that when the cursor is over the first image it is replaced by the second. The first image should be restored when the cursor moves away.

2 Create an XHTML form containing a single text field, labelled **email address**. Write a script that checks the value entered in the field whenever it loses focus to see whether it includes an @ sign. (You can access the text in the field by way of the **input** object's **value** property. If **s** is a string, **s.indexOf("@")** returns the position of the first @ in **s**, or −1 if **s** does not contain an @ character.) If it doesn't, the script should write a warning message beside the field. What additional checks would you need to make to be sure that the value entered in the field could be a legitimate email address?

3 An alternative way of organizing the style-switching script would be to use a single event listener, permanently attached to the **span** element, which changed the **class** attribute and the control's text, using the current values to determine what to change them to. This way, it would not be necessary to change the event listener every time the style was switched.

Rewrite the style-switching script along the lines just sketched.

4 Calling an event listener directly, with **null** instead of an **Event** as its argument, as we did on page 574 might be considered bad practice. Reorganize the code of that example to avoid doing so.

5 The **follow_rotator_drag** and **move_rotator** event listeners are particularly simple because we arranged that the number of distinct values in the slider was equal to the number of frames in the movie. Rewrite these methods so that they work correctly no matter what the slider's minimum and maximum values and the length of the movie are.

6 Modify the Flash document for the geological slide player (which you can download from the book's Web site) so that the angle display field is editable. Extend the script so that a user can type an angle into the field and the slide will rotate to that angle (or as near to it as possible).

7 Create a second 150-frame movie the same size as the sample slide (it doesn't have to be realistic) and import it into the library. Modify the scripts so that the button labelled with an X switches between our original slide and yours. You should ensure that the rotation of the two slides remains in sync.

15

XML and Multimedia

■ **Syntax and DTDs**

Well-Formed Documents. DTDs.

■ **Namespaces**

Preventing Name Clashes. Attributes.

■ **SVG**

Shapes. Stroke and Fill. Transformations. Other Features.

XML (eXtensible Markup Language) is the basis for XHTML and a host of other languages that have been proposed, if not actually used, for marking up different types of content on the Web. XML is the format used to deliver RSS feeds and podcasts. Almost all the formats and languages proposed for implementing the W3C's "Semantic Web" are based on XML. In particular, XML can be used as a concrete syntax for RDF (Resource Description Framework), which is intended to provide a standard for metadata on the Web. It is also used as a format for exchanging data between Web applications, and has found many applications off the Web. XML is used to define ODF (OpenDocument file format) and Microsoft's OOXML (Office Open XML), both of which are used as formats for office documents, and provides the syntax for Apple's property list files, used to record preferences on Mac OS X. Adobe used XML to define MXML, the layout language for Flex, and XFL, for exchanging Flash documents.

At its simplest, XML can be used as a markup language, like XHTML, to apply tags to documents so as to identify their structural elements. Unlike XHTML, though, XML does not provide a fixed set of elements. In effect, it lets you make up your own. For simple purposes, such as exchanging data between a blogging application and a desktop blog editor, this is adequate, but for more important tasks it is helpful to be able to impose constraints on which elements may be used, what attributes they may have and which elements may be contained in others. This allows a program that processes the XML data to verify that it is correctly formed and includes everything it should and nothing it shouldn't.

A formal definition of a set of elements and their attributes, together with constraints on the way they may be combined, can be created in the form of an XML **Document Type Definition (DTD)**. In effect, a DTD defines a specialized markup language. XHTML is defined by a DTD, for instance. You can therefore consider XML not just as a markup language, but also as a markup *metalanguage* – a language for defining markup languages.

Languages defined by XML are often called **XML-based languages**. They all share the basic notation for writing tags and entities that we described for XHTML, but have different sets of elements and their own rules about how these elements can be used. The common syntax makes it feasible to mix elements from several XML-based languages in the same document.

XML 1.0 was adopted as a World Wide Web Consortium Recommendation early in 1998. It was intended to provide a new foundation for the Web, which would be built by mixing XML-based languages including XHTML, SVG, MathML (Math Markup Language) and SMIL

(Synchronized Multimedia Integration Language). Metadata would be added using RDF and the semantics would be described for processing by machines using OWL (Web Ontology Language). Improved linking would be provided by XLink and better forms by XForms. XSL (the eXtensible Stylesheet Language) would allow radical restructuring of documents to be performed, which in turn would allow more extensive control over appearance than CSS provides. XML would even bootstrap itself: DTDs would be replaced by "schemas" which would define XML-based languages using XML syntax.

Things haven't worked out that way, though. The XML-based Web has been met by a mixture of indifference and incomprehension by the majority of the Web design community, and by positive hostility from the Web browser makers. The leading proposal for a successor to XHTML 1.0 is HTML 5, which can be "serialized" as XML, but can also be serialized using a custom syntax based on HTML 4, which is recommended instead. XForms has attracted little attention and HTML 5 includes an alternative extension to the existing form elements. The metadata formats considered essential to the Semantic Web are only used in small specialized communities. The XML-based languages specifically concerned with the subject matter of this book are being little used. SVG is finally being implemented, at least partially, in most browsers, but continues to be overshadowed by Flash as a vector format. SMIL's only popular application to date has been the embedding of advertisements in media streams.

Despite all this, XML is worth knowing about. Certain features of XHTML only make sense if you understand the relationship between XHTML and XML. Some XML-based languages for Web metadata are likely to become increasingly important, even if others continue to be seen as irrelevant. XML's role in Web services, allowing data to be exchanged between Web applications, is firmly established. Although the dramatic change to a Better Web built on XML may not have occurred as foreseen, XML's other uses continue to grow. Furthermore, because XML is easy to read, looking at an XML-based language, such as SVG, can provide insight into the way media are represented.

Syntax and DTDs

To begin with, you will get quite a long way if you think of XML as being the same as XHTML except that you can make up your own tags and attribute names. In fact, it would be more accurate to say that XHTML is XML with a fixed repertoire of tags and attributes. Therefore, you already know that tags are written between angle brackets, as in `<tag>`, and, unless the element is empty, must be matched by a closing tag, which has a / before the element name, as in `</tag>`. Attributes' values are written enclosed in double quotes and assigned to attributes following the element name using an = sign. Empty elements can be written like a start tag with a / before the closing >. Elements must be properly nested. Character and entity references beginning with an & and ending with a ; can be used for certain characters that are hard to type or, like <, are reserved for a special purpose.

Well-Formed Documents

Simply following the rules we just summarized allows you to write what are called ***well-formed*** documents. Being well-formed simply means that a document obeys the rules of XML syntax that allow it to be parsed correctly. For many purposes, this is adequate: it lets us create documents whose structure is expressed with markup tags, which can be processed by a computer program.

The following XML document shows you what well-formed XML looks like.

```
<books>
    <book id = "dmt">
        <title>Digital Media Tools</title>
        <author>Nigel Chapman</author>
        <author>Jenny Chapman</author>
        <price sterling="34.99" euro="47.30" />
        <publisher>John Wiley &amp; Sons</publisher>
        <numberinstock current="1" ordered="6" />
    </book>

    <book id = "perl">
        <title>Perl: The Programmer's Companion</title>
        <author>Nigel Chapman</author>
        <price sterling="38.99" euro="52.70" />
        <publisher>John Wiley &amp;Sons</publisher>
        <numberinstock current="0" ordered="0" />
    </book>

    <book id = "dmm">
        <title>Digital Multimedia</title>
        <author>Nigel Chapman</author>
        <author>Jenny Chapman</author>
        <price sterling="29.95" euro="45" />
        <publisher>John Wiley &amp;Sons</publisher>
        <numberinstock current="12" ordered="20" />
    </book>
</books>
```

The document provides a list of books, with their basic bibliographical details. It might be part of the stock inventory of an online bookshop, so the data also includes the current prices in two major currencies and a record of the stock situation.

The XML markup imposes a structure on the data, but it has no semantics. We have chosen element names that make it clear to an English-speaking reader what each element is supposed to represent, but the actual names have no formal significance. We could just as easily have used **aardvark** elements to record the authors' names. The meaning only resides in what is done to the document by software.

A little thought will tell you that there is considerable scope for choice in representing a particular set of data as XML. In particular, there is no clear-cut criterion for deciding whether to use an element with an attribute to record values such as, in this document, the publisher's name, or an element whose content is the value. For example, `<publisher>John Wiley &amp; Sons</publisher>` or `<publisher company="John Wiley &amp; Sons" />`.

Here, we have used a mixture: the price and number in stock are recorded using attributes; this has made it easy for us to combine two different values in both cases: the price in sterling or in euros, the number in stock currently and in a few days' time. Using attributes avoids multiplying the number of elements. On the other hand, placing the author in the content of an element has made it possible to have two author elements for the jointly written books. This would help indexing and searching software to identify the book from either author. The decision to use element content to record the values of the remaining fields is somewhat arbitrary.

We showed in Chapter 14 how the structure of an XHTML document could be displayed as a tree. The structure which XML markup imposes on any document can equally well be represented in the form of a tree, sometimes called a *structure model* in this context. The structure model is essentially an abstract representation of the way in which document elements are ordered and contained within each other. Figure 15.1 is a picture of the structure model of the document for books shown earlier. (Compare it with Figure 14.2.)

The methods of the Core DOM can be used to traverse any XML document's tree structure. Unlike the methods of the HTML DOM, those of the Core DOM do not embody any assumptions about which elements are being used, or what attributes they have. They allow a program to traverse and alter the tree of any XML document in a consistent manner. This means that if data is formatted as XML the repetitive operations used to extract individual items, such as the price of a particular book, can be performed using library routines that build a tree and implement the DOM methods, leaving only the operations specific to the particular application to be implemented from scratch.

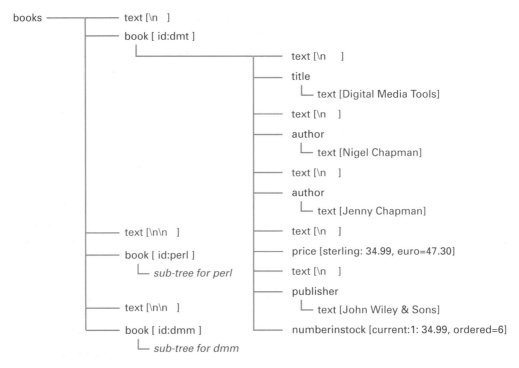

Figure 15.1. *The structure model of an XML document*

Implementations of the DOM are available for all the major programming languages, not just JavaScript, so XML data can be processed in a uniform way irrespective of the language being used. Not all programmers find the DOM convenient to use, so several other libraries have also been created for dealing with XML. The result of the attention that has been paid to XML processing is that if you use it as a data format, it is going to be relatively easy to read and write the data.

IN DETAIL

Although the DOM is described in terms of a tree structure, the DOM standards do not actually require an implementation to build the tree explicitly. Equivalent operations may be performed on an implicit representation. However, it will always be necessary to parse the XML, that is, to analyse its structure.

DTDs

You can use any elements and attributes you like in a well-formed XML document, providing you obey the simple rules of XML syntax. If, however, you supply a specification of a set of permitted elements, the attributes each may have and which elements they can contain, and require that your document conforms to the specification, you can ensure that it belongs to a class of documents with a well-defined structure. (The set of XHTML pages is an example of such a class of documents.) This means that any software that processes documents knows from the specification what tags to expect and how they will be related to each other. It can check that documents do indeed conform to the specification, thereby catching a whole class of possible errors, and it can provide specific functionality based on the document class's structure. For example, a browser can provide default formatting for each element, or an editor can show a list of all the permitted attributes when you type an opening tag. If a well-formed document has a specification attached to it and conforms to the rules in that specification, the document is said to be *valid*.

In XML, there are two ways of providing such a specification. The older, better-established method is by means of a DTD; a newer method, which is gaining in popularity, is by an XML **Schema**. Schemas are somewhat more powerful than DTDs, and provide means akin to the type-definition facilities of modern programming languages for specifying more elaborate constraints on document content. ("Schemas" is the officially endorsed plural of "schema" in the context of XML, rather than the formally correct "schemata".) They use the same syntax as well-formed XML documents, instead of the specialized notation required by DTDs. Because of this, schemas are usually more verbose than DTDs, which often makes them harder to read. We will concentrate on the DTDs, as they are still the more widely used way of defining XML-based languages.

Formally, a DTD defines a set of legitimate documents. For instance, the XHTML DTD tells us which documents are legal XHTML. We can therefore take the DTD to be the definition of the XHTML language, on the grounds that the language is the same as the set of all legitimate documents. It is in this sense that XML is a metalanguage. In practice, the rules of a DTD are used to check whether a document is legal, or as a guide for creating legal documents.

A DTD may be included within an XML document, but it is more common, especially where the DTD defines a complex language like XHTML, to store the DTD in a separate file, and reference it from within documents that use it. Two pieces of XML boilerplate are required for this to happen. They both use a slightly different syntax from the elements and attributes with which you are familiar. First, there should be an XML declaration, which usually takes the form:

```
<?xml version="1.0" encoding="UTF-8" ?>
```

The **version** attribute specifies the XML version number. Presently, the only possible values are "1.0" and "1.1". (The only differences between these two versions concern Unicode character codes.) The value of the **encoding** attribute specifies the character set used in the document – in this case it is UTF-8-encoded ISO-10646 (see Chapter 9).

An XML declaration is, strictly speaking, optional, but it may assist XML parsers to do their job, and should normally be included – the XML specification states "XML documents should begin with an XML declaration which specifies the version of XML being used". However, in the case of XHTML, including an XML declaration causes Internet Explorer to misbehave, so it should be omitted. (If there is no XML declaration, the version number is assumed to be 1.0, so an XML declaration is necessary if you are using XML 1.1.)

If it appears, the XML declaration must be the very first thing in the document.

If a DTD in an external file is being used, the XML declaration should be followed by a DOCTYPE declaration resembling the following:

```
<!DOCTYPE books PUBLIC "-//DMM//BOOK Bibliographic
information 1.0//EN" "http://www.digitalmultimedia/DTDs/books.dtd">
```

Note the use of <! and > as delimiters. These are used in those parts of XML concerned with the DTD, in much the same way as < and > are used in markup. (Another example of a DOCTYPE declaration appears in every valid XHTML document, as we illustrated in Chapter 10.)

The DOCTYPE declaration declares two separate things. First, the name of the document element, which will contain the document's entire content, is given after the keyword DOCTYPE. In this case, we have specified the element books, since our entire document is delimited by <books> and </books>, just as an XHTML document is delimited by <html> and </html>.

After this comes a specification of where the DTD is to be found. The keyword PUBLIC is followed by two different specifications of the DTD's location. The first, "-//DMM//BOOK Bibliographic information 1.0//EN", is the DTD's public name. Its peculiar syntax is a relic from XML's SGML ancestor. The public name identifies the organization responsible for the DTD – here a fictional enterprise, DMM – the name, a description and version number of the DTD, and its language (the natural language used for comments, element names, and so on, not the language of the DTD itself, which is always XML, of course).

The public name is followed by a conventional URL, at which the DTD is located. This URL is known as the DTD's system identifier. XML processors that read DTDs may look for the DTD here, or they may use some implementation-dependent mechanism to find it somewhere else using the public name. If you are using a publicly supported XML-based language, such as XHTML or SVG, the language's specification will include the appropriate public name and a URL for the DTD. Note that, although you have to provide these in the DOCTYPE declaration, there is no implication that any program that processes your XML document will actually fetch the DTD and use it in its processing. Normal Web browsers, for example, don't fetch the XHTML DTD before processing a Web page; the DTD's rules are built in to the browser's code.

We will not go into the full details of what might be in a DTD, since we do not expect many of our readers will be writing their own DTDs, and the more obscure features involve some wearisome details and specialized jargon. The following brief introduction should convey the essence of how a DTD can specify a markup language.

An external DTD (one stored in a separate file from the document) is itself an XML document, so it begins with an XML declaration. After this, though, instead of marked-up text there are special markup declarations, which provide the definitions of the set of elements and attributes, and constraints on how they may be combined. A markup declaration begins with <!, followed by a keyword that specifies the kind of markup being defined. After this comes some information that depends on the kind of declaration, and then the declaration is closed with a >.

We will only consider elements and their attributes.

An element declaration gives the element's name and specifies what may appear in the element's content. For instance,

```
<!ELEMENT price EMPTY>
```

This is about the simplest element declaration, which says that the element **price** is an empty element (can have no content). Note the use of upper-case letters for the keywords in the DTD.

EMPTY is an example of what is known in the XML standard as a content model. Other content models may appear in the corresponding place in the element declaration. The next most simple is (#PCDATA)* (the brackets are required), which is an obscure way of referring to textual content. The authors' names in our example are of this type, so the declaration of the corresponding element is:

```
<!ELEMENT author (#PCDATA)* >
```

The **book** and **books** elements are more complicated, because they can contain other elements, and we need to specify which ones, the order they can occur in, and how many of each there may be. Actually, with a DTD we cannot specify exactly how many times an element may occur within another; we can only state broadly whether it may occur once or several times. In the case of **books**, for example, the content must consist of one or more **book** elements. This is expressed in the following element declaration:

```
<!ELEMENT books (book+) >
```

The + following **book** indicates that the preceding element occurs one or more times. If the + was omitted, there would have to be exactly one **book** element inside **books**. You can also follow the element with a * indicating zero or more occurrences, or a ? indicating zero or one (an optional element). These notations may be familiar to you from regular expressions, as used for pattern matching in text editors and programming languages such as Perl and Ruby.

Where a sequence of elements must occur in order, they are written one after another, separated by commas, as in:

```
<!ELEMENT book (title, author+, price, publisher, numberinstock) >
```

which you should be able to see correctly specifies the structure of a **book** element. Note the way that you can use repetition (**author+**) within a sequence. Note also that this specification fixes the order of the elements within the **book** element. In a DTD it is not possible to specify that every element of a set must appear without also specifying the order they appear in (but you can do this in a schema). For more complicated constraints, you can use brackets for grouping. (Note that the brackets surrounding all the content models except **EMPTY** are required, even for trivial cases, such as the declaration of **books**.)

An additional possibility for content models is the use of the | operator to indicate a choice. Suppose, for example, a book could have some authors or some editors, but not both. Then, assuming an element **editor** had been declared somewhere, the declaration of **book** could look like this:

```
<!ELEMENT book (title, (author+ | editor+), price, publisher, numberinstock) >
```

(Note the use of brackets to delimit the choice.)

In a DTD, an element's attributes are listed in a separate attribute-list declaration. This is introduced by <!ATTLIST, followed by the name of the element whose attributes are being declared. Following this is a sequence of declarations, one for each attribute, declaring the attribute's name and specifying the type of values it may contain, and whether it is compulsory or optional. For example, the attributes for the **price** element could be declared like this:

```
<!ATTLIST price
  sterling CDATA #REQUIRED
  euro CDATA #IMPLIED >
```

For each attribute, its name is followed by a keyword declaring the type and a specification of the default behaviour. Some new keywords are used in attribute-list declarations: **CDATA** indicates that the attribute takes values which are character data (strings). Note that, in XML, numerical values are represented as strings, so there are no number data types.

As an alternative to **CDATA**, an attribute's type can be an enumerated list of possible values. This would be used where it only makes sense for an attribute to have certain specific values. For instance, if an element had an attribute **day**, which could only be assigned the abbreviated name of a day of the week as its value, the corresponding part of the attribute-list declaration would be:

```
day (mon|tue|wed|thu|fri|sat|sun) #REQUIRED
```

There are several special types which are also sometimes required. The most common is **ID**, which is used for attributes that serve as identifiers, like the **id** attribute of any XHTML element. Although values of type **ID** look like strings, the XML processor must ensure that **ID**s are always unique within a document, so that they can be used to address an element uniquely, in a script for example. **ID** would be the appropriate type for the **id** attribute of our **book** element.

```
<!ATTLIST book
  id ID #REQUIRED >
```

The meaning of **#REQUIRED** following the type in these declarations and that of **sterling** above should be evident: the attribute must be given an explicit value in the start tag of the element it belongs to, so <book> would be an invalid start tag. **#IMPLIED**, as used for **euro** in the attribute-list declaration for **price**, means that the attribute is optional and that no default value will be assumed, so in this declaration we are saying that it is all right to specify a price just in sterling, without giving the euro equivalent.

For some attributes, it makes sense to specify a default value, meaning that the attribute may have a value assigned to it, but if it does not, the default specified in the DTD will be used. For example, we might assert that, unless we are told otherwise, there are no copies of a book on order, in which case the **ordered** attribute of the **numberinstock** element could be left out, and the value "0" would be assumed. That is,

```
<numberinstock current="1"/>
```

would be equivalent to

```
<numberinstock current="1" ordered="0"/>
```

This would be declared as follows:

```
<!ATTLIST numberinstock
  current CDATA #REQUIRED
  ordered CDATA "0" >
```

Note that we are still requiring the number currently in stock to be explicitly specified, even if it is zero.

The preceding description should be sufficient to enable you to read the following complete DTD for our books example.

```
<?xml version="1.0"?>
<!ELEMENT title (#PCDATA)* >
<!ELEMENT author (#PCDATA)* >
<!ELEMENT editor (#PCDATA)* >
<!ELEMENT publisher (#PCDATA)* >

<!ELEMENT price EMPTY>
<!ATTLIST price
  sterling CDATA #REQUIRED
  euro CDATA #IMPLIED >

<!ELEMENT numberinstock EMPTY>
<!ATTLIST numberinstock
  current CDATA #REQUIRED
  ordered CDATA "0" >

<!ELEMENT book (title, (author+ | editor+), price, publisher, numberinstock) >
<!ATTLIST book
  id ID #REQUIRED >

<!ELEMENT books (book+) >
```

We must emphasize that although we have covered all the basic aspects of DTDs, there are additional features, which are important for the DTDs used to define large-scale languages like XHTML, and which are not entirely straightforward. If you need to write or understand more realistic DTDs you should consult a specialized reference work.

KEY POINTS

XML-based languages all use the same syntax for tags, attributes and entities.

Documents that obey the basic syntax rules of XML are well-formed.

The tree structure of any well-formed XML document can be traversed and modified using the methods of the core DOM.

A Document Type Definition (DTD) provides a specification of a set of permitted elements, the attributes each may have and which elements they can contain.

Schemas are a more recently developed alternative to DTDs, which do not need any special syntax in the specifications.

A well-formed document is valid if it declares a DTD and conforms to it.

An XML document may begin with an XML declaration specifying the XML version and the character set used in the document.

The DOCTYPE declaration declares the name of the document element and the location of a DTD, by its public name and system identifier (URL).

A DTD consists of markup declarations, enclosed between <! and >, which provide the definitions of the set of elements and attributes.

An element declaration declares the name and content model of an element.

Content models include EMPTY, (#PCDATA)* and the names of other elements.

A list of content types separated by commas means that the corresponding elements, etc. must appear in the given order.

Postfix operators +, * and ? indicate one or more, zero or more, or zero or one occurrences. The | operator represents a choice between two alternatives.

Each element's attributes are listed in a separate attribute-list declaration.

An attribute-list declaration begins <!ATTLIST followed by the element name, and a list of attribute specifications, terminated by >.

Each attribute's specification consists of its name, its type and an indication of whether it is compulsory or optional.

Types include CDATA (characters), an enumerated list of values and ID, for identifiers which must be unique.

Compulsory attributes are specified as #REQUIRED, optional attributes as #IMPLICIT. A default value may be provided instead.

Namespaces

By writing a DTD or schema you can create a specialized XML-based language for a particular class of documents, but this is not always the most sensible thing to do. For instance, XHTML is a markup language for Web pages, and MathML is a markup language for mathematics. If you wanted to make a Web page containing some mathematical equations, it wouldn't be very efficient to create a new markup language for mathematical Web pages. You would want to be able to combine XHTML and MathML instead. Since they are both XML-based languages, this would seem to be a reasonable thing to do, but in general, combining different XML-based languages raises some issues which must be addressed before this can be done safely.

Preventing Name Clashes

The most serious problem is the potential for name clashes. That is, the languages you wish to combine may use the same name for element types, but with different meanings. To see how this might come about, and how the problem is resolved, consider a simplified version of a possible real scenario.

Imagine that an XML-based language called BiblML has been devised for recording bibliographical data. (Several such languages do exist, but none is standardized.) A BiblML document might look like this (omitting the prologue):

```
<bibliography>
  <article>
    <author>H.Z. Hackenbush</author>
    <title>Bilaterally anomalous hypertension in wealthy females</title>
    <journal>Veterinary Dissimulation</journal>
    <volume>23</volume><pages>14–16</pages>
    <date>1939</date>
  </article>
  elements for other items in the bibliography
</bibliography>
```

Now suppose that an academic institution sets up documents containing the personnel records of its staff, using another XML-based language, StaffML. A typical staff record might be similar to the following:

```
<member>
  <surname>Hackenbush</surname>
  <forenames>Hugo Z</forenames>
  <title>Dr</title>
```

```
<post>Head of Sanitarium</post>
</member>
```

Finally suppose that it became necessary to produce a document listing the publications of all the members of staff. The natural way to do this would be by adding a bibliography element to each member element, like this:

```
<member>
  <surname>Hackenbush</surname>
  <forenames>Hugo Z</forenames>
  <title>Dr</title>
  <post>Head of Sanitarium</post>
  <bibliography>
    <article>
      <author>H.Z. Hackenbush</author>
      <title>Bilaterally anomalous hypertension in wealthy females</title>
      <journal>Veterinary Dissimulation</journal>
      <volume>23</volume> <pages>14–16</pages>
      <date>1939</date>
    </article>
  elements for other publications by Hackenbush
  </bibliography>
</member>
```

As you can see, we now have two **title** elements, shown highlighted, performing quite different functions. Such name clashes will always be possible when the vocabularies of separately developed languages are combined. It is easy for a human reader to see what is going on, but a computer program needs some explicit indication that these two elements are different. The solution is to allocate names to ***namespaces***, which are just identifiable collections of element and attribute names, and to add a mechanism for indicating which namespace a name belongs to.

Although it is not practical to demand that names used in XML documents are unique, there is a mechanism in place that allows us to generate unique identifiers. Domain names are unique, and the method by which they are administered ensures that they will remain so. It is reasonable to suppose that organizations or individuals that register a domain name can maintain control over the path components of any URLs belonging to that domain. In other words, URLs can safely be assumed to be unique. Thus, if a namespace is associated with a URL, element and attribute names could be prefixed with this URL, and they would, in turn, be guaranteed to be unique. URLs are, however, long and unwieldy to use in this way; they also may include characters that are not allowed in names in XML. The solution is to allow an arbitrary short prefix to be defined, which stands in for the full URL.

The chosen prefix can have the same form as a legal XML name, though usually short strings of two or three lower-case letters are used. (You cannot use xml as a prefix name, however, because some predefined names use the xml prefix. These are not actually in a namespace, but have fixed meanings in any XML-based language.) A colon is used to separate a namespace prefix from the rest of a name.

To make this clearer, suppose that the URL http://www.biblml.org/bibns is used for the BiblML namespace. In our document that uses BiblML with StaffML, we might decide to use the prefix b to designate names from the BiblML namespace. The journal element's name would be written b:journal, and the title element, for the title of the article, would become b:title.

To associate a prefix with the namespace's URL, it is necessary to declare the namespace by assigning the URL as the value of an attribute with a special name, consisting of the string xmlns followed by a colon and the chosen namespace prefix. Hence in this case, we need to assign the BiblML namespace URL to the attribute xmlns:b. If we preferred to use the prefix bbl, we would have to assign the URL to xmlns:bbl, and so on. The attribute that defines a namespace prefix can be used with any element. Its effect extends throughout that element. In our example document, a good place to declare the namespace is the bibliography element, since all the BiblML names are contained within it. Thus, the publication details could be written like this:

```
<b:bibliography xmlns:b="http://www.bibml.org/bibns">
 <b:article>
   <b:author>H.Z. Hackenbush</b:author>
   <b:title>Bilaterally anomalous hypertension in wealthy females</b:title>
   <b:journal>Veterinary Dissimulation</b:journal>
   <b:volume>23</b:volume><b:pages>14–16</b:pages>
   <b:date>1939</b:date>
 </b:article>
   ...
</b:bibliography>
```

Notice that we have used the b prefix on the bibliography element itself; the start and end tags are part of the element, so the prefix is defined within them.

If, at the same time, the developers who created StaffML had chosen to identify their namespace with the URL http://www.staffml.com/staffns we could use a prefix p for the StaffML element names, so that there would no longer be a clash between the two uses of title. The combined document would now look like this:

```
<p:member xmlns:p="http://www.staffml.com/staffns">
  <p:surname>Hackenbush</p:surname>
  <p:forenames>Hugo Z</p:forenames>
  <p:title>Dr</p:title>
  <p:post>Head of Sanitarium</p:post>
  <b:bibliography xmlns:b="http://www.bibml.org/bibns">
    <b:article>
      <b:author>H.Z. Hackenbush</b:author>
      <b:title>Bilaterally anomalous hypertension in wealthy females</b:title>
      <b:journal>Veterinary Dissimulation</b:journal>
      and so on
  </b:bibliography>
</p:member>
```

At this point, most people ask what is stored at the URL associated with a namespace, expecting that there is some sort of "namespace declaration" stored in a file there. There isn't (although in principle there could be). A URL is used simply because it is easy to ensure that it is unique. It is not being used as a pointer to a resource, the way it is in a link. There is no need for a namespace URL to point to anything at all.

It is the author of the document who decides what prefixes to use, so these can always be chosen to be unique within a document. If prefixes were chosen by the developer of the language, we would still have the possibility of name clashes, since language developers working independently might chance upon the same prefix and the same element or attribute name. By using URLs to identify namespaces, this possibility is avoided; by letting the author of the document choose prefixes to stand in for namespace URLs, a manageable notation is achieved, which still guarantees freedom from name clashes.

There is one additional complication to the use of namespaces. Where a document is predominantly or entirely marked up with elements from a single namespace, it is tiresome to have to add a namespace prefix to every name used in the document. This can be avoided by declaring a *default namespace*. Any names that do not have a namespace prefix are taken to belong to this namespace. A default is set by assigning its URL to the attribute xmlns, with no suffix. Thus, if we wanted to use the names from the BiblML namespace without prefixes within the bibliography element, we would use the following start tag:

```
<bibliography xmlns="http://www.bibml.org/bibns">
```

Within the bibliography element, title would mean the title from the BiblML namespace, and so on.

Where all the elements in a document belong to the same namespace, as they do when only a single markup language is used, it is natural to use a default namespace. This is the case for most Web pages written in XHTML. All the names in XHTML belong to the namespace with URL http://www.w3.org/1999/xhtml, so the start tag for the html element usually declares this as the default namespace:

```
<html xmlns="http://www.w3.org/1999/xhtml">
```

allowing all the familiar XHTML tags to be used without any prefix. The namespace declaration becomes another piece of housekeeping syntax, which will usually be inserted into your documents automatically by any editor used to create them.

Where languages are combined, the situation gets more complicated, because there is no way to declare a namespace inside a DTD, so various unsatisfactory expedients must be employed. The only satisfactory solution is to move to schemas to define XML-based langugages intended to be combined with each other, and this is gradually happening with XML-based languages defined by W3C. (This excludes HTML 5.) Whereas DTDs and namespaces have an uneasy relationship, schemas and namespaces have been integrated from the beginning. The full details lie beyond the scope of this book, but the important fact is that the author of a schema may define (within the schema itself) a "target namespace", to which all the names defined in the schema are allocated. A document that uses the schema can then declare the namespace and use all the names from the schema.

Attributes

The names of attributes do not have to be unique: different elements can have attributes with the same name. In effect, an element defines its own local namespace for its attributes, so there is usually no need for attribute names to belong to a namespace or be qualified with a prefix. However, sometimes it is convenient to use an attribute originally defined in one language to perform the same function in another.

For instance, XHTML 2 allows any element to have a role attribute, whose value indicates the purpose of a particular occurrence of the element. (For example, a ul element used as a navbar might have role="navigation".) The role attribute is defined in the XHTML namespace. It could equally well be used for similar purposes in other XML-based languages. By declaring a prefix, such as xh, for the XHTML namespace, any document can use the role attribute as xh:role.

A namespace may also be used to identify a collection of related attributes. For instance, the XLink Recommendation defines a collection of attributes which can be used by any element type that performs a linking function. The names of these attributes are contained in a namespace, so any document that uses them must declare this namespace. The effect is that any program that processes such a document can easily recognize the XLink attributes and process them accordingly, irrespective of the names of the elements used as link anchors.

Namespaces have also been proposed as a way of classifying attributes' values when the set of possible values is limited. The most highly developed example of this use is **_RDFa (Resource Description Framework attributes)_**. The idea behind RDFa is that, by adding metadata to the elements of a document in attributes, the existing structure and content can be reused as metadata, without having to duplicate it and define special metadata elements. RDFa uses several XHTML attributes to hold metadata. (Some of these attributes are only defined in XHTML 2, but may find their way into HTML 5.) In particular, the **property** attribute can be used to label an element as a metadata item whose value is the element's content.

When we introduced metadata in Chapter 2, we described various standard metadata specifications, which define named fields for various purposes. Programs that process metadata can identify fields if they use the names defined in one of those standards. The value of the RDFa **property** attribute should therefore be a standard field name, if possible.

RDFa allows a prefix to be used to identify values as belonging to a standard such as Dublin Core using the namespace mechanism we have described. For instance, suppose a learned paper had been made available on the Web as an XHTML document with the following body:

```
<body>
    <h1>Bilaterally anomalous hypertension in wealthy females</h1>
    <h2>H.Z. Hackenbush</h2>
    <p>Veterinary Dissimulation, 2314–16 </p>
    <p>1939</p>
    marked-up text of the paper
</body>
```

There is nothing here to indicate to a computer program that the top heading is the title of the paper, the second-level heading is its author, and so on. We could add class attributes and style the elements so that a human reader would be able to understand that this was the case, but for machine processing it is necessary to mark the elements explicitly, using a standard format.

Dublin Core defines the fields needed. RDFa allows us to use the Dublin Core fields by declaring a prefix for the Dublin Core namespace in the **body** element. The Dublin Core namespace URL is http://purl.org/dc/elements/1.1/. We'll declare the prefix to be dc and then use it in the values we assign to the property attribute.

```
<body xmlns:dc="http://purl.org/dc/elements/1.1/">
    <h1 property="dc:title">Bilaterally anomalous hypertension in wealthy females</h1>
    <h2 property="dc:creator">H.Z. Hackenbush</h2>
    <p property="dc:source">Veterinary Dissimulation, 2314-16</p>
    <p property="dc:date">1939</p>
    marked-up text of the paper
</body>
```

Since property is not defined in XHTML 1.0 you must use a special DTD if you want to use RDFa in valid documents. The necessary DOCTYPE declaration is:

```
<!DOCTYPE html PUBLIC "-//W3C//DTD XHTML+RDFa 1.0//EN"
   "http://www.w3.org/MarkUp/DTD/xhtml-rdfa-1.dtd">
```

Values that use a namespace prefix are sometimes called **CURIEs (Compact URIs)**, which draws attention to the fact that such a value is an identifier for some resource, just as a URL is.

KEY POINTS

Namespaces are collections of element and attribute names, which are used to prevent name clashes when XML-based languages are combined.

Namespaces are identified by unique URLs.

A prefix is associated with a namespace's URL within an element by assigning the URL as the value of an attribute consisting of the string xmlns: followed by the namespace prefix in the element's start tag.

Assigning to xmlns with no prefix defines a default namespace.

A name with a prefix and colon at the beginning (e.g. px:elname) belongs to the namespace with which that prefix has been associated. Names without prefixes belong to the default namespace.

Attributes do not need to be in a namespace to avoid name clashes, but if an attribute name is used for the same purpose in more than one language, placing it in a namespace makes it easy to process in the same way in each language.

Namespaces can be used to classify the set of values an attribute may have.

RDFa allows a prefix to be used to identify values of the property attribute as belonging to some metadata standard, such as Dublin Core.

SVG

XHTML is the most-used XML-based language in the area of multimedia. As we mentioned at the beginning of this chapter, many others have been proposed but none has achieved the same level of use as XHTML. The only other example of an XML-based language for multimedia that is attracting much support is the *SVG (Scalable Vector Graphics)* language, which provides a way of describing two-dimensional vector graphics using XML. In the words of the SVG specification:

> "SVG allows for three types of graphic objects: vector graphic shapes (e.g., paths consisting of straight lines and curves), multimedia (such as raster images and video) and text. Graphical objects can be grouped, styled, transformed and composited into previously rendered objects."

This should sound familiar, since (with the exception of video) these are the types of object that can be manipulated by vector graphics packages such as Illustrator, and which we described in Chapter 3. Indeed, the usual way of producing SVG documents is by exporting them from such a program.

IN DETAIL

If you want to examine some SVG code that has been generated by a program, you can export any drawing from Adobe Illustrator by choosing the Save As… command from the File menu, and choosing SVG from the pop-up menu of file types. When the options dialogue appears, make sure that the option Preserve Illustrator Editing Capabilities is off, otherwise a lot of confusing extra data will be generated.

In reality, vector graphics on the Web are rare, and when they are used instead of bitmapped images, they are almost invariably realized by way of Flash. However, Flash uses a proprietary, binary format, whereas the less-used XML-based SVG is an open W3C standard with a textual representation. This means that, by examining the structure and contents of SVG documents and reading the relevant standards, it is easy to see how concepts such as filled and stroked shapes can be represented in a way that can be processed by computer programs. This should provide an indirect insight into their representation in other formats, including Flash.

Our purpose in describing SVG here is thus not to enable you to write SVG by hand but to show you how vector graphics objects and transformations can be represented in a format that can be processed by a computer. For this reason, we will make no attempt at completeness in our account.

The simplest way to introduce SVG's manner of representing vector graphics using XML constructs is with a trivial example, which defines the image shown in Figure 15.2.

```
<?xml version="1.0" encoding="utf-8"?>

<!DOCTYPE svg PUBLIC "-//W3C//DTD SVG 1.1//EN"
   "http://www.w3.org/Graphics/SVG/1.1/DTD/svg11.dtd">

<svg version="1.1" xmlns="http://www.w3.org/2000/svg">

   <rect x="4" y="4" fill="#E53930" stroke="#0066B3" stroke-width="8"
    width="126" height="126"/>

</svg>
```

Figure 15.2. *A simple SVG drawing*

The first line is the familiar XML declaration, which you should have expected. This is followed by a DOCTYPE declaration, declaring svg as the document element, and showing the public name and system identifier for the SVG 1.1 DTD. These lines are just the usual XML red tape. After them comes the document proper, which is contained in the svg element. Unlike XHTML documents, SVG documents are not divided into a head and body.

In this example, the only attributes we have provided for svg are version, whose meaning is obvious, and xmlns, which declares the SVG namespace as the default namespace, so within the svg element we can use SVG element and attribute names without a prefix.

This example illustrates the normal arrangement for SVG documents that are intended to stand alone. In browsers that implement SVG, a document such as this can be treated as an image, and embedded in an XHTML document using an img or object element. SVG images can also be used in CSS, as backgrounds and so on. It is also possible to embed SVG fragments inside other types of XML document, in which case it is necessary to use a namespace prefix, usually svg:. It is also a good idea to specify the height and width of the resulting graphic, otherwise it will occupy 100% of the space of its enclosing element. If this is the document, or some element within that inherits its dimensions, the entire window will be used, which is rarely what is required.

For example, if the following markup appears in a document, it will cause the square from Figure 15.2 to be drawn as the content of the div element within a block 200 pixels square. The enclosing div element can, of course, be floated or absolutely positioned using CSS to place the SVG image anywhere on the page.

```
<div>
    <svg:svg xmlns:svg="http://www.w3.org/2000/svg"
      version="1.1" width="200px" height="200px">
    <svg:rect x="4" y="4" fill="#E53930" stroke="#0066B3
      stroke-width="8" width="126" height="126"/>
    </svg:svg>
</div>
```

This combination of languages within the same document only works when the content is treated as XML, which means that the media type must be application/xml or a related type such as application/xhtml+ xml. If the code just shown appeared in a document that was delivered using the media type text/html – which most Web pages still are – the SVG code would be ignored. In that case, SVG images must be treated like any other and embedded using img or object elements. (Similar considerations apply to including other XML-based languages, such as MathML, in XHTML documents.)

Following a growing trend among XML-based languages defined by W3C, SVG's definition is modular. That is, it has been broken into pieces which may be used in different combinations. This modularity has been exploited to create two "mobile profiles" – basically subsets of the full SVG 1.1 language – known as *SVG Basic* and *SVG Tiny*. These subsets are designed to provide a set of vector graphics facilities suitable for mobile devices. Their implementation should not impose too great a burden on the limited facilities of such devices, but are sufficient to bring the advantages of vector graphics, especially low bandwidth requirements, to PDAs and mobile phones.

Shapes

Returning to our small SVG example, the representation of graphic objects – the real business of the document – appears within the svg element. In this case, there is only one, the coloured square shown in Figure 15.2). This shape is described by a single element, of type rect, whose attributes provide all the pieces of information necessary to draw the square in its chosen position. The x and y attributes' values are the coordinates of the upper left corner of the rectangle; the height and width attributes set its dimensions. The remaining attributes specify the presentation (i.e. appearance) of the rectangle; they use the same names and values as corresponding CSS properties. Here, we have set the stroke and fill colours, using the attributes stroke and fill, and the width of the stroke, using stroke-width.

We described most of SVG's shape elements briefly in Chapter 3. As we mentioned there, their attributes (or sometimes the element's content) hold the same values as are set, implicitly or explicitly, when drawing the corresponding object in an illustration program.

Element Name	Attributes	Notes
rect	x	coordinates of top left corner
	y	
	width	
	height	
	rx	x and y radii of rounded corners
	ry	
circle	cx	coordinates of centre
	cy	
	r	radius
ellipse	cx	coordinates of centre
	cy	
	rx	x and y radii
	ry	
line	x1	coordinates of end points
	y1	
	x2	
	y2	
polyline	points	list of points – see text
polygon	points	

Figure 15.3. *SVG shape elements*

The expected repertoire of simple shapes – rectangles, circles, ellipses, lines, polylines and polygons – each have their own element. These elements have attributes controlling their appearance in common; each has its own distinctive attributes for specifying the shape and its position. Figure 15.3 summarizes these elements and their attributes. Figure 15.4 is a rendering of the following SVG document, which uses some of the shape elements and their attributes. (We have omitted the XML and DOCTYPE declarations, and will do so in the remaining examples. They are always the same as in the previous example of an SVG document.)

```
<svg version="1.1" xmlns="http://www.w3.org/2000/svg"
    width="110px" height="110px">
<polygon fill="#6B90C4" points="50,10 66,10 76,27 66,42 50,42 40,25 "/>
```

```
<polyline fill="none" stroke="#98B0D6"
  stroke-linecap="round" stroke-linejoin="round"
  points="40,25 1,50 50,99 99,50 76,27 "/>
</svg>
```

Note the form of the **points** attribute values for the polygon and polyline. Strictly speaking, these values may comprise a sequence of coordinate values, separated by whitespace, commas or both. Here, we have adopted a convention whereby two coordinates that should be understood as points are separated by a comma, and each pair is separated from the next by a space. This convention is merely intended to improve readability; whichever separators are used, the coordinates are always examined from left to right, and considered as alternating x and y values. (This example also illustrates some further presentation attributes, which we will explain shortly.)

Figure 15.4. *Shapes*

In vector graphics, shapes are special cases of a path consisting of a sequence of lines and curves, as we described in Chapter 3. SVG provides a **path** element for the general case. The description of the path is given as the value of the element's **d** attribute, which is a string containing the path data. The path data consists of a set of instructions for drawing the path, as if with a pen. These instructions are written in a special compact notation. Each instruction is represented by a single letter, which is followed by a series of coordinates; the number and interpretation of these coordinates depends on the instruction they belong to.

Every path begins with an **M** instruction; M is short for "move to". The following two values are taken as the coordinates of the point at which the path begins, and the instruction establishes a "current point". In other words, they tell you where to move the pen to before you start drawing with it. Straight line segments are drawn by the **L** instruction. This instruction is also followed by a pair of coordinates, separated by whitespace or a comma. Its effect is to draw a straight line from the current point to the point specified by those coordinates, which then becomes the new current point. Sometimes, it may be more convenient to specify the end of the line as an offset from the current point. This is done using the **l** command. The two coordinates that follow it are treated as offsets in the horizontal and vertical directions from the current point. The polyline in Figure 15.4 could have been drawn using the following path element (see Figure 15.5):

```
<path fill="none" stroke="#99A6CF" stroke-linecap="round"
      stroke-linejoin="round"
      d="M40,25l-39,25l49,49l49-49l-23-23"/>
```

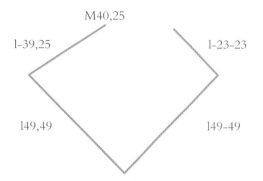

Figure 15.5. *A polyline as a path*

Here we have used an additional notational shorthand: whitespace can be omitted where doing so causes no ambiguity. The reason for this is that, when SVG documents are generated from complicated graphics by a program, it is likely that the path data will be the single largest contributor to the size of the resulting file. Since SVG is a Web format, it is desirable to keep the file size to a minimum, and condensing the path data in this way helps do so.

Horizontal and vertical lines are more common than lines at any other orientation in some types of graphic illustration, so there are special instructions for these. H and h are each followed by a single value, and result in a horizontal line from the current point to a point with the same y coordinate and the specified x coordinate. In the case of H, the value is treated as an absolute coordinate; for h it is an offset from the current point. Similarly, V and v are absolute and relative instructions for drawing vertical lines; the coordinate following them gives the y coordinate or offset of the end point. (In general, as you will no doubt have guessed, an instruction with a lower-case letter is a version of the instruction with the same letter in upper-case, which uses relative coordinates instead of absolute ones.)

In Chapter 3, we described how Bézier curves are used to construct smooth flowing paths and outlines, since they can be combined without discontinuities. SVG supports Bézier curve segments within a path. The C instruction is followed by six coordinate values; call them x_2, y_2, x_3, y_3, x_4 and y_4. These are interpreted as the coordinates of three points, $P_2 = (x_2, y_2)$, $P_3 = (x_3, y_3)$ and $P_4 = (x_4, y_4)$, corresponding to the two control points and the end point of a Bézier curve segment that begins at the current point. If you let P_1 be the current point, then the naming of the points corresponds to Figure 3.9 from Chapter 3. The c instruction is used to specify a Bézier curve using relative coordinates. That is, the pairs of coordinates represent displacements, not positions.

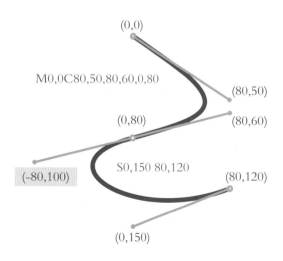

Figure 15.6. *Smoothly joined Bézier curves*

The typical way of combining curve segments into a smooth path, is by using the end point of one segment as the start curve of the next, keeping the gradient constant by using control points that are placed symmetrically.

This construction is optimized in SVG with the S and s commands, which each take just four coordinates. In the notation used in the previous paragraph, these are $P_3 = (x_3, y_3)$ and $P_4 = (x_4, y_4)$. The missing control point P_2 is taken to be the same as the second control point on the preceding curve segment, reflected in the current point. Figure 15.6 illustrates how C and S instructions may be combined to produce smoothly joined curves. The **path** element for this curve is:

```
<path fill="none" stroke="#99A6CF" stroke-width="2"
     d="M0,0C80,50,80,60,0,80S0,150 80,120"/>
```

The highlighted control point at (-80,100) is implicit in the use of S, being the reflection of (80,60) in (0,80), those two being the final pair of values in the preceding C command

Stroke and Fill

The examples given so far illustrate the way in which simple stroke and fill properties are represented: the various shape elements and the **path** element can all have **stroke** and **fill** attributes to specify the stroke and fill colours. Their values may be given in any of the forms used in CSS for colour properties; SVG offers an extended range of named colours, but since SVG is almost always automatically generated, colours can just as well be specified as hexadecimal colour codes, which we have used in our examples.

Naturally, the width of a stroke can also be specified. This is done using the **stroke-width** property. Stroke widths are specified by default in pixels.

When a path is painted with colour, the colour is applied symmetrically about the zero-width path that the pure geometrical specification of the corresponding document element describes. Hence, the **rect** element we used in our first example specifies a square whose exterior height and width are 134 pixels:

```
<rect x="4" y="4" fill="#E53930" stroke="#0066B3" stroke-width="8"
  width="126" height="126"/>
```

The **width** and **height** attributes specify a 126-pixel square, and the coloured stroke extends four pixels each side of this.

The way in which lines are terminated and joined can be specified using the **stroke-linecap** and **stroke-linejoin** attributes. The former may take any of the values "**butt**", "**round**" and "**square**", while the latter has the possibilities "**round**", "**bevel**" and "**miter**" (sic). For this last case, there is also a **miterlimit** attribute to restrict the length of projecting mitred joints. These attributes' values correspond to the properties of line ends and joins described and illustrated in Chapter 3. (See Figure 3.20 in that chapter.)

Both stroke and fill can be made partially transparent. The attributes **stroke-opacity** and **fill-opacity** are used for this purpose. A value of zero makes the stroke or fill completely transparent, a value of one makes it completely opaque. Values between these extremes are used to produce partially transparent strokes and fills. We will use these attributes in some later examples.

By default, all fill and stroke attributes are inherited from enclosing elements, in the same way as the similar properties are inherited in CSS.

The case of gradient fills is more interesting, both in the way gradients are defined and in how they are used. SVG supports linear and radial gradients, with the **linearGradient** and **radialGradient** elements, respectively. Both of these elements have some attributes that are used in a technical way to map the gradient onto the area it is used to fill, but we can safely ignore these and concentrate on the elements' content, which is where the gradient's colours and spacing are specified. It is important, though, to provide an **id** attribute value for gradients, since, as we will see, these are used to identify a particular gradient when it is applied.

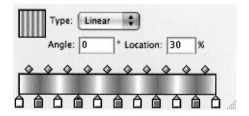

Figure 15.7. *Illustrator's* Gradient *panel*

The content of a gradient element of either sort consists of **stop** elements. These correspond directly to the gradient stops used in drawing programs to define gradients interactively. Figure 15.7 shows the **Gradient** panel in Adobe Illustrator, for example. Each of the little tabs underneath the gradient sample is a point at which a colour value is set. Between the tabs, the colours blend gradually to form the gradient. Here we have created a gradient in which white alternates evenly with a blue-grey colour.

This gradient could be represented in SVG with the following element:

```
<linearGradient id="SVGID_1_">
    <stop  offset="0" stop-color="#FFFFFF"/>
    <stop  offset="0.1" stop-color="#8191A6"/>
    <stop  offset="0.2" stop-color="#FFFFFF"/>
    <stop  offset="0.3" stop-color="#8191A6"/>
    <stop  offset="0.4" stop-color="#FFFFFF"/>
    <stop  offset="0.5" stop-color="#8191A6"/>
    <stop  offset="0.6" stop-color="#FFFFFF"/>
    <stop  offset="0.7" stop-color="#8191A6"/>
    <stop  offset="0.8" stop-color="#FFFFFF"/>
    <stop  offset="0.9" stop-color="#8191A6"/>
```

```
    <stop offset="1" stop-color="#FFFFFF"/>
</linearGradient>
```

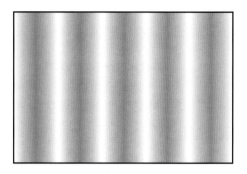

(The curious value for the id attribute here was automatically generated.)

For each stop, the offset attribute's value specifies the position of the stop as a number in the range 0 to 1, which is interpreted as a proportion of the length of the gradient. The stop-color attribute specifies the colour at that point, in the same way as fill and stroke colours are specified.

Figure 15.8. *Linear gradient fill*

The linearGradient element does not cause anything to be drawn, it merely defines the gradient. To use it, the fill attribute of some shape or path must be set to a value of the form url(#*idref*), where *idref* is the value of a gradient's id attribute, as in url(#SVGID_1_). Thus, the following element produces the rectangle shown in Figure 15.8.

```
<rect x="0.5" y="0.5" fill="url(#SVGID_1_)" stroke="#000000"
  width="170" height="113"/>
```

The value of several SVG attributes, including in particular fill, may be a "URI reference", which usually takes the form url(*URL*), where the URL may have a fragment identifier appended. If, as in this example, the URL proper is omitted, leaving just a fragment identifier, the notation refers to an element, such as our gradient, defined elsewhere in the same document. By specifying a relative or absolute URL it is possible to refer to gradients defined in other documents (although this may not be very efficient).

Radial gradients are defined using a radialGradient element, which contains stop elements in the same way as linear gradients are. If the example just given is modified as follows:

```
<radialGradient id="SVGID_2_">
    <stop offset="0" stop-color="#FFFFFF"/>
    <stop offset="0.1" stop-color="#8191A6"/>
    eight more stop elements, as before
    <stop offset="1" stop-color="#FFFFFF"/>
</radialGradient>

<rect x="0.5" y="0.5" fill="url(#SVGID_2_)"
  stroke="#000000"
  width="170" height="113"/>
```

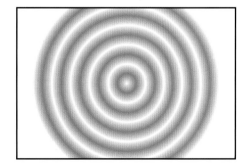

Figure 15.9. *Radial gradient fill*

it produces the result shown in Figure 15.9. The gradient stops run from the inside out in a radial gradient.

Transformations

In Chapter 3, we introduced a collection of transformations that can easily be performed on vector graphic objects: translation, scaling, rotation, reflection and shearing. Four of these transformations can easily be expressed in SVG. Reflection is the odd one out, which requires a little more work. The others are all applied using the **transform** attribute, which can be used with any graphic element.

The value of **transform** is a string consisting of transformation specifications, separated by whitespace or commas. Each specification consists of a transformation name, followed by some arguments in brackets. The available transformation names are **translate**, **scale**, **rotate**, **skewX** and **skewY**, whose meanings should be apparent. The arguments to each are interpreted according to the transformation.

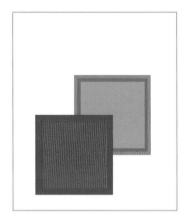

For a translation, one or two arguments may be supplied. The first is the amount by which the object should be moved in the *x* direction; if the second is present, it is the amount by which it should be moved in the *y* direction (downwards). If the second argument is missing, it is taken to be zero.

Figure 15.10. *Translation*

Figure 15.10 illustrates the effect of translation. The dim rectangle was drawn to serve as a reference with the following element. Notice the use of **fill-opacity** and **stroke-opacity** to fade it down.

```
<rect x="50" y="50" fill="#E53930" fill-opacity="0.6"
  stroke="#0066B3" stroke-width="5" stroke-opacity="0.6"
  width="55" height="55"/>
```

The other rectangle is obtained by adding a transform attribute, and leaving the default opacity.

```
<rect x="50" y="50" fill="#E53930" stroke="#0066B3" stroke-width="5"
  width="55" height="55"
  transform="translate(-30,30)"/>
```

The transform value for scaling is similar: one or two arguments may be supplied. The first or only argument is a horizontal scale factor. If the second is present, it is a vertical scale factor. If it is omitted, it is taken to be equal to the first argument. That is, if only a single argument is provided, the object is scaled uniformly. Figure 15.11 shows the effect of changing the rect element in the previous example as follows:

```
<rect x="50" y="50" fill="#E53930" stroke="#0066B3"
  stroke-width="5"  width="55" height="55"
  transform="scale(1.1,1.4)"/>
```

You can see from this example that scaling is performed by multiplying all the object's coordinates by the specified scale factors, so that the object moves as well as getting bigger. To scale an object in place, the scaling transform would have to be followed by a translation that moved the top left corner of the object back to its original position.

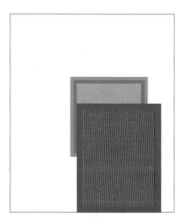

Figure 15.11. *Scaling*

The rotate transform takes either one or three arguments. The first argument is an angle in degrees, by which the object is rotated. If there are no other arguments, the rotation is around the origin. Hence, changing our rect element as follows produces the result shown on the left of Figure 15.12.

```
<rect x="50" y="50" fill="#E53930" stroke="#0066B3"
  stroke-width="5"  width="55" height="55"
  transform="rotate(45)"/>
```

If you wish to rotate an object about a different point, you specify two additional arguments, which are the coordinates of the centre of rotation. The effect of the following transform is shown on the right of Figure 15.12.

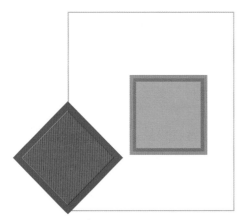
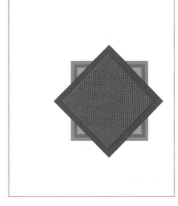

Figure 15.12. *Rotation about the origin and about a point*

```
<rect x="50" y="50" fill="#E53930" stroke="#0066B3"
  stroke-width="5" width="55" height="55"
  transform="rotate(45, 77, 77)"/>
```

Finally, both the skew transform functions take a single argument, the skewing angle in degrees. You must specify skewing along the *x* and *y* axes separately. To produce a combined skew, such as the one shown in Figure 15.13, you must combine two transforms. This can be done, for any number of transforms of any type, by including them all in the same transform specification string, separated by whitespace or commas. Figure 15.13 was produced by the following, for instance:

```
<rect x="50" y="50" fill="#E53930" stroke="#0066B3"
  stroke-width="5" width="55" height="55"
  transform="skewX(-30),skewY(-45)"/>
```

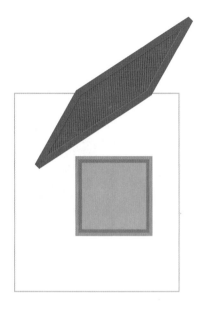

Figure 15.13. *Skewing*

You can see from the illustration that, as with scaling, skewing moves the object as a side-effect of the transformation. A translation could be combined with the **skewX** and **skewY** transforms to move it back to its original position.

IN DETAIL

If you have studied computer graphics, you will be familiar with the idea, mentioned in Chapter 3, that any transformation can be expressed as a 3×3 matrix, three of whose coordinates are constant. Hence, six numbers suffice to express a transformation or combination of transformations. SVG supports this notation, allowing you to use matrix(a,b,c,d,e,f) in the value of the transform attribute. Among other things, this allows you to specify the missing reflection transformations. A reflection in the vertical axis is matrix(–1,0,0,1,0,0), a reflection in the horizontal axis is matrix(1,0,0,–1,0,0), a reflection in the line $x = y$ is matrix(–1,0,0,–1,0,0), and so on.

You may want to apply the same transformation to several objects at once. In Illustrator, you would do this by grouping the objects and then applying the transformation to the group. You can do just the same in SVG. The **g** element forms a group; its content comprises the objects in the group. A **g** element can have a **transform** attribute, and the transformation will be applied to all the child elements of the group. For instance, to rotate and enlarge the polygon and polyline in Figure 15.4, you could group the elements and transform the group, in the following way:

```
<g transform="scale(2), rotate(90),
  translate(-50,-100)">
  <polygon fill="#6B90C4"
    points="50,10 66,10 76,27 66,42 50,42 40,25 "/>
  <polyline fill="none" stroke="#98B0D6"
    stroke-linecap="round" stroke-linejoin="round"
    points="40,25 1,50 50,99 99,50 76,27 "/>
</g>
```

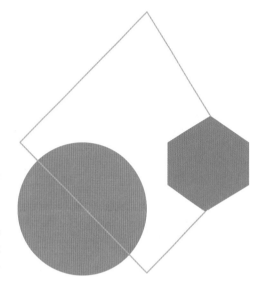

Figure 15.14 shows the result – the circle is not part of the group so it stays where it was.

Combined transforms, such as this one, can be confusing, since their effect is cumulative. Using groups can make it clearer what is going on. The example just given is equivalent in effect to the following:

Figure 15.14. *Transforming a group*

```
<g transform="scale(2)">
    <g transform="rotate(90)">
        <g transform="translate(-50,-100)">
            polygon and polyline elements
        </g>
    </g>
</g>
```

That is, the scaling is applied to the rotated group after it has been moved. In other words, the transformations are applied from the inside out in nested groups, and hence from right to left when they are combined.

Other Features

The preceding descriptions of shapes, paths, fills and transformations should have demonstrated that it is possible to use XML's syntax to represent vector graphics. It is unlikely that you would ever write SVG by hand, so we will not go into any other aspects in detail. We will just briefly describe a handful of noteworthy features that show some more of the potential of XML-based graphics.

SVG documents may incorporate links. SVG provides an a element, by analogy with XHTML, for creating links to other resources on the WWW. Unlike XHTML, SVG takes the attributes it uses for linking from the XLink namespace. XLink defines several attributes which could be used to implement elaborate types of link, but in practice, the only links that are actually used are the simple uni-directional links which are familiar from XHTML. Usually, therefore, an href attribute whose value is the destination of the link is all that is required.

However, because of the use of namespaces, a namespace declaration for the XLink namespace must be present to make the names of the XLink attributes available in an SVG document. To make it possible to use links anywhere in the document, this would be attached to the svg element, which would therefore normally look like this:

```
<svg version="1.1" xmlns="http://www.w3.org/2000/svg"
  xmlns:xlink="http://www.w3.org/1999/xlink">
```

The first namespace declaration makes the SVG namespace the default, so SVG names can be used without a prefix. The highlighted second declaration declares xlink: as the prefix for XLink attribute names, so that the attribute xlink:href can be used in a elements to point to a URL.

As in XHTML, the content of an a element acts as the link source. In SVG, elements typically represent graphical objects, so the usual effect of enclosing an element in an a is to make the graphical object it represents into a hot spot, like an area element on an image map. For instance, wrapping an a element around the polygon in our example of shapes (Figure 15.4), as shown below, has the effect of making the hexagon into a hot spot. Clicking on the shape will cause the *Digital Multimedia* support site's home page to be retrieved and displayed.

```
<a xlink:href="http://www.digitalmultimedia.org/">
    <polygon ... />
</a>
```

We described in Chapter 9 how text can be readily integrated with vector graphics. Their text manipulation facilities are a major feature of illustration programs. Hence, SVG must provide support for text.

Since SVG is XML, the only sensible way of representing text is as XML characters inside a suitable element. This means that any Unicode characters can be used in text, but that character entities must be used for ampersand and angle brackets. The text element is used to hold text strings that are incorporated in an SVG document. It has several attributes, the most important of which are x and y, which hold the coordinates of the string's "anchor point" (usually its left end), and a collection of attributes with the same names and semantics as CSS's font properties: font-family, font-weight, and so on. The fill attribute is used to set the colour, since vector glyphs usually have no stroke. (One is sometimes added to create a special effect.)

SVG does not support automatic wrapping and line breaking. Blocks of text that occupy more than one line must be created a line at a time, so it is up to the program generating the SVG to perform the block-level formatting. Within a **text** element, the **tspan** element can be used to change the styling of selected spans of text. It, too, takes font and appearance attributes, so it can be used, for example, for setting part of a string in italics or boldface for emphasis.

The full range of attributes available for **text** and **tspan** elements provides a high degree of typographical control over text in SVG. Kerning and baseline shift can be controlled to arbitrary accuracy, allowing fine typesetting within an SVG illustration. Text may also be set on a path.

The possibility of including text in SVG documents raises the question of fonts. We saw in Chapter 10 that CSS allows you to specify a list of fonts for the **font-family** property, so that a user agent can select whichever is available. This is all right for XHTML's model of text display, but SVG's precise typography could get messed up if a different font from the one you intended was substituted. To preserve the appearance of text, it is necessary to make fonts available for downloading, or to embed them in the SVG document. SVG supports both these possibilities, but for practical reasons it is usually better to embed the fonts. SVG fonts are outline fonts whose glyphs are described using SVG elements. The **font** element may include **glyph** elements describing the glyphs and other elements providing information about the font. SVG fonts are usually generated automatically from fonts in some other format, such as Type 1, when the document is exported.

So far, we have concentrated on showing how vector graphics can be represented as XML. XML offers more than just a syntax for marking up documents, though. Any XML document can be represented as a tree whose nodes can be manipulated using the methods of the Core DOM. In other words, SVG is scriptable. Just as the Core DOM is extended by objects and methods that are specific to XHTML documents in the HTML DOM, which we used in Chapter 14, it is extended by objects and methods that are specific to SVG documents in the SVG DOM. The SVG DOM makes it possible for scripts to operate on objects that represent SVG elements, so, among other things, a script can create objects corresponding to elements and thus draw shapes dynamically, and apply transformations to them, which has the effect of moving and otherwise changing the appearance of the shapes on the screen. SVG DOM scripting thus provides one way of creating vector animation. Because the DOM supports events, SVG animations can be interactive.

Scripting is not an easy way to go about animation. SVG provides animation elements for some simple types of motion graphics. These elements provide a means of defining motion paths, creating fade-in or fade-out effects, and making objects grow, shrink, spin or change colour. They are wholly inadequate for any serious animation. Unless interactive graphical animation tools that generate scripts that operate on SVG objects become available, SVG is unlikely to challenge Flash as a format for animation on the Web.

KEY POINTS

SVG (Scalable Vector Graphics) is an XML-based language for two-dimensional vector graphics.

An SVG document begins with the usual XML and DOCTYPE declarations. The graphic content is contained in the svg element, which must declare the SVG namespace.

SVG fragments can be embedded in documents that use other XML-based languages, provided the document is treated as XML.

SVG Basic and SVG Tiny define SVG profiles suitable for mobile devices.

The rect, circle, ellipse, line, polyline and polygon elements represent the basic shapes. Attributes define the geometry, position, stroke, fill and other properties of each shape.

The path element represents a sequence of lines and curves. Its d attribute's value is a string containing a sequence of instructions for drawing the path.

Path instructions include M (move to), L (draw a line to an absolute position), l (draw a line to a relative position), H, h, V, v (draw horizontal and vertical lines), C, c (Bézier curves), S and s (curve segments). Each instruction is followed by an appropriate number of pairs of values, to be interpreted as coordinates.

Stroke colour and width are specified by the stroke and stroke-width attributes. Line joining and end styles can be specified with stroke-linejoin and stroke-linecap.

Gradients are defined by linearGradient and radialGradient elements, which may contain stop elements, each specifying the colour at an offset.

Gradients are applied by setting the fill attribute of a shape to the URL of a gradient element, usually just a fragment identifier referring to its id.

Any element may have a transform attribute, whose value is a string of transformation specifications. The available transformation names are translate, scale, rotate, skewX and skewY. Appropriate arguments appear in brackets.

The g element may be used to combine elements into a group, which can be transformed as a whole.

Links (hot spots) can be created with the a element. The XLink namespace must be declared so the xlink:href attribute is available.

The text element is used to hold text strings. Text may be set on a path.

The SVG DOM makes it possible for scripts to perform dynamic drawing and programmed animation by operating on objects that represent SVG elements.

CHAPTER 15

Exercises

Test Questions

1   Rewrite the example XML books document, (a) using no attributes, and (b) using nothing but empty elements. Discuss the relative merits of these two versions and our original.

2   In Chapter 14 we described the use of the getElementById method to access elements in an XHTML document. Can this method be used with any XML document? Explain your answer.

3   Is every well-formed XML document valid? Is every valid XML document well-formed?

4   A valid XHTML document begins like this:

```
<!DOCTYPE html PUBLIC "-//W3C//DTD XHTML 1.0 Strict//EN"
  "http://www.w3.org/TR/2000/REC-xhtml1-20000126/DTD/xhtml1-strict.dtd">
<html xmlns="http://www.w3.org/1999/xhtml">
```

Explain carefully what each part of this rubric means, and why it must be present. What would you expect to find after the closing </html> tag in such a document? What could appear before the DOCTYPE declaration?

5   In our description of DTDs, we only describe how elements and their attributes may be specified. What else would you expect to find specified in a DTD for a language such as XHTML?

6   Why is it necessary to define namespace prefixes instead of using a full URL to distinguish names from different namespaces?

7   How does the use of namespace prefixes on attributes differ from their use on element names?

8   Write SVG elements to draw a 300×400 pixel rectangle with a red fill and no stroke whose top left corner is at (150,200) using:

(a)   a rect element;

(b)   a polygon element;

(c)   a polyline element;

(d) a path element using only M and L instructions;

(e) a path element using only M and l instructions;

(f) a path element using M, h and v instructions.

9 Show how you can use a combination of transforms in SVG to scale a 300×400 pixel rectangle in place. Can you write a general transform which will scale any object in place?

Discussion Topics

1 Investigate the arguments that have been put forward against the use of XML on the Web. Do you think they are outweighed by the advantage of having a single basis for the syntax of all the markup languages on the Web?

2 Does it follow from part (a) of Test Question 1 that attributes are unnecessary?

3 In XHTML, any element may have a class attribute, and the values of these attributes can be used to distinguish different ways of using the same element. Discuss whether this provides an adequate alternative to XML as a way of defining document structures to cope with different sorts of content. Could class be used to define metadata instead of RDFa?

4 If all the markup languages used on the World Wide Web were XML-based, would it be practical to base a Web browser on an XML parser, which downloaded the appropriate DTD, instead of creating parsers for each language? (You may assume – unrealistically – that documents are always delivered with the correct media type.)

5 Is describing XML as a markup metalanguage justifiable, when the syntax of DTDs is different from the syntax used for marking up text?

6 What methods of avoiding or resolving name clashes might be used as an alternative to XML namespaces?

7 SVG has facilities for setting type. Could SVG be used as a substitute for XHTML for creating Web pages?

Practical Tasks

1 Devise a simple XML-based language for marking up documents containing a collection of recipes. For each recipe you would have to be able to represent its name, a list of ingredients, a method (this could be a list of separate steps), a cooking time, oven temperature or gas mark, and the number of people the given amounts will serve. Add any other information or metadata (such as the source of the recipe) that you think would be useful. (Some elements or attributes may be optional.) Consult a good cookery book for ideas and recipes.

Start by creating a marked-up document with two or three recipes, then write a DTD that describes its structure. Try to validate your document against the DTD.

2   Write SVG code to draw a smiley face, in appropriate colours. If you have it, draw the same face in Illustrator or a suitable alternative, and export it as SVG. Compare the machine-generated code with the code you wrote by hand.

16

Multimedia and Networks

■ **Networking Fundamentals**

Clients and Servers. Protocols. Multicasting.

■ **Delivering Multimedia**

HTTP. Caching. RTSP. Quality of Service.

■ **Distributing Media Files**

RSS and Podcasts. BitTorrent.

■ **Server-side Computation**

The Common Gateway Interface. Alternatives to CGI.
AJAX.

The preceding chapters have shown that multimedia places considerable demands on resources – files are often very large, complex processing such as decompression may be required, tight, sometimes complex, synchronization constraints must be respected, and response times must be short. Networks are particularly poorly placed to satisfy these demands, because of the inherent limitations of present-day technology, and because of the complex and unpredictable effects of the interactions between network components and patterns of network traffic. At the same time, it makes a great deal of sense to maintain multimedia data in a central repository, to be accessed over a network instead of using a physical medium, such as a CD-ROM, for distribution. More importantly, the combination of networks and multimedia is what makes the World Wide Web and new applications – such as video-conferencing and live multimedia presentations – possible. The benefits to users of these applications are so compelling that they outweigh the technical difficulties that networks present.

In this chapter we will take a closer look at the mechanisms that are provided to make it possible to deliver multimedia over a network. This material is among the most technical in the book, and you probably won't find it of much interest unless you have some knowledge of how computer systems and networks operate. Readers without this technical background may prefer to skim the opening paragraphs of each section to get some idea of what is involved in meeting the demands of distributed multimedia. Computer scientists and engineers will be able to appreciate why the main thrust of academic and industrial research in multimedia is concentrated on the matters covered in this chapter.

We will concentrate exclusively on TCP/IP networks. Bear in mind that this includes not only the Internet – although that was where these protocols were developed – but also "intranets" – that is, local area networks utilizing the same set of protocols. Because of their generally higher speeds and more centralized management, intranets are better able to support some of the distributed multimedia applications, such as video-conferencing, that can be implemented using the real-time protocols we will describe. For the Internet, universal high-quality deployment of these applications is still in the future, although the growth in broadband means that they are beginning to become more widely enjoyed.

Networking Fundamentals

Modern computer systems rarely operate in isolation. *Local area networks (LANs)*, usually employing some form of Ethernet or wireless technology, are used to connect computers within a small organization – even a single home – or within a single site belonging to a large one.

Local area networks are connected together in turn by routers, bridges and switches. The **Internet** is a global network of networks, communicating via a standard set of protocols loosely referred to collectively as **TCP/IP**. Most of these networks are operated by commercial **Internet Service Providers (ISPs)** who lease access to other organizations via dedicated lines and routers, and to individuals via the telephone or cable TV networks. The growth of the Internet since the removal of restrictions on its commercial use in 1991 has been more than adequately described and commented on elsewhere. Although its ubiquity can be exaggerated, in developed countries and the major developing nations the Internet is rapidly achieving the status of a public data network, analogous to the public communication network of the telephone system.

Networks, and the Internet in particular, offer valuable opportunities for distributing multimedia, but they also present formidable technical difficulties. In the case of the Internet, an additional factor to be considered is the presence of a largely technologically unsophisticated community of users, who have high expectations of technical quality based on their experience of film, videos, television, photography and print media. Where multimedia content delivered over the Internet attempts to compete with traditional media – as it does in news or sports coverage, for example – it must provide some additional value (usually in the form of interactivity or social interaction) to compensate for inferior picture and sound quality.

Broadband Internet access is available in most developed countries and, as shared resources, in some developing countries. 256 kbps is the minimum speed offered under the name of broadband (though it's stretching the definition), with higher speeds being available at a premium. 8 Mbps (megabits per second, where a megabit is a thousand kilobits) is presently a common speed for domestic broadband in many countries, although there are places where speeds up to 100 Mbps are routinely offered to domestic users. The extent to which broadband is available and its rate of adoption by consumers vary widely from country to country.

Currently, **ADSL (Asymmetric Digital Subscriber Line)** is the leading method for broadband access over existing copper telephone wires. Its speed in the downstream direction, from the Internet to the user, is usually about 10 times as fast as the upstream speed (hence "asymmetric"). This makes a lot of sense for typical domestic and small business users, who will normally spend most of their time downloading Web pages and other files over the network, and relatively little time, if any, uploading anything other than email attachments and updates to their Web sites. Other DSL technologies, including **Symmetric DSL (SDSL)**, provide higher upstream data rates, and are becoming more widely available.

Technical restrictions mean that ADSL cannot reach remote homes (more than 5 km from an exchange), and the cost of enabling exchanges for ADSL has meant that in many countries, telecoms companies have only considered it financially viable to provide ADSL in cities and large towns.

The perceived economic importance of the Internet has led governments in some countries (for example, Scotland) to subsidize the provision of broadband to rural communities.

In areas where cable TV is available, **cable modems** permit data to be transferred over the cable TV network at rates from 500 kbps to 30 Mbps. For remote users, broadband services using geo-stationary satellites are available, but at a cost well in excess of ADSL and cable. (Satellite connections also suffer from latency – the delay that results from the long distances that signals must travel.) Still more broadband technologies are in various stages of development, including delivery of data over the electricity supply network and the use of high-altitude tethered balloons as an alternative to satellites. Nevertheless, a significant proportion of domestic users still connect to the Internet using V.90 modems, which provide speeds well below the meanest broadband.

Access to the Internet by mobile devices, such as smart phones, is becoming increasingly important and widespread. "Third generation" (**3G**) phones are the first mobile devices capable of Internet access at broadband speeds. Unlike previous generations, which were optimized for speech transmission, 3G systems were designed for both voice and data from the start. The International Telecommunications Union has specified a system called **International Mobile Telecommunications (IMT2000)**, which was supposed to provide a global 3G standard. In practice, six different variants have been developed in different parts of the world, but all offer bit rates for data from just under 2 Mbps up to 10 Mbps.

Commercial Internet users, especially those operating their own Web servers (see below), usually prefer to lease dedicated lines to provide a fixed connection to ISPs. T1 and T3 lines provide 1.544 Mbps and 44.736 Mbps, respectively. T1 and T3 lines are also used by small local ISPs to connect to the larger ISPs who are directly connected to the Internet backbone.

Figure 16.1 shows the typical times taken to transfer different media elements over various types of connection, assuming the maximum speed is attained. For comparison, we have included times for old-fashioned dial-up connections (V.90 modems) and the experimental Abilene network, a high-speed network that uses technology which might develop into a successor to the Internet.[†]

Although the comparison is striking, it tells only part of the story. The connection between the user and their ISP is not always the factor that limits the speed of data transfer over the Internet. The capacity of the connections between ISPs' networks, and the computing power of the machines from which data is being downloaded may be just as important.

---

† *When looking at these numbers, don't forget that the k and M in kbps and Mbps stand for 1000 and 1,000,000, respectively, but in kB and MB they stand for 1024 and 1,048,576.*

Connection Type		Speed	Text 20 kB	Graphics 100 kB	Multimedia 2 MB
Dial-up (V.90)		56 kbps	2.9 s	14.6 s	5 min
ADSL	basic	512 kbps	320 ms	1.6 s	32.8 s
	typical	2 Mbps	82 ms	410 ms	8.4 s
	premium	8 Mbps	20.5 ms	102 ms	2.1 s
Cable	typical	512 kbps	320 ms	1.6 s	32.8 s
	premium	2 Mbps	82 ms	410 ms	8.4 s
Satellite†		512 kbps	860 ms	2.1 s	33.3 s
Leased line	T1	1.5 Mbps	109 ms	546 ms	11.2 s
	T3	44 Mbps	3.7 ms	19 ms	381 ms
G3 phone		2 Mbps	82 ms	410 ms	8.4 s
Abilene		100 Mbps	1.6 ms	8.2 ms	168 ms

† *Includes latency.*

Figure 16.1. *Typical download times*

Clients and Servers

Online distribution of multimedia over LANs or the Internet is almost always based on the *client/server model* of distributed computation. In this model, programs called *servers* "listen" on a communication channel for *requests* from other programs, called *clients*, which are generally running on a different machine elsewhere on the network. Whenever a server receives a request, it sends a *response*, which provides some service or data to the client. Requests and responses are collectively known as *messages*. Here, a message is a structured collection of data transmitted over the network. The messages exchanged by a client and server conform to a *protocol* – a set of rules governing the format of the data and the actions to be taken by a server or client when it receives a request or response.

The most popular form of online multimedia delivery is the World Wide Web, whose implementation is an example of the client/server model. Web servers and clients communicate with each other using the *HyperText Transfer Protocol*, abbreviated to *HTTP*. HTTP is a very simple protocol designed for the fast transmission of hypermedia in the form of HTML or XHTML documents and CSS stylesheets, as described in Chapter 10, and the graphics, sound, video, animation and other sorts of data that go with them to make up Web pages.

HTTP provides communication between Web servers and their clients. A client first contacts a server, and then (usually) sends a request for a Web page. The identity of the server and the location of the file containing the Web page's data are normally extracted from a URL, the familiar "Web address" described in Chapter 10. The initial prefix http:// in a Web page URL such as http://www.digitalmultimedia.org/DMM2/index.html is what tells the client to use the HTTP protocol to retrieve the document. The domain name www.digitalmultimedia.org identifies a server (roughly speaking). As we will see shortly, servers cannot be directly addressed using their names, so the client has to look up the corresponding numerical IP address, which is does using a facility known as the **Domain Name Service (DNS)**. Once it has the IP address, the client is able to send an HTTP request, asking for the file /DMM2/index.html. The server responds by sending the contents of the designated file, if it exists, wrapped up in the form of an HTTP response with some extra information, such as the Internet media type of the data it is sending (in this case text/html). We will describe the format of HTTP messages in more detail later in this chapter.

World Wide Web clients are usually browsers, such as Firefox, Safari or Internet Explorer, which allow us to access Web pages interactively. Despite the foregoing description, Web browsers are usually multi-protocol clients, which can communicate using other protocols, too. (Hence the need for the URL prefix identifying the protocol.) Nearly all browsers allow you to download files using the File Transfer Protocol (FTP), for example, although the interface to that protocol is integrated transparently into the Web browsing interface used for HTTP. Modern browsers also support real-time data streaming for audio and video using several special protocols for this purpose.

Web servers often run on powerful dedicated machines, usually running a special server version of Windows or Unix, to enable them to cope with heavy traffic. A common arrangement is for ISPs to provide Web space on one or more of their machines running a server for the benefit of their customers; small companies and individuals wishing to put up personal Web pages can use the ISP's facilities. Larger companies maintain their own sites and servers. It is possible to run a Web server on a desktop machine, provided that only a reasonable number of hits are expected. The machine running the server must be permanently connected to the Internet, which usually implies that a broadband connection is necessary.

Most servers augment their basic Web page serving function with interfaces to other programs running on the same machine. This allows them to generate Web pages dynamically, incorporating information retrieved from a database, for example, and to perform computations based on information supplied through a form on a Web page. The Common Gateway Interface (CGI) is a *de facto* standard for such interfaces, but other proprietary mechanisms, such as Microsoft's Active Server Pages, and open standards such as PHP and JSP are increasingly preferred, largely because of efficiency and their tighter integration with database management systems.

Protocols

Protocols are the rules governing the exchange of data over networks. They are conceptually organized into "layers", stacked on top of each other, with the lowest-layer protocols dealing with the actual physical signals transmitted over wires, radio waves and optical fibres. Above these, slightly higher-level protocols handle the transfer of packets of raw data, and ensure that they reach their correct destination. The highest layers implement more application-oriented services, such as file transfer or Web browsing. The protocols on each layer are implemented using those on the layer below.

When a Web server and client exchange information using HTTP, for example, it appears as though the client sends HTTP requests to the server, which replies with HTTP responses, as we just described. To the Web software, no other protocols appear to be involved, but in fact, what actually happens is that the HTTP messages are translated into streams of TCP packets, which are themselves translated into the format of the actual networks over which the data must pass. At the receiving end, these packets are used to reconstruct the incoming HTTP message. Thus, we need some understanding of the lower-level TCP/IP protocols before we can appreciate the characteristics of the application-oriented protocols that are used for multimedia.

TCP/IP networks are *packet-switched* networks, which means that all messages transmitted over the network are split into small pieces, called *packets*, which are sent separately. This enables network bandwidth to be shared efficiently between many messages, since, if the rate at which packets are generated for one message is lower than the available carrying capacity, packets belonging to other messages can be transmitted at the same time; we say messages are *multiplexed*. Contrast this with the telephone network, where a connection is established between the caller and the person being called, and this connection is held open for the exclusive use of their conversation until the caller hangs up, whether or not anybody is speaking. The advantages of this "circuit-switched" approach, which can be used for data exchange as well as spoken conversations, are that there is no need to distinguish between packets belonging to different messages on the same circuit – there is only ever one message – and that the two parties can rely on the availability of all the bandwidth provided by their circuit. On a packet-switched network, neither of these is the case: packets must carry additional information identifying (at least) their source and destination, and the rate at which packets can be transmitted between two points will depend on what other traffic the network is carrying. For real-time distributed multimedia applications this last factor is particularly problematic.

IP is the **Internet Protocol**, both in the sense that that's what IP stands for, and in the more fundamental sense that it's what makes internets and the Internet possible. IP defines a basic unit of transfer, called a *datagram*, and provides a mechanism for getting datagrams from their source to their destination through a network of networks. The machines that actually exchange datagrams are called **hosts**. Each host will be connected to one of the networks making up the internet. It is identified by its **IP address**, a set of numbers uniquely identifying the network and host, which is used by IP to send datagrams to the right place.

Datagrams belong to the category of data structures comprising a header, containing administrative information about the datagram, followed by the actual data. The header contains the source and destination IP addresses, as well as some additional information concerning routing and optionally security. The detailed layout of an IP datagram depends upon the version of IP being used. IPv4 is the "classical" IP that has been in use for many years. IPv6 is a newer, more flexible, version. An important difference is that, whereas IPv4 addresses are 32 bits long, IPv6 addresses are 128 bits long, so the new version can accommodate many more hosts and networks. A datagram may be made up out of several packets on the underlying physical network that is carrying it.

As well as hosts, an internet includes machines called **routers**, connected between its component networks, which maintain information about the network topology so that they can work out where to send a datagram to. In general, an IP datagram may have to pass through several routers during its travels over several networks. By inspecting the destination address in a datagram's header, a router can determine whether or not the datagram should be sent to a host connected to the same network as it is. If it should, the router translates the IP address to the native address format of the network, if necessary, and sends the data to its destination. Otherwise, the datagram is passed on to another router. Dynamically updated tables are used to determine which of the accessible routers a datagram should be forwarded to.

IP treats each datagram individually, recognizing no connection between the datagrams that make up a Web page, for example. Furthermore, it cannot identify the application that generated a piece of data, nor the one that should receive it. All that IP does is attempt to deliver individual datagrams from one host to another. It doesn't even guarantee to succeed. In particular, if some datagram has failed to reach its destination after a certain length of time, it will be discarded. This is more efficient than continuing to try to deliver it – its destination is probably unreachable for some reason – and it has the beneficial side-effect of preventing rogue datagrams going round and round forever. It follows, though, that if an application sends a stream of data, it may arrive at its destination with some pieces missing. It is also possible for some pieces to arrive in the wrong order. Since IP treats each datagram individually and calculates routes dynamically, it is possible for a packet to overtake others sent before it. For example, a router that was down, forcing data to be sent round by a long route, may come back on line so that later packets will take a shorter, faster route to their destination, arriving earlier than the packets sent before them.

The majority of applications that communicate over TCP/IP networks require the data they send to arrive intact and in the right order at the receiving end. Consider an email system, for example.

If we send you an email message, you won't consider it very satisfactory if it arrives in your mailbox with key passages missing, and others in the wrong order. If applications had to rely on IP alone, this could happen, so, to provide the required service, the application would have to implement some mechanism for putting packets back in order and requesting the retransmission of any that are missing. It would be unreasonable to expect every application to implement these functions. Instead, a reliable transport protocol, **TCP (Transmission Control Protocol)**, is layered on top of IP.

TCP provides reliable delivery of sequenced packets. It does this using a system of acknowledgement. A simplified version of the protocol would work as follows. When the destination receives a packet it sends an acknowledgement, and the sender does not transmit another packet until it gets the acknowledgement. If the acknowledgement is not received within a specified period of time (the time-out), the packet is sent again.

The algorithm as just described is prohibitively slow, and TCP actually uses a more sophisticated technique, based on the same principle, using a "sliding window" of unacknowledged packets. Instead of sending a single packet and waiting for an acknowledgement, it sends several – let's say eight for concreteness. As each packet is received it is acknowledged. Because of the time packets and acknowledgements take to traverse the network, the acknowledgement of the first packet will probably not reach the sender until several others have been sent. That is, there may be several unacknowledged packets in transit at one time. If the acknowledgement of the first packet has not been received by the time the eighth packet has been sent, the sender waits, and retransmits as before if the acknowledgement does not come in time. On the other hand, once the acknowledgement of the first packet is received, the limit on the number of packets to send before waiting is incremented, so the sender will send up to the ninth packet before waiting for the acknowledgement of the second, no matter at which point in the transmission of the first eight the acknowledgement arrives. Once the second acknowledgement has been received, the limit is advanced to packet number 10, and so on (see Figure 16.2).

Notice that retransmitted packets may arrive out of sequence, and also that the possibility exists for packets to be sent twice, if an acknowledgement goes astray, for example, or a packet turns up long after it should. TCP thus introduces new opportunities for packets to arrive out of sequence. However, the finite number of packets that can be transmitted without acknowledgement imposes an upper bound on how far out of sequence a packet can be.

An analogy that is often used to describe the difference between IP and TCP concerns pouring water onto a burning building. IP is like a bucket brigade – water (data) is poured out of a hydrant into buckets (datagrams) that are carried by a disorganized crowd of volunteers (the network). A bucket may be carried some distance, then passed from hand to hand to the next volunteer.

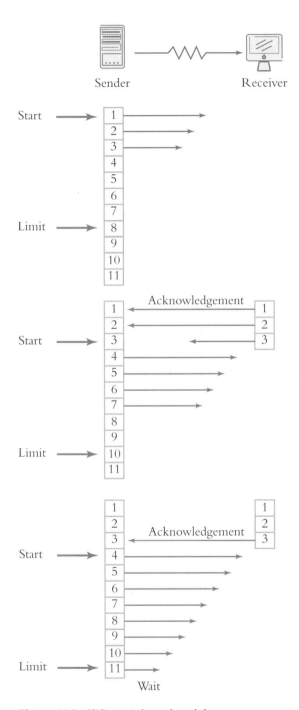

Figure 16.2. *Sliding window acknowledgement*

Some buckets will get dropped in the process. Others will work their way through the crowd at different speeds, so that the order in which they arrive at their destination bears little resemblance to the order in which they were filled up and sent on their way. In contrast, TCP is like a firehose that carries the water straight from the hydrant to the fire – the water just goes in one end and comes out the other in an orderly stream, without loss.

The analogy is not perfect. A firehose is a much more efficient way of transporting water than a crowd of bucket carriers, but TCP is less efficient than IP, because it is actually implemented using IP, but then adds extra overheads with its system of acknowledgements and retransmission.

Besides the overhead incurred by acknowledgement, TCP also incurs a cost in setting up a connection. This is necessary, in order for the acknowledgements to work, and in order to ensure that packets are sent to the appropriate application. Recall that IP addresses only identify hosts, and that IP accordingly only attempts to transport data between hosts. In order to identify a particular application running on a host, the IP address must be extended with a number, called a **port number**. Ports are associated with applications according to the protocol they use. For example, programs communicating via HTTP conventionally use port 80. The combination of an IP address and a port number is called a **transport address**, and enables the protocols running on top of IP to provide communication facilities between programs running on different hosts. TCP uses a pair of transport addresses to set up a connection between two programs, and subsequently these can communicate as if there was a reliable data conduit between them.

For some networked multimedia applications, the possibility of lost packets is more acceptable than the overhead of TCP. Streamed video and audio are the prime examples. Suppose, for example, a speech is being transmitted live over a network. If the video data were sent using TCP, then every frame would arrive complete and in the correct order, but the rate at which they would arrive would be unpredictable. Jerks and pauses might occur as packets were retransmitted and acknowledgements were awaited. Almost inevitably, the display of the picture would fall behind the actual delivery of the speech. The transient glitches caused by the occasional loss of a frame or fragment of audio would be less intrusive if they permitted an otherwise steady frame rate to be maintained instead. An alternative to TCP is needed to transport data with these characteristics.

The *User Datagram Protocol (UDP)* is built on top of IP, like TCP, but is much simpler, doing little more than ensure that datagrams are passed to the correct application when they arrive at their destination host. Like IP, UDP only tries its best to deliver datagrams, it does not offer the reliable delivery provided by TCP. Nor does it set up connections – port numbers are included in the source and destination fields of every UDP packet to ensure data finds its way to the right place. UDP does perform some elementary error checking that is not provided by IP, to help ensure that datagrams are not corrupted. These features of UDP make it a suitable basis for building protocols for delivering data such as streamed video and audio, for which real-time constraints are more important than totally reliable delivery.

The low-cost delivery of UDP is not enough, on its own, for such purposes. The *Real-Time Transport Protocol (RTP)* typically runs on top of UDP, adding extra features that are needed for synchronization, sequencing and identifying different types of data – or payloads as they are called in this context. RTP itself still does not guarantee delivery or prevent packets arriving in the wrong order, but it does enable applications to reconstruct a sequence of packets and detect whether any are missing. It does this by including a sequence number in the header of each packet belonging to a particular stream – RTP sets up connections between applications, so that the stream of data belonging to a particular connection is an identifiable entity. Each time a packet is sent over a connection the sequence number is incremented. This makes it clear to the receiver what order the packets should be in. Depending on its requirements and the way in which it treats data once it has arrived, a receiving application can reconstruct the correct sequence, discard packets that are received out of sequence, or insert them in their correct places in some data structure being built from them.

An RTP packet's header also identifies the payload type – whether it is video, audio, and so on – which determines, by implication, the format of the data contained in the rest of the packet. This allows different payload types to employ formats that are optimized for their special characteristics. In particular, it allows appropriate forms of compression to be applied to images, video and sound. Where several different media types are being transmitted – typically video with accompanying sound – they must be sent over separate RTP streams with different payload types. It is therefore necessary to synchronize them when they are received. A timestamp is included in the header for this purpose. It records the instant at which the first byte contained in a packet was sampled. This can be collated with the timestamps in other related streams, to ensure that simultaneously sampled data is played back at the same instant.

RTP can be tailored to different applications' requirements and extended to cope with new types of payload – it is a framework for an entire family of protocols, rather than a protocol in the traditional sense. RTP profiles define subsets of the protocol's features that are suitable for particular applications. In particular, the audio-visual profile is intended for use with audio and video streams.

A complementary protocol, the **RTP Control Protocol (RTCP)**, can be used in conjunction with RTP to provide feedback on the quality of the data delivery – statistics such as the number of packets lost and the variance of the time between packets' arrival. This data can be used by the application sending the data – for example, to adjust the rate at which it sends.

Multicasting

Users' connections to the Internet, via ADSL or cable and so on, are usually the slowest link in the communication chain, but the high-speed networks that provide the skeleton of the Internet are also of finite bandwidth. Here, too, new technologies are leading to increased speeds, but traffic is also growing at a considerable rate, and new types of traffic – especially that associated with bulky time-based media such as video – are adding to the demands placed on the Internet as a whole. Speeding up the network is one way of coping with these demands. Reducing the volume of traffic by eliminating duplication is another.

A common situation where data is unnecessarily duplicated arises when a group of Internet users require access to the same resource at the same time. This situation is often associated with multimedia. Suppose, for example, a well-known musician – let's call him Tim Linkinwater – has arranged to transmit a live video feed from a concert over the Internet. Every Tim Linkinwater fan with Internet access will want to watch this Webcast. The data being sent to every fan is identical, but conventional (**unicast**) transmission will require that the server from which the video is being streamed sends a copy of it to everybody who has set up a connection to watch this concert. If the concert is taking place in New York, but Tim Linkinwater is popular in Europe, many copies of the video data will be sent across the Atlantic, putting a strain on both the transatlantic links and the video server. This strain could be reduced by sending a single copy over the Atlantic and not duplicating it until it became necessary to do so in order to distribute the data to all the people in Europe who wanted it.

The scenario just outlined is the basis of *multicasting*. Figures 16.3 and 16.4 illustrate the difference between unicasting and multicasting. In unicasting, a separate packet is sent to each user. In multicasting, a single packet is sent, and is duplicated along the way whenever routes to different users diverge. Many distributed multimedia applications, including live video streaming and conferencing, have characteristics that make them suitable for multicasting.

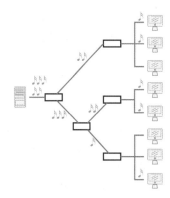

Figure 16.3. *Unicast transmission*

For multicasting to be possible, hosts must be assigned to *host groups*, with certain network addresses identifying groups instead of single hosts. A range of IP addresses is reserved for this purpose. From the sender's point of view a multicast address behaves rather like a mailing list – although mailing lists are implemented quite differently (using unicast). One difference is that the sender does not know who – if anybody – belongs to the host group.

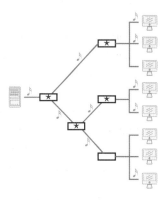

Figure 16.4. *Multicast transmission*

A packet that is intended to go to a group is sent to the appropriate multicast address. Routers must be enhanced to cope with multicast addresses, duplicating packets where necessary. They must also be able to perform the routing calculations necessary to determine optimal routes – which may be different from optimal unicast routes. These technical issues, while difficult, are amenable to technical solutions. Other problems that arise when multicasting is attempted on the scale of the Internet are less straightforward.

The main problems concern management of host groups. These will typically be spread across different networks, so the information about which hosts belong to a group must be distributed to routers. Group membership has to be dynamic, to accommodate applications such as the Webcast described earlier, so a mechanism is required for a host to join and leave a group. Routers must then be able to adjust to the new state of group membership. At a still higher level, some mechanism is needed for users to find out about the existence of host groups, what their multicast addresses are, and how to join them. Essentially, when a multicast session is set up an address must be chosen from the available range and then advertised – by email, newsgroup, Web site, or a dedicated application that serves the function of a listings magazine.

KEY POINTS

The Internet is a global network of networks, communicating via TCP/IP.

ADSL, cable modems and the 3G mobile phone networks are among the technologies used for broadband connections to the Internet.

Online distribution of multimedia is based on the client/server model of distributed computation. Servers listen for requests from clients and send responses, providing some data or service to the client.

Protocols are sets of rules governing the interactions between servers and clients.

HTTP (Hypertext Transfer Protocol) is a simple protocol designed for the fast transmission of hypermedia between Web servers and clients (e.g. browsers).

DNS (Domain Name Service) translates domain names to numerical IP addresses.

Protocols are organized into layers, with each layer providing services to the layer above, which are implemented using the services of the layer below.

TCP/IP networks are packet-switched, so messages are multiplexed.

IP (Internet Protocol) only provides a mechanism for getting datagrams from their source to their destination through a network of networks.

Each host is identified by a unique IP address.

TCP (Transmission Control Protocol) is layered on top of IP to provide reliable delivery of sequenced packets, using a system of acknowledgements with a sliding window of unacknowledged packets.

TCP uses transport addresses, consisting of an IP address and a port number, to provide connections between programs running on different hosts.

UDP (User Datagram Protocol) only tries its best to deliver datagrams. It does not offer reliable delivery, so it has less overhead than TCP, which makes it more suitable for streamed video and audio.

RTP (Real-Time Transport Protocol) runs on top of UDP, adding features for synchronization, sequencing and identifying different payloads.

Multicasting may be used to send the same data to many users: a single packet is sent, and is duplicated along the way whenever routes to different users diverge.

Multimedia applications such as live video streaming are suited to multicast.

For multicast, hosts must be assigned to host groups. Certain IP addresses identify groups instead of single hosts.

Delivering Multimedia

The network and transport protocols we have described do no more than deliver packets of data – more or less reliably – to their designated destinations. Higher-level protocols must run on top of them to provide services suitable for distributed multimedia applications. We will describe two such protocols: HTTP, which is the basis of the World Wide Web, and **RTSP (Real Time Streaming Protocol)**, a protocol designed to control streamed media. Our description is not exhaustive, but is intended to show what is involved in mapping the requirements of some kinds of distributed multimedia applications on to the transport facilities provided by the protocols described in preceding sections.

HTTP

Interaction between a Web client and server over HTTP takes the form of a disciplined conversation, with the client sending requests which are met by responses from the server. The conversation is begun by the client – it is a basic property of the client/server model that servers do nothing but listen for requests, except when they are computing a response.

To start things off, the client opens a TCP connection to a server. The identity of the server is usually extracted from a URL. As we explained previously, the domain name in the URL is translated to an IP address by DNS. This translation is done transparently, as far as HTTP is concerned, so HTTP can always work in terms of names. By default, Web servers listen to port 80, so this will normally be the port number used when the connection is opened.

Originally, prior to version 1.1 of HTTP, a connection was used for one request and its response only. That is, the client opened a TCP connection and sent one request; the server sent a response to that request and closed the connection. This way of using connections is very efficient from the server's point of view. As soon as it has sent the response and closed the connection it can forget about the transaction and get on with something else, without having to keep the connection open and wait for further requests to come over it, or close the connection if it times out. The disadvantage is that accesses to Web servers tend to come in clusters. If a page contains 10 images most browsers will make 11 requests in rapid succession – one for the page itself and one for each image – so 11 connections between the same pair of hosts must be opened and closed. For technical reasons, to help minimize packet loss, a TCP/IP connection starts out at a slow rate and gradually works up to the best speed it can attain with acceptable losses in the existing state of the network. Hence, in our example, the data for the page and its images will not be sent as fast over the 11 connections as it would over a single connection, since each new connection has to start over and work up to speed. HTTP version 1.1 has therefore introduced the possibility of a persistent connection, which must be explicitly closed by the client (although the server will close it after a specified time has elapsed without requests).

Nevertheless, the structure of an HTTP session retains the form of a sequence of requests that evoke responses. No state information is retained in the server, which is therefore unaware of any logical connections between any requests.

Each HTTP message (request or response) consists of a string of 8-bit characters, so it can be treated as text by programs that read HTTP messages (and can be read by humans if they have a program that can eavesdrop on them). Messages conform to a simple rigid structure, consisting of an initial line (the *request line* for a request, the *status line* for a response) containing the essential message, followed by one or more headers, containing various parameters and modifiers. These may be followed by the message *body*, which contains data – such as the contents of a file being sent by the server – if there is any. Headers are separated from the data by a blank line. (The line terminator is always the combination of a carriage return followed by a linefeed, irrespective of the conventions of the operating system running either the server or client.)

A request line comprises three elements. The *method* is a name identifying the service being requested: the most commonly used methods are GET, which is used to request a file or other resource, and POST, which is used to send data from a form. The *identifier* comes next, and tells the server which resource is being requested, for example by giving the path name of a file. Finally, the HTTP *version* indicates which protocol version the client is using.

For example, if a user clicked on a link with its href attribute pointing to the URL http://www.webdesignbook.org/Info/index.html, their Web browser would connect to the host with name www.webdesignbook.org, using port 80 so that communication would go to the Web server on that machine. It would then send an HTTP request, whose request line was:

GET /Info/index.html HTTP/1.1

The headers that may follow a request line all take the form of a header name followed by a colon and some arguments. For example, the following two headers can be found after the request line shown above:

Host: www.webdesignbook.org
User-Agent: Mozilla/5.0 (Macintosh; U; PPC Mac OS X 10.5;en-GB; rv:1.9) ↩
Gecko/2008061004 Firefox/3.0

(The User-Agent header has been split over two lines to fit on the page here, as indicated by the ↩ symbol.)

The Host header tells the server the host name that the request is directed at. This is necessary, because nowadays it is common for several host names to correspond to a single IP address, using a mechanism known as "virtual hosting", which is implemented by most important Web servers, and this might make request identifiers ambiguous. The User-Agent header identifies the Web browser (or other user agent) that is making the request. This should allow the server to make allowances for any known problems with this particular browser, if it chooses to. However, it is common for Web browsers to send User-Agent headers that falsely identify them, so the information in this header is often unreliable.

One of the most commonly seen headers in GET requests is Accept. Its arguments indicate – using Internet media types – the range of types of data that the browser can deal with. For example,

Accept: image/gif, image/x-xbitmap, image/jpeg

is sent by a browser to indicate that it is able and willing to display GIF, JPEG and X bitmap images. Browsers may send several Accept headers instead of combining them. Web servers will only send them data that is of an acceptable type. In a media type used in this way, a * can be used as a wildcard character, so

Accept: image/*

indicates that the browser will accept any image format, and

Accept: */*

that it will accept any type of data for which there is an Internet media type.

Two similar headers, Accept-Charset and Accept-Language, are used by browsers to inform servers about the character sets and languages they will accept. The following would be typical of the headers sent by a browser set up in an English-speaking country where British usage is preferred:

Accept-Language: en-gb,en
Accept-Charset: UTF-8

Since a GET request does not send any data, its body is empty – the message terminates with the blank line.

The first line of an HTTP server's response is the status line, indicating how it coped with the request. This line begins with the protocol version, telling the client which HTTP version the server is using. Next comes a numerical status code, whose meaning is defined by the HTTP standard, followed by a short phrase, explaining to human readers what the code means. If all goes well, the code will be 200, which means OK, as shown:

HTTP/1.1 200 OK

Just as the client told the server who it was in the **User-Agent** header, the server introduces itself in the **Server** header. It also dates and times the response, and uses the **Content-type** header to inform the client about the media type of the data being returned. For example:

```
Server: Apache/2.2.0 (Fedora)
Date: Mon, 16 Jun 2008 15:17:06 GMT
Content-Type: text/html; charset=UTF-8
```

Typically, a server's response does contain some data. In the case of a response to a **GET** request, for example, this will be the contents of the file that was requested. In this example response, after any other headers there would be a blank line, followed by the XHTML document itself – the contents of a text file, encoded using UTF-8, containing the markup and text of the Web page in question. Any images and other embedded material would not be returned at this point, but the browser would send additional requests when it encountered markup referring to an external resource.

For instance, if the document that was returned in response to the request we have just described included a **style** element that referenced a stylesheet called **styles.css**, the browser would fetch it by sending another request, which included the following:

```
GET /styles.css HTTP/1.1
Host: www.webdesignbook.org
User-Agent: Mozilla/5.0 (Macintosh; U; PPC Mac OS X 10.5; en-GB; rv:1.9)↵
Gecko/2008061004 Firefox/3.0
Accept: text/css,*/*
Accept-Language: en-gb,en
```

The server should send a response with the following headers (plus some others):

```
HTTP/1.x 200 OK
Date: Mon, 16 Jun 2008 15:17:06 GMT
Server: Apache/2.2.0 (Fedora)
Content-Type: text/css
```

Again, the headers will be followed by a blank line and then the stylesheet itself. Similar requests will be made for the images in the page, and similar responses will be used to return them. The interaction is illustrated in Figure 16.5.

We will describe some other noteworthy headers shortly.

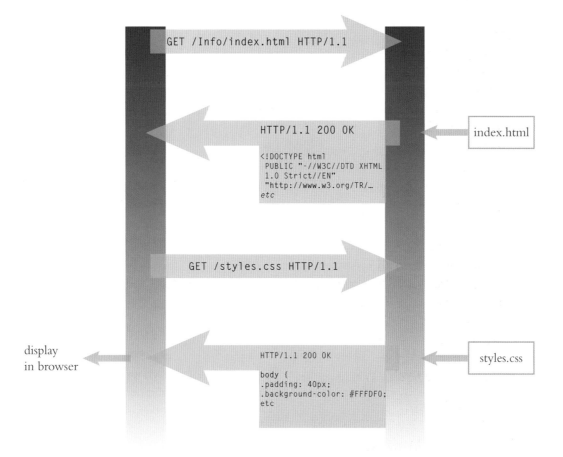

Figure 16.5. *HTTP requests and responses*

The status code in a response is not always 200, unfortunately. The HTTP 1.1 standard defines many 3-digit return codes. These are divided into groups, by their first digit. Codes less than 200 are informative; the only such codes presently defined are 100, which means "continuing", and is only applicable to persistent connections, and 101, which is sent when the server switches to a different protocol, for example to stream some real-time data.

Codes in the range 200–299 indicate success of one sort or another. The most frequently used response code is 200 ("OK"). Codes in the three hundreds are used when the server must redirect the request to a different URL. For example, a code of 301 ("moved permanently") indicates that the resource identified by the URL in a GET request has been permanently moved to a new location (the server sends a Location header giving the new URL).

Codes that begin with a 4 or a 5 represent errors, by the client and server respectively. Probably the two most commonly encountered error codes are 400 and 404. 400 means "bad request" – the request was malformed in some way. This error usually occurs when requests are manufactured by programs other than Web browsers. Error code 404 is "not found" – the URL in a request does not correspond to any resource on the server. This is the code that results from broken links. Error code 403 ("forbidden") corresponds to requests for services that are denied by the server, such as attempts to access protected files. Another interesting code is 406 ("not acceptable"), which is sent if the requested resource's media type is not listed in the Accept headers of the request.

Server errors include 500 ("internal server error"), which should never happen. If it does, it usually indicates a programming error in some server-side script that has been called by the server. Error code 501 ("not implemented") is sent when the server does not know how to implement a requested method, and 503 ("service unavailable") means that the server is temporarily unable to respond, usually because of system maintenance of some sort, but sometimes because it has been overloaded by requests.

Caching

The World Wide Web has made information accessible over the Internet in a way that it never had been previously. This has led to an increase in network traffic as people take advantage of this new-found accessibility. The growing popularity of video and other multimedia content with high bandwidth requirements only adds to the traffic. In order to help alleviate the strain this could cause on the network, HTTP provides support for a system of *caching*, which allows copies of pages that have been received to be kept on a user's machine, and on other intermediate machines between it and the server from which they originate. When a page is requested more than once, it can be retrieved after the first time from a cache instead of from the server. If the cache is on the local machine, this may not require any network access or action by the server at all.

The full extent of HTTP 1.1's support for caching is quite extensive, supplying several alternative mechanisms; we will only describe a subset.

The characteristic trouble with any caching scheme is that a version of the requested resource which is newer than the version in the cache might have appeared on the server. In that case, the new version should be retrieved, and the old one in the cache should be discarded. This should be obvious, but leads to the question "How can a client discover whether that is the case?" The simplest way is for the client to ask the server whether it has a version of the resource that is newer than the one in the browser's cache. It does this by sending an If-Modified-Since header, giving the date and time of its cached copy (which it knows from the Date header in the response to its original request). The request is then said to be "conditional", and the server only sends the requested page if the condition is satisfied – that is, if the page has been modified since the date specified in the header. If it has, the server sends a response containing the modified page, as before. If not, it sends a response with status code 304, which means "not modified". On receiving this code, the browser displays the page from its cache.

Conditional requests of this sort eliminate the need for servers to send complete responses in some cases, thus reducing the volume of data transmitted. A further facility potentially eliminates the need for servers to send any response at all, by eliminating the need for clients to send requests. A server can include an Expires header in its response to a GET request, indicating the date and time after which the data it returns should no longer be considered up-to-date. Until that time, the client is free to use a cached copy of the data to satisfy any subsequent requests for the same resource. Thus no network activity at all is required to obtain the same page until it reaches its expiry date.

While this mechanism is sound, it begs the question of how servers are to assign expiry dates to arbitrary pages. Most of them appear not to try, although one can imagine tightly controlled environments in which it would be known how long a page would remain valid. In the absence of any widespread use of Expires headers, Web clients fall back on their own ad hoc devices for avoiding unnecessary network accesses. For example, Firefox and other browsers offer an offline browsing mode. When this mode is selected (using a menu command in the browser) all requests are met from the local cache, if possible. This allows previously visited Web sites to be accessed without the user even being connected to the Internet. However, sites that are not in the cache cannot be visited in offline mode – the browser displays a message offering to go back online if the user tries to reach a page that has not been cached.

So far, we have assumed that a cache is maintained on a user's machine. There are other places that data can be cached, though, sometimes more effectively. In particular, **Web proxies** usually maintain large caches. A proxy is a machine that handles requests directed to some other server. So when a client that is configured to use a proxy sends a request, the request is sent to the proxy, which then forwards it to its designated destination, receives the response and passes it back to the client. This apparently pointless exercise is often needed when clients are operating behind a "firewall" – a specially modified router that filters packets to provide additional security. Firewalls prevent users inside them from making HTTP requests, so a proxy is used, which has access to the outside world and the protected machines. Security can be added to the proxy to prevent unauthorized access across the firewall, in either direction. All responses to requests sent by any machine inside the firewall must pass through the proxy, which means that a cache on the proxy will end up holding a pool of data that is of interest to people in the organization maintaining the firewall. This is likely to mean that many requests can be met from the proxy's cache.

Proxies can provide effective caches whenever they are placed somewhere that many requests pass through. ISPs, in particular, can employ proxies with extremely large caches to intercept a high proportion of their customers' requests.

Caching of pages that are dynamically generated must be done with care, to ensure that pages are not cached if they depend on data on the server that changes over time. For such cases, it is better to generate unnecessary requests than to return invalid data. Caching doesn't help users who never visit the same page twice unless it has been updated, of course, and caches are finite, so that, sooner or later, cached copies of pages must be discarded, and retrieved again if they are requested subsequently. Nevertheless, they are widely considered to be making a useful contribution to keeping network traffic within bounds.

RTSP

HTTP provides the services necessary for implementing a distributed hypermedia system. It should be easy to see in principle how HTTP requests can be constructed in response to mouse-clicks on links, and how a browser displaying the data in their responses can provide the experience of following a link to a new page. HTTP can cope with embedded images, sounds and video, by downloading a complete data file. Streaming audio and video require a different treatment, though.

In the first place, HTTP runs on top of TCP, and, as we explained earlier, the overheads incurred by the reliable delivery that TCP provides are unacceptable for streamed media, which are better served by a less reliable but more efficient protocol. Its use of TCP also makes HTTP unsuitable for multicasting. RTP, as described earlier, is adequate for carrying streaming media data, and can be used for multicasting, but it does not provide all the necessary functionality required by streams of such data. We usually want to be able to start, stop and pause them, and possibly (for streams that are not being transmitted live) go to a particular point in the stream, identified by a timecode. For live streams, we might want to schedule a time at which to start the display. For example, if a concert was being transmitted over the Web, we might want to skip the support band and start listening when the headline act was due to go on stage.

RTSP is intended to provide these services. It is often described as an "Internet VCR remote control protocol", which conveys much of the flavour of what it does (as well as dating its origin). Syntactically, it closely resembles HTTP, with request and status lines and headers, many of which are the same as in HTTP, but there are some differences. In particular, RTSP uses ISO 10646 (with UTF-8 encoding) as its character set, unlike HTTP which is restricted to ASCII in its messages (but not in its data, of course). In RTSP requests that include an identifier, an absolute URL must be used, instead of the pathname that may be used in HTTP. Consequently, RTSP does not need a separate Host header. Most importantly, RTSP responses do not carry the media data, in the way that HTTP responses carry Web page data. Instead, the data is transmitted separately, often using RTP. RTSP merely coordinates the transmission.

Before an RTSP session can be set up, the client must obtain a *presentation description*, which contains information about the data streams that are to be controlled, which make up a multimedia presentation. The RTSP specification does not stipulate the format of a presentation description. The *Session Description Protocol (SDP)*'s format is commonly used, but the prevailing applications using RTSP (Streaming QuickTime and RealPlayer G2) take advantage of that format's extensibility to customize it to their own requirements, so, in effect, presentation descriptions largely conform to proprietary formats.

A typical description will include one or more media announcements, including the transport address and protocol (e.g. RTP) of one of the session's component streams, and information about the encoding used, including the type of compression, if any. Each stream will have an rtsp:// URL. It is quite possible for different streams to be served from different hosts. The presentation description will also provide a *connection address*, to which subsequent requests are addressed. This is necessary because RTSP does not specify the mechanism whereby presentation descriptions are to be retrieved. There is a DESCRIBE request that is often used for this purpose, but it is permissible for the presentation description to be retrieved using HTTP, or even sent to a user by email.

In practice, both RealPlayer and Streaming QuickTime use DESCRIBE requests, but need a bootstrapping step before they can find out where to send it to. Typically, HTTP is used to obtain the URL of the presentation description – this will begin with rtsp://, to indicate that it can be accessed using RTSP. QuickTime uses a self-contained approach: a small movie containing URLs for different versions of a session corresponding to different connection speeds is presented as the representation of a streamed movie – for example, it might be embedded in a Web page, where a user can click on it, causing it to be retrieved by HTTP. RealPlayer uses a small file with a distinctive extension for the same purpose, although it does not provide for different versions.

Once the necessary URLs have been obtained by the client, it sends a DESCRIBE request, to which the server responds with a message containing the required presentation description. The client's request can include an ACCEPT header, indicating the description formats it understands. Once it has a presentation description, the client can send a SETUP request. The server responds with a message that includes a *session identifier*, an arbitrary string that is used by both client and server to identify messages associated with the same session. (RTSP does not use connections in the way TCP does, partly because the actual streamed data is sent over a separate transport protocol, and partly to enable it to be used for controlling multicast streams.) Everything is then in place for the streaming to begin.

In the simplest mode of operation, an RTSP client sends **PLAY** requests to cause the server to begin sending data, and **PAUSE** requests to temporarily halt it. A **PLAY** request may include a header specifying a range within the duration of the stream – SMPTE timecodes or clock values in a standard format may be used for this purpose. A session is ended by the client sending a **TEARDOWN** request, which causes the server to deallocate any resources associated with the session. It is, of course, conceivable that something might go wrong. Status codes are used in responses to indicate any errors that might occur, just as they are in HTTP. Indeed, wherever it makes sense, RTSP uses the same status codes as HTTP.

We emphasize that RTSP messages travel separately from the streamed data they relate to. Usually, RTSP will operate on top of TCP, so that it can rely on delivery of its messages, although it can as easily run on top of UDP if efficiency is important. For the streamed data, there is no such choice. As we explained previously, TCP is not suitable for carrying the streamed data itself, and this will usually be carried over RTP, which in turn runs on top of UDP. Nevertheless, there is always a logical connection between the streamed data and the RTSP messages. For example, RTSP supports the same headers for controlling caching as HTTP does, but, although the headers are transmitted as part of RTSP messages, it is the streamed data that is cached, not the messages.

RTSP can be used for unicast and multicast streams. Where unicast is used, it provides services such as video on demand. A client requests a movie to be streamed from a server, for example, and the data is sent exclusively to the client, who controls its playback with RTSP requests. Multicasting provides services more like conventional television broadcast. A client joins a multi-cast session that has been set up beforehand – to transmit a concert, for example. Where RTSP is being used with a multicast service, the main difference from the client's point of view is that the server has to tell it the multicast address for the transmission, whereas, in the unicast case, it is the client that has to tell the server where to direct the data stream.

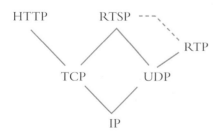

Figure 16.6. *Relationships between TCP/IP protocols used for multimedia*

Figure 16.6 summarizes the relationships between the protocols we have described. Video-conferencing and similar applications require additional protocols for session management and the equivalent of rules of procedure. We will not describe the protocols presently available for these purposes, since they take us too far away from our main concerns.

Quality of Service

Normally, when data is being transmitted over a packet-switched network, it is subject to the vagaries of network performance, which depends on many factors, most of them unpredictable. This can interfere with the satisfactory streaming of media in several ways.

First, delays can be introduced. There is always some delay due to the distance signals must travel at a finite speed. The operations that must be performed by routers contribute additional delays. Whereas traditional network applications, such as email and file transfer, can tolerate considerable delays, real-time and streamed multimedia are much less tolerant. You are probably familiar with the slightly disconcerting effect of the transmission delays that occur when live interviews are conducted over transatlantic links for television news bulletins. The effect of similar, or longer, delays on a real-time application, such as a video conference, can seriously interfere with its effectiveness. Streamed applications can tolerate longer delays, although the appeal of live streaming often lies in its immediacy, which is compromised by excessive delays.

Typically, the delay experienced by a particular stream of data will not be constant, but will vary continuously. The variation in delay is called *jitter* – it means that the time between the arrival of successive packets will vary. Jitter causes two kinds of problem for multimedia. First, the variation in the time between packets can result in **time base errors** – that is, samples will be played back at the wrong time. This is most likely to affect audio streams, where it manifests itself as noise. Second, where a presentation comprises several streams that are transmitted independently, as they will be over RTP, for example, the streams may jitter independently, resulting in a loss of synchronization between them (see Figure 16.7). Unless this can be corrected at the receiving end, disturbing – or unintentionally comical – effects may occur, since people are sensitive to tiny errors in lip-sync. As with delay, different applications can tolerate different amounts of jitter. For example, a video application might buffer incoming data streams, so that it could smooth out jitter and synchronize video and audio streams, provided the jitter was within certain limits.

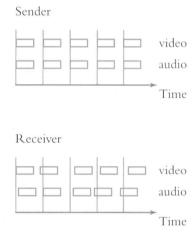

Figure 16.7. *Effect of jitter on synchronization*

In addition to delay and jitter, there may be packet loss, since, as we explained earlier, streamed media cannot be sensibly transported using a reliable protocol such as TCP. Once again, different applications can tolerate different amounts of packet loss.

Delay, jitter and packet loss are measurable quantities. Therefore, we can quantify the amounts of each which a particular application can tolerate. The values of these parameters, together with the bandwidth it needs, define the *quality of service (QoS)* required by an application.

Established types of network service do not require much in the way of quality of service. Mostly, they are based on the transfer of entire files, such as a mail message or the XHTML and embedded images of a Web page. They can tolerate as much delay as users' patience allows, and jitter is irrelevant, since nothing will be done with the data until it has all arrived. However, it is generally the case that packet loss is completely unacceptable. These characteristics led to the development of transport protocols like TCP that are reliable but pay no other attention to the requirements of applications. On the contrary, their performance is driven by the availability of bandwidth, and their objective is to make the best use of that bandwidth – which is how delay and jitter are introduced, since the bandwidth available to any one connection is not constant or guaranteed. Integrating support for streamed and real-time applications with their more demanding requirements for quality of service is thus quite a challenge.

New high-speed network technologies are coming into use which are able to reserve resources for individual connections. The best known of these is *ATM*, which stands for *Asynchronous Transfer Mode*. A pure ATM network can offer guarantees about the quality of service it will provide. Applications can reserve resources to satisfy their requirements, and the network will honour those reservations, so that the application can be assured that delay, jitter and packet loss will be kept within tolerable limits. In order to maintain the quality of service to some applications, the network may have to restrict the resources it allocates to others, perhaps even refusing to accept any new traffic after a certain point. The network is thus behaving much more like a circuit-switched network, such as the telephone system, than an ordinary packet-switched network.

Making an open heterogeneous network of networks, such as the Internet, behave in the same way, while still providing the traditional services that users have come to expect, is problematic. Parts of the Internet are presently ATM networks, but other parts are not, so the quality of service support has to be implemented at a higher level, by way of protocols. A framework known as the *Integrated Services Architecture* has been developed for this purpose. It defines different classes of service, such as "best effort", which is the traditional IP approach to delivery, and "guaranteed", where an absolute upper bound is imposed on the delay of packets. Several mechanisms for controlling network traffic to ensure that specified classes of service are actually provided are defined, together with a protocol for reserving resources, *RSVP (Resource Reservation Protocol)*. Some effort has been made to ensure that the facilities of the Integrated Services Architecture work with multicasting, since it is expected that many applications, such as video-conferencing and live video streaming, requiring guaranteed quality of service will employ multicasting.

KEY POINTS

Application protocols run on top of the network and transport layers to provide services for delivering multimedia.

HTTP clients send requests to and receive responses from HTTP servers.

An HTTP request starts with a request line, containing the method (GET, POST, etc.), identifier (path to the resource) and a version number. This is followed by some headers, such as Host, User-Agent and Accept.

The response begins with a status line, containing a version number and a status code. This is followed by some headers, such as Server and Content-Type, and a blank line followed by the response data (the requested resource).

Status codes beginning with 2 indicate success. Those beginning with 3 are used when the request is redirected. Codes beginning with 4 indicate client errors and those beginning with 5 indicate server errors.

Caching reduces network traffic by keeping copies of pages that have been received on a user's machine, or on Web proxies.

Conditional requests may include an If-Modified-Since header; if the requested resource is no newer than the date in the header, a response with status code 304 (not modified) is sent instead of the data.

RTSP is an "Internet VCR remote control protocol", resembling HTTP syntactically, but RTSP responses do not include data, which is carried separately over RTP.

A presentation description containing information about the streams to be controlled and a connection address for subsequent RTSP requests must be obtained before setting up an RTSP session.

An RTSP client sends a SETUP to set up a session, PLAY and PAUSE requests to control the data stream, and a TEARDOWN request to end the session.

RTSP can be used for unicast and multicast streams.

Networks may introduce delays in transmission. Jitter is a variation in delay, which may cause time-base errors and loss of synchronization.

The Quality of Service (QoS) required by an application is a function of the delay, jitter and packet loss it can tolerate, and the bandwidth it requires.

TCP is designed to eliminate packet loss, but allows for much delay and jitter, making it unsuitable for streamed media.

ATM networks are able to provide a guaranteed QoS, and allow applications to reserve resources.

Distributing Media Files

If you just want to transfer a video or audio file, without streaming or embedding it in a Web page, you don't need HTTP, RTSP, or any other special multimedia protocol. ***FTP (File Transfer Protocol)*** has been used since before the World Wide Web to transfer files efficiently between hosts on the Internet. Although there are many FTP clients with graphical interfaces that make transferring files in this way relatively straightforward, FTP still demands more technical sophistication than many computer users possess. To transfer a file from an FTP server, you need to know the server's URL, and be able to connect to it, usually supplying a user name and password, and navigate through its file system to find the file you want. While this is not much more demanding than copying a file from one place to another on your hard disk, it lacks the convenience of clicking on a link, which the Web has made everyone accustomed to.

RSS and Podcasts

In contrast to FTP, *podcasts* offer the sort of simplicity that is appreciated by many casual computer users. Unlike any of the other mechanisms we have looked at in this book, downloading a podcast requires no deliberate action, once you have subscribed to a feed – which is usually just a matter of clicking on an appropriately labelled link on a Web site. Once this has been done, a suitably enabled Web browser, email client or specialist reader will check periodically for new podcasts and download them for you, using HTTP.

Podcasts are an application of ***RSS (Really Simple Syndication)***. RSS is just a file format, based on XML, developed for packaging information about frequently updated Web sites, such as blogs and news sites in a form that can easily be checked and downloaded. The subscription links for RSS feeds are just XHTML a elements that point to a file in RSS format. (They are often labelled with a standard icon, but this is just convention.) For example, here is part of the RSS feed for a blog (reformatted slightly to make it easier to read):

```
<?xml version="1.0" encoding="utf-8"?>
<rss version="2.0" xmlns:dc="http://purl.org/dc/elements/1.1/"
  xmlns:content="http://purl.org/rss/1.0/modules/content/">
<channel>
  <generator>http://textpattern.com/?v=4.0.4</generator>
  <title>The Web Design Book Blog</title>
  <link>http://www.webdesignbook.org/textpattern/</link>

  <pubDate>Wed, 11 Jun 2008 14:16:18 GMT</pubDate>
  <item>
    <link>http://www.webdesignbook.org/textpattern/index.php?id=45</link>
    <pubDate>Wed, 11 Jun 2008 12:56:55 GMT</pubDate>
```

```
<dc:creator>Nigel Chapman</dc:creator>
<title>HTML 5 differences from HTML 4</title>
<description>
   <![CDATA[<p>A <a href="http://www.w3.org/TR/2008/WD-html5-diff-
20080610/">new W3C Working Draft document</a> provides an outline of the differences
between <span class="caps">HTML</span> 5 and <span class="caps">HTML</span> 4.
It&#8217;s worth looking at before you try to tackle the full <a href="http://www.w3.org/
TR/html5/"><span class="caps">HTML</span> 5 specification</a>.</p>]]>
   </description>
   <guid isPermaLink="false">tag:www.webdesignbook.org,2008-06-
11:5894e687682de58d1bda6bed72720544/ab4687fedd7d4cb3bd19cb311dcc5226</guid>
   </item>

   more item elements

</channel>
</rss>
```

Even if you skipped the detailed description of XML in Chapter 15 you should be able to understand this fragment just by considering it to be like XHTML, but using different elements. For instance, here the rss element serves as a container for all the other content, just as the html element does in an XHTML document. The rss element just carries the version number and namespace; the actual content of the feed is contained in the single channel element.

At the top of this element is some information about the feed itself: its title, a URL that points to the Web page from which it is derived – in this case a blog – and a URL that identifies the software that created the feed data. The pubDate element's content is the date on which the feed was most recently updated. This value can be used by a feed-reading program to determine whether any new material has been added since the last time it downloaded the feed.

Following these elements that describe the feed as a whole, there is a sequence of item elements (we have only shown one). Each item corresponds to whatever unit of information makes up the feed. For blog feeds, each item will be a blog post; for news feeds a news story; and so on. Each item has its own link and pubDate elements, and a dc:creator element is used to identify its author. (The prefix dc: identifies this element as belonging to the Dublin Core metadata namespace. Such elements may be used in RSS provided an appropriate namespace declaration appears in the start tag of the rss element. Consult Chapter 15 for an explanation of XML namespaces.)

The description element contains the actual content of the item – in this example, a synopsis of a blog entry. Here, the content of the element is XHTML markup. It is essential that this not be confused with the tags delimiting the elements of the RSS feed itself (channel, item, description and so on); these XHTML tags will only be interpreted when the content of the item is displayed. The ![CDATA[and]] are sequences used in XML to delimit text that should not be considered as XML itself, even if it contains XML tags.

The last element occurring within the item, guid, provides a globally unique identifier for this item. This can be used for various purposes by software that processes RSS data. If the isPermaLink attribute is set to "true", the GUID will be a URL that is guaranteed to point forever to the blog entry, news story, or whatever the item refers to. Such a URL is said to be a *permalink* (permanent link) for the item.

Blogging software and other programs used to generate content on a server usually update an associated RSS feed automatically whenever the Web site is changed. Thus, by subscribing to an RSS feed with a program that checks it periodically, you can be notified of such changes soon after they occur, and see the synopses of any new posts or stories. The popularity of RSS has grown in parallel with the rise of blogging, because the sort of automatic notification RSS provides is a perfect match for the characteristic way blogs are updated.

IN DETAIL

RSS isn't just a single format, it is a family of formats, with an involved history that has led to several different incompatible versions. The different versions even ascribe different meanings to the initials RSS – they have stood for Rich Site Summary, RDF Site Summary and Really Simple Syndication, in different versions of RSS. The latest and most widely used version is RSS 2.0, and it is now generally allowed that RSS stands for Really Simple Syndication.

No version of RSS has ever been any sort of official standard. The IETF has defined a standard format, related to RSS, called Atom. Atom looks more like other XML formats than RSS itself does. For instance, the link element in Atom is empty, with an href attribute, instead of having the URL in its content, as it does in RSS. Most importantly for readability, Atom elements may have a type attribute. If its value is "xhtml", the content may contain XHTML markup without being surrounded by the CDATA markers. Atom is also more robust, since important elements, such as the title and publication date of each individual item, which are optional in RSS, are compulsory in Atom.

The name RSS is used loosely to include Atom as well as all versions of RSS itself. Fortunately, almost all systems that handle RSS at all can handle all versions of it and Atom, so users don't really need to know which format is being used when they subscribe to a feed. The subscription links to many Atom feeds are labelled RSS, simply because the latter name is better known.

What has all this got to do with multimedia? Any item element may contain an enclosure element, which has three attributes (and no content): url points to the location of the enclosure, length specifies its size in bytes, and type is an Internet media type. If the type is an audio or video type, such as audio/mp3 or video/mp4, the feed can be used to periodically deliver files containing these media in a convenient way.

A podcast is just an RSS feed whose items have media enclosures. The mechanism for subscribing and checking podcast feeds is the same as it is for checking news feeds – you subscribe and then your software will check periodically for new content and download it. The same software that is used for reading textual RSS feeds can often be used for subscribing to podcasts, but a dedicated class of podcast clients – sometimes called *podcatchers* – which make receiving podcasts more convenient, can also be used. Apple's iTunes is widely used as a podcatcher (although that is not its primary function); Juice Receiver is an Open Source alternative.

Most podcasts contain audio enclosures, which allows podcasting to be used to create feeds that are much like radio programs. A new episode is posted at regular intervals, and subscribers will find it downloaded to their systems when their podcatcher next checks the feed. Podcasts can also include video, but the extra complexity of video production and the greater bandwidth requirements mean that the majority of podcasts are still primarily audio. (A podcast channel may include an image element. This is often used like a CD cover, to supply a visual identity for the podcast – when scaled down it may be used as an icon. Individual items may also include short text descriptions of their audio content.)

The name "podcast" is an amalgam of "iPod" and "broadcast". The broadcast part is derived from the analogy between podcasts and radio broadcasts; the iPod refers to Apple's portable music player. The connection is that, if iTunes (the software normally used for managing the contents of an iPod) is used to subscribe to a podcast, the enclosures can easily be transferred to an iPod. This makes podcasts something that can easily be carried about, to be listened to on buses or trains and so on. Other podcatchers can be used in a similar way with other makes of music players, or they may just save files to a specified location on disk.

Apple defined a collection of extra elements, with names that have the prefix itunes:, which allow additional metadata to be added to podcasts. The values of these elements are used by iTunes when it displays the podcast. In particular, the element itunes:category may be used in a channel element to assign the podcast to one or more iTunes categories, to make it easier for subscribers to find when browsing. The itunes:keywords element can be used for adding keywords, or tags, within an item, for further ad hoc classification of each episode. The iTunes store (used for selling music downloads) provides a classified database of podcasts, which can be subscribed directly from iTunes. Podcast feeds are also available on many Web sites; they are generally made compatible with iTunes. The Open Source community has defined a set of additional attributes, which are contained in the podcast namespace. Their main function appears to be to make it possible to integrate podcasts with peer-to-peer file-sharing protocols, such as BitTorrent (described below).

In itself, a podcast is nothing more than a way of wrapping up a collection of URLs in a format that can easily be checked for new additions. The success of podcasting is attributable to the convenience which this simple idea brings to distribution of audio (and video) over the Internet. There is no need to be concerned about integrating time-based media content into a Web page. If bandwidth is limited, downloads can be scheduled for times when the network connection is not otherwise busy and, most importantly, people like the familiar, radio-like format.

BitTorrent

HTTP and FTP are both based on the client/server model. There are several advantages to this arrangement, including increased security and availability, easier maintenance and a clear division of functions between the client and the server. However, because data is stored centrally on a server, all requests for a particular resource must be processed by the same server. This can place a burden on the server. If many requests are received for a popular file the server may become overwhelmed – it may take an unacceptably long time to process requests, or it may even crash.

Multimedia data is particularly susceptible to these problems. The files are often large, especially, as we have seen, in the case of video. People like to download music and video, and both are subject to fashion, so it is quite likely that particular files may suddenly become very popular.

An alternative to client/server systems, which can avoid some of their problems, is provided by *peer-to-peer (P2P)* systems, in which no single host is distinguished as a server. Any computer on the network can function as both server and client. BitTorrent is one of the most successful applications of the peer-to-peer approach.

BitTorrent is most easily introduced by contrasting it with a more conventional client/server system. Figure 16.8 shows

Figure 16.8. *Distributing a file from a central server*

a centralized server being used to distribute a large popular video file, using FTP or HTTP. It receives requests from many clients and sends a separate copy of the movie in response to each request. The arrows on the diagram, indicating the direction of responses, all go away from the server to the clients: the system is essentially asymmetrical. As more and more requests are received by the server, it must send more and more copies of the file. These multiple copies must all be transferred over the network, placing a load on the available bandwidth.

Figure 16.9 shows how the same file might be distributed using BitTorrent. Here most of the arrows between hosts go in both directions, to indicate that each machine is both downloading and uploading the file. Thus, it makes no sense to talk about a "BitTorrent client" (though people often do so). This is the essential feature of BitTorrent – when you download a file, you make your machine available as a source for others to download it from. Your BitTorrent program operates as both a "downloader" and an "uploader".

To make this process efficient, files are split into pieces. Typically, when a torrent is first started the entire file will be available on one machine, which will be the only place it can be obtained from, just as in the client/server case. Such a machine is called a *seed*, since the whole process grows from it.

To begin with, all requests for the file must go to the seed. Instead of returning the whole file in its response, the seed just sends a piece of it. BitTorrent downloaders request the pieces of a file in a random order, so each request probably asks for a different piece. After a while, therefore, copies of parts of the file are available on several machines. By arranging for these machines to communicate directly with each other – as peers – the file can be distributed to all of them efficiently.

Suppose we just have three machines, *A*, *B* and *C*, and a seed *S*, and our file has been divided into six pieces. (This is an unrealistic value for illustration only. It is usually recommended that files be split into between 1000 and 1500 pieces.) After a few requests, suppose that *A* has pieces 1 and 4,

Figure 16.9. *Distributing a file using BitTorrent*

B has 5 and C has 2 and 3. If A next requests piece 5, the response can be sent by B. Similarly, if B requests piece 1, it can get it from A. Only piece 6 must be sent by S. In general, as more machines start to download the file, more requests can be exchanged between peers, so fewer must be satisfied by the seed. This is in contrast to the client/server case, where as more requests are sent, the load on the server goes up. Furthermore, once every piece of a file has been downloaded by some machine, the seed is no longer really necessary. If it goes down for some reason, it will still be possible for the file to be downloaded. Again, this contrasts with the client/server approach, where if a server goes down, its resources become inaccessible.

To enable downloading to begin, a "torrent file", which provides a description of the file to be downloaded – primarily its whereabouts and the number of pieces it has been broken into – must be obtained. This is usually done through a Web browser – torrent files are posted to Web sites that act as indexes for BitTorrent downloads. The torrent file is usually passed to a dedicated program, which then performs the downloading and uploading of the pieces of the file. (Some Web browsers have BitTorrent support built in, while others use a plug-in to eliminate the need for a separate program.)

Evidently, the file transfers require coordination, so that requests can be sent to the most appropriate place. This coordination is performed by a program called a "tracker". Usually, the tracker runs on the machine used to host the original seed, though some sites provide freely available tracker services. When a downloader wants a piece of the file, it sends a request to the tracker to find out which other machines it can request the piece from. This has the effect of making it a peer in the process. Requests are also sent while the download proceeds, which include information about the status of the download and any uploads being performed by the same machine, so that the tracker can know what pieces are available where.

Another essential requirement of this type of file transfer is security. When you are downloading a file, you are allowing any computer to send you data, without having any idea whether you can trust it. It would require considerable ingenuity to insert malicious code into a torrent in such a way that it could be executed, but it would be rash to say that it was impossible. To help prevent any such possibility, and to check the integrity of the downloaded data, the pieces of the file carry a hash value computed from an identifier in the torrent file, which can be checked to provide an assurance that the downloaded data really belongs to the file it claims to.

Much of the BitTorrent protocol is concerned with preventing machines becoming overloaded with requests and with optimizing the use of the available bandwidth. The issue is a complex one and we will not describe the solutions adopted by current implementations in any detail, beyond noting that they appear to work and do not require any intervention from users.

BitTorrent is used for transferring entire files, so it must provide reliable transmission. It therefore runs on top of TCP connections. Unlike HTTP messages, BitTorrent messages are in a format that is not easily readable by people.

If you recall from our earlier description of ADSL that the upstream speed of most domestic broadband connections is much slower than their downstream speed, you will see that even though peers act as downloaders and uploaders at the same time, the downloading will go much faster than the uploading for most of them. This asymmetry seems to undermine the basis of BitTorrent. If the peers download 10 times as much as they upload, the original seed will end up behaving like a server most of the time. At present, the only way of avoiding this is for BitTorrent programs to be left running after a download completes, so that the uploading can catch up. Programs usually display the ratio of uploading to downloading, so users can see when they have performed their share of the upload, but the smooth operation of the system relies only on courtesy and a sense of fairness.

┌─IN DETAIL─

BitTorrent isn't the only P2P method of file-sharing in use. Others, including Kazaa and Gnutella, don't break the files into pieces and mix uploading and downloading. Instead, they arrange for the information about where a copy of a file is available to be distributed to a network of peers, either by keeping a central directory, or by letting peers identify themselves to each other and announce which files they have available dynamically. To download a file, a machine just makes a connection to one of its peers that has indicated it is willing to make it available, and downloads it using HTTP. P2P networks of this kind include search facilities to make it possible to find files to download.

BitTorrent and other P2P file-sharing technologies have acquired a bad reputation. They are widely associated with illegal activities, particularly the exchange of bootlegged software and copyrighted music and video, such as episodes of TV programmes. The absence of any easily identifiable central source for the material makes it easy to hide its origin. This has led to calls from large copyright owners, such as record companies and television networks, for P2P traffic to be banned from the Internet. More recently, though, some publishers have started to look at the possibility of using P2P distribution themselves, because of its technical virtues. Proposals usually include stringent DRM (Digital Rights Management) controls, or demands that ISPs filter out illegal traffic – no simple task when files have been broken into hundreds of pieces.

P2P transfers are unpopular with ISPs, too, in countries where it is customary to allow customers unlimited bandwidth. P2P transfers use the ISPs' bandwidth, instead of that of the people providing the content. This may lead to caps on bandwidth, and charges for exceeding them, becoming more widespread, which will be unpopular with customers in countries where such charging is not presently common practice. At present it seems likely, though, that P2P transfer will play an increasing role in the distribution of media files over the Internet.

KEY POINTS

RSS is an XML-based file format for packaging information about frequently updated Web sites in a form that can easily be checked and downloaded.

An RSS file contains some metadata about the feed and a sequence of item elements, each of which has a publication date and a description element, containing text corresponding to a blog post, news item, etc.

The RSS feed is updated whenever the Web site is, and can be checked periodically by a feed reader.

A podcast is an RSS feed whose items contain an enclosure element with a URL pointing to an audio or video file. Podcasts are used to distribute regular episodes, like weekly radio programmes.

Peer-to-peer (P2P) systems, in which no single host is a dedicated server, overcome some of the problems of centralized client/server applications.

A machine downloading a file using BitTorrent simultaneously uploads it to other machines.

BitTorrent files are split into pieces, so parts end up on different machines. A downloader requests a part which it is missing from some machine that has it.

The BitTorrent process is started by a seed which has a complete copy of the file.

A torrent file containing metadata must be downloaded before a machine can join in the process.

A tracker is used to coordinate the interactions between peers.

Machines should continue uploading after they have finished downloading, to compensate for the asymmetry of most broadband connections.

Server-Side Computation

In previous sections we described protocols that allow multimedia data to be carried over a network, but we have not yet considered where that data ultimately comes from. Consider the World Wide Web, in particular. Using client-side scripting, as described in previous chapters, we can produce Web pages that are responsive to user input in a limited way, but they must be made up from a fixed collection of elements – typically stored in files accessible to a server, although video and audio streams can also be incorporated by a server that understands the appropriate protocols. Using this approach, we cannot even embed the time of day in a Web page.

Server-side scripting is used to enable an HTTP server to communicate via other programs with external resources, such as databases, and incorporate data obtained from them into its responses. (Remember that, although the term "server" is often used loosely to refer to the machine it runs on, a server is really the program that accepts requests and sends responses.) In particular, server-side scripts are used to enable a server to construct Web pages dynamically from time-varying data. Popular facilities of the sort you find on photo- and video-sharing sites, such as file uploading, tagging and commenting, are all dependent on server-side computation to process and store information. User registration, which is a pre-requisite for most sites that allow users to contribute to their content, is also carried out by server-side scripts. Blogs are almost always driven by server-side scripts that allow the articles, embedded media and attached comments to be held in a database to be retrieved in different arrangements, searched and used to populate RSS feeds. In fact, none of the facilities that go under the vague name of "Web 2.0" could exist without server-side scripting. Nor could e-commerce, online music and video stores, or any really interesting or useful Web sites.

In contrast to **client-side** scripts, which are invariably written in JavaScript, server-side scripts use many different languages – anything that will run on the same machine as the server can be used, provided it has some way of exchanging data with the server itself. Popular choices include PHP, Python, Ruby and Perl.

There are several different mechanisms in place to perform the exchange of data. The oldest is known as the **Common Gateway Interface (CGI)**. Although CGI itself is not used much any more, the mechanism it provides for moving data between the server and some other program has influenced all subsequent interfaces, so we will begin by examing CGI.

The Common Gateway Interface

Earlier in this chapter, we described how a client sends HTTP requests to a server, which sends responses back. The Common Gateway Interface provides a mechanism for the server to pass on data in a client's request to a script[†] – referred to as a **CGI script** – running on the server's machine, and for the script to pass data back, which the server then sends on to the client. It is important to realize that the communication between the client and server takes place using HTTP, so the output of a CGI script must be something from which the server can construct an HTTP response. Some scripts – technically known as "non-parsed header" scripts – actu-ally generate complete HTTP responses, but more often a CGI script produces the response body and a few headers, such as Content-Type, which describe the data generated by the script,

---

† Or program, but most server-side computation is done using scripting languages.

and leaves the server to add the status line and other headers, such as **Server**, which it is better placed to generate.

CGI is a mechanism for communication in both directions between client and CGI script, via the server. A CGI script is called by the server when the identifier in the request line denotes a script (usually because it refers to an executable file in a designated script directory). How does the client send data to the script? There are four possible mechanisms. First, there are the headers in the HTTP request. Some of these might contain information that is useful to a CGI script. Second, the path part of the URL may be extended with extra components, which may be passed on to a script. Third, as we mentioned in Chapter 10, a query string may be appended to the end of the URL – it is then added to the identifier in the request line. Finally, a similar string can be sent as the body of a request whose method is **POST**. The last two are by far the most common, so we must begin by looking at the format of these query strings, and how they are constructed by browsers.

A query string assigns values to named parameters. It consists of a sequence of assignments of the form name = value, separated by & characters. Within the value, spaces are encoded as + signs, and other special characters are replaced by code sequences in the same way as they are in URLs (see Chapter 10). Thus, an HTTP request for a CGI script called **register.cgi**, with a query string setting the value of a parameter called **Name** to the string **MacBean of Acharacle**, and that of **Profession** to **Piper** would look like this:

```
GET /cgi-bin/register.cgi?Name=MacBean+of+Acharacle&Profession=Piper HTTP/1.1
```

Such a request can be generated by any program that has opened an HTTP connection, but HTTP requests are usually constructed and sent by Web browsers. URLs with fixed query strings can be used in anchors like any other URL. This is useful for embedding links to pages that are generated by retrieving information from a database.

Often, query strings need to be constructed dynamically from user input, either to allow the retrieved data to be determined by a value that is provided by the user, or to allow such data to be stored in a database. It is unreasonable and impractical to expect users to construct query strings themselves. The traditional way of constructing them is by using XHTML's facilities for constructing and submitting forms, which we described in Chapter 12.

You will recall that each element within the form has a **name** attribute. Its value is used as a parameter name when the browser constructs a query string. The value of the parameter is taken from the user's input in the **form** element. For instance, a simple form that was used to elicit a user's name and profession for registration purposes might be constructed in the following way:

```
<form method="get" action="cgi-bin/register.cgi">
  <p><label for="Name">Your name:</label>
   <input type="text" name="Name" id="Name" size="54" />
  </p>
  <p><label for="Profession">Your profession:</label>
   <input type="text" name="Profession" id="Profession" size="49" />
  </p>
  <p>
   <input type="submit" name="Submit" value="Submit" />
  </p>
</form>
```

The method attribute of the form element is used to determine the method in the HTTP request
(GET or POST), and its action attribute is what identifies the CGI script. Clicking on the Submit
button causes the browser to send an HTTP request with the request line shown earlier to the
server, which in turn passes the parameter values and request headers to the script register.cgi.

More often, though, the method attribute's value will be POST. The same query string will be
sent to the server, but it will be sent in the body of the request, instead of being incorporated in
the request line. This method is less vulnerable to abuse, and permits larger amounts of data to be
sent from a form.

CGI specifies a mechanism for passing data from an HTTP request to a separate program invoked
by the HTTP server. The specification makes the assumption that this program will run as a separate process, which will be started up by the server. Most values sent in the request, including form
data and the request headers, are copied into environment variables, which can be accessed by the
program. Any data sent in the body of a POST request is passed in the standard input stream. The
standard output from the program is normally passed back to the server process, where HTTP
response headers are added to it before it is sent to the client. The flow of data is illustrated in
Figure 16.10.

Although environment variables and standard input and output streams are system-dependent
concepts – the CGI specification appears to assume that all HTTP servers run on Unix – CGI
scripts can run on almost any platform and interact with almost any HTTP server.

CGI places most of the burden of deciphering the data from the request on the CGI script. Any
query string appended to the path of a GET request is passed exactly as it is in a single environment
variable. The script must replace + signs by spaces and URL-encoded sequences by the characters
they represent, and split the string at & characters to access the name/value pairs sent by a form.

Client   Server

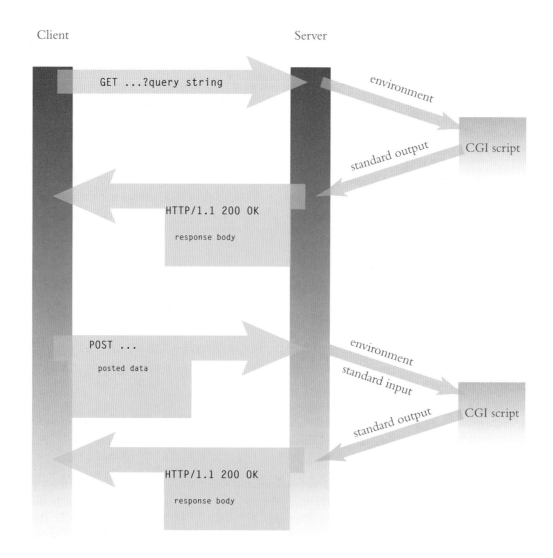

Figure 16.10. *The Common Gateway Interface*

POST data is similarly sent to the CGI script's standard input exactly as it is received by the server, and so this must be deciphered in the same way.

Because almost any CGI script must decipher query strings, programming languages commonly used for CGI scripting usually provide a higher-level interface to the CGI data. Generally, an object or associative array is created, either automatically by the run-time system or explicitly using some library call, which allows the script to look up the value of any variable sent in the request.

IN DETAIL

> The use of extra path components to pass values to server-side scripts allows "clean" URLs to be used in place of ones with an appended query string. One place where this is often used is in creating permalinks to blog entries. If an entry is retrieved by looking up its date, for example, a URL with a query string, such as http://www.someblog.com/entries?date=2008-06-25 might be used to identify an entry.
>
> A clean URL for the same entry would put the date in a path component, giving http://www.someblog.com/entries/2008-06-25, which looks as if it is pointing at a file. URLs of this form may be rewritten by the Web server into an equivalent URL with a query string, or interpreted as they are by a script that understands the significance of the extra path component.

Alternatives to CGI

CGI is implemented by creating a new process every time a request for a script is received. This is inefficient: the overhead of creating and destroying processes is considerable. Since the processes for each request are separate, a great deal of memory may be allocated to running multiple copies of the same script. If, as is usual, the script is written in an interpreted language, each process will need a copy of the interpreter. A script that is part of a popular site may be requested many times a second, so the overheads may place a considerable load on the server machine.

FastCGI is an extension to CGI, which avoids this overhead. Instead of processes starting up when a request is received and terminating when they have dealt with it, FastCGI processes are created when the HTTP server is started, and continue running all the time. When a request is received by the HTTP server, it opens a connection (e.g. a pipe in Unix) to the appropriate FastCGI process. This connection is used to pass the information that a CGI process would receive in environment variables and its standard input. The FastCGI process sends its output back over this connection to the server, which passes it on to the client in the form of an HTTP response. After sending the output, the FastCGI process closes the connection and then waits for another request. FastCGI can be significantly faster than CGI, but this additional speed is obtained at the expense of keeping a pool of running processes, one for each Web application hosted on the server.

The widely used Apache Web server provides another way of avoiding the overhead of creating and destroying processes incurred by CGI. It supports the use of dynamically loaded modules. Rather like browser plug-ins, these are loaded into the server itself when they are needed. A module of this sort can include an interpreter, so that instead of spawning a new process with its own copy every time a CGI script is requested, the script can be run inside the server, thus avoiding the overhead of starting up the process and the memory requirement associated with it. Once a script has been compiled, it can be kept in memory for subsequent requests.

A script running inside an Apache module does not have access to environment variables – these are created for a process, and the script is running as part of the Apache process, so the actual CGI mechanism cannot be used to pass data to the script. However, various expedients are available to make it appear to the script as if the environment variables had been set up, so that scripts can run more efficiently in a module and use the same interfaces for accessing the data passed in the request.

Microsoft's ***ASP.NET*** framework does something similar. ASPX documents, the equivalent of scripts, can be compiled into dynamically loaded libraries (DLLs), which are then loaded into the server. Typically, compilation occurs the first time a document is requested, and then the compiled version can be executed rapidly on subsequent requests. One of the strengths of ASP.NET is that it allows almost any programming language to be used, although Visual Basic and C# tend to be preferred by programmers using this technology.

An alternative strategy is to bypass CGI and HTTP entirely, by using a special-purpose server to implement Web applications written using some application framework. A popular example is the Tomcat "servlet container", which executes applications written in Java, or as Java Server Pages (JSP), in which Java code is embedded in XHTML documents. Web browsers may send their requests directly to Tomcat or it can be arranged for a conventional Web server to forward requests to it. The latter option is complicated, but is necessary if applications built in JSP must co-exist with more conventional scripts written in PHP, for example.

AJAX

XHTML forms provide a familiar and effective interface for eliciting user input, and you can use stylesheets to format them in a way that harmonizes with the rest of your page (up to a point – not all browsers implement styling of form controls properly). However, forms have two shortcomings. First, they only provide a limited reportoire of controls. Many types of interaction that are familiar from desktop applications – such as drag-and-drop, in-place editing and auto-completion – are missing. Second, the only way in which data can be sent from a Web page is by submitting a form, which causes an HTTP request to be sent and a response containing a new page to be returned. Hence, the browser window will be refreshed with a new page every time data is sent. This is often appropriate for sites that are simply presenting content, but where a site is functioning as a Web application, allowing its visitors to work with data in roughly the same way as they do when using desktop applications, it would often be preferable to change just part of the page. In this way, a page would become a dynamic interface to the data.

These shortcomings can be overcome by the use of JavaScript. We showed in Chapter 14 how scripts attached to Web pages can be used to alter the contents of a page in response to input from users. An extension to the DOM (presently being standardized by W3C) makes it possible for a script running in the browser to request data from the server, which it can then use to change the page in a similar way. The request is sent by way of an object called an XMLHttpRequest, which can be used to send any HTTP request to a server. Usually, such objects are used in conjunction with server scripts that return responses containing XML data, hence the name.

The requests sent by XMLHttpRequest objects are processed asynchronously. That is, the request is sent to the server, and then the script that sent it carries on doing something else. When the data is received an event occurs, and the script can then process the XML it has been sent. The abbreviation *AJAX* – standing for Asynchronous JavaScript and XML – is often used to describe Web applications that make use of this technique of fetching data using scripts.

As an example of the use of AJAX, imagine a Web site used as a showcase for video clips. A user can select a clip from a catalogue and go to a page for that particular clip, where it can be displayed. Suppose that the site allows people who have looked at a clip to post a review of it. The natural place to show the reviews of a clip is on the page where it can be viewed. However, popular clips may have many reviews, and visitors might not want to read all – or any – of them.

Without using AJAX, there are really only two ways of presenting the clip and its reviews. Either the two must be separate, with a link from the clip's page to a separate page containing the reviews, or they must all be on a single page. (In that case, it would be possible to hide reviews using CSS and use a script to reveal them, but it would be necessary to download all the text of all the reviews, even if a visitor to the page never chose to look at them.)

AJAX provides another alternative. The page can be displayed without reviews. Some controls will be provided to request that they be shown. Possibly, some filtering criteria could be applied, so that only reviews by respected reviewers would be displayed, for example. Instead of sending the data from these controls directly to a server-side script, causing a separate page to be loaded, they could be processed by a client-side script, which would build an XMLHttpRequest object and use it to send the request. The response would be passed to this script, not to the browser itself. The script could then use DOM methods to insert the reviews into the page. If somebody preferred not to look at reviews, no data would ever be sent. If they did choose to read them, the reviews would be displayed *in situ*, so that they appeared to be an integral part of the page.

This example is just one simple illustration of the potential of AJAX. The technique has already been applied in many different ways, and as the technology becomes standardized it will become a standard part of Web development. Several powerful JavaScript libraries and frameworks are now available to make it easy to add features that depend on AJAX to Web applications.

There are some disadvantages. Most importantly, it is always necessary to ensure that sites still work – even if they don't work so smoothly – for people whose browsers don't support JavaScript. This is still the case with some mobile devices and certain types of assistive technology. Some people simply choose to disable JavaScript in the browsers. In addition, creating pages dynamically in the browser – which is effectively what AJAX does – makes it impossible to bookmark pages or even to use the browser's Back button without using some messy expedients. Careless use of AJAX may lead to excessive numbers of requests being sent to servers. Nevertheless, the richer applications that can be created by using AJAX are generally considered to outweigh these disadvantages.

ActionScript provides a URLLoader class. Objects belonging to this class serve the same purpose as XMLHttpRequest objects do in JavaScript. They can be used in a similar way to load XML data dynamically into a Flash movie from a server.

> **KEY POINTS**
>
> Server-side scripting is used by HTTP servers to incorporate data from external resources in its responses, thereby building Web pages dynamically.
>
> Server-side scripts are written in many different languages, including PHP, Python, Ruby and Perl.
>
> The Common Gateway Interface is the oldest mechanism for the server to pass data in a request to a CGI script, and for the script to pass data back.
>
> Data is taken from the request headers, extra path components in the URL, a query string appended to a GET request, or the body of a POST request.
>
> Query strings and POST data consist of name = value pairs. Spaces are replaced by + signs. Other special characters are URL-encoded.
>
> Data is usually sent from an XHTML form.
>
> Query strings and header information are passed to the script in environment variables. POST data is sent in the standard input stream. The script's standard output is used to construct the HTTP response.
>
> More efficient alternatives to CGI include FastCGI, Apache modules and dedicated application servers.
>
> XMLHttpRequest objects can be used to send requests from JavaScript and receive XML data that can be used to rewrite parts of the page without fetching a new one.
>
> AJAX is a technique for creating interactive interfaces to Web applications using scripts in the browser.

CHAPTER 16

Exercises

Test Questions

1 Why are technologies such as ADSL, where the downstream speed is much higher than the upstream speed, appropriate for domestic Internet connections?

2 What is the difference between a transport address and an IP address? Why are both needed?

3 Must file transfer applications such as FTP always run on top of a reliable transport protocol such as TCP?

4 Why are timestamps needed as well as sequence numbers to synchronize RTP streams?

5 Which of the following potential Internet applications would benefit from multicast?

   (a) Video on demand.

   (b) Internet radio.

   (c) Automatic distribution of operating system upgrades.

   (d) Online photo editing.

6 What are the advantages and disadvantages of using persistent connections for HTTP?

7 Give an example of a Web page (real or fictitious) for which a Web server could accurately supply an Expires header. Would the use of this header be likely to reduce network traffic?

8 Why must an RTSP client obtain a presentation description before a session can be set up?

9 If new entries to a blog are displayed on its front page as soon as they are posted, is there any advantage in providing an RSS feed for the blog?

10 ISP *A* charges its customers a flat monthly fee for unlimited data transfers. ISP *B* charges a lower fee that allows each customer to transfer 10 GB each month, and then charges an additional amount (20% of the standard fee) for each extra GB. Which of the two is more likely to be opposed to P2P file transfer and why?

11 Many Web sites include image galleries: a collection of small thumbnail images is shown on a page together with a single large image. Clicking on a thumbnail causes the large image to be replaced with a full-sized version of the corresponding picture. Such a gallery might be implemented by generating separate pages on the server for each image, showing that image at full size, or by using AJAX to download the image when the user clicks on a thumbnail. Describe any differences that a user would perceive between the two implementations, and the pattern of HTTP requests generated in each case.

Discussion Topics

1 What sorts of program, besides Web browsers, might send and receive HTTP messages?

2 Since the Internet is a network of networks, packets often travel over networks belonging to several different ISPs. Normally, ISPs operate "peering agreements", whereby they provide their services free to other ISPs of roughly the same size, in return for reciprocal services. This way, ISPs don't have to keep track of where packets come from and go to, or charge each other for carrying them. Discuss how the commercial provision of multicasting may affect such arrangements.

3 The HEAD method of HTTP is much like GET, except that it causes the server to return only headers, and no body, in its response. What might this method be used for?

4 Why do Web browsers sometimes send User-Agent headers that provide false identification?

5 Discuss the feasibility of using BitTorrent, or some similar protocol, for streaming media.

6 Video streams are often described as "bursty", that is, the data rate is not constant, but exhibits bursts or intermittent peaks. Explain why this pattern occurs, and describe the problems it presents to networks.

Practical Tasks

1 There are many programs and browser extensions available which allow you to see HTTP requests and responses as they pass between your Web browser and servers on the Internet. Install one or more of these, and visit a simple Web page. Observe the requests that your browser sends and explain why each one is being sent. Refresh the page and explain the resulting sequence of requests and responses.

2 Create a podcast for distributing some simple instructional material, such as a set of tutorials for using some computer program. You will probably need to use a combination of software to create the content, prepare it for distribution and add the RSS metadata.

3 Design – and implement, if you have the skills and resources – a Web application that could be used in conjunction with a college course on multimedia, to allow students to upload images, video and Flash movies that they have created for course assignments so that other students on the course can look at them and provide comments and criticism. List the facilities you would provide and describe any security measures you think would be necessary. Assess the hardware and software requirements of the application, and the effort needed to implement it.

Appendix

Standards and Multimedia

The International Organization for Standardization (ISO)[†] offers this description of standards:

> "Standards are documented agreements containing technical specifications or other precise criteria to be used consistently as rules, guidelines, or definitions of characteristics, to ensure that materials, products, processes and services are fit for their purpose."

Since standards are agreements, we can assume that things that conform to the same standards are interchangeable. For example, an important set of ISO standards is concerned with screw threads. Any manufacturer's standard screws can be fitted in place of any other manufacturer's standard screws, which means that equipment assembled using standard screws is not tied to the products of one screw manufacturer. In a market economy, this is supposed to lead to healthy competition. In practical terms, it means that the bankruptcy of one screw manufacturer does not imply that everything built with their screws becomes irreparable. However, only some standards have any legal status, so conforming to a standard is not something that anybody can usually be compelled to do. Nor does conforming to a standard necessarily mean doing something the best way; it just means doing something the standard way.

In multimedia, standards define interfaces, file formats, markup languages, network protocols, and so on, in precise, and usually formal, terms. The role of these standards is broadly analogous to that of the standards for screw threads. If we have a standard file format for image data, for example,

---

† *ISO is not a mistyping of IOS, and it does not stand for International Standards Organization. ISO is not an acronym, but a play on words on the prefix iso- meaning "the same".*

then we can incorporate images into a Web site or Flash movie without having to worry about which program was used to prepare them originally. Similarly, standards for all the other media types enable multimedia authoring systems to be constructed independently of the applications used to prepare the individual media elements. The alternative would be for each manufacturer of multimedia software to produce a system that could only use its own formats. Whereas this may be attractive to some manufacturers, such closed systems are unacceptable in a world where several different hardware and software platforms are in use, communicating with each other over networks. Open systems that can accommodate data from any platform or source are needed.

Standards are of particular importance in networking, precisely because a modern network should be capable of connecting different makes of computer running different operating systems. It is only by conforming to standards for protocols and for electrical connections agreed to by all the manufacturers that this can be possible. Because modern networks cross national boundaries and carry data all over the world, international standards are essential.

Three organizations are involved in making international standards that are relevant to multimedia: **ISO**, the **International Electrotechnical Commission (IEC)** and the **ITU (International Telecommunication Union)**. ISO takes responsibility for formulating standards in all technical fields except electrical and electronic engineering, which are the responsibility of the IEC. Information technology defies categorization, and is dealt with by a joint ISO/IEC technical committee. ISO works through the national standards bodies of its member countries – ANSI (the American National Standards Institute) in the United States, BSI (the British Standards Institution) in the United Kingdom, DIN (Deutsches Institut für Normung) in Germany, and so on – who administer the committees that formulate standards, with ISO itself largely operating as a coordinating agency. The IEC operates in a similar way with the relevant national bodies responsible for electrotechnical standards.

Whereas ISO and the IEC are non-governmental agencies – commercial companies, in fact, albeit of a rather special nature – the ITU is an agency of the United Nations. It has a more regulatory function than the other two international standards bodies. For example, it is the ITU that allocates frequencies to radio services; these allocations must be followed to prevent interference, so they have a mandatory status according to international treaty. ITU standards covering video formats and telecommunication are those most relevant to multimedia.

Although there is broad agreement on the desirability of standards, the process of agreeing standards through these official bodies is a fraught and often a long drawn-out one. Since standards will only be observed if there is a consensus among the concerned parties, a great deal of politics and compromise may be involved in the production of a standard. The major standards bodies require extensive consultative procedures to be followed – to ensure that a standard has the broadest possible support – before a draft document can be endorsed as a full standard. These procedures work well for such things as screw threads, where a standard may be expected to remain relevant for very many years after it has been created, but in the rapidly changing environment of computers, networks, and multimedia, standards are often obsolete before they have passed through all the necessary stages and national and international committees. Furthermore, international standards bodies derive some of their income from the sale of standards, and are therefore reluctant to make their documents freely available. This causes some resentment in the computing community, which has become used to free documentation on the World Wide Web – and the high prices charged for some standards put them out of the reach of small software companies. As a result, semi-formal standards and ad hoc arrangements play a greater role in these areas than they do in more traditional fields of engineering.

Internet standards are a prime example of this semi-formal standardization. Since the Internet is, by definition, an open network architecture, it relies on standard protocols to enable different networks to be interconnected. The Internet grew out of Arpanet and NSFNET, which had some degree of central administration; the TCP/IP protocols could be imposed in the early days of internetworking and were inherited as the basis of the Internet. Responsibility for the further development of protocols, and for administering information required for the protocols to operate, now resides with the *Internet Architecture Board (IAB)* and its subsidiaries, including the *Internet Engineering Task Force (IETF)*, which deals with technical development, and the *Internet Assigned Numbers Authority (IANA)*, which registers Internet media types, language codes, and so on. These bodies have no formal standing outside the Internet community, and no statutory powers – IETF documents, including Internet standards, are even called "Requests for Comments".

Similarly, the organization responsible for defining World Wide Web standards, the *World Wide Web Consortium (W3C)*, has no official status but its "Recommendations" are treated as standards. As you would expect, these bodies make use of the Internet as a means of disseminating standards, both after they have been adopted and during the standardization process, thereby providing an opportunity for a wide audience to comment on drafts and proposals.

The advantage of such an ad hoc approach to standards is that it accommodates rapid change. The disadvantage is that manufacturers feel less compunction in ignoring, adapting, or extending standards. There is a fine line between such behaviour and legitimate experimentation aimed at advancing a standard. This is illustrated by the history of HTML, where, during the initial period of rapid development of the Web, the two main competing browser companies, Netscape and Microsoft, each implemented their own extensions to HTML 2.0, leading to incompatibilities, but ultimately most of the extensions were incorporated into later versions of the HTML standard. However, Microsoft's Internet Explorer browser's support for standards remained poor until the release of Internet Explorer 8 in 2008. The broad use of older versions of Internet Explorer, which do not conform to Web standards, is a long-standing source of unnecessary difficulties for Web designers.

Sometimes, standards are established without the intervention of standards bodies of any sort. One company's product may come to dominate the market to such an extent that it becomes a standard in all but name. In some cases, a *de facto* standard of this sort may be more widely used than a competing official standard. For instance, at the time of writing the W3C's standard for vector graphics on the Web, SVG, is rarely used in comparison with Adobe's Flash format, which is implemented by almost all browsers and is in wide use as the "standard" Web vector format. Often, such an ad hoc standard is eventually handed over to one of the official standards bodies for adoption and subsequent development. This has happened in the case of PDF, for example.

KEY POINTS

Sharing multimedia between programs and platforms requires standards.

International standards are the responsibility of ISO (working through national standards bodies), IEC and ITU.

Internet and Web standards are relatively informal. They are developed and maintained by IETF, IANA and W3C.

Glossary

24-bit colour

A digital colour representation using 3 *bytes* (24 *bits*) to represent each *pixel*; one byte for each of the red, green and blue components.

3-D graphics

Three-dimensional graphics. Applied to genuinely three-dimensional models, images generated by those models, or applications for the production of such models, but also to two-dimensional images giving an impression of depth (using perspective, stereographic projection, shading, etc.).

3DMF

A 3-D image file format capable of storing representations of 3-D objects and scenes.

3G

Third generation mobile devices capable of Internet access at *broadband* speeds.

4:1:1 sampling

Chrominance sub-sampling where *co-sited* $B-Y$ and $R-Y$ samples are taken from every fourth *pixel* on each line.

4:2:0 sampling

Chrominance sub-sampling where the $B-Y$ and $R-Y$ samples are not *co-sited* and are sub-sampled by a factor of 2 in both the horizontal and vertical directions.

4:2:2 sampling

Chrominance sub-sampling where *co-sited* $B-Y$ and $R-Y$ samples are taken from alternate *pixels* in each line.

A-law

A standard *companding* function used for audio compression in telecommunications outside North America.

AAC

Advanced Audio Coding. An improved version of *MP3*, used to compress audio in *MPEG-4*.

absolute positioning

In *CSS*, the use of combinations of the top, bottom, right and left properties, with the position property set to absolute, to place boxes at arbitrary positions on the page.

absolute URL

A complete *URL*, with all its components present, which therefore always refers to the same *resource*, no matter where it appears.

accessible, accessibility

Fully usable by everyone, irrespective of any physical or mental limitations they may suffer from.

ActionScript

The *Flash scripting language*, based on *ECMAScript*, used for the creation of interactive features in Flash movies.

ActiveX control

Modules based on Microsoft's Active X component technology which may be loaded by the Internet Explorer *Web browser* to display content types which are not handled natively. See also *plug-in*.

ADC

Analogue-to-digital converter. A hardware device that performs *digitization* of analogue signals.

additive primary colours

Three colours of light, usually red, green and blue which, when combined together in differing amounts, can produce all the colours in a *colour space*, such as *sRGB*.

address

A numerical value used to identify a *byte* by its position in the linear sequence making up the memory of a computer.

adjustment layer

In Photoshop, an extension of the *layer* metaphor that provides a way of applying adjustments to an image non-destructively. Adjustment layers alter the appearance of layers beneath them, without permanently altering the *pixels* of the image, and can be hidden to turn the adjustment off temporarily.

ADPCM

Adaptive Differential Pulse Code Modulation. A digital audio compression technique, which is a refinement of *DPCM*, using a dynamically varying step size to represent the quantized differences between samples and predictions.

ADSL

Asymmetric Digital Subscriber Line. A high-speed data connection for *Internet* access, using existing copper phone lines. Upstream data rates are typically significantly slower than downstream rates.

Advanced Simple Profile

An *MPEG-4 Part 2* profile that uses *B-pictures* as well as *P-pictures* for *compression* of video frames.

Advanced Video Coding (AVC)

See *H.264/AVC*.

affine transformations

In *vector graphics*, transformations which preserve straight and parallel lines and therefore maintain the fundamental shape of an object.

AJAX

Asynchronous *JavaScript* and *XML*. A technique for creating JavaScript applications embedded in *Web pages* that fetch data without refreshing the page, in order to provide a seamless user experience.

aliasing

A type of distortion that occurs in digital representations of analogue information when the number of different digital values is not sufficient to distinguish between all possible analogue signals. In graphics, it shows itself in the form of jagged edges or *jaggies*, especially when images are resized. See also *anti-aliasing*.

alpha channel

In computer graphics, a *greyscale* mask used to specify different degrees of transparency in a *bitmapped image*. (Also used in digital video processing.)

alphabet

In formal language theory, a set of symbols. Usually a collection of characters to which a *character set* assigns codes. See also *character repertoire*.

anchor points

In *vector graphics*, the points where segments of a *path* meet.

animated GIF

A *GIF* file that contains more than one image. Because *Web browsers* and other programs will display each image in turn, this format is suitable for *animation*. Animated GIF is the only *file format* for animated sequences which does not require a browser *plug-in* for playback on *Web pages*.

animation

The creation of the illusion of movement by the rapid display of a succession of still images created artificially, not captured from live action. See also *cel animation*, *clay animation*, *stop-motion*.

anti-aliasing

The replacement of *pixel* values at a contrasting edge in an image (especially a diagonal edge) with values between the original extremes. This softens the coarse, step-like appearance (*pixellation*) often seen in low-resolution images and type, which is caused by *aliasing*.

API

Application Programming Interface. A set of objects, classes or functions provided to allow a script or program to manipulate some system or service. See also *DOM*.

arguments

Values which are passed to a *method* when it is called. The arguments are assigned to the method's *formal parameters*.

arithmetic coding

A form of *lossless compression* that is more effective than *Huffman coding*. Used to compress quantized coefficients in *JPEG2000*.

array

In programming and *scripting languages*, a sequence of values, each of which can be identified by a numerical *index*, which is its position in the sequence. In some languages, indices may also be strings, in which case the array is said to be an *associative array*.

ascender

In typography, a *stroke* that rises above the *x-height*, such as the initial stroke of an h.

ascent

In typography, the height above the *x-height* of the tallest *ascender* in a font.

ASCII

American Standard Code for Information Interchange. A seven-bit *character set* providing a standard for the interpretation of bit patterns to signify 127 letters, digits, punctuation and control operations.

ASF

Advanced Systems Format. The container format for Microsoft's *DirectShow*, used to hold *WMV* data.

ASP.NET

A Web application framework developed by Microsoft.

assignment

In programming, a fundamental operation where the value stored in a *variable* is replaced by a new value.

assistive technologies

Devices designed to help people with access difficulties to use computers and access information. For example, voice input software, Braille writers, large character displays, etc.

associative array

An *array*-like data structure indexed by strings instead of integers. Also called a dictionary or look-up table.

asymmetrical codec

A *codec* that takes longer to perform *compression* than *decompression*.

ATM

Asynchronous Transfer Mode. A high-speed network technology, which is able to reserve resources for individual connections and offer guarantees about the quality of service the network will provide.

Atom

An *XML-based* format used as an alternative to *RSS*.

attribute

A named *property*, in particular, a named property of an *element* in an *XML-based language*. For example, in *XHTML*, elements of different types have named attributes such as class, alt, and so on.

B-picture, B-frame

Bidirectionally predictive picture. In video *compression*, a difference frame based on the previous or next *I-pictures* or *P-pictures*, or both.

base URL

The *URL* used to supply missing parts of a *relative URL*. Usually the URL of the document in which the relative URL occurs.

baseline

In typography, the horizontal line on which characters are set.

Baseline Profile (BP)
An *H.264/AVC* profile that is suitable for video-conferencing and mobile devices with limited computing resources.

Basic Multilingual Plane (BMP)
The subset of *UCS* defined by the plane $(0,0,\star,\star)$, which is identical to *Unicode*.

Bézier curve
A curve specified by an ordered set of control points, the first and last of which are the curve's end points. The entire curve will lie within the polygon constructed by joining the control points with straight lines. The most common type of Bézier curve used in *vector graphics* has four control points, so it can be defined by two end points with a pair of direction lines at each end to indicate the directions and rates at which the curve leaves the two end points. Bézier curves are particularly useful because they may be connected smoothly.

bi-directional links
In *hypertext*, *links* that can be followed in either direction.

bicubic interpolation
An algorithm used in *resampling* of *bitmapped images* that uses information from neighbouring *pixels* to produce better results than simpler algorithms, but at the cost of added computational complexity.

bilinear interpolation
An algorithm used in *resampling* of *bitmapped images* that produces better results than *nearest-neighbour interpolation* but not as good as *bicubic interpolation*.

binary
In arithmetic, numbers represented using base 2; arithmetic operations performed on such numbers.

bit
A *binary* digit; the smallest unit of digital information, taking one of the values 0 and 1.

bitmapped fonts
Fonts in which the *glyphs* are stored as *bitmapped images*.

bitmapped graphics, bitmapped images
A method of representing images, in which the colour of every *pixel* is recorded in an *array*. The term bitmap is often used to refer to the image itself, and is contrasted with *vector graphics*. Bitmapped images are typically complex and have large file sizes; images from a scanner, camera or video source (whether originally digital or not) are all represented by bitmaps in a computer.

block element
An *XHTML* element which by default is displayed as a block, that is, with a new line before and after it.

block-level formatting
Formatting applied to entire paragraphs, for example, alignment and justification.

BMP
See *Microsoft Windows Bitmap* or *Basic Multilingual Plane*.

body (1)
In a *valid XHTML* document, the second top-level *element* within the document, to be displayed in a browser window. The body follows the *head* and contains the document's *content*.

body (2)
In *HTTP*, the part of an HTTP *message* following any *headers*, containing the message's *content*.

body size
In typography, the smallest height that could accommodate every symbol in the *font*, hence the font size. The body size is the distance between the tallest *ascender* and the longest *descender* in the font.

bold, boldface
In typography, a *font* with a heavier *weight* than the regular form of the same *font family*.

border
In *CSS*, an area between the *padding* and *margin* of a box, which may have a colour or a style (such as dash or dot) applied to it to provide a visible outline to the box.

broadband
An adjective used to describe network connections providing broad bandwidth, typically 500 kbps or greater over, for example, *ADSL*, *cable modems* or *3G*.

bump mapping

In *3-D graphics*, mathematically wrapping a picture over the surface of an object to apply bumpiness or roughness.

button symbol

A type of *symbol*, formerly used for adding interactivity to *Flash movies*, now superseded by *UI components*.

byte

A data storage unit comprising an ordered sequence of eight *bits*.

byte codes

Bit patterns that cause some operation to be performed by an interpreter for a virtual machine. Programs written in *scripting languages* are often compiled into byte codes for execution.

cable modem

A device that allows a computer to connect to the *Internet* using the cable TV networks.

caching

Keeping copies of recently used data that can be accessed more rapidly than the original values. In particular, in *HTTP*, keeping copies of pages that have been received on a user's machine, or on other intermediate machines between it and the *server* from which they originate. When a page is requested more than once, it can be retrieved after the first time from a cache instead of from the server.

calligraphic font

A *font* based on handwriting styles.

camera raw

The unprocessed data from a digital camera's sensor before it has undergone the processing that rearranges it into an image. See also *DNG*.

cap height

In typography, the height of capital letters in a *font*.

Cascading Style Sheets

See *CSS*.

cel animation

A traditional *animation* technique, in which elements or characters that were intended to move in a scene were drawn on sheets of trans-parent material known as "cel", and laid over a background which was drawn separately.

centred

A style of aligning paragraphs, with both margins ragged and the text ranged symmetrically about the centre line.

CGI

The Common Gateway Interface. A mechanism for an *HTTP server* to pass data contained in a client's *request* to a *script* running on the *server* and for the script to send back results to be incorporated in the *response* dynamically.

CGI script

A *server-side script*, often written in Perl or Python, that uses *CGI* to exchange data with an *HTTP server*.

channel

In computer graphics, each of the separate *greyscale* images making up a colour image. For example, the red, green and blue channels of an *RGB* image. See also *alpha channel*.

character entity reference

In *XML-based languages*, a symbolic reference used to insert characters which would be hard to type, which are not available in the chosen *character set encoding*, or which form part of an *XML tag*, for example < for the < symbol.

character formatting

Formatting applied to spans of characters within paragraphs, for example, italicization.

character repertoire

The alphabet (set of symbols) which a *character set* maps to integers.

character set

An association between a set of characters and the integers used to represent them.

character set encoding

A mapping which transforms a *code value* into a sequence of *bytes* for storage and transmission.

character style

A named set of *character formatting* properties that can be applied consistently to text in a word processor or page layout program.

check box

In user interfaces, a *control* that allows users to turn an option on or off.

chroma keying

In video post-production, designating a colour to be transparent when *composited* with another scene.

chrominance sub-sampling

A method of image *compression*, especially video, by using fewer samples for colour than for brightness. See also *4:2:2 sampling*.

CIE XYZ colour space

A device-independent *colour space*, which uses three components *X*, *Y* and *Z* to approximate the three stimuli to which the colour-sensitive parts of our eyes respond. The *XYZ* colour space is impossible to realize with physical light sources.

CJK consolidation

A process used in the definition of *Unicode*, whereby characters used in writing Chinese, Japanese and Korean are given the same code value if they look the same, irrespective of which language they belong to and whether or not they mean the same thing in the different languages. Also known as Han unification.

class (1)

In *XHTML*, a subset of all the *elements* of a particular type, whose class *attribute* has a particular value.

class (2)

In *object-oriented* programming, a set of *objects* that all have the same *methods* and *properties*.

clay animation

A form of *stop-motion animation* using a malleable modelling material such as Plasticine.

click repairer

A specialized audio filter, intended to remove clicks from recordings taken from damaged or dirty vinyl records.

client

See *client/server model*. Also used to mean a *host* on which a client is running.

client-side script

A *script* downloaded as part of a *Web page* and executed in the client (*Web browser*). Client-side scripts are written in *JavaScript*.

client/server model

The model of interaction in a distributed system such as the *Internet* in which a *client* program running on one computer sends a *request* to a *server* program, usually running on another computer, which listens for *requests* and sends *responses* to them according to some *protocol*.

clipping

A form of audio distortion which occurs when the amplitude of the signal being recorded exceeds the maximum value that can be represented.

closed path

A *path* that joins up on itself, i.e. its start and *end points* are the same.

CMY colour model

A *colour model*, based on subtractive colour mixing, in which each colour is represented by three values denoting the proportions of cyan, magenta and yellow light it contains.

CMYK colour

A *colour model* based on *CMY*, in which black is used as a fourth primary, to reflect the properties of colour printing processses.

co-sited samples

In *chrominance sub-sampling*, values that are *sampled* at the same point.

code point

An integer in the set of values to which a *character set* maps its *character repertoire*.

code value

The *code point* to which a character is mapped by a *character set*.

codec

A component performing the *compression* and *decompression* of video signals (the term is a contraction of compressor/decompressor).

colour depth

In computer graphics, the number of *bits* used to represent each *pixel* in an image.

colour management system
Software which compensates for variations in device-dependent colour handling to try to achieve accurate and consistent colour reproduction.

colour model
Any means of representing colours numerically, especially a *colour space*.

colour picker
A dialogue for choosing colours, which shows the colours that can be represented in a specific *colour model* in a graphical form.

colour profile
A description of the colour characteristics of a device used for mapping between colours and *colour values*, used by a *colour management system*.

colour space
A means of representing colours numerically as a tuple of *n* components, for instance, the 3-tuple of red, green and blue values in the *RGB* colour space.

colour table
A *data structure* used to map small colour index values to full 24-bit *colour values*.

colour wheel
A circular arrangement of colours, with primaries equally spaced around the perimeter and secondaries in between them such that each one is opposite its complementary primary. Used as the basis for rules of colour harmony and in *colour pickers* for some *colour models*.

comment
In programming, an annotation added to a program, set off by special delimiters, that has no effect on the computation but is provided for the benefit of people reading the program.

Common Gateway Interface
See *CGI*.

companding
A form of audio *compression*, applied especially to speech, using non-linear *quantization levels*, with the higher levels spaced further apart than the low ones, so that quiet sounds are represented in greater detail than louder ones.

compilation
The process of translating a program written in a high-level language into an equivalent sequence of machine instructions.

compiler
A program that performs *compilation*.

complementary colour
The colour obtained by subtracting light of a specified colour from white light.

components
In *Flash*, reusable *movie clip symbols* with parameters that allow you to modify their appearance and behaviour.

compositing
Combining *layers* to create a composite image.

compression
An operation performed on data to reduce the amount of storage required to represent it, for reasons of economy or efficiency. Used very frequently with *bitmapped images*, with sound, and in all but the highest-end video work. See also *lossless compression*, *lossy compression* and *decompression*.

compression artefacts
Unwanted visual features that occur after an image or video sequence that has been lossily compressed is decompressed.

condensed font
In typography, a *font* that appears somewhat squashed horizontally, compared with the normal proportions of most fonts.

conditional statement
In programming languages, a *statement* that is used to select a statement to execute depending on whether some condition is true or false.

connection address
An *address* provided as part of the *presentation description*, to which subsequent *RTSP requests* are sent.

constructive solid geometry
An approach to *3-D* modelling, in which complex objects are constructed by combining a few primitive geometric solids, such as the cube, cylinder, sphere and pyramid, which are combined using union, intersection and difference operations.

constructor

In *object-oriented* programming, a function or method that creates new *objects*.

content (1)

In an *XML* document, the text and any *elements* between the start and end *tags* of an element.

content (2)

In *Web* design, the text, images and *time-based media* displayed on a *Web page*.

context-sensitive selector, contextual selector

In *CSS*, a *selector* that causes a *rule* to be applied only to *elements* that occur in particular contexts, such as within another specified element.

control

In user interfaces, an element, such as a text field, used to enter data in a form.

control character

Code values corresponding to *bit* sequences, such as form-feed, carriage return and delete, which have traditionally been used to control the operation of output devices and are not printable. Now mostly used for special purposes by programs.

control points

In two-dimensional graphics, the points which define a *Bézier curve*.

convex hull

The polygon constructed by joining a *Bézier curve's* control points with straight lines. The curve will be entirely enclosed by this polygon.

convolution kernel

The set of *pixels* used to compute a pixel's value by a filter based on *pixel group processing*.

convolution mask

An array of weights applied to the values in a *convolution kernel* to compute the result of a filter based on *pixel group processing*.

coordinates

In two-dimensional graphics, a pair of numbers which give the horizontal and vertical distance of a point from the *origin*.

CSS

Cascading Style Sheets. A language defined by a *W3C* Recommendation for specifying the formatting and layout of the elements of *XHTML* and *XML* documents.

CURIE

Compact *URI*. A value that uses a *namespace* prefix to identify it as belonging to some well-defined set, such as the set of terms in a controlled vocabulary.

data structure

In computer programming, an organized collection of values, that can be manipulated as a composite value.

datagram

The basic unit of data transferred over the *Internet* by *IP*.

DC component

The component of a *frequency spectrum* with a frequency of zero.

DCT

Discrete Cosine Transform. A mathematical operation which transforms a two-dimensional waveform into the collection of its frequency components. Used as a step in *JPEG compression*.

de-esser

A specialized audio filter, intended to remove sibilance from recordings, for example, when a speaker talks too close to the microphone.

de-interlacing

In *video* processing, the separating of the two *fields* of an interlaced video *frame*. See also *interlacing* and *progressive scanning*.

declaration

In *CSS*, part of a *rule* which describes how *elements* matching the *selector* should be displayed, by giving a value to some *property*.

decompression

An operation performed on previously compressed data to restore it as far as possible to its original, pre-compressed state. Used frequently in *bitmapped image* and video processing. See also *compression*, *lossless compression* and *lossy compression*.

default namespace

In an *XML* document, the *namespace* to be used for all *element* and *attribute* names that do not have an explicit namespace prefix.

deflate

A *lossless compression* algorithm, based on *LZ77* and incorporating *Huffman coding*.

degree (of a Bézier curve)

One less than the number of *control points*, e.g. a curve with four control points has degree three.

derived

In *object-oriented* programming, a *class* is said to be derived from its *parent class* (if it has one).

descender

In typography, a *stroke* that extends below the *baseline*, such as the tail of a y.

descent

In typography, the depth below the *baseline* of the longest *descender* in a font.

detail coefficients

In computing a *Haar wavelet*, the stored value of the magnitude of the difference between two values and their average.

device control

In digital video recorders and camcorders, the ability for the tape to be stopped, started and moved to a specific position by signals sent from the computer by software.

dictionary-based

A term describing a class of *lossless compression* schemes, including *LZW*.

digitization

The construction of a digital representation of an analogue signal. See also *quantization* and *sampling*.

dingbat font

A *font* consisting entirely of graphic images such as arrows or pointing hands, for example.

direct colour

The technique of storing full *24-bit colour* values for each *pixel* of an image. See also *indexed colour*.

directed graph

In graph theory, a finite set of *nodes* connected by *edges*. An abstract model of network structures.

direction lines

In *vector graphics*, the lines connecting the *end points* and *direction points* of a Bézier curve. They

define the direction and rate at which the curve leaves the end points.

direction points

In *vector graphics*, two of the four *control points* of a cubic *Bézier curve*. They fix the ends of the *direction lines*, which start from the *end points*.

DirectShow

Microsoft's *multimedia architecture* for Windows operating systems.

displacement vector

In video *compression*, a record of the relative displacement of objects in the difference frames of video compressed using an algorithm that incorporates *inter-frame compression* with *motion compensation*.

display font

A *font* that is suitable for headlines, advertising and other short pieces of text that need to have a high visual impact. See also *text font*.

dithering (1)

In *bitmapped image* processing, a method based upon the principle of optical mixing which uses patterns of *pixels* of available colours to simulate missing ones. Often used in conjunction with *indexed colour*. Dithered images often have a "dotty" appearance.

dithering (2)

In digital sound processing, the addition of small amounts of noise to mitigate the effects of an inadequate number of *quantization* levels.

DNG

Digital Negative. A *bitmapped image* format intended to serve as an archival format for *camera raw* data.

DNS

Domain Name Service. The means by which human-readable *domain names* are resolved into numerical *IP addresses*, which can be used to send *packets* to their correct destinations over the *Internet*.

document type declaration

Part of the prologue of an *XML* document, which usually points to a *DTD* defining the allowable *markup* for the document.

DOM

Document Object Model. An *API* defined by W3C standards specifying an interface between the components of a *Web browser* and objects representing the elements of an *HTML* or *XML* document.

domain name

A readable name that corresponds to one or more *IP addresses*.

dominant wavelength

The wavelength at which most of the energy of the light in a particular colour is concentrated

downsampling

In computer graphics, changing the *resolution* of a *bitmapped image* to a lower value in order to restrict data size or to match the image *resolution* to that of a display or other output device. In audio, the process of changing the sample rate of digital audio to a lower value. See also *upsampling* and *resampling*.

DPCM

Differential Pulse Code Modulation. A digital audio *compression* technique, based on storing the differences between *samples* and a value predicted for them from preceding samples.

DRM

Digital Rights Management. Technology applied to digital media which aims to prevent it from being used for any purpose not approved by the copyright owners.

DTD

Document Type Definition. A specification method for *XML* which defines the grammar for a class of documents. See also *schema*.

Dublin Core

A general *metadata* standard that defines 15 kinds of metadata item which can be applied to describe most types of media data.

DV

A popular consumer and semi-professional digital video standard.

DWT

Discrete Wavelet Transform. A mathematical operation which computes a *wavelet decomposition* of a signal. Used as a step in *JPEG2000 compression*.

easing in

In *animation*, the technique of making an object whose motion is being *tweened* appear to accelerate from rest by using smaller, slowly increasing, increments between the first few frames of the motion.

easing out

In *animation*, the technique of making an object whose motion is being *tweened* appear to decelerate to a stop by using larger, slowly decreasing, increments between the last few frames of the motion.

ECMAScript

A core *scripting language* which provides computational facilities that can be augmented with *objects* to control host environments such as *Web browsers* and *Flash* movies.

edges

In graph theory, the connections between the *nodes* of a *directed graph* or *tree*.

elastic layout

In *Web* design, a layout in which all the elements maintain their relative sizes at any *font* size.

element

In an *XML* or *HTML* document, the basic logical unit used to define its structure.

element node

A node in an *XML* document's *structure tree* corresponding to an *element* in the document. See also *text node*.

em

A unit of measurement in typography. One em is equal to the size of the *font*, so in a 16 pt font, 1 em equals 16 pt.

embedded video

Video added to a *Web page* in such a way that the movie file is transferred from a *server* to the user's machine, and not played back from the user's disk until the entire file has arrived.

empty element

In *XML-based languages* an *element* without any *content*, e.g. an empty element with name ee is written <ee/>.

encoding

See *character set encoding*.

end points

The first and last *control points* defining a *Bézier curve*: the points where the curve begins and ends.

end tag

In *XML-based languages*, the sequence that marks the end of an *element*, e.g. for an element with name el, the end tag is </el>.

envelope shaping

Audio processing operations which change the outline of a *waveform*.

escape sequence

A sequence of characters, introduced by one or more special escape characters, which alter the way the characters in the sequence are interpreted. For example, in *URLs*, certain characters that may get corrupted, removed or misinterpreted must be represented by escape sequences, consisting of a % followed by the character's *ASCII* code in *hexadecimal*.

even–odd rule

In *vector graphics*, a rule for determining whether a point lies inside or outside a *path*, by determining whether the number of path segments crossing a line drawn from the point is even (outside) or odd (inside). See also *non-zero winding number rule*.

event

In an interactive system, an occurrence, such as a mouse click, that can trigger an action, usually by causing an *event listener* to be executed.

event listener

In object-oriented interactive systems, a *method* attached to an *object*, which is triggered by an *event*.

event target

An *object* which is notified of an *event* when it occurs.

exdented line

In typography, a line that is indented by a negative amount relative to the rest of the paragraph, so that it sticks out into the left margin.

Exif

Exchangeable Image File Format. A standard for image *metadata*, which records details about how a digital photograph was taken: exposure time,

focal length and so on, together with some information about when it was taken.

extended font

A *font* that is stretched out horizontally, making it suitable for headings and other isolated text elements.

extended links

Types of *link*, including *bi-directional links*, *regional links* and *multi-links*, which extend the concept of *simple uni-directional links*.

Extended Profile (XP)

An *H.264/AVC* profile that is intended for streaming video.

extrusion

In *3-D graphics*, a method of generating 3-D objects from 2-D shapes, by extending a plane surface into the third dimension by sweeping it along a *path*. The simplest form of extruding extends the surface along a straight line perpendicular to the (x, y) plane, so the object grows outwards, as though it had been squeezed out of a shaped nozzle.

FastCGI

A mechanism for executing *scripts* on a *server*, and passing *request* data to them, which provides a more efficient alternative to *CGI*.

ffmpeg

An open source command-line tool for video capture, *compression* and format conversion and its supporting libraries.

field

In most video (but not in film) each *frame* is composed of two *interlaced* fields, transmitted one after the other (but see also *progressive scan*).

file format

A specification of the internal structure of a class of files, often forming part of a standard (e.g. *JPEG*, *GIF*, *MP4*). File formats are understood by the set of applications which read or write that class of file.

fill

In *vector graphics*, the colour, gradient or pattern applied to the interior of a shape.

FireWire

A high-speed serial data bus, defined by the IEEE 1394 standard, used to connect video equipment and other peripherals to a computer.

fixed-width font

In typography, a class of *fonts* in which each *glyph* occupies the same amount of horizontal space, as though it was typed on a typewriter.

Flash

An Adobe application for the creation of *animation* and front ends to Web applications.

Flash movie

The format of movies generated for playback by the Flash Player or plug-in, formerly known as SWF.

Flex

A framework for building *Flash movies* which act as small applications with an interactive multimedia interface, without using *Flash* itself.

FLV

Flash Video. A video format associated with *Flash* that may be streamed and viewed in a *Web browser* using the Flash Player plug-in.

font

In typography, a collection of *glyphs* sharing the same basic design so that they are visually related and work well together for the display of text.

font family

A set of *fonts*, comprising several variants, which share some fundamental visual characteristics, so that the variants will look good together on the same page.

font metrics

In typography, the set of measurements which describe the size of individual characters in a *font* and the spacing between them.

for loop

A statement provided in many programming languages, including *ECMAScript*, for describing a computation consisting of some initialization followed by a *loop* that repeats as long as some condition is true with an incrementing operation at the end of each repetition. Often used for loops controlled by a counter whose value is increased every time the loop is executed.

formal parameter

In programming, an identifier declared in the head of a *function* or *method* definition, which is assigned the value of one of the function's *arguments* when it is called.

Fourier Transform

A mathematical operation which transforms a periodic waveform into the collection of its frequency components (i.e. maps it from the *time domain* to the *frequency domain*).

fractals

Loosely speaking, in *vector graphics*, shapes that exhibit the same structure at all levels of detail.

fragment identifier

A name appended to a *URL* after a # to identify a location within a document. The fragment identifier should match the value of the id or name *attribute* of some *element* in the document.

frame

In *video*, *animation* or film, each discrete photograph or image in a sequence, and therefore the smallest possible unit available in editing (but see also *field*).

frame grabbing

Capturing *animation* using a video camera by only storing the digital version of a single frame each time a shot has been set up.

free form modelling

In *3-D graphics*, a type of modelling using a representation of an object's boundary surface as the basis of its model.

frequency domain

A mathematical space in which periodic waveforms are represented by the amplitudes of their frequency components. See also *time domain*.

frequency spectrum

A representation of a signal in the *frequency domain* as a graph, with the horizontal axis representing frequency and the vertical axis amplitude.

FTP

File Transfer Protocol. One of the *TCP/IP* family of *protocols*, used for transferring files.

function

In programming and mathematics, an operation or sub-routine which maps *arguments* to a result. See also *method*.

function body

The part of a *function's* definition consisting of the code that will be executed when the function is called.

fusion frequency

The minimum frequency at which a sequence of still images must be presented to the viewer in order to create the illusion of motion as a result of *persistence of vision*.

gamma

A single number used to approximate the relationship between input *RGB* values and the intensity of light emitted by a monitor.

Gaussian blur

A blurring filter used in *pixel group processing* in which the coefficients of the *convolution mask* fall off gradually from the centre of the mask, following the Gaussian "bell curve".

General MIDI

A standard assignment of 128 voices to correspond to the values used by "Program Change" *MIDI messages*.

gestalt

In visual communication, principles of visual organization derived from the theories of *gestalt psychology*.

gestalt psychology

Psychological theories developed in Germany in the early twentieth century, which were particularly concerned with the way the human brain tends to organize the visual information that reaches the eyes.

GIF

Graphics Interchange Format. An 8-bit *bitmapped image file format* using *indexed colour*, which can permit one arbitrary colour to be defined as transparent. One of the three image file formats natively supported by *Web browsers*. See also *animated GIF*, *JPEG* and *PNG*.

Gimp, The

An Open Source *bitmapped image* processing program.

Global Motion Compensation

A technique used in video *compression*, for compressing static scenes with conventional camera movements, such as pans and zooms. The movement can be modelled as a vector transformation of the original scene, and represented by the values of just a few parameters.

Globally Unique Identifier

A meaningless codename, which is guaranteed to be unique, used to identify *ActiveX* controls.

glyph

In typography, one of the individual character shapes making up a *font*.

GOP

Group of Pictures. In *MPEG* video *compression*, a sequence, which always begins with an *I-picture*, that is repeated to form the encoded compressed video stream.

Gouraud shading

In *3-D graphics*, a shading algorithm applied to objects whose surfaces are defined by polygons, in which the colour across each polygon is interpolated on the basis of colour values calculated at the vertices.

gradient

In *vector graphics*, a type of *fill* in which colours, specified at gradient stops, gradually blend into each other. In *SVG*, the blending may be *linear* or *radial*. More advanced programs and formats support other options.

graphic equalization

In audio processing, an effect which transforms the spectrum of a sound using a bank of filters, each controlled by its own slider and each affecting a fairly narrow band of frequencies.

graphic symbol

A type of *symbol* used in *Flash* for reusable graphic content. Graphic symbols may be animated, but they cannot be controlled by scripts. See also *movie clip symbol*.

greyscale

A range of colours comprising shades of grey from white to black, in graphic applications generally restricted to one *byte* per *pixel*, i.e. 256 greys.

grouping

Perception of a collection of discrete objects as a whole. Grouping is determined by the *gestalt* principles of visual organization.

gTLD

Generic top-level domain. A top-level domain, such as .com, used as the final component of a *domain name*, which does not identify a specific country.

H.264/AVC

A video *codec*, defined in the *MPEG-4* Part 10 standard, which produces high-quality video at low data rates by using a combination of advanced intra- and inter-frame *compression* techniques. Often known simply as H.264.

Haar wavelet

A mathematical operation for transforming a sequence of values into a set of *detail coefficients*. See also *wavelet decomposition*.

hanging punctuation

Extending lines of text that begin or end with a punctuation mark so that the punctuation moves outwards into the margin to counteract the impression of unevenness caused by the size and shape of punctuation marks.

HD, HDTV

High-definition television. Any television system providing significantly higher resolution than standard definition.

head

In an *XHTML* document, the first top-level *element* which precedes the *body* and contains *metadata*, which is not displayed in a browser window.

headers

In an *HTTP request* or *response*, lines containing various parameters and modifiers to the *message*.

helper application

An external program that may be called by a *Web browser* to display content that the browser does not display on its own or by using a *plug-in*.

hexadecimal

Numbers represented using base 16; arithmetic operations performed on such numbers. Often abbreviated to hex. Hex numbers are commonly used to specify *colour values* in *CSS*.

hidden surface removal

In *3-D graphics*, determining which surfaces of an object are visible, using the coordinates of corners of objects, and hiding the others, to present a two-dimensional view of the object.

high-pass filter

In signal processing, a filter which passes the high frequencies and blocks the low ones. Used in audio processing to remove rumble.

High Profile (HIP)

An *H.264/AVC* profile used for *HDTV* and Blu-Ray DVD.

Hijax

A technique used to increase the *accessibility* of *Web pages* using *AJAX* by using *scripts* to create any controls that depend on scripting support and to override the default behaviour of *links* and input elements so that the page will still be usable without scripting.

host

Any computer which is connected to the *Internet*.

host group

A collection of *hosts*, identified by a single *address*, to which *multicast packets* are sent.

HSL

Hue (H), *saturation* (S) and *lightness* (L). A *colour model* in which hue is modified by white and black. Geometrically, the HSL model is a double cone.

HSV, HSB

Hue (H), *saturation* (S) and value (V), or (synonymously) brightness (B). A variation of the *HSL colour model* in which the geometry is distorted to be a cylinder, to make the colour space easier to present on screen.

HTML

HyperText Markup Language. A document *markup language*, defined by *W3C* standards, used to create *Web pages*. See also *XHTML*.

HTTP

HyperText Transfer Protocol. A simple *protocol* for the fast transmission over the *Internet* of *hypertext* information, usually documents marked up in *HTML* or *XHTML*.

HTTP streaming

See *progressive download*.

hue

A pure colour. In the *HSV* model of colour, hue is equated with position around the rim of the *colour wheel*.

Huffman coding

A *lossless compression* technique, based on the use of variable-length codes, with the shortest codes being used to represent the most common values. Huffman coding is often used as the final phase of *JPEG compression*.

hypermedia

A collection of different media elements such as text, graphics, sound and video connected by *links*. The *World Wide Web* is the best known example of hypermedia.

hypertext

Text augmented with *links* which are pointers to other pieces of text, either elsewhere in the same document, or in another document, possibly stored at a different location.

I-pictures, I-frames

A term used in *MPEG* standards to refer to *frames* which are compressed in their entirety as still images. They are used as the base values for *inter-frame compression*. See also *key frames*.

IAB

Internet Architecture Board. International organization with responsibility for the development of *Internet protocols*, and for administering information required for the protocols to operate. *IETF* and *IANA* are subsidiaries of IAB.

IANA

The organization that administers the use of *IP addresses* and *domain names*.

ICC

International Color Consortium. A group set up in 1993 to promote the standardization and evolution of an open, cross-platform *colour management system* architecture and components.

identifier

In *HTTP*, the second element of an HTTP *request* line, which identifies the *resource* being requested from the *server*.

IEC

International Electrotechnical Commission. An organization with responsibility for formulating international standards in the field of electrical and electronic engineering.

IETF

Internet Engineering Task Force. A subsidiary organization of *IAB*, which deals with technical development of the Internet.

image coding

Alternative name for image *compression*.

image histogram

A visual representation of how different brightness levels are distributed among the *pixels* of an image (or selection). The horizontal axis represents the different possible brightness levels, with black (zero) at the left, and white (255) at the right. The height of the graph at each point indicates the number of pixels with that brightness.

Image Magick

An Open Source suite of programs and libraries that can perform common operations on *bitmapped images*, including format conversions, from a command line or using *API* calls.

image map

An interactive image which contains active areas known as hot spots.

IMT2000

International Mobile Telecommunications. A system specified by the *ITU*, which was supposed to provide a global *3G* standard offering bit rates for data from just under 2 Mbps up to 10 Mbps. Several variants have been implemented in different parts of the world.

in point

In video editing, a designated *frame* where a clip should begin. If the in point is not the first frame, material before it will be trimmed off.

indent

In typography, the space between the left edge of a block, such as a paragraph, and the edge of the page or window.

index

In programming, a numerical value used to identify an element of an *array* by its position. Also used as a verb, to access using an index.

indexed colour

A method of representing colours indirectly. Each *pixel* holds a value which is used as an index into a table (colour mapping) holding the *colour values* to be used.

inheritance

In *object-oriented* programming, the organization of classes into a hierarchy, with properties and methods being *inherited* from *parent classes*.

inherited

In *object-oriented* programming, defined in an object's *parent class*, or one of its ancestors.

inline element

An *XHTML* element which by default is displayed as part of an enclosing *block element*, without a blank line before and after it.

Integrated Services Architecture

In computer networks, a framework which defines different classes of service and provides ways of specifying *QoS*.

inter-frame compression

A video *compression* technique, in which, for most *frames*, only data about the difference between that frame and some other frame is stored explicitly. See also *motion compensation*.

interlacing

In video, a standard for the scanning of each *frame* such that the two *fields* are displayed alternately, giving a set of odd and even raster lines. See also *de-interlacing*.

Internet

A huge, world-wide network of computers, communicating with *TCP/IP protocols*, now principally used for access to the *World Wide Web*.

Internet Media Type

A specification used on the *Internet* to describe the type of data; for example, an Internet Media Type is used to specify the type of data contained in an *HTTP response*. Often referred to inaccurately as MIME type.

Internet Protocol

See *IP*.

Internet Service Provider

See *ISP*.

interpolation

The calculation of additional, approximate values between known values in a set, typically used in the *upsampling* of *bitmapped images*, where additional *pixels* are required, and in the calculation of in-between *frames* in digital *animation*.

interpretation

Executing programs by means of an *interpreter*.

interpreter

A program that reads the source or *byte code* version of another program, and carries out the operations it specifies.

intra-frame compression

In video, *compression* applied to a single *frame*, which usually serves as an *I-picture* for *inter-frame compression*.

intranet

A *LAN* which uses the same *TCP/IP protocols* as the *Internet*.

Inverse Discrete Cosine Transform

A mathematical operation that computes the inverse of the DCT, mapping a collection of frequency components to a two-dimensional image.

Inverse Fourier Transform

A mathematical operation that computes the inverse of the Fourier Transform, mapping signals from the frequency domain to the time domain.

IP

Internet Protocol. The set of rules governing the interaction at the Internet Layer between *hosts*.

IP address

A set of numbers that identifies a *host*. IPv4 addresses (the standard most widely used at present) are usually written as four sets of three-digit numbers, separated by dots.

IPTC Core

A trade standard for image *metadata*, defined by the IPTC (International Press Telecommunications Council), that provides a uniform way of recording information about an image's creator, its copyright status, and various other information that helps to classify it.

ISO

International Organization for Standardization. Responsible for setting international standards in all technical fields except electronic and electrical engineering. In information technology ISO works together with the *IEC*.

ISO/IEC Motion Picture Experts Group

See *MPEG*.

ISP

Internet Service Provider. A company providing *Internet* services such as dial-up access, domain name registration and *Web site* hosting.

italic font

A *font* in which the letters are slanted to the right and share some of the characteristics of italic handwriting.

ITU

International Telecommunication Union. An agency of the United Nations, which defines international standards for telecommunications.

jaggies

An informal name for the visible effect of *aliasing* in *bitmapped images*.

JavaScript

A *scripting language*, based on *ECMAScript* and the *DOM*, used to add interactivity to *Web pages*.

JFIF

JPEG File Interchange Format. The file format most commonly used for storing *JPEG* image data. See also *SPIFF*.

jitter

The variation in delay experienced by *packets* in a stream of data transmitted over a network.

JP2

The standard file format for images compressed with *JPEG2000*.

JPEG

Joint Photographic Experts Group. Usually used to refer to the JPEG algorithm for *lossy compression* of *bitmapped images*, and to images compressed using it. JPEG is widely used on *Web pages*. One of the three image file formats natively supported by *Web browsers*. See also *GIF* and *PNG*.

JPEG2000

A successor to the *JPEG* standard, which aims to provide better quality at higher *compression* ratios. JPEG2000 uses a compression algorithm based on *wavelet decomposition*.

JPX

An extension to the *JP2* file format.

justified

In typesetting, justified type is set by adjusting the spacing between words so that both margins are straight.

kerning

In typography, the technique of moving certain pairs of letters, such as AV, closer together to maintain an optical illusion of uniform spacing.

key

In *JavaScript* and other programming languages, a string used to index an *associative array*.

key frame

In digital *animation*, a *frame* whose contents are fully specified by drawing and/or by the setting of precise parameters, as opposed to those in-between frames which are *interpolated*. Also used as a synonym for *I-picture* in video compression.

keying

In video post-production, any method for selecting transparent areas.

kilobyte

1024 bytes.

Kuler

An online application for creating and sharing colour schemes.

LAN

Local area network. A network used to connect computers within a small organization or on a single site, usually based on Ethernet or wireless connections.

lasso tool

A tool for making selections, of objects or *pixels*, by drawing a freehand outline.

lathing

In *3-D graphics*, a method of generating 3-D objects with radial symmetry by sweeping a plane surface around a circle.

layer

A means of organizing complex images, by separating them into independent sub-images stacked as if they were printed on sheets of clear acetate material so that lower layers show through the transparent areas.

layer mask

In Photoshop, a *mask* that is attached to a *layer*.

layout grid

In graphic design and *Web* design, a geometrical, usually rectilinear, division of a page, which can be used to control and organize the placement of text blocks and images.

leading

The distance between consecutive baselines in typeset text. (Pronounced to rhyme with "heading".)

left-aligned

A style of aligning paragraphs, with a straight left margin and ragged right.

left side bearing

In typography, the distance between the glyph origin and the bounding box of a *glyph*.

letter spacing

See *tracking*.

levels adjustment

A form of image adjustment, in which the end points of a linear mapping function are adjusted to set the white and black levels.

ligatures

Composite *glyphs* used to replace sequences of two or three letters which are difficult to set in a pleasing way individually.

lightness

A measure of how light or dark a colour is. One component in the *HSL colour model*.

linear gradient

A *gradient fill* in which the colours are arranged in a straight line across the filled object.

Linear Predictive Coding

A form of audio *compression* using a mathematical model of the state of the vocal tract as its representation of speech.

link

In *hypermedia*, a pointer or reference to a location in a document. Usually, links are embedded in documents as distinguished text or in *navbars*, for example to connect locations in two documents, and may be followed using some interface gesture such as clicking with a mouse.

link type

In *XHTML*, a string designating a type of relationship, which can be used as the value of the rel *attribute* of a link or a element.

liquid layout

In *Web* design, a layout in which the proportion of each element's width to the width of the window remains the same if the window is resized.

listener

See *event listener*.

live-action

Video captured by a camera recording motion taking place in the real world. See also *animation*.

logical pixels

The stored *pixel* values of a *bitmapped image*. See also *physical pixels*.

loop

In programming, any *statement* used to execute a series of statements repeatedly. See also *for loop*.

lossless compression

Any fully reversible data *compression* technique which permits the original values of the data (before compression) to be recovered exactly after *decompression*.

lossy compression

Any data *compression* technique which cannot be exactly reversed, so that *decompression* restores only an approximation to the original data.

low-pass filter

In signal processing, a filter which passes the low frequencies and blocks the high ones. Used in audio processing to remove hiss.

luma keying

In video post-production, designating a brightness threshold to determine transparency.

luminance

A precise measure of brightness, defined by a formula expressing its value as a weighted sum of the *R*, *G* and *B* components of a colour.

LZ77

A *dictionary-based* algorithm for performing *lossless compression*.

LZ78

A *dictionary-based* algorithm for performing *lossless compression*.

LZW

Lempel-Ziv-Welch. A *dictionary-based lossless compression* algorithm used in *GIF* files.

machine instruction

A bit pattern which causes a computer to execute some operation that is built into its hardware.

macroblock

A block of *pixels* (usually 16×16) in a video *frame* to which *motion compensation* is applied by *MPEG codecs*.

magic wand

A tool for selecting *pixels* or objects that share some attributes. For example, in Photoshop, all pixels of the same colour (within a specified tolerance) as the one clicked on with the magic wand are selected.

magnetic lasso

In Photoshop, a tool for making selections by drawing roughly round the area to be selected. As the tool is dragged, the selection boundary snaps to the nearest clearly defined edge.

Main Profile (MP)

An *H.264/AVC* profile for general use.

Main Profile at Main Level (MP@ML)

The combination of parameters and profile most commonly used by *MPEG-2* video for DVD and broadcast television.

margin

In *CSS*, the transparent region outside the *border*, which separates a box from its neighbours. See also *padding*.

markup

Instructions, often in the form of *tags*, inserted into a document to specify its structure or control its formatting.

markup language

A language consisting of a set of *tags* and rules governing their usage, for applying *markup* to computer-readable text documents.

marquee tools

In Photoshop, a set of four selection tools, with which areas of *pixels* that lie within a geometrical shape (rectangle, ellipse, single-pixel row or single-pixel column) can be selected.

mask

In *bitmapped image* processing, including video, a *greyscale* image which defines an area to be excluded from processing or considered transparent. A mask may be saved as part of another image as an *alpha channel*, or it may exist independently.

masking curve

In audio, the modification of the threshold of hearing curve in the region of a loud tone.

matte

In film and video, a *mask* used for compositing.

megabyte

1024 *kilobytes*.

messages

In computer networks, the structured data exchanged between *hosts* using certain high-level *protocols*. Specifically, the *requests* and *responses* exchanged between a *client* and *server* using *HTTP*.

metadata

Data consisting of information about data. In particular, the information about an *XHTML* document included in its head, or the data attached to a digital photograph with details of how and when it was taken.

metalanguage

A language for defining other languages.

method (1)

In *JavaScript* and other *object-oriented* languages, a function called through an *object*, which implements some behaviour characteristic of the object.

Usually methods alter the value of some of the object's *properties*.

method (2)
The first element of an *HTTP request* line, which specifies the operation being requested, such as GET or POST.

Microsoft Windows Bitmap
A *bitmapped image* file format used on Windows operating systems. Usually abbreviated as BMP.

MIDI
Musical Instruments Digital Interface. A standard for communicating between electronic musical instruments and music software such as sequencers.

MIDI message
An instruction that controls some aspect of the performance of an instrument using *MIDI*.

MJPEG
Motion JPEG. A largely obsolete form of video *compression* that works by applying *JPEG* compression to each frame.

monospaced
In typography, an alternative term for *fixed width*.

morphing
See *shape tweening*.

motion compensation
A technique used in video *compression*, where a record of the relative displacement of objects is incorporated in the difference *frames*.

motion estimation
Another name for *motion compensation*.

motion graphics
Animated graphic design.

motion path
In *animation* applications, a Bézier *path* along which an object or layer can be made to move.

movie clip symbol
A type of *symbol* in *Flash* which may be animated and controlled by scripts. See also *graphic symbol*.

MP3
A popular audio *compression* algorithm, defined in Part 3 of the *MPEG*-2 standard, which uses *perceptual coding*.

MP4
The standard file format for *MPEG-4* data.

MPEG
Motion Picture Experts Group. Usually used to refer to the set of standards for video and multimedia defined by this group. These include MPEG-2, the *compression* method used for DVD video and MPEG-4 Part 10 (*H.264/AVC*), a high-quality, low *bit rate codec*, increasingly used on the *Internet*.

MPEG-2
An *MPEG* standard defining the video *codec* used for DVDs. Also includes the definition of *MP3*.

MPEG-4
A multi-part standard, including several video and audio *codecs* and a file format, designed to support a range of multimedia data at bit rates from 10 kbits per second to 300 Mbits per second or higher.

MPEG-4 Part 2
A video *codec* that is a refinement of *MPEG-2*, now superseded by *H.264/AVC*.

MPEG-4 Part 10
See *H.264/AVC*.

MSAA
Microsoft Active Accessibility. An *accessibility* technology for Windows that can act as a bridge between programs, such as the Flash Player, and screen readers, so that the contents of a *Flash movie*, for example, can be made available in spoken form.

multi-links
In *hypertext*, links that connect more than two locations.

multicast
In computer networks, a method of transmission to multiple *hosts*, in which a single *packet* is sent, and is duplicated along the way whenever routes to different hosts diverge.

multimedia

The combination of different media, usually with interactivity.

multimedia architecture

A combination of an *API*, one or more *codecs*, a file format and some software for the creating, storage and display of *multimedia*.

multiplexed

Sharing a network connection.

MXML

An *XML-based markup language* for arranging *components* when creating *Flash movies* with *Flex*.

namespace

In *XML*, a collection of *element* and *attribute* names, identified by a *URL*. Namespaces are used to prevent name clashes when different *XML-based* languages are combined.

navbar

Navigation bar. A set of *links*, often incorporating *rollovers*, placed on a collection of *Web pages* to provide standard navigational access to each page.

nearest-neighbour interpolation

The simplest algorithm used in the *resampling* of *bitmapped images*; nearest neighbour is efficient but produces poorer results than more complex algorithms.

nodes

In graph theory, the points in a *directed graph* or *tree* which are connected by the *edges*.

noise gate

In audio processing, a crude filter that removes background noise by eliminating all samples whose value falls below a specified threshold.

non-linear

A term primarily used in *multimedia* and *time-based* media to describe any sequential production which is not played back or experienced in an order predetermined by the producer(s). This normally implies some measure of user control or interactivity, although we sometimes speak of a non-linear narrative or structure within a linear work such as a book or film.

non-visual user agent

A *user agent*, such as a screen reader, which presents *Web pages* in some form other than a visual display.

non-zero winding number rule

In *vector graphics*, a rule for determining whether a point lies inside or outside a *path*, by determining whether the number of times the path crosses a line drawn from the point from left to right is equal to the number of times it crosses it from right to left. If so, the point is outside, if not it is inside. See also *even–odd rule*.

notch filter

In audio processing, a filter that removes a single narrow frequency band.

NTSC

National Television Standards Committee. More usually used to refer to the composite colour video standard which that committee devised for use in the USA, consisting of 29.97 *interlaced* frames per second, each with 480 lines of vertical *resolution* out of a total of 525.

numeric character reference

In *XML-based languages*, a numerical (decimal or *hexadecimal*) reference to a character's *Unicode* value, used to insert characters which would be hard to type, which are not available in the chosen *character set encoding*, or which form part of an XML *tag*, for example < for the < symbol.

NURB

Non-rational B-spline. In *3-D graphics*, a surface that can be used to model complicated 3-D objects. Patches defined by NURBs can be fitted together in 3-D much as *Bézier curve* segments are fitted together in 2-D.

Nyquist rate

The minimum frequency at which a signal must be sampled to allow it to be reconstructed perfectly. The Nyquist rate depends on the highest-frequency component in the signal being sampled.

object

In *object-oriented* programming, a collection of *properties* and *methods* which can be treated as a single entity.

object-oriented

An adjective applied to programming languages which provide facilities for the creation of *objects* as instances of *classes*, hierarchically organized using the principle of *inheritance*.

ODF

OpenDocument file format. An *XML*-based language for representing office documents, such as spreadsheets, charts, presentations and word processing documents. ODF is an *ISO/IEC* standard.

Ogg

A *multimedia* file format associated with various Open Source multimedia projects coordinated by the Xiph.org foundation.

Ogg Theora

An Open Source video *codec*.

Ogg Vorbis

An Open Source audio *codec*.

On2 VP6

A video *codec* used for encoding Flash Video (*FLV*).

onion-skinning

An *animation* aid provided by *Flash* and other digital animation programs, for showing dimmed versions of previous *frames* to help the animator position objects in the current frame.

OOXML

Office Open XML. An *XML-based language* defined by Microsoft for representing documents created by the programs in their Office suite.

open path

A path that is not *closed*.

OpenType

An *outline font* format providing advanced typographic features, such as extended *ligatures*, swash capitals, alternative *glyphs* and positioning options.

optical margin alignment

See *hanging punctuation*.

optical printer

A device used in film post-production for creating transitions and special effects by optical means. Now superseded by digital effects.

origin

In two-dimensional graphics, the point from which *coordinates* are measured.

out point

In video editing, a designated *frame* where a clip should end. If the out point is not the last frame, material after it will be trimmed off.

outline font

A digital *font* in which the *glyphs* are stored as *vector graphics*.

overshoot

In typography, the amount by which the curved tops of certain lower-case letters extend through the *x-height*. Overshoot helps make the letters look more uniform in size.

P-picture, P-frame

Predictive picture. In *video compression*, a difference frame based on preceding *I-pictures* or *P-pictures*, or both.

P2P

Peer-to-peer networking. An approach to distributed computing in which no single *host* is distinguished as a *server*. Any computer on the network can function as both *server* and *client*.

package

In ActionScript, a collection of *classes*.

packet

In communications, one of the small pieces into which messages are split when transmitted over a network such as the *Internet*.

packet-switched network

A type of computer network in which all messages are split into *packets*, which are sent separately.

padding

In *CSS*, the region between a box's content region and its *border*.

PAL

Phase Alternate Line. A composite colour video standard consisting of 25 *interlaced frames* per second, each with 625 lines of vertical *resolution*, of which 576 carry picture information. PAL variants are used in most of Europe, Australia, New Zealand, China and some other areas.

palette

The set of colours contained in an image.

Pantone

A colour matching system, widely used in the printing industry, based on swatches of standard colours that can be reproduced accurately, each of which is identified by a unique number.

paragraph formatting

See *block-level formatting*.

parent class

In *object-oriented* programming, a *class*'s parent in the *inheritance* hierarchy, the class in which any *derived methods* and *properties* are defined.

partial URL

See *relative URL*.

path (1)

In *vector graphics*, a connected sequence of curve and line segments.

path (2)

The third component of a *URL*, which defines the location of a document within a hierarchy (which is often a sub-hierarchy of the file system of the *server*).

pattern fill

In *vector graphics*, a type of *fill* made up of regularly repeated tiles.

pc

Pica. A typographical unit of size, equal to 12 *pt*.

PDF

Portable Document Format. A file format capable of displaying graphics and text, developed by Adobe for transferring and presenting electronic documents in a way independent of the original hardware, software or operating system used to create them.

perceptual coding

Audio *compression* based on discarding insignificant information. See also *lossy compression*.

perceptually uniform colour model

A *colour model* in which a certain change in one of the values produces the same change in appearance, no matter what the original value was.

permalink

Permanent link. A *URL* that is guaranteed to point to the same *resource* forever.

persistence of vision

A lag in the eye's response to visual stimuli, which results in "after-images" being seen briefly when the stimulus is no longer present, so that a sequence of still images presented in rapid succession will appear to be moving. See also *animation*, *video*.

Phong shading

In *3-D graphics*, a shading algorithm applied to objects whose surfaces are defined by polygons, in which the colour across each polygon is interpolated on the basis of colour values calculated at the vertices, taking account of specular reflection so that highlights are rendered convincingly.

physical pixels

The dots of light on a screen or ink on paper making up the displayed or printed version of a *bitmapped image*. See also *logical pixels*.

pi font

A *font* consisting of *glyphs* for non-alphabetic symbols, such as mathematical symbols.

pitch alteration

In audio processing, changing the pitch of a note without altering its duration. See also *time stretching*.

pixel

The smallest element of a *bitmapped image*, capable of displaying a single colour. Pixels are usually square, except in video, and are assembled into images in rows and columns.

pixel density

The number of dots per unit length that a device can display or sample, often what is meant by the device's *resolution*.

pixel dimensions

The width and height of a *bitmapped image* or video frame, measured in *pixels*.

pixel group processing

In *bitmapped image* processing, a class of transformations in which each *pixel*'s new value is computed as a function of its old value and the values of neighbouring pixels.

pixel point processing

In *bitmapped image* processing, a class of trans-formations in which each *pixel*'s new value is computed as a function of its old value.

pixellation

In *bitmapped image* processing, including video, a visible "blockiness", usually the result of *aliasing* following *downsampling* or *lossy compression*. So named because it seems as though the individual *pixels* are themselves visible, though usually they are not.

plain text file

A file whose contents are interpreted as characters, which does not contain any layout information.

playhead

In the Flash Player, a notional device that keeps track of the current *frame* in a movie as it plays.

plug-in

A small computer program that can be attached to a larger program in order to execute specific functions, such as the display of a certain type of file. Plug-ins are frequently used with *Web browsers* to display file formats not supported directly by the browser itself.

PNG

Portable Network Graphics. A *bitmapped image* file format that uses *deflate* compression. One of the three image file formats natively supported by *Web browsers*. See also GIF and JPEG.

podcast

An *RSS* feed with an audio file enclosed, which allows users to subscribe to regularly updated episodes.

podcatcher

A dedicated *client* for subscribing to *podcasts*.

pop-up menu

A *control* that allows a user to select one of several alternatives from a list which is normally collapsed to a single entry, but appears in full when clicked on.

port number

In computer networking, a number which identi-fies a communication channel on which *servers* listen for incoming *packets*.

posterization

In computer graphics, a form of artefact which occurs when images are reduced to a small number of colours, resulting in a greatly simpli-fied appearance resembling cheaply printed posters, with blends and gradations replaced by hard-edged areas of a single colour.

PostScript font

A popular *outline font* format, in which the *glyphs* are stored as images in the PostScript language.

POUR

The four principles of *accessibility* defined in WCAG 2.0: perceivable, operable, understandable and robust.

presentation description

A document that must be obtained by the *client*, before an *RTSP* session can be set up, which contains information about the data streams that are to be controlled.

procedural modelling

In *3-D graphics* an approach to modelling in which objects are described by an algorithm or procedure.

progressive download

A method of playing video over the *Internet*, where the movie starts to play as soon as the time it is calculated it will take the remainder of the data to arrive is shorter than the time it will take to play the movie through to the end.

progressive scanning

In a video system, the display of all the raster lines in each *frame* in consecutive order, instead of alternately as *interlaced fields*.

property

In *object-oriented* programming, a named value stored as part of the state of an *object*.

proportional font

In typography, a *font* in which characters occupy differing amounts of horizontal space, depending on their shape, in contrast to *fixed-width* fonts.

protocol

In computer networking, a set of rules governing the exchange of data between programs over a network.

pseudo-classes

In *CSS*, names such as first-child, which are treated as classes in *selectors*, but depend on properties of the document, not on the value of the class *attribute*.

psycho-acoustical model

A mathematical description of aspects of the way the ear and brain perceive sounds, used as the basis of *perceptual coding*.

pt

Point. In typography, a unit of measurement, also used in *CSS*. In digital typography, 1 pt is defined as $\frac{1}{72}$ inch.

PTP

Picture Transfer Protocol. A *protocol* for transferring images from a digital camera to a computer and controlling the camera from the computer.

QoS

Quality of service. A measure of the amount of delay, *jitter* and *packet* loss that a network application can tolerate, and the bandwidth it requires.

quantization

In signal processing, the restriction of any continuously varying signal to a finite set of discrete values.

quantization levels

The levels to which a signal is *quantized*.

quantization noise

A form of distortion that occurs when sound is *quantized* to too few amplitude levels.

QuickTime

A *multimedia* architecture developed by Apple, available on Macintosh and Windows platforms, most widely used as a cross-platform video format with synchronized sound.

radial gradient

A *gradient fill* in which the colours are arranged in concentric circles inside the filled object.

radio button

In user interfaces, a *control*, which can only occur in sets of two or more, used to select exactly one option from a set.

radiosity

A rendering technique for 3-D models which attempts to model the complex reflections that occur between surfaces that are close together to provide an accurate representation of scattered and ambient light.

raster graphics

Alternative name for *bitmapped images*, used most commonly in North America.

ray tracing

A *rendering* technique for 3-D models that produces photo-realistic results.

RDF

Resource Description Framework. An abstract language, standardized by *W3C*, which is intended to allow *metadata* to be specified in a standard way.

RDF/XML

An *XML-based language* providing a concrete syntax for *RDF*.

RDFa

Resource Description Framework attributes. A collection of *attributes*, whose values can be *CURIEs*, that may be added to any *XML-based language* to embed *RDF metadata* directly in the *markup* of documents.

reflection

In *vector graphics*, an *affine transformation* in which an object is reflected in a line, as if in a mirror.

reflection mapping

In *3-D graphics*, mathematically wrapping a picture over the surface of an object to modify its shininess.

regional links

In *hypertext*, links that connect areas on pages.

relative URL

A *URL* with one or more leading components missing, which identifies a *resource* relative to the location of the document it appears in.

remote rollover

An effect used on *Web pages*, usually implemented with *JavaScript*, in which the appearance of an element is made to change when the cursor moves over some other element on the page.

render

In computer graphics, to convert a 2-D or 3-D *vector graphic* to *pixels*, a process which may introduce *aliasing*.

rendering engine

A software module optimized to perform *rendering* of *3-D graphics*.

request

In communication *protocols*, a *message* sent from a *client* to a *server*.

request line

The first line of an *HTTP request*, which specifies the operation and *resource* being requested.

resampling

In computer graphics, the process of changing a *bitmapped image*'s *resolution*. In audio, the process of changing the sample rate of digital audio. See also *upsampling* and *downsampling*.

reserved word

In programming languages, a name used by the language as part of its syntax, which cannot be used as a *variable*'s name.

resolution

The number of horizontal and vertical *pixels* in a *bitmapped image* or *frame* of video, or the number of *pixels* per unit length stored in a *bitmapped image* file.

resource

In the context of the *Internet*, a file, program or other entity that can be identified by a *URL*.

response

In communication *protocols*, a *message* sent from a *server* to a *client*.

return statement

In programmming languages, a statement used to indicate the value to be returned by a *function* or *method*.

reverb

In audio processing, an effect produced digitally by adding copies of a signal, delayed in time and attenuated, to the original, to simulate the acoustics of enclosed spaces.

RGB colour model

A *colour model*, based on additive colour mixing, in which each colour is represented by three values denoting the proportions of red, green and blue light it contains.

RGB gamut, RGB colour gamut

The set of colours that can be represented in the *RGB colour model*.

right-aligned

A style of aligning paragraphs, with a ragged left margin and straight right.

RLE

Run-length encoding. A *lossless compression* technique which replaces each run with a single copy of the repeated string, together with a repeat counter.

rollover

In user interfaces, an image or a piece of text which changes its appearance when the cursor moves over it, usually to indicate that it will respond to a mouse click. Often used to give a visual indication of *links*.

rotation

In *vector graphics*, an *affine transformation* in which an object is rotated about a point.

rotoscoping

In *animation*, the technique of tracing selected elements from a *live-action* video clip. Also used to mean combining animation with live action.

router

A machine connected between component networks of the *Internet*, which uses information about the network topology to determine where to send a *datagram* to.

RSS

Really Simple Syndication. An *XML-based* format for packaging information about frequently updated *Web sites*, such as blogs and news sites in a form that can easily be checked and downloaded.

RSVP

Resource Reservation Protocol. A *protocol* forming part of the *Integrated Services Architecture*, used to reserve network resources.

RTCP

RTP Control Protocol. A *protocol* that can be used in conjunction with **RTP** to provide feedback on the quality of the data delivery

RTP

Real-Time Transport Protocol. A *protocol* used on the *Internet* for the delivery of streamed media. RTP does not guarantee reliable delivery of *packets*.

RTSP

Real Time Streaming Protocol. A *protocol* used on the *Internet* to control streaming media, sometimes described as an "Internet VCR remote control protocol".

rule

In *CSS*, a specification of how certain *elements* should be displayed, comprising a *selector* and some *declarations* to be applied to elements matching the selector.

samples

The values recorded during *sampling*.

sampling

In signal processing, the recording of values at discrete intervals in time. Part of the process of *digitization*. See also *quantization*.

sampling rate

In *digitization*, the number of samples in a fixed amount of time or space.

Sampling Theorem

An important theoretical result in signal processing, which states that, if the highest-frequency component of a signal is at f_h, the signal can be properly reconstructed if it has been sampled at a frequency greater than $2f_h$. See also *Nyquist rate*.

sans serif font

In typography, a class of *fonts* whose *glyphs* do not have *serifs*.

saturation

One of the three components used to specify a colour in the *HSL* and *HSV colour models*. As saturation of a colour is reduced the colour becomes greyer; a fully desaturated colour will be a shade of grey, tending to white at high brightness values and black at low brightness values.

scaling

In *vector graphics*, an *affine transformation* in which the dimensions of an object are multiplied by a constant.

schema

In *XML*, a specification method which defines the grammar for a class of documents. Unlike a *DTD*, a schema is itself a *valid* XML document.

screen reader

An example of *assistive technology*, a program that turns text, such as the text on a *Web page*, into speech.

script

A program written in a *scripting language*.

scripting language

A programming language, often with a restricted syntax, used to manipulate the facilities of an existing system. For example, *JavaScript* is used to manipulate a *Web browser*.

SD

Standard Definition. In video, the original resolutions for **PAL** (768×576) and **NTSC** (640×480) frames.

SDP

Session Description Protocol. An extensible *protocol*, often used as the format of *presentation descriptions* for **RTSP** sessions.

SDSL

Symmetric Digital Subscriber Line. A high-speed data connection for *Internet* access, using existing copper phone lines. Upstream data rates are as fast as downstream rates. SDSL is less widely available than *ADSL*.

SECAM

Séquential Couleur avec Mémoire. A composite colour video standard, similar to *PAL*, used in France, Eastern Europe and countries of the former Soviet Union.

secondary colours

The *complementary colours* of the primaries in a *colour model*.

seed

A *host* that holds a complete copy of a file being distributed as a torrent over a *P2P* network.

segment

In vector graphics, a line or curve forming part of a *path*.

selector

In *CSS*, the part of a *rule* which determines which *elements* the *declarations* should be applied to.

semiotics

The study of systems of *signs*. Also known as semiology.

sequencer

A program or hardware device that can be programmed to send out sequences of *MIDI* instructions to control instruments.

serif

In typography, one of the small decorative strokes on the ends of letter shapes.

serifed font

A *font* whose glyphs have *serifs*.

server

See *client/server model*. Also used to mean a *host* on which a *server* is running.

server-side script

A *script* running on the same machine as an *HTTP server* that communicates with external *resources*, such as databases, so data obtained from them can be incorporated into the server's *responses*. See also *CGI script*.

session identifier

An arbitrary string that is used by both *client* and *server* to identify *messages* associated with the same *RTSP* session.

shade

A colour obtained by adding black to a pure *hue* (but sometimes used to mean the same as *tone*).

shading algorithm

In *3-D graphics*, an algorithm used during *rendering* to produce an image that is consistent with the lights and materials that have been used in the model.

shape tweening

In *Flash*, transforming one shape into another by *tweening*, for instance, transforming a square into a circle. Outside Flash this kind of transformation is often called morphing.

shearing

In *vector graphics*, an *affine transformation* in which the opposing sides of an object are moved in opposite parallel directions.

shuffling

In *DV compression*, an elaborate process of rearrangement applied to the blocks making up a complete *frame*, to make best use of the space available for storing coefficients.

SIF

Source Input Format. The typical format for *MPEG*-1 video, having a *frame* size of 352×240, at a frame rate of 30 fps, using 4:2:0 *chrominance sub-sampling*.

sign

In *semiotics*, the whole that results from the association between the *signifier* and the *signified*. The term is often used (incorrectly) to mean just the signifier.

signified

In *semiotics*, the object or concept which a *signifier* stands for or points to.

signifier

In *semiotics*, a symbol which, within a system of *signs*, arbitrarily stands for or points to an object or concept. The form which the sign takes.

Simple Profile

An *MPEG-4 Part 2* profile that uses only *P-pictures* for *inter-frame compression*.

simple uni-directional links

In *hypertext*, a *link* that connects two locations and can only be followed in one direction, from its source to its destination.

skip link

A *link* from the beginning of a document to the start of its main *content*, which allows *screen reader* users to by-pass the *navbar* and other secondary material, such as a logo, at the beginning of a *Web page*.

slanted font

A *font* in which a *shear* transformation has been applied to upright *glyphs*, formerly used as a substitute for *italic* fonts.

SMPTE timecode

The most commonly used *timecode* format.

Sorensen Spark

A video *codec* used for encoding Flash Video (*FLV*).

span

A sequence of characters to which *character formatting* may be applied.

spatial compression

An informal name for *intra-frame compression*.

SPD

Spectral power distribution. A description of how the intensity of light from some particular source varies with wavelength.

SPIFF

Still Picture Interchange File Format. The official ISO standard file format for storing *JPEG* image data. See also *JFIF*.

sRGB

A standard *RGB colour space*, defined by the *W3C*, used for colour values in *CSS*.

stage

In *Flash*, the main window in which the contents of a *key frame* can be created and edited. The contents of other frames can be displayed on the stage.

start tag

In *XML-based languages*, the sequence that marks the start of an *element*. For an element with name el, the start tag is <el>.

statement

In programming languages, the primitive pieces of executable code from which programs are constructed.

static media

Any form of media, such as still images, that is not *time-based*.

status line

The first line of an *HTTP response*, which indicates how the *server* dealt with a *request*. It includes a status code and a short readable description.

stop-motion, stop-frame

In traditional *animation*, a technique in which objects or characters are photographed one *frame* at a time, being moved or altered a small amount between each frame so that an illusion of motion is created when the frames are subsequently played back in sequence.

streamed video

Video which is transmitted over a network and played back as soon as it arrives.

stroke

In *vector graphics*, the colour or pattern applied to the outline of a shape.

structural markup

Markup in which *tags* are used purely to identify logical elements of a document, such as headings, lists or tables, not their appearance. See also *visual markup*.

structure model, structure tree

An abstract representation of the tree structure of an *XML* document.

stylesheet

In *CSS* or some other stylesheet language, a specification of how each of the *elements* in a document should be displayed.

sub-class

In *object-oriented* programming, a *class* that is *derived* from another.

sub-pixel anti-aliasing

A technique for improving the appearance of type on LCD screens by adjusting the relative intensities of the individual colour components of each *pixel*. See also *anti-aliasing*.

sub-pixel motion compensation

In video *compression*, the use of *displacement vectors* for *motion compensation* which record movement to an accuracy finer than a single *pixel*.

subtractive primaries

Three colours of pigment, usually cyan, magenta and yellow, which when mixed in differing amounts can produce all the colours in a *colour space*, such as *CMY*.

SVG

Scalable Vector Graphics. An *XML-based language* for *vector graphics* for use on the *Web*.

SVG Basic

An *SVG* profile for moderately powerful mobile devices.

SVG Tiny

An *SVG* profile for mobile phones.

SWF

See *Flash movie*.

symbol

In *Flash* and some other *vector graphics* programs, a reusable graphic or animated object, which can be stored in a library and instantiated multiple times.

symbol font

Alternative name for *pi font*.

symmetrical codec

A *codec* that takes the same time to perform *compression* as *decompression*.

tag

A character sequence used in a *markup language* to mark the beginning or end of an *element*. See also *start tag* and *end tag*.

tagging

Attaching words or phrases to items in a collection to form the basis of a classification scheme. Used to refer to the classification of *content* in this way by visitors to a *Web site*.

TCP

Transmission Control Protocol. The *protocol* used at the Transport Layer in the *Internet* for the reliable transmission of streams of data.

TCP/IP

Loosely used to refer to all of the *protocols* used on the *Internet* and *intranets*. *TCP* and *IP* are the lowest-level protocols used to communicate between applications and *hosts* respectively.

temporal compression

An informal name for *inter-frame compression*.

tertiary colours

The colours produced by mixing primaries and secondaries.

text area

In a user interface, a *control* which provides a space for users to enter text that occupies more than one line.

text font

A *font* that is suitable for setting continuous text, such as the body of a book or article. See also *display font*.

text node

A node in an *XML* document's *structure tree* corresponding to a sequence of text in the document. See also *element node*.

texture mapping

In *3-D graphics*, mathematically wrapping a pattern representing some particular sort of surface's appearance, such as fur, bark, sand, marble and so on, over the surface of an object.

threshold of hearing

The minimum level at which a sound can be heard, which varies non-linearly with frequency.

TIFF

Tag Image File Format. A cross-platform *bitmapped image* file format, in which the image data is usually uncompressed.

time base errors

Errors that occur when playing back a digitized signal caused by samples being played at the wrong time. Often caused by *jitter* in streamed media.

time-based media

Any media that exhibits intrinsic variation over time, for example video, *animation* and sound.

time domain

A mathematical space in which periodic waveforms are represented by the variation of their amplitudes over time. See also *frequency domain*.

time stretching

In audio processing, changing the duration of a note without altering its pitch. See also *pitch alteration*.

timecode

A notation for precisely identifying a *frame* in a video sequence, also used to specify time within an audio track in an editing application. Timecode enables frame-accurate editing and is used to synchronize picture and sound. When written to tape, it permits logging and offline capture of clips.

timeline

A simplified graphical representation of the extent in time of any time-based media, which usually reads from left to right. In *Flash*, the sequence of *frames* in a *Flash movie*, normally shown above the *stage* in the Flash workspace.

tint

A colour obtained by adding white to a pure hue.

tone

A colour obtained by adding black and white to a pure *hue* (but sometimes used to mean the same as *shade*).

tracking

In typography, increasing or decreasing the spacing between all the letters by a fixed proportion. Also called letter spacing.

transfer characteristic

The relationship between the light intensity emitted by the screen of a CRT and the voltage applied to the electron gun.

translation

In *vector graphics*, an *affine transformation* in which an object is moved to a different point.

transparency mapping

In *3-D graphics*, mathematically wrapping a picture over the surface of an object to modify its opacity.

transport address

The combination of an *IP address* and a *port number*, which enables the *protocols* running on top of *IP* to provide communication facilities between programs running on different *hosts*.

tree

A hierarchical structure, a *directed graph* in which each *node* has exactly one ancestor.

tristimulus theory

The theory that any colour can be specified by just three values, giving the weights of each of three components.

TrueType

An *outline font* format.

tweening

In digital *animation*, the *interpolation* of additional *frames* between *key frames* to complete the illusion of motion or action.

UCS

Universal Character Set. A *character set* using 32-bit character values, defined by the standard ISO-10646.

UCS-2

A *character set encoding* of *UCS* using only two *bytes* to represent a 16-bit subset of the full character set. UCS-2 is identical to *Unicode*.

UCS-4

The trivial *character set encoding* of *UCS* using four *bytes* for each character.

UDP

User Datagram Protocol. A simple communications *protocol* used on the *Internet* for transmitting *datagrams* between *hosts*. UDP does not guarantee delivery of individual *datagrams*.

UI components

Flash components implementing user interface *controls*.

undersample

To *sample* a signal at less than the *Nyquist rate*.

unicast

In computer networks, the conventional method of transmission to multiple *hosts*, in which separate *packets* are sent to each host. See also *multicast*.

Unicode

A 16-*bit* subset of the ISO 10646 *UCS* which represents text in most of the written languages of the world.

unsharp masking

In *bitmapped image* processing, a sharpening operation performed by constructing a copy of the original image, applying a *Gaussian blur* to it, and then subtracting the *pixel* values in this blurred mask from the corresponding values in the original multiplied by a suitable scaling factor.

upright font

A conventional *text font* with characters whose vertical strokes (stems) are truly vertical, unlike *slanted* or *italic fonts*.

upsampling

In computer graphics, changing the *resolution* of a *bitmapped image* to a higher value by means of *interpolation*. This may be in order to match the image *resolution* to that of an output device, or to increase the number of *pixels* for use in further processing. In audio, the process of changing the sample rate of digital audio to a higher value. See also *downsampling* and *resampling*.

URI

Uniform Resource Identifier. A *URL* or *URN*.

URL

Uniform Resource Locator. A means of identifying a resource on the *Internet*, comprising a *protocol*, *domain name* and a *path*.

URN

Uniform Resource Name. A name that identifies a *resource* on the *Internet* in a location-independent way.

user agent

A generic name for any program that interprets or displays the data in *HTTP responses*. *Web browsers* are the best-known examples of user agents.

UTF

UCS Transformation Format. A *character set encoding* applied to *UCS-2* values.

UTF-7

A *UTF* encoding which turns *Unicode* characters into streams of 7-bit values in the set of *ASCII code points*, so they can be transmitted safely through networks that are only equipped to deal with ASCII text.

UTF-8

A *UTF* encoding for representing single *Unicode* characters by variable-length sequences of up to six *bytes*. Values in the range 0–127 are sent as single bytes, which are identical to the *ASCII* codes for the corresponding characters.

UTF-16

A *UTF* encoding which allows pairs of 16-bit values to be combined into a single 32-bit value, to extend the *character repertoire* of *Unicode* beyond the *BMP*.

valid

In *XML*, a document is valid if it is *well-formed* and conforms to the rules in an associated *DTD* or *schema*.

variable

In programming languages, a named container that can hold an *object* or value.

variable-length coding

A technique used in several *compression* algorithms, including *Huffman coding*, where strings are replaced by code values, such that the shortest values are used for the most common strings, and longer values are used for less common ones.

VC-1

A video *codec*, identical to that used in *WMV*-9, standardized by the Society of Motion Picture Engineers (SMPTE).

vector

A tuple of n values, specifying a displacement in n-dimensional Cartesian space. In particular, a 2-D vector is a pair of values used to specify a displacement having direction and magnitude.

vector graphics

Images displayed by rendering a description comprising mathematically defined shapes and *paths*, which can nevertheless be very complex visually. Vector graphics are compact, scaleable and *resolution*-independent.

version

In *HTTP*, the final element on an HTTP *request line*, indicating which version of the *protocol* the *client* is using.

video

Moving pictures stored as a sequence of *bitmapped images*, usually compressed and often with a synchronized soundtrack.

visual hierarchy

The hierarchical structure of a visual field caused by particular elements dominating others, often a result of deliberately violating *gestalt* principles of visual perception.

visual markup

Markup in which *tags* are used purely to describe the intended appearance of elements of a document. See also *structural markup*.

visual user agent

A *user agent*, particularly a *Web browser*, which display *Web pages* visually on a screen.

W3C

World Wide Web Consortium. The organization that creates *Web* standards and oversees the evolution of the Web.

WAI

Web Accessibility Initiative. A *W3C* programme which develops guidelines for enhancing the *accessibility* of *Web pages*.

WAI-ARIA

WAI Accessible Rich Internet Applications Suite. A *W3C* standard intended to enhance the *accessibility* of *AJAX* applications on the *Web* by providing a way of communicating information about page updates to *assistive technology*.

waveform

A plot of an audio signal's amplitude against time, showing how its *frequency spectrum* varies.

wavelet decomposition

A sequence of *detail coefficients* which describe an image, for example, in increasing levels of detail. Used in *JPEG2000* compression.

WCAG

Web Content Accessibility Guidelines. *W3C* Recommendations defining guidelines and conformance levels for assessing the *accessibility* of *Web pages*.

Web

See *World Wide Web*.

Web browser

A program for displaying *Web pages* visually. The most common type of *user agent*.

Web page

The smallest unit of the *Web* that can be displayed in a single browser window. Usually held as a collection of resources, including an *HTML* or *XHTML* document, on a remote *server* and accessed with a *Web browser*.

Web proxy

A machine that handles *requests* directed to some other *server*, forwarding them to their intended destination. Used to provide security in the form of a firewall, and to improve performance, since proxies usually maintain a cache.

Web site

A collection of *Web pages* with a common theme, a coherent structure and a home page.

weight

In vector graphics, the width of a *stroke*. In typography, the thickness of the strokes making up the *glyphs* in a *font*.

well-formed

In *XML*, a document is well-formed if it conforms to the basic syntactic rules of XML, concerning the form of *elements*, *attributes* and *character entity references*. A well-formed document need not include a *DTD* and may or may not be *valid*.

white point

The value of pure white displayed on some device, specified in a *colour space*, used as a component of a *colour profile*.

Windows Media

A Microsoft *multimedia* format widely used for *Web* video.

wire frame

In *3-D graphics*, a form of *rendering* performed by joining the vertices of objects with lines, making no attempt to shade the faces or perform hidden surface removal. Used as a preview mode, because of its relative efficiency.

WMV

See *Windows Media*.

word

In computing, a unit of storage, usually equal to four *bytes*.

World Wide Web

The global distributed *hypermedia* system hosted on the *Internet*.

WYSIWYG

What You See Is What You Get. A style of working, especially in word processors, in which text appears on the screen laid out just as it will appear when it is printed or displayed.

x-axis

In coordinate geometry and *vector graphics*, the horizontal line through the origin, from which *y* coordinates are measured.

x-height

In typography, the height between the *baseline* and the top of a lower-case letter x in a *font*.

X3D

An *XML-based language* for representing 3-D objects and scenes.

XHTML

A version of the *HTML markup language*, defined using *XML*.

XLink

A means of specifying *links* in *XML* documents, using a collection of *attributes* defined in a dedicated *namespace* for the purpose.

XML

Extensible Markup Language. A *markup language* with facilities for defining *tags* and specifying restrictions on their usage; hence XML may be considered a *metalanguage* for defining other markup languages.

XML-based language

A language defined by a *DTD* or a *schema*, which shares the basic syntax of *tags*, *attributes*, and so

on of *XML* but has its own specified collection of *elements* and attributes, with constraints governing how they may be used.

XMP

Extensible Metadata Platform. A subset of *RDF/ XML*, defined by Adobe for adding *metadata* to files created by their applications. XMP can be used to add *Dublin Core*, *Exif* and *IPTC Core* metadata.

y-axis

In coordinate geometry and *vector graphics*, the vertical line through the origin, from which *x* coordinates are measured.

YUV colour

A notation used to refer loosely to any component video system using a luma (Y) and two colour difference (U, V) components.

z-axis

In 3-D coordinate geometry and *vector graphics*, an axis perpendicular to both the *x-axis* and *y-axis*.

zig-zag sequence

In *compression*, the order in which the coefficient array is traversed during the final phase of *JPEG* compression, in which *lossless compression* is applied to the quantized coefficient values.

Index